EL GENERALÍSIMO

EL GENERALÍSIMO
A BIOGRAPHY OF FRANCISCO FRANCO

GILES TREMLETT

OXFORD
UNIVERSITY PRESS

Oxford University Press is a department of the University of Oxford.
It furthers the University's objective of excellence in research, scholarship,
and education by publishing worldwide. Oxford is a registered trade mark of
Oxford University Press in the UK and in certain other countries.

Published in the United States of America by Oxford University Press
198 Madison Avenue, New York, NY 10016, United States of America.

© Giles Tremlett 2025

All rights reserved. No part of this publication may be reproduced, stored in a retrieval system,
transmitted, used for text and data mining, or used for training artificial intelligence, in any form or
by any means, without the prior permission in writing of Oxford University Press, or as expressly
permitted by law, by license or under terms agreed with the appropriate reprographics rights
organization. Inquiries concerning reproduction outside the scope of the above should be sent
to the Rights Department, Oxford University Press, at the address above.

You must not circulate this work in any other form
and you must impose this same condition on any acquirer.

CIP data is on file at the Library of Congress.
ISBN 9780197832318 (hardback) | ISBN 9780197832332
(updf) | ISBN 9780197832325 (epub) | ISBN 9780197832349 (online)

Printed by Marquis Book Printing, Canada

The manufacturer's authorized representative in the EU for product safety is
Oxford University Press España S.A. of Parque Empresarial San Fernando de Henares,
Avenida de Castilla, 2 – 28830 Madrid (www.oup.es/en or product.safety@oup.com).
OUP España S.A. also acts as importer into Spain of products made by the manufacturer.

For Katharine, Lucas, Samuel and Jara

Content

	Introduction: A Military Messiah	1
1	El Desastre	14
2	Cadet	29
3	Without Africa, I Can Scarcely Explain Myself	36
4	The Girl Behind the Lattice Screen	48
5	Los Novios de la Muerte	56
6	A New Disaster	62
7	Fame	68
8	My Mussolini	74
9	Retreat and Revenge	82
10	Hero Brothers	88
11	Out with the Old – The End of Monarchy	97
12	¡Viva la Republica!	104
13	Rebels in Asturias	117
14	The Pendulum Swings	124
15	The Popular Front – The Left Returns	128
16	The Big Decision	135
17	Insurrection	149
18	Fascism's Tailcoat	162
19	Fighting at Last	166
20	Absolute Power	171
21	Holy War	181
22	Attack on Madrid	189
23	The Absent One	199
24	Enforced Unity	206
25	Slow War	213

26 A New Regime	222
27 The Three Dictators	231
28 Victory and Repression	239
29 The World at War	247
30 My Friend Hitler	252
31 Famine	259
32 The Race	265
33 The Wrong Side of History	271
34 End of Empire, Again	280
35 Post-War Pariah	287
36 Great Poisons	297
37 The Sleeper Prince	304
38 The Grey Fifties	315
39 Take-Off	327
40 Change	341
41 Lost Years	350
42 ¡Viva Franco!	358
43 Operation Ogre	370
44 He Listens but Does not Hear	375
45 Last Gasp	384
Epilogue: Franco's Funerals	387
Acknowledgements	405
Notes	407
Bibliography	463
Index	489
Image Credits	505

Introduction: A Military Messiah

On 19 May 1939 a small man dressed in the khaki uniform and red sash of a Spanish army general stepped out of an open-topped car on Madrid's broad Castellana Avenue to climb onto a two-story dais placed before a towering victory arch. The strides of Generalísimo Francisco Franco were short, as befitted a 48-year-old man measuring 5 feet 4 inches and whose waist and belly had thickened to give him a pear-like profile. His unimposing presence, accentuated by a reedy, high-pitched voice, was deceptive. It hid a steely and cold-blooded self-confidence that was underpinned by preternatural calm. Many had underestimated him. Yet now there could be no doubt about his ambition or ability to achieve his aims. He was here to celebrate his absolute personal and political triumph as the generalísimo who had won a three-year civil war. A 36-year dictatorship was just beginning in Europe's sixth most-populous country.[1]

Franco was far more than a victorious general. He agreed with his adulators, who were busy describing his triumph in biblical terms. He was the Redeemer. He had drawn the bad blood out of the sickly body of Spain and poured it into the gutter. It had cost half a million lives, but it was worth the price. The enemies who had poisoned and weakened the nation over 125 years, since Liberals first came close to power, had not just been vanquished, but politically annihilated. He was comparable only to the great heroes of Spanish history – El Cid, Columbus or the sixteenth-century conquistadors who captured much of the Americas for Spain.

Decline was finally over. Spanish pride had been restored and glory awaited. That was the message, at least, being broadcast this day on the magnificent Castellana Avenue (soon to be renamed 'Generalísimo' after Franco himself). A million or so people lined the streets, though Franco's propagandists would claim double that. It did not matter that a similar number had been imprisoned or exiled, at least not to Franco.[2] Now there would be peace. It would be his peace, built on enforced, unbending terms.

The contrast between Franco's uncharismatic presence and his absolute hold on power remains one of many puzzling contradictions. In person, he could be mild-mannered, shy, courteous, sometimes humorous and often tediously dull. As a leader, however, he was cold and ruthless. One of Mussolini's ambassadors, like many who met him, was confounded. The caudillo, or military strongman, as Franco was also frequently called, was 'hard in a way that is not brash, but rather smooth and flexible, like a well-shined stone' and combined 'chilliness and gentility [with]... a measured way of saying the gravest things'.

In fact, there were two Francos: the soldier and the civilian. Soldier Franco was confident and decisive. Civilian Franco was calculating, slow and cautious.[3] He never admitted to mistakes. In both guises, his defining characteristic was his obstinate pride. His political motivations were reactionary and ultranationalist, embedded in what one British ambassador termed a 'heavy mist of self-complacency'. His regime became, above all, about imposing control and the rigid social conservatism of religion and gender that ruled in his own home. His greatest weakness was an outsized, thin-skinned ego.

Much of his rule was to prove disastrous, paid for by ordinary Spaniards with hunger, misery and the stultifying greyness of a society beholden to priests, soldiers or bureaucrats. Yet he refused to stand down, even when his personal status as an international pariah brought hardship to the whole country. Events impacted Franco's actions, but never dented his core beliefs or limitless self-regard. The narrative of his rule, indeed, is more about Spaniards adapting to Franco than them changing him. They were only liberated by his death, in a hospital bed further up this same tree-lined boulevard, in 1975. By that time, Francoism was all most people knew. Yet it had gone through markedly different phases.

Spain was unrecognisable from the country Franco had finished conquering in 1939. A decade and a half of remarkable, if belated, economic growth before his death meant Spaniards had recently lived through the kind of material changes that today only people in, say, Vietnam or China are equipped to understand. The countryside had given way to the city. Electricity, running water and schooling had reached into most people's homes. Cars, tractors and television sets were normal. The contrast with the famine, hunger and vengeful repression of Franco's early years – when many struggled just to survive – was stark. In comparative terms, Spain was still a western European laggard, but people did not always know that. Growth provoked optimism, excitement and ill-informed gratitude.

Franco's death produced a genuine outpouring of grief, provoking unsettling questions about autocracy. Why weren't more people openly overjoyed to be rid of him? The answers to that, part-excavated from the murk of propaganda and censorship, are often awkward. The recent economic boom and the optimism it engendered was partly to blame. Some people, however, either did not want freedom or rated it below other desires. They feared change, preferring enforced stability or to wilfully impose their worldview on others. Many others simply acquiesced. They justified this to themselves as consent, in order to retain a sense of agency and self-worth. Franco gave the Spanish people no other option. An early investment in terror paid dividends for decades, even as it disappeared from open sight. Franco shaped Spaniards – whether in acquiescence or opposition. Some loved him. Most knew nothing else. They had, quite literally, been schooled in Francoism.

None of this could have been imagined on the overcast day of Franco's 1939 victory parade. The vast stage was divided into two main levels, with seated dignitaries and bishops spread along the broad lower tier. Prominent amongst them were representatives of his fascist allies Adolf Hitler and Benito Mussolini, while France's ambassador Marshal Philippe Pétain looked more glumly over his walrus-like white moustache. Of the six most populous countries in Europe, Pétain's France and Britain were the only democracies left standing as fascists and right-wing autocrats drove the world's still-dominant continent towards a new world war. A second level of the stand was reserved for Franco's senior generals and admirals, standing pressed together as if on the bridge of a warship. Above that, a tiny platform with room for little more than two people stood like a pulpit or a guard post, looking out over the boulevard. Franco's personal guard of white-caped, white-turbaned 'Moors' – as he called his Moroccan mercenary troops – had trotted along beside his armour-plated car and now lined the street below him.

Along the boulevard and in the fields to the north of the city, 120,000 troops waited under grey clouds to march past the man who had led the battle to overthrow a young democracy. First, however, a fellow general climbed into the pulpit with Franco and pinned onto his chest the Laureate Cross of San Fernando – Spain's greatest military honour. Franco had coveted this medal for a quarter of a century as he rose through the army's ranks. Now he could award it to himself.[4]

Franco's supporters believed he deserved this shiny prize. After all, no Spanish general in recent history had achieved a victory quite as absolute. The large star, with its four twin-pointed arms sat pinned to his left breast in the space above the sash. His simple military attire, topped by the red beret favoured by his most reactionary Catholic allies and worn over the blue shirt of Spain's home-grown breed of fascists, reflected the trinity of overlapping social and political world views that underpinned his nascent regime: reactionary Roman Catholicism, martial nationalism and fascism. Despite their contradictions, he had used a shared fear and hatred of Leftists to cement them into a platform from which to impose his view of how Spaniards should live and be governed.

Although Franco himself, later that day, spoke of Madrid as a victim – a city of martyrs to the communist-inspired 'Red' fury that supposedly ruled his enemy's hearts – this march past was a celebration of conquest rather than liberation. Spain's capital had been meant to fall soon after he joined a military insurrection against an elected left-wing government in July 1936. Instead, Madrid resisted Franco's armies, who called themselves 'nacionales', Nationalists, for three years.[5]

This five-hour parade was designed, amongst other things, to drive home a message of total, unbending and irreversible triumph of one part of Spain over the other. Franco's fractious alliance of conservatives, reactionaries and fascists had imposed itself on an equally diverse mix of liberals, leftists, anarchists, communists and regionalists.

Franco himself saw it as the defeat of history or, rather, of the previous century and a quarter of Spanish history. 'The nineteenth century was the negation of the Spanish spirit, and something we would like to erase from history,' he would say later.[6] That century had been contaminated by foreign impurities – the Enlightenment, liberalism, democracy, Freemasonry, Marxism and the denigration of a Roman Catholic church that, to his mind, defined the Spanish race. Later that day he would denounce the 'Jewish spirit' behind all this.[7] To Franco this was a triumph of purity and a return to a natural religious and social order that had spawned the sixteenth-century heroes who conquered a great empire in the Americas for Spain and its Christian God. Franco was thus both the dazzling new man and the recommencement of Spain's interrupted glory, a new conquistador. His name was emblazoned on the arches behind him, three times on each pillar – 'Franco! Franco! Franco!' He would hear and see that triple repetition of his name, painted on walls or shouted by crowds, continuously from now on as a cult of personality was carefully curated.

Providence had brought him here, he thought. In reality, his personal triumph was the product of ambition, military competence, ruthlessness, violence, unbounded self-esteem, clear-headedness, a sinuous ability for self-interested scheming and a naturally untrusting, authoritarian nature. Luck had also played a large part. He had been a methodical commander-in-chief, although frustratingly slow, to Hitler and Mussolini, as they intervened crucially on his side with men, weapons, armaments and aircraft. But, unimpeded by self-doubt, Franco refused to be rushed. Instead, in his frigid fashion, he set about slowly eradicating the enemy on the battlefield and extirpating it behind the lines. Even close collaborators and family were amazed by his cold nature, which chilled further over time. Little moved him beyond a personal desire to climb the ranks and the idea that Spain was a scorned country whose reputation had to be defended at all costs. In this he was like a Regency duellist demanding respect above all else, including his own life. Indeed, his was an essentially old-fashioned mindset, a throwback to the nineteenth century or beyond.

Franco was an autocrat. He did not, however, have to impose himself on all of Spain. One part of the country had backed the insurrection and overthrow of democracy. This may not have been the majority he claimed, but it did represent a significant section of Spanish society. None had backed the rebellion imagining it would produce a 36-year personal dictatorship, or even that Franco would become their generalísimo and caudillo. On his own side, however, he also imposed absolute authority. Over the decades of indoctrination, demographic churn and the numbing of Spaniards into a state of passivity and political apathy, many more were converted to the rigid social conservatism that underpinned Franco's own mindset. Even a broad section of those who remained unconverted to Francoism feared the uncertainty of a future without him.

Historian Antonio Cazorla Sánchez, an otherwise deeply critical biographer of Franco, believes that a majority of Spaniards came to support him, at least passively. 'His political rise and exercise of government were a tragedy for the country,' he writes. 'Yet it would be disingenuous and self-comforting to think that he remained in power for forty years only by force and trickery.'[8]

The exact size of Franco's support is impossible to measure. That is part of the autocrat's playbook. They claim to speak for a majority but do not consult them (except under heavily circumscribed or corrupt circumstances, as Franco did occasionally). It is also true that the tyranny of a sizeable minority – or even of a majority – is still a tyranny.

Franco's gift was to convert Spanish social conservatism into autocratic imposition. At its harshest, he turned it into a murderous machine. Opposition, unsurprisingly, remained cowed. The enigma of how he could do that and garner support is best explained by his use of another autocrat's trick – blaming all setbacks on the enemies of the nation. Perhaps his most unique talent, however, was to persuade a significant number of Spaniards that they were incapable of governing themselves or living peacefully without him. His view was simple and condescending. The Spanish people were naturally great but, like the troops he led as a young officer, they could only realise that greatness under his firm and sometimes violent discipline.

Franco's political ideas were not yet apparent on the day of his victory parade, in part because he had so few. He had long hidden behind a calculated ambiguity that some put down to the slippery wiliness – or 'retranca' – of a native from the rainy, north-western region of Galicia. As a young man that had acted as a disguise for his ambition. In the long-term, it also helped him project himself as a benevolent pragmatist. However, the endless display of stiff-armed salutes and the swastikas and other symbols on the uniforms of the many German and Italian officers on his dais showed where his sympathies lay. The *ad hoc* regime installed early in the war – compared to a 'military encampment' – now seemed set on a course towards fascism. In reality, the Francoist state was in its infancy. It would have plenty of time to mutate.

If Spaniards were unsure of what motivated Franco in 1939, he did little to help those who study him today. His inner thoughts and feelings are largely invisible. His writing mainly takes the form of baroque speeches laden with patriotic slogans and epic-sounding but unrevealing phrases. His prejudices – against leftists, liberals, Jews and, most intensely and bizarrely, against Freemasons – were clearly visible there and, especially, in newspaper columns he wrote under the pseudonym Jakim Boor. But the letters and diaries penned by other leaders who felt a need to dialogue with themselves or others simply do not exist. Franco never knew that need, not least because self-doubt rarely disturbed his mind. For insight into his emotional or intellectual life we must turn to the diaries and memoirs of those who worked alongside him. They often admit that his legendary, impenetrable coldness forced them into guesswork.

A rare glimpse of the dictator's inner thoughts appeared in Spanish cinemas in 1942 with the film *Race* (*Raza*), based on an outline written by Franco himself. The title summed up his political preoccupations. The Spanish 'race' could, simply by remaining true to itself, achieve anything it wanted, he argued. It did not need the rest of the world. Indeed, it was only when contaminated by foreign ideas that the race failed. This had been happening ever since French Enlightenment thought had spread to Spain, followed by its bastard offspring: liberalism, democracy, Freemasonry and Marxism.

Race also revealed Franco's mystical embrace of martial martyrdom, with war as the forge for a new nation – a view honed as a colonial army officer in the Spanish protectorate in Morocco. Filmgoers watched a saccharine version of Spanish domesticity in which virile men fought and died defending the nation's reputation, while women supported them, prayed and raised children. Before the father sets off to fight in the then-Spanish colony of Cuba in 1898, one of his sons comments: 'I don't understand how death can be beautiful.' The father answers with a line that expresses Franco's own thoughts: 'Well, it can be. The greater sacrifices are involved, the more beautiful it is to do your duty.'[9] It was revealing that Franco should associate this idea with the most traumatic moment in recent Spanish history, when it lost the remains of a once-great empire in 1898. Returning Spain to lost greatness, indeed, was his primary mission.

Franco's turn to film-making was typical of his wide-ranging, and sometimes catastrophically misplaced, belief in his own knowledge and capacities. Yet it also showed that he was capable of imagining a story and inventing a narrative, even though this always took one form: the hero who wades into danger, ready to give up his life to defend his own and the nation's honour, emerging from it in a state of near saintliness. In fact, this was the narrative he would tell Spaniards about himself. He had previously shown, with a book published in 1922 about his military exploits, *Moroccan War Diary*, that he had the discipline, desire and capacity to write. The book is full of clichés and hackneyed heroics but also reveals an icy emotional switch that served him in battle and in politics. 'In war you must close your heart!' he declares.[10]

Thanks to the survival of guerrilla bands, he did not fully lift Spain's state of war until 1951, giving him ample excuses for keeping his heart closed for many years. In fact, some supposed war measures, like rigid, prepublication press censorship, remained in place until the mid-1960s. His regime continued to execute people until the very end.

His inability to admit to ignorance on matters of which he had no experience was his greatest weakness. This led to terrible economic decisions during his rule, while also making this otherwise untrusting man an easy mark for misguided or fraudulent miracle projects, like the mining of allegedly rich gold seams under Spain or the existence of a secret formula for creating synthetic fuel.

Although Franco did not establish full power over the whole of Spain until 1939, the Francoist era starts in 1936, since its self-defining inaugural event is the armed insurrection which he helped to lead and which sparked the Spanish civil war. Francoism became a mutable concept, but was always driven by the twin aims of returning Spain to greatness and keeping Franco in power. Mostly, it failed at the former. In comparative terms, Spain remained poor and powerless. For the first half of his dictatorship, it was an economic disaster. The later years of the so-called 'Spanish economic miracle' never made up for that. Both Italy and Portugal, the nations to his east and west, outstripped Francoist Spain in per capita GDP growth between 1936 and 1975.[11] Yet two things remained absolute. The regime proclaimed not just that Spanish pride had been restored, but converted that unthinking pride into a virtue. It also made that pride conditional on a single man – Francisco Franco himself.

Franco did, however, successfully impose his peace for over three decades. His Spain was mostly tranquil, at least for those not forced to struggle with violent poverty or purged (like the 15,107 out of 15,860 public servants sacked in Catalonia) and punished for belonging to the losing side.[12] Political and social earthquakes might rock the rest of the world, but life in Francoist Spain – however squalid it was for some – barely seemed to shake. This was partly because Franco's regime, having abandoned other aims, became mostly about the imposition of order, conformity and social conservatism. Otherwise, its main objective was to maintain Franco as a lifelong dictator.

Obedience to church and state produced a remarkable about-turn in piety. Historians looking for a way to describe his sparse political philosophy eventually called it 'National Catholicism'. Decades of control of schools, newspapers, broadcasters and the output of novelists, film-makers and others worked to spread political apathy. Censorship removed public disturbances from sight, even those as banal as routine thuggery on the football pitch.[13] An individual desire to rebel against the moral, sexual and cultural strictures of Franco's regime – which were a faithful reflection of his own extraordinarily conservative home life – lived on in many people but society as a whole was tamed, even subjugated, by the cultural, social, religious and legal imposition of Francoist mores. Nobody in Franco's Spain felt that as keenly as women, whether in their imposed dependency on fathers and husbands, their wider embrace of religiosity, their need to navigate regime rules for the benefit of their children or the punishments meted out to them (but not to men) for adultery.

Franco's own implicit and arrogant claims to be the most important person to bestride the Spanish stage for at least three centuries are right. It is difficult to name others who rival his impact without reaching for the extraordinary string of early modern monarchs who gave Spain the world's first global empire in the fifteenth and sixteenth centuries.

It is tempting to see Franco, with his petty, reactionary mindset and lack of intellectual rigour, as a quirk of history – a mediocre man who got lucky. Yet there was nothing mediocre about the Franco family. A single shared childhood bedroom that produces a national aviation hero (his brother Ramón was a European equivalent to Charles Lindbergh) and a dictator is far from normal.

In fact, Franco can only be understood in the broader context of Spanish history. The 'Two Spains' of conservatism and liberalism that emerged from Spain's War of Independence against Napoleon Bonaparte (1808–1814) were at loggerheads in his childhood home. They were represented by a pious mother and a domineering but politically liberal father who refused to ever be impressed by his own son, however remarkable his feats. A popular poem by Antonio Machado had already claimed that the sometimes bloody stand-off between the Two Spains would 'freeze the hearts' of young Spaniards.[14] The conflict between them was heightened by the acute humiliation – felt especially by Franco's naval family – after a once glorious navy was sunk by the United Sates in brief battles off Cuba and the Philippines in 1898. That was also the end of empire.

Franco's journey from childhood to deathbed is easier to make sense of in terms of this history than as the path taken by an inspirational leader of a modern political project. He was, rather, a reflection of what happens to nations everywhere when they fall from a very great height. Empire is addictive, creating a sense of God-given power, wealth and superiority. Spain is by no means the only nation to have clung to ideas of exceptionality once the empire has gone, as any British-born writer must admit. In that sense, Franco both explains and is explained by Spain's history. He personifies its final, losing battle with colonial decline.

That battle was fought without a firm guiding idea beyond holding on to power. Franco's early expressed enthusiasm for fascist-style totalitarianism would be discarded, though not all the power structures established to promote it were set aside.[15] That said, Franco's early public embrace of totalitarianism was heartfelt, leading his initial regime to be variously described as 'fascist', 'semi-fascist' or 'pseudo-fascist'. In fact, his slow-changing personal dictatorship was always in some way 'fascistised' (as historians of Spain now put it), even if the strength of that gradually diminished. His dictatorship also had plenty of time to evolve, lasting almost twice as long as Benito Mussolini's and three times longer than that of Adolf Hitler.[16]

This biography seeks to understand not just Franco the man, but also to explain Francoism as a society-shaping phenomenon that reflected the dictator's own character and interests above the influence of the factional ebb and flow around him. His personal views on virility, hierarchy, religion or women arguably had a greater and longer impact on the daily lives of Spaniards than his cack-handed dabbling in economics or even his more successful grand agricultural, hydrological or tourism schemes. At its most incongruous, this meant imposing Victorian-era mores and ideas on Spain while the rest of the western world indulged in the social revolution of the swinging sixties and the youth-led political upheavals of the same decade. The widespread existence in Spanish society of something called 'sociological Francoism', a mindset which outlived the dictator, can also not be denied.

Life went on, as it does in authoritarian and dictatorial regimes everywhere. Francoism could be easy to navigate if you were not amongst the impoverished, purged or punished. Indeed, the narrative splits here between civil war winners and the losers for whom life was often far tougher under Franco's vengeful regime. If you did not rock the boat, however, you might easily get by. If you had money then, as always, that became easier. If you sympathised with some of Francoism's core ideas – like religion, nationalism or the importance of obedience to hierarchy – then it became easier still. You could grumble about Francoism, just not too loudly and certainly not if you were preaching its overthrow. 'Most people lived in a state of daily ambiguity towards the regime, with rejection, resignation and passive acceptance of the regime mixed up in each individual,' wrote historian Francisco Sevillano Calero.[17]

The regime often applied its own rules selectively, reflecting Franco's own natural ambiguity. As a result, Spaniards across the decades learned to steer their way through – or past – Francoism, reading its mood, playing at cat-and-mouse and self-censoring. That could also be exhausting. In private, they laughed at its absurdities. Yet they never fully rebelled and even those who chafed against the regime were shaped by it, if only by opposition.[18]

In short, Franco bent Spaniards to his will. They moaned, but mostly did not revolt (a small elite of students, convinced activists and some late-appearing terrorist groups were the exceptions). They had little choice and, at the end of his time, were thrust into a giddying upward spiral of economic growth that meant many were more interested in managing their growing personal prosperity, or release from poverty, than in politics.

In fact, rule-breaking in the form of corruption greased the machinery of Francoism. The caudillo was unconcerned, to the dismay of purists in his own regime. This created an uneven playing field in which the honest and the poor lost out, and others were driven to corruption by need or ambition. All that makes Francoism more like the later dictatorships of Latin America than the more ideologically coherent and coercive totalitarian regimes of Nazi Germany, say, or Stalin's Soviet Union.[19] It is hardly surprising that Chile's General Augusto Pinochet – another ambitious military officer turned dictator – was one of the few heads of state to attend Franco's funeral.

The dictator imposed himself so thoroughly that Francoism could remain almost invisible to foreign visitors unless they themselves broke rules of public decorum (as bikini-clad women in the 1960s did) or chanced upon police exercising their unrestricted and unaccountable power. Visiting statesmen – especially American presidents, for whom massive popular receptions were always organised – were surprised that the dictator could expose himself publicly without fear of assassination.

Freedom is never absolute, nor is repression. One of Franco's tricks was to hold out the idea that some restrictions might be softened (but not lifted entirely) at any time. Given his sluggish decision-making, such promises hung in the air for years. If a softening eventually happened, as with censorship, the opposite threat immediately existed. Restrictions could be reapplied if anyone went too far. In the final decade of Franco's life, faced with outbursts of violence, he declared several states of emergency and issued decrees in which already restricted liberties were suspended.[20]

In those troubled but prosperous years before his death, the Francoist state began creeping back towards where it had started – as a hard-hearted machine for imposing Franco's ideal of order. In most other senses, the Francoist project had been emptied of ideological content to become what one historian called 'bureaucratic authoritarianism'. Even the Vatican turned against the reactionary strain of Catholicism that Franco had made a pillar of his regime.

In the end, then, Francoism was about constraint – of freedom, debate and behaviour – and maintaining the generalísimo's power. Loudly proclaimed ideals – of empire-building, say, or economic autarky – had to be jettisoned, though nobody was permitted to point out that this was exactly what had happened. It is understandable that the initial horror, mid-term greyness and, eventually, tedium of the Franco regime saw Spaniards bury ideas of their own exceptionalism. They knew that Spain was not a leading nation. Franco had failed, at least on his own terms. After the generalísimo's death, however, this realisation helped them shun all kinds of political extremism. So, too, did his successful depoliticisation of Spaniards. The Francoist period thus stilled some of the more destructive passions of the Two Spains, including those embraced and inflamed by Franco himself.

That is the most positive result of Franco's 36 years in power. In fact, the culture of apathy and obedience produced entirely unintended consequences. Since they never rebelled, Spaniards were led into the ensuing democratic transition by their own elites – including many who had served Franco. In that, they were remarkably successful, taking just three years to convert the country into a proper democracy. It also meant Franco's people could ensure their own continued prosperity. In an act of generosity and tolerance by democrats and leftists, they even won guarantees that nobody would judge or blame them for what they had done.

It is remarkable that the only significant apology for its role in the imposition of Francoism through a civil war came from the same Roman Catholic church that, due to its thousands of murdered priests, was also the clearest victim of Leftist excesses during the same war. In death, however, it was as if Franco alone had been responsible for a 36-year dictatorship. Elsewhere, there was no question of recognising errors or accepting personal guilt for aiding in the restriction of liberties or the mass shedding of Spanish blood. In life, famously, Franco did not make mistakes. His changes of direction were presented as proof of infinite wisdom rather than the failure of what he had done before.

The generalísimo certainly never felt a need for contrition. Instead, at his death he pardoned 'those who declared themselves my enemies' and warned that 'the enemies of Spain and of Christian Civilisation are on alert.' In his belief that Spain was under constant assault from foreigners trying to grind it down with their poisonous ideas or threatened violence, he remained utterly unchanged and unapologetic.[21]

I

El Desastre

FERROL, GALICIA, 3 JULY, 1898

Naval supply officer Nicolás Franco's three-storey house in the narrow, elongated grid of streets inside the walled Atlantic port of Ferrol, north-west Spain, was solid but unexceptional. With its granite exterior and glassed-in top-floor gallery jutting above the street, this was a good middle-class dwelling in a modest town. Inside, however, it was far from usual. By 1898, the narrow building squeezed between similar blocks at 136 Maria Street housed a collection of children with remarkable futures: Spain's national leader for 36 years; a pioneering hero of transatlantic aviation; an ambassador; and a bossy sister who, despite being third in age, sometimes imposed her will on the rest. The children were overseen by their conspicuously pious mother, Pilar Bahamonde, and by the family's brilliant, mercurial and authoritarian patriarch, Don Nicolás - whose courtesy title 'Don' reflected his social standing. A fifth child, a green-eyed girl called Paz, was still in her mother's womb and would die five years later, afflicted by an illness that doctors could not identify, but which made her lungs wheeze. A stricken Pilar Bahamonde was temporarily 'mad with grief', according to her daughter.[1]

Outwardly, the least remarkable member of this household was the short and stick-like future dictator, Francisco Franco Bahamonde. In such a small town, people knew that the two surnames he received from his parents reflected the fusion of two families who had long provided senior officers to the navy administrative corps. Such things mattered in Ferrol, which lay at the end of a fourteen-kilometre-long sea loch of the kind that punctuate the Atlantic seaboard of Galicia, in Spain's rain-lashed north-west corner. The drab, granite-coloured town, encased in a six-kilometre wall, was a military ghetto where everything revolved around the Spanish navy. Ferrol had become one of its three major mainland bases and shipbuilding centres early in the eighteenth century, and the Franco family had been there ever since, as Ferrol developed into an important naval facility surrounded by a provincial town that now shared national delusions about Spain's global power and importance.

Ferrol was unaware on 3 July 1898 that dramatic events elsewhere were reshaping the future of Spain, of its once glamorous navy and of the family at 136 María Street. This was the day that, in waters off Cuba, the country's most potent naval flotilla was destroyed by the world's upstart power, the United States of America. In this navy town, it was also the day where many lost the heads of their household, friends and close relatives.

That morning, Admiral Pascual Cervera had ordered his flotilla to flee Cuba's Bay of Santiago. He knew his vessels could neither outgun nor outrun the Americans who stood off its narrow entrance, but still hoped that some might escape. The admiral had long realised the futility of fighting the Americans. 'We are heading towards a useless sacrifice,' he wrote to a friend before leaving Spain. 'If I should die, as seems probable, please look after my wife and children.' Such worries were overridden by those who clung to ideas of Spanish exceptionality. The navy's Quixotic concept of honour did not help. A few years earlier, Admiral Castro Méndez Núñez had been applauded for declaring that it was 'better to save your honour and lose your boats than to lose your honour and save your boats'.[2]

The battle became what Americans already called a 'turkey shoot', when birds were tied up and shot at in fairgrounds. Commodore William Sampson's fleet sat off the mouth of the bay, shelling the thinly protected Spanish vessels and hunting them down as they struggled to pick up steam. All six warships were lost and 343 men died. Admiral Cervera, despite his prediction, did not, becoming one of many who, exhausted, swam to the shore.[3] Most vessels were run aground by their crews to disable them before capture. Only one American sailor died.

Spain's most important colony, sugar-rich Cuba, was lost. The action was a near-repeat of the sinking of the Pacific squadron in Manila Bay two months earlier, on 1 May 1898, which soon led to the loss of Spain's other major colony, the Philippines. In that case, Commodore George Dewey sank eight of thirteen Spanish boats in a few hours (reportedly with a pause for breakfast) at the cost of just eight American sailors injured. Spaniards had blamed the commander, Rear Admiral Patricio Montojo, for that. The Cuban defeat, however, was incontrovertible proof of a deeper malaise. It also meant the certain loss of neighbouring Puerto Rico and the end of empire altogether.

Spain's self-esteem sank with its navy. Five centuries of imperial glory were gone. The fall from such giddy heights was hard and poisoned politics for decades. The Franco children were acutely aware of this and the idea of returning this fallen Spain to greatness shaped young Francisco's future.

In a few short hours, a new world order had been confirmed. It had taken a concerted effort by politicians like Theodore Roosevelt, along with newspaper magnates William Randolph Hearst and Joseph Pulitzer, to whip up war fever. Hearst's newspapers turned the mysterious but probably accidental sinking of the USS *Maine* cruiser (and deaths of 268 sailors) in Havana's port into a Spanish attack. Americans soon rallied to the cry: 'Remember the *Maine*! To hell with Spain!'[4]

Spanish newspapers had been similarly boosterish, deriding the 'backward and uncivilised' Americans and driving politicians towards fatal misjudgements. Initially, almost all Spain backed war. 'Spain made America, as God made the world,' wrote the former president Emilio Castelar. 'America will be Spanish forever.' A young diarist, María de Echarri Martínez, noted that the 'Yankee pig' would be savaged by 'the Spanish lion'.[5]

With up to 200,000 Spanish troops in Cuba and the pre-war US standing army at just 28,000 men, such optimism had seemed justified. Few people were aware of the navy's weakness – including the lack of armour-plating that protected its vessels – or of the depths of Cuban desire for independence. Yet even those who foresaw defeat preferred this to a surrender that might destroy a fragile Spanish monarchy led by 12-year-old King Alfonso XIII under the regency of his mother

Maria Cristina and a top-heavy social order which feared revolution. Cervera himself declared it 'an honourable disaster', returning to the idea that honour was more valuable than victory. At a time when western nations arrogantly claimed a duty to civilise the world by colonising it (while conveniently extracting wealth), Spain no longer had a role.

Spaniards had been wallowing in what a contemporary termed 'a tub of romantic history'. From the legendary medieval knight El Cid to Columbus, the conquistadors of Latin America and the centuries of empire, Spaniards had seen their greatness as divinely ordained. 'It was axiomatic that God, with inexhaustible largesse, had given us all that is magnificent and desirable on earth; riches, fertility, a delicious climate, the gift of fruit, illustrious talent, courage and beauty, everything except good government,' according to one Spanish writer.[6] With that image now shattered, a fuse was lit that turned the house in María Street into the explosive origin of some of Spain's most remarkable twentieth-century stories.

'The hangover from the loss of colonies accompanied me through that [early] part of my life,' Francisco Franco said later, referring to 'the unjust criticisms of '98' and the ensuing disparagement of the army and navy. More explicitly, he blamed this on foreigners, 'foreign ideas' and, somewhat bizarrely, on Freemasonry – which had attracted a small membership that included some influential Spanish liberals but in the rest of the world had largely stopped being the centre of wild conspiracy theories.[7]

The combined events became known as El Desastre, 'the disaster', of 1898. Between them, they crystallised the long decline of a proud global superpower that had spent much of the century arguing over why other countries were leaving it behind. That this argument greatly exaggerated the degree to which Spain lagged in terms of economic and social development was beside the point. The impassioned breast-beating and bitter disagreement amongst Spanish elites over how to revive the nation's fortunes exposed older fault lines provoked by the Enlightenment's clash with tradition. It mattered little that many, if not most, Spaniards did not really care or that Madrid's bullfights had continued without incident after the Manila news.[8]

Cuba's sugar industry had been one of the motors of the Spanish economy, part-financing the industrial revolution at home. The

Caribbean island felt so close that the six-time prime minister Antonio Cánovas del Castillo had declared it 'Spain's Alsace-Lorraine'. The *La Epoca* newspaper had foreseen in 1897 that 'Spain without Cuba ... would enter a period of rapid and inevitable decadence.' But the struggle to keep Cuba had been costly. One early calculation estimated that a third of the 200,000 Spanish troops sent to fight Cuban insurgents died, mostly from yellow fever or other illnesses. Battlefield encounters accounted for just one in fifteen deaths in an army where corruption was rampant and medical services worse than basic.[9]

On the field, however, Spanish officers were expected to lead from the front and, if necessary, die gloriously. A 20-year-old British subaltern called Winston Churchill briefly joined the Spanish side to observe the campaign against insurgents seeking Cuban independence in December 1895. He was impressed by their disdain for danger. Churchill watched as the general in command, Alvaro Suarez Valdés, rode to within 500 yards of the enemy. 'The General, a very brave man – a white and gold uniform on a grey horse – drew a great deal of fire onto us and I heard enough bullets whistle and hum past to satisfy me for some time to come,' he wrote. Churchill was awarded Spain's Military Medal for his brief intervention.[10]

For young Francisco Franco and his friends, the Disaster was shockingly real. One of Francisco's childhood companions and future ministers, Camilo Alonso Vega, lost his father on the cruiser *Vizcaya*. The injured and maimed were disembarked in Ferrol. Franco's second cousin, neighbour and future aide-de-camp, Francisco Franco Salgado Araujo – known as Pacón (big Francisco) to differentiate him from Paquito (little Francisco, as the future caudillo was known) – turned eight years old in 1898, the year his cousin turned six. He recalled 'my own terrible sadness, a reflection of my hometown, where most of the crew of those [defeated] naval squadrons were from'.[11] In María Street, Cuba felt closer than parts of mainland Spain. It was now a source of bemused conversation. Where had Spain gone wrong?

'The Navy is dead... What remains of it is, with a few exceptions, useless,' Franco's conservative great-uncle Manuel Baamonde, another navy supply officer, wrote in a book published the following year that must have sat on a shelf in María Street (it was dedicated to Franco's maternal grandfather, Don Ladislao, who eventually occupied the ground floor).

Baamonde blamed weak-willed politicians (and was amongst the last in the family to consistently spell his surname without the 'h'). In 1899, when he was writing, just over 50 fighting vessels were left, mostly poorly armoured and of limited range. As popular opinion turned against the military, Baamonde warned that if politicians left Spain 'without an army or navy, we risk losing the few things that we still have.' Like many conservatives, he feared Spain was on a path to further disaster as nationalists in Catalonia and the Basque Country also threatened it from inside. The country was destroying the legacy of Isabella of Castile, the remarkable fifteenth-century queen 'who unified Spain and gave it the New World'. Young Francisco imbibed this reactionary mindset, which blamed meddling politicians for betraying a country of God-endowed greatness.[12]

In fact, to live in Ferrol was to bear daily witness to Spain's dwindling stature. Almost a hundred vessels had to be decommissioned (or were sunk or grounded) between 1898 and 1900. Some had been built in Ferrol's shipyard, which struggled to produce the era's new armoured vessels but still did repairs and fitted out vessels built elsewhere. The fleet's most prestigious vessel, the protected cruiser *Carlos V*, failed to join the international flotilla in Portsmouth harbour for Queen Victoria's funeral in 1901. It broke down on the way, and had to return to Ferrol. 'Everything is broken in this unhappy country; there is no government, no electorate, no political parties; no army, no navy; all is fiction, all decadence, all ruins,' the *Correo* newspaper wrote on 7 February that year.[13]

The Disaster augmented the yawning political divide between the Two Spains that had emerged earlier in the nineteenth century. On one side stood supposedly progressive liberals who wished to imitate the thrusting, secular, industrialised and rapidly-modernising 'western' states of the age. On the other side were conservatives who believed Spain had turned soft under the influence of the ideas of semi-pagan foreigners and that it urgently needed to rediscover its true, historic and religious soul. 'Here lies half of Spain, the other side killed it,' the acerbic journalist Mariano José de Larra had written in a biting graveyard sketch marking All Saints Day in 1836. The Two Spains were starkly present inside the Franco house, where the abrasive and intelligent Commissar Franco was notoriously 'liberal in ideology and behaviour', according to his daughter. This contrasted with his pious wife's clasping to the old certainties of tradition and church.[14]

The house itself originally belonged to Francisco's paternal grandfather, who rose to the top of the navy's supply arm, as '*intendente general*', equivalent to a vice-admiral. On the other side of the family, the maternal grandfather Don Ladislao Bahamonde had done exactly the same. The tall-tale-telling Ladislao eventually died as the oldest admiral in Spain, aged 93, after eating so much chorizo sausage in a local taberna that it 'burst his blood vessels', according to Francisco's bossy sister Pilar. After the death of their maternal grandmother, Don Ladislao occupied the ground floor, surrounded by his collection of armour and the books carefully kept in a glass cabinet. He was a steady, conservative contrast to the father: so contrasting, indeed, that the wild and rebellious Ramón felt particularly close to him.[15]

The family lived on the upper two floors, furnished in what Spaniards call, after the mid-nineteenth-century Queen Isabella II, the 'Isabelline' style – heavy, dark wooden furniture, with chairs and sofas in red brocade. Flowers from the market, which were cheap in well-watered Galicia, decorated the house for much of the year. A fully stocked kitchen housed a wood-fired stove and two 25-litre wooden water casks which were filled at the public fountain. Unlike other Spaniards of their time, the family suffered no shortages, but there was little luxury. An officer's salary did not run that far, at least not with four children to raise – though there was an ounce of chocolate each twice a week. A seamstress visited to make or repair clothes and washerwomen took away the laundry. Francisco shared an upstairs room with his young brother Ramón. On the frequent rainy days, the children played hide and seek or *policías y ladrones* (cops and robbers) in the huge wardrobes or in the attic, which looked out over tiled rooftops and chimneys. It was packed with trunks full of old navy uniforms that served for dressing up and, presumably, for Francisco to fantasise about the day when he, too, might wear the crisp white or blue outfits.[16]

The navy elite was close-knit, with the Franco family a perfect example of its intense endogamy. Such was the genetic entanglement that Pacón, who was two years older, was both a second cousin and a cousin once removed to little Francisco. The family was not, however, as elite or glorious as Francisco would have liked. *Intendentes* were pen-pushing accountants, not fighting men. Nor were they especially wealthy, unless corrupt. Like generations of Spanish hidalgos ('sons of someone') they could also count their riches in social prestige. The Disaster of 1898, however, and the humiliation of the navy reduced their status considerably.

Small and thin, Francisco Franco was known by diminutives like Paquito, Franquito or *cerrillito* ('little matchstick'). He navigated the stormy, bruising atmosphere imposed on the house by his father by staying out of trouble. Don Nicolás was 'always excessively demanding and severe with his children' as well as 'very clever but eccentric', according to Pacón, who spent much time in the house after his own parents died young. 'He never boasted about his children's merits, nor gave much importance to their successes, despite the fact that they often gave him reasons to feel proud.'[17] In fact, Don Nicolás resolutely refused to be impressed by Francisco, whose maternally induced narrow-mindedness offended him. This paternal disdain pursued Francisco through his life.

Don Nicolás lost his temper easily, especially when contradicted.[18] The most violent clashes were between his father and the 'quick-witted but inattentive' elder brother, also called Nicolás, who would reputedly be forced to lie under a sofa if he brought bad marks back from school. The bright, rebellious and outgoing younger brother Ramón was the garrulous father's favourite. Francisco could not compete. According to their sister Pilar, Nicolás was 'brilliant, intelligent and a good student' if also 'very naughty and very lazy', while Francisco (also known as 'Paco') dutifully got by at school. 'The truth is that there was nothing brilliant about Paco,' she said. 'He was meticulous; good at drawing but otherwise quite average, quite ordinary ... a nice lad, of a happy disposition, thoughtful; he took his time answering questions but was playful,' his cousins recalled. He and the 'naughty madcap' Ramón fought so fiercely that Francisco allegedly bore a mark on one ear left by his younger brother's teeth. Pilar considered herself a figure of authority. 'I ordered them around like the commander-in-chief and smacked anyone who misbehaved and didn't do what I said,' she admitted later. Her mother, on the other hand, had been 'the best and most patient person in the world' with her children.[19]

Francisco was his mother's boy, accompanying her dutifully to Mass (without showing signs of being especially pious himself) and becoming the child most attached to her. Pilar was handsome, devout, sweet-natured, kindly and energetic. 'He adored her,' Pilar said. 'Our mother had far more influence on his upbringing ... they were very close.' That did not make him weak or malleable, nor did he specially enjoy praying. Francisco was 'obedient, well-behaved and affectionate ... [and] quiet, which doesn't mean he was timid', according to his sister. He was also, Ramón would say later, 'a prig' and a 'goody-goody'.[20]

Don Nicolás felt shackled by a wife whose pious religiosity (she attended two masses a day) must have filled him with scorn. His high opinion of himself, meanwhile, meant he cared little about others, which made him unpopular in the navy.[21] For young Francisco, he was that endlessly frustrating target of ambition – the person who resolutely refuses to be impressed. Right until his dying day, indeed, Franco's father remained far more pleased with himself than with his high-achieving son.

Obedience, respect and an ability to dissemble became the survival tools of a straw-weight boy with jug ears who stood just 5 feet 4 inches tall. Francisco must have emerged from adolescence weighing barely 100 pounds. A congenital defect – a narrow palate and a deviated septum – gave him a weak, high-pitched voice that stayed with him for life and added to his weedy image.[22]

The dramatic contrast between Franco's physique and the way he later imposed himself on Spanish history has tempted observers to see a lifelong attempt to compensate for humiliations inflicted by his own body. Yet turn-of-the-century Spaniards were not tall, and Ramón was even shorter at 5 foot 2 inches (though his green eyes would later dazzle female admirers). A slight palate defect was a relatively minor disadvantage at a time when – like Franco's youngest sister Paz – a good number of children did not survive infancy.[23] Humiliation and its poisonous sibling, vengeful pride, were more likely to have been generated by his father than by his body.

Francisco was tougher than he looked. Pilar ('who would have made an excellent commander-in-chief if she had been a man', according to their cousins) recalled him stoically standing the pain of having a red-hot pin applied to his skin during a childish game of physical endurance. When he fell off a cupboard and knocked himself out, the first thing he said on coming back to consciousness was: 'You all seem terrified. I'm not dead yet.' She admired his pluck.[24]

Francisco showed a modest talent for problem-solving, drawing and mathematics, but never amazed anyone with his intellect or creativity in the small private schools run by former navy officers in Ferrol. That naval emphasis on problem-solving, however, was better than the rote-learning favoured in other Spanish schools.[25]

In fact, it was the energetic and demanding father who personally ensured his children had a broader education than their peers. At weekends, he forced them out of the house and took them on long, exhausting walks up the green hills above Ferrol and its rugged bay. He talked non-stop, spewing information and explaining everything from soil types, trees, plants and birds to electricity, telegraphs or telephones. Vessels of all kinds populated the bay, from twelve- or fourteen-oar wooden *trainera* fishing boats to the latest iron-clad battleships. Don Nicolás gave them 'magnificent lessons on the naval history of Ferrol', according to Pacón, who tagged along with the man who was now his own guardian. He also provided detailed descriptions of the vessels they could see, full of technical explanations of how everything worked. Much of it may have stuck in Francisco's mind since he was later deemed to have 'an astonishing memory', according to one of his doctors.[26]

Pacón lived at the maternal grandparents' house a few streets away and was part of a wide but close-knit network of uncles, aunts, cousins and grandparents, most of whom lived in Ferrol. They were part of the Franco children's everyday lives, but his childhood was not something Franco later dwelled on. 'That was not the period of his life that he looked back on with the greatest affection,' his daughter Carmen said. Only his intense dislike of his eccentric, well-read father – the domestic version of an enlightened absolutist despot – can explain this. In this scenario, Francisco became his mother's impotent protector, storing up hatred for his father.[27]

We do not know when he first became aware of his father's pursuit of other women, but this realisation, whenever it came, can only have increased his disdain. Francisco had certainly not yet discovered that his father also had a secret fourth son, an elder boy who was born after Don Nicolás got a 14-year-old girl pregnant in the years before his marriage. He would eventually consider loose morality and political liberalism two of his, and Spain's, greatest enemies.

In Ferrol, as Francisco later pointed out, 'all the children of our age were friends': by which he meant those of his class. In fact, Ferrol's population of 25,000 was divided into distinct social ghettoes. Franco and his like did not mix with the children of the town's fishermen, skilled dock-workers or non-ranking sailors. 'Anyone who wasn't from the navy, or a navy family, faced a kind of discrimination,' said his niece, Pilar Jaraiz, who remembered that girls of six or seven would refuse to play with the daughters of shopkeepers or merchants. Ferrol had 'more hierarchy than [the saints in] heaven', according to another contemporary.[28]

In the summer, the children rented rowing boats to fish in the bay or a launch to take them to the beach. They played catch, hide-and-seek, kite-flying, spinning tops and fought mock battles with slings and stones in the streets and squares of Ferrol. One square was overlooked by a statue to Cosme Churruca, a heroic Spanish captain who had died fighting the Royal Navy at Trafalgar in 1805 (nine of the fifteen Spanish vessels involved had been based in Ferrol). The Franco family claimed blood ties to him and to another famous martyr from the same engagement, Dionisio Alcalá-Galiano.[29] Dying in battle, young Franco learned, was a glorious thing.

He also learned to take pride in the way Spaniards, who had been dragged into the Trafalgar debacle by a dominant Napoleon Bonaparte, had joined together to eject the French in a successful war of independence between 1808 and 1814 (known as the Peninsular War to the British, who sent troops led by Sir John Moore and the future Duke of Wellington, Arthur Wellesley). Yet that victory had also exposed deep fissures. Spaniards had fought and died for the return of Ferdinand VII, known as El Deseado, 'The Desired One'. In his absence, they had drawn up a radically ambitious constitution – the Constitution of Cadiz – in which sovereignty was no longer exercised exclusively by the monarch. Instead, it resided in 'the nation', meaning the Spanish people.[30] On his return, Ferdinand VII threw out the constitution and returned to royal absolutism. The constitution's supporters became known as *liberales* and were persecuted or forced into exile. The ensuing decades saw the pendulum of Spanish politics jerk violently back and forth between various forms of absolutism and liberalism amid dozens of 'pronunciamientos', attempted military coups. In the meantime, countries from Argentina to Mexico followed the logic of the Cadiz constitution to proclaim, with their own *gritos* ('shouts') of independence, that they were now sovereign. These losses were widely seen as the monarch's problem: the idea that Spain and its empire belonged to the people, rather than the monarch, had not yet taken sufficient root for them to feel a personal sense of loss. They were the monarch's lands, and he had lost them.[31]

In the meantime, Spain had moved from monarchy to Republic and back again, amidst crumbling faith in key institutions. Three devastating civil wars during the nineteenth century saw the Enlightenment-hating, red-beret-wearing Carlists rebel in an attempt to impose strict Catholicism and a different royal line on the throne (nominally as a result of an argument over whether a woman, Isabel II, should be allowed to sit on it). Those wars provoked some 200,000 deaths across Spain.

Since 1876, in an attempt to bring stability, the two main political parties and the restored monarchy had run a sham democracy known as the 'peaceful turn', based on fixed elections which allowed them to take turns in government. Thuggish provincial bosses known as *caciques* used bribery, fraud, strong-arming and ballot-stuffing to ensure the 'correct' results. This provided stability but promoted cynicism about politics. Opponents resorted to violence. Anarchism became the sometimes violent expression of working-class grievance as smoke-stack industries and urban poverty spread through cities like Barcelona, Bilbao and Valencia. When anarchist Santiago Salvador hurled two bombs during a performance of Rossini's *William Tell* at Barcelona's Liceu Opera House in 1893, he killed some twenty members of the city's burgeoning bourgeoisie. In 1897, anarchist gunman Michele Angiolillo killed prime minister Antonio Cánovas del Castillo, the chief architect of the corrupt 'peaceful turn': he was one of four prime ministers to be assassinated between 1870 and 1921.[32]

Other non-conservative credos were spreading. The Socialist Workers Party (PSOE) and its trades union, the General Workers Union (UGT), had both been formed over the previous two decades by Pablo Iglesias, a man born into Ferrol's working class a generation before Franco. The young Francisco may also have been aware of growing working-class militancy, since a wave of strikes spurred by the Disaster began in Ferrol and Valencia in 1899, subsequently spreading to the country's major cities over the next few years; by 1902, martial law had been declared in several provinces and battleships were being used as jails after a general strike in Barcelona.³³

Ferrol's poor barely scraped a living, as Francisco knew. 'I remember the impact on me as a child of seeing the extremely low standard of living of the water women,' he wrote later. 'After standing in long lines before the fountains in public squares, in every kind of weather, they earned only fifteen céntimos for bearing twenty-five-litre jars of water on their heads up to apartments. Or the example of the women in the port who unloaded coal from ships for a peseta a day.'³⁴

Two-thirds of Spaniards were illiterate and most lived in country towns and villages where the high politics of Madrid or distant naval battles barely touched their existence. In some parts, the power of landowners over people's lives dwarfed that of the state. Yet by 1898 Spaniards generally believed sovereignty resided in the nation and its people, not just in the king. That idea extended to Spain's few remaining colonies, meaning that Cuba now seemed like part of their communal property. Its loss, unlike that of the earlier colonies, felt shared and personal.³⁵

While the sensation of national crisis and division was abundantly apparent in Ferrol, the fractious Two Spains were also present in the domestic dramas of the Franco household. Much later, during one of his few autobiographical musings, Franco described his parents as 'typical of their time: when the men were severe, exacting, authoritarian and cold about religion, which they deemed a female affair; [while] the women were virtuous, believers, faithful ... and protectors of children for whom they often had to perform the role of both mother and father.' At home, this meant Sunday Mass with their mother ('an old-fashioned lady, of the kind who have their name on a prayer-bench in church', according to Franco's daughter Carmen) followed by long, vigorous walks with their father.³⁶

Little Francisco shared some of his mother's religiosity, even weeping at his own first communion – the start of a tendency towards public lachrymosity as a rare, if sometimes performative, display of emotion. Occasionally, he was punished by his father, who thought nothing of clipping a child, and Francisco would become furious if he thought it was undeserved. Don Nicolás had served in the Philippines and regaled his children with stories about the country as he pumped them full of knowledge during their long walks.

While Nicolás Franco stretched his children's minds, their mother taught them to live in 'holy fear of God'. Although he was not yet pious, Francisco was the only son to take this to heart. In fact, he became easily the most socially conservative of them, a direct consequence of also being the one who most doted on her. From their mother's side of the family, he also learned that there were three demons, listed by his sister Pilar as: 'Atheism, Freemasonry and communism ... [which] are, basically, the same.' The obsession with Freemasons – long cast as enemies of Spain's Roman Catholic church – was primitive and impulsive. Yet from an early age, Francisco Franco 'saw something in that [Freemasonry] which repulsed him', Pilar claimed.[37]

Nicolás Franco's impatience with his wife matched that of anti-clerical liberals with Spain itself. As they looked around Europe, they saw countries that had embraced industrial innovation, adventurous capitalism, empire-building, state secularism and social modernity. The might of nations was measured by their colonies. Even Spain's much smaller Iberian neighbour Portugal had swathes of Africa, including Angola, Mozambique and Guinea Bissau, and Asian outposts in Goa and East Timor. At home, liberals saw a nation hobbled by a fossilised social hierarchy, monarchy and the church. Outside the big cities, change came at a snail's pace. Film-maker Luis Buñuel, speaking of his hometown of Calanda in Aragon, claimed that 'the Middle Ages only ended with the First World War'.[38]

At exam time in the years up to 1907, Franco travelled by boat with his classmate and elder cousin Pacón to nearby La Coruña – a bigger port city where schools could oversee public examinations – and stayed with Don Nicolás's eccentric, cultured and famously miserly sister, Gilda, whose lady servant walked a couple of steps behind her. Gilda was also Francisco's godmother, though that did not stop her making him and Pacón sleep on a mattress on the floor. Another aunt was abbess at one of the city's convents, where abundant teas were to be had. Francisco passed the exams, allowing him to apply to military cadet academies. Pacón flunked.[39]

When Franco's father was posted to Madrid in 1907, his wife stayed behind. In moving, Nicolás abandoned his family to live with his mistress – a woman whom his daughter Pilar called 'a certain Agustina'. This was schoolteacher Agustina Aldana, described as 'a modest village woman ... of infinite patience', whose 'niece' shared their apartment in Fuencarral Street amid rumours that she was another illegitimate half-sibling to the future dictator. In conservative Ferrol, it was a major scandal and a humiliation to young Francisco. He was acutely aware that it publicly shamed his mother – a social, personal and moral cross that she bore with dignity. The maids gossiped about how Don Nicolás had informally 'married' his lover during a party in the garden of a popular Madrid tavern. Other children teased them about having no father. We do not know how Francisco reacted, but he was developing a thin-skinned pride that was easily wounded. His little brother Ramón hated it, forever deeming Ferrol a mean and gossipy place.[40]

Either way, the battle lines were drawn. Francisco's exuberant brothers were closer in character to their father, but it was clear which Spain Francisco belonged to. His father represented betrayal, liberalism and admiration of evils like Freemasonry: everything Francisco came to hate. As he approached manhood, Francisco Franco would seek his role models elsewhere.

2

Cadet

ALCÁZAR DE TOLEDO, JULY 1907

In July 1907, fourteen-year-old Francisco Franco once again caught the boat out of Ferrol's sea loch to La Coruña, this time accompanied by his father Nicolás. From there, they travelled by train to Madrid and then on to the infantry cadet college housed in the Alcázar castle in Toledo, central Spain, where he took and passed the college's entry exam. Young Franco had wanted to follow family tradition by joining the navy, but by the time he wanted to apply for the navy cadet school in Ferrol, that was no longer an option. The aftershocks of 1898 were still rippling through the armed forces, and admissions to the cadet school were restricted by an impecunious government.[1]

Francisco thus became the first to break family custom, applying for a place at the Toledo infantry school. He was one of the youngest applicants – a sign of a talent for passing exams, even if he never did so brilliantly.[2] An infantry career considerably increased his chances of experiencing real warfare, an exciting thought that soon shaped his ideas of virility and patriotism. For all their social airs, intellectual arrogance and impressive ranks, after all, his *intendente* father and forebears were really just uniformed accountants.

Initially, however, Franco was resentful. He had already imbibed the military's knee-jerk dislike of the politicians who controlled them and their funding. That was the standard mindset of Ferrol's frustrated navy elites who, with officer recruitment now slowed, suddenly saw their children's futures disrupted. 'No-one could understand why, since the country was at precisely that moment building a new squadron, which meant there would be a need, in the short-term, for more officers,' Franco said later.³

For the young Francisco Franco, the country beyond his home province remained a mystery. Like most people in a land traversed by wide rivers and high mountain chains, he had barely travelled beyond it. Indeed, as his train climbed onto the high Spanish flatlands known as the 'meseta', he discovered that much of the country was hot and dry, with the summer sun burning into a dusty landscape. It was very different to the rain-fed Atlantic greenery of home. At Toledo, he would soon learn that the meseta's bitter winters are even harsher than the summer and that the climate switches rapidly from one to the other.⁴

The journey was not fun. His father's lack of 'intimacy and attentiveness' made it emotionally uncomfortable, he said later. Perhaps Francisco also intuited that his father's move to Madrid from El Ferrol that year was more than just a temporary departure. Carriages, pulled by six horses, awaited them at Toledo's station, the only transport strong enough to cope with the city's steep streets. Father and son spent two weeks there while Franco completed his exams and cadet uniforms were ordered. They wandered Toledo's narrow streets and visited its historic cathedral, decorated with trophies from medieval battles. There is no evidence of young Franco appreciating Toledo's wealth of religious art – epitomised by the mystical work of El Greco – but he must certainly have sensed the weight of history in Castile's early-medieval capital.⁵

The infantry school occupied the austere and imposing sixteenth-century Alcázar fortress that loomed above the city and the curling River Tagus and had been recently restored after a fire gutted the building in 1887.⁶

In the bumptious and bullying atmosphere of a military academy, Franco was a child among men. Of the 350 cadets in his year, only about forty were aged under sixteen. Some students were already in their twenties. Given his height, he was handed a Mauser rifle with fifteen centimetres of its barrel sawn off to drill with. He felt humiliated by the child-sized weapon and borrowed proper rifles whenever he could. Hazing was standard, and fellow pupils picked on him. He was tied to his bed, or thrown out of it and had this books hidden. Cadets rose early and were often sleep-deprived. Petty rules meant they were continually punished. He had few friends. It was, he recalled later, 'a true Calvary'.[7]

The small, frail-looking boy drew on personal arrogance and the resilience acquired under the roof of a despotic patriarch in order to survive, though he never forgot the cruelty and humiliation. His pride was frequently wounded, not least because, as his cousin Pacón later commented, 'he had such a high opinion of himself.' Like father, in this case, like son. The academy was also a rite of passage. The one time he reportedly responded to taunts with violence, he found himself in front of the commander, but refused to name anyone else, accepted his punishment and won respect. Franco thus entered his adulthood in uniform and in adversity. For good or for bad, the army became his family.[8]

Training was mostly carried out by young lieutenants who served as 'assistant' instructors to lazy and largely absent senior officers. One instructor, the military intellectual and writer Antonio García Pérez, urged cadets to 'think each day about what the patio arches of the barracks represent, about the bronze inscriptions that adorn the walls, about the past glory once present in the very rooms in which you now walk'. They should 'capture the spirit and let it take you through history, revering and admiring those who in this very Alcázar earned worldwide respect'. The cadet school, in other words, was a place where Spain's once magnificent empire lived on – if only in the imagination.[9]

Franco's own words, written down decades later, echoed this uncannily. 'These glorious places, with their ancient stones, lifted my spirit and overwhelmed me,' he said. 'Right there, in the birthplace of the Spanish infantry and faced with its glories, my previous dreams of the navy drifted way and I felt that I would be doing something important with my life.'[10]

Franco learned not just the history of recent wars between French and Germans or Russians and Japanese, but also the great legends of Spanish military history – from Hannibal's campaigns to the feats of the sixteenth-century general Gonzalo Fernández de Córdoba, known as the Great Captain, who had led triumphant Spanish armies across Italy.[11]

Yet if Franco's spirit was inspired, his brain was not. Little was done to encourage practical thinking. Instead, students had to memorise and repeat sections from their textbooks. After Franco went to the library and read up on fortifications in order to give a fuller presentation than was available from his textbook, he was scolded for not following the correct text. Rote-learning was dull but not difficult for someone who prepared each lesson in case he was called on to regurgitate a list of facts, rules or approved battlefield tactics. He studied just enough to pass exams, wanting 'to learn, but not go too far', he said.[12] One cadet recalled him as 'taciturn, quiet, not at all brilliant … with a squeaky voice.'[13]

The only instructor he expressly admired taught law, providing a simple clarity on both military and civilian rules which he relied on later in life. Apart from that, the most exciting moment was the visit of a hero of either the Cuban or Philippines wars who had won a medal that Franco himself later coveted with passion, the Great Laureate Cross of San Fernando. 'He had fought hand-to-hand with the enemy and conserved on his head glorious scars from machete strikes,' Franco recalled later.[14]

The curriculum showed that little had been learned from fighting such insurgents in Cuba and the Philippines, where guerrilla-style opponents had inflicted serious damage. This was despite the fact that these problems were not merely historical: Spanish troops were now engaged in a similar struggle in the mountains of northern Morocco, trying to impose their authority on the Riffian tribesmen there as part of a wider European carve-up of north-west Africa. The Rif Mountains were an inhospitable place whose war-like inhabitants reacted angrily to the Spanish presence. Franco saw it as an opportunity to restore the military pride lost in Cuba and the Philippines and, he wrote, to 'repair the unfair criticism over 1898'.[15]

This so-called 'pacification' campaign in Morocco provoked excitement amongst the Toledo cadets, with Franco earnestly hoping 'that we might soon become combatants' (since, in earlier wars, cadets had been sent into battle before completing their training). At the academy, however, Franco still learned the traditional dogma, soon practised to disastrous effect in World War I, of frontal attacks in formation on fortified positions. Later, he observed that such tactics turned Spanish soldiers in Morocco into 'highly desirable' targets.[16]

The values he acquired were, in the long run, more impactful than the skills. Ideas of heroism and patriotism shaped him most, though the hard grind of surviving adversity and upholding personal pride were also crucial. Love of the fatherland and military obedience substituted the flawed paternal role model of Don Nicolás. García Pérez urged them to bring 'to your sentiments something beyond reason and inspiring in your will something that intelligence cannot elucidate'. In other words, men enamoured of their own cleverness, like Don Nicolás, were inferior to those who made a spiritual leap of faith to love their *patria*. War itself was noble, purifying and necessary.[17]

It was not a uniquely Spanish sentiment: similar ideas would soon propel millions of Europeans to their deaths in the trenches of the First World War. Yet Spain's historic view of itself as forged in the armed defence of Christianity made this semi-mystical idea of war especially enticing. Franco learned from men like García Pérez that, for centuries, Spain had been a 'nation of perpetual Crusade, the sentry of Christian civilization'.[18]

This was not the only viewpoint available to cadets, however, and other instructors drew from Spain's long nineteenth-century liberal tradition – in which generals had also played a major part. Citizenship, progress, reason and science, for example, were the cornerstone beliefs of another instructor and prolific writer, the anti-monarchist Enrique Ruiz-Fornells – a man who could see that the officer class's belief in courage above all else was also a path to disaster. Franco, in other words, could choose between pro-democratic liberalism and authoritarian, mystical soldiering. He preferred the latter.[19]

The spindly and immature Francisco's only attempt at wooing girls came in the childish poems he sent home to some of his sister Pilar's girlfriends – which they read together, laughing at his soppiness. 'We teased him a lot for that,' she said, recalling how this provoked the rage of her thin-skinned brother. During the holidays, he returned to Ferrol along with the other young men at officers' academies around Spain. He did not talk much about Toledo, preferring to slip into the intimacy of home life, returning to his role as the obedient, dutiful son.[20]

Another Spanish military catastrophe, this time inflicted by poorly armed Riffian tribesmen in Morocco, dominated conversations amongst the young cadets in the summer of 1909. That July, the Riffians killed 153 Spanish soldiers and wounded 599 more at the Barranco del Lobo near Melilla – one of two military emplacements, along with Ceuta, on the north coast of Africa that had belonged to Spain for centuries.²¹

At Barranco del Lobo, or Wolf's Ravine, officers blundered around the unmapped countryside shouting 'Follow me if you are a man!' as they led badly trained troops into gulleys where they became sitting targets. That same week, departing reservists and their families in Barcelona became so angry about the pointless dangers that, after metal workers called an anti-war strike, riots broke out. These lasted for an entire week, with rioters burning churches and fighting police and soldiers in what became known as the 'Semana Trágica', or Tragic Week. Violence against the church already had a long tradition in Spain, ever since mobs killed priests during the civil wars against the ultrareligious, liberal-hating Carlists in the 1830s. More than 100 civilians and eight soldiers were killed. It served as a lesson for Franco, who learned that 'during a state of exception, it was the ungrateful task of the army to guarantee order, defend the Constitution and uphold rule of law.'²² The army could be called on, in other words, to act against its own people.

Franco was aware, however, that those now being forcibly shipped to Morocco had a right to complain, since wealthier Spaniards could buy themselves out of any military draft. 'Let the rich go too,' had been a rallying cry during the disturbances. Indeed, a wealthy man from Ferrol had created a special fund which allowed anyone from the town to buy themself out. 'We really couldn't understand why an out-dated law like that still existed – exchanging service in the army for money,' Franco recalled later (he was similar angry that wealthy cadets at his own school could live in private lodgings outside the Alcázar).²³ That did not stop him viewing the rioters as 'subversives' and the Tragic Week as proof that politicians should treat the army better.

With the patio of the Alcázar dressed up with crowns of laurel bearing the names of recent battles in Morocco, tapestries from the cathedral and an altar covered with yellow damask, Franco became second lieutenant at a passing-out ceremony on 5 June 1910. His cousin Pacón, who despite being sixteen months older had needed to repeat his school exams and did not enter the academy until the year after Francisco, was present when the 17-year-old became one of the youngest officers in the Spanish army. 'His physique made him seem even younger, but his great desire to study and the seriousness with which he carried out any official task made him seem older,' said Pacón.²⁴

Wearing his full dress uniform, with a sword strapped to his waist, Franco heard the officer in charge of the ceremony ask: 'Do you swear to God and your king that you will diligently rally to their flags, defending them with the last drop of your blood and never abandon those who you lead into action or prepare for war?'²⁵

'Yes, we swear!' he replied with his fellow cadets.

The prematurely serious teenage officer had made little impact, finishing in 251st position out of a cohort of 312. His younger brother Ramón entered the academy a year later and, despite indulging in all the excesses of alcohol, gambling and brothel-visiting that Francisco shunned, ranked 37th out of a class of 413.²⁶

Francisco may simply have been satisfied with surviving the academy. He had not enjoyed it, but he had developed a capacity to cope with adversity.²⁷ He was also now an adult and the army, which had shaped his views of manhood with its exaggerated cult of 'virility', was his life.

3

Without Africa, I Can Scarcely Explain Myself

MOROCCO, 1912–1917

Francisco Franco was too young for war but old enough for the dull chores of provincial garrison life. The slight second lieutenant, now sporting a wispy teenage moustache, was sent home to Ferrol to join a small, undermanned unit, the Eighth Regiment of Zamora. This was boring and frustrating, though he surely enjoyed having a salary, wearing his well-pressed uniform and being home with his mother Pilar. With 150 pesetas a month, you 'lived very well in Ferrol', his cousin Pacón recalled. His mother now stood out amongst her peers as an abandoned woman, though she initially refused to recognise that her husband had left her, saying he had simply been posted to Madrid. She would later excuse his absence to her grandchildren by claiming he was terribly busy in the capital.[1] She continued to be 'the best and most patient person in the world', according to her daughter Pilar. Her stoicism provided a strong contrast to the man Francisco and his siblings blamed for her suffering.

Francisco Franco later recalled scrambling up a steep hill above Ferrol with his mother to worship before the image of the Virgin Mary at the Chamorro chapel, part of the routine of pious locals – who, in moments of fervour, climbed the slope in bare, bleeding feet. Pilar sometimes scaled the rocky hillside path to give thanks for the miracles that kept her adventurous, risk-loving sons alive.[2]

Franco was as disheartened by garrison life as Pacón, who arrived the following year to join a company of just 50 men, or a dozen per officer, instead of the regulation 240. 'Was this why I had spent three years studying the campaigns of Hannibal, the Great Captain, Napoleon, the Franco-Prussian and Russo-Japanese wars, along with logistics and the joint tactical use of the three service arms?' Pacón asked himself.[3]

His youth and low rank meant Franco could not fight in Morocco, where officers accelerated careers by winning promotions for battlefield prowess as Spain set about 'pacifying' what would soon be formally recognised as a protectorate in the country's rugged north. For men like Franco, Spain was not just finally joining the European carve-up of Africa but also recovering the spirit of conquest by which empires were built. Eager young officers were alleged to cry 'Promotion or death!' on graduating from Toledo. Both he and Pacón were desperate to join the fighting.[4]

Spain already had a foothold in Africa: it had held an outpost on the north African shore at Melilla (120 miles across the Mediterranean from the Spanish port city of Almería) since the fifteenth century and another at Ceuta (just 17 miles across the mouth of the Mediterranean from the British-held territory of Gibraltar) since 1668. When Spanish workers unwittingly desecrated a holy tomb at Melilla in 1893 it took 15,000 men to prevent the people of the rugged Rif region from tearing down a new fort there in response. In 1904, at the insistence of Britain – which wanted to limit French power in the region – France invited Spain to join it in the task of 'protecting' Morocco's sultan Abd al-Aziz. His Alaouite dynasty had ruled the country, or parts of it, since 1631 and had never asked for this help.[5]

In fact, the Morocco campaign was a poisoned chalice which frequently provoked domestic turmoil in Spain over its cost in blood and money. With European capitalists also offering huge rewards for mining rights, the fragile stability of the tribes had been shattered. This was replaced by a combustible, shifting panorama of alliances and enmities, adding to what one army report called 'the absence of a regular and defined enemy'.[6]

Jingoistic Spanish newspapers boasted of Spain now joining the club of European colonial powers in Africa and suggested that the young king, Alfonso XIII, should be known, like the Roman general and victor in the Second Punic War, Publius Cornelius Scipio, as 'Africanus'. The meddling Alfonso was, in the words of one historian, a constitutional monarch 'who enjoyed many of the attributes of an absolute one'. In 1904, still aged just 18, he had appointed a new head of the General Staff without consulting the government, thereby obliging the prime minister to resign.[7]

In 1906, Spain hosted a summit at the southern port of Algeciras, during which colonial powers decided the future of Morocco. Spain was definitively handed the most difficult, dangerous and least wealthy part - the Rif and its proud, indomitable population of Berbers. 'Because we are weak, we have to content ourselves with the crumbs,' the *Correspondencia Militar* newspaper, which officers like Franco read, complained. Spain's protectorate amounted to little more than five per cent of Morocco but included its Mediterranean coast and a small stretch of Atlantic as far as Larache, which became the protectorate's second city after its capital, Tetouan. It had a population of 400,000. A second sliver of land, the Cape Juby Strip, lay farther south, adjoining the Spanish Sahara, a block of harsh Atlantic coastline and barren desert that Spain had claimed in 1884.[8]

The outspoken Republican writer Vicente Blasco Ibáñez (whose novels the *Four Horsemen of the Apocalypse* and *The Temptress* became Hollywood films starring Greta Garbo and Rudolph Valentino) blamed the 20-year-old monarch for leading Spain into an African quagmire:

> He accepted the Protectorate of the Rif – that is to say, a land belonging supposedly to Morocco but over which the Sultans of Morocco have never been able, in spite of centuries of warfare, to establish their authority. This is the bone that was offered our poor Spain at the diplomatic banquet at Algeciras! Needless to say it was a gift nobody else wanted. Alfonso XIII accepted it joyfully, however. Here was an opportunity to show he, too, was a 'war lord!' And straightaway he entered upon that most incomprehensible and senseless struggle of all history – the Spanish-Moroccan war.[9]

Franco shared his king's passion for this colonial adventure and when second lieutenants were finally allowed to volunteer in February 1912, he and Pacón travelled to Melilla.[10] They were accompanied by officers returning after recovering from wounds. This was proof, if needed, that they had volunteered for danger. Indeed, that shared experience was turning the officers who fought there into a distinct and tight-knit group, the so-called 'Africanistas', who viewed themselves as a military elite. Some saw Morocco as a forge, creating iron-cast patriots who might finally restore the nation to greatness. Franco, still just nineteen, embraced that idea passionately while enjoying a brilliant career as a young officer.

The two cousins were sent to separate units. Franco joined a regiment led by his former commandant at the Toledo academy, Colonel José Villalba Riquelme. His first piece of advice to the smartly turned-out second lieutenant was to cover his sword scabbard, since this glistened in the sunlight, making him a sniper target. Spanish conquest (euphemistically termed 'pacification') was unwelcome and Moroccans felt free to kill Spaniards at will. 'The enemy is a thousand times more difficult than you would find in any other fight,' Franco said later, expressing himself in typically epic terms. 'It is a war in which cruelty stalks and you pay dearly for your mistakes.'[11]

Riffian snipers, known as pacos because of the 'pac!' sound of their shots and the softer, drawn-out echo that hummed across the countryside, acted much like bandits. 'Their technique was simple. Towards dawn they used to hide in a gully with their rifles loaded, and wait for the first lonely soldier. They would kill him, rob him, and disappear,' the socialist writer Arturo Barea, who served as a sergeant in Morocco for three years, explained.[12] 'It's better to die once, than die a slow death under the foreign yoke,' went a Berber saying that circulated among the Spanish troops. Another was that 'victory comes not from the quantity of enemy deaths, but rather the number of frightened enemy forces'.[13] In practice, that meant torturing captives and mutilating bodies. While frightened Spanish soldiers cowered behind the barbed wire and walls of their compounds at night, Berbers moved freely around them.[14]

Spaniards thought the Riffians were breaking the rules of civilised killing. 'When they want to they accept battle, or seek it out; but when they don't want to, they run away and flee in disorder without fear that their honour might suffer, because they do not know what honour is,' wrote one Spaniard, as if this was somehow unfair.[15] The Riffians, needless to say, did not let the invaders set the rules of engagement.

Simple, sensible fieldcraft to deal with this sort of irregular warfare had not been taught at Toledo. The traditional tactic of frontal bayonet charges immortalised in the motto *'el rifle es la locura, la bayoneta la cordura'* ('the rifle drives them mad, the bayonet delivers the final blow') proved suicidal. Young officers like Franco had to learn in the field, which explains why so many died on their first forays into battle – even if Franco put this down to 'fate'.[16]

He experienced own baptism of fire at an advanced post near the Kert River, on the eastern edge of Spain's zone, when a reconnaissance group he led into enemy territory on 19 March 1912 came under fire. Later that month he joined an attempt by several columns to trap a harka (war party) of Moroccans, only to experience the realities of warfare in a region where mapless Spanish units often got lost. Ambushes halted the advance, leading to numerous losses and more debate about why Spain's army was in Morocco.[17] Such 'unpatriotic' questioning outraged Franco.

On 15 May 1912, he led his platoon during the attack by 14,000 men on the stronghold of Riffian leader Mohammed Amezian at the village of Haddu-Allalu-Kadur. He was beginning to show remarkable fearlessness and won the first of many medals.[18]

Officers were often uncaring about their conscript troops 'who were themselves overwhelmingly poor, unmotivated, illiterate, and poorly trained', according to one military historian.[19] Young Franco so mistrusted his men that on his first night in the field, he reportedly slept with a pistol in his hand – fearing they might attack him. He was strict, cautious and yet ambitious, gaining a reputation for having the best-organised and best-instructed platoon, whose soldiers knew that breaking rules brought certain punishment.[20]

By contrast, many officers were lazy and corrupt. Arturo Barea, arriving in 1920 as a sergeant to oversee road-laying, was expected to syphon off money for himself, for his captain and the contractor. There were reports of supplies sold to smugglers and cartridges filled with sawdust. 'Everyone in Northern Morocco knew that many of the Spanish officers spent their time whoring and gambling ... [and] knew what happened to stores and the fate of the men's pay,' said a British observer.[21]

The enemy, on the other hand, was highly-motivated. Franco eventually concluded that, so long as the 'Moors' (or *moros*, as he and Spaniards of his generation still called the Riffians and all other Moroccans) were allowed weapons, they would always fight. 'The Moor is born a warrior. He fights through instinct. Pillaging runs in his blood. That is the inheritance of so many years of barbarity,' he proclaimed with colonial certainty. 'The Moor will sacrifice anything for his rifle – his mother, his father, his peace, his life. He loves his rifle like a God.' Even the women were frightening: 'Their ferocity amazes us, and their lack of feminine sentiment, finishing off the wounded with rocks while the poor men are crying out.'[22]

Like colonial officers from other European countries, he felt disdain for their culture, religion and 'primitiveness'. 'I don't think they have a right to demand respect,' he said. 'If we are not allowed to teach them the morality of Christ, I cannot see any way to civilise this people.' Islam, indeed, was 'the key to the problem ... in mosques they preach holy warfare ... saying that all Mohammedans are obliged to fight the unfaithful Christians.'[23]

The regular army shut itself into barracks or blockhouses strung along key roads, leaving the dangerous work to indigenous police units or indigenous regiments known as 'regulares', led by Spanish officers. Staff officers were slow to take decisions and unwilling to adapt to a form of warfare they had not trained for. That, at least, is how Franco came to see it. Nor did he fool himself that 'pacification' was welcomed. 'The hatred that race feels [for us] stays alive, its coals whipped into flame by the first wind that blows in ... all it needs is some prestigious chief or long-haired preacher to stir them up.'[24]

It was only nine months after Franco arrived, and thanks to a treaty signed with France, that the Spanish zone formally became a protectorate covering 28,000 square km (10,800 sq miles). It is difficult to overstate the problems of turning this theoretical protectorate into reality. Effective communication was mostly by sea, since the landscape was mountainous and roads were either nonexistent, terrible or made seasonally impassable by rains. Mountain peaks rose to almost 2,500 metres amid what one Spanish doctor called 'a mad geological configuration' of broken terrain. Deep ravines and high mountains provided perfect cover for ambushes and sniping. The plains were exposed to freezing winter nights, baking summer heat and lightning enemy attacks. Much of the area was unmapped.[25]

Spain's Army of Africa, as the force in Morocco became known, eventually amounted to more than 40,000 men – or one soldier for every ten inhabitants.[26] The enterprise was costly and pointless as anything more than a limited statement of power, though Franco was always an enthusiastic supporter.

In the spring of 1913, Franco applied to join a unit of indigenous shock troops, the Regulares Indígenas de Melilla. These units, referred to by the regulares officer Emilio Mola – an archetypical Africanista and future coup plotter – as 'mercenaries', had been formed two years earlier, partly to reduce Spanish casualties. They were used on the most difficult, dangerous missions, gaining a fearsome reputation akin to the British army's Nepalese Gurkhas. They also provided an opportunity for ambitious officers like Franco to win promotions for battlefield merits. This came with considerable risk: the highest casualty rate amongst officers was in the regulares.[27]

The unit Franco joined in April 1913, then, pushed him deeper into war. The regulares were courageous when forced to fight, but could flee when they sensed danger. Officers sometimes stood behind them, pistols in hand, in case they turned. Their exotic uniform included a tasseled red fez, or tarbush, and a thick Moroccan wool 'selham' cape, sometimes thrown over a thinner, white 'alquicel' cape. Franco commented that they needed strong leadership but 'were apt for all tasks'.[28]

In June, Franco's unit was sent to Tetouan, the newly established capital of the Spanish protectorate, where troops under Colonel Dámaso Berenguer were building fortified positions as they slowly extended the zone under their control. Every two weeks or so, Franco found himself being shot at, and his unit joined several assaults through the summer.[29]

By September, he was being noticed by superiors like Berenguer as they sent units on more ambitious missions into the unconquered countryside. Franco's cool in the fierce fighting on 22 September, where he led his platoon of thirty to forty men as it flanked a dangerous enemy position and helped recover the corpse of a certain Captain Angel Izarduy, was probably worth a battlefield merit promotion, but his commanders preferred to wait. This may have been because he was so young, or perhaps because there was no vacancy for a new captain in the regulares.[30]

In December 1913, he was sent back to Melilla for three weeks, having spent most of the year in the field. It was a chance to relax, but he was a prim and stuffy young man compared to most fellow officers, who let off steam in bars and brothels. He attended, instead, the Friday afternoon parties held by the military governor of Melilla and set about trying to woo Sofía, the green-eyed fifteen-year-old daughter of the governor's brother-in-law and aide-de-camp Colonel Subirán. He pursued the girl in a clumsy, joyless but relentless fashion. That meant bombarding her with postcards, seeking her out as she walked through the park with a chaperone or applauding her turns on the piano and her singing. He also appeared at her window, chatting until her father arrived – at which stage he would, sensibly, run off. It became a Quixotic pursuit in which he endowed her with the imaginary virtues of his perfect woman, with his own 'saintly' mother as an obvious role model. Unfortunately, Franco danced badly, his conversation was prolific but dull and he was incapable of realising that it was a lost cause. He was faultlessly, stiffly polite, but also – as Sofía Subirán herself recalled later – 'overly attentive, to the extent of wearing you out' and in his conversation there was 'never any witticism, and much less any fun'. In other words, the pedant with the thin moustache was what Spaniards (and Sofía Subirán) call a 'pelma', or a tiresome bore. 'He was far too serious for someone so young.'[31]

She also noticed his strong, bristling ego. Over six months, he sent hundreds of postcards and letters full of quaint, antique phrases but little punctuation. In his final postcard he insisted that 'I love you a fair amount, in fact a lot.' Sofía had had enough. He seemed incapable of understanding that she was not interested. 'In fact, I didn't like Franco.'[32]

His military career was more successful. In January 1915 he was praised for 'distinguished' behaviour during the attack on a Riffian hilltop called Beni Hosmar, winning another Military Merit Cross specifically for that action. Promotion eventually came in March 1915 for his bravery in an action 13 months earlier, with the rise to the rank of captain backdated to that moment.[33] Aged 22, Franco was now amongst the top ten ranking infantry officers of his age, with a company of 120 men under his command. The merit system of promotions based on participation in battlefield engagements placed the Africanistas apart from officers based in Spain, who were promoted purely and ploddingly on seniority, and made Franco part of a small club of ambitious, dynamic and successful young officers united by an impatience for action and a high degree of self-regard. They were sure that they deserved their rewards, not least because they put themselves in danger. In short, they felt themselves superior, more patriotic and better equipped to 'resolve' problems than most other people, whether inside the army or out.[34]

He was also made his unit's paymaster, probably because he was unlikely to steal. He was an unusually honest but priggish officer with an icy nature and a stickler for discipline. A soldier who served in one of his units, quoted by Barea, later remarked:

> And he's fussy! God save you if anything's missing from your equipment, or if your rifle isn't clean, or you've been lazy. You know, that man's not quite human and he hasn't got any nerves. And then, he's quite isolated. I believe all the officers detest him because he treats them just as he treats us and isn't friends with any of them. They go on the loose and get drunk – I ask you, what else should they do after two months in the firing line? – and he stays alone in the tent or in barracks, just like one of those old clerks who simply must go to the office, even on Sundays. It's difficult to make him out and it's funny because he's still so young.[35]

Franco also gained a reputation for luck. By the end of 1915, having won several medals, he was one of just seven out of 42 officers in the regiment who had not been wounded or killed, according to an early hagiography. Although willing to lead from the front, he was also a careful tactician and planner, which helped explain his good fortune.[36]

His luck ran out the following year, during an attack on the mountain village of El Labyout in the steep hills that separate Tangiers from Ceuta. On 29 June 1916 he was leading his company of 113 men towards a crest known as the Hill of Trenches when he was shot in the stomach as he crouched to pick up an abandoned rifle.[37]

The unit's doctor did not expect Franco to survive. 'Will I die?' Franco asked him. The doctor lied, saying he certainly would not. The priest at the aid station administered the last rites, seeing just another young officer on his way to death. The bleeding was staunched and morphine relieved the pain, but he was initially too weak to be transported to hospital. In fact, the bullet had missed his vital organs. Franco had been breathing in when the bullet struck him, lifting his diaphragm and liver just enough for it to pass straight through him. Had he been breathing out, his doctor said, the bullet would have killed him.[38]

'A famous Moor called El Ducali picked me up in his arms, while part of my Moorish soldiers charged the enemy with bayonets, while other surrounded me to protect me from the considerable enemy fire,' Franco recalled later. His soldiers later gifted him the coloured leather bag belonging to the enemy commander, who they killed.[39]

It was a bloody encounter with 247 dead or wounded on the Spanish side, including half of Franco's company and all three officers under his command. Of the twelve wounded officers who made it to the aid station, only five survived. They included Franco and Lieutenant Juan Salafranca, who was the hero of the day. Salafranca was a contemporary from the same cadet class at Toledo and almost certainly seen as a rival by the ultra-competitive Franco. He had led the final successful charge despite having been wounded twice himself and having had his horse shot out from under him. As a result, Salafranca was also promoted to captain.[40]

Franco's elder brother Nicolás rushed to visit the wounded Francisco at the military hospital in Ceuta and his mother Pilar travelled from Ferrol, reportedly convinced that he was dying. Pilar took him home to Ferrol on 10 August 1916 – where he enjoyed two months' sick leave before returning to take command of his company in Tetouan. His main battle now would be to leverage his wound and his glory to win medals and promotion.[41]

Africa was a factory for military heroes and Franco was by no means the most decorated. He was, however, one of the most ambitious. Wounds often brought rewards, in the form of decorations or promotion. Yet only one of the three surviving captains from his tabor, Fernando Lías Pequeño, was promoted after El Labyout, having taken command after the tabor's commanding officer was killed. Salafranca, meanwhile, had been proposed for the highest gallantry medal of them all, the Cruz Laureada of San Fernando – the Laureate Cross of San Fernando – which Franco of course craved. Franco was outraged, though military authorities eventually decided against awarding Salafranca the medal.[42]

It was becoming clear that the ambitious Captain Franco sought not just glory, but also fame and rapid advancement. Franco lobbied hard to win either the San Fernando Cross or a promotion for this action, petitioning King Alfonso XIII directly. It is not clear whether his petition reached the king but, if it did, this would not be the only time that he pressed him to accelerate his career. Indeed, Alfonso XIII later recalled that no officer ever petitioned him more insistently.[43]

As part of his lobbying campaign, Franco claimed to have stayed in command of his company until the position was taken. In fact, the report on his petition for the bravery medal cited military doctor Captain Enrique Blasco Salas as saying that 'he was the first officer to be treated at the [medical] post ... it was absolutely impossible that he could have been capable of commanding afterwards.' The soldier who had picked him up, El Ducali, agreed, insisting 'that Captain Franco was the very first to fall and that he was in no state to issue commands, since he did not have the strength to do so, and that he was injured 15 minutes into the action, not having had time to do anything distinguished or heroic, and that the other 58 losses [in his company] came afterwards.' Franco had undoubtedly been valiant, but he was lying about having stayed in command. So, too, were the officers whom he cajoled into supporting his claim.[44]

The episode reflected the wider anxiety for promotion and, with it, improved pay in the poorly remunerated army. Arturo Barea recalled seeing a general receive reports from his officers, after taking a small village. '[They] entered his tent one by one, each reporting his casualties in dead and wounded. Every officer had two or three dead, ten or twelve wounded to his credit,' he wrote, highlighting the fact that the greater the losses, the more likely they were to be decorated, receive financial rewards and boost their career. 'The General's adjutant noted them down. The General offered each officer a glass of wine. They went away dreaming of the decoration which the list of dead would bring them.'[45]

The idea that glory and reward came from leading men to their deaths was part of the military culture that marked Franco's life permanently. For example, regulations stated that the San Fernando Cross, which brought lifelong pension payments, could be won by an officer who lost a quarter of his men during a fighting retreat as a rearguard unit, a third of them while taking an enemy position, or half while defending a position on flat land. Franco's fellow officers had suggested in their evidence about the attack at El Labyout that he deserved a medal for losing one-third of his men. The medals committee disagreed, but it is not surprising that disregard for the human cost of war became a defining characteristic of Franco and other Africanistas. Nor, in his typically stubborn fashion, would Franco ever give up on this medal.[46]

His petition to the king worked to his advantage in other ways. Franco was promoted to comandante (equivalent to major) in February 1917, backdated to the previous June. He was now 24 years old and one of the three youngest infantry comandantes (though, annoyingly for such a competitive man, Comandante Luis Pareja was three months younger). All three were regulares.[47]

These years in Morocco transformed young Franco. In a contest between fear and ambition, the latter clearly won. He had found a talent for warfare, leading men and planning. Those who had underestimated the prissy young officer with the reedy voice were left in no doubt about his zeal, discipline and self-confidence. He also craved recognition. Indeed, the ranking of officers on the promotion scale became a personal obsession as he sought to rise to the top over the next two decades.

As his success grew, so too did his ego. Franco himself was clear that Morocco, to which he would return over the coming years, was where he forged his adult personality. It was also where he began to build an idea of grandeur for Spain and himself. 'My years in Africa live within me with indescribable force. There was born the possibility of rescuing a great Spain. There was founded the idea which today redeems us. Without Africa, I can scarcely explain myself to myself.'[48]

4

The Girl Behind the Lattice Screen

OVIEDO, MAY 1917

By May 1917 Franco had recovered from his wounds, his promotion to comandante had come through and he was given command of a small garrison in the northern city of Oviedo, the provincial capital of coal-rich Asturias. Before he travelled to Asturias, his classmates from Toledo, whom he now outranked, hosted a dinner for him at the Palace Hotel in Madrid, just a hundred yards from the parliament building. This being the army, there was no question of Franco being a 'first amongst equals'. He must have felt glee at rising above those who had bullied him a decade earlier in Toledo.[1]

A short column on the dinner in Madrid newspaper *El Día* was a first sign that his fame might spread beyond the army. 'The youngest comandante in the Spanish army', as the newspaper called him, thanked his companions with a speech about military fraternity, monarchy and the fatherland.[2] Franco must have been delighted to see that the article also mentioned his nomination for the Cross of San Fernando. He was as yet unaware that his version of events at El Labyout would be rejected.

In Oviedo, he commanded a battalion of 500 men from the Third Prince's Regiment. This part of Asturias was somewhat like Franco's childhood home in verdant Galicia: gently sloping hillsides around the city were covered with meadows, apple groves and maize-patches, bordered by chestnut and oak trees, and dotted with white farmhouses or summer villas. Oviedo was still the dull, self-important provincial city that novelist Leopoldo Alas had sarcastically called 'the city of heroes' in his scandalous novel *La Regenta*, published in 1884. The cathedral's priests were, according to Alas, the real masters of a city dominated by 'the monotonous drone of the hour-bell high in the graceful tower of the Holy Cathedral'.[3] Sleepy, bourgeois Oviedo was far from the battlefields of Morocco, but suited Franco. He was, after all, a provincial boy and his expanding ego matched the haughtiness of a host city which prided itself on having been capital of the first Christian kingdom to emerge in Iberia after the Moslem conquest of 711. The city's buoyant bourgeoisie now added a real, if minor, hero to its ranks.

Like much of Spain, Asturias was living though a boom. Elsewhere in Europe, the First World War had been going for three years and all sides needed the products of the local coal mines and steel mills. These lay elsewhere in the province, meaning Oviedo enjoyed the wealth they generated without the dirt and disruption. Franco may not have been blind to what Alas called the 'distributive injustice' of the old quarter, where vast convents and ancient palaces with gardens sat beside whitewashed hovels of mud and their poor, 'unhappy plebians'. He would not, however, have agreed that they had been 'elbowed aside by the egotism of nobility and Church'. He was far too conservative for that.[4]

Initially, there was little to do. Soldiers had to be trained and the basics of garrison life attended to. During exercises, Franco was a demanding commander who obsessed about tactics. Officers knew they would be interrogated closely about their movements. 'It was like sitting a permanent exam,' said Pacón, who, in the first of Franco's many nepotistic appointments, became one of his company commanders.[5]

There was plenty of leisure time and locals were happy to entertain the adolescent-looking comandantín, or 'little major', as some still called him. There was also the local Royal Automobile Club, a gentleman's club overlooking the central San Francisco Park, where he and Pacón socialised, read and played games. Members soon learned that Franco was competitive to the point of bad manners. 'Losing at chess put him in an extremely bad mood,' recalled Pacón. 'He had a very high opinion of himself.'[6] That made him more like his father, Don Nicolás, than he might have liked.

Franco could also prove childish and thin-skinned, teasing companions but exploding with rage if they did the same in return. He also seemed envious of those who had more success with women. On one occasion, he organised a group of friends to wait outside the house of a woman who was entertaining a fellow officer late into the evening. They dressed as muggers and hid behind trees in the park, jumping out and brandishing knives as Franco cried 'Get him! Get him!'[7]

It was a vicious prank and the victim soon exacted revenge. Sometime later, an ecstatic Franco opened a telegram from Madrid which informed him that he had finally won the Cross of San Fernando. He whispered the news excitedly to Pacón, ordering him not to tell the same 'big mouth' officer they had played the trick on. Yet, when they met him, the officer already knew. In fact, he had sent the telegram himself. He had identified Franco's most tender, ambitious spot and pricked it. 'Franco was indignant and got very angry, calling him a bad friend, saying that you couldn't compare a small scare with a soldier's dream of winning such a valued medal,' recalled Pacón. 'You're not a real soldier!' Franco fumed. 'Our friendship is over!' It took him several days to calm down.

With the First World War raging, conversation within the regiment and the club revolved around the largely theoretical issue of whether one wanted the Entente allies led by France and Britain to win the war or backed Germany's Kaiser Wilhelm II and his Central Powers coalition. This was further complicated by the fact that King Alfonso, who stood in shiny riding boots, sword and gala uniform in a signed portrait hung on the club's wall, had both a British wife (Queen Victoria's granddaughter, Victoria Eugenia) and an Austrian mother. For a soldier like Franco, there were practical lessons too – from the use of aircraft, tanks, trenches and gas to the defeat of supposedly sophisticated European forces by a mostly Asian country, Turkey, at Gallipoli.[8]

Closer to home, Franco lived through the roiling political summer known as the Crisis of 1917. This saw three of the stresses on Spanish society flare up simultaneously: firstly, workers organisations demanded better conditions (or revolution) and lower prices for basic goods impacted by inflation; secondly, mainland infantry officers formed their own 'unions', or *juntas de defensa*, aiming to influence politics, dismantle the 'battlefield promotions' system that had served Franco so well and improve pay; and, finally, regionalist and separatist factions in Catalonia and the Basque country grew rapidly. The army formed part of all three of these stresses, since it policed workers' strikes and felt a duty to prevent Catalans or Basques splitting off from Spain.[9]

A general strike in the sweltering days of August 1917 finally ignited the crisis. The officers had by now won their battle for better conditions and were happy to assume the task of policing. In fact, many officers supported calls for an autocratic 'Iron Surgeon' to impose order on a fractious nation.[10]

The strike dwindled quickly in most places as its leaders were arrested, court-martialled and jailed, but it lasted a whole month in Asturias. Socialist unions were strong there, especially amongst the miners. Amongst those tasked with policing the strike was the young comandante Franco. The military governor of Asturias, Ricardo Burguete, declared martial law and warned that his troops would treat strikers 'like wild beasts'. This some of them duly did, as troops and Civil Guard militarised police units were dispatched into the mining valleys, killing 80, wounding 150 more and detaining 2,000, many of whom were brutally beaten. A train that ran regularly between Lena and Ablaña was armed with soldiers who gained a reputation for shooting at anything – including cows and children. Miners' leaders spoke of the 'African hatred' directed against the strikers by officers blooded in Morocco.[11]

In Oviedo, soldiers patrolled the streets and charged protesters. For sixteen days 'Oviedo felt like an army stronghold, given the large number and variety of soldiers in the streets, as well as regimental trucks, carts, and automobiles,' according to one newspaper report.[12]

Franco led a unit of soldiers, including an infantry company, a machine-gun group and some Civil Guards to the Falla de los Lobos, above a crucial mountain pass east of Oviedo. His orders were, in Franco's own words, to 'hunt down workers like vermin'. When he sent scouts into the valleys, however, they found 'absolutely nothing ... People were out on walks, and the children going to school.' The danger was, at best, exaggerated, without a single clash between his men and the workers. Socialist mayors, he noted, 'received me with great courtesy'. The strikers gave up. One hundred were jailed in the city while many were forced to emigrate, joining the 1.5 million, or 8 per cent of all Spaniards, who had left sluggish Spain for the booming countries of Latin America between 1885 and 1913 (at a time when millions of people from the impoverished parts of southern European countries like Spain, Italy and Portugal were crossing the Atlantic). Burguete was sacked.[13]

Franco later told a biographer that he started reading up on politics and economics in order to understand what was happening. He discovered 'the appalling conditions under which employers were making people work' but concluded that solutions 'put forward by socialists and anarchists could lead only to chaos'. But his reading seems cursory and he never said which authors or books he had read. His wife later declared that, while her husband read almost daily, his books 'all deal with the same subject: the army'.[14]

Across much of working-class Spain, interest had suddenly switched to Russia as the Bolsheviks grabbed power, but Franco was already on the other side of the debate. In a speech to Asturian miners given many years later, Franco complained that it made no sense to 'give workers the right to strike' and then 'turn the Civil Guard and army on them to hunt them down'. The original sin, he meant, was the right to strike.[15]

***

Not everyone in Spain was delighted to see such a young comandante. As noted, the practice of promoting officers for battlefield bravery, rather than years served, had been the chief complaint of mainland officers who created the Juntas de Defensa. They claimed the system was corrupted by favouritism and that some promoted officers had been nowhere near a battlefield. They complained, too, that it rewarded failure and high casualties, with 61 officers promoted for taking part in the self-inflicted Wolf's Ravine disaster of 1909. That set them against Africanistas like Franco. On a visit to a garrison in Coruña, Pacón recalls Franco being mobbed by the young lieutenants while 'some of the senior men said he was too young' to be a comandante.[16]

Garrison life also gave Franco another chance to look for a girlfriend. His behaviour with women was still stiff, sentimental and old-fashioned. Given this attitude, it was no accident that his next target could often only be seen through the latticed screens of a convent chapel.

Carmen Polo had just turned 17 and was the eldest of the four children of local businessman Felipe Polo Flórez. He had been widowed young, which is why she boarded at the convent school of the Salesas order in Oviedo. Relatives wondered whether, like most of her classmates, this pious girl would become a nun. Bourgeois women were expected to devote much of their energy to religious devotion, and be guided by priests or nuns. Elsewhere in Spain, a handful of early feminists and, especially, anarchist women were pushing for change, but none of that would have reached Carmen Polo. A contemporary put it this way: 'If a woman belongs to the upper class, she is a simple luxury object with very restricted rights. Her education and instruction are rudimentary. Reading, writing, a bit of history and geography, painting, a couple of languages, music, dance, a bit of embroidery and sewing and a large dose of religion. With all that she is on her way to shining in the saloons of marriage making.'[17]

Carmen Polo was tall, thin and dark, with a well-burnished pedigree. The Polos were one of the city's wealthier families, with English or French nannies to help raise the three daughters, overseen by their father's sister, Isabel. Aunt Isabel had married the nephew of a count and liked to tell her charges, and others, that the Polo family was descended from Castilian nobility. She filled the girl's heads with notions that, in the words of Carmen's biographer, 'they were destined to be the wives of wealthy and important men, reaching the highest ranks of Oviedo's stuffy society.' Meanwhile, their French nanny, Madame Claverie, told stories about women who became empresses, including the Spaniard Eugenia de Montijo, wife of Napoleon III.[18]

Given her background and aspirations, it is perhaps surprising that Carmen showed interest in the little comandante, who she outranked in terms of wealth and class. The couple first met during the summer holidays at a romería, one of the popular outdoor festivals attended by all classes. Young Franco probably rode the horse that he exercised daily. But Carmen's father was a liberal and her aunt a snob. Neither saw promise in a young military officer whose long-term destiny was to become one of the many not very well-off retired officers who dotted Spain's landscape or, worse still, to die young, leaving a widow and her children on a meagre pension. He may just as well marry her to a bullfighter, Felipe Polo liked to say. In the words of one of her childhood friends: 'Felipe Polo couldn't set eyes on Franquito and wouldn't let his daughter see him.' Nor, initially, was Carmen terribly interested. One fellow officer recalled her asking him to dance with her at a social event 'so that the comandante could not.'[19]

Franco was not deterred. He set about wooing her with the same determination that he applied to military manoeuvres. After she returned to school, he would rise early and assiduously attend mass at the convent in order to prove his devotion, though the girls sat behind latticed screens. Everyone knew why he was there. Even the nuns, one of whom described the devout Carmen as 'decisive and energetic', were excited by the unusual sight of a young major at 7 a.m. mass. Spanish army officers were not famed for their religiosity. They intercepted his letters, however, delivering them to Carmen's family instead.[20]

The courtship was as old-fashioned as a medieval knight's tale, which helps explain why Franco liked it so much – though rigidly-patrolled relationships with heavily protected young women were common enough at the time. On days away from the convent, Carmen occasionally stood on a friend's balcony, while Franco stood on a balcony down the street. Secret letters were smuggled to her. The son of a society doctor who had been a Toledo cadet with Franco eventually arranged encounters at his family's country house. Her father continued to protest for two years until, worn down and displeased, the family accepted the inevitable. Franco's mixture of devotion, conservatism and ambition had won Carmen over. The young man may not have been tall, deep-voiced or particularly 'manly' in his bearing, but he was active, sporting, relentlessly optimistic and had remarkably lively eyes that suggested a curiosity about all he saw. In 1920, with Carmen now 20 years old, they became engaged. He was 27. She had been his first and only girlfriend.[21]

A visit to the relatively drab Franco house in Ferrol did not impress a fiancée used to large, airy homes with ballrooms, ancestral portraits, crystal chandeliers and exquisite décor. Franco's niece Pilar Jaraiz saw someone 'with the air of a French woman, distinguished and beautiful, as if from a higher place'. His mother apparently declared her to be 'like a fairy princess'. His forthright and judgmental sister Pilar was less impressed, finding Carmen superior and snobbish. 'I'm not going to say she was beautiful, which would be going too far, but she was attractive and dark, just as Paco liked them,' she said later.[22]

Franco was undoubtedly impressed by the Polo family's wealth, but there was nothing culturally exotic about Carmen. She belonged, indeed, to the same stultifying bourgeoisie of Oviedo that one translator of *La Regenta* described as an 'absurd, unchanging world of mediocrity, pretence, hypocrisy, boredom and quirkiness'.[23] That suited Franco well. Carmen Polo was devout, like his mother, but a class above him. His engagement was a form of social climbing and another expression of ambition, but also confirmation of his conservative, traditional tastes. His wife-to-be carried the social confidence of her upbringing, but also brought the pious traditionalism that he had admired in his mother. Carmen Polo aspired to social success, but she knew her place in a marriage and would neither cross nor embarrass her husband. Her innate snobbishness did not put him off. In fact, it matched his own ambitious nature. Her choice would eventually pay off and she carried the same mixture of rigid conservatism, religious piety and haughtiness into Franco's home, including during his almost four decades as a dictator. In that sense, she also became a model of womanhood in Franco's Spain. Her values, indeed, informed the sort of society that he himself eventually sought to impose on Spaniards.

Franco had hoped to wed quickly, but he soon put off marriage for a more enticing invitation. Morocco beckoned again, this time to help create a fearsome and controversial unit that would soon make its mark on history – the Spanish Legion.

5

Los Novios de la Muerte

MOROCCO, 1918–1921

In September 1918, while attending an obligatory marksman's course for majors near Madrid, Franco met one of the most remarkable and outrageous characters in the Spanish army. José Millán Astray was thirteen years older, had been wounded several times and was intelligent, eccentric and energetic. One of his interests was France's Foreign Legion, which he received permission to study as the model for creating a similar outfit in the Spanish army.[1]

Millán Astray later claimed that he spoke to Franco about this during their marksman's course and sought him out to become second-in-command after obtaining permission to create a Spanish Foreign Legion in 1920. 'Franco possesses all the characteristics of a good military man, which are: valour, intelligence, martial spirit, enthusiasm, love of work, spirit of sacrifice and virtuous living,' he declared a few years later.[2]

Franco tried to persuade Pacón to join him, but his cousin refused. He did not trust Millán Astray to be honest with money, and he himself was a stickler for rules. 'Millán Astray had a reputation for doing whatever he wanted,' he explained.[3] Franco obviously did not mind. For such a stickler, indeed, he remained remarkably tolerant of corruption of all kinds during his life.[4]

The Spanish Legion, also known as the Tercio de Extranjeros, was formally founded on January 31, 1920. In the hands of Millán Astray, who moulded it according to his personal values, it would soon become the most influential force in the Spanish army. These, in the words of one military historian, included 'fervent Catholicism, duty until death, honour above everything [and] love of the fatherland'. The Legion's founder was also a fervent admirer of Japan's samurais. Franco shared Millán Astray's ideas of duty, honour and patriotism absolutely.[5]

The Legion was created to compensate for heavy losses amongst Morocco's indigenous regulares. It was to be a similar unit of shock troops, thrown always into the heaviest fighting. Like the French Foreign Legion, it offered amnesty, anonymity and redemption to men with terrible pasts. One potential recruit, or so Franco claimed, arrived from a monastery, where the prior had ordered him to do penance with four years in the Legion.[6]

Paying for earlier sins through absolute obedience and, if necessary, death, was part of the Legion's ethos. Unruly recruits were to be tamed through cruelty and harsh discipline before being unleashed into battle by those who had gifted them a fresh start. They nicknamed themselves the Novios de la Muerte, or Bridegrooms of Death and had battle cries, penned by Millán Astray, that included '¡Viva la Muerte!' ('Long live death!') and '¡Legionarios, a luchar; legionarios, a morir!' ('Legionnaires, to battle! Legionnaires, to die!').[7] 'There is something akin to the Japanese in their indifference to death, though the Spanish legionnaires face it with a cold, individual contempt, as though death were something to be spat on disdainfully,' said an early observer who had served in the French Foreign Legion.[8]

Recruitment started in a handful of cities on 20 September 1920 and exploded. Two hundred men joined immediately in Barcelona alone and, though he had nowhere to house them, Millán Astray's cabled instructions were: 'Let them come!' Franco took charge and his contingent boarded a ferry in the southern port of Algeciras on October 10.[9]

In his own version of this moment, Franco sees this bunch of ne'er-do-wells and thugs as 'sun-tanned, blond, foreign-looking men and young devil-may-care lads ... emotion mists our eyes, it is the dawning of our legionnaire spirit!' More sagely, he also notes that 'their former lives [are] consigned to oblivion: it is as if they are children again.'[10] In fact, Franco's initial group of 200 men had just twenty foreigners, and non-Spaniards were always a minority in the

Spanish Legion, but they did join, coming from as far away as Japan and including a White Russian prince and the African-American William Brown, who arrived wearing a red-and-white striped soccer shirt.[11]

Franco recalled with enthusiasm how Millán Astray greeted them with promises of a 'hard and terrible life' while pledging 'anonymity, honours, Glory … always in the thick of it, many, perhaps all, will die.'[12] Recruits were allowed to use false names. When it came to picking up their pay, some had forgotten the names they gave or had to read them off pieces of paper pulled from pockets. They included Pedro Calderón de la Barca, a seventeenth-century playwright, and Rodrigo Diaz de Vivar, the medieval Spanish hero and mercenary known as El Cid.[13]

Franco was already a famously cold-blooded and harsh disciplinarian, but these characteristics reached fresh heights in the Legion. The first recruits immediately lived up to their dubious pasts. A near-riot over pay was averted by heaping money on tables in the barracks courtyard, so they could see it. During the few days before he could house them at a new camp outside Ceuta they drank their way through the port city and got into lethal fights. 'The first thing we did in Ceuta was to bump off three or four people,' said one Sanchiz, a friend of the socialist sergeant Arturo Barea who had joined the Legion to seek death and an escape from his pain at sudden widowhood after failing to find either at the bottom of a bottle.[14]

Franco glosses over this period, observing only that the men now had money and over 'a few orgiastic days say goodbye to the pleasures and attractions of garrison town life'. Sanchiz believed the shocking behaviour of the first recruits scared the officers and turned them into savage disciplinarians who rewarded disobedience with 'two bullets in his head'.[15]

Whereas Millán Astray was a grandstanding braggart, Franco's men discovered a cold, discipline-obsessed martinet who inspired fear and respect. 'The Tercio is rather like being in a penitentiary. The most courageous brute is the master of the jail. And something of this sort has happened to that man,' Sanchiz told Barea. 'He's hated, just as the convicts hate the bravest killer in their jail, and he's obeyed and respected – he imposes himself on all the others – just as the big killer imposes himself on the whole jail.'[16]

While officers risked being shot in the back by their own legionnaires if they led them too obviously towards death, nobody dared challenge Franco. 'Not one of them has the courage to do it. They're afraid that he might turn his head and see them just when they have taken aim… Believe me, it's sticky going with Franco… He simply looks blankly at a fellow, with very big and very serious eyes, and says: "Execute him," and walks away, just like that. I've seen murderers go white in the face because Franco had looked at them out of the corner of his eye.'[17]

The shooting of disobedient legionnaires was not routine, but nor was it rare.[18] Franco himself admitted having one man shot for hurling his food at an officer:

> I was informed about it and ordered everyone to form up, checking to see what had happened by asking eyewitnesses. Then I ordered a firing squad of legionnaires to shoot their rebellious comrade and the Legion was marched past the corpse.[19]

His matter-of-fact retelling of this event revealed to what extent he was now capable of switching off any emotions produced by violence or his own exercise of it. It also captured the ethos of the Legion and the importance of discipline and obedience in the mindset of hard-core Africanistas, who did not shrink from imposing them with cold brutality.

Franco was given charge of the First Bandera (a small battalion of some 450 to 600 men), which marched out of Ceuta towards the protectorate's capital at Tetouan in November 1920, to be placed in a defensive position at the mouth of the Lau River. It would soon be joined by two other Legion banderas.[20]

This, however, was an elite shock regiment, trained to attack, and officers like Franco hated being sent to defensive positions. They wore better uniforms, carried better weapons and ate better than most Spanish soldiers. It was not, however, until April 1921, when a supply column accompanied by a Legion patrol was attacked, that Franco's new outfit was able to fight. Rather than scramble for cover, it counterattacked, with the commanding officer leading from the front and being killed.[21]

In May 1921, Franco and the Legion joined an assault on the positions of a powerful Moroccan chief called Ahmed er Raisuni in the mountainous Jebala region. They quickly impressed. Over the next few months, the 2,000-strong Legion grew in the estimation of senior officers. It eventually found itself where Millán Astray and Franco had wanted to be – in the vanguard of the attack. Sanchiz witnessed Franco's legendary coolness under fire. 'I've seen him walk upright in front of all the others, while they hardly dared to lift their heads from the ground, the bullets fell so thick,' he said. 'That man's not quite human and he hasn't got any nerves.'[22]

If arrogance and disdain for death were legionnaires' defining characteristics on the battlefield, it was perhaps inevitable that some of that attitude should spill into the rest of their lives – including for Franco and Millán Astray. In May 1921, Franco wrote a provocative opinion article called 'The Rewards of Campaigning' which the editors of the infantry's own magazine, *Memorial de Infantería*, deemed too risky to print. Now aged 27, Franco believed his readiness to sacrifice his life gave him a right to opine about how politicians should run the army, and how the army should inspire politics. The spark for that was his outrage at calls for the creation of a separate colonial officer corps to detach the Africanistas – with their love of action and battlefield promotions of the kind that had catapulted Franco up the ranks – from the plodding, mainland regular army.[23]

The proposals, wrote Franco, 'sentence those in Africa never to return to Spain, so depriving the Peninsular Army of its best practical school'.[24] He also saw envy of the way he and other young officers who gained promotions for battlefield merits were leap-frogging over their colleagues on mainland Spain:

> The Army fails to comprehend the weight of the pain and sufferings of a forgotten campaign, and of the great number of officers who heroically die for their country thereby adding to the glory of the Infantry. They are the ones who forge a nation! ... One day, this officer corps fighting in Africa must become the backbone and soul of the peninsular army. In order not to destroy this enthusiasm, this spirit which must be guarded like a precious jewel, it is indispensable that such worthy campaign service be recognised and rewarded.[25]

Franco here provides a first glimpse of his idea that the army must rescue and 'forge' Spain. Africanista officers are the model for Spaniards to follow, while hierarchy, sacrifice, obedience and colonial ambition are crucial national values. He is also bitter. His sacrifice, and that of his fellow Africanistas, is not being recognised – adding to the list of slights to himself or to the nation by weak-willed colleagues and politicians that already populated his mind.[26]

He already saw propaganda and the press as crucial battlefields. 'By bringing together the pen and the sword ... we conduct our most virile battles in the press and in the field,' he would say later.[27] On this occasion, he had overstepped the mark with his criticisms, which is why his article was not published. The Legion was gaining respect and fame, but was still politically powerless. That was about to change. In July 1921, the main Army of Africa was to suffer a major disaster at a place called Annual, near Melilla. Comandante Franco and the Legion would be sent to the rescue. Few officers were shrewder at generating personal advantage out of that than Francisco Franco.

6

A New Disaster

ANNUAL, 22 JULY, 1921

Franco was awoken shortly after 2am on 22 July 1921, while campaigning in the Jebala highlands, and ordered to urgently march his First Bandera the 65 kilometres to the coast. He was not told why. 'The truth is, nobody knows anything,' Franco recorded in his diary. Setting out in the dark, he led his men on a 27-hour march punctuated by just four hours of sleep during which two soldiers reportedly died from exhaustion. His weary troops eventually reached Tetouan at 9.30am the following day.[1]

Spain was fighting several enemies at once in Morocco. While its army had been advancing against Raisuni in western Morocco, an even more formidable Riffian leader – Mohammed ibn Abd el-Krim – had emerged in the east. His men had fallen on the Spanish position at Annual, 60 km west of Melilla, and a bloody rout was under way. The commanding officer there, General Manuel Fernández Silvestre, had already died, probably by suicide. Melilla looked as though it might fall for the first time since Spain claimed it in 1497. With that shocking news ringing in his ears, Franco put his men on a train to Ceuta, where they boarded a steamer for Melilla. 'No one suspects the size of the disaster,' Franco recalled. Nor could he or anyone else imagine just how transformative the next few months would prove for Franco, the Legion and for Spain.[2]

Poor leadership had provoked disaster. Silvestre was a cavalry officer and favourite of the ambitious King Alfonso XIII. He had driven his troops far to the west as Spain sought to join up its two principal blocks of land – around Ceuta and Tetouan in the west and Melilla in the east. The rugged, inhospitable Rif mountains rise sharply from the coast between the two blocks. From his steamer, Franco saw a coastline that was 'dark and clifflike, steep and closed off by high mountains'. This mountainous landscape provided cover for Abd el-Krim's forces as they fell on Silvestre's overstretched army, which was scattered around poorly connected outposts.[3]

Abd el-Krim came from a powerful local family and had studied engineering in Madrid before working for the colonial administration in Melilla. There he had discovered the value of Moroccan mining rights being squabbled over by Spanish and German companies. He began agitating for Riffian independence, was detained by the Spanish and then broke out, walking thereafter with a limp after falling from a rope during his escape. During the First World War, Germany had paid his family to disrupt French colonial activity. By 1921, he was a formidable leader whose well-motivated army defeated a Spanish force four times its own size. His men were armed with rifles and artillery smuggled in by the Germans during the First World War or bartered away by corrupt Spanish troops.[4]

Silvestre ignored requests that he slow his advance to the west as Abd el-Krim's men began attacking supply convoys. Isolated positions were besieged. At one of these, called Mount Igueriben, much of the garrison died of thirst as they licked the underside of rocks, or drank ink, vinegar, cologne and their own urine. Silvestre's attempt to relieve the position by personally leading cavalry charges withered under machine-gun fire. The general believed that Spanish 'guts' would prevail but these were no match for Abd el-Krim's brains. Soon Silvestre himself and 5,000 men were trapped at Annual, while thousands more were scattered at vulnerable outposts across the territory. Accepting the inevitable, they began a chaotic retreat on the morning of July 22. Officers and men threw away their weapons and an 'every man for himself' mindset swept the army as it turned into a bloodbath.[5]

Fleeing Spanish troops were still being slaughtered when the steamer carrying Franco and his men reached Melilla on 24 July. The task of calming the city's panicked civilian inhabitants began even before the dirty, smelly contingent of legionnaires could disembark.

From the gunwale, Millán Astray harangued the waiting crowd. His melodramatic style, for once, matched reality. 'People of Melilla: the Legion which comes to save you, greets you. We are ready to die for you... Forget fear! The chests of the Legionnaires stand between you and the enemy!' As a military band played, the legionnaires marched through the town in their peculiarly theatrical manner – heads thrown back, with an exaggerated swing of the arms.[6]

Franco recalled being 'welcomed with applause, hugs, kisses, and gifts from the grateful populace. Women, men, and even Legionnaires all wept.' 'These are soldiers! How dark and unshaven they come,' Franco remembered them shouting in his cliché-ridden memoir of that period, *Morocco: Diary of a Bandera*. 'Look at the officers, how careless they are, with their discoloured uniforms smelling of war. These men will avenge us!' The legionnaires immediately took up defensive positions on the east of the city.[7]

Arturo Barea, whose engineering unit joined the new arrivals as the defenders were boosted by eight more infantry battalions over the next 24 hours, recalls an altogether different atmosphere.[8] The city was charged with violent fear and into it 'poured those thousands of seasick, drunken, over-tired men who were to be its liberators':

> We set up camp, I don't know where. We heard guns, machine guns, and rifles firing somewhere outside the town. We invaded the cafes and taverns. We got drunk and rioted in the brothels. We challenged the frightened inhabitants: 'Now you'll see! Now we're here and that's that. Tomorrow not a Moor will be left alive.' The Moors had disappeared from the streets of Melilla; after the ship had anchored alongside the jetty, a legionary had cut off the ears of one of them and the authorities had ordered all Moors to stay indoors.[9]

Outside the city, the massacre continued. Stragglers appeared. 'Men with terror-stricken eyes who fearfully tell of being hunted, of Moors who chased them and of Moorish women who finished off the wounded,' as Franco recalls. 'They come in naked or in shirttails, bewildered, like pathetic madmen.'[10]

Twelve thousand Spanish soldiers and indigenous troops had been killed. European colonialists had not suffered such a catastrophe in Africa since Ethiopians routed the Italians at Adowa in 1896. Fifty thousand square kilometres of land, which had taken a dozen years to occupy, were lost in a week. Abd el-Krim's forces captured some 20,000 rifles and 200 artillery guns. In Spain's parliament, the episode was soon compared to the losses of Cuba and the Philippines during the Disaster of 1898. Deputies clamoured for the military culprits to be punished.[11]

The events of the coming months had a profound impact on Franco and Spain. The day after disembarking, legionnaires and other troops began to cautiously expand the area they were defending. This soon brought Franco within sight of Nador, a neighbouring town which was still being sacked by Abd el-Krim's men. Franco could only watch, since it would have been foolhardy to attempt a rescue.[12]

It took almost two months to build a force of 47,000 men who could go on the offensive, with Franco leading his bandera into some of the most dangerous work. As they slowly retook old positions, they found the festering bodies of Spanish soldiers who had been tortured and butchered. 'Corpses had been defiled and barbarously mutilated,' Franco recalled.[13]

In October, Franco's men reached Mount Arruit, where a force of Spaniards had held out into early August.[14] Up to 3,000 bodies were found. 'It is so difficult to identify these naked bodies, with their heads crushed in! We leave that place with a desire to punish those criminals in the most exemplary way seen for generations,' wrote Franco.[15]

Given the background of many legionnaires and the belligerence of officers like Franco, it was a short step to start repaying the enemy in kind – marking the Legion out as not just the boldest, but also the cruellest, unit in the Spanish army. Franco and his bandera were transformed. Barea's friend Sanchiz, who was in Franco's bandera, described the process.

> You know, barbarism is surely one of the most contagious things in life. When the First Standard [Bandera] went to Melilla, we attuned ourselves to the bestiality... They cut off the genitals of Spanish soldiers and stuffed them into their dead mouths and left the corpses rotting in the sun. You've seen it yourself. Then we cut off the heads of the Moors and put them on the parapet of our position in the mornings. Well, you've seen that too. Anyhow, that's what the Legion was like from the beginning. And there is no remedy.[16]

As Melilla held and the defensive circle widened, the Legion's reputation for fearlessness and efficacy grew. Millán Astray travelled to the mainland temporarily in mid-August to form two new banderas, increasing the Legion's strength to around 3,000 men. Franco was left in command at the youthful age of just 28. He found himself involved in what, essentially, was the creation of a new Army of Africa – one that was militarily effective and driven by revenge. A visiting delegation of Red Cross women, led by a duchess, was reportedly gifted a basket of roses that held the severed heads of two Moroccan fighters. Newspapers called on the army to 'ruin the land, exterminate the race'. There was nothing uniquely Spanish about this. Winston Churchill had recently declared himself 'strongly in favour of using poisoned gas against uncivilised tribes [of Kurds in Iraq, in order to] ... spread a lively terror'.[17]

According to Franco's own writings, he himself also showed little mercy, on one occasion recording that: 'At midday, I receive authorisation from the General to punish the villages from where the fire is coming... While one platoon provides enfilading fire, the other climbs down by a small ravine and surrounding the houses, punishes the people inside; flames belch from the roofs as the legionnaires seek out their owners.' When a legionnaire-manned blockhouse near Dar Drius was surrounded, he personally led a dozen volunteers to relieve the men. They returned bearing the hacked-off heads of a dozen tribesmen.[18]

Casualties were high, with one battle seeing a third of 300 legionnaires lost. New recruits replaced them. Praise also came. 'With your indomitable valour, admirable patriotism and incomparable skill, you struck the enemy one of the mightiest blows that he has suffered during all our campaigns, causing him innumerable casualties,' an Army General Order from Melilla from 10 September read. 'In the name of all your comrades in the Army of Africa, who take pride in you, I warmly congratulate you.'[19] The Legion was just a year old, but it had already become a weighty institution within an Army of Africa that, with the salvation of Melilla, was growing in self-confidence.

On 17 September 1921 Franco took over from Millán Astray as temporary commander of the Legion again, after the latter was wounded. The two men had been discussing tactics mid-battle. 'Just as he [Millán Astray] is pointing out to me our place in the attack order, the characteristic crack of a rifle bullet knocks our beloved commanding officer to the ground. Blood pours from his chest,' Franco recalled.[20] His tone suggests that, rather than being tragic, such events add glory to a soldier's reputation. Millán Astray reportedly cried 'They've killed me!' before sitting up and shouting 'Long live the King! Long live Spain! Long Live the Legion!'[21] They had not, in fact, killed him: he survived and resumed his fighting career, later losing an eye and an arm to separate wounds.

Despite the Legion's successes, though, Spaniards were tiring of the costly colonial adventure in Morocco. The government declared in November 1921 that it planned to withdraw the army to the coast. The campaign to recover lost positions was halted. Africanistas were outraged and Franco's intense dislike of politicians grew accordingly. He was coming to an entirely different conclusion about Morocco. It was here that leaders like him were showing the way forward for Spain, by offering to sacrifice their lives while creating a spirit of optimism, pride and obstinate defence of the country's reputation amongst their men.[22]

It could have been much worse. Melilla had been saved. The Legion, now associated not just with Millán Astray but increasingly with Franco, was fast attaining legendary status. Barea found that normality had returned to Melilla almost as suddenly as it had disappeared when Abd el-Krim's troops had threatened to take it:

> One day at dawn we came back to the city. It was filled with soldiers and with people who were no longer besieged. They lived and laughed. They stopped to speak to each other in the streets and sat down in the shade to take their vermouth. The bootblacks worked their way through the crowds in the cafés. A silvery airplane traced circles overhead. A band was playing in the park.[23]

7
Fame

MADRID, 22 FEBRUARY 1922

On 22 February 1922, Francisco Franco discovered that the Legion's military successes could also be a vehicle for personal fame. That day, the popular conservative newspaper *ABC* wrote a fawning profile headlined 'The "Ace" of the Legion'. Journalist Gregorio Corrochano claimed to have bumped into Franco in the street during his first leave in ten months. Franco was passing through on a visit to Ferrol 'to calm my mother', who now had all three sons serving in Morocco. For Corrochano, the young major evoked the whole of Spanish military history. 'He is the Disaster [of 1898], the Reconquest, and the military spirit of the army.' The journalist, who knew Franco from Morocco, claimed the young major had fought in fifty engagements over ten months.[1]

Corrochano told his readers that Franco's success as a commander was based on a battlefield personality that remained 'serene and reflexive':

> Monitoring the action closely, he solves military problems by eliminating risk, or rather by accepting it as a necessary factor without fretting too much and instead weighing it up so that there are no surprises, nor a looming sense of fear that overly influences the outcome.[2]

The piece claimed General Sanjurjo had once been obliged to threaten Franco in order to prevent him leading his troops into the attack in person, mounted on a horse that marked him out for snipers. 'You won't be sent to hospital by a Moor's rifle shot,' Sanjurjo reportedly said, 'but rather because of the rock I will hurl at you if I see you amongst the skirmishers on horseback again.' It was a piece of hagiography that nevertheless reflected how Franco's closest admirers and the Legion's growing band of enthusiastic supporters saw him. It was also the kind of glowing report that a doting father might have enjoyed reading, but there is no record of Don Nicolás congratulating his son or, indeed, of Franco ever visiting him when in Madrid. It is probable, in any case, that he did not want to meet his father's live-in girlfriend and the rupture appears to have been complete. Franco's siblings, however, were not so strict, and maintained a relationship with their father.[3]

For the first time, Franco's name was being broadcast beyond the army. The profile also provides an appraisement of Franco from the conservative, militaristic viewpoint which *ABC* represented. Given the Spanish army's dire performance in Morocco and the now dwindling public support for the protectorate, conservatives, royalists and militarists who backed the venture needed a hero.[4] Franco fitted the bill. In fact, the glowing profile seems to have been stage-managed. It was accompanied by a photograph of Franco visiting the *ABC* print plant and was published on a day when he was to be received by Alfonso XIII. The monarch too, the young major discovered, was a Franco enthusiast, congratulating him on his successes with the Legion.

Journalists were waiting for him after he visited the king, anxious to ask about the now famous Legion. 'We had to show the Moors how a Spaniard can fight, and now they really know,' he told them. 'The Legionnaires know what awaits them: death, if necessary.' When journalists pointed out that many officers were dying too, he agreed. 'Quite so! That may well be Spain's proudest thing, to see how officers die and how the numbers who want to replace them grows continually. Every officer wants to join the Legion.'[5]

Corrochano described Franco as extremely modest. 'What has been said about me is somewhat exaggerated. I merely fulfil my duty. The soldiers are the brave ones. You can go anywhere with them,' he said after meeting the king.[6] The journalists at the palace considered him tight-lipped. In fact, he suffered the kind of shyness that can hide thin-skinned pride. Amongst other military men, this was not a problem: rank and the rules of the obedience provided clear parameters. The civilian world was harder to navigate. He knew, however, that royal approval boosted an officer's career and image. His fiancée's family in Oviedo, or other friends, appear to have made sure his visit to the king appeared in the local *El Carbayón* newspaper. In Ferrol, he was met by military bands, the mayor and a crowd who accompanied him to his mother's house, obliging him to express his thanks from her balcony.[7]

Millán Astray was back commanding the Legion by this stage. It had grown to 5,800 men and five banderas, with Franco effectively in charge of two of them, returning from home leave at the end of March and provoking 'widespread joy', according to his cousin Pacón, who now commanded a Legion company. Again, Franco's style of leadership in the field when under fire was described by his cousin as 'serene'. Orders were clear and concise with subordinates left to use their own initiative to carry them out as effectively as possible.[8]

Franco continued to lead his two banderas into engagements, frequently being praised for his willingness to take them into the most difficult spots. He displayed 'quite brilliant military qualities', according to one official dispatch, and inspired his men 'with his military spirit and [by] directing them according to the very best techniques'. It was just one of many paeans to the young major in dispatches that year.[9]

By the end of 1922, though, overall public enthusiasm for Morocco had reached its lowest point. The Riffian army had not murdered all the Spanish soldiers they found: 534 prisoners, including many officers, were being held in dire conditions, and pressure grew for a ransom to be paid. There were calls, too, for most of the army to be withdrawn so that tens of thousands of soldiers could go home. Meanwhile, attempts were made to hold those responsible for the Annual disaster to account.

Franco found this shameful and yet another example of political disdain for the supposedly heroic Africanistas. Elsewhere, the decade during which military governors had held all power in Spanish Morocco was now deemed a disaster. It had cost too much Spanish money and blood. Civil governors arrived in 1923, immediately complaining that the army was corrupt and given to colonial overreach.[10] The antagonism between the new civilian administrators and the Africanistas became so acute that one civil governor described Ceuta and Melilla as 'subjected for centuries to an exclusively military regime, where interests of all kinds have been created that need war to continue'.[11]

Franco's decision to publish *Morocco: Diary of a Bandera* at the end of 1922 can be seen, in part, as a response. His praise of 'virile' martial heroism and unconcealed resentment of critics was a challenge to the naysayers. The inclusion in the book of the article censored the previous year by the infantry magazine *Memorial de Infantería* showed a newly emboldened Franco.[12] It also helped turn him into an Africanista figurehead, ready to publicly challenge their opponents. All this reflected the rapidly growing self-confidence of the Legion, which was tipping into arrogance. A celebrated picture of Franco and Millán Astray, heads thrown back and chins jutting as they presumably sang one of the Legion's anthems, captures the swagger of the moment. He was also learning, as the *ABC* profile showed, to become a self-publicist. If part of Spain wanted military heroes, he was happy to fill the role.

Franco's public profile still paled, however, beside that of his commander, the exuberant Millán Astray. When Astray was sacked as commander of the Legion in November 1922 after publishing a letter criticising the government for kowtowing to the juntas, who were deemed cowards by the Africanista faction, it seemed Franco's turn had come. Franco expected to be handed command, but this was apparently stymied by those who saw him as sharing Millán Astray's arrogant impetuousness. The government turned instead to a respected regulares officer, Lt. Col. Rafael Valenzuela. In a considerable display of power by the Africanistas, the juntas were suppressed in November 1922, but it was too late for Franco.[13]

In January 1923, the now multi-decorated Franco was posted to a mainland regiment in Oviedo, where his fiancée awaited. Just before he left, the king appointed him a 'gentleman of the chamber', an honorary title that confirmed him as a royal favourite. He seems to have felt emboldened.[14] That month, while passing through Madrid and visiting the king, he was interviewed by the Madrid press again – this time for *Nuevo Mundo* by the journalist Julián Fernández Piñero, who used the byline Juan Ferragut. Franco claimed that he had left Morocco because he was bored. 'We aren't doing anything there.

There's no fighting. The war has become a job like any other, just more tiring. All we are doing now is vegetate.'[15]

He described himself as a man of action. 'I think that a soldier has two periods: one for war, the other for study. I've done the first of those and now I wish to study. War used to be a lot simpler. You just applied resolve. But now it is far more complex,' he said. Ferragut was gushing in his praise of the young officer as amongst 'the best, the caudillos [the first time Franco is publicly described this way, as an absolute military leader], those who knew how to be strong, heroic and Spanish'. He still, however, comes across as publicly shy and modest. Ferragut claimed that he responded to praise by blushing 'like a flattered girl'. His social timidity, indeed, made him childlike. 'His brown face, shiny dark eyes, curly hair, short answers and modest hand gestures, together with a quick, full smile seem to infantilise him.'[16]

This timidity contrasted with his obvious fearlessness, which Franco wrote off by saying: 'I've done nothing really. The dangers are fewer than people imagine.' He may have been particularly honest when he declared that he did not actually know 'what courage and fear are': someone whose mind does not conjure up fear has no need of courage to overcome it.[17]

In Oviedo, people were so impressed by his status as a gentleman of the chamber that they collected money to present him with a symbolic golden key. Wedding plans were sketched, with the ceremony to be held in the summer. Yet Franco barely had time to get used to the sedate garrison life of Oviedo or the company of Carmen Polo. Africa once more got in the way. On 4 June 1923, Rafael Valenzuela died leading his men in a bayonet charge that claimed the lives of 58 legionnaires. Four days later Franco was finally promoted to lieutenant colonel (as he had long been expecting), back-dated to January. It was another war merit promotion, for his six-month spell after the Annual disaster, rushed through so that he could take command of the Legion. It was the first time an officer had been promoted for battlefield merits in two years. Franco, in other words, was a special case. Four days later he left for north Africa. 'If I do not die, I promise we will marry this year,' he reportedly told Carmen Polo.[18]

But marriage could wait, he told a newspaper in Oviedo. 'Plans?... I am a simple soldier who obeys orders. I will go to Morocco. I will see how things are. We will work hard and as soon as I can get some leave I will come back to Oviedo … to do what I thought was virtually done… [but] when the fatherland calls, we have only rapid and concise response: Here I am!' ("¡*Presente!*")[19]

Franco must have enjoyed the adulatory tone taken by the press. The Legion had made a huge impact in its short lifetime. Far more than any other regiment, its commander was a celebrity. A week later Franco was in Madrid, on his way to Morocco. At a goodbye dinner, a priest called for him to be buried beside St James in the cathedral at Santiago de Compostela – the assumption being that, like Valenzuela, he would die in action.[20]

Franco returned to Morocco in the same week that the *Diario Oficial* published the royal authorisation needed for him to marry Carmen Polo. His brother Ramón, who was making a name for himself as a daring military pilot, flew the seaplane in which they flew on to Melilla so that he could review the Legion's banderas there.[21] They greeted him with a new ditty:

> El coronel Franco es un gran militar
> que aplazó su boda para ir a luchar
>
> ('Colonel Franco is a soldier of might
> who postponed his wedding to go and fight')[22]

Right-wing Africanista cheerleaders now began to hold Franco up as an example of a mystical Spanish heroism that could transform a crestfallen nation. At a time of national pessimism, personal egoism and spiritual vacuity, wrote Luis Galinsoga in *Las Provincias*, Franco represented hope for the future. People knew, he said, of Franco's heroism but not of the 'saintly abnegation' he displayed when patriotic duty called – even if it meant putting of his wedding. 'Franco stands out as a symbol of the immortality of the race, as a relic [of greatness] who will be the seed for a new generation in which we will find virtues that seemed extinct, a faith that seemed to have died and the patriotism that we thought had disappeared.'[23] This was exactly how Franco would eventually come to view himself. A leader, in other words, was in the making.

8

My Mussolini

MOROCCO, JULY 1923

Ten weeks after Franco returned to Morocco to take command of the Legion, he received some startling news. Spain's shaky democracy had collapsed, and a military dictator was in charge of the government – even though the the king remained the head of state. On 13 September 1923, backed by most of the military and by Alfonso XIII himself, General Miguel Primo de Rivera had launched a peaceful coup. The Moroccan war and, especially, the Annual catastrophe had dealt a death blow to the status quo. For the previous half-century this had been based on the 'peaceful turn' agreement between liberals and conservatives to take it in turns to govern via rigged elections. This phony democracy, supported by the monarchy, had been in crisis for over a decade. Now it was dead.[1]

The new arrangement twinned two of Franco's loves – the army and the monarchy. The coup was backed by a bourgeoisie that was terrified of revolution. In Barcelona, where Primo de Rivera was captain-general of Catalonia, industrialists had been using hired gunmen to fight in a bloody, tit-for-tat game of assassinations with armed anarchists. Faithful monarchists like Franco were happy to follow King Alfonso's lead as an enthusiastic backer of the shift towards authoritarianism.[2] Just the previous year, his Italian counterpart Victor Emmanuel III had appointed fascist leader Benito Mussolini to head the government as a 'strong man' who would impose 'order'. Monarchs and dictators, in other words, could work together.

Widespread disillusionment with the old system, which the workers detested, meant few people bothered to defend it. As a result, virtually all Primo de Rivera had to do was declare a state of war in Catalonia, publish a manifesto, wait two days and then catch a train to Madrid.[3] The army in which Franco served was now a political power with a royal-approved right to take control of the nation when it wanted. For politician-hating Africanistas like Franco that seemed entirely right. Primo de Rivera's main concerns – fixing Morocco and defending the army while repressing left-wing revolutionaries and separatists – exactly matched those of men like Franco.

Alfonso XIII praised his new strongman as 'my Mussolini', thus introducing the idea that Italian-style fascism might cure Spain's ills. Yet there was no radical lurch towards totalitarianism. Mussolini was just starting out in power and Adolf Hitler had not yet provided a monstruous model to imitate. Primo de Rivera was a strongman and an authoritarian, but he was not a fascist: in fact, he wielded power in a way that eventually came to seem too weak to Franco. For the time being, however, opposition was desultory. Even the Socialist Party worked with him, seeing an opening to improve workers' conditions. With no great ideology to promote, Primo de Rivera was a pragmatist who headed a 'directorate' of nine fellow generals and admirals which ran the country until December 1925, when he replaced it with a civilian one.

Franco approved of the change, but disagreed fervently with the new dictator about how to resolve the problem of Morocco. Primo de Rivera had served there, but not since 1913, and he was not a true Africanista. His brother Fernando, a lieutenant colonel, had died at Annual. As a highly decorated officer who had fought in Cuba, he was dismissive of Africanista portrayals of their fighting as especially courageous. To him, the Rif war was little more than 'skirmishes, surprises, aggressions, and ambushes'.[4]

The Moroccan venture, Primo de Rivera had argued after Annual, was actually a danger to Spain and the army should withdraw. He had even wanted to swap Ceuta for Gibraltar. More important to Africanistas, though, was Primo de Rivera's desire to silence criticism of the army for Annual. Indeed, one of his first acts was to suppress the Picasso Report – drawn up by Lieutenant General Juan Picasso, a great-uncle of the celebrated painter, who had been charged with investigating the calamity. The army could now close ranks. Men like Franco approved of that.⁵

Franco himself returned to Oviedo to be married on 22 October 1923. He stopped off in Madrid to see the king, who became the official padrino of the wedding. Franco's falling-out with his own father meant the latter did not attend the ceremony at Oviedo's San Juan el Real church. The 30-year-old Franco wore his Legionnaire uniform and medals. The organist played military marches and a military chaplain conducted the ceremony. Carmen, now aged 21, walked into the church on the arm of the region's military governor, who represented the king. Two local aristocrats served as witnesses. Since the governor was representing royalty, they walked in under a canopy born by four bearers. 'It was as if I was dreaming,' Polo recalled later.⁶

A cheering crowd greeted them outside and followed them to their banquet, disrupting the city's traffic. Local and national newspapers took note, with their photograph on the front page of the Asturian daily *El Comercio*. The many admirers of the 'brave and popular' commander of the Legion were overjoyed that 'a love which had been so mistreated by fate could finally receive divine sanction', as one local newspaper reported. The couple left for Morocco, stopping for lunch with the king and queen. The queen remembered an awkward, dumbstruck young man sitting at their table, while Franco claimed to have spent the meal vigorously urging the king for further action in Morocco. They moved on to north Africa. Carmen did not enjoy it: luxuries were scarce and she had to learn how to console the wives and families of Legion officers who died in action. She herself was once told, incorrectly, that her husband had died in battle.⁷

Primo de Rivera no longer wished to abandon Morocco, but planned a withdrawal to tighter defensive lines, believing he could then bomb or gas the Riffians into submission and negotiate agreements with them. Franco disagreed with the strategy. With the army now in charge of Spain, he joined the political fray by angrily confronting the high commissioner, General Luis Aizpuru, about the withdrawal plans. 'If this order or line of thought was made public, it would provoke a rising against us across the whole zone, creating such a grave situation that it could provoke a second Annual [massacre],' he said. Aizpuru reminded him that he was obliged to follow orders.⁸

In January 1924, the rebellious attitude of Franco and other officers led General Manuel Montero Navarro, the military commander of Ceuta, to demand that they swear to obey orders if told to abandon positions.[9] Franco replied that he was ready to obey, but not to relinquish an officer's right to be guided by his sense of honour at a moment of doubt. In Franco's later retelling, other officers immediately followed his example. His fellow Africanista Emilio Mola called Primo's withdrawal plans 'a whip-blow to the face'.[10] The normally cautious and disciplined Franco was now caught up in the indignation he could see all around him.

On the streets of the Protectorate's cities, the Legion looked rebellious. The British consul in Tetouan, C. G. Hope Gill, claimed that Legion officers allowed men to loot shops and stab shop-owners in Ceuta. Gill watched in disgust as they ignored Aizpuru when he demanded that drunken legionnaires be arrested in the town square:

> He [Aizpuru] turned on the groups of officers sitting in the surrounding cafes and harangued them. Then seeing Major Villalba of the Legion, a notorious character against whom the Moors have a detailed list of rapes committed in the Melilla area, he called him forward but the Major strolled away through the crowd advising them not to listen to the 'old man'... The officers make no attempt to control their men.[11]

Africa was far from the seat of power, but Franco was by now also involved in a separate initiative for the Africanistas to influence politics. In August 1923, he had joined with other officers to launch a magazine designed to educate the Army of Africa and exert pressure on the government. In his own words, they vowed to fight the chaotic policies 'that have turned what should have been a two- or three-year campaign into a chronically painful war'. The mastermind and editor-in-chief was the forthright, belligerent (and, in his younger years, duel-fighting) Brigadier General Gonzalo Queipo de Llano. They named their magazine the *Revista de Tropas Coloniales* (*Review of Colonial Troops*).[12]

The first issue appeared in January 1924. It contained just two dozen pages of text. Queipo de Llano's editorial was a proclamation of how Africanistas, including Franco, viewed Spanish history and their own role as saviours of the nation. Decline had set in, he said, because self-centred politicians had brought decadence and anarchy (presumably by letting workers and separatist movements spread). Africanistas, he declared, were among the 'few men of heart who, risking everything, confronted the arduous task of resurrecting the spirit of Spain'. For that task, they enjoyed the support of the king and those who 'love our country and conserve intact faith in our race'.[13]

Right-wing journalist and contributor Ramiro de Maeztu declared military bravery the highest of all virtues and denounced the 'hostility of intellectuals to heroism'. He insisted that the occupation of northern Morocco was to 'civilise a backward nation', following the standard European colonialist justification of the time. Additionally, Ramiro de Maeztu praised the army's eruption into politics because only it could stop separatists from tearing the nation apart. 'The army is the great unifier of Spain,' he declared.[14]

On the same page, in a piece nominally about the role of commanders, Franco began his own personal campaign to shape opinion. His sinuous, baroque style mixes fawning praise for superiors with criticism of those who 'look down on the Moroccan problem' and fail to see it as 'the task of giants'. The sacrifice of patriots, Franco exclaimed, was being met with 'the indifference of the country!'[15] Franco's criticisms, though, were often more veiled, revealing a man keen not to damage his future prospects. Calculated ambiguity, indeed, became a notable feature of his political machinations from now on.

Patriotism and colonialism were clearly tied together in Franco's mind. In wider European terms, that merely made him a man of his time. Franco's insistence, however, that those fighting Spain's colonial war were moral giants (and, by inference, superior to their countrymen) took this argument into new and potentially dangerous terrain, especially since other Africanistas clearly agreed. It was as if this class of supermen, and they alone, could save the nation.

The new magazine was deemed a great success and the tone of the next edition, in February 1924, was euphoric. 'This is not the triumph of a group of authors, most of them beginners; it is the triumph of the feelings and ideas of the entirety of Spain,' its editors boasted. 'Every Spaniard finds in our pages something intimate about their own spirit.'[16] Franco and his fellow founders were becoming military messiahs, expounding a millenarian view of change and the recovery of national pride based on war and the virile embrace of danger – an obviously authoritarian path.

Franco's own piece in the second issue is a call for officers to learn the art of manoeuvres, which he also uses to lambast those who fail to 'live for the army, or do not feel the glory of sacrificing themself for the Fatherland'. His was not the only family by-line. His younger brother Ramón, by now a celebrated military aviator, wrote about his own groundbreaking flight from mainland Spain, via Morocco, to the Canary Islands. He was also making a name for himself as the wildest member of the Franco family, carousing late into the night and – especially after he jumped naked onto the stage of a cabaret club – scandalising people.[17]

By the next edition, in March, Franco's name was on the masthead as part of the two-man editorial council, effectively becoming deputy editor to Queipo de Llano. The two men seem to have egged each other on and by April an article by Franco about the dangers of keeping the Army of Africa idle provoked an angry reaction from Primo de Rivera's government. 'It is impossible to remain immobile and carrying out the eternal parody of the protectorate, which needs authority and strength,' Franco wrote.[18] His fellow Africanistas were a special caste 'born to the profession' of war. Ignorant and indecisive leaders should not stand in their way:

> The period when politics, time and money helped our work, and when those who were prudent or timid seemed correct, has given way to a time when passivity and inaction may provoke upsets and setbacks.[19]

It was a direct challenge to Primo de Rivera's government and the edition was sequestered before it could be distributed. Franco later complained about 'outside pressures and the red pen of the censor'.[20] It was also a sign of the Army of Africa's growing boldness and, within it, that of the impudent Legion – which demanded the right to speak its particular version of the truth to power. The article, however, received tacit backing from the king. One of the *Revista's* civilian contributors, the journalist Víctor Ruiz Albeniz, took him a copy of the banned edition and watched as the king made a point of slowly reading 'Franquito's article':

> On finishing the article, he goes back to read selected paragraphs. He finishes, he smiles again, looking straight at us. It seems that there is now a special shine in his eyes.[21]

The monarch liked Franco's militant tone. 'I cannot hide the fact that the desires of my colonial troops coincide with my own,' Alfonso said in an interview published in the May 1924 edition. That helped push Franco further into confrontation with Primo de Rivera, especially after he ordered a withdrawal from parts of Morocco on 30 May 1924. Franco was outraged.[22]

Shortly thereafter, in July, Primo de Rivera travelled to Morocco, where Franco hosted a dinner for him at the Ben-Tieb military camp outside Melilla, home to three banderas of his Legion. Francoist mythology claims eggs were served because in Spanish slang *huevos* (or eggs) also mean 'balls', which the 'virile' Legion possessed and, by inference, Primo de Rivera lacked. Franco's speech was incendiary.

'How we would have liked for this first visit to the Legion by a head of the government to fill our hearts with serene joy,' Franco told Primo de Rivera in a room decorated with rousing Legion slogans. 'Unfortunately, we have to admit that a terrible worry has invaded our souls.'[23]

> Legion officers reject the idea of a retreat. The soil of Morocco is to us the same as the soil of Spain, and we have paid for it in blood! We want, General, to reach the last crag of the Rif, to be worthy of the affection of our fatherland and to extol those who died… We want to go forward bare-chested, facing glory, and, since we believe the honour of Spain comes before the convenience of government, the Legion awaits your word.[24]

Honour, in other words, ranked above national interest (and by 'honour' he meant respect, rather than doing the right thing). A livid Primo de Rivera reminded Franco that Africanistas did not have 'a monopoly on patriotism' and were obliged to obey orders. His comments were received icily and when one of his aides shouted 'well said!', a young Africanista officer called José Enrique Varela replied 'badly said!' Another of Primo's aides claimed to have silently checked his pistol in case shooting started.[25]

Primo berated Franco in turn. 'You should never have invited me to something like this,' he said.[26] According to Franco's later version, he retorted that he had only invited him because he had been ordered to. In fact, such forthrightness was unlikely from a man in awe of military hierarchy. When other officers fretted that it had all gone too far, Franco claims to have calmed them – saying he would shoulder the blame. Primo then sat down with him for a two-hour private conversation in which, according to Franco, he thanked Franco for his frankness and pledged to keep Africanista officers abreast of his plans.[27]

Days before the visit, Franco and his main rival in the race up the ranks – the equally youthful Lieutenant Colonel Luis Pareja Aycuéns – had agreed to demand mainland transfers if withdrawals started. In a letter to Pareja, Franco claimed many officers would follow them. After the dinner, which he attended, Pareja remained true to his word and demanded the transfer. Franco did not. His career was too important.[28]

9
Retreat and Revenge

CHEFCHAOUEN, 18 NOVEMBER 1924

On 18 November 1924, old Legion uniforms were stuffed with hay and left on the walls of the Moroccan hill town of Chefchaouen while the garrison, along with their civilian Arab and Jewish collaborators, prepared to abandon the emblematic city. Franco had led part of a fighting relief column to the town and was now obeying Primo de Rivera's orders to evacuate the city as his partial withdrawal plan was executed. Primo had even appointed himself high commissioner in October 1924 in order to take direct command of the Army of Africa and oversee the operation, further obliging men like Franco to obey orders. Queipo later claimed that, two months previously, Franco had proposed launching a coup against a dictator who planned to withdraw from 400 hard-won outposts in the interior. That is unlikely, but men like Queipo certainly did want a coup and Franco, with his sinuous ambiguity, had a gift for letting people imagine he was on their side.[1]

Franco wandered the narrow streets of Chefchaouen as workmen removed the 'Plaza de España' sign and other names imposed by the occupiers. Beds, chairs, pots and pans were sold off at cut-rate prices in the square since there were not enough buyers for everything that was being left. Crowds of Spanish prostitutes and hangers-on milled around, begging for places on the convoy of trucks before they set off down windy tracks. An old shopkeeper who Franco described as 'maybe more than 100 years of age' asked why the Spaniards had bothered coming in the first place. Franco blamed the Riffian people's ingratitude. 'It's your fault,' he claims to have replied. 'You will weep over our departure and eventually you will understand that we were right.'[2]

Franco commanded part of the fighting rearguard as, over a month, the evacuation column battled through rain, mud and ambushes towards the coast. The retreats proved costly, with casualties reaching anywhere between 2,000 and 18,000 men, including to sickness. Exact figures were not released and returning soldiers were banned from talking about it in public. In the meantime, gas, explosives and incendiary bombs were dropped on the insurgents by, amongst other, Franco's brother Ramón. In fact, Abd el-Krim's growing 'Rif Republic' now occupied more than half of the Spanish protectorate. He styled himself 'Emir of the Rif' and even applied to join the League of Nations.[3]

Once more, Franco was frequently praised in dispatches throughout this chaotic period. By February 1925 he had been promoted again for battlefield merits, this time to full colonel,. In January 1925, Franco became the main editor of *La Revista de Tropas Coloniales*, with his name prominently placed below the masthead. The 'modest' Franco of Ferragut's 1923 article was disappearing. In the March 1925 edition, the magazine devoted its front page (along with page two and part of page three) to his promotion, with a fawning piece by the influential far-right monarchist Antonio Goicochea.[4]

Goicochea compared Franco to the conquistador of Mexico, Hernán Cortés, calling him a caudillo who embodied 'a romantic attachment to the cult of high and noble ideas'. With his small frame and high-pitched voice, Franco had rarely, if ever, been considered charismatic. Yet this was what Goicoechea claimed to have seen during a dinner in Franco's honour in Madrid in October 1924. Goicoechea found a simple authenticity and a 'look in his eyes that was both somewhat childlike and challenging'. In response to the after-dinner toasts, Franco had given 'a vibrant speech, overflowing with inflamed passion, more like a harangue than a toast'.[5] He had spoken, in other words, as if the audience was standing before him on a parade ground.

Primo de Rivera kept Franco as head of the Legion and, in May, handed him a letter from the king: 'the beautiful history that you are writing with your lives and your blood is a constant example of what can be done ... you know how much you are loved and appreciated by your most affectionate friend who embraces you. Alfonso XIII.'[6] Despite his meteoric career and socially superior wife, Franco had not shed his small-town, provincial awe of the monarchy and aristocracy. He must have been delighted.

Commanders also continued to praise him. 'Calm during action, serene when taking decisions, with an ability to weigh-up the tactical situation with great precision, bold and risk-taking when moving up if he deems it necessary to see for himself the situation that his troops find themselves in before taking a decision, this is an exceptional leader,' reads a report from the Military Headquarters in Ceuta on 31 July 1925. It was a succinct and accurate precis of Franco's considerable military virtues.[7]

Having given up the exposed and militarily extravagant outposts so ardently defended by Franco and his 'no-step-back' Africanistas, Primo de Rivera now drew up a bold plan to defeat the overambitious Abd el-Krim by striking directly at his heartland with a beach landing at Alhucemas Bay. The French offered support and warships while promising a strong, coordinated attack from their protectorate in the south.

Franco later claimed to have been the first to propose a bold new plan to attack the Alhucemas beaches to Alfonso XIII and Primo de Rivera while on the mainland for his own wedding in the autumn of 1923. 'We take the war right into the heart of the enemy territory and we capture his capital,' he claimed to have told the monarch.[8] Primo de Rivera was too drunk by the end of their dinner to take his advice in, according to Franco, but he had repeated it during the general's infamous Moroccan visit in July 1924. 'Primo de Rivera promised to study the matter further,' he claims. At some stage, Franco sent a more detailed proposal to Alfonso XIII, which included the use of massive force and poisoned gas.[9]

In fact, similar proposals had been around for years. With the Annual defeat in mind, however, it was a risky decision. Franco was tasked with leading advance units onto the beaches. The landings at Gallipoli during the First World War had shown that such assaults could be fraught with danger, even against a less sophisticated enemy.[10]

On 8 September 1925, Franco rode in some of the first landing crafts to approach Alhucemas Bay. These secondhand craft, bought off the

British, had in fact previously been used at Gallipoli. The attack was preceded by naval and aerial bombardment, including mustard gas attacks. Franco's brother Ramón was again amongst the pilots in this first coordinated beach landing involving all the three arms (air, sea and land armies) of any country's military.[11]

War destroys the best-made plans. The creaky, fat-bellied landing craft struggled against the wind and a string of explosives on the target beach prevented them landing at their chosen spot. Sea currents then helped push them to a beach further west of the bay, leaving them stuck in water that was too deep for pack animals, vehicles or heavy weapons. Orders arrived for the landing to be aborted, but Franco commanded his bugler to sound the command to attack. The water was, he reasoned, shallow enough for a man to jump into if he carried his equipment above his head. The men jumped out and waded ashore under fire. By night-time Franco's men had carved out a workable beachhead.[12]

Franco was especially proud of the fortifications that his men built overnight, which kept them safe from anything but direct artillery hits, and for which he was applauded. His decision to ignore orders and storm the beach, he said, had been taken to prevent his men's morale from collapsing after so many hours sloshing around in boats and because military rules allowed 'an officer in command to use their initiative at crucial moments'. The move likely saved the day for Spain, which established a wider bridgehead over the next three days for a total cost of only 11 dead and 89 wounded. From there, they marched on Abd el-Krim's hometown and headquarters at Ajdir, taking it on October 1 and driving his forces towards the French who – in a campaign carefully coordinated by the two countries – were approaching from the south.[13]

For Franco, who published a dramatic four-part description of the battle in the *Revista de Tropas Coloniales*, this victory must have seemed like further proof of his long-held vision of the war as a forge for the rebirth of a nation. Yet he did not express political ambitions and espoused no greater ideology. In his colourful telling, he is more interested in the exemplary character of those involved. Stretcher-bearers scuttle around carrying 'their glorious, pain-wracked cargo' and the dead are all 'heroes'. These deaths are examples of 'the spirit of the race'. His overwrought descriptions, indeed, are a clear attempt to use the landings to generate popular support for the Africanistas.[14]

Despite the old-fashioned imagery, the use of fast-moving mobile units, radio communications, air support and naval guns had now changed the way Spaniards fought. The credit for that belonged to officers senior to Franco, including Primo de Rivera himself.[15] It also, however, matched the changes in battlefield culture that Franco had called for in the *Revista de Tropas Coloniales* two years earlier.

A French liaison officer reported that his country's previously damning judgement of the Spanish army would need revising. 'The officers have learned from the hard lessons of [earlier] defeat,' he said. The French were, nevertheless, shocked at the Spanish determination to 'punish, disarm and dominate' by shooting prisoners and allowing their indigenous allies to pillage at will.[16] Not for the last time, the harsh military culture that both shaped Franco and which he now promoted repulsed observers from other European nations.

Franco remained as head of the Legion through 1925 and continued his meteoric ascent – at the rate of a promotion every other year – to reach brigadier general in February 1926. He was 33 years old and was hailed as the 'youngest general in Europe'.[17] It was an extraordinary achievement.

It meant, however, that he now had to leave Morocco to take up a position that matched his rank. Franco was returning to what had become a relatively mild and stable government in Spain, with Primo de Rivera's popularity boosted by success in Morocco. He had replaced his governing Military Directorate with a Civilian Directorate that was seen as a step towards consolidating a dictatorship. He also, cleverly, drew the socialist UGT trades union close, giving it a role in a system of labour committees while banning anarchist unions.[18]

Franco was therefore not in Morocco to see Primo de Rivera's strategy, which he had criticised so bitterly before the Alhucemas operation, reach fruition after the joint campaign with the French resumed in the spring of 1926. Abd el-Krim surrendered to the French, who acclaimed his 'dignity' and 'greatness'. On 10 July 1927, the Spanish army declared victory over the entire protectorate. This, it claimed, was a way 'to maintain the legacy of pride and valour left us by our ancestors, the conquerors of a World'.[19] The small, rugged territory that Spain now controlled – nominally on behalf of a Moroccan Sultan – was thus compared to the conquest of the New World five centuries earlier.

Thirty years after the loss of Cuba had cast a shadow over the military world into which Francisco Franco had been born, a sliver of pride had been recovered. Final victory had been the result of Primo de Rivera's astute decision-making, with his tactical withdrawal allowing him to prepare a massive blow at Alhucemas. Intelligence had won out over Africanista bravado. Yet boosterism turned an often disastrous campaign into a military epic which Africanistas held up as a moral exemplar. Franco was amongst their most distinguished and successful representatives: given his age, he was also the one with the most promising future.

10

Hero Brothers

MADRID–ZARAGOZA, 1926–1930

Europe's youngest general's fame was quickly eclipsed by that of his very own brother. Ramón Franco's timing could not have been more extraordinary. The day after Francisco was promoted to general, Ramón landed his Dornier Do J Wal seaplane, baptised *Plus Ultra*, in Rio de Janeiro. It was the first transatlantic air crossing from mainland Spain to South America – a feat celebrated in much the same way that Americans would rejoice after Charles Lindbergh's non-stop solo flight to Paris the following year.[1]

Long-distance aviators were the astronauts of the time and Spain embraced Ramón Franco with passion. The daring, rule-breaking and unconventional younger brother of the Franco clan also became the most famous. Foreign newspapers followed his progress almost daily, with the *New York Times* hailing Ramón as the 'Columbus of the air' and praising 'a boldness and skill in air navigation that have not been excelled by aviators of other nations'.[2] Francisco was pleased by Ramón's success, later saying that his arrival in Brazil was one of the greatest days of his life, along with the Alhucemas landing and his wedding. His younger brother now joined him as one of the monarch's gentlemen of the chamber – a sign of their combined social prestige. The Franco brothers, indeed, were suddenly public figures. But in the military terms that mattered most to him Francisco still ranked far above his brother, however much glamour Ramón now added to the Franco surname. In fact, one of Franco's obsessions was now where he stood in the ranking of active Spanish generals, a group of 150 men.[3]

By the time war in Africa officially ended in July 1927, Franco was established in Madrid, commanding the illustrious First Brigade of the First Division. He had also been placed in charge of the committee that was to organise a new General Military Academy. In Madrid, however, he was just one of many generals. He was pleasant enough but conversationally pedestrian, reedy-voiced and could not dance. Without the physical activity of campaigning, he began to fill out and develop the pear shape of a man whose ample hips and buttocks eventually earned him the military nickname 'Paca la culona', or Fat-Arsed Franny. As a brigadier general in what was mostly an office job, he was earning less than a colonel on the front line. His wife's family wealth probably helped, but at the many receptions for his bohemian and boisterous brother, he and Carmen were extras. The star was the outgoing Ramón, who increasingly enjoyed his hero status. 'Whenever we walked into a new place, people would just stand up and applaud,' his wife said, as they began a new life of partying and expensive restaurants.[4]

Even in El Ferrol, where a crowd gathered outside the house in María Street and a *Te Deum* was celebrated in the church of San Julián to celebrate the brothers' achievements, Francisco took second place to Ramón. On the outside wall of the first floor of the family house, the town mayor unveiled a bronze plaque bearing the sculpted images of both Ramón and Francisco (with a dagger in his hand), but the town's joy was mostly in response to the younger brother. María Street was packed, with their mother and grandfather Ladislao leaning out of second-floor windows as speeches were made from the first-floor balcony.[5]

Franco, though, did not mind his brother's popularity, and knew that it added too to his own prestige. One ardent speechmaker suggested that Francisco's rise to brigadier general meant he was 'writing on the clouds ... the programme of a new patriotic union'.[6] With a general running the country as a dictator, commentaries like that took on a new, political meaning.

In uniform, Franco commanded huge respect. His peers from the cadet academy in Toledo presented him with a new sword and a text claiming that, when the history of the period was written, 'there will endure the memory of the sublime epic written by the Spanish Army in the development of the nation. And the glorious names of the most important caudillos will be raised on high, and above them all will be lifted triumphantly that of General Francisco Franco Bahamonde … [like] Hernán Cortés.'[7] If Ramón was the daring explorer being compared to Columbus, in other words, then Francisco was being compared to one of the bloodiest and most successful of Spain's sixteenth-century New World conquistadors.

With the army's reputation restored in Morocco and Franco's unique status as a young general established, it was a fine moment to be a senior officer in Madrid. Primo de Rivera had squashed the more radical and violent anarchist workers' movements and would-be separatists in Catalonia, two phenomena that irritated officers like Franco immensely. With his mind freed from the day-to-day intensity of a soldier on campaign, he began a transformation. The ambitious but outwardly modest officer who explained himself in terms of duty and patriotism began to find his feet in the complex world of Madrid society and politics.

Although his civilian social skills needed working on, Franco could always expect an attentive audience of fellow officers at La Gran Peña, the conservative gentleman's club he frequented on the Gran Vía. Other Africanistas gathered there. Victory had increased their public standing. Outside the military world, however, Franco made little impact on Spain's socially vibrant capital city – though there was an undoubted cachet to being such a young general. Natalio Rivas, a wealthy liberal businessman and author, was his main cheerleader, introducing him to Madrid society at the 'tertulias', or informal debates, over which he presided. Franco acquired a taste for theatre and cinema, and even had a bit part in a film shot at Rivas's house, playing a returned Africanista. He appointed his cousin Pacón to stand by his side as his aide-de-camp. The two men would rarely be separated from then on.[8]

He claimed also to have begun reading intensely, this time on history, and learning about economics through conversations with the manager of the local branch of the Banco de Bilbao, which held his wife's savings. 'He was a friendly and intelligent man who, little by little, encouraged my passion for economics,' Franco recalled later.[9] Evidence of this supposed expertise does not appear in his speeches or writing, making it difficult to guess exactly what books he obtained. Yet Franco still exhibited no overt political ambition at this time, perhaps because he felt Spain was already in good hands under a military dictator. His true obsession was his army career.

He devoured military history and could sketch out, say, Napoleon's manoeuvres in the battle of Austerlitz, or the Spanish naval victory at Lepanto in 1571. His future brother-in-law Ramón Serrano Suñer complained that he bored people with endless battle descriptions. His wife Carmen later accused Franco of 'reading books that I do not understand'.[10]

There was a singular problem in their marriage. Carmen was not pregnant. 'The normal thing was for people to have a child by their first wedding anniversary, and if that did not arrive, gossip started,' remarked one of Carmen Polo's later biographers.[11] It was not until September 1926, three years after the wedding, that a child was born – leading to a lifetime of rumours that the little girl, also christened Carmen and known as Carmencita, had been secretly adopted.

The theory behind these rumours was that Franco's wounds prevented him fathering children, with unsubstantiated gossip claiming that he had only one testicle. An estranged cousin even claimed the child was actually Ramón's, again without evidence. The fact that the baby girl was an only child was held up as further support for the theory. However, two witnesses – Franco's sister Pilar and his wife's niece – recalled seeing Carmen pregnant.[12] She gave birth in Oviedo, having left Madrid four months earlier to visit her dying father, which only added to the intrigue. Franco was smitten by his daughter, though he was a traditional, hands-off father – sentimentally-attached rather than involved in her day-to-day life. 'When Carmencita was born, I thought I'd go mad with joy,' he claimed, though nothing seems to have disturbed his usual outward immutability.[13]

Primo de Rivera had early on sounded out Franco about the new cadet college he planned for army officers in Zaragoza. The General Military Academy was to replace the separate colleges for the infantry, cavalry, engineers and artillery. The idea was to improve training but, most of all, to resolve the historic infighting between these branches. That was something that Franco felt strongly about, seeing a divided army as weak. Indeed, when artillery officers locked themselves into their barracks to complain that they were being mistreated by Primo,

Franco was indignant. 'They should all be shot!' he said. This commonplace Franco expression of frustration would have sounded less menacing were it not for his sincere belief in the usefulness of the firing squad.[14]

By this time, Primo de Rivera had shifted his personal support to the Africanistas and they now backed him. Franco was now clearly on his side and the bond was mutual. 'He has a great future, not just because of his military abilities but because of his intellectual ones,' Primo de Rivera said of his 'formidable' young general.[15]

Franco was sent to study the French École Militaire at St Cyr for a time, to examine its methods, and on 4 January 1928 was formally named director of the new cadet school in Zaragoza. 'The future officers will first of all receive an intense education in values,' he told *Estampa* magazine in May 1928. Intense physical training and a planned altar to the Virgin of Pilar (patron of the militarised Civil Guard) in the academy's central patio would help turn out 'physically and morally robust' young officers. The interviewer, Luis Franco de Espes, Baron of Mora, came away with the sensation that Franco would transform his young officers into 'a military priesthood'.[16]

In fact, Franco had not made a show of his religiosity in the army. He had often accompanied his mother to church, but treated this more like a filial duty than something which added great meaning to his life. In the Legion, indeed, he was known as the 'officer of the three M's', reflecting that he had no fear (*miedo*), no women (*mujeres*) and did not go to Mass (*misa*). He only mentioned religion five times in his *Morocco: Diary of a Bandera.* But Carmen Polo was changing that, bringing daily religious practice into his home. Spain, Franco increasingly believed, was born out of Christianity, making the Roman Catholic church a cornerstone of its identity. In fact, it was becoming a core belief, adding a sanctimonious and mystical edge to his belligerent Africanista patriotism and placing the church's social conservatism at the centre of his ideas about how proper Spaniards should behave.[17]

The three-page interview in *Estampa* included photographs of Franco with Carmen Polo in a chintzy apartment furnished with heavy wooden desks, chairs, rugs and drapes, and a cabinet full of delicate fans. 'I, who admire and know the general well, can assure Spaniards who read these pages that nobody is better suited to the sublime and delicate mission of educating the hearts of our future officers,' the author said.[18]

That October, Franco welcomed the first officer cadets to his academy. 'Military life is not a bed of roses ... it brings huge work, sacrifice and difficulties: it also brings glory, which grows amongst thorns, like roses. Do not forget that he who knows how to suffer wins, and that this ability to resist and defeat every day is the school of triumph and the path to heroism.'[19] Like anything that shaped the quarrelsome army, his appointment was strongly political, but he was curt with *Estampa* when it asked if he now considered himself a politician. 'I am a soldier,' he said.[20]

Franco was a pragmatic director, insisting not just on fitness and military manoeuvres but also that cadets carry condoms (to avoid that traditional scourge of armies, venereal disease). He banned the hazing that had made his own cadet years so miserable. Recalling the turgid texts that he had memorised in Toledo, he made instructors teach practical skills by demonstration. Unknowingly reflecting the influence of the despised father who he largely ignored when in Madrid, he insisted they learn to think for themselves. 'They came to us accustomed to the awful parrot-like methods of Spanish schools,' he complained.[21]

What made Franco's academy stand out, however, was his insistence that cadets were making a sacred and spiritual pact with the army, which was itself the maximum expression of virtue, 'virility' and patriotism. The emphasis on martial virility contrasted with the impression visitors to Franco often took away after meeting him close up or in private – of a man who was physically unimposing, soft, timid, even slightly effeminate. His own embrace of military life, based on hierarchy, discipline, an ability to cope with hardship and unquestioning acceptance of the two-way consequences of patriotic violence, allowed him to superimpose the first personality without destroying the other.[22] It was now becoming clear that there were two very different sides to Francisco Franco. One was a hardened and occasionally mystical warrior. The other was a cautious, courteous and sometimes ingratiating part of the civilian world.

Instructors were chosen for war experience, ensuring that Africanistas and their belief system predominated. One in seven were from the Legion. Franco was building a young officer corps, in other words, in his own image. Having set out his beliefs, he was a hands-off manager, letting instructors work with little interference. This reflected his belief that officers needed room to use their own initiative. Franco also delegated the day-to-day running of the academy to his energetic, loyal and intelligent number two, Colonel Miguel Campins. They were friends, but the latter knew his place and made it his task to deliver Franco's desires.[23]

In other ways, Franco's academy was very conservative and his brother Ramón – who was veering rapidly towards the antimonarchical Left – complained of its 'caveman' style. 'It pains me that they will be such poor citizens,' he wrote to Francisco in April 1930. 'They need classes in that.' Ardent Republican officers like General Enrique Ruiz-Fornells fretted that officer cadets were now being educated by an 'ignorant warmonger'.[24]

In his speech to the 1929 intake, for instance, Franco railed against how Britain, France and others exercised power through the League of Nations, pretending that their aim was to avoid another world war. Pacifism, he warned, was a trick played on weaker nations like Spain to keep them down. He had clearly not lost his idea that war offered a chance to 'forge a nation'.[25] Pacifism, he warned his cadets, was a Utopian delusion 'which contradicts the history of the world and the laws of nature'. It was the very same thing that Mussolini was saying in Italy.

Once established in Zaragoza, Franco and his family felt at ease in a provincial city where they had significantly more social cachet than in Madrid. They mostly socialised with the academy's staff, including Franco's loyal head of studies Colonel Campins and his wife, but were also wooed by local high society. His wife's siblings liked to stay, finding the larger Zaragoza more stimulating than Oviedo. Game-shooting became Franco's favourite pastime, thanks to the many invitations to the estates of local elites. He even had a street named after him.

In Zaragoza, Franco made friends with a clever and ambitious government lawyer called Ramón Serrano Suñer, who would play a crucial role in his later life. 'He still had some of that youthful look that had been broadcast in the press during the African war; he wasn't much different from the tiny officer who had graduated from the Academy in Toledo,' Serrano Suñer recalled many years later.[26] The two men spoke at length about politics, which drove Serrano Suñer's passions and about which Franco knew little, his own interests centring on army intrigues and the bickering over promotions as he climbed towards the top.

Franco's ego had grown to match his rank. Serrano Suñer was surprised by the way in which he pronounced firm ideas on subjects about which he knew little, especially economics.[27] (At a chance meeting with finance minister José Calvo Sotelo, he even criticised his foreign exchange policy. 'What stupidities are you saying?' the minister retorted.)[28] They were not, however, the musings of a man with a grand political project for Spain or an expressed desire to lead the country, but rather the incontinent opinions of someone unused to being challenged. The young general, Serrano Suñer noted, was given to wide-ranging monologues full of personal anecdotes and military tales. 'He rarely showed much admiration of other people, rather tending to think of himself as unique,' said Serrano Suñer after the two men had fallen out years later. 'He was beginning to show a tendency to consider other people – for the moment other officers – as good or bad, depending purely on whether he believed that they were favourable or friendly towards his own plans and ambitions. Those who looked like they might get in his way were enemies.'[29]

Although garrulous, opinionated and critical in private, Serrano Suñer noticed, Franco was circumspect in public and slow to make difficult decisions away from the battlefield or barracks. For the moment, however, Serrano Suñer was delighted by his new acquaintance and they spent many hours together.[30]

In February 1931, the two men became brothers-in-law when Serrano Suñer married Carmen Polo's sister, Zita. At their wedding in Oviedo, Franco was a witness, alongside José Antonio Primo de Rivera, the son of the military dictator – who was a close friend of his new brother-in-law. The two men never got on well at a personal level, but the suave and charismatic José Antonio Primo de Rivera would soon found Spain's most important fascist party, the Falange, becoming a major influence. In the coming years, indeed, Serrano Suñer acted as the funnel through which the ideology of fascism reached Franco, and the Falange, in time, would become a crucial part of his regime.[31]

Franco was already showing signs of a radical anti-communism that drifted easily into imagined conspiracies. In 1929, he had begun to receive regular editions of the bulletin published by the International Anticommunist Entente (IAE), a Swiss-based group that attracted the support of Benito Mussolini and, later, Adolf Hitler. He even wrote to the secretary expressing his 'admiration for your great work'.[32] Fear of communism was widely felt in the army and dictator Miguel Primo de Rivera was another IAE supporter. In fact, the defence ministry paid for Franco's subscription. From now on, he received a drip-drip of alarming articles that saw Bolshevism hiding in every corner, intent on destroying 'Christian civilisation'. 'It allowed me to see that communism was already at work in Spain,' he said later.[33] In fact, communism had made very little impact – with Spanish workers and Leftists mostly drawn to either socialism or anarchism.

Other forces were also at work, however, with Primo de Rivera failing to cement an opportunistic dictatorship that had always lacked a defining ideology and was riddled with corruption. In fact, Primo de Rivera still needed the king's support and he had lost that by January 1930 when Alfonso XIII accepted his resignation. Franco's admired commander in Morocco, General Dámaso Berenguer, was appointed to lead what became known, in a play of words, as not a 'dictadura' but a 'dictablanda', a 'soft' dictatorship, rather than a 'hard' one.

Franco was upset. Primo de Rivera had triumphed in Morocco and silenced separatists in Catalonia. Franco believed the dictator had raised the nation at all levels, but that the king had mistreated him. Nevertheless, Spain had tasted dictatorship and many on the far right liked the idea, even if they felt it could be done better. Franco later identified one great failing in the outgoing dictator – he had allowed people to know he did not plan to govern forever.[34]

11
Out With The Old – The End Of Monarchy

ZARAGOZA, 1930–31

Francisco Franco was extremely young for his military rank but decidedly old-fashioned and reactionary in his ideas. This contrasted with the increasingly dramatic and rebellious behaviour of his brother Ramón, who was caught up in a wave of anti-monarchist fervour sweeping across Spain as it struggled to find a new path after Primo de Rivera. In fact, the brothers stood on opposite sides of a growing split between those loyal to Alfonso XIII and those who saw an interfering and inept monarchy as Spain's biggest problem.[1]

The impulsive and impassioned Ramón was furious with the monarch and the entire establishment. To his conservative family's chagrin, Ramón had married the French-educated daughter of a Spanish engineer, Carmen Díaz, in July 1924, bypassing the usual formality for an officer of seeking royal permission. Instead, they flitted across the border to France to marry. 'He was not punished for that,' Díaz noted later. 'Only his brother Paco [Francisco] criticised him, because it had an element of indiscipline.' In fact, the two brothers had a difficult relationship, not least because they had dramatically different personalities, with Ramón 'liking to do the opposite to everyone else ... things that nobody else dared to do', according to his wife. His dislike of the monarch had increased after the latter gifted his *Plus Ultra* aircraft to Argentina in 1926 and ordered him to return by boat. In June 1929, he announced another trans atlantic flight, promising to show off Spain's aircraft- building capacity by flying a Dornier

Wal seaplane built under licence in Cádiz to the Americas. Instead, he cheated. The aircraft was not up to the task, so he took another Wal, built in Italy, and repainted its numbering to match the Spanish one.[2]

Cloudy skies meant Ramón's crew became lost over the Atlantic after take-off and, after seven days bobbing in the ocean with no petrol, had to be rescued by the British aircraft carrier HMS *Eagle*. Over that week, the disappearance of the famous aviation hero became a national drama. Francisco followed it closely, sending his mother upbeat telegrams of reassurance as navy vessels from several countries searched for Ramón. 'I was always optimistic, given the fine condition of the aircraft,' he told journalists. 'I told my mother it could stay afloat not just for days, but for months.'[3]

News of the rescue provoked an outpouring of popular joy. An emotional Francisco joined a march through Madrid's streets to the embassies of Great Britain, France and Italy – all of which had taken part in the search. To everybody's shame, however, Ramón's cheating was soon discovered and he was forced into a form of retirement on the reserve officers list, with a large salary cut.[4]

'He was his own greatest enemy,' Ramón's wife said. 'Vain, brave and generous; always facing death in the face, he was never at peace.'[5] An angry and erratic Ramón both joined the Freemasons and consorted with anarchists in Barcelona. He became an ardent and active Republican, plotting the monarchy's overthrow. He was by no means the only Spaniard to have tired of the monarchy.

Politically, in other words, the brothers could not have been further apart. On 8 April 1930, Franco wrote to warn Ramón that he was under surveillance and risked arrest as he travelled around trying to persuade military officers to back a republic. 'Your every move and exhortation is known,' he wrote in an admonishing, elder brother tone. If Ramón was jailed, his many admirers would drop him instantly, he added. Berenguer's government was legal and the army would defend it against 'those who want to inflict so much damage on the fatherland'. It was Ramón's patriotic duty to do the same. He should also think of their mother and the 'great sadness' that she and the whole family would feel if this became public. 'Your brother loves and hugs you,' he finished.[6]

Ramón was not impressed. In his written reply, he raged against the 'nobles who think they are superior, but are mostly the bastard offspring of other nobles' and the high clergy whom, he said, lived well on public money while children had no schools to go to. In its anxiety to serve the monarchy, the army had become 'the nation's executioner', while its generals guzzled up the budget and placed themselves above the people. A 'moderate Republic' would do so much better and keep the 'radical elements' that Francisco so feared under control. Otherwise, Ramón warned, revolution was around the corner. 'Today it is more patriotic to be Republican than to be a monarchist.' That was Alfonso XIII's fault, he insisted. By trampling over the constitution to appoint a dictator, thereby breaking his vows, the king had given everyone else permission to do the same – including Republicans.[7]

'If you get down from your little general's throne and walk amongst the captains and lieutenants, you will realise that few think like you,' Ramón wrote.[8] It was now Lent, he added sarcastically, so perhaps his elder brother might study his own conscience before lecturing others. Adding insult to injury, Ramón gave copies of the letter to a friend, allowing them to circulate widely. At this stage Franco still had a reputation for keeping his opinions to himself, with the writer José María Pemán meeting him and declaring that he was probably 'the man who best holds his tongue in Spain'.[9] That made the publicity especially loathsome to him. The fact that both brothers were gentlemen of the chamber to the king only added to the scabrous interest.

The differences between the brothers were underscored in June 1930 when Alfonso XIII visited Franco's academy in Zaragoza during a week of intense contact with the monarch. Three days later Franco himself rode his horse at the head of a parade in Madrid as his cadets filed past Alfonso to swear allegiance to the flag. On the following day, he joined the king on the royal balcony as he waved to a crowd of monarchist youths and his 130 cadets mounted guard at the palace.[10]

Berenguer's director-general of security was Franco's old Africanista friend Emilio Mola, who was now a general. In October 1930, he warned Franco that he would almost certainly have to arrest his brother for plotting against the king. Francisco travelled to Madrid and dined with Ramón on 10 October, urging him to desist. He had no luck. To his embarrassment, Ramón was indeed arrested the next morning. Mola said publicly that the arrest of the popular aviation hero was for breaking an unspecified army regulation. It was an attempt to save face, perhaps because that afternoon he again had met with Francisco.[11]

Further shame came the following month. Ramón escaped jail early on 24 November, reportedly armed to the teeth and having sawn through his bars. He left behind a letter to Berenguer. 'Today you are the hammer, and I am the anvil; the day will come when you are the anvil and I am the sledgehammer,' he said. 'And if I am killed, it won't matter. My name will join the martyrs of freedom.' His brother can only have felt humiliated by what Mola called an escape worthy of 'a petty crook who had broken into someone's home'.[12]

Republicanism had now become a glue that bound together a broad alliance of those seeking profound change, who stretched from the centre-right to the far-left. The centrist Republican Alejandro Lerroux sounded out Francisco Franco to see if he might back a move against the monarchy. Franco said no, suggesting only that he would help impose order if a popular rebellion provoked chaos or what he called 'power in the street'.[13] Serrano Suñer recalled Franco's violent indignation when told that the plotters wanted to meet him, but this contrasted with the extreme courtesy with which he eventually treated their emissaries and the fact that, despite his outraged private assertions that he would report them to police, he did not. Franco, in other words, hedged his bets and protected his career prospects. Either way, he seemed too wrapped up in his academy to notice that support really was draining radically away from the monarchy.[14]

Soon Ramón was a major part of an even wider plot that pitted him directly against Francisco. A meeting in the northern seaside city of San Sebastian that summer had brought together the many disparate groups intent on ousting the monarchy. A coup was eventually organised for mid-December. Ramón was in hiding in Madrid and eager to help lead the rebellion in the capital. His wife Carmen Díaz drove back and forth to San Sebastian and the border town of Irún in her Chrysler, ferrying arms back to Madrid and burying them in their garden.

The conspirators, however, lost control of their own plot, which began earlier than planned with a violent insurrection in Jaca, near the city of Huesca and just 140 km north of Francisco's academy in Zaragoza, on 12 December. Two decorated infantry captains who had served under Franco in the Legion – Fermín Galán and García Hernández – raised the gold, purple and red flag of Republicanism in Jaca, before gathering 600 men and marching on Huesca. The two officers were friends of Ramón, but Francisco too knew Galán as a subordinate and considered him 'brave, but excitable and ambitious'. Those marching with them were told a Republic had been declared across Spain, but this was wrong. In fact, Galán and company launched their rebellion three days before the wider coup involving Ramón was due to start. They also spilled blood, wounding the military governor of Huesca (who died of an infection on 26 December) and killing a Civil Guard sergeant and two policemen.[15]

When news of the uprising reached Francisco, he prepared his cadets to stop the rebels if they advanced past Huesca. The column, however, was halted before that became necessary. Galán and García Hernández were captured, court-martialled and shot on 14 December.[16]

But the rebellion was not over. It was a sign of Alfonso XIII's declining reputation that a significant minority of army officers had also turned Republican. This included not just Ramón, but also Francisco's old friend and editor-in-chief at the *Revista de Tropas Coloniales*, the almost permanently rebellious General Gonzalo Queipo de Llano. He had previously been involved in attempts to topple Primo de Rivera. In Madrid, even though Mola had started arresting people, Queipo de Llano and Ramón took control of the Cuatro Vientos military airfield in a chaotic attempt to fulfil at least part of the original plan on 15 December. While Queipo de Llano read out a manifesto on the radio, Ramón Franco took to the skies, ready to drop leaflets on the capital and bomb the royal palace. On seeing, however, that the general strike that was meant to accompany the uprising had not happened, he returned to base. The plotters then flew together to Portugal.[17]

Francisco was incandescent. 'He's completely mad and there is no cure. He lost his sense some time ago,' he wrote to his friend and fellow Africanista José Enrique Varela. 'Many families produce a kid who takes the wrong path without the parents realising. My brother Ramón was just such a case. For his mother and for me, his behaviour could not have been more upsetting,' Franco said later. Serrano Suñer recalled him being far more belligerent and succinct in the moment. 'Ramón ought to be shot,' he raged.[18]

Soon Ramón was stuck, out of money and unable to pay his passage to France from Portugal. Francisco sent him 2,000 pesetas, writing once more on 21 December 1930 to his 'dear, misfortunate brother', warning that his 'latest crazy act' could have ended before a firing squad. The family, he added, was immensely hurt to have a fugitive brother whose inglorious death would have provoked, at best, indifference amongst other Spaniards. Such military uprisings were a thing of the mid-nineteenth century, he claimed. Democratisation, if sought, could be achieved through slow change within the law, rather than 'extremist, violent revolutions that produce the most odious of tyrannies'.[19]

Franco called the Jaca rebellion 'disgusting'. 'The army is so full of cuckoos and cowards, that an overexcited madman was able to drag people along with him in the most abominable fashion,' he wrote to Varela.[20]

The events presaged the fact, however, that Spain was on the cusp of major change. Alfonso XIII and Berenguer had imagined they could wind the clock back in time and return to the old, pre-dictatorship system of fixed elections overseen by the monarch. The philosopher and writer José Ortega y Gasset was not the only person to think this ridiculous, though he had expressed it better than most in *El Sol* newspaper on 15 November 1930. The king, Berenguer and the entire monarchist regime thought Spaniards 'sheep-like, putting up with any sort of suffering without reacting', he wrote.[21]

Franco had been furious with Ortega y Gasset and lambasted his brother-in-law Serrano Suñer for admiring a philosopher intent on 'demolishing the monarchy'. Serrano Suñer recalled him reading out whole paragraphs of the article, his rage growing. Franco had stopped liking Berenguer, however, after he broke a pledge to promote him to major general in favour of an old friend who needed it more, arguing that young Franco could wait. His career, for the time being, was still more important to him than anything else. Franco, meanwhile, felt an ambitious young man's disdain for his elders: 'I don't trust much in those who lived through or took part in the events of 1898. The Cuba generation must go,' he wrote to a friend in December 1930 as they discussed army reforms.[22]

Ortega y Gasset's argument had been that there was nothing revolutionary about wanting to get rid of the monarchy, since so many ordinary people wished it. With public opinion against him, Berenguer was forced to resign in February 1931. Another military figure, Admiral Juan Bautista Aznar took over and called municipal elections for 12 April 1931. These were to be the first elections in eight years and soon came to be seen as a plebiscite on the monarchy.[23]

In March, as campaigning was under way, Franco served on the court-martial board for some of those involved in the violent Republican uprising which his brother had joined the previous December. He was fully prepared to impose 'strict justice', Pacón observed. Indeed, a death sentence and five life sentences were amongst those passed, but they would soon be commuted.[24]

On 12 April 1931, Franco voted in a working-class Zaragoza neighbourhood where, Pacón observed, he probably deposited 'the only monarchist vote'. At his Zaragoza academy, some officer instructors now openly declared themselves republicans.[25]

The following night, the correspondent for Britain's *Daily Telegraph* newspaper, Henry Buckley, stood outside the royal palace in Madrid's Oriente Square in his overcoat. Inside, the lights were still burning and a uniformed doorman informed him that King Alfonso XIII and his family were 'attending a cinematographic performance in the salon recently fitted up with a sound apparatus'. But just a mile away in the Puerta del Sol crowds were gathering to celebrate the end of the monarchy. Republicans had won massively in the large cities – where elections were freer than in a countryside still in thrall to the vote-fixing local powerbrokers. Monarchists won more council seats overall because of their power in rural areas, where a councillor represented far fewer voters, but socialists and Republicans had clearly won most votes. 'The result could not have been worse for us monarchists,' acknowledged one of their leaders, the Count of Romanones. It could not be whitewashed, he admitted.[26]

The king found himself abandoned. 'Where are Spain's four hundred generals? Where are the two hundred Grandees?' Buckley asked himself. 'What of this Spain which we are told is so Catholic; where are Bishops, friars and the faithful tonight?'

They never appeared. On April 14, Alfonso XIII fled the country and the Second Republic was proclaimed. 'Spain went to bed as a monarchy, and awoke as a Republic,' admitted Aznar.[27] It was an extraordinary change.

12

¡Viva la Republica!

ZARAGOZA-MADRID, APRIL 14, 1931

Four months earlier, Francisco Franco had been ready to use his cadets to crush the Jaca rebels and prevent an overthrow of the monarchy. Now he had to rethink. Should he be loyal to the new Republic? Franco's bold and decisive side had always been reserved for the army (even his confrontations with Primo de Rivera and more belligerent writing were within the military estate or its publications). 'Off the battlefield his behaviour was almost always the opposite – to lower his head, be prudent, not run risks and be very, very calculating,' according to one biographer.[1] However, it was not now clear what course of action best suited his own self-interest. The Franco who saw himself as a patriotic defender of the national interest and loyal servant to the king was cast into conflict with the careful, ambitious man determined to climb to the top of the army hierarchy. A difficult balancing act lay ahead.

Overnight, the outcome that Franco's brother Ramón and other plotters had tried to achieve with armed revolution had happened peacefully. Yet this was still revolution, in the sense that it upturned the status quo by allowing Spain's first experiment in proper democracy to begin, while leaving the economy largely functioning as before. 'How the commentators of Spain have aged!' the Catalan writer Josep Pla said.[2] 'In a single day they have all turned unbearably gaga.' Franco liked the simple, stable hierarchy of monarchy. He had especially enjoyed being close to Alfonso XIII. Now the cautious and reactionary sides of Franco's nature were thrown into conflict, since defending the monarchy would mean taking dramatic and audacious decisions.[3]

In fact, Franco felt sure most army officers would have happily defended the monarchy by force. He considered arming his cadets but, after consulting with Millán Astray (who was in Madrid), realised that was futile. He blamed the commander of the militarised Civil Guard police, General José Sanjurjo, for refusing to deploy his men. Yet the streets of Zaragoza, like most cities, were full of joyous crowds and cars draped with gold, purple and red Republican flags. The conservative *Correspondencia Militar*, an influential daily newspaper for army officers which Franco read, reported a festive atmosphere of 'indescribable enthusiasm' in the city. Crowds cheered the police for not stopping them and even Pacón, a fervent monarchist, found that 'the demonstrators were well-behaved.'[4]

New times had come and new men were required. Women, too, began to find a role in the public sphere and would soon be allowed to stand for parliament (though only three would become deputies and even they would argue about whether women should be allowed to vote). On 16 April 1931, the *Correspondencia Militar* declared the army would support a Republican government that guaranteed peace and order. A provisional government had already been formed by those who had been plotting against the monarch.[5] It brought together left and centre Republicans with socialists.

The monarchist *ABC* newspaper soon claimed that this government planned to appoint Franco as its High Representative in Morocco, provoking his angry response. Franco wrote, saying that he would not accept a job that made it look as if he might have conspired against the king. He did not want people to think him 'indulgent' towards the new regime or weak 'in the loyalty that I owed and showed to those who, until very recently, embodied the representation of the nation under the regime of monarchy'. Not for the first time, he reached for a deliberately ambiguous expression to state his desire to 'observe and obey, as I have always done, national sovereignty' which he hoped would be 'expressed through the correct legal means'.[6] He did not explain what legal means he was referring to.

At the Zaragoza Academy, Franco kept the monarchist flag flying for five days, until ordered to take it down. A cautious ambiguity continued to guide his actions. He told his instructors, for example, that it was everyone's duty to cooperate 'so that peace reigns and the nation can orient itself through the natural legal means'.[7] Again, he did not say what those 'legal means' were. He advised fervently monarchist officers not to resign since the army and country needed 'patriots' more than ever: presumably in case they had to step in to restore order.[8]

When a government decree was published on 23 April 1931 obliging officers to swear loyalty to the Republic or retire within four days, he did not complain. 'I pledge on my honour to faithfully serve the Republic, obey its laws and defend it with arms,' he swore. Some more principled officers resigned, but Franco argued that they should stay as a buttress against what might come, meaning the chaos of communism. Years later he claimed to have told fellow officers that 'so long as the Republican regime can prevent anarchy and does not surrender to Moscow, we have to support a Republic that was accepted first by the king, then by his government and, after that, by the army.'[9]

Honour was one of Franco's military obsessions and he had now given his word, along with most officers. Given his later behaviour, it is valid to ask whether he committed perjury. In fact, he almost certainly believed his oath could be overridden, allowing him to strike against a real or imagined threat to the nation. He had already argued, when obliged to reaffirm his obedience to General Montero during the retreats in Morocco in 1924, that it was an officer's duty to be guided by his sense of honour at a moment of doubt.

Ramón put Franco's acquiescence down to ambition. Asked what Francisco really thought of the new Republic, his brother reportedly replied: 'His ambition is such that [if necessary] he would murder our mother while his arrogance means he would also kill our father.'[10] Ramón had returned on 15 April to an exultant welcome at a Madrid railway station and was immediately appointed Head of Military Aviation, temporarily becoming a prominent figure on the far left of republican politics.[11]

Over time, Francisco Franco concluded that power had been usurped and the army should have quashed the change. He also convinced himself (by counting councillors rather than votes) that the municipal elections had been 'easily won [by monarchists] in most of the country'.[12] Yet on 3 June, a further general election in which women could finally stand (but still not vote) produced a massive Republican victory. The Spanish Socialist Workers Party (PSOE) founded by another son of Ferrol, Pablo Iglesias, became the largest party in a heavily fragmented parliament, taking a quarter of the vote. The moderate Niceto Alcalá-Zamora, of the Liberal Republican Right, led a provisional government that included several socialist ministers until October and then, after a new constitution was approved unanimously by parliament in December 1931, became president. He was replaced as prime minister by Manuel Azaña of the progressive Republican Action party, whose government included three socialists. Was this the 'legality' that Franco had sought? His view on that proved changeable.[13]

For some time now, Franco had been gathering material on Freemasons, whom he saw as a dangerous, powerful and anti-church secret sect intent on controlling the country In Franco's mind, they were at the root of most of the country's ills. He even blamed them for the phenomenon of the Two Spains, with Britain introducing Freemasonry into Spain with the idea of turning 'Spaniards against Spaniards' and provoking the downfall of an empire that allegedly 'overshadowed it'. This had worked so well that it provoked the rebellion of most of Spain's colonies and brought a nineteenth century replete with coups and civil wars. 'No one can deny that freemasonry was the undermining force in our Empire,' he wrote later in one of many newspaper columns he devoted to Freemasonry. 'It started the wars in our colonies and converted the nineteenth century into an endless procession of revolutions and civil conflicts.'[14]

Such ideas reflected Franco's suspicious nature, but also the fact that Spanish priests viewed Freemasons as the guiding force behind the spread of anti-clericalism since the early nineteenth century. That anti-clericalism was now embraced by the far Left and seen by Franco as a threat to Spain's very identity.

Franco's personal archives later came to contain material on Freemasons stretching back to the 1910s, intensifying from 1930. His animosity likely started with his Masonic father Don Nicolás, though there were many Freemasons in the army and amongst the monarchists.[15] With the Republic, however, he decided that they had achieved their aim. 'The country fell into the hands of people, a great majority of whom were Freemasons – which in Spain are the embodiment of atheism, anti-Catholicism and the persecution of the [Roman Catholic] church,' he wrote later.[16] With Catholicism increasingly a crucial part of his personal identity and his view of Spain itself, this was like surrendering the country to its enemies.

Franco could see that 'the Republic was greeted with great hopes by large sectors of the population', but still mistrusted it deeply. He blamed 'the spectacle provided by political parties' who he claimed had been 'unable to pardon the King for collaborating with the dictatorship'.[17] They bore the blame for creating a crisis that brought the expulsion of his admired Primo de Rivera and turned city voters into republicans.

Much later in life, Franco claimed the Republic 'lost all its credit in just a few days'. He summed up its achievements as 'the burning of churches and monasteries, persecution of religious beliefs, shredding of the army, giving in to the freemasons, social disorder and anarchy in the countryside'. Tensions rose in Madrid in May when false rumours spread that a group of monarchists had killed a Republican taxi driver. On 11 May, radicals set fire to a dozen religious buildings, forcing the government to impose a state of war in the city and its province. The church-burning spread, however, with more than 100 buildings damaged across the country. For a soldier like Franco, who saw maintaining public order as the army's job, this was shocking.[18]

Franco also believed Republicans sought to dismember Spain by allowing Catalans to split off and provoke social revolution. Change was certainly afoot, though not as radical as he made out: Catalans would gain a degree of self-government and the new government sought to improve the lot of workers and peasants while taming the power of army officers and priests.

Franco's chagrin reached an early crescendo for highly personal reasons. Manuel Azaña was minister of war in both the provisional government and the one he subsequently led as prime minister. He had long proposed reforms to depoliticise the military, take away its remaining powers over civilians and make it more efficient. However, there was little parliamentary debate and Azaña's reforms were originally passed as a series of decrees, making him a hate figure for those who opposed them, especially impassioned Africanistas. A third of officers retired from the army, partly because Azaña offered generous terms to slim their bloated ranks. His reforms also demoted Franco on the scale of brigadier generals, moving him down from near the top of the ranking towards the bottom, thus damaging his prospects of promotion. This was because, in a move that Franco labelled 'an injustice', Azaña invalidated the dictatorship's reinstallment of war merit promotions. He also suppressed the rank of lieutenant general, to which Franco aspired.[19]

Azaña noted in his diary that Franco was angry about this, though the young general did not mention it when they met. 'I never heard him complain about a measure that inflicted such damage on his career possibilities,' said Franco's cousin Pacón. 'But inside he naturally felt embittered.'[20]

Another personal blow came on 30 June 1931, when Azaña ordered the closure of Franco's academy in Zaragoza, arguing that it was overblown for the new, smaller army. Sanjurjo warned Azaña that Franco was now 'like a child who has had his toy snatched away' and doubly aggrieved by his slide down the ranking of brigadier generals. Since the term ended on 14 July, Franco had to shutter his own beloved invention within just two weeks. Africanistas like Emilio Mola were outraged. 'It will have to be restored if we ever want an army again,' he huffed.[21]

Franco's speech to his cadet officers at their passing-out ceremony was laden with phrases that could be taken as criticism of the new regime, or not. He spoke of 'times like this, when gentlemanliness and nobility suffer constant setbacks ... we must rise above it all, silencing the inner hurt.'[22] Afterwards, Pacón found him distraught, a rare break from his usual demeanour. 'He made no attempt to hide his emotions, or his pain,' he said, after saying goodbye to the downcast general. 'His great work had been clumsily and brutally destroyed.'[23]

The speech earned a formal reprimand from Azaña, who accused Franco of indiscipline. 'This affair might bring consequences later,' Azaña noted in his diary, aware that Franco was a natural leader for any military rebellion. Franco tried to wriggle out of the problem, insisting that his speech had been misinterpreted and, in a letter, protesting his 'loyal commitment' while pointing out that the Republican flag had been dutifully flown and its anthem played.[24] His career, at this stage, remained the most important thing to him.

Not only had Franco's job disappeared, but the Republic initially found nothing else for him to do. He spent eight months without a posting, an enforced rest that chafed for someone so ambitious and high-achieving. Resentment grew, apparently fuelled by his wife and the damage to her own social ambitions which depended to a large degree on her husband's status. 'They destroyed a brilliant and much-deserved military career earned by risking his life over many years,' Pacón observed, noting that it was the worst thing you could do to an officer.[25]

To begin with, Franco went to the Polo family estate in Asturias. In the meantime, monarchists gathered funds and plotted. Some hoped – even assumed – that Franco would lead a coup. 'It would only be to impose social discipline with a new military dictatorship, carried out and led, of course, by General Franco, the caudillo who is so admired,' the writer Cipriano Rivas wrote to Azaña on 17 August 1931 after meeting a wealthy Basque plotter. The coup, he warned, would be 'massive and decisive'.[26]

When Franco travelled to Madrid in August, he was tailed and had to wait a week before seeing Azaña. 'He protested his loyalty and, though he has been sought out [by conspirators], says he respects the current regime just as he respected the monarchy,' Azaña noted. Franco also pointed out that Azaña himself must know he had not conspired in Madrid since 'the police follow me everywhere in their car!' Azaña, who had indeed asked police to watch him, reprimanded them for being overzealous. The tail was removed but Azaña was already convinced that Franco was one of the few generals capable of raising the army in rebellion. 'Franco is the most dangerous,' he wrote in his diary. He saw, too, hypocrisy in Franco's overstated claims to be frank and straight-talking.[27]

In February 1932, Franco was finally given a brigade to command in La Coruña. He appointed his cousin Pacón once more as his assistant. The new job came with a large house and the social cachet that his wife sought, and Franco was happy to be near Ferrol, where he spent weekends. Other Africanistas felt sidelined. 'Those who acted with such great success [in Morocco] have been persecuted with rancorous savagery,' said Mola in 1933. Franco was more sanguine. If the aim had been to rid the army of monarchists, it had not worked. 'Most of us stayed,' he commented.[28]

The Republican parliament also turned a sometimes-vengeful gaze on the past, punishing those who helped install the Primo de Rivera dictatorship, which was deemed anti-constitutional and illegal. It declared Alfonso XIII an outlaw for perpetrating 'high treason' and a handful of ex-officials and generals were jailed or went into exile. In December, Franco was himself called before a parliamentary commission to be quizzed on the court martials that followed the Jaca uprising, whose executed officers were now Republican heroes. He delivered an impassioned defence of military neutrality, arguing that it was 'criminal at any time and in any situation' for soldiers to rise against the state.[29]

In March 1932, Franco and Pacón travelled to Madrid to find horses for his new brigade. Fellow officers asked insistently about whether they were there to organise a coup. Sanjurjo had by now fallen out with the Republic and everybody seemed to know that he was now plotting with those monarchists who always wished to overthrow the Republic. As a result, Franco was once more tailed by police.[30]

Franco responded to the tail with elaborate precautions. It was probably during this Madrid trip that Franco entered the Baviera restaurant on Alcalá street, a few hundred metres uphill from the central Puerta del Sol square, as part of an elaborate plan to meet Sanjurjo. The monarchist plotter Pedro Sainz Rodríguez arranged to 'bump into' Franco at the restaurant and, after the requisite public play-acting, they crossed the street to the grandiose Bellas Artes cultural club, quickly exiting from a side door where a car awaited. From there they were driven to a night club frequented by Sanjurjo, a syphilitic lover of Madrid's nightlife and brothels, who met other plotters in his box during intervals at the Comedia Theatre.[31] Sainz Rodríguez recalled:

> He explained his plan to Franco who replied, in my presence: 'I won't promise to join; I'll see what I can do in the moment. What I can promise you today, and I give my word of honour, is that if the Government organises a repressive force I will do my best to ensure that nobody joins it.'[32]

Once more, Franco told Pacón that the Republic needed to establish 'order and peaceful coexistence' within a legal framework. Since, by now, Spain had an elected Republic government and a constitution, it remained unclear what legal framework might satisfy him. In any case, Franco observed, people still liked the Republic. Any attempt to overthrow it would fail.[33]

He was right. On 10 August 1932, a coup partly led by Sanjurjo from Seville duly collapsed in less than 24 hours, with ten people killed in clashes in Madrid. 'I would only rise against the Republic if it tries to disband the army or Civil Guard, or if I saw clearly that communism had arrived. In that case, I'd rebel with whoever wished to follow me,' Franco told Pacón. He also observed that any uprising would need the crack troops of the Army of Africa with no surrender possible. 'You fight until you win or die,' he said.[34]

The government's heavy-handed reaction to the Sanjurjo revolt saw 114 newspapers temporarily closed, including the influential *ABC*, and the arrest of more than 5,000 people. Sanjurjo asked Franco to visit him in jail and then to act as his defence lawyer in the court martial (just as Franco had agreed to do for Berenguer at his trial for his role during the dictatorship, though he was barred on a technicality).[35] Franco refused. In later life he claimed his reply had been: 'I cannot do that. Having failed, you have gained the right to die.'[36] He felt absolute disdain for Sanjurjo's pathetic preparations.

Sanjurjo was duly tried and a death sentence passed, but Azaña successfully argued that it should be commuted, ignoring Mexican president Plutarco Elías Calles's prescient warning that his execution would 'avoid a bloodbath' later.[37] Azaña reasoned that if he shot Sanjurjo, he would also have to execute half a dozen more army officers. Instead, he moved to weaken the army further. Both the Civil Guard and the frontier guards, or Carabineros, were transferred out of the military – to the interior and finance ministries respectively – while a new urban police corps known as the Guardias de Asalto was boosted in size.

Franco was not yet rebellious, but his dislike of the Republic was obvious. In February 1933, he was made commander general of the Balearic Islands – which many interpreted as a move to keep him away from mainland Spain and prevent him joining or leading a rebellion. It was a promotion of sorts, but he felt deliberately sidelined.[38] That month he published his last article in his old magazine, the *Revista de Tropas Coloniales*, now renamed *África*, recalling its foundation, and warning that communism was the new threat in Spanish Morocco. 'It is no secret that communism shows a special interest in trying to promote insurrection in protectorates,' he claimed. 'Many have seen how the communist seed is disseminated by attaching itself to nationalism.'[39]

Although Spain's politics were a product of its own history and culture, the wider political and moral panics generated by fascism in Italy and Germany and communism in the Soviet Union cast a shadow over the Republic. Neither communists nor fascists held any real sway in Spain in 1933, but scare-mongering saw the flags of antifascism and anticommunism agitated in a dramatic, end-of-the-world rhetoric.[40] They stoked the sort of fears that generate aggression camouflaged as self-protection and can ignite a spiral of tit-for-tat violence. Franco himself, with his reading from the Anti-Communist Entente, was an early and willing victim of this – his mind already prepared by anti-Masonic paranoia.

Others, too, were thinking along these lines. In October 1933, Primo de Rivera's charismatic son, José Antonio, delivered a speech in the Comedia Theatre in Madrid which acted as the founding moment of Spain's first significant fascist party, the Falange. There was to be 'no shrinking from violence' and he called for the use of 'fists and pistols when justice or the Fatherland is offended'. The Falange was not properly constituted until the end of the year but embraced a cult of violence from the start, pledging 'holy civil war to rescue the Fatherland'. Militants were to be 'half-monk, half-soldier'. To foreign observers they were simply 'fascists'. Some prominent Africanistas were early recruits. Franco's aide-de-camp and cousin, Pacón, was enthralled and became, in his own words, 'one of the most fervent admirers of that brave politician'.[41]

Before coup plotters could strike again, democracy intervened. Elections were called for November 1933 as the government fell apart, with women voting for the first time. Liberal Republicans from centrist parties had tried to block the reform, claiming that women were in thrall to priests and would vote for right-wing parties. 'The Spanish woman is politically retarded, a retrograde; she still has not separated herself from the influence of the sacristy and the confessional, and giving women the vote is to hand them a political weapon that could bring the Republic to its end,' one deputy had argued in parliament.[42] Shocked by their rout in the previous elections and with the Left now split, Catholic rightists joined to form the Spanish Confederation of Autonomous Right-wing Groups (CEDA). With the church's help, this quickly became a mass party which claimed 700,000 members. Catholicism did indeed form a crucial part of many people's identity, daily existence and communal life. It was present in the family home, village fiestas and rituals of birth, growing up, marriage and death. Petty Republican restrictions on the parading of saints' effigies, bell-ringing and other age-old customs helped drive voters towards CEDA.[43]

Leader José María Gil Robles vowed to defend the Roman Catholic religion and declared that 'democracy is not an end but a means ... either parliament submits, or we will eliminate it.'[44] CEDA admired corporatist regimes like that installed in Portugal by dictator António de Oliveira Salazar. Fascist attitudes seeped into its radicalised Juventedes de Acción Popular (JAP), or Popular Youth Action movement, which sent study groups to Hitler's Germany and Mussolini's Italy. JAP youths imitated the latter's supporters by greeting Gil Robles with cries of 'Jefe! Jefe! Jefe!' (Duce! Duce! Duce!).[45]

Franco was approached. Would he join them, and stand for parliament? He was not interested, but did vote for CEDA – reflecting his basic dislike of the Republic. So did many Spaniards, making it the party with most parliamentary deputies, with 115 seats out of 472. Lerroux's centre-right Radical Republicans took a further 102 seats in scrupulously clean elections. A mosaic of other rightists parties (with just one Falange deputy) meant the majority lay comfortably on the right. Many blamed the new women voters, who were mostly conservative. In fact, the swing was not that violent. The left had crumbled, but the centre remained strong.[46]

Just as the 1931 proclamation of the Republic had immediately sparked plotting on the right, so leftists now began to talk of violent uprisings. Parliament opened on 8 December, with anarchists launching a simultaneous but easily quashed 'social revolution' that claimed 89 lives. The most dramatic event was the derailing of the Barcelona to Seville express train which killed 23 people. Soon 15,000 anarchists were in jail and their organisation broken.[47]

A centre-right minority government took office under Alejandro Lerroux of the Radical Republican Party. His minority government depended, however, on the parliamentary votes of the militantly Catholic CEDA. CEDA was the larger party, but President Alcalá-Zamora would not allow the Republic to be run by people who did not seem to believe in it.[48]

The new government was born under a twin threat. The greatest of these came from the left, as socialists increasingly embraced the idea of armed revolution. On the right, Gil-Robles constantly demanded to be allowed into the government and menacingly warned of seeking 'other solutions'. Meanwhile, the fascists of the Falange – now known as the Spanish Falange of the Juntas of the National Syndicalist Offensive, or 'Falange Española de las JONS' - sought to attract a militant working class. 'We do not seek votes, but audacious and valiant minorities,' José Antonio Primo de Rivera said. It seemed also to consciously court the Africanista officer class, claiming to embrace 'a military sense' of life. Young Falangists and socialists, meanwhile, soon found reasons to inflict violence on one another.[49]

But to those army officers who had seen the Republic as a threat, it suddenly seemed workable. Why rebel when your own side was in power? Even Franco's politically erratic brother Ramón, who was no longer in parliament, now declared that Spain needed 'eight years ... of conservative government.'[50] He would soon move to Washington as a military attaché.[51]

In December 1933, Franco travelled to Madrid on sick leave apparently for complications to the wound received in Morocco – dividing his time between his family and Africanista friends. The Spanish capital was a strange place to choose for a rest and it seems likely that his real aim was to cultivate the new government in order to advance his career. Whenever his wife and daughter were away in Oviedo, he spent the evenings in cafés with other officers, journalists and hangers-on. Franco led the conversations, which invariably revolved around military reform and lasted until well after midnight.[52]

He was in Madrid again in February 1934 to see his mother, now aged 68, as she passed through on a pilgrimage to Rome, staying at her daughter's apartment in the city. She got no further. Pilar Bahamonde caught pneumonia, spent ten days in bed, then suffered a stroke during a coughing fit and died before a doctor could arrive. Franco was heartbroken.[53]

The death meant a forced meeting with his father while the will was read out. Don Nicolás inevitably upset his son again, this time by being rude to his brother-in-law Serrano Suñer, who was presented as the family lawyer. Don Nicolás dismissed the famous parliamentarian as a *picapleitos*, or shyster. Franco returned to Palma de Mallorca but in March was promoted by Minister of War Diego Hidalgo (from Lerroux's Radicals) to major general, effectively returning to his position as an army prodigy. Hidalgo recalled Franco's responding with stiff formality, though he must have been inwardly delighted. 'I never saw him either joyful or depressed,' he said.[54]

Franco remained in the same job but now also rented an apartment in Madrid where he and his family spent much of their time. Although claiming to remain distant from politics, he tried to influence army legislation, visiting the far-right monarchist deputy Sainz Rodríguez and sending Pacón to knock insistently on his door early in the morning with notes and suggestions. Sainz Rodríguez passed these to the relevant committees, thereby allowing Franco to both play at politics and publicly distance himself from it.[55]

Franco was in Madrid in October 1934 when the CEDA party finally joined the government, tilting it further to the right and sparking angry reaction from the increasingly radical Spanish Socialist Workers Party (PSOE) and its associated General Workers Union (UGT) which had already threatened a revolutionary strike in response to such a move. It became Franco's task to stop that. It was also an opportunity to present himself in a new and glamorous light as 'Franco, the Saviour of Spain'.[56]

13

Rebels in Asturias

MADRID-ASTURIAS, OCTOBER 1934

Franco must have heard the gunshots that rang across Madrid on the night of 4 October 1934 as the socialist-led uprising against the new government began. Sporadic firefights broke out through the night as police and armed strikers clashed. The following day, with shops staying shut and trams being driven by soldiers with armed guards, Franco was called in by Minister of War Diego Hidalgo to oversee the military response. Hidalgo did not trust the senior staff of his own ministry, who were sidelined. It was a mission that Franco was delighted to carry out, not least because the uprising fed straight into his growing belief that communists were plotting to take over Spain. Freemasons, he felt sure, lurked somewhere in the background.[1]

Franco installed himself in the War Ministry, housed in the Buenavista Palace overlooking the Cibeles fountain, from where he continued to hear rifle shots. He gathered a small staff, made up of two navy officers and Pacón. They operated, in effect, as the army high command. Franco enjoyed immense power, operating as *de facto* chief of the defence staff. This involved, in his own words, 'talking frankly to the minister, explaining his responsibilities in this matter'.[2]

The uprising was alternately dramatic, tragic and pitiful. In Madrid alone, the socialists claimed a militia of 2,500 members, though it was poorly armed and absurdly overconfident. Attacks on public buildings, ministries, police stations and army barracks all failed. Fifty people, nevertheless, were killed in the city over the first four days of the rebellion. Shoddy organisation and a naïve assumption that the rank-and-file of the army would rise in support made it nothing like the popular revolution its leaders dreamed of, though a general strike sputtered on for a week.[3]

Despite the initial flurry of gunfire, Madrid was an easy win for Franco. On 7 October, indeed, members of his staff watched admiringly from their windows as the Falange marched through Madrid, with José Antonio Primo de Rivera declaring 'Long live Spain! Long live national unity!' That same day, the national government had taken over the city administration, sacking its left-wing mayor. Primo de Rivera had written to Franco in the days before the revolt and was obviously aware, like the government, that it was likely to happen. He had even asked the government to arm his men. His letter to Franco said, in essence: 'If you need me, I am here.' Franco did later claim to have told the Falange founder to 'await with attention but without losing faith in the Army' and to volunteer at his nearest barracks if a proper revolution broke out.[4]

The formerly pragmatic, reformist Socialists were not always clear about why revolution was suddenly needed. Sometimes their reasons were defensive: to prevent a hijacking of democracy like that carried out by Adolf Hitler in Germany or Engelbert Dollfuss in Austria. The arrival of the authoritarian-minded CEDA in the government was deemed the tipping point since, the argument went, they planned to imitate Hitler and Dollfuss. Other times the reasoning was offensive: to impose themselves through violence. In short, the socialists did not trust Spain's young democracy if they could not control it. For Franco, the warnings that Spain was the target of the global conspiracy of godless Marxists which he had read about in the International Anticommunist Entente publications now made absolute sense.[5]

The revolution was poorly planned, especially in Madrid.[6] Nevertheless, it was a complex situation that, if mishandled, could easily have spun out of control. Franco had shown in Morocco that, at moments of intense decision-making, he maintained an icy cool. Again, he impressed with his calm and decisive manner. He worked incessantly, dictating orders via Pacón and absorbing information as it arrived from the rest of Spain by phone or telegraph. Neither he nor Hidalgo showed any sign of fear that they would lose control of the situation.[7] Franco's presence, however, was not well received by other officers in the ministry or by some in the government who fretted about the sudden appearance of a famously belligerent Africanista in such an important post at such a crucial time. 'The president [Alcalá-Zamora] has an aide spying on my movements all day long,' Franco claimed.[8]

The chaotic and doomed uprising in Madrid set the overall pattern, but two exceptions stood out. The first was Catalonia, where Republican sentiment had flourished ever since Primo de Rivera's regime had, to the relief of conservatives like Franco, annulled a small degree of administrative self-government won by the Catalans in 1914. In 1932, the first left-wing Republican government had awarded them a far broader charter of self-government, which some now feared losing under a right-wing government. On 6 October, Catalan regional premier Lluís Companys took advantage of the situation to go much further and declare 'a Catalan state' which would be part of an as yet non-existent 'Federal Republic of Spain'.[9]

Given the size and importance of Catalonia, that sounded dramatic and destabilising. In fact, Companys's new state was a rhetorical fantasy and the Catalan nationalists who backed it were crushed within hours. Franco's calm was such that, according to Hidalgo, he sent the minister to bed while he dealt with Catalonia. 'I obeyed and managed to sleep despite my state of restlessness... I woke to the news that the government of the Generalitat [the Catalan government] had surrendered and been placed in jail,' Hidalgo said. A military officer was appointed to run the region instead.[10]

In this hotchpotch up rising, Asturias was the only area where workers united to create durable danger. Trades unions had already created a well-organised industrial workforce, especially amongst miners, but Asturias was also where socialists and anarchists showed a rare ability to work together, presenting an effective, united front.[11]

Across Asturias, more than 20,000 well-armed men joined the militias.[12] Dynamite from the mines, weapons taken from ransacked police stations and, eventually, the capture of an arms factory (with 29 artillery pieces) made them a formidable, if untrained, opponent. Soon they occupied a third of the Asturias region and successfully marched on Oviedo, occupying most of it on 6 October. Sticks of dynamite were used as hand-grenades, adding a destructive power that frightened opponents and left its mark on buildings. The events also unshackled the violent anticlericalism latent in part of the radical left, with up to 37 clergymen ruthlessly assassinated across Spain.[13]

In September, a ship called the *Turquesa* had unloaded arms onto launches off the coast of Asturias. Once ashore, they were picked up by socialists, some of whom were in turn picked up by police.[14] Franco later deemed the *Turquesa* shipment proof that the Soviet Union was the driving force behind the failed revolution. 'It was deliberately prepared by Moscow's agents,' he wrote.[15] 'The socialists thought that they could use the experience and technical leadership of the communists to install a dictatorship.' Given that those involved were all Spaniards (or Portuguese) and that the communists had only joined the Workers Alliances that helped organise the uprising at the last moment, this was highly unlikely, but his conspiratorial paranoia did not end there, since he also detected the Freemasons' black hand. 'Freemasonry thought that it could use the workers as cannon fodder in order to grab power,' he wrote.[16]

He did not see his task as a mere policing exercise. This was war, just as in Morocco. 'This is a frontier war, and the frontiers are socialism, communism and all other things that attack civilisation in order to replace it with barbarism,' he told a visiting journalist.[17] The idea liberated him from any qualms about fighting fellow Spaniards. If overwhelming force was the way to achieve a rapid victory, that is what he would employ. If the barbarous practices employed in Morocco were used by some of his troops, he did not seem worried.

Franco chose his dynamic, bellicose friend and fellow Africanista Lt Colonel Juan Yagüe Blanco to lead the two Legions banderas and two battalions of Moroccan regulares, flying him into Gijón in an autogyro, a Spanish-designed precursor to the modern helicopter. Yagüe was an early Falange supporter. Tall, strong and bullish, his personality was summed up by Serrano Suñer as 'violent and generous'. Franco also removed his own cousin and childhood friend, the pro-Republican Major Ricardo de la Puente Bahamonde, from his post as head of the air base in nearby León, suspecting that he sympathised with the rebels.[18]

Yagüe's legionnaires and Moroccan mercenary battalions worked their way south from the port city of Gijón as a separate column led by General Eduardo López Ochoa (who was nominally overall commander on the ground, but under Franco's orders) approached from

Galicia to the west. In the meantime, Franco ordered aerial bombing and naval cannon fire against rebel areas, personally coordinating fire from the cruiser *Libertad* by phone. The air force killed 10 people with a bomb that landed in Oviedo's main square. On 11 October, the revolutionaries began to abandon the city. The heaviest fighting started three days later as the burgeoning army columns (now some 18,000 trained men) battled their way into the mining areas. The revolutionaries sued for peace on 18 October, and the army and police moved into the mining zones – though some rebels refused to give up.[19]

López Ochoa was appalled by the savagery of Yagüe's troops, who brought with them the ethos of the war in Morocco. 'They cut off their feet, their hands, their ears, their tongues, even their genitals!' a shocked López Ochoa reported later.[20] 'One of my most trusted officers told me that there were *legionarios* wearing wire necklaces from which dangled human ears.' The hatred was mutual. Yagüe was appalled to hear that negotiations with rebel leader Belarmino Tomás were progressing well because of Lopez Ochoa's 'gentlemanliness and humanity'. Like Franco and other Africanistas, Yagüe favoured strong and exemplary punishment. 'To defeat an enemy is completely useless while his morale has not been broken,' he said.[21] Franco too had little respect for López Ochoa, deeming him a Freemason and complaining later of his 'slowness and [frequent] halts, as if he did not want to get there'.

On 22 October, Franco and his team left the ministry that had been their home for two weeks, their job done. Franco nevertheless stayed at Hidalgo's side as a special advisor for five months. Some 1,300 rebels had been killed, mostly in Asturias, while 450 members of the army and police also died. A further 450 civilians were victims of so-called 'red terror' killings by militiamen. Franco's wife's family, like most of the rest of the Asturian bourgeoisie, was presumably thankful that the rebellion had been put down. Indeed, Franco now found himself acclaimed as a protector of his own class. In Washington, his brother Ramón began to notice that he was no longer the most famous of the brothers.[22]

Thousands of Asturian rebels were arrested and, under the supervision of the notoriously sadistic Civil Guard commander Lisardo Doval, men were beaten, tortured or, sometimes, killed. Franco carefully vetted senior officers and he either chose Doval personally to become the ministry's special 'delegate for public order' or approved his appointment. When journalist Luis Higón tried to investigate atrocities, he was arrested. A Legion officer then walked into the barracks where Higón was detained and shot him eight times, killing him. By December, the terror stories from Asturias were such that Doval had to be posted elsewhere.[23]

The crackdown was widespread, with more than one out of eight Spanish mayors removed from their posts and up to 30,000 people arrested. Repression was sometimes indiscriminate, with anarchists also rounded up even though they mostly played no part. Azaña, who had not joined the uprising, was imprisoned for 90 days before the case against him was thrown out.[24]

Martial law across Spain was not lifted until three months after the rebels had been crushed. It continued, however, in the populous regions of Madrid, Cataluña, Asturias and in four northern provinces until mid-April. Yet death sentences handed down to rebels were mostly commuted. Franco opposed such leniency, which he saw as undermining his victory. He was a stickler for the law, especially for martial law, and was outraged by any hint of benevolence. However, President Alcalá-Zamora and Prime Minister Lerroux were moderates who did not want to inflame the extremism that might kill off the Republican project. Their attitude mirrored the earlier leniency of Azaña towards Sanjurjo's monarchist rebels after their failed uprising in August 1932.[25]

While the revolution was a resounding failure, it had a long-lasting impact on everyone involved, including Franco. He felt validated in his hatred of the left and Freemasons. He had also tasted the power of having Spain's entire armed forces (since the navy and air force had been used) answer to him.[26] Later in life, Franco wrote that the uprising amounted to 'a declaration of war, with all its consequences' in which the revolutionaries had failed to consider one important thing. 'In the War Ministry they were going to come across a Captain who was an expert [in war],' he wrote.[27] He was referring to himself – a sign that his ego had been given a further boost by a victory that he attributed, in large part, to his own skills.

An idea of himself as a providential saviour of Spain, then, may now have been forming in his mind. After all, he argued later: 'If we hadn't done what we did, the revolution would have triumphed.' He was not alone in this view. Right-wing newspapers called him the 'Saviour of the Republic'.[28]

Four years later, in the middle of a civil war that he helped provoke, Franco would declare that this was 'the continuation of bloody revolutionary events of 1934'.[29] In that sense, it had set a tone for the next major uprising – in which Franco himself would eventually play the leading part.

14

The Pendulum Swings

MADRID, 1935–6

In May 1935, Franco was offered the most important job in the army, as Chief of the General Staff. Franco later claimed to have argued that – given the way in which chiefs of the general staff were constantly changed by ministers – 'it was important to the country' that he remain in Morocco, where he had been sent only three months earlier to head the Army of Africa. Although Franco later protested that only a duty to obey orders prevented him turning the job down, his brother-in-law Ramón Serrano Suñer could see that the appointment was 'rather the result of a concerted effort on his part.' The rest was fake humility. In fact, Franco was delighted by his new status as Spain's most powerful general. 'It satisfied his sense of self-worth,' commented Pacón, who continued as his aide.[1]

The appointment was made against considerable opposition. President Alcalá-Zamora even warned the new Minister of War, José María Gil Robles, that 'young generals are aspirants to fascist strongmen'.[2] Gil Robles claimed the entire army supported the appointment, while Queipo de Llano said the exact opposite. Franco's appointment was part of a shift towards the right in the government, after Prime Minister Lerroux invited Gil Robles's CEDA to join it again, with more ministers. If suppressing the Asturian miners had already placed Franco in the ranks of Spain's right-wing – at least in the general imagination – his appointment by Gil Robles appeared to confirm people's suspicions. In public, however, he continued to avoid making political statements.

Franco later claimed that his close-up view of politics made his heart sink.

> The coalition government of centrist and right-wing parties was being ferociously combatted by the Left, with their press campaigns creating a morbid popular romanticism about the Asturian revolutionaries... The lack of a solid majority party in parliament made inevitable these hybrid coalition governments which lacked unity and mutual trust. Given the president's pledge to the Left not to allow the party with most parliamentary seats [CEDA] to hold power, however, there was no solution.[3]

Franco now consciously shaped the army to put down unrest. He made sure that Emilio Mola, who as spy chief had arrested his brother Ramón, was appointed as commander in Morocco. Mola was given 'the secret mission of having the colonial Army ready in case it was needed by the Fatherland one day'.[4]

Franco and his minister leant on two men who viewed the Republic with deep suspicion, Generals Joaquín Fanjul and Manuel Goded. Garrisons were armed to put down unrest and commands given to 'officers who would be crucial pawns' on the Rightist side in the future Civil War, as Franco himself noted later.[5]

The government, however, soon fell apart. In December 1935, Gil Robles made another bid to force President Alcalá-Zamora to appoint him prime minister. Instead, he was sacked and the country prepared for another general election.[6]

When Gil Robles left the ministry, Franco gave what Pacón considered his most heartfelt speech since closing down the Zaragoza Academy, saying the army had never been so well led. 'Honour and discipline, and the other key concepts, have been reestablished,' he claimed with tears in his eyes. He likely thought that the merit for that belonged to him as well. Franco remained as chief of the general staff, while elections were called for 16 February 1936.[7]

He began discussing a coup with other generals on the very same day that Gil Robles was sacked, but Franco was the most cautious. He believed that, between the Civil Guard, police, socialists and anarchists, their chances of success were slim. 'The usual generals and especially the Galician [i.e. Franco] say that they cannot guarantee their people and that the moment has not yet come,' a monarchist emissary reported.⁸ A coup, everybody seemed to accept, could not be carried out without Franco, and he was only interested if success was highly probable.

The ferocious repression unleashed after the October revolution encouraged the Left towards unity once more, while the right fractured. The Left gathered together in a broad Popular Front alliance that included moderates, the powerful socialists and a smattering of small communist or other revolutionary groups. It offered a return to the reformist policies of the first government of the Republic and amnesties to those jailed, while the Right painted the opposition as bloodthirsty revolutionaries and made 'For God and Spain!' a unifying call. In fact, the division between Spaniards remained broadly as it had been before the previous elections – with liberals, urban workers and the destitute rural poor backing the Left while conservatives and devout Catholics fretted about the coming end of their precious social, economic and cultural traditions.⁹

As the political temperature rose and coup rumours featuring Franco spread, a senior government official was sent to talk to him. Franco assured him the rumours were false. 'I won't conspire while there is no communist threat to Spain,' he said. 'I give you my word of honour on that.'¹⁰

In fact, Franco thought that moment was imminent. In late January he was sent to London as a Spanish representative at the funeral of King George V. Few observers paid much attention to what *Life* magazine later called 'the dumpy Spanish general' in khaki uniform with a scarlet sash who stood behind the more imposing Marshal Tukhachevsky from Stalin's Red Army. On the ferry taking them back across the English Channel, he deliberately took the Spanish military attaché in Paris, Major Antonio Barroso, onto the deserted deck to speak confidentially. He claimed that Spain's Popular Front was the brainchild of Comintern, the Stalinist international organisation run from Moscow. He was talking to other generals, he explained, and planned to take charge of the Army of Africa if a coup became necessary. 'If you hear of me going to Africa, you'll know we have decided there is no other way but a rising.'¹¹

That same month, President Alcalá-Zamora complained in his diary about just how far 'reactionary sectarianism' had gripped the

War Ministry when Franco was the senior officer, amounting to 'a takeover of the Army by the extreme right'.[12] He had called fresh elections in the hope that the pro-Republican centre might finally come together to achieve victory. That proved naïve.

The election campaign showed, if anything, increasing radicalisation. The far-right monarchist leader José Calvo Sotelo spoke openly of using the army. 'When the red hordes of communism are advancing, one can only think of a single brake: the strength of the army and transfusion of military virtues – obedience, discipline and hierarchy – into society itself,' he told a January rally. On the left, Socialist leader Largo Caballero declared that 'if the right wins, we'll have to go to a civil war.' As the rhetoric heated up, so did the violence, with Falangists, Socialists and others fighting with one another or the security forces, claiming 37 lives in the seven weeks prior to the 16 February 1936 elections.[13]

Franco returned to Madrid on 5 February, just eleven days before the elections. He was convinced that the army had to be prepared to react. If the Left won, communism would be hammering at Spain's door.[14]

15

The Popular Front – The Left Returns

MADRID, 16 FEBRUARY 1936

On the night of 16 February 1936, Franco sat up fretting. Voting in the general election had passed off with few incidents. Indeed, it was only when the results came through that Franco began to feel alarmed. Outbursts of violence began in which twelve people died across Spain. The early results showed that the Popular Front had won a narrow victory, but one that translated into an absolute majority of seats in parliament. The pendulum of power had swung back and Franco was now on the losing side. The victory, in part, came about because many of those who had responded to an anarchist call to boycott the 1933 previous elections had voted this time.[1]

Jubilant leftists and Republicans took to the streets, while extremists occupied a handful of town halls and rumours once more spread that Franco and other generals were preparing a coup. He was soon visited by General Joaquín Fanjul, who claimed Leftists were now terrorising people across Spain.[2]

At three o'clock in the morning, Franco woke the minister of war and asked him to declare a state of war, citing reports of disturbances in various parts of Spain. 'Just as the monarchy had been overwhelmed by the Republic, so the Republic could be overwhelmed by communism,' he later recalled warning the minister. 'It was his job to take measures to prevent a catastrophe.' It was, he explained, much like when the overconfident Kerensky government had been caught out by the Bolsheviks and their October Revolution in 1917. He could not conceive of a government supported by the Spanish Socialist Workers Party [PSOE] – which had led the October 1934 rebellion – that was not an imminent threat to the nation.[3]

Franco viewed the Popular Front as a Trojan horse for communism, on which he considered himself an expert. 'For those of us who had followed the process of communism... it was clear,' he wrote many years later. 'The revolution in Spain was to be carried out from the top. It was all going exactly to plan and there could be no doubt about where this would lead.'[4] He was referring to the Comintern decision for communist parties in Europe to join or back left-wing 'popular front' coalitions, taken in August at its Seventh World Congress in Moscow. Franco was parroting what he had read in the *International Anticommunist Entente*. In fact, the Comintern decision was a retreat which reflected communism's failure to impose itself anywhere in western Europe as well as Stalin's insularity, lack of interest in world revolution and prioritising of 'socialism in one country'. What was more, both Stalin and the democratic left could see they might need each other in a fight against fascism.[5]

Franco had already rung the head of the Civil Guard, according to a version that he gave a few years later to an early hagiographer, to warn him that 'the masses are in the streets'. He began to lobby hard for a declaration of an 'estado de guerra', or martial law.[6]

Franco was told that only Prime Minister Manuel Portela Valladares – the stop-gap centrist appointed by President Alcalá-Zamora to oversee elections – could order a state of war, so he arranged a meeting on 17 February. Any attempt to persuade Portela that a revolution was effectively underway clearly failed, despite his promises that the Legion could deal with dissenters if the army was called out. In fact, a less repressive 'state of alarm' was decreed that day with the president signing a martial law decree that Portela could use if needed. That did not stop some regional commanders declaring a state of war, presumably encouraged by Franco, before they had to backtrack. Franco returned to Portela's offices two days later, claiming again to speak for the army and ambiguously offering its 'support' at a time when the prime minister was also under pressure from the Right to declare himself dictator. Franco was spotted by the press, adding fuel to the coup rumours. The message passed to journalists was that these were 'absurd rumours' since he 'lived completely detached from politics and solely occupied with military duties'.⁷ He made similar protests to government officials.

That was not true. Already on the afternoon of 18 February, he had met again with Fanjul and two other notoriously rebellious generals – Goded and Angel Rodríguez del Barrio – to discuss a possible coup. Franco told them to sound out military commanders, but most said they would not support such a thing. Goded's attempt to bring out the troops garrisoned in the massive Cuartel de la Montaña by the Plaza de España in Madrid was met with refusal from the senior officers.⁸

Franco's thesis was now that any coup attempt needed massive support within the army and would be justified by either a communist takeover or rampant disorder. In his own mind, this was inevitable, if not already happening. A coup would also need to be well-planned and ruthless. The position of the Civil Guard police worried him especially, since they were 'the most numerous in quality [sic] and of legendary good morale'.⁹ The planning was still missing, as was the support of enough of the military: the time was not yet right.

In fact, revolution had not broken out. However, there were riots in jails in Bilbao, Burgos and Valencia, as well as reports that demonstrators had opened the doors to the Lepers Hospital at Fontilles in Alicante – meaning that patients were wandering free. In some places, including the suburban Madrid towns of Chamartín and Vallecas, workers had occupied town halls. Attempts had also been made to burn religious buildings and peasants were occupying olive groves. Violence did generally increase, with at least 31 people dying over the week to 23 February.¹⁰

An accelerated handover of power saw Portela Valladares resign and Azaña's new Republican Left party form a government three days after the elections. This excluded the more belligerent Socialists even though, like the CEDA before them, they had most seats in parliament and could bring down the government if they wished.¹¹

Franco came to believe that the Left had snatched victory by falsifying the vote. 'The election results were falsified by extremist parties; they won votes by threats and terror, either through demanding that people voted for them, or that they abstained from voting against,' he said.¹² With control by the outgoing government crumbling during the final stages of vote-counting in some districts and the Left already in power by the time counting finished, this was as easy for someone like Franco to believe as it was impossible to prove.[13]

Either way, it was clear that Franco was radically opposed to the new government, which reacted by immediately posting him to the Canary Islands as military commander. The intention was to get him as far away as possible from Madrid and the plotting against the new government. General Goded was similarly sent to the Balearic Islands. The Canary archipelago lay off the west coast of Africa and more than 1,000 kilometres south of mainland Spain, just 100 km from where the Sahara Desert meets the Atlantic Ocean. With the eight inhabited islands, some of them with still-live volcanoes, linked only by ferries, it was a difficult place to organise even a local plot.

In his old job as head of the general staff, Franco had been in a position to direct the repression of left-wing extremists (if asked to by the government) or to head a coup. He was now convinced that Spain was on the precipice of communism, even though the Spanish Communist Party (PCE) had won just 17 seats in parliament and 3.5 per cent of the popular vote.[14] A move to the Canary Islands would leave him powerless: unless he joined a coup. That option was fraught with uncertainty and danger. He considered requesting leave of absence or going abroad to avoid getting mixed up in something he could not control. He even asked his astonished brother-in-law Serrano Suñer if he might be able to oversee a coup from France, presumably to avoid prison or the firing squad if it failed.[15]

Over the two and a half weeks before he left Madrid, Franco met with potential plotters like Mola, Varela, Fanjul and Orgaz. A crucial meeting at the house of Lt Col Delgado Brackenbury saw them all agree that the Republic was heading towards 'revolution and communism'.[16] Pacón was also there. 'We calculated what forces and material we could count on and instructions were given to maintain contact between the organisers,' he said.[17]

Franco also went to see the Falange leader, José Antonio Primo de Rivera. They were both invited to the apartment of the family of Serrano Suñer, who recalled the meeting as 'hard-going and uncomfortable'.[18] José Antonio urged rebellion, but Franco was evasive, rambling and cautious. He chattered interminably in his high-pitched voice about army gossip, the qualities (or, more usually, lack) of fellow officers and the minutiae of artillery guns while avoiding mention of plots or politics. He refused, absolutely, to engage in talk about his own political beliefs or intentions. It was a classic, wily Franco performance, revealing nothing at all about himself and boring the sophisticated, intelligent and impassioned Falange leader to death. As soon as Franco walked out of the door, the Falange leader let loose a torrent of splenetic scorn. The young Primo de Rivera had watched his own father become a military dictator and now seemed persuaded that army officers were unsuited to politics, with Franco a prime example. 'My father, for all his faults and lack of political direction, was something else – humane, decisive and noble. But these people…!' he complained. Serrano Suñer was shocked by quite how thoroughly Franco had driven his friend to despair.[19]

Franco told any retired officers who asked him that, should an uprising occur, they had best report immediately to their old barracks. Otherwise, he warned, the Marxists would get them. He continued to conspire with Mola, meeting in Madrid cafés. Serrano Suñer recalled Franco's disquiet when he passed on a message that General Miguel Cabanellas, a formerly Republican-supporting Freemason and military governor of Aragon who now disliked the Popular Front, was ready to join them. He clearly neither liked nor trusted him.[20]

In the meantime, Pacón sat down with General Varela and two other key plotters, lieutenant colonels Juan Yagüe and Valentín Galarza, to work out a code by which Franco could communicate with them. They based their code on two identical editions of a storybook, with each word in a message identified by a code that referred to a particular word in a particular page and line of the book. It stopped working when Yagüe swapped to a new edition of the same book with a different layout.[21]

When Franco visited President Alcalá-Zamora before setting out for the Canary Islands early in March 1936, he warned that a Marxist revolution was about to happen. 'The revolution was defeated in Asturias,' Alcalá-Zamora replied.[22] 'Whatever happens, there will be no communism under me.' When Franco went in turn to see Azaña, the recently appointed prime minister warned him against coups, referring back to Sanjurjo's attempt to grab power in 1932. 'I knew about that beforehand and I could have stopped it, but I preferred to let it fail,' Azaña reportedly said.[23]

Shortly before leaving Madrid for his new posting, Franco once again met with Mola and other would-be coup plotters. They decided that their leader would be the exiled General Sanjurjo, but could not agree on whether to restore the monarchy or remain a Republic, or whether it was best to target Madrid or the provinces. A council of generals formed by those remaining in Madrid was to oversee planning. Franco did not commit himself. The tipping point for rebellion, he argued, would be outbreaks of anarchy, uncontrolled rioting or the appointment of a government headed by the Socialists. He also suggested, however, that an uprising did not need the monarchy – it was enough to take control of the country and decide on the new regime later.[24]

Franco clearly did not think that the moment of anarchy had arrived yet. Rightists and bourgeois Spaniards, however, were becoming increasingly worried. The liberal feminist Clara Campoamor's memory of those days reflects both the reality of the growing hostility to landowners and the church, along with the wilder rumours that began to circulate:

> In the countryside, attacks by revolutionary elements against the right, the agrarians and the radicals, and in general against landowners and employers, increased. Land was seized, enemies were beaten, all adversaries were branded as 'fascists'. Churches and public buildings were set on fire, cars were stopped on the roads in the South, as in the days of banditry, and travelers were required to pay a contribution to the International Red Aid.[25]

On 8 March 1936, Franco and his family boarded an express train heading for Cádiz, on the south coast. From there, they were to catch the *Dómine* packet boat to their new home on the island of Tenerife. At stations along the way, ticket collectors and railway engineers exchanged left-wing raised fist salutes. Church-burnings continued across the country amid outbursts of anticlerical fury. Violence against the church had existed in Spain ever since mobs killed priests during the civil wars against the ultrareligious, liberal-hating Carlists in the 1830s, but this kind of public disorder was anathema to Franco, who thought the army should be called on to quell them. When they reached Cádiz, smoke was drifting from soot-stained churches. The local commander explained that a monastery in front of his garrison had been set afire. Franco demanded to know why his troops had not stopped the arsonists, to which the local commander said he had orders not to intervene. 'No officer should obey an order like that,' Franco retorted.[26]

On the quay the following day, Franco found a crowd sending off the new civil governor of Las Palmas and occasionally singing the global leftist anthem 'The Internationale'. As the boat pulled away, Franco's group, including Pacón, felt 'sad and downcast'. To make things worse, they sailed straight into an Atlantic storm that churned the sea and left them groaning in their bunks with seasickness – except for Franco, who always had good sea legs. For the government, however, it was a relief to know that Franco was on a packet boat that would transport him 1,300 km from mainland Spain. To them, he was the most dangerous general in Spain – not because he was the most ardent anti-Republican in the army but because of his potential for persuading others to follow him.[27]

16

The Big Decision

SANTA CRUZ DE TENERIFE. MARCH 12, 1936

Franco and his family were met at the quay in Santa Cruz de Tenerife by a divided crowd – some were noisy and hostile, while others cheered enthusiastically. For someone used to respect and adulation, the island of Tenerife was a testing place to be. Men, women and small children who saw Franco's official car often responded by shouting 'UHP!', for '¡Uníos Hermanos Proletarios!' (Unite, Working-class Brothers!). On one trip to the cinema to see a film about his beloved Legion, he was both cheered and booed.[1]

Elsewhere, the Azaña government was greeted with a rise in political violence, including tit-for-tat killings between parties. Shootings by Falangists, socialists, anarchists or police claimed two lives a day over the next five months. This provided a bloody backdrop to a period of mostly peaceful strikes, protest marches and land occupations that some on the political right found more frightening, because they were more popular and visible. By mid-May the opposition in parliament was complaining that 178 buildings belonging to the church or others had been attacked by arsonists in the first three months of the new government. Clara Campoamor reported that one burst of violence against the church was provoked by rumours that 'Catholic ladies and priests were killing children by gifting them poisoned sweets.'[2]

In everyday terms, Tenerife was a relaxing posting. Franco often worked only in the mornings (sometimes only for part of them) and spent much time on the golf course, refining the technique of his latest passion. The daily horse-riding of his younger married days continued at a lesser pace with outings to the steep hills north of Santa Cruz, accompanied by Pacón. He saw an English tutor for an hour on three mornings each week, handing in written exercises based around golf, complaining about the influence of Moscow on the Popular Front, damning 'materialism and socialism' and expressing nostalgia for his military academy in Zaragoza. 'Nothing can be done for the moment,' he replied when asked if all that could be changed. He was a diligent student but only learned to read basic English in his few months of lessons. French, spoken poorly, remained his sole foreign language.[3]

The level of political violence dipped, but remained above a killing a day for all but three of the weeks through to mid-July.[4] As Falangist and Leftist gunmen struck against one another on mainland Spain, the man deemed by some 'the butcher of Asturias' was reportedly warned of a plot on his own life. Franco's first hagiographer, Joaquín Arrarás, claimed that 'paid assassins hovered and spied... he was watched night and day, his mail was censored, his telephone messages were intercepted, and he was surrounded by a veritable ring of spies organised by the hostile authorities on the island.'[5] One melodramatic conversation reported by Arrarás, in which Franco improbably claims that the USSR wants him dead, went like this:

A friend warned the general. 'There are plans afoot to take your life.'
'Two years ago,' he answered, 'Moscow sentenced me to death.'[6]

Franco joked to his family that the government might arbitrarily detain him, thereby giving him more time to study English, but told them he saw no real threat to his life. However, his wife was sufficiently alarmed to make sure that, when they drove off to play golf most afternoons, they were followed by a security escort of junior officers in a separate car. When Franco realised, he complained that people would say he was 'scared and a coward' but Carmen Polo and Pacón prevailed.[7]

Graffiti appeared on walls. 'Death to Franco!' read one. When Franco complained to civil governor Manuel Vázquez Moro, the latter replied that he had seen posters proclaiming: 'Death to the governor!', 'Long live Franco, our future dictator!', 'Up with Fascism!' and

'Death to the Republic!'. It was in both their interests, he said, not to stir up trouble.[8]

The fact that Franco was now being publicly named as a potential dictator, despite having given no public clues about his intentions or political priorities, showed just how far the coup rumours flying around Madrid had travelled. Franco's fellow plotters in Spain's capital city, meanwhile, urged for an immediate uprising. Some insisted that victory would be quick and simple. Franco disagreed, spelling out the dangers to his cousin and aide-de-camp Pacón:

> It will be very difficult and very bloody. You must understand that we barely have an army, that the support of the Civil Guard is more than doubtful and that there are many generals and other officers who will stick by the current regime – some out of self-comfort and others from conviction and ideals.
>
> No one should forget that a soldier who rises against the constituted regime can never go back on that, nor can they surrender, since they will be shot by a firing squad in any case. What happened to Sanjurjo [in 1931] with the death sentence commuted to jail is not a desirable end and in a similar situation I will do my best to ensure that the said death sentence is actually carried out.
>
> I would conduct my own defence and say: 'Gentlemen of the court, when I rose up I did so in order to save my Fatherland; I knew that should I fail then by law the death sentence should be applied and so I ask you to carry out what is dictated.'[9]

This conversation, remembered years later, may have been embellished to burnish Franco's reputation, but the core is undoubtedly true and Franco was right. An uprising was an all-or-nothing affair. Anyone involved should realise that it would claim the lives of many Spaniards.

Franco was less worried about the human cost of an uprising than he was about the likelihood of failure. Nor did he now seem concerned about showing more blatantly where his political sympathies lay. On 14 April, during the anniversary commemorations for the Republic, he made no attempt to keep his voice down as he praised Mussolini's invasion of Abyssinia. Separately, he told the Italian consul in Tenerife that he hoped his country could impose itself as a 'young, strong new power in the Mediterranean, which has been treated up to now like a lake under British control'. If Italy wanted to oust Britain, he suggested, then it would be easy for either Italian planes or Spanish artillery (or both) to suppress Gibraltar.[10]

That same day in Madrid, during the march-past to mark the Republic's anniversary, fighting broke out between groups cheering or booing the Civil Guard. Then someone detonated a firecracker by the tribune, provoking panic. In the ensuing mayhem an off-duty Civil Guard officer was killed: his funeral procession two days later attracted groups of angry Falangists and leftist gunmen who fired at them. Eventually a group of pro-government Assault Guards led by Lieutenant José del Castillo opened fire to disperse the protesters. At least three (some reports say five) people were killed, including a cousin of the Falangist leader Primo de Rivera.[11]

The main coup plotters in Madrid were still mired in uncertainty they set a date for 20 April but postponed it after realising they did not yet have sufficient support. The government found out and broke up the group, either by sacking them or moving them away from Madrid. General Mola, based in Pamplona, now took control of the planning. He would be known as 'the director'.[12]

In the meantime, Franco shed his public aversion to politics. When his brother-in-law Serrano Suñer suggested he stand for a parliamentary seat in the central Spanish province of Cuenca – where voting for the general elections had to be re-run – he initially said yes. The move had two potential advantages. It would take him back to Madrid, where the coup was being organised. Parliament would also offer an alternative to the army, if he needed one in the coming turbulent times.[13]

Vanity and family might also have played a part. His brother Ramón had already been a radical left-wing parliamentarian while his elder brother Nicolás, a naval engineer, was secretary general of the conservative Spanish Agrarian Party and had served the previous government as director general of the Merchant Marine. This was a chance for Franco to prove his personal popularity.

The presence of a celebrated military leader, and the man who had put down the Asturias rebellion, as a candidate on the right-wing slate looked politically astute, but Falange leader José Antonio Primo de Rivera successfully nixed the idea, arguing that Franco was politically unsophisticated and was needed for the longer-term plan of violently overthrowing the Republic. 'This is not his world,' he said.[14]

Franco's political priorities, indeed, remained a mystery. He had served the Right during the 1934 rebellion and as chief of the general staff, but had said very little about his own views in public. Caution guided him, while hierarchy, obedience, order and patriotism were his keystones. He had never publicly proposed anything like a vision for Spain beyond the belief that Africanistas like himself – men prepared to risk their lives and exercise violence on behalf of the nation – were a model to follow.

Nobody wanted to deliver the message that he was not wanted as a candidate for parliament to such a prominent, proud and thin-skinned man. In the end, Serrano Suñer flew to the Canary Islands and persuaded him, apparently pointing out that he might be overshadowed in a debating chamber. Franco would never admit that he had been ousted by Primo de Rivera, however, and both he and his official hagiographers later gave differing versions of him standing down. None mention him being rejected.[15]

In the meantime, Spanish politics moved on. President Alcalá-Zamora, who had always appointed relatively moderate prime ministers on both the right and the left, was ousted and eventually replaced as president by Azaña on 11 May 1936. Azaña then invited Santiago Casares Quiroga, of his own progressive Republican Left party, to take over as prime minister and run the government.[16]

The coup plot continued to progress. By 25 May, Mola had the blessing of the man the plotters wanted to impose on Spain as a new dictator, the exiled General Sanjurjo. Mola was, in turn, formally confirmed as 'director' of the plot by Sanjurjo. Franco remained an important piece in the puzzle, but had not given a definitive 'yes'. Left-wingers nevertheless saw him as the greatest threat. 'General Franco, because of his youth, abilities and friendship network within the army, is the man who, at a given moment, would have the best chances of leading a movement of this kind, thanks to his personal prestige,' the leader of the socialists' pragmatic wing, Indalecio Prieto, observed at the time. Other people had wanted him in Madrid for precisely that reason, he suspected.[17]

The plotters' political programme was deliberately broad and fuzzy. It was neither monarchical nor necessarily Republican (nor anti-Republican). Sanjurjo would lead a military directorate, the Left would be repressed and order enforced. Beyond that, it was essentially an 'anti' movement which justified itself as stopping a potential communist revolution. That was something that could be supported by military reactionaries like Franco, monarchists, fascists and even the still strong Carlist movement – described by one historian as 'indisputably the oldest continuously existing popular movement of the extreme right in Europe'.[18] The Carlists had lost three civil wars in the nineteenth century but they still boasted an 8,400-man militia in their northern stronghold of Navarre and had supporters scattered around the country. In an attempt to explain the Carlists' apparently anachronistic survival, a British diplomat called them 'medieval reactionaries'.[19]

With such a broad and varied alliance, there could be no agreed plan for what kind of regime would follow or what its policies would be. It was obvious, however, that even the mildest option would be authoritarian and repressive. Beyond that, each faction had its own dreams about what should happen, while making these secondary to the task of overthrowing the elected government.

Franco had agreed with Mola, in principle, that he would travel to Morocco to lead the mighty Army of Africa – with its hardcore of Africanista officers, legionnaires and local mercenary units - into rebellion. The idea was that the Army of Africa would rise first, inspire the rest of the armed forces to do the same and then cross to mainland Spain to take a lead role in any fighting. Franco's prestige would not only guarantee the adhesion of the Army of Africa, but also that of many other units. That made him a crucial part of the plot, or so it seemed to Mola. Yet Franco ignored four separate messages sent to him by Mola in June. It was as if Franco had been teasing him – both encouraging the plotters and then disappearing completely when asked to commit. 'This isn't working. No-one is pushing,' Mola complained.[20]

In fact, Franco was hedging his bets. On 23 June he wrote to prime minister Casares Quiroga, both protesting about the way the army was being treated and assuring him of its loyalty. Typically, the letter could be read two different ways – either as an expression of loyalty or as a threat. 'Those who paint the army as being against the Republic are not telling the truth and those who invent plots are trying to fool you,' Franco insisted. Mola was furious when he found about the duplicitous letter some months later.[21]

According to Pacón, Franco was also sounding out military commanders in various places about whether they were prepared to rebel. These included his deputy at Zaragoza, General Miguel Campins, and the chief of staff of the Army of Africa, Colonel Martín Moreno. 'Dissimulating as much as possible ... he explained that the army might be obliged to intervene,' Pacón says. Martín Moreno suggested he would only join an uprising led by Franco, while Campins reminded him that they were sworn to obey the Republic. Either way, Franco's dissimulation left them uncertain about his true intentions, just as Franco himself was. 'Not even Hamlet was that indecisive,' his brother-in-law Serrano Suñer commented later.[22]

The Casares-Quiroga government seemed convinced that, after the failure of the Sanjurjo uprising in 1932, military rebellions were no longer a threat, despite insistent rumours to the contrary. It failed to detect growing unrest amongst army officers as pardons were issued to the revolutionaries they had fought against in Asturias during the October 1934 uprising. With the government needing the parliamentary votes of the same Socialist Party that had led the uprising, some feared revolution by stealth. 'Extremist elements of the Popular Front were preparing a Soviet-style communist revolution in order to grab power and exterminate their enemies,' Franco himself reasoned a few months later.[23] Some officers did not need such an excuse. They were already diehard authoritarians or fascists.

In fact, Casares and his government were ingenuous left-wing moderates, which is why they missed several opportunities to quash the coup. The prime minister personally interviewed Lieutenant Colonel Juan Yagüe, the chief plotter in the Army of Africa, to test his loyalty on 12 June. 'Yagüe is a gentleman and a good soldier, who I am sure will never betray the Republic. He has given me his word ... and men like Yagüe keep their word,' he said. In fact, Yagüe was amongst those pushing hardest for the coup.[24]

Yagüe almost certainly used the same trip to visit the Franco family apartment on Jorge Juan street in Madrid, then occupied by Serrano Suñer. 'What that man [Franco] has to do is speak out loud and clear, which is what Spain demands, even if he gets put in jail, because that is how you earn and deserve the leadership of a movement,' Serrano recalls him saying, before he pulled a photograph of Falange leader José Antonio Primo de Rivera from his wallet, saying most officers in Morocco now carried one. 'Like him! You have to commit, you have to take the risk, the situation is so grave that this cannot wait.'[25] On being informed that General Mola was in a secret enclave with the heads of various northern garrisons three days later, Casares Quiroga was similarly dismissive. 'General Mola is a loyal Republican who deserves the respect of the authorities,' he insisted.[26]

By now, the plotters had realised that their coup would provoke a civil war. Madrid and Barcelona were unlikely to fall instantly, given the strength of workers' organisations and the loyalties of local police. So, they began preparing for a short war with garrisons rising in smaller provincial cities and then falling rapidly on the biggest cities in columns. Both Franco and Mola thought such a war might be won in two weeks.[27]

On 1 July, Mussolini agreed to back, with aircraft sales and munitions, the far-right monarchists who were now the most belligerent public opposition to the Republic. Led by José Calvo Sotelo of the Spanish Renovation party, the monarchist faction (which wanted to restore Alfonso XIII) had many supporters in the army officer corps. On 16 June Calvo Sotelo told parliament that he wanted to ban strikes, lockouts, usury and 'abusive financial capitalism'. 'If that is a fascist state, then I agree with that concept of the state and I, who believe in it, declare myself fascist,' he added. In private, he was also asking Serrano Suñer about Franco: 'What does your brother-in-law think and what will he do? What are the generals up to? Don't they realise what is coming?'[28]

Meanwhile, the real fascists of the Falange boasted that they could raise a militia of 10,000 men. José Antonio Primo de Rivera finally confirmed the group's backing for the coup on 29 June, adding a crucial piece to the jigsaw coalition of Rightist factions. By this stage he was operating from a prison cell, having been arrested in March and sentenced for illegal possession of several pistols. Either way, the Falange was expected to provoke a breakdown in public order by increasing its attacks. This was seen by Mola as a vital precursor to a coup – since disorder gave the army an excuse to step in.[29]

Franco followed the plotting at a distance from the Canary Islands, deliberately not committing himself to an uprising in which he was meant to take a major role. He could see that the plans were not yet ripe. On 1 July, for example, Mola admitted that he still had not struck a deal with the ultra-conservative Carlist movement whose militia, the Requetés, were being helped by rebellious army officers like Varela.[30]

The plotters fumed at Franco's ambiguity, coquetry and what Yagüe called his 'hesitation and parsimony'.[31] Some referred to him as 'Miss Canary Islands' since he needed such intense wooing. 'With or without Franquito, we can save Spain,' Sanjurjo had already grumbled after his previous failed coup, seeing a 'crafty' general who preferred to live 'in the shadows'.[32]

Franco's reticence was a mixture of self-interest, fear and extreme caution. 'He was a cold man, who lived in his own world. Everything began and ended with him,' his brother-in-law Serrano Suñer remarked.[33] Franco knew that his participation in the uprising was important, even vital, because so many officers would follow him. At the same time, as plotters worked out the likely level of resistance, the Army of Africa grew in importance. By 24 June Mola was telling Yagüe to expect the arrival of a 'prestigious general' (meaning Franco) who would lead them onto the mainland. The aim was to ship two troop columns based on Legion units to the southern mainland ports of Málaga and Algeciras before marching on Madrid. They were to use 'great violence' and intimidate the government into surrender.[34]

In fact, the Army of Africa and its militant Africanista officers now became so important that the date for the uprising had to be altered to allow it to finish manoeuvres in Morocco on 12 July. The new date was set for 17 July in north Africa and 18 July elsewhere – giving Franco and the Army of Africa the task of initiating it. During the manoeuvres, Yagüe's tent was a centre of plotting for what he already called 'the Crusade'. At a farewell dinner, drunken young officers allegedly shouted thinly coded Falangist greetings like 'CAFÉ!' - an acronym for '¡Camaradas! ¡Arriba Falange Española!' ('Comrades, up with the Spanish Falange!'). When the exercises finished, it took the 18,000 men of the Army of Africa two hours to march past their commanders. It was a massive display of the manpower that the plotters planned to put to good use.[35]

On paper, Franco was now central to the whole operation. It was his task to start the rebellion, gain control of Spain's most potent fighting force, lead the Army of Africa onto the mainland and, if necessary, fight his way to Madrid. Yet he continued to dilly-dally. Despite this, on 5 July plans were made in England to charter a civilian aircraft that could take him from the Canary Islands to Morocco to start the violent uprising against what were now generically and scornfully called 'the Reds'. Over lunch at Simpson's restaurant in London's Strand, plotters asked Catholic publisher Douglas Jerrold to charter an aircraft that could fly from England to the Canary Islands. This was meant to appear like an innocuous tourist jaunt, so they added a request for some English 'platinum blondes' to travel with it. Jerrold rang a pilot called Captain Cecil Bebb, whose passengers included retired army major Hugh Pollard, his 19-year-old daughter Diana and her friend, Dorothy. They set off from Croydon airport in a de Havilland Dragon Rapide on 11 July, stopping off at Bordeaux and in Portugal.[36]

Yet by the time the Dragon Rapide landed in the Moroccan city of Casablanca on 12 July, Franco had cold feet again. Already, on 8 July he had told plotter General Alfredo Kindelán that he was not yet fully committed. On 12 July he sent a coded message that read 'the geography is not very broad', meaning conditions were not yet right. When Mola was told this on 14 July, just four days before the coup date, he hurled the belt containing the message brought to him by a young female intermediary to the floor and changed the plans so that Sanjurjo would replace Franco in charge of the Army of Africa.[37]

Franco was in a multi-layered quandary. On the one hand, he was a regimented, conservative army officer who had sworn loyalty to the Republic. On the other hand, he feared that Leftists and freemasons would deliver Spain to communism. He had been conspiring for months and agreed wholeheartedly with the objective of overthrowing the government and eradicating the Left, but was not sure it would succeed. Apart from that, he had no specific political ideology. He also knew that an uprising needed to be well-planned and well-timed. The price of failure was death by firing squad.

Franco's brother Ramón had already given his own version of what should happen to those who tried to overthrow the Republic. 'If a group of generals tries to establish a new dictatorship or fascist regime, then they should be dragged out and lynched. And if a group of colonels meets up to make threats or with the aim of acting against the people, then they should be burnt or blasted to death in their hideaway,' he said.[38]

Yet those who did not join the uprising also risked being shot by the right-wing insurrectionists. 'The timid and uncertain must be warned that whoever is not with us is against us, and will be treated accordingly,' Mola had written to his fellow plotters, adding that the reaction would be 'inexorable'.[39] Franco was still in the group of 'the timid and uncertain'.

Franco's greatest advantage, in terms of personal safety, was that the Canary Islands lay off the west coast of Morocco and far from mainland Spain. If he could successfully take control of the Canary Islands, he and his family would be safe. If he flew to the Spanish protectorate in Morocco, he could also be sure that the Army of Africa's officers would be the most enthusiastic participants in the uprising. That gave him not just personal security, but also considerable firepower. In other words, he would not be risking death to the same degree as the mainland plotters. Nor would he be putting his family in peril. If all failed, exile remained a possibility – if not a happy one.

By 12 July, the coup had become an inevitability. Yet one part of the plan had already failed. Factional street violence had not yet reached such an extreme that the coup could be launched under the desired pretence of restoring order. 'Attempts have been made to provoke a state of violence between two political sectors so that, on the basis of this, we could proceed. This has not yet happened, despite the help provided by certain political elements,' Mola wrote on 1 July in reference to violent provocations by the Falange. Although political and police violence had caused an average of eleven deaths a week over the previous four weeks, this had not brought a sensation of chaos. Life in most Spanish cities, towns and villages continued largely as normal, though a creeping tension appeared to spread though Madrid and other major cities as coup rumours grew. With left and right so bitterly confronted, it was clear that this would provoke considerable bloodshed.[40]

In the week before the coup date, however, the victims suddenly became far more prominent.

On 12 July, Rightist gunmen killed José del Castillo, the left-leaning lieutenant from the Assault Guards police force who acted as an instructor to the Socialist Youth militia, and whose men had previously opened fire at the Falangist funeral crowd. Married three weeks earlier, Castillo's bride had apparently received a letter saying: 'Why marry a man who will soon be a corpse?' Castillo was reportedly second on a list of Leftist officers put together by a clandestine far-right organisation of army officers who Pacón was in close contact with, the Spanish Military Union (UME). Early on 13 July, in a fit of vengeful fury, a gang of Castillo's colleagues and socialist youth friends kidnapped and shot José Calvo Sotelo, leader of the militant monarchist Right. In terms of the importance of those killed, this was a major escalation. Calvo Sotelo's death provided what *Daily Telegraph* correspondent Henry Buckley called the 'big dramatic act on which to hinge the coup which had been constantly postponed since February'.[41]

When Franco heard the news later that day, he reportedly exclaimed: 'The Fatherland has a new martyr. We cannot wait any long. This is the sign!'[42] The following morning, Franco's English teacher Dora Lennard claims to have found a changed man. 'He looked ten years older, and had obviously not slept all night. For the first time, he came near to something like losing his iron self-control and unalterable serenity,' Lennard, who became a pro-Franco propagandist, said later.[43] 'He was obviously moved to the very depths of his being. It was with visible effort that he attended to his lesson.' Given Franco's nonchalance about other people's deaths, it is likely that Franco's state of disarray meant he had spent the night struggling with his decision.

He now sent a telegram to Mola, finally confirming his role in the rebellion. Fortunately for him, the Dragon Rapide from England was already on its way. He ordered Pacón to buy his wife and daughter tickets on a German freighter, the *Waldi*, so they could flee the country on 19 July.[44]

While his propagandists later presented the Calvo Sotelo killing as proof of a Bolshevik plot to takeover Spain, Franco himself claimed it had been 'carried out on the orders of the Secretariat General of Masonry in Geneva'. Even more bizarrely, Franco believed that international Freemasons and communists were in cahoots. 'It was one of a series of crimes that were meant to be the prelude to the proclamation of a Soviet state in Spain. We knew that at the time.'[45] He claimed to possess documents proving this communist-style state had first been due to be proclaimed in May 1936, then postponed to the end of July and that the uprising had been specifically timed to prevent that happening.

Franco's decision to rejoin the uprising brought the plotters reassurance, but not organisational serenity. 'There were no detailed instructions; there could be none, for it was impossible to foresee the course of events,' explained Luis Bolín, the monarchist journalist from the *ABC* newspaper who had chartered the Dragon Rapide and flown with the crew as far as Casablanca, in Morocco. The confusion was not helped by the fact that the Dragon Rapide eventually landed on a different island, Gran Canaria, at Las Palmas. This was apparently because the Tenerife air strip was either prone to mist or too easily associated with Franco.[46]

Pollard, his daughter and her friend took a night ferry to Tenerife in order to deliver a coded three-word message to a local physician, Doctor Gabarda, who was a friend of one of the Madrid plotters. He was by now fed up with the bizarre, coded messages that various strangers kept asking him to recall. When Pollard rang on the doctor's bell early in the morning and uttered the words 'Galicia Saluda Francia' ('Galicia greets France'), the doctor angrily threw him out, thinking it was a prank.[47]

The message nevertheless found its way to Franco. It meant he urgently needed an excuse to travel to Las Palmas. That would normally have required him to inform the War Ministry, which might find such a movement suspicious, since he had been there on official business two weeks earlier. However, a tragic but timely excuse was suddenly created by the military commander of Gran Canaria, General Amado Balmes, who was shot in the stomach at a firing range on 16 July and died. This was almost certainly a self-inflicted accident but it was also amazingly fortuitous, since it resolved Franco's problems over the Dragon Rapide. That evening, Franco and his family caught a boat to Las Palmas in order to attend the funeral the following morning.[48]

It was a hot, sweaty night, despite the cooling effect of the Atlantic Ocean. They reached Gran Canaria early in the morning of 17 July and Franco oversaw the 11am funeral. During the day, Franco was handed a fake diplomatic passport with his photograph inside it, since the Dragon Rapide would have to stop off in French Morocco to refuel. That evening, Franco, his family and Pacón ate supper in a restaurant in the Plaza San Telmo.[49]

Confusion over the exact timings for the coup was widespread, partly because these were rejigged to give Franco more time to reach the Army of Africa in Morocco. The final version of the plan was for the uprising to start at 5am on 18 July in Africa before spreading to mainland Spain the following day.⁵⁰

In fact, while the Franco family lingered over dinner and the heat of the day subsided, the uprising was already underway. Spooked by news that their plot had been discovered, the Army of Africa garrison in Melilla had brought forward the timing. The plot had been discovered earlier in the day by General Manuel Romerales, commander of the Army of Africa and memorably described as 'the fattest of Spain's 400 generals and one of the easiest fooled'. The local Falangist leader, Lieutenant Colonel Juan Seguí, went to Romerales' office to find the general dithering about whether to start arresting people. Seguí resolved the matter at pistol-point, arresting Romerales himself. By 4pm, the rebellion was under way in Melilla and phone calls were being made to plotters in Tetouan and Ceuta so that the rest of the Army of Africa rebelled. They were acting, the rebels claimed, in the name of Franco as 'Head of the Armed Forces in Africa'.⁵¹

Franco himself only discovered that he had already nominally led a military uprising when he was woken up by Pacón in his room at the Hotel Madrid shortly after 3am the following morning.⁵² It was Saturday, 18 July, and the Spanish Civil War – widely viewed as the opening act of World War II – had just begun.

17

Insurrection

LAS PALMAS, 18 JULY 1936

As Franco slept in his hotel room in Las Palmas, bodies piled up in the morgue at Melilla's Hospital O'Donnell, mostly of men in uniform whose insignia had been torn off – meaning soldiers or police who had refused to rebel. Orders sent by General Mola to legionnaire Lt Colonel Juan Yagüe called for 'extreme violence ... exemplary punishment... Eliminate leftist elements: communists, anarchists, unionists, Freemasons etc...' That night 189 people were killed across Spain's protectorate and north African enclaves: the following morning bodies could be seen on streets and beaches. This was as many as had died in political violence across Spain over the previous two months in the so-called 'chaos' the plotters claimed to be resolving.[1]

The heavily militarised protectorate was in rebel hands by the end of 18 July. A small number of poorly armed workers fought back in Melilla and Ceuta, with the support of just a handful of loyal army officers, including Franco's cousin and childhood companion Major Ricardo de la Puente Bahamonde, whose men defended Tetouan's Sania Ramel airfield. He swore to fight 'to the last bullet' but eventually surrendered after disabling the seven airplanes there. Captain Virgilio Leret Ruíz, aged 34, did the same at the Atalayón seaplane base in Melilla. He was captured, summarily tried and shot.[2]

For the moment, however, Franco had to organise his own insurrection in the Canary Islands. At 4am he set out from the Hotel Madrid with Pacón for the military governor's office, bumping into a drunk who had heard about the uprising in Morocco and exhorted him to be 'hard on them - they don't deserve any compunction'. It was unclear whether the drunk thought Franco was setting out to defend Spanish democracy or destroy it.[3]

It was a sign of how small the group of plotters was, and how much they leant on the prestige of generals like Franco, that his first task was to ring local commanders and ask them to join him. The head of the local garrison immediately agreed, adding a battalion of infantrymen and their weaponry to his cause. Franco failed, however, to persuade numerous Civil Guard officers. They argued that they only took orders from Madrid, despite Franco's pleas that – should the uprising fail – they could blame him. 'I am the only one responsible,' he insisted. The Assault Guards also declined to join Franco, though the captains of two small gunboats in the port and the coastal artillery unit agreed to obey him. The docks were soon occupied by rebel soldiers and a flurry of orders were issued so that the telephone exchange, water deposits, electricity stations and other crucial bits of infrastructure were in the rebels' hands.[4]

At 5am that morning Franco unilaterally declared a state of war in the Canary Islands. He ordered an infantry company accompanied by trumpets and drums to make the announcement in Las Palmas. At 5.15 a pre-prepared, if somewhat garbled, communiqué was read out in his name over the radio. It contained a long list of reasons why Franco was rebelling – from anarchy on the streets and the weakness of elected politicians to disrespect towards the army, Catalan nationalism and the supposedly growing influence of the Soviet Union.[5]

Franco gave no clues about what might replace all that beyond making airy promises about 'peace and love between Spaniards'. Above all, the rebels would enforce what Franco called 'order' and he vowed to outdo the violence of anyone who opposed his men. He promised a country 'without hatred or revenge' but also 'pitiless war against those who exploit politics, trick the workers and bring foreign ideas with the intention of destroying Spain'. They were contradictory ideas, and it was already clear from the shootings of opponents in north Africa that revenge would play a large part in the conflict. Less clear was what the rebels stood for beyond hatred of the Left, or how they would be led and organised. To confuse things further, Franco's communiqué ended with a version of a very foreign revolutionary cry, taken from the French, 'Fraternity, Liberty and Equality!' Franco did not write this text himself but must have approved it and reportedly added a postscript: 'Damn those who instead of carrying out their duty, betray Spain.'[6]

Shortly after 7am, Franco sent a telegram to the main military commands in Spain itself. 'Glory to the Army of Africa. Spain above everything. These garrisons send enthusiastic greetings to you and our other companions on the peninsula at this historic hour. Blind faith in victory! Long live an honoured Spain. General Franco.'[7] Four days earlier, he had been doubtful about joining the rebellion. Now it was Franco who, at least to those ignorant of the original plot, had fired the starting gun.

Soon an angry crowd gathered outside the Military Governor's headquarters in Las Palmas. Another crowd was gathering a few hundred metres away in front of the offices of Civil Governor. Pacón ordered the infantry unit at the military governor's headquarters to fire its small cannon in order to keep the two crowds apart. A cornet sounded as the soldiers advanced and exchanged fire with the few armed members of the crowd, which rapidly dispersed. Franco embraced Pacón, later claiming 'a catastrophe' had been averted – though the imbalance in firepower was huge and a serious battle was never a real possibility. In the meantime, the building filled with retired army officers, Falangists and other supporters, who were all given a rifle and ammunition. With their opponents so poorly armed, they looked set to gain control quickly – though it took a week to definitively capture all of the scattered Canary Islands.[8]

Franco did not wait for this, however. At around 11am on 18 July, Franco handed command of the uprising in the Canary Islands to his co-plotter, General Luis Orgaz. Even though the insurrection there was not yet fully secured, he felt it more important to travel to the Army of Africa in northern Morocco. His wife Carmen Polo and daughter Carmencita were taken to the docks to sail for Le Havre, France. Polo told her daughter they were escaping an outbreak of scarlet fever. 'I'm not sure she believed it,' she said later.[9]

Franco boarded a separate launch with Pacón and sailed 20 kilometres south to the Gando aerodrome, carrying his false diplomatic passport. From the sea, they spotted machine guns mounted by Republican loyalists on the roof of the Civil Governor's building.

They were carried ashore by sailors at the beach beside the aerodrome. There Franco was met by the Dragon Rapide's pilot Bebb, who had been given half a playing card that he was meant to match with one Franco was carrying, though in the excitement everyone forgot about that. They climbed into the Dragon Rapide at 2pm, with the two cousins changing out of their uniforms and Franco at some stage shaving off his moustache. The acidly witty General Queipo de Llano, who was leading the insurrection in Seville, later quipped that this was the only thing Franco had personally sacrificed for Spain.[10]

The journey was interrupted by a fuel stop in Agadir, in French Morocco, and a late, overnight stop in Casablanca. In the latter city, after a fraught landing at an airstrip where a blown fuse had switched off the runway lights, they were met by co-plotter and journalist Luis Bolín. He was the man who had originally hired the Dragon Rapide. Bolín led them to a shabby beach hotel. Given the constant ringing on the doorbell during the night, Pacón suspected it doubled as a brothel.[11]

A nervously garrulous Franco stayed up until 2 a.m., chatting excitedly to Bolín. He was in other people's hands and seemed unable to exercise the sort of calm self-control that came to him whenever he was in command of events. In fact, he didn't shut up even when the lights in their room were turned off and Bolín was trying to get to sleep. According to the admiring Bolín the general knew that a tough fight awaited. 'In the last resort we would take to the hills and from there carry on the kind of guerilla warfare at which my men excel. The enemy could never beat us,' he said.[12]

After just two hours' sleep and a quick breakfast, they returned to the aerodrome (where, conveniently, they had arrived after border officials left for the night) and pushed the Dragon Rapide out of its hangar. With Bebb at the controls, they headed north, eventually spotting the Mediterranean Sea and the Rock of Gibraltar. After two further stopovers, taking an entire day and night, Bebb brought Franco and his entourage to the Sania Ramel aerodrome which Franco's cousin Major Ricardo de la Puente Bahamonde had tried to defend the previous day. As they flew a reconnaissance run over the aerodrome, unsure if it was now in their hands, Franco spotted his friend Colonel Eduardo Saenz de Buruaga amongst the officers waiting for them. They were safe.

In fact, Franco had arrived in Morocco too late to take part in the uprising. It was already over. Franco greeted the waiting officers with a short speech in which he declared 'Spain needs saving and here I am.'[13] He was then driven in an open-top car to the city, hearing for the first time cries of 'Long live Franco!'. Those cheering him were probably unaware that the formal figurehead of the movement was not yet Franco, but rather the exiled General Sanjurjo. Once established in the High Commissioner's office, Franco gave another speech during which he suddenly found himself overcome by either emotion, nervous exhaustion or a mixture of both. Bolín recalled watching the scene:

> When he referred to the present ignominious state of affairs and the depths to which the Reds had lowered Spain — 'We can no longer hold our heads up and feel proud of being Spanish'— the intensity of his feelings dried up his throat, and he tapped the floor with his foot for some seconds before being able to continue.[14]

He seemed overwhelmed by emotion, once more, when driven out to the Legion's base at Dar Riffien, where several banderas awaited in formation. 'Here are your legionnaires, my general, just as impossibly magnificent as when you left them. May you, who have led them to so many victories, take them to more,' Yagüe told him. They marched smartly past Franco with the Legion's exaggerated, theatrical arm swing and shouting '¡Viva España!'[15]

Franco's job now was to oversee local repression, to organise the Army of Africa to cross to the mainland and to coordinate with the other leading plotters. The repression eventually included shooting two pro-Republican soldiers accused of plotting to assassinate Franco in Ceuta.[16] During the journey from the Canary Islands, Casares Quiroga had resigned as prime minister in Madrid. His place was taken by Diego Martínez Barrio, who refused to arm the workers and was trying to parlay with Mola. 'If you and I should reach agreement, both of us will have betrayed our ideals and our followers,' Mola was reported as saying. Tellingly, he also added: 'I am at the orders of my general, Francisco Franco.'[17] Martínez Barrio resigned after just a few hours.

By the time Franco landed in Tetouan, a government led by the Republican Left's José Giral had been installed.[18] This finally began distributing arms to the workers (which, in effect, meant to left-wing parties and trades unions). Soon, a mass of people were armed, including socialists, anarchists, orthodox Stalinist communists, Trotskyists, Catalan separatists, Basque nationalists – as well as loyal army units, Assault Guards and part of the Civil Guard. The impact on the streets of major cities like Madrid and Barcelona was remarkable and the coup failed wherever workers were armed in time.

In these cities, and many other parts of Spain where the coup failed, a left-wing counter-revolution was breaking out, with extremist factions grabbing control of cities and country areas. Ironically, Franco's uprising had provoked exactly what he most feared, leaving the Republican government with the task of imposing control in these places. In Barcelona, some 30,000 rifles were distributed as the insurrectionists were halted and 'syndicalist' anarchists began patrolling the city in requisitioned cars. 'Many of the Syndicalists' automobiles have rough-looking women in them accompanied by armed men and the sign given by those who pass, on foot or in automobiles, is the raised fist,' the US consul in Barcelona reported.[19] Bernie Danchik, an American wrestling coach in Barcelona for an international left-wing Popular Olympics tournament, jotted approvingly in his papers: 'Sunday – Comes the revolution!'

The right-wing insurrectionists fared better in Seville and nearby cities in Andalusia. A Spanish navy destroyer, the *Churruca*, had delivered a first battalion of Moroccan troops from the Army of Africa to the southern port city of Cádiz early on the morning of 19 July. Another unit reached the port of Algeciras. Franco, however, now faced a problem that threatened to derail the entire rebellion. After dropping the Moroccan regulares at Cádiz, the *Churruca's* crew had forcibly taken control of the vessel, arresting its officers and declaring for the Republic.[20]

Across most of the navy, the same thing was happening. A naval radio operator in Madrid called Benjamin Balboa López had refused to retransmit Franco's original message announcing the rebellion, arresting at gunpoint the officer who ordered him to do so and warning crews that their officers were set to rebel. In a single-handed strike against Franco's side, the low-ranking Balboa also established a code system by which radio operators on navy vessels could indicate whether officers had forced these to join the insurrection.[21]

Since most officers did indeed side with the insurrection, crews took control of many vessels. In some cases, that involved storming the bridge or exchanging fire with officers. The crew of the *Jaime I* messaged the marine ministry saying they had overcome their officers by force. 'Urgently request instructions as to bodies,' they said. 'Lower bodies overboard with respectful solemnity,' was the reply.[22] The captain of the cruiser *Libertad* was Franco's cousin (and Pacón's brother) Hermenegildo. He and his officers were detained by their crew and would eventually be shot and tossed into the sea. In fact, several Republican destroyers controlled by their crews were on their way to the Moroccan coast, blocking the sea route to mainland Spain. Franco's army, in other words, was stuck on the wrong side of the Strait of Gibraltar.[23]

In the meantime, Franco sent Bolín back in the Dragon Rapide to Portugal. The idea was that he would visit General Sanjurjo there to inform him that Franco was now safely with the Army of Africa. Then he would go on to Italy or elsewhere to seek the aeroplanes that they now desperately needed to transport the Army of Africa to the mainland. Franco wanted bombers, which could both transport troops and bomb opponents.

> 'Could you write out something for me?' I asked Franco. 'It might be as well to carry some sort of credentials.' He called for a piece of notepaper and wrote down with a firm hand: 'I authorise Don Luis Antonio Bolín to negotiate urgently in England, Germany or Italy the purchase of aircraft and supplies for the Spanish non-Marxist Army, Tetouan, 19 July 1936. The Commander-in-Chief, Francisco Franco.' 'What kind of aircraft and supplies?' I asked, and the General added a footnote in pencil: '12 bombers, 3 fighters, with bombs (and bombing equipment) of from 50 to 100 kilos. 1000 50-kilo bombs and 100 more weighing about 500 kilos.[24]

By signing with the grandiose title of 'commander-in-chief', Franco was elevating himself above his fellow insurrectionist generals. It is possible he simply meant he was commander-in-chief of the Army of Africa, though he did not think to write that down. For the *Times* of London, reporting on the still confusing uprising and the unfamiliar Spanish generals behind it, Franco was still best described to its readers as 'brother of the well-known airman'.[25]

Just as Bolín set out, a famously dashing Spanish pilot called Juan Antonio Ansaldo reached Portugal in a lighter and flimsier aircraft – a three-seater de Havilland Puss Moth. Ansaldo had been sent to collect the uprising's real leader, General Sanjurjo. In Estoril, on the coast 20km west of Lisbon, Ansaldo grandiosely hailed Sanjurjo as head of the insurrection amid theatrical applause from his monarchist hangers-on. He informed the general that he was to be flown to Burgos, where the rebel generals had established a headquarters. Portuguese government nerves about being seen as supporting the uprising meant they had to leave from an improvised landing strip at a horse-racing track called A Marinha. The corpulent Sanjurjo clambered into the small airplane with a large, heavy suitcase into which he had packed uniforms and medals for his expected triumphal entry into Madrid. The Puss Moth struggled to climb as it headed towards a line of trees just outside the racetrack, snagged a tree-top and fell straight back down to earth. Ansaldo survived with barely a scratch but Sanjurjo was killed, leaving the uprising without an overall leader.

On mainland Spain, meanwhile, the insurrection was struggling. The swift war in which rebel columns would fall on and capture Madrid had not materialised. The rebel commander in Barcelona, General Goded, surrendered on 19 July. Already 450 people had died in the city. 'Luck has gone against me and I am now a prisoner; if you wish to avoid further bloodshed, I release you from your pledge to me,' he said on a radio broadcast heard across Spain.[26] In Madrid, the rebellion only started properly on 20 July as General Fanjul holed up with several hundred rebels in the Montaña barracks. When a mob of armed workers and regular soldiers broke into the imposing building, they arrested some defenders and killed others. Writer Arturo Barea saw a giant militiaman hurl rebels from the upper galleries into a courtyard, recording that one 'fell through the air like a rag doll, and crashed onto the stones with a dull thud'. The ground was littered with corpses. A group of officers who had committed suicide were found lying around a mess table. 'At the head was a major with a bullet hole through his heart; all the others were slumped with similar bullet holes,' a Republican soldier who found them said.[27]

As news reached Franco in cables, he read them quickly and stuffed them into his pockets without sharing the flow of bad news.

When Pacón insisted on knowing what they said, the reply was brief and gruff.

'Very bad,' he answered me. In Madrid we had failed and also in Barcelona.[28]

Fanjul and Goded were both jailed and eventually shot by the Republic. The three senior generals in the uprising, including Sanjurjo, were thus out of action within three days. Of those left, Franco outranked Mola (a brigadier general) and was junior to his fellow major general Gonzalo Queipo de Llano, whose enthusiastic backing for the ousting of Alfonso XIII in 1931 had damaged his reputation amongst the monarchist faction of the insurrectionists. Above them all sat Cabanellas and the 59-year-old General Andrés Saliquet, one of many officers who had come out of retirement to join the coup. But no politicians were charismatic enough to fill Sanjurjo's role apart from Falangist leader José Antonio Primo de Rivera, who remained in a Republican jail in Alicante. Who now would lead the insurrection?[29]

Within two days of Sanjurjo's death, Franco's co-plotter in Morocco Lt Col Juan Beigbeder was sending messages that spoke of 'General Franco's National government'. That was a breathtaking assumption of importance given the Army of Africa's failure to participate in the real fighting on mainland Spain, where columns were moving towards Madrid from the north and Queipo de Llano held the area around Seville. Yet many observers already saw Franco as the natural head of the insurrection. Some foreign diplomats started referring to a 'Francoist' army, introducing a new term that was not yet used in Spain. British newspapers were calling Franco 'the leader of the militarists' by July 21 and, over the next few days, 'principal plotter' or 'principal rebel leader'. By 25 July *Chicago Tribune* journalist Jay Allen, one of the great chroniclers of the developing war, was mentioning reports of the 'hardboiled, ambitious general' having 'dictatorial calibre'.[30]

There were other setbacks. Republican loyalists in major cities like Bilbao in the north, Valencia in the east and Málaga in the south all defeated the right-wing insurrectionists. But other large cities did fall, including Seville, Zaragoza and, in Franco's home region of Galicia, both La Coruña and Ferrol. Many provincial capitals in the northern part of Castile also fell quickly. Especially important was the Navarrese capital of Pamplona, which was quickly occupied by the insurrectionists' Carlist allies and their requeté militia.[31]

Unlike elsewhere in Europe where young democracies had been easily erased by the authoritarian or totalitarian Right over the previous decade, Spanish resistance was so strong that success soon began to seem either difficult or unlikely. On 25 July, Franco and Pacón listened to Indalecio Prieto – a leading socialist – declare that the insurrectionists stood no chance. Pacón recalled that his arguments were sound.

> Everything the socialist leader said was resoundingly logical. They had all of Spanish industry, the main ports, the state gold, the support of all democratic governments etc. However, he forgot that in the matter of morale, which is so important in any war, we were ahead... Our army had inherited the virtues of Spain's national army... We were convinced that we were fighting for God and Spain. Our ideal was to prevent Spain becoming a communist country and we believed that only our armed intervention could save it from such a disaster.[32]

In fact, the major difference was in the quality of each side's army, with fewer than one in five officers available to the Republic, where the emerging and shambolic militia groups raised by unions and left-wing political parties lacked military skills, training and leadership.[33]

While his troops were stuck in Africa, all Franco could do was make stirring radio speeches and send envoys abroad to beg for aircraft. He broadcast propaganda to mainland Spain daily, boldly claiming that victory was in sight. Soviet Russia featured prominently, while Franco himself claimed to be on a crusade. 'You are either with communism and Moscow, sacrificing Spain and its Christian civilisation, or with the crusaders for a great, powerful and respected country,' he said on 25 July.[34]

For Franco, however, the situation was bitterly frustrating. A proper war was being fought in mainland Spain and he was not there. Just over two dozen Army of Africa soldiers were making it to the mainland every day in small Dornier and Fokker aircraft while other commanders were gaining all the glory. In northern Spain, Mola's forces had taken Zaragoza, Pamplona, Logroño, Burgos and Valladolid. By 22 July his columns were fighting at the Alto de León mountain pass, just 45 km north-west of Madrid.[35]

In Valladolid, the repression of opponents was such that 448 men who had held out in a socialist clubhouse were all tried – with only 19 escaping death or prison sentences of over 20 years. The elected socialist mayor and other officials were amongst those shot at the Campo de San Isidro park outside the city, where coffee and fried churro stands were set up for spectators. The new civil governor verbally reprimanded those who took wives and children to watch.[36]

Mola was still adding 'Viva la República!' to his proclamations and even Franco used the phrase in at least one message during the first week of the uprising. It was a reflection of confusion amongst the plotters, who had failed to agree on what model of state they were fighting for.[37]

Crucially for Franco and his Army of Africa, the fact that the insurrectionists had won in the southern Spanish cities of Seville, Cádiz and Algeciras created a solid launchpad for a strike towards Madrid from the south – if only his men could cross the sea. All these places would be subjected to the terror tactics of the insurrectionists, with the Falange headquarters in Cádiz used as a torture centre. Some were forced to swallow a mixture of industrial alcohol, castor oil and sawdust. An ad hoc tribunal selected 25 people to be shot every day.[38]

Yet the radical left-wing counter-revolution led by anarchists and others in parts of Republican territory also produced terror. Anticlericalism ran rife. Priests and prisoners were shot, while shadowy death squads knocked on doors, taking away men whose corpses appeared in parks and ditches. Even Clara Campoamor, a feminist and former liberal parliamentarian who had campaigned for women to vote, decided to flee Madrid and Republican Spain because of what she called 'the absolute lack of personal security, even for liberals – or perhaps especially for them'.[39] Red terror allowed the insurrectionists to put out propaganda laced with blood-curdling tales of murder and rape. While behind-the-lines violence would be worse on the insurrectionist side, it often did not seem like that in foreign news coverage. 'Red terror' atrocity stories, indeed, helped tilt government opinion in France and Great Britain away from aiding what had been a ragged but functioning democracy. Hubert Renfro Knickerbocker, a star correspondent for Hearst newspapers who accompanied the insurrectionist army, reported that fifty aristocrats were said to have been shot in the northern city of San Sebastian alone, while hundreds of people in the city were tortured in what, without further explanation, he called 'the approved Ethiopian manner'.[40]

Franco also set about wooing the Italian consul and military attaché in Tangiers as he sought a way to transport his troops to the mainland. He bombarded Mussolini's government with requests for arms and aircraft. Mussolini was wary. Even though he had previously pledged to help monarchist plotters overthrow Spain's Republic, he now worried that this might force him into a fight with France and Great Britain. Mussolini turned down Franco's first two requests. On 22 July, armed with a letter from the exiled Alfonso XIII – now living at the Grand Hotel in Rome – Bolín met the foreign minister, Mussolini's son-in-law Count Galeazzo Ciano, but still Mussolini would not cede.[41]

At the same time, Franco pressed Adolf Hitler. On 22 July, the German consul in Tangiers forwarded a message requesting 'ten troop-transport planes with maximum seating capacity... Transfer by air with German crews to any airfield in Spanish Morocco. The contract will be signed afterwards. Very urgent! On the word of General Franco and Spain.' German diplomats were not impressed, recommending the request be turned down 'at this time'. They fretted that the insurrectionists lacked popular support and that the factions involved had no 'ideological unity and objectives'.[42]

The Germans had good reasons to worry. Quite how the diverse factions of the right-wing insurrection might ever govern together remained a mystery. These were divided into four separate groups with different aims: militant monarchists wanted a reinforced, more authoritarian-minded monarchy led by Alfonso XIII; the fast-growing Falange wanted Spanish fascism; the Carlists wanted a pre-Enlightenment ultra-religious monarchy, but not from Alfonso XIII's line; and the army's now Africanista-dominated officer class wanted a hierarchical regime based on order, obedience and martial values, though its members also often belonged to one of the three other groups. Moderate conservatism was completely sidelined by the violent and vengeful atmosphere of a civil war. Even the well-supported ultraconservative CEDA was deemed suspect for having participated in Republican politics before the war. At a time when soldiers who stood by their pledge to support the Republic were being shot, moderates risked being seen as traitors.[43]

With German diplomats so utterly unimpressed, Franco turned instead to the Nazi party via its overseas 'Auslands-Organization' (AO) in Spanish Morocco. This was led by businessmen Johannes Bernhardt and Adolf Langenheim. Franco now either claimed to Langenheim, or allowed him to believe, that he was the head of a military directorate, with Mola and Queipo de Llano as his juniors. This extraordinary claim, at a time when he had still not taken any part in the fighting, may have added clout to his demands but suggests that the always ambitious Franco already saw himself as the natural commander-in-chief of the insurrectional army.

A chain of Nazi party friendships led from Langenheim to Hitler's deputy, Rudolf Hess. A Lufthansa postal plane was requisitioned in the Canary Islands to fly Bernhardt, Langenheim and the head of Franco's tiny air force, Captain Francisco Arranz, to Berlin on 23 July. Government officials there still wanted nothing to do with Spain. Senior Nazis, however, arranged for them to travel to Bayreuth, where Hitler was attending the music festival dedicated to the work of his composer hero, Richard Wagner.[44]

On 25 July, Mola was so worried about the missing Army of Africa, without which he would be attacking Madrid with no support from the south, that he thought it best for his own troops on the mountains near Madrid to retire to a line behind the River Ebro. Franco's abundant self-assurance now shone through. His telegram in response read: 'Stay firm, victory assured.'[45] Considering he still had no way of transporting his army across the sea, this was a bold statement – reflecting both the 'all or nothing' nature of the venture and Franco's long-held aversion to retreats of any kind.

Fortune, however, was on his side. Over the next three days, Hitler and Mussolini came to his rescue, changing the course of events not just in Spain – but for the rest of the world.

18

Fascism's Tailcoat

BAYREUTH, GERMANY
25 JULY 1936

Franco's dogged pursuit of Adolf Hitler through his Nazi party contacts finally bore fruit when the Führer received Bernhardt and Langenheim after a performance of Wagner's opera *Siegfried* on the evening of 25 July. Hitler had been watching events in Spain unfold over the previous year, sharing the European far right's paranoia about a Bolshevik takeover. The Führer was at first doubtful about backing Franco's side, seeing the Spanish uprising as messy and poorly funded. Apparently fired up by the opera he had just seen, he perorated at length about the dangers of Bolshevism before finally agreeing to help.[1]

Luftwaffe chief Hermann Göring joined the meeting as it continued into the early hours of 26 July. 'The Führer thought the matter over,' Göring explained at a war crimes trial a decade later. 'I urged him to give support under all circumstances: firstly, to prevent the further spread of communism; secondly, to test my young Luftwaffe.' It was a first chance to engage in real warfare as Germany pursued a massive expansion of its military. Hitler agreed to send Franco transport and other aircraft. The Führer dubbed it Operation Magic Fire (*Unternehmen Feuerzauber*) after a passage in which Siegfried battles through flames to rescue Brünnhilde. With that, Nazi Germany's first foreign military intervention was launched.[2]

On 29 July, the first of twenty Junkers Ju-52/3m took off from Stuttgart and flew to Spanish Morocco. 'Today the first transport aircraft arrives!' Franco telegraphed excitedly to Mola. 'Two more will arrive every day until there are twenty. I'm also awaiting six fighters.' Hitler later declared, with some reason, that Franco should erect a monument to his Junkers.[3]

It was a major coup for the insurrectionists and also for Franco himself, since both Queipo de Llano and the National Defence Junta set up by the rebel generals in Burgos on 24 July to oversee the insurrection had failed to get Germany to send aircraft. The junta was headed by two major generals and three brigadier generals, including Mola. Franco was not a founding member, probably because he was so far away and not involved in the fighting. 'We are not rebels, because we are obeying the supreme duty of patriotism,' the council had insisted in its first declaration. 'We have not usurped power, but have recovered the authority that had been abandoned in mud and blood.'[4]

Securing Hitler's ear was also a way for Franco to start establishing personal pre-eminence in a movement that now lacked an overall figurehead. It helped that Hitler's regime had decided German arms were to be sent to Franco and no-one else.[5]

Hitler's Junkers were not the only aircraft to arrive on 29 July. By now, Mussolini had also changed his mind. It was clear that the British conservative government of Stanley Baldwin wanted nothing to do with the Republic – especially as it watched the chaotic formation of militia units by Leftist political groups and trades unions. The *Guardian* explained Baldwin's position succinctly: 'It is doubted here whether arms could be supplied to the Spanish Government as such, or to troops that are indubitably under its control. The view taken is that the arms would probably pass into the hands of extremists who, although fighting against the insurgents, are under no central authority.'[6]

The British position, in turn, helped persuade France's government to stand back, though it also had a Popular Front government led by Socialist Leon Blum. Even the Soviet Union, Mussolini was told, was wary of being sucked too far into supporting the Republic in what could become a full-blown European war.

As a result, Mussolini now joined Hitler in backing the right-wing insurrection. His senior officials already considered Franco the de facto leader. A dozen Savoia SM.81 bombers piloted by Italian officers took off for Spanish Morocco on 29 July. Due to strong headwinds, only nine aircraft finished the journey. One crashed into the sea, another crashed in French Morocco and a third aircraft made a forced landing there. As a result, the rest of the world quickly learnt that Mussolini's fascist Italy was now actively involved in the war. 'The incident confirms beyond doubt the complicity of Italy in the Spanish rebellion,' the *Guardian*'s Paris correspondent commented in a dispatch sent on 30 July. That day, the Italians promised an additional twelve Fiat C.R.32s fighters for what it now called 'the Franco movement'.[7]

Germany was more subtle. In order to distance the Nazi regime from the deal, Bernhardt set up a transport company called HISMA in Tetouan on 31 July to act as a facade. The Spanish-speaking head of Germany's Abwehr military intelligence service, Admiral Wilhelm Canaris, became involved, building a close and long-lasting relationship with Franco's regime. Half the aircraft were flown over from Stuttgart while the rest were put on a cargo ship in Hamburg, reaching Cádiz on 6 August. The cargo included six He.51s fighters, twenty anti-aircraft guns, munitions and 85 military 'volunteers' under Major Alexander von Scheele to operate them. Reports of the first arrivals – and that 20 German aircraft were due – appeared on 29 July in the French press. In a single day, Franco had acquired the foundations of a proper air force. Air power from Italy and Germany would now play a crucial role in the war.[8]

American journalist Jay Allen interviewed Franco in Tetouan on 27 July, finding him in 'full uniform with a red and gold tasselled sash'. Allen was not impressed. 'He is surprisingly small – another midget who would be a dictator,' he reported, 'His eyes are gentle, his nose is hooked, his hands and feet are tiny. He will soon have a paunch.' He also noticed, however, that Spain's 'baby' general was adored by his men.[9]

Franco insisted to Allen that the insurrectionists were neither fascist nor monarchist, calling them Nationalist Spanish (though the *Tribune* routinely called them 'fascists'). The term 'Nationalists' would slowly spread as a description of Franco's side, with Hitler's propaganda chief Josef Goebbels already embracing the term, though most foreign newspapers called them 'rebels' or 'insurgents'. Asked what regime they would install, Franco replied: 'A military dictatorship and, later on, we would have a plebiscite for the nation to decide what it wanted.' Before that could happen, he added, Spain must be cleansed of the threat of communism.[10]

'I will save Spain from Marxism whatever the cost,' he told Allen. 'And if that means shooting half of Spain?' he was asked. 'As I said, whatever the cost,' he replied.[11]

By 4 August, Hitler's Junkers – along with the Italian aircraft – had flown some 5,600 men from the Army of Africa to the mainland. It was the first major air bridge in military history, with the number transported reaching 24,000 men by October. 'If I had not decided in 1936 to send him the first of our Junker aircraft, Franco would never have survived,' Hitler boasted later. Franco, he said, was now part of the 'great European family' of those opposed to 'Jewish bolshevism'. The course of the war certainly changed dramatically. In his later notes for a memoir, Franco deemed the arrival of arms from Germany and Italy – which continued throughout the war – a 'miracle' that proved that a 'guardian angel was with us'.[12]

Franco himself had already flown across the sea on two overnight visits to the mainland. On 27 July he flew to Seville to see General Queipo de Llano, whose brash and extrovert character made him very different to Franco. Little is known about this visit or the next one, on 2 August, though Franco may have been starting a campaign to impose himself as overall coup leader, reinforced by his deal-making with Hitler. Franco had already accused Queipo of over-using the two Army of Africa battalions who reached the mainland in the first days of the uprising. They had been used to secure the major Andalusian cities of Cádiz, Granada, Córdoba and Huelva. Since these were amongst the best troops in the insurrectionist army, Franco wanted them for himself. 'Better to use artillery against buildings, which has a great impact on morale and can save many casualties,' he wrote.[13]

On his second trip to Seville, with the airlift already several days old, Franco sent two columns of troops on a march towards Madrid. It was only on 7 August, that he finally moved permanently to mainland Spain. He installed his headquarters in the palace of the Marchioness of Yanduri in Seville, well behind the front lines.[14]

The imposing building was 'more solid than luxurious', according to one visitor, but connected directly to the ancient royal palace in Seville, the Reales Alcazares. The proximity of history and grandeur suited Franco's view of Spain and, it was becoming apparent, of himself.[15]

19

Fighting at Last

SEVILLE-BADAJOZ-CÁCERES, AUGUST 1936

The news reaching Franco about the columns that he had dispatched from Seville filled him with hope for a rapid victory. The two motorised flying columns of up to 2,500 men each had achieved a spectacular initial advance as they headed north on the first leg of their march towards Madrid. They were under the overall command of one of Franco's favourite officers, the ardent Falangist, legionnaire and coup plotter Lt Col Juan Yagüe. As the former commander of the Army of Africa contingent during the Asturian rising of 1934, he had experience of turning legionnaires and Moroccan mercenary units against Spanish workers. Their savagery in Asturias was a precise indicator of how they now behaved as they covered 80 kilometres in the first two days.[1]

The speed of advance reflected both Franco's excitement at finally deploying his own forces and a desire to prove his prowess as insurrectionist generals jostled for glory and position. The flying columns, which moved in a mix of military vehicles, requisitioned trucks, buses and cars, looked shambolic but were light, mobile, well-trained and far superior to any opposition. One column commander travelled in a limousine loaned by a local aristocratic landowner. The ragged, impromptu Leftist militia units were no match. They had weapons, but little idea about how to use them effectively. Sometimes they were armed with nothing more than hunting rifles and shotguns. They were easily outmanoeuvred or fled when targeted by modest field artillery or one or two of Franco's Italian and German bombers. 'They know how to burn priests alive, but they don't know how to fight trained soldiers,' Queipo de Llano said scornfully.²

Town after town fell and the city of Mérida was taken on 10 August, allowing Franco's southern army to join up with Mola's Army of the North – thus cutting off the important city of Badajoz, which lay to the west by the Portuguese border. His men had covered 190 kilometres in a week, carrying out mass executions of suspected or real Leftists along the way.³

With the two main insurrectionist armies now joined up, Franco and Mola were able to talk by telephone on 11 August. They agreed not to duplicate their attempts to find arms abroad, with Mola ceding this role to the more successful Franco. Mola's own international arms go-between, the right-wing newspaper editor José Ignacio Escobar, warned that he had ceded the most valuable chess piece when it came to deciding who would be their leader now that Sanjurjo was dead. Mola dismissed his concerns. 'There is no battle between Franco and me,' he said. Neither harboured personal ambitions, Mola added. The question of overall command could be dealt with later. On 23 August Franco's own press office suggested this was not how the matter was viewed in his headquarters, calling him 'Head of the Movement of Salvation of the Fatherland'.⁴

Franco, meanwhile, told a Portuguese newspaper that the overall aim was for a military dictatorship to oversee a rapid and 'complete transformation' of Spain by technocrats. It still remained unclear, however, what Spain was to be transformed into. Nationalism, authoritarianism and Catholicism would obviously play important roles, but nobody could say how. When Franco flew to Burgos to meet Mola in person a few days later, they stood together on a balcony to wave at cheering supporters, undoubtedly giving Franco the warm rush that comes with public adoration. The two men swapped stories about the previous month, apparently oblivious to the anxiety of many officers who still wondered if victory was possible.⁵

The assault on Badajoz on 14 August was the bloodiest and most difficult action yet. Yagüe's men took most of the day to break into the walled city. The vengeful bloodletting reflected the barbarism that Franco had learned in Morocco. 'Anyone who had political literature or insignia, or just the bruise of a rifle butt on their shoulder, was ordered to be shot,' a young socialist called María Mejías Correa noted down. The Army of Africa's Moroccan mercenaries were considered especially terrifying. 'The Moors searched and sacked houses and shops, stealing and raping the women,' she said.[6]

The 24-year-old Portuguese journalist Mario Neves of *Diario de Lisboa* was traumatised by what he encountered. Bodies of those shot lay in the sand of the city's bull-ring and a column of thick smoke rose above the white-walled cemetery, where he found 300 smouldering corpses. More corpses were being taken off trucks or brought in on wheelbarrows. 'They deserved this,' an eager priest accompanying him said. Neves asked Yagüe if it was true that 2,000 people had already been shot. 'It can't be that many,' he replied, beginning years of obfuscation about what really happened. In fact, numbers continued to rise, reaching some 3,800 in a city of 44,000 inhabitants.[7] Neves's final despatch was censored by the pro-insurrectionist Portuguese regime of dictator António de Oliveira Salazar. It read:

> I am going home. Cost what it may, I want to get out of Badajoz as quickly as possible, and make a solemn promise to myself that I will never come back. For all the many years that I remain a journalist, I do not believe that I will ever see a sight as affecting... This is no ridiculous extravagance, no excess sentiment. Even the most modest education in morality... is enough to make it impossible to remain calm in the face of these horrible scenes.[8]

Franco's headquarters denied the killing had been quite so extensive but when Yagüe was asked about it by American journalist John Whitaker, he was brutally honest. 'Of course, we shot them. What do you expect? Was I supposed to take four thousand Reds with me as my column advanced racing against time? Was I expected to turn them loose in my rear and let them make Badajoz Red again?'[9]

Executing opponents was now so routine that Franco failed to stop two people he was close to from also being shot by his side. The first of these was his Republican cousin, Major Ricardo de la Puente Bahamonde, who had defended the airbase in Tetouan. The cousins had been playmates as children – not least because the de la Puente family had a beachside summer house at La Graña, near Ferrol - and 'were almost like brothers', according to Pacón. 'He was a fine officer and honourable person, serious and faithful to his ideas,' admitted Pacón. De la Puente was shot early in August. Franco might have stopped it, but did not try. Instead, he asked General Orgaz to sign the death sentence that should have carried his own signature. He considered all officers who remained loyal to the Republic to be traitors – even if this particular death was 'hard and painful' to him, in Pacón's words.[10]

Elsewhere, Franco's friend and faithful number two in Zaragoza, General Miguel Campins, had failed to rise immediately on Queipo de Llano's instructions and had been arrested in Granada. In this case, Franco did try to persuade Queipo not to shoot him, but could not sway him. Campins wrote protesting against the 'irregular' trial, pointing out that he had eventually joined the rebellion on 20 July and had refused to send troops to fight against the insurrectionists before that. 'I am not trying to defend a life that I long ago offered to the Fatherland, but rather my honour as a gentleman, which is so much more valuable, as well as the good opinion that you may feel,' he wrote to Franco. If he had been forewarned, he might have acted differently. 'Nobody spoke to me ... about the preparations for the carrying out of this patriotic military movement,' he protested.[11] In other words, Franco had not been clear enough about his intentions when he spoke to Campins. His self-protective ambiguity (which permitted denial if the plot was broken up in advance) had exposed an old ally to danger.

Franco's brother-in-law Serrano Suñer saw a man of absolute personal loyalty abandoned by his former commander. 'Campins knew of the bitter, disparaging dislike that Franco felt towards Queipo,' he said. How was he meant to know that this rebellion was any different to the one led by Sanjurjo in 1931, which Franco had scorned? Franco's attitude, Serrano Suñer said, showed not just hypocrisy but 'coldness and indifference to a former underling and friend'.[12]

Campins was shot by a firing squad beside the city walls of Seville's Macarena neighbourhood at 6.30am on the morning of 16 August before a crowd of curious locals. He refused to wear a blindfold or turn his back to the firing squad. We do not know Franco's reaction to a letter from Campins' widow Dolores Roda, whom he and Carmen had also befriended in Zaragoza. 'Franco, Franco. What have they done to my husband? Who killed him? What crime had he committed?' she asked. 'Please say something, I beg you.'[13] The reply came, instead, from Pacón, who expressed 'the sadness of General Franco' but told her that in this Civil War everyone was suffering.[14] Privately, probably like Franco himself, he thought Campins had lacked decisiveness when the rebellion broke.

It is likely that Carmen Polo also received letters from Campins' wife, since she later wrote to her sister Zita. Carmen was no stranger to the entreaties of friends or relatives whose husbands or sons were threatened with the firing squad. She is recorded as saving just one person – the poet Leopoldo Panero, who was a cousin's son. A letter from her husband was all it took.[15]

The business of approving death sentences became a banal part of Franco's daily routine. Often when taking a coffee after lunch, his legal advisor Lorenzo Martínez Fuset brought a list of the newly condemned so Franco could give his approval, or, less often, his refusal, saving someone's life. He disliked personal appeals for clemency, resisting the entreaties of Cardinal Gomá, Queipo de Llano and Cabanellas when General Domingo Batet – who had put down the October 1934 revolt in Catalonia on Franco's orders – was shot for failing to support the insurrection. Batet's crime, like all soldiers who opposed the insurrection, was deemed to be 'rebellion'. Even Serrano Suñer admitted that this was an absurd inversion of the law when they had merely stuck by their oaths to defend the Republic.[16]

For Franco, the taking of Badajoz was a major triumph. His men had overcome one of the toughest obstacles yet encountered, securing the Portuguese border and the road to Madrid. Over 15 days they had covered 20km a day. The Spanish capital lay 350km to the east. If they progressed at the same speed, they would reach it in two and a half weeks.[17]

Franco had also made a point with the repression that followed. The message for his opponents was that they should fear not just his military might, but also his vengeful wrath. Both things could now be turned on the mission of taking the greatest 'red' stronghold of all, the city of Madrid.[18]

20

Absolute Power

TALAVERA-TOLEDO-SALAMANCA, SEPTEMBER 1936

Franco believed in righteous willpower as a weapon. He was sure this had delivered victory at Badajoz and been crucial in the war in Morocco. 'Blind faith, no doubts, energetic firmness of purpose without wavering, this is what the Fatherland demands,' he had said in one of his first messages from Tetouan. This faith was grounded in values honed as an Africanista colonialist – pride, moral superiority, the defence of reputational honour and a version of virility expressed as disdain for death itself. It was also a way of maintaining that precious but slippery military resource, good morale.[1]

All this was already crystallised in his own creation, the Spanish Legion, where casualties in the Rif war had reached 38 per cent and an astonishing 46 per cent amongst its lead-from-the-front officer corps. Perhaps only the Japanese military – soon to be fighting a war of aggression against China – shared such an extravagant glorification of martyrdom for the Fatherland.[2]

There was no question of Franco exposing himself to the dangers of the front line, however. Commanding generals in most armies avoid that, since their leadership is too valuable. Also, he believed firmly in leaving field commanders to decide how their targets should be conquered. His job was to choose those targets and ensure there were enough men and arms to capture them, while also overseeing the subsequent occupation and purging of enemies. It was his task, too, to coordinate with other insurrectionist generals over aims and strategy.

His army, now headed by three flying columns of two battalions each, set out eastwards towards Madrid. Within five days, they had covered half the distance to reach Navalmoral. A mostly straight and gentle road stretched ahead of them to Spain's capital city. If Franco's columns could maintain that speed, they would be in Madrid by the end of August.[3]

On 26 August, he moved his headquarters to Cáceres – once more finding a city palace for his new home, in this case the impressive sixteenth-century Palacio de los Golfines de Arriba. It was here, finally, that Carmen Polo joined him from France on 23 September, though she was kept waiting an hour before she was permitted to see him.[4]

Shortly after installing himself in Cáceres, on 6 September 1936, Franco was surprised by an envoy from Hitler, Lieutenant Colonel Walter Warlimont (using the nom de guerre 'Guido Waltersdorff'). The visit was the final stage of a trip that had begun in Rome with Warlimont accompanying Hitler's spymaster Admiral Canaris to meet Mussolini and his military intelligence chief General Mario Roatta. Warlimont and Roatta then travelled to Seville to meet Queipo de Llano before flying to Cáceres. They told a surprised Franco that Hitler had unilaterally decided to increase his involvement. He would supply large amounts of equipment, especially aircraft, and training staff, but minimal support by German field troops. 'Franco apparently knew nothing about our mission,' Warlimont recalled later.[5] 'He received us in a rather reserved manner.' Franco's churlishness reflected his hatred of others making decisions on his behalf. He thought he was in absolute control of foreign aid to the rebels, which is what a German intermediary had suggested to Mola on informing him that he was to receive a cargo of machine-guns. 'I have received orders to tell you that you do not receive these arms from Germany, but from the hands of General Franco,' he had said.[6]

A first proper test of the advance came on 3 September when Franco's columns attacked the large Tagus River town of Talavera de la Reina, 125 km from Madrid. By now the defenders were better organised. They were still no match for the Army of Africa, but the pace of the advance was slowing. Supply routes were longer, and the enemy was more numerous and closer to its own Madrid headquarters. Units of foreign volunteers who mostly defined themselves as anti-fascists had also arrived, often proving better fighters than the militia. Small groups of Italian, Polish and French volunteers, for example, fought outside Talavera while French writer André Malraux had helped form a squadron of donated aircraft with foreign pilots.[7]

In fact, Spain occupied an ever-expanding space in the minds of fellow Europeans, especially those worried about Nazi rearmament. Mussolini, meanwhile, was also fighting wars of colonial occupation in Ethiopia and Libya. It seemed that fascism and national socialism could not be contained by the borders of the countries where they already ruled.

As the insurrectionist armies became better coordinated, people on Franco's staff manoeuvered for him to take overall command. Franco must have wanted this position ever since Sanjurjo died. Given the size of his ambitions and his ego, it is impossible to imagine him accepting second place to any of his rival generals. It was not his way, however, to make this obvious – especially since the National Defence Junta was presided over by its most senior officer, the 64-year-old General Miguel Cabanellas. In many ways, the white-bearded Cabanellas was exactly the sort of soldier that Franco hated – liberal, anti-monarchist and a Freemason. His adhesion to the uprising had surprised many people, since he had always seemed a faithful Republican. It was a sign that even some Republicans had mistrusted a minority government that depended on the same Socialists who led the October 1934 uprising. Such moderates, however, thought of the uprising as a short-term solution or, at the most, the start of a period of soft dictatorship like that led by Miguel Primo de Rivera. Franco felt very differently: not only did he want control, he wanted it to be absolute and indefinite in time.

Another rival was Queipo de Llano, the so-called 'viceroy' of southern Andalusia – where he was beloved by aristocrats, landowners and relieved right-wingers in one of Spain's most left-wing regions. The two men scorned one another with martial cordiality and subtly vied for overall control, with their diplomatic advisor José Antonio Sangróniz shuttling daily by airplane between their headquarters 'until this is sorted out'. Franco could not forgive the extravagant Queipo for wanting to overthrow the monarchy. Queipo saw Franco as 'selfish and devious'.[8]

Indeed, Franco played a subtle game, suggesting both that he did and did not want the job. The cool, calculated ambiguity that overlaid his indecisiveness was now an advantage. So was the fact that he was not strongly associated with any of the competing factions in the insurrectionist camp. Formerly avid Republicans like Cabanellas and Queipo, Carlist allies like Mola and even out-and-out Alfonsine monarchists like the deceased Sanjurjo were all likely, at some time, to have offended at least one other faction. It was impossible, however, to pin any strongly held previous political position on Franco beyond his conservative and martial Africanista culture. Even that was tempered by his calm, unexcitable manner. In short, he was more of a clean slate – politically dull and militarily competent – than others with their conspiratorial backgrounds or penchant for bold public outbursts. He was also receiving strong hints from the Germans by mid-September that they wanted a single leader and would back him. In fact, their aid might depend on exactly that.[9]

Timing was important. Up to now, there had been no point pushing for a job that did not exist. There can be little doubt that Franco saw himself as a first amongst equals, but he was also concerned about what powers a commander-in-chief might have. Would they just be military? Or political as well? Could the new caudillo make decisions alone and about everything, or would he be constrained? Would these powers be open-ended or only held for a limited period?

The task of winning Franco overall command was delegated to General Alfredo Kindelán, now his air-force chief. Kindelán believed a single commander-in-chief was a military necessity. Franco warned him to be discreet and not to push before the prize was ripe. Another key player was his elder brother Nicolás. His career had blossomed under the Republic, especially during the period of right-wing government.[10]

Nicolás now functioned as Franco's general secretary and was effectively his right-hand man in administrative affairs. He showed little affinity for the Falange or, indeed, for political manoeuvring beyond helping his brother, whom he expected to lead a Primo de Rivera-style military dictatorship. Although clever, energetic and effective, Nicolás had inherited his father's dissoluteness and, as a result, worked eccentric, erratic hours. He was famed for his long meals as well as for arranging to see visitors at half past two o'clock in the morning or making them wait for hours. In Franco's otherwise austere headquarters, he stood out as an inveterate and sometimes ill-disciplined pleasure-seeker. He was regularly the centre of the nightlife at Salamanca's Gran Hotel, where sybarites, drinkers, high-class prostitutes, Italian officers and suspected spies gathered. Late, wine-drenched dinners at the hotel were often followed by a return to the office to meet visitors. He was also a consistently pro-German influence, not least because numerous members of his wife's family had escaped Republican Spain thanks to the German consul in Alicante, who dressed them up as sailors so they could board a German navy vessel.[11]

Behind-the-scenes preparations involved several of Franco's other closest advisors in Cáceres, including his flamboyant former Legion commander Millán Astray, who was in charge of propaganda and already called Franco 'Generalísimo' to denote his ascendancy over everyone else.[12]

These men must have consulted continually with Franco, not least because Kindelán spent several hours a day in his office. But just as with his adhesion to the insurrection, Franco dithered and fretted over the timing. In the second half of September, Kindelán and the others persuaded him that the moment had come.[13]

On 21 September, Franco called a meeting of the National Defence Junta, now made up of nine generals and two colonels, at a bull ranch with a landing strip outside Salamanca. During a morning going over various aspects of the war, Kindelán felt the others were deliberately avoiding the issue. It was only after lunch that he managed to formally propose a unified command with a single commander-in-chief, or generalísimo. This, he argued, was standard military doctrine and would improve their chances of victory. To the surprise of many, Mola was amongst the most enthusiastic. He did not want the position himself but threatened that 'if a generalísimo is not appointed within eight days, I'm leaving.'[14]

Cabanellas was the main objector, saying that a war council could do the same job. When it came to voting, however, he was the only opponent. Franco's name was then put forward and approved unanimously with Cabanellas abstaining. Mola told his aides that Franco was the better candidate than himself, because 'he is younger, superior in rank, has a huge amount of support and is well-known abroad.' It was decided not to make the appointment public yet, though Franco seems to have expected a formal National Defence Junta announcement shortly.[15]

While the generals were voting for Franco as their commander-in-chief, the Army of Africa was tidying up the conquest of Maqueda, a town just 75 km from Madrid. Franco would soon visit, congratulating his men for taking for the first time a town defended by concrete bunkers and barbed wire – a sign that the Republican army was improving rapidly.[16]

Instead of heading for Madrid, however, the columns that left Maqueda turned south-east for Toledo. Franco had decided that the capital could wait. First he wanted to lift the siege of the building where he had trained as a cadet, the Alcázar in Toledo. This had resumed its role as the Infantry and Cavalry Officers Academy after Franco's Zaragoza academy was closed and it was where local insurrectionists had retreated after their uprising failed across the rest of the city.[17]

Franco had lived there as a 14-year-old cadet, but it was now the summer holiday, so only nine cadets were at the academy when the Civil War broke out. Some 1,000 insurrectionists led by Colonel José Moscardó – mostly Civil Guards, soldiers and Falangists, alongside some 600 women and children – had retreated into the Alcázar with a large haul of arms and twenty Republican hostages, including the civil governor.[18]

In a famous exchange, the head of the militias telephoned Moscardó to say his son Luis had been captured. According to one contemporary version, this is what happened:

> At 10am, the militia leader called the military commander [Moscardó] to notify him that he had one of his sons and would shoot him within ten minutes if we did not surrender and, to show this was true, he handed the telephone to the son who, with immense calm, told his father not to worry, with father and son exchanging goodbyes laden with great patriotism and religious fervour. When the commander spoke again to the militia leader, he told him that he did not have to wait ten minutes to shoot his son, since there was no way the Alcázar would surrender.[19]

In fact, the son was not shot at that moment, though militiamen killed him a month later after insurrectionist aircraft bombed the city. The Alcázar's walls were slowly, but only partially, destroyed by artillery as the defenders ran short of food and water. Supplies were dropped by insurrectionist aircraft, including the DC-2 flown by Franco's personal pilot, Captain Carlos de Haya González. On at least one occasion they included a note from Franco himself, urging them to hold on. 'We are getting closer to rescuing you,' he had written on 22 August. A month later he decided to do exactly that.[20]

This was a calculated risk on Franco's part. It gifted Madrid's defenders time to organise themselves, receive fresh arms (which the Soviet Union had now agreed to send) and be reinforced with troops sent from elsewhere in Spain. These included the first units of the newly founded International Brigades, a shock force of foreign volunteers of varying political outlooks, largely recruited by the Comintern, with undercover Red Army officers leading some units.

But Toledo was a sentimental matter for Franco. It also offered rewards in terms of morale and propaganda – both of which he rated highly. Toledo had been the Visigoth capital of Christian Spain before Muslim invaders swept across Iberia in 711. Its recapture in 1085 was a legendary reconquista event and Toledo's cathedral was the seat of the primate of Spain, making it the symbolic capital of the Roman Catholic church in the country. Its conquest would increase his personal reputation, just as the insurrectionists chose a new generalísimo and decided on the extent of his powers.

Pacón, Yagüe and Kindelán all disagreed with Franco's Toledo detour, even though he assured everyone that 'eight days after taking Toledo, I will be in Madrid.'[21] The Germans were astounded. 'After overcoming considerable difficulties of terrain west and south of Madrid, Franco is now in the open plain where he should be able to advance easily,' their Chargé d'Affaires on the Republican side reported. 'Every day lost brings the [Republican] Government an abundance of new war material. Ultimately, superiority in material will be decisive.' American and French military observers were equally astonished, deeming the switch to Toledo 'a massive mistake' or the abandonment of 'good strategy for a plan based on sentiment'.[22]

Franco, however, stood to gain from slowing the campaign down. He was eager to impose himself on the rebel side and unify it politically before Madrid was taken. If the capital fell, that would end the war and allow the factions to start scrapping for power, or so Franco told a senior German diplomat two weeks later. Despite the decision taken on 21 September, the National Defence Junta led by Cabanellas (who mistrusted Franco) had yet to make public his new appointment. It was also still not clear exactly how much power he might be given.[23]

The Alcázar siege was finally lifted on September 27. Two days later, Franco made a set-piece arrival in the city, clambering up the rubble into the building's courtyard. This was filmed and edited as though he was personally leading the liberation, with film sent around the world. The streets were still full of corpses, not least because of the now-routine barbarity of the Army of Africa whenever it made a conquest.[24]

Friendly newspapers like the *Daily Express* in Britain received colourful reports from their correspondents:

> Those human spectres, half-starved, holding weapons that were no longer of any use. They had nothing. They had to learn how to live all over again, and they had not yet decided to leave the scene of their martyrdom. Then they saw Franco. Many of them did not know him, but upon hearing the cry 'General Franco!' those people began to come to life again, as though they had been revived by some drug. The name of Franco meant everything to them, and they were united in their feelings. It was the name which they had awaited as they resisted. They cried out in shrill tones to express their diverse sentiments. They cheered, wept, and embraced the soldiers. It was an unforgettable spectacle in which it seemed that some had lost their minds completely.[25]

A few months later Franco told a Portuguese journalist that he had committed 'a deliberate mistake' by diverting his troops from Madrid, calling his decision 'political'. He told Pacón, in slight contrast, that the decision was 'spiritual'. Either way, it cemented his prestige just as final negotiations about appointing a commander-in-chief were reaching their climax. Franco's staff organised a second meeting at the Salamanca ranch to settle the matter a week later.[26]

On the evening of 27 September, with the Alcázar siege just lifted, Franco had been acclaimed by a crowd in Cáceres, with Yagüe by his side addressing him as 'head of state'. That was a considerable leap from a purely military generalísimo or commander-in-chief. It was a first clear and public suggestion that he harboured dreams of adding political power to military power. The following day, Franco,

Kindelán and Yagüe flew to Salamanca together, determined to push through the acquisition of absolute military and political power. His brother Nicolás made sure that young Falangist and Carlist supporters were there to cheer his arrival, underscoring a moment of huge personal popularity. Once more, though, it seemed Franco himself remained silent at the meeting. Instead, a draft decree drawn up by Nicolás Franco and Kindelán was read out by the latter. It now included a clause that read: 'The position of Generalísimo will carry with it the role of Head of State for as long as the war lasts and, as such, all national action will be dependent on this: political, economic, social, cultural etcetera.' For the first time, it was clear to everyone that Franco wanted not just military command but also full power over the entire state. This was personal dictatorship.[27]

'That was received badly,' Kindelán admitted later. Now it was not just Cabanellas but Mola, Queipo and others who looked worried. Most rebel generals were monarchists who wanted Alfonso XIII to return as head of state. The insurrection had been open-ended and based on the idea of saving Spain from communism. That had allowed different generals to harbour differing ideas about who would be in charge when it all ended. Pacón recalled 'long faces' around the table.[28]

The final decision was handed to Cabanellas. He spent that night consulting by phone with Mola, Queipo and others. Queipo was at his most acerbic. Cabanellas's son Guillermo reported that the expletives used to describe Franco were too obscene for him to write down.[29] 'We'll have to play his game until it all explodes,' Queipo added, before letting loose another tirade of swear words. Mola's eventual approval came with the proviso that 'this will all have to be reviewed at the war's end.'[30] Like them, however, Cabanellas could see no other option. After all, this was only for the duration of the war, and many expected that to last just a few more weeks with the conquest of Madrid. Yet Cabanellas was so alarmed that, according to his son, he warned one of Franco's backers:

> You don't realise what you have done because you don't know him as well as I, who had him under my command in the Army of Africa... If, as you now wish, you are going to give Spain to him, he will think it belongs to him and will not allow anyone to substitute him during the war, or afterwards, until his own death.[31]

On 30 September, Franco's appointment was finally published in the rebel zone's Official Bulletin, with one key difference. The words 'while the war lasts' had disappeared. Nobody knows who removed them, though suspicion obviously has fallen on Franco, his brother or his staff. He was now simply 'head of the government of the Spanish state ... who will assume all the powers of the new State'. Franco's power grab was as complete as it was breathtaking. In just nine days, he had elevated himself from one general amongst others to commander-in-chief of the army, head of state and finally to dictator for as long as he wished.[32]

'My guiding aim was to win the war,' Kindelán explained apologetically later. The wording of the final decree, he insisted, 'was not what I had proposed' and not his fault. Like everyone else, he had been blindsided. While Spain and the world were dazzled by the bloody events in Toledo, Franco had pulled off what one Spanish historian called 'a step-by-step [internal] coup'. Franco later admitted that he was only interested in power if it was absolute: 'I would never have accepted a political mandate accompanied by conditions,' he said.[33]

Franco was now the generalísimo or caudillo of insurrectionist Spain. He had an autocrat's powers, though neither he nor his followers approved of the term 'dictator'. In fact, Spain now had its equivalent to a Duce or Führer – an equal to Hitler or Mussolini.

With all power in his hands, it seemed that Franco could be elevated no higher. On the very same day that this power grab was made public, however, Spain's Roman Catholic church did exactly that. The new dictator, it believed, was doing God's work. He was a holy crusading knight.

21

Holy War

SALAMANCA-BURGOS, 30 SEPTEMBER-1 OCTOBER 1936

Religion had not featured as a major part of Franco's public life, though the domestic piety of Carmen Polo meant that rosary beads and smaller daily observances of his faith were increasingly present in his life.[1] Before marriage he had confined his Roman Catholicism to the dutiful obedience of a Spanish conservative man – at most, weekly attendance at Mass. His early morning visits to Carmen's convent school chapel while courting her were, in that regard, an exception. There was a widespread belief in conservative families that observance was largely women's business while men were, in his own words, 'cold about religion'. His own mother, for example, had regularly attended Mass and scrambled up the Ferrol hillside to the Chamorro Chapel to give thanks for answered prayers. Priests did the rest of the work. This attitude was particularly common amongst army officers – especially amidst the extreme martial virility of, say, the Legion.[2]

Yet just as Franco achieved the secular superlatives of 'generalísimo' and 'head of state', so the Bishop of Salamanca, Enrique Pla y Deniel, placed him on the same level as a Crusader knight in a pastoral letter published on 30 September 1936. 'The Spanish uprising is not a mere civil war, but is substantially a crusade on behalf of religion, the fatherland and civilisation against communism,' he proclaimed. Spain, he added, was now clearly divided between good and evil.[3]

Pla y Deniel was one of the Spanish church's most brilliant intellectuals, so when he appropriated the idea of a crusade (already used by Franco's Carlist allies, who went into battle carrying cloth scapulars or Sacred Heart medallions) and formally pinned it to Franco's cause, it was as if he had awarded another title to Franco himself. This was now holy war. That placed it on the same level as the so-called reconquest of Muslim Spain that had finished in 1492 with the fall of Granada to Isabella of Castile and Ferdinand of Aragon. Those empire-founding joint monarchs best represented, in Franco's mind, the greatness that Spain had lost and should reclaim. The Pope had awarded them the title of 'the Catholic monarchs' for their defence of Christendom. Franco could – and from now on would – claim to be doing the exact same thing.[4]

Franco's followers digested this concept eagerly. When the insurrectionists captured a small village in the south in January 1937, for example, Franco's picture was placed on the church altar alongside the Virgin Mary. Franco also internalised the idea, as his self-image shifted from successful soldier to God-chosen saviour of Spain. When a relic of part of the arm of Saint Teresa of Ávila was found in Málaga and sent to him in February 1937, Franco held on to it. He became superstitiously attached to this gnarled and desiccated piece of Spain's most revered female saint. The wizened, tan-coloured stretch of arm, bent into a V-shape at the elbow with the two forearm bones exposed and the upper arm skin hardened by four centuries of exposure, was conserved in a thick crystal glass container. It lived in his bedroom and travelled with Franco on his trips away from home, reminding him that, according to Spain's bishops, he was embarked on a divinely sanctioned crusade. Providence, in other words, was on his side.[5]

His wife Carmen had always put Franco's survival during his time in Morocco down to her own 'blind faith in the Virgin of Covadonga'. Following the apparently traumatic death of his beloved mother two years previously, she had encouraged him into a more religious state of mind. A personal chaplain called José María Bulart was installed on 4 October 1936 and remained with the family until after Franco's death. As a result, Franco attended Mass every morning. Carmen insisted that he also join her when she said the rosary in the evening. He now heard Mass almost wherever he was, including amid air-raid warnings or when camped out in his mobile headquarters, which became known as Términus.[6]

Bulart would go on to praise the 'devotion to the eucharist' of his 'fervently Christian caudillo', noting that he followed Mass properly in his missal without distraction and almost always took communion. Bulart was another person struck by Franco's preternatural calm and the fact that untrammelled power did not provoke any sort of angst. 'If he was suffering inside, I never noticed it,' said Bulart, before adding mysteriously that 'perhaps he was cold, as some people say, but he did not show it: in fact, he never showed anything.' Carmen Polo agreed. 'This man is unshakeable,' she said. 'He is never upset by anything.'[7]

Pla y Deniel gifted Franco a clear and simple moral ideal that elevated his insurrection above the mucky mundanity of politics and power, while sanctifying bloodshed. It also provided a welcome distraction from the ideological messiness of an insurrection that joined the ultra-modern fascism of the Falange with the archaic ideas of the Carlists and the indignant, violent and class-based conservatism of many monarchists. It also, however, gave the mass of Spanish voters who had backed Catholic parties during the Republic a rationale for supporting him. Pla y Deniel ignored the fact that some priests and bishops in the Basque Country and Catalonia had sided with the Republic.

A few weeks later Franco received a leaflet written by Cardinal Isidro Gomá, the primate of Spain, in which he explained 'The Spanish Case' to the faithful. Gomá falsely claimed that thousands of Russian troops were disembarking in Barcelona. He also pointed to 'thousands of priests and monks and nuns that have been killed', which was no invention. No mention was made of the insurrectionists' own horrific killings or of eleven Basque priests who were amongst their victims, though Gomá had already complained to Franco about the latter (his reply was 'Your Eminence can be assured that this will stop immediately', but at least one Republican Basque priest would be shot after that). Franco immediately ordered that Gomá's leaflet be translated in English, French and Polish.[8]

On 1 October, Franco travelled to Burgos, where the National Defence Junta had its headquarters, to receive formally all the powers of the state. A crowd packed the square in front of the city's military headquarters, where an honour guard made up of the Falange, the Legion and the Carlists awaited. Fellow rebel generals and other dignitaries squeezed into the building's throne room to anoint him as dictator. 'In the name of the National Defence Junta, I hand you the absolute powers of the state,' said Cabanellas. Franco adopted his characteristic haranguing posture, his shoulders thrown back and head tilted upwards as if imitating Mussolini, and replied: 'Victory is on our side. You have placed Spain in my hands and I assure you that my hand will not tremble.'[9]

The broadly smiling Franco was clearly delighted, though one disenchanted contemporary later reported that he looked like a swaggering Lilliputian:

> General Francisco Franco appeared, his stomach pushed forward, showing its increasing prominence, and his back leaning rearwards, which also serves to accentuate its existing roundness. Given his small height, this stance makes him seen like a deformed ball of fatty tissue. He has a round face, incipient double chin, black hair, with strong eyebrows, straight nose, with his moustache shaved off and a bald patch that is spreading at a gallop ... his clothes seem too small for him.[10]

To the rest of the world there was no longer confusion about who was in charge. British cinema-goers who saw the Movietone News report from Burgos learned that Franco was now the 'dictator-like ... head of state' of the 'rebel' part of Spain.[11]

In a rambling balcony speech delivered to people giving fascist salutes in the square, Franco glorified war and proclaimed that the Republic was now dead, but gave no clues about what lay ahead. 'War unites and brings together those who the political system had artificially separated,' he told them. That same war would be the crucible of his 'New Spain', he added, with patriotism forged in the trenches.[12]

Franco was more explicit in a speech delivered later over the rebel Radio Castilla station, which he filled with sentimentalism about Spanish history and dark warnings about how foreign ideas had poisoned the national character (echoing Pla y Deniel's warning that the evil Republic was the offspring of the French Revolution and 'freedom of thought'). 'Communism', now a catch-all for all left-wing ideas, was wrecking Spain's economy, unity and spirit. Capitalism, on the other hand, would be controlled so workers did not become its 'slaves'. The only clue about how this might happen came with the use of a single word that he never seems to have uttered publicly before and which many Spaniards would have found new: 'totalitarian'.[13]

After acquiring the powers of a dictator and declaring himself a totalitarian, Franco immediately wrote to Adolf Hitler stressing that they were now equals. 'Upon assuming the leadership of the Spanish State and the office of Generalísimo of the Nationalist troops, I have the honour to convey my warmest wishes,' he wrote in the 3 October telegram. 'We are united by so many bonds of sincere friendship and deep gratitude.'[14]

Hitler immediately sent an envoy, Count Du Moulin-Eckart, to see him. Franco met Du Moulin on 6 October, the day he moved his headquarters into the episcopal palace in Salamanca, lent to him by Bishop Pla y Deniel. Hitler's representative thus became the first foreign diplomat to meet Franco as head of state. According to Du Moulin's report, the unctuous dictator 'expressed his veneration for the Führer' and was eager to reassure Hitler that he understood that the time was not yet right for formal recognition of his government. In fact, Hitler had decided to hold off until Madrid fell. Franco also boasted that his army was killing ten Republicans for each man he lost to death or injury – with machine guns and artillery doing the most damage.[15]

Franco insisted he did not want to return to a Spain run by church and aristocracy, saying that his most urgent aim was to bring the rebel factions together in a 'unification of ideas'. That was an obvious challenge, since the revolutionary and fascist Falange, for example, was very different to the ultra-Catholic, reactionary Carlist movement who, in turn, had fundamental disagreements with the Alfonsine monarchists. He also sounded dubious about restoring the monarchy, insisting that a 'common ideology' was more important, even if the task of bringing together the Army, Falange, monarchists and Catholics needed "kid gloves".' All this, nevertheless, had to be done before he occupied Madrid. Postponing the Madrid attack by taking Toledo, in other words, had also bought him time to impose himself on the disparate factions.[16]

For this task, and this period, he needed men he could trust. For such a naturally suspicious man, this meant either his own family or obedient career officers who would unquestioningly carry out orders.

Du Moulin noted that the most powerful figure outside the army was now that 'untiring worker', Franco's brother, Nicolás. 'I hear consistently that he possesses great influence with General Franco, who, too much occupied in the past by purely military tasks, has had little time for decisions in the field of internal policy,' he added. Du Moulin could see that Nicolás also felt in debt to Germany for rescuing his wife's family in Alicante.[17]

Close family was so important that the usually strict rules of revenge on those with a Republican or leftist past were suspended when his brother Ramón appeared in Salamanca at the end of October 1936. Ramón was not marched off to jail or put before a firing squad. Instead, he was given command of the insurrectionist's air base in the Balearic Islands. Ramón had crossed over the Portuguese border, avoiding the frontiers controlled by Queipo de Llano and Mola – both of whom might have had him shot. He had not been informed of the uprising and had had no contact with Francisco since he left for Washington three years earlier. In fact, Ramón had since divorced, remarried in a Spanish civil ceremony and recognised his new wife's 7-year-old daughter as his own – his behaviour again contrasting with that of a caudillo who soon struck out divorce and civil marriage laws and would refuse to acknowledge this niece. When quizzed by American journalists as the Civil War broke out, Ramón had affirmed that, whatever happened, Spain would not return to monarchy.[18]

Franco foisted Ramón's appointment on air-force chief General Kindelán, who wrote expressing 'deep concern and disgust'. Kindelán pointed out both his own 'personal mortification' and wider dismay. 'The measure, my general, has been very badly received by the airmen.' They saw Ramón as a Freemason and a communist who had personally turned many air-force personnel into ardent Republicans who eventually had to be shot. Some officers, he added, believed Ramón deserved the same treatment. 'In his new command post, his subordinates obey but repudiate him,' General Cabanellas's son Guillermo reported. 'When he enters the mess, they stand up, salute and leave.'[19]

One of Franco's first acts as head of his own state was to annul the constitution of the Republic. 'Democratic liberalism' had been an aberration that, combined with Freemasonry, had spawned communism, or so he reasoned. Such democracy, indeed, was now an ill on a par with Freemasonry or liberalism. When asked, six months later, by a British journalist why he thought democracy could never work in Spain, he answered that it would also be the downfall of Great Britain. Franco enjoyed the attention of foreign journalists, though he was rarely straight with them. 'Although effusively flattering, he gave me no frank answer to any question I put to him; I could see that he perfectly understood the implication of even the most subtle query,' the American John Whitaker recalled. 'A less straightforward man I never met.'[20]

In fact, Franco did not yet have much of a state or regime to run. While his part of Spain included around half of the country, it lacked the country's major industrial zones. The government bodies (or quasi-ministries) set up to run his ill-defined 'New State' had little autonomy. Power sat in Franco's own office, allowing him to rule like 'an absolute monarch', as one historian put it. He governed by edict, issuing decrees via his War Secretariat, Diplomatic Office or the General State Secretariat, run by Nicolás. These occupied a large room on the ground floor of the bishop's palace in Salamanca, divided by screens – but with only a handful of staff. The diplomatic office was 'a table and two or three chairs', according to one visitor.[21] Franco's office was on the first floor. Amongst those helping him was the Civil Guard major Lisardo Doval, the infamous repressor Franco had sent to Asturias after the revolutionary strike, who now ran his intelligence service. Franco's old mentor in the Legion, Millán Astray, headed Franco's aggressive press and propaganda service.[22]

Some previously ardent Republican intellectuals had backed the insurrection as a way of imposing order, but this could also turn to regret once they saw what was happening. The philosopher Miguel de Unamuno, perhaps Spain's greatest intellectual at the time, was one of the first to complain. His rapid change of heart was, in part, because some of his own friends, especially the episcopalian minister Atilano Coco, were being rounded up. (Protestants like Coco tended to be Republican and found themselves targeted by the behind-the-lines repression.) Unamuno, then the rector of Salamanca University, believed Franco had introduced a 'stupid regime of terror'. When he gave a speech warning that the insurrection had become 'an uncivil war' and that crude conquest could not replace winning hearts and minds, he was publicly threatened by Millán Astray. 'Death to intellectuals!' Millán Astray shouted. Franco's wife Carmen had to escort the 72-year-old philosopher out of the building as angry army officers and Falangists barracked him. Unamuno was sacked and died two months later, shortly after his friend Coco was shot.[23]

In the meantime, Franco was expected to take Madrid within a few weeks – a move that would likely end the war or, at least, bring recognition from Germany, Italy and other crucial countries. Germans and Italians were working together closely, with their frequent conversations about Spain helping solidify an alliance with broader aims that took formal shape with the creation of the Axis entente on 23 October 1936. Their aim in Spain was to coordinate their help, keep France and Britain out of the fight and jointly recognise a Franco regime at the same moment. More globally, they also wanted to hide their own imperialistic plans – in Africa, for Mussolini, and central and eastern Europe for Hitler – behind a veil of 'anti-communism'. Franco's war, launched under the same pretext, fitted that aim perfectly.[24]

Franco's 'political' decision to take Toledo first had won him international fame and bought him time to take absolute power. It also showed that he was no longer thinking in purely military terms. Not least, the conquest of the emblematic city added to his credentials as a Christian crusading warrior. It remained to be seen whether it had been wise to gift his enemy added time to organise the defence of Spain's capital city, Madrid.[25]

22

Attack on Madrid

OUTSKIRTS OF MADRID, NOVEMBER 1936

Franco did not reach the gates of Madrid until the first week of November 1936. He arrived convinced of an easy victory. Up to now, every village, town and city attacked by the Army of Africa had fallen quickly. After the Getafe aerodrome, 14 kilometres south of Madrid, was taken, the *ABC* newspaper in Seville boasted on 4 November that the generalísimo's troops were just a 4.60 peseta taxi ride away from the city's central Gran Vía. He was expected to celebrate Sunday Mass in the capital that week, turning the attack into an easy coronation. He even had a list of supporters who would become city councillors and mayor. 'My general had no doubt that his troops would crush all resistance,' Pacón said.[1]

Such was Franco's confidence that he had also foreseen the repression that he would impart after taking the capital. 'Numerous executions are inevitable,' he told one visitor. He did not say how many, but excitable members of his staff had proposed up to 50,000 people. In the meantime, a part of Madrid's communist- and socialist-led Republican internal security force had decided to pre-emptively liquidate many of the prisoners who Franco hoped to free. Over the next few weeks, at least 2,400 prisoners – many of them army officers – would be removed from jails and shot at Paracuellos de Jarama and other places in the war's largest single example of 'red terror'.[2]

Much had happened since Toledo fell. Just the previous day, for example, Madrileños had spotted snub-nosed Russian Polikarpov fighters in the sky above a city where Italian 'Black Bird' Caproni bombers and German Ju 52s had begun the first regular aerial bombardment of a European capital at the end of October. On 4 November they watched as the Russian aircraft tussled with German and Italian fighters, performing well. Franco would soon have the opportunity to see this for himself on trips to the Madrid front and the attacking army's headquarters nearby in Leganés.[3]

It was the first visible proof that Stalin's Soviet Union really had sent arms – along with pilots, tank-drivers and military advisers – to Spain. It was also evident that, by diverting his troops to Toledo, Franco had made a great tactical mistake. Major arms deliveries had now reached the other side, just in time to defend Madrid.

With France and Britain embracing non-intervention, Republican Spain had few options. Mexico and the Soviet Union were the only countries willing to counter Hitler and Mussolini's presence on Franco's side. Turning to Stalin was, Hitler himself later reasoned, a decision not made 'on ideological grounds, but rather [something the socialist-led Republican government had] been forced into ... dragged into a political current not of their own choosing – simply through lack of other support.' After all, he reasoned, it was clear that not all the people Franco called 'reds' were really communists. British elites were not so certain about that, with Madrid ambassador Sir Henry Chilton terming the war a battle between 'rebels and rabble' while considering that Franco defended the interests of 'our class'. British-led non-intervention, indeed, would seriously hobble the Republic's war effort.[4]

Stalin nevertheless waited to send aid, not committing until mid-September. He did not want to upset Britain and France, for which reason the USSR had joined the non-intervention pact.[5] Yet proof that Germany and Italy were brazenly flouting the pact kept appearing. This was provided by, amongst others, the Hungarian writer, polyglot and Comintern agent Arthur Koestler, who used his press credentials to roam the Francoist zone and enter one of Seville's most expensive hotels on 28 August:

> Hitler was denying having dispatched aircraft to Spain, and Franco was denying having received them, while there before my very eyes fat, blond German pilots, living proof to the contrary, were

consuming vast quantities of Spanish fish, and, monocles clamped into their eyes, reading the *Völkischer Beobachter*... Their uniforms consisted of the white overall worn by Spanish airmen; on their breasts were two embroidered wings with a small swastika in a circle.[6]

Stalin signed off on an arms and aid program called Operation X and, on October 4, the steamship *Campeche* docked with the first arms. For this, he overcharged the Republican government, who used up a considerable part of the Bank of Spain's gold reserves paying for these arms. But soon Soviet T-26 tanks were proving superior to Franco's German Panzers, while the Polikarpov bested the German and Italian fighters. Some 330 tanks and 746 aircraft would eventually be delivered, with the time lag provided by Franco's Toledo attack proving crucial.[7]

On 6 November, a black limousine slipped out of the Madrid heading for the eastern coastal city of Valencia. Prime minister Francisco Largo Caballero, a militant socialist who had taken charge on 4 September, sat in the back. His government was fleeing the capital and leaving the bald and bespectacled Republican general José Miaja behind to defend the capital at all costs. The arrival that same day of 2,000 foreign volunteer fighters would be greeted by Franco as proof that Spain really was the objective of a global leftist conspiracy. The idealistic, antifascist fighters were the vanguard of the International Brigades, whose numbers eventually grew to 40,000. Once again, Franco's diversion to Toledo had bought the recently arrived and poorly trained volunteers time to join the defence of Madrid.[8]

Their weapons had only just arrived in wooden crates stamped with exotic bills of lading. 'Some were in Arabic and one case was branded with the letters IRA,' recalled British volunteer Bernard Knox, who later became a World War II Special Operations Executive officer and then a Yale and Harvard classics professor. 'They contained American '03 Springfields, the rifle carried by the Doughboys in the Great [First World] War.'[9]

The International Brigades were, nevertheless, an improvement on most regular Republican units and their arrival provoked a certain gloom in Franco's headquarters. In Madrid, the mysterious foreigners were greeted by a bewildered crowd who cried: 'The Russians have come! The Russians have come!' They soon discovered that the new arrivals were from all around the world – providing a fillip for those *madrileños* who, after seeing the government flee, had concluded that defeat was imminent. A French member of the brigades, nevertheless, still felt they were viewed like a 'straw plug brought in to stem the flow of water into a ship that had already been ripped open'.[10]

Back in Franco's camp, there were still many factions to be balanced against one another. When the Carlist envoy, the Count of Rodezno, asked why the plans being drawn up to celebrate his inevitable triumph did not include placing altars in every city square, Franco warned that displays of piety would jar at a time of maximum bloodshed as firing squads started work. He appeared to suggest, indeed, that those same squares might be used for shooting people. 'Implacable justice will require the imposition of the most severe punishments,' he explained. Franco obviously delivered this information to Rodezno in his usual calm and unexcitable fashion, since Rodezno left thinking this was a 'serene, cautious, friendly but reserved man'.[11]

Rodezno also admitted, however, that he had left the meeting 'with no idea about his beliefs'. That partly reflected Franco's natural ambiguity but also the fact that he had no real political programme. For the moment, his reactionary revolution was mostly social and cultural. It was intent on establishing a society of order based on obedience, hierarchy, Roman Catholicism and a nationalism that supposedly reflected a naturally Spanish way of being. Apart from that, nobody yet knew what 'Francoism' was supposed to be. Nor, in fact, did Franco.

By the following day, 7 November, Franco's troops were in the outer suburbs south-west of Madrid. A tiny Italian Fiat-Ansaldo tank – with two crewmen squeezed inside and only a mounted machine gun as a weapon – reached the banks of the river Manzanares, where it was ambushed. Both crewmen were killed and one was found to be carrying the Francoist plan of attack. These showed that they planned to enter from the west, crossing the shallow river Manzanares.[12] Crucially, that gave General Miaja twenty-four hours to place his troops accordingly.

Foreign correspondents accompanying Franco's columns were infected by their optimism. The headline in the London *Times* on 9 November read 'Last Hours of Madrid', while the Hearst newspaper group's Hubert Renfro 'Red' Knickerbocker listened to Francoist radio and filed an entirely fictional 'eyewitness' account of the generalísimo leading his men into Madrid with a dog trotting along beside them. In fact, the International Brigades and other units were digging in to resist the Francoist charge, while Soviet aircraft flew overhead and Red Army advisors helped organise the defence. All this was the price Franco now had to pay for his 'political' timewasting at Toledo.[13]

Franco's North African mercenaries first crossed the Manzanares on 9 November, but were immediately beaten back by – amongst others – a unit of International Brigaders. Six days later, they crossed again to establish a bridgehead in the University City, an as yet unused campus that was close to completion. They got no further, despite multiple attempts throughout November and December. These were accompanied by city-centre bombardments meant to destroy morale. *Paris-Soir* correspondent Louis Delaprée found a young woman dying amid the rubble while 'under a pile of glass, her small, flattened child' lay on the corner of Gran Vía and Alcalá. He angrily accused the world of being less interested in this than the ongoing drama of the affair between Britain's King Edward VIII and American divorcée Wallis Simpson.[14]

The failure to capture Madrid was a huge embarrassment to Franco, especially given the boastful tone used before the attack. 'They were days of great anxiety,' his cousin Pacón admitted later. 'The generalísimo's telephone conversations with General Varela and the other column commanders were full of angst.' Franco received confusing reports about the strength of his own forces and those he faced. 'He was upset and worried,' said Pacón, who listened as his cousin struggled to make decisions.[15]

According to Pacón, an obviously partial witness, the only choice left was to destroy the capital – since the Republicans had pledged to fight to the death – and Franco was not prepared to do that. Reuters, however, quoted Franco as saying: 'The bombardment started yesterday will be continued until Madrid surrenders. Madrid will have to be destroyed district by district no matter how much I regret it.'[16] In fact, he had misjudged the situation: he could neither destroy Madrid, nor capture it. The Republicans were better fighters than he thought and had benefitted from the extra weeks of preparation. His own attack army was now too small for the task.

John Whitaker, embedded with Franco's men, found them in a state of confusion. 'In war it is extremely difficult to change the psychology of troops from offensive to defensive operations,' he commented. 'Franco's men could not understand the need for their own entrenchment. They lay in shallow ditches, expecting always to crash into Madrid the next day or the day after that ... Franco's Moors died by the thousands.' As a result, Whitaker concluded that Franco was now 'a caudillo without an army and without a country'. He bumped into a German military advisor who was convinced that only 20,000 German troops could save the situation. 'Franco is finished,' he said. 'He cannot stand against red counterattacks now or later. I am going to Salamanca to telephone the Führer and ask for the immediate dispatch of German infantry.' German diplomats wrote worried reports about a frivolous atmosphere of over-optimism.[17]

Franco blamed the International Brigades, even though they defended only a third of the bulge his troops had created in the University City. From now on, however, he welcomed any opportunity to raise the subject of the International Brigades and Russian arms in public. It meant he could respond to any complaint about Germany and Italy flouting the non-intervention pact with counter-claims of Soviet interference. He saw a racial aspect in this, identifying the communism of the Soviet Union with 'the Orient and the steppes of Asia'.[18]

Both Hitler and Mussolini had planned to formally recognise the Francoist government as soon as it captured Madrid, but that had not happened. Eventually, on November 18, they recognised his regime anyway. Franco thought this only right, given that 'in Spain the battle is being fought not just in defence of the Spanish nation but of the essence of western civilisation.' A secret treaty signed by Franco and Mussolini ten days later saw both men pledge never to enter an alliance against the other and to oppose the League of Nations' sanctioning of aggressor states (meaning support for Mussolini's wars of colonial conquest in North Africa).[19]

The lines around Madrid quickly became fixed. Franco toured the front on 22 November, quizzing officers and ordinary soldiers. That day he ordered that frontal attacks, which were causing his first major losses, must stop. He was running out of men. 'You don't win [the war] by occupying the capital city if you don't have enough reserves for the job,' he told Pacón.[20] This was a concession that the Civil War would last much longer than they expected. For the majority of Spaniards who were neither from the radical right or the extreme left, that was terrible news, as one Andalusian soldier on Franco's own side recalled later.

> On top of all the disasters a war brings to the civilian population, the hunger and hardships, a civil war is a struggle between brothers. One was on the nationalist side and one's brother was on the red side and you never knew if it wasn't your brother you were shooting at. It happened to me – I served in the nationalist army; it happened to the majority of Andalusians. What can be worse than thinking: 'Am I shooting my brother?' Almost everyone had someone on the other side; the immense majority didn't want to fight for one side or the other, I believe.[21]

In Salamanca, German and Italian advisors were scathing. In reports home, they suggested Franco was not up to the job of securing victory in a war so much bigger than anything he had experienced in Morocco. In fact, the war had reached a new and different phase. Foreign observers, seeing Franco's lightly armed flying columns and ragged opponents, had commented that this was not a properly 'modern' war. It lacked the latest technology, large armies and intense firepower.[22] Madrid changed that, as Franco now realised.

When Hitler sent his first ambassador to the Franco regime a week later, he reported that Franco needed at least two divisions of foreign troops – one German and one Italian – to break into Madrid. Although Germany and Italy had already agreed that they should make a 'joint military effort' in Spain, this idea provoked horror in Berlin. If anyone was to send troops on that scale, officials said, it should be Mussolini. In fact, the Italians had already unilaterally decided the situation was so dire that they would indeed send thousands of their own soldiers to fight. But when Franco was informed that 3,000 Italian black-shirt fascist militiamen were on their way, the Spaniard was outraged. 'And who asked you for them?' he demanded. 'When you send troops to a friendly country, the least you can do is ask permission.'[23]

It was a sign of how badly Franco needed help, however, that he could not refuse Mussolini. His anger was not about the quantity, but the form. He wanted mixed units of Spaniards and Italians commanded by his own senior officers. Mussolini, however, was sending a semi-independent army of his own – with salaries paid in Italy. Franco's need was greater than his outrage and on 12 January 1937 he asked Mussolini to increase his force to 9,000 men. These soon began to reach the southern Spanish cities of Cádiz, Huelva and Seville.[24]

Hitler also repeated his commitment to Franco's cause. At the meeting in his Berlin villa with Mussolini's foreign minister Ciano, where the so-called Axis alliance that would fight World War II was formed, he boasted that they were already digging 'the first trench against Bolshevism' in Spain. Hitler boosted his force there, adding 40 tanks, anti-tank gun units and more aircraft in what was now dubbed 'Operation Guido'. Up to twice a week, Warlimont (in civilian dress or disguised in a borrowed Italian uniform) accompanied Franco to the front to see how the new arms were performing. Franco was dismayed by the German tanks, which were little more than armoured cars mounted with machine guns, complaining that they were inferior to the Republic's Russian tanks. Warlimont explained that Hitler's rearmament push in Germany had yet to produce anything better. In fact, Franco did not know how to use tanks. A German commander, Colonel Wilhelm von Thoma, had to teach him. 'General Franco wished to parcel out the tanks among the infantry – in the usual way of generals who belong to the old school,' commented Thoma, who became one of the Second World War's most prestigious tank commanders. 'I had to fight this tendency constantly in the endeavour to use the tanks in a concentrated way. The Francoists' successes were largely due to this.'[25]

By November, General Hugo Sperrle was commanding a German contingent with 100 aircraft and 5,000 men, now baptised the 'Condor Legion'. Once again, decisions were being made for Franco, who was simply informed that this unit was on its way. Twenty-five vessels carrying Condor members and equipment reached Franco's ports in November. They returned laden with the copper, iron and other minerals that Hitler, seeing Franco's Spain as a promising source of raw materials for his expanding Third Reich, sought in return. Access to

Spain's natural resources, indeed, was one of the main reasons why Hitler had decided to back Franco.[26]

Franco was building an air force that would be one-third made up by Luftwaffe pilots and aircraft, one-third by Mussolini's Italians and one-third by Spanish pilots flying German or Italian aircraft. While there were never more than 6,000 German troops in Spain at any one time, Göring deliberately rotated 20,000 men through the Condor Legion in order to give them combat experience. Hitler, meanwhile, repeatedly told his staff that he wanted to 'distract the attention of the western powers to Spain, and so enable German rearmament to continue unobserved'.[27]

On 14 January 1937, Göring and Mussolini met in Rome. They were frustrated with Franco, whose advances had slowed dramatically since reaching Madrid. They agreed to apply 'energetic pressure on Franco to speed up his operations and fully use all the vast material placed at his disposition'. They also decided to set up a joint Italian-German high command to pressure him into 'carrying out military operations in an opportune way'. Franco was dismayed by their growing lack of faith in his abilities. In a telegram to Rome on 27 January 1937 he expressed his 'decisive and firm intention' to go on the offensive and bring the war to a speedy end.[28]

Franco quickly sent Mussolini's troops into action. By 18 January 1937 a full brigade of 6,000 Italian troops was in Seville, with numbers growing to 43,000 over three months. The Italians led the successful expulsion of Republican defenders from Málaga, pushing tens of thousands of refugees on a deadly march towards Almería. The Italians assumed Franco would be vociferously grateful, but that was not his way. When the Italian commander visited him a week after Málaga fell, the generalísimo neither congratulated him nor thanked him for sending the relic of Saint Teresa of Ávila's arm.[29]

'The first sentence we shall pass in Málaga is the death sentence,' Queipo de Llano had pronounced in one of his buffoonish, rambling and inflammatory radio broadcasts. The threat was carried out as soon as the Italians handed the city over to Franco's men, who shot at least 804 people over the next six weeks.[30]

Italians and Germans were shocked. The overwrought Italian consul in the city, Tranquillo Bianchi, now found women and priests waiting at his hotel door every morning, begging him to intercede in farcical 'trials carried out with primitive means and out of hate'. Firing squads worked three shifts a day to shoot people at dawn, 8 a.m. and midnight. Even Franco's brother-in-law Serrano Suñer admitted that military tribunals churned out death penalties like a machine. Mussolini worried that Franco was preparing to 'plant his flags in a cemetery'.[31]

23

The Absent One

SALAMANCA, NOVEMBER–DECEMBER, 1936

José Antonio Primo de Rivera was everything that Francisco Franco was not. Handsome, charismatic and cultured, the slick-haired, green-eyed Falangist lawyer exuded a personal magnetism and social ease that Franco could only envy. 'He is the most handsome man I have met in my entire life,' Queen Victoria Eugenia had been heard to exclaim. Even Manuel Azaña, who hated his politics, liked the man. He also had a clear political doctrine which placed him closer to Hitler and Mussolini than Franco, whose unformed political beliefs were still those of a simple, militaristic reactionary. José Antonio had visited both Hitler and Mussolini, finding the latter especially inspiring. His occasional encounters with Franco, however, had ended badly. Primo de Rivera found him indecisive, evasive and uninspiring.[1]

When the insurrection broke out, Primo de Rivera was already in jail, having been arrested in March. He had conspired from his prison cell, finally bringing the Falange into the uprising at the end of June – before Franco committed himself. A suspicious Republican government moved him to Alicante on the east coast, meaning that, when the insurrection started, he was deep inside enemy territory. He continued to charm people from his prison cell, including the left-leaning American journalist Jay Allen who – as the US ambassador put it – 'liked the young man, as everyone does who knows him'. With his many adherents in the army, the Falange's swelling militia, his natural charisma and the death of Calvo Sotelo, the young Primo de Rivera had looked destined to play a crucial part in the uprising. Serrano Suñer claimed that only the move to Alicante had stopped Franco being secondary to José Antonio.[2]

Franco himself helped stymie several attempts to release Primo de Rivera, either by springing him from jail with the help of the German consul, negotiating a swap or mounting an international campaign. Typically, Franco never gave an outright 'no': he just added so many conditions as to make each course of action impracticable. Franco even suggested that Primo de Rivera might be untrustworthy or mentally unstable, insisting that he would have to be interrogated fully by one of his own people before being allowed into the part of Spain that many now called the 'Nationalist' zone. In short, he saw no urgency about having this charismatic rival freed from a Republican jail cell.[3]

With Primo de Rivera imprisoned, the fast-growing Falange was governed by a weak Junta that met only occasionally. The Falange had swelled from 10,000 members at the start of 1936 (and 0.4 per cent of the vote at February elections) to one that could have won 50 seats by November just with the votes of those wearing its uniform. 'Never in Spanish history has a party grown so quickly,' says historian Javier Tusell. Manuel Hedilla, a 34-year-old mechanic, emerged as a leader but a tussle soon broke out for the party's future in which the cleverest participants realised that Franco would choose the winner.[4] The Falange was barely three years old, with Italian fascism as its clearest lodestar and a 27-point set of principles that were not just expressly totalitarian, but also corporativist in the economy, imperial in ambition and with a strongly Roman Catholic identity. It was avowedly both anti-Marxist and anti-capitalist, seeking a centrally-coordinated economy where capital still flowed and private property was respected but workers and bosses belonged to syndicates, or unions, that shared the same nationalistic aims. Although it declared itself revolutionary, this ultranationalist, disciplinarian credo was meant to make class warfare pointless by resolving the needs of workers itself and reducing the gap between rich and poor. Its anti-capitalism was mostly directed against finance, with banks and public services meant to be nationalised and jobs for all men of working age. Of course, it also brooked no dissent. The Falange's idealism was accompanied by a boastful, blustering and belligerent manner which meant some leaders were temperamentally incapable of the sycophancy that worked best with Franco. Hedilla, especially, failed at this by referring to José Antonio Primo de Rivera, rather than Franco, as Caudillo.[5]

Primo de Rivera, meanwhile, was tried by the Republic for abetting military rebellion, found guilty and shot in the courtyard of Alicante prison on 20 November 1936. It was a messy execution, with the Republican firing squad reportedly shooting at will and out of time. Franco found out about his death very quickly, since it was announced prominently in Republican newspapers and the Italian press. Yet neither the Falange nor Franco mentioned his death publicly until almost two years later.[6]

This extraordinary state of affairs may have started as an attempt to avoid demoralising Falange fighters, but its continuity over time only benefited one person – Franco. As long as José Antonio's return was formally awaited, the Falange leadership could only be provisional and weak. Serrano Suñer even accused Franco of fanning rumours that Primo de Rivera had been secretly taken to Russia and castrated.[7]

In the words of one Falange leader, they had now gone from being 'a small body with a big head to a monster-sized but headless body'. They were also, as one Italian fascist in Spain commented, 'a party without a leader' while Franco was 'a leader without a party'. That was an opportunity. In the meantime, Franco paid lip service to the growing cult around José Antonio, but also found it annoying. It was as if, one Falangist writer later said, he had married a widow, only to hear her speak relentlessly about how wonderful her deceased husband had been. After all, Franco himself was meant to be the adored Caudillo. Instead, he made speeches praising José Antonio, while Falange leaders were encouraged to say that 'his work is continued by the victorious work of Franco'.[8]

The Falange recruited volunteers quickly in part because membership was a way of escaping retribution for previous left-wing sympathies. In practise, it was divided into local power hubs, some of which ran death squads that targeted suspected Republican sympathisers.

Fourteen-year-old Obdulia Camacho was arrested with her socialist-supporting mother Pilar Espinosa on 29 December 1936 by a Falangist gang in Poyales del Hoyo, a village nestled in the foothills of the Sierra de Gredos, 140 kilometres west of Madrid. That night they and two other women – one of them a Protestant – were bundled into a lorry and driven towards the neighbouring village of Candeleda. Halfway there, Obdulia was told to get out and run back to the village. The three others were shot and their bodies left at the side of the road. It was both a punishment and a warning. Falange gangs across the country were operating in much the same way. The playwright and poet Federico García Lorca, author of works like *Blood Wedding* and *The House of Bernarda Alba*, was amongst those shot by a death squad in Granada.[9]

The Falange's thuggish ascendancy behind the lines was made apparent when Franco's former boss as war minister, José María Gil Robles, reached Burgos. Gil Robles had been helping Franco from abroad but Falangists in Burgos tried to arrest him and threatened to beat him up, apparently because he had once taken part in the now discredited game of parliamentary politics. He also felt cold-shouldered by Franco, eventually concluding that the generalísimo did not like working with someone who had once been his superior.

Nor did Franco want to work with another potential source of rivalry – the exiled Alfonso XIII or his family. The monarch's son and heir, Don Juan, had tried to volunteer for the insurrectionist army in August 1936. He was stopped and sent back across the border in his chauffeur-driven Bentley. When he instead asked Franco for permission to join the crew of the cruiser *Baleares* in December 1936, arguing that 'all good Spaniards of my age should be in combat posts' he was again rebuffed. This was, at least in part, because of Alfonso XIII's tepid support for Franco himself. 'He is a great man for war, but one cannot be sure that he will be capable after the victory of governing the country,' he said. Worse still, he shared these thoughts with his Italian hosts, who passed them on to a 'hurt and surprised' dictator. Franco rarely forgave those who crossed him. He wrote to Alfonso accusing him of being out of touch. Alfonso was furious. 'I picked out Franco when he was a nobody,' he told American journalist John Whitaker later. 'He has deceived and double-crossed me at every turn.' That did not stop him from profusely congratulating Franco when he conquered major cities, or Franco from writing to tell him about them.[10]

Alongside Falangists, hardline monarchists had joined the uprising with enthusiasm, especially those close to the authoritarian Renovación Española party, formerly led by the assassinated Calvo Sotelo. Whitaker was scathing about them. 'If I could sum up their social philosophy it was simple in the extreme. They were outnumbered by the masses: they feared the programme to educate the masses and they proposed to thin down their numbers.'[11] Hubert Renfro Knickerbocker, from Hearst newspapers, found himself forced to spend many hours in the company of an impoverished but castle-dwelling, multilingual count and army major who viewed the workers not just as another class, but as an entirely different and inferior 'slave' race. The unnamed count was furious when, in November 1936, he received instructions to stop routinely shooting all prisoners. Echoing Franco's occasional outbursts, one of his favourite expressions was: 'Take them out and shoot 'em!''[12]

These reactionary monarchists also expected to share Franco's power or, at least, to influence it heavily. The Caudillo initially turned to them to staff the upper echelons of his regime. Men like the diplomat Sangróniz wielded great power, but if monarchists thought this meant Franco was on their side, they were fooling themselves. There was, after all, a glaring contradiction in their support for Franco in that, ultimately, they wanted someone else as head of state.[13]

Just as Franco's ambitions, culture and expertise were initially constrained to his army world, so he saw his dictatorship in mostly military terms. To friends and collaborators, he talked about 'command' rather than 'power'. While dictator Miguel Primo de Rivera had, in Franco's mind, been the best governor of Spain during his own lifetime, he had committed one great error. He had said his hold on power would be temporary. 'That is a mistake. If you take command, you have to do so as if it was for your whole life,' he said.[14]

Few people outside Franco's inner circle could imagine such statements were anything more than a necessary bluff. Those who knew his idea of military command, however, were not surprised by his determination to impose discipline and suppress internal opposition. Franco had, after all, helped create the Legion, described by one Welsh recruit as 'one of the few military forces where men are drilled by the use of whips'.[15]

A German diplomat who arrived late in November 1936 found Franco's Spain even more divided and factional than the notoriously fractious Republic – where disagreements raged between socialists, communists, anarchists, Trotskyists and Catalan or Basque nationalists and their militias. 'Sharp differences have arisen between the

Fascist Falange and the monarchist-clerical [Carlist] Requeté... There is also rivalry amongst the leading generals,' he reported.[16]

The Carlists were the first to challenge Franco's position as master-of-all. In December 1936, they decided to set up their own officer training school, in part because so many officers had died that chaplains occasionally took command of units. The Carlists' Requeté militia saw itself as a semi-independent army whose soldiers had 'one hand holding a grenade, the other a rosary'. The unilateral decision to set up a training school, grandly published as a decree in the Carlists' own official bulletin, was a clumsy challenge to Franco's power since it suggested that they were a sovereign entity.[17]

From Franco's new-found height as dictator, this was intolerable. His power was absolute and unquestionable. He called the Carlists' representative in Salamanca, the Count of Rodezno, to see him personally. 'Without losing his calm, he politely but firmly expressed the disgust that this decree had provoked,' Rodezno recalled. As the conversation progressed, however, Franco's controlled rage became apparent. 'He spoke of this as a coup d'état, as an act of treason, or the kind of behaviour expected of an anarchist.'[18]

As his behaviour in the Legion showed, Franco believed discipline must be visibly punitive. He considered shooting Carlist leader Manuel Fal Conde for 'high treason' and only restrained himself since 'that would have produced a bad impression among the Requetés at the front, who were fighting bravely'. Instead, he banished Fal Conde from Spain. This was an extraordinary punishment for the man who had guaranteed the success of the insurrection in Pamplona and Navarre while providing a large and well-trained militia in the early days of their precarious uprising.[19]

It was characteristic of Franco that he did not carry out, or convey, this punishment himself. Whenever bad news had to be imparted, he delegated. Instead, the message was delivered by General Fidel Davila, who made it clear to Fal Conde that his crime was political, for encouraging Carlists to think that they owed allegiance not to Franco but to their own exiled pretender to the throne, Don Javier de Borbón-Parma.[20]

All this came at a time when the war effort was paramount and Carlists had little room for protest. In this case, Franco's failure to take Madrid and end the war the previous month played to his own advantage. The Carlists could not even announce Fal Conde's banishment, since the press was under strict censorship. A requeté soldier was more likely to hear the news on Republican radio. Don Javier deemed Franco's move 'treachery'. 'We are not fighting for the benefit of Franco,' he said. In fact, they were.[21]

When Carlist emissaries delivered a furious letter from Don Javier, Franco gave them five minutes of his time, was 'violently' angry and dismissed them in such a peremptory manner that they worried they would be arrested. The Carlists' were thus the first to learn that a Francoist dictatorship meant even allies must bend to the dictator's will or face punishment.[22]

There was more. Six days after Fal Conde was banished, all militias were brought under the central authority of the army. This was logical, but also bold. One in four soldiers on the insurrectionist side belonged to either the Requeté or the Falange militias. If the Falange was already missing its charismatic head, then Franco had to all effects decapitated the Carlists. Now they and their militias were all under Franco's control.[23]

24

Enforced Unity

BURGOS AND SALAMANCA, 1937–8

On 20 January 1937, a man dressed in women's clothing left a private clinic in Madrid and made his way to the Belgian embassy to join those seeking protection from Republican police and militia death squads. This was Franco's brother-in-law, Ramón Serrano Suñer, who had been in Madrid when the insurrection started. He had been arrested and survived the raids on the notorious Modelo prison by left-wing death squads, but saw several friends (including José Antonio Primo de Rivera's brother Fernando) removed from the jail to be shot. Elsewhere, his own brothers José and Fernando were detained and also shot.

The well-connected Serrano Suñer had eventually been allowed to leave jail to be treated for a gastric ulcer at the clinic, with a special permit signed by a Republican minister. It was an easy place to begin his escape, starting with the trip to the Belgian embassy from where, via a roundabout route, he was eventually able to reunite with his family and cross into the part of Spain controlled by Franco. On 20 February 1937, Serrano Suñer reached Salamanca and immediately began to work directly with his brother-in-law, in whose house they now lived.

For a man so mistrustful of others, family remained of vital importance to Franco. Close relatives such as Pacón and his brother Nicolás served as refuges of dependability. Carmen Polo's brother, Felipe, now also worked for him as one of his secretaries. Even within the military, he seemed to trust and promote people he knew from his childhood in Ferrol above others. Notably, Franco had never included Serrano Suñer in the lists of prisoners to be exchanged even though Nicolás Franco was constantly adding the names of friends and family. That reflected more his unwillingness to bargain about anything than a dislike of Serrano Suñer, who soon became a major influence on his politically unsophisticated brother-in-law.[1]

Membership of the family allowed him to overcome Franco's naturally suspicious and peremptory nature. The *cuñadísimo* (or 'super brother-in-law'), as Serrano Suñer was soon known, lived with his wife and three children at the Franco residence, first in a small room in the Bishop's Palace in Salamanca and then in a summer mansion built by a wealthy financier, the Palacio de la Isla in Burgos, where they all moved in July 1937. They lunched daily with Franco's family and aides, including Carmen's other siblings Isabel and Felipe. Carmen Polo claimed this was the only moment of relaxation for a husband who rose at 7.30 am and started work immediately, often not finishing until late into the night. By now his routine included morning Mass, being at his desk by 9.30am and working through until a lunch that sometimes did not start until 3pm. A stroll around the garden with his next visitor preceded a return to his desk until late evening. After dinner he often went back to work. Given the state of war, there were few luxuries. Carmen Polo could sometimes be found with a sewing needle in her hand, mending his uniforms.[2]

Serrano Suñer was intense and clever, crushed by the death of his brothers and obsessed by his mission. Politics became a way to anaesthetise the pain. The devout Serrano Suñer had now also turned to Italian fascism for inspiration, preferring it to Hitler's National Socialism because of the latter's dislike of the church. As an intellectual and ideologue, he was very different to his military-minded brother-in-law, but the two men shared a mistrustful mindset, constantly imagining plots against them, as well as holding an increasingly Messianic belief in their own importance for Spain's future. Franco's brother-in-law lived in a state of constant tension that left him thin and unwell. Mussolini's foreign minister Ciano saw the 'skinny and sickly' Serrano Suñer as 'one of those people better suited to study and reflection: all consciousness, honesty and enthusiasm... But he is always overcome by his emotions. He hates and loves with great force.'[3]

Carmen Polo took a motherly interest in her tortured brother-in-law, who soon began to act as Franco's unofficial 'political secretary' (as Italian diplomats saw him). She liked him, in fact, a lot more than Nicolás Franco – whose freewheeling, *bon vivant* lifestyle she frowned upon. Neither Carmen nor Franco detected Serrano Suñer's intellectual disdain for the simplistic political mindset of the man whom he wanted to make head of a totalitarian state modelled on Mussolini's Italy. In fact, he very quickly became the chief architect and second most powerful person in what could now be called 'Francoist Spain'.[4]

Yet it was still not clear early in 1937 what Franco stood for. On the one hand, he realised that the monarchy had always benefitted 'the privileged classes, something without popular roots'. Yet while fascism 'was a respectable form of government' he did not want his regime to be 'exclusively fascist'. When asked by another Italian envoy about a new king, he gave an evasive reply. 'First I must create the nation; and only then will we decide if it is a good idea to name a monarch,' he said. The royal 'we' showed that he thought the position was, at least symbolically and for the moment, filled – by Franco himself.[5]

In an opinion article for the Italian *La Stampa* newspaper on 26 February 1937 he claimed disingenuously that 'I have never been interested in politics; nor has it ever crossed my mind to take absolute power.' He added that Spaniards would choose a new regime once war was over, with a 'military dictatorship' until that happened. 'Will it be monarchy or Republic? I can't say. I repeat: it will be up to Spain to choose. Whatever is decided, we will respect.'[6] As if to reaffirm this, an accompanying piece signed by his wife Carmen added: 'Politics never attracted him and we can say right now that in the future, just as in the past, it will never attract him. When the current task is accomplished, when he is able to look upon a peaceful and joyous Spain, then we will return to our normal lives.'

It was one of the last times either would suggest publicly that his time in power might be short and temporary. When articles started appearing in the insurrectionist press in February 1937 talking, for the first time, about 'Francoism', he was upset. His Press and Propaganda Delegation immediately put out a communiqué stating that: 'Press articles talking about Francoism in the sense of a [political] party, have not been authorised nor suggested by any authentic representative [of

Franco] and do not respond to the impersonal concept of patriotic idealism which drives the Caudillo.'[7]

Franco struggled to think outside his usual, military mindset. A Fascist envoy from Mussolini, Roberto Farinacci, found 'a beginner at politics' with no clear ideas about the future beyond the need for a long dictatorship.[8] Obedience, hierarchy, unity and blind nationalism – all military credos – remained, as ever, his core values, along with an embrace of law and order. Beyond that, his ideology was framed in reactionary terms – against communism, liberalism, Freemasonry, 'foreign' ideas and any religious belief outside the Roman Catholic church.

Serrano Suñer quickly set about persuading Franco that the Falange was the party closest to this way of thinking. With its glorification of a single leader, mystical attachment to the nation, love of action and embrace of violence or self-sacrifice, it coincided with many of Franco's core beliefs. It also provided a forward-looking ideology that did not simply dwell on past glories or lost traditions.

Franco's obsession was to create unity and engender obedience, as his disciplining of the Carlists had shown, but that clashed with the multi-factional nature of the uprising. He had begun to study the credos of both the Falange and the Carlists. To the disbelief of many in both groups, he soon concluded that they could be fused into a single political entity (or 'movement', as he preferred to say). Franco performed mental gymnastics to convince himself that the two movements could be merged. He would bolt modern Falange ideas about the future onto reactionary Carlist values about history, morals and religion. Both ideologies hated liberalism and required an autocratic leader. If Falangism needed a Duce, Carlism sought a catholic prince. Franco found little trouble imagining himself as the hybrid incarnation of both.[9]

The ideological underpinning of his new state, in other words, was to be a combination of two very different ideologies supported by very few Spaniards at elections just a year earlier. It would also, inevitably, be a fusion created around his own person, allowing a military-style hierarchy of control and discipline.

Carlist leaders told him the merger was impossible. The Falange leadership, meanwhile, split into rival factions who actually confronted one another with pistols and hand grenades in normally peaceful Salamanca on 16 April. Two Falangistas were killed and Franco saw even greater reason for him to take direct control.[10]

On 19 April, the unification decree was proclaimed. Essentially, it was foisted on both sides. Franco was contemptuous of the leadership of both organisations. 'There is no way to change this man's mind,' the Carlist leader Rodezno now discovered.[11]

The merger created the tortuous-sounding FET y de las JONS, or Spanish Traditionalist Phalanx of the Council of the National Syndicalist Offensives (inserting the Carlist term 'traditionalist' into the already long-winded full name of the Falange to create what one wag called 'the longest name for a political party in history'). This was the Francoist state's new single party also commonly known as 'the Movement', though many people continued to call it 'the Falange' and its members 'blue shirts', since they conserved that part of the Falange uniform. It recognised only one leader.[12]

Franco announced the unification in a radio speech, a piece of baroque, detail-free rhetoric written in his own hand. Franco stated that he was founding 'a movement' rather than launching a programme. He promised 'a union of all Spaniards in service of the Fatherland' and to make Spain 'worthy of the respect of other nations'. His guiding principles were 'authority, glorification of the Fatherland and social justice'. What people really wanted, Franco said, was 'to see and feel themselves governed'. He was the man for that.[13]

Concrete measures could not yet be revealed, he claimed, since they were 'in a process of elaboration'. This allowed both Falangists and Requetés to imagine he was speaking principally to them. Amidst the bombast and historical romanticism, however, Franco gave a crucial indication of his priorities. There was, he said, nothing 'fleeting' about this new regime. The creation of what some now called 'el partido único', or the 'single party', was not a war measure, but something permanent.[14]

When the text of Franco's new decree was published two days later, the reach of his takeover became starkly clear. A long, heroic preamble was followed by three simple articles. 'Falange Española and Requetés ... are now integrated under my leadership into a single political entity of national reach,' the first article read. The new organisation's main mission was 'communicating to the state the encouragement of the people and to transmit the state's thinking... All other organisations and political parties are dissolved.'[15] A single state party, in other words, was being formed, with Franco as absolute and unchallengeable leader. Its members were mostly there to listen, applaud and obey. They would also staff the great bureaucratic backbone of the state, providing everything from town mayors to their own intelligence network.

The second article explained that Franco's regime would now embark on 'the definitive organisation of the totalitarian New State'. In the language of the time, that indicated a Spanish version of Mussolini's Italy or Hitler's Germany. The Falange's 'twenty-six points' were to serve as the party's initial programme while the totalitarian state was built (a twenty-seventh point that had existed previous to the merger – and stated that such a thing could never happen – was removed). This looked much more like the fuzzy totalitarianism of Mussolini – which Umberto Eco, then a child in Italy, called a 'beehive of contradictions' – than Hitler's relentless Nazi programme.[16]

The Carlist movement was reduced to little more than a handful of symbols. Its only significant contribution to the new regime of Francoism would be a ferocious embrace of reactionary Roman Catholic doctrines.

The Falange was no longer the party founded by Primo de Rivera. The young Falangist intellectual Dionisio Ridruejo called it 'a reverse coup d'état' in which the head of state captured the mass party, rather than the party imposing itself on the state. One angry Falangist called it 'a monster that killed two authentic bodies in order to create an artificial one'.[17]

In the shadows, Serrano Suñer pulled the political and ideological strings trying to create a Spanish form of totalitarianism for Franco at a time when the dictator was more interested in war than politics. The cuñadísimo worked with a small, loyal team of young Falangists and continually overruled Franco's other advisors, administrators and ministers. He would soon be considered, by others in government, 'the most hated man in Spain'.[18]

One of the first measures was to officialise the stiff-armed 'Roman' salute, already used by Italian fascists and German Nazis. The adoption of the yoke and bundle of arrows symbols used by Queen Isabel and King Ferdinand in the fifteenth century appealed to both Falangists and reactionaries. In the uniform of the new 'single party', the Carlist red beret was added to the Falange's blue shirt. Photographs of Franco were to be hung in all its offices. He was now 'the supreme *caudillo* of the movement' who exercised 'the most absolute authority' and answered only 'to God and history'.[19]

The Falange's list of twenty-six principles remained the guiding framework. It is easy to see why these appealed to Franco. The first five principles were grouped together under the title of 'nation, unity and empire' – his three obsessions. Individual, group and class interests were subordinate to the nation. Empire, military might and maritime power were its aspirations. Totalitarianism, corporatism and national syndicalism (by which workers and employers were forcibly brought together under state guidance) were the path to achieving them. Private property was sacrosanct, but finance and public services needed to be run or overseen by the state. Spanish tradition required that the nation be Roman Catholic, but the state came first.

Beyond that, Franco showed little interest in the political direction of his new mass party. Some found his political naivety and ignorance endearing, mistaking it for humility. 'His simplicity and clearness of mind are admirable,' said the writer José María Pemán. 'He does not realise how strong he is now or the unanimity with which he is followed.' Even the admiring Pemán, however, worried that Franco lacked the talents of a charismatic leader. 'He has a poor ear for oratory and doesn't deliver the rhythms of his sentences,' he said after hearing him harangue a youth meeting in Burgos. Propagandists, meanwhile, worked hard to endow Franco with a crusader's halo.[20]

Serrano Suñer co-opted the Falange's leaders, who took the crucial roles within the new party. All military officers were obliged to join, differentiating it from fascist parties of other nations. When Carlist leaders tried, once more, to argue that they had been short-changed, Franco cut them off angrily. The single party, also known as 'the Movement', had been founded precisely to end such bickering. The previous liberal regime had allowed debate. His regime did not. How, otherwise, was unity to be achieved? 'It is I who, answering only to God and history, decide what position everyone should hold,' he angrily informed one recalcitrant Carlist.[21]

It was the clearest statement yet of what Francoism really meant - a personal dictatorship led by a man convinced of his own providential nature. Franco's image of himself had passed onto a higher plane. Only God and history outranked him.

25
Slow War

JARAMA AND GUADALAJARA, FEBRUARY–MARCH 1937

The long queue of Italian tanks and trucks lined up on 8 March 1937 at the town of Algora, along the highway connecting Madrid to Zaragoza and Barcelona, was meant to be living proof of the superiority of Mussolini's army and of the new tactic of 'guerra celere' or rapid warfare. It was also evidence that Franco's military machine was increasingly dependent on foreigners and was not just the army of divinely-backed Spanish patriots that his propaganda machine talked about. With tanks and flame-throwers clearing obstacles along the way and warplanes flying above them, the 35,000-strong Italian army planned to fall first on Guadalajara and then Madrid. This lay 100km south-west from their starting point. 'Tomorrow Guadalajara, the day after Alcalá de Henares. Madrid in three days' time!' General Roatta wrote in his instructions to his four divisions before they launched themselves along the road from Algora as cold, wet weather closed in.[1]

The Italian attack was a further sign of Franco's growing reliance on Mussolini and Hitler. After his failed head-on assault on Madrid in November 1936, Franco had tried to isolate the capital city, first cutting roads to the north and then attacking over the Jarama River on February 11. Franco's overoptimistic command staff had claimed they would cut Madrid off in five days. His Moroccan mercenaries slipped across the fast-moving Jarama and surprised the Republican guards on a river bridge, allowing his army of 20,000 men to start crossing.

Soon, however, the attack was halted as his men failed to take the hill crests east of the river. Losses were steep at 6,000 men.[2]

As a result, Italian officers had begun sarcastically complaining that while Franco had been a 'magnificent battalion commander', he was a useless commander-in-chief. General Roatta, in particular, treated Franco and his military staff in a way that, one Italian diplomat recorded, was 'high-handed, distant and cold'. At Guadalajara, Roatta assumed, Italians would teach Franco and the rest of the world how a modern war based on the idea of guerra celere should be waged.[3]

Instead, they found themselves bogged down in mud and their vehicles snarled up on the roads, sitting targets for Republican aircraft while the men froze in the snowy weather. The Italians' aircraft remained mud-bound on primitive air strips. A small Italian civil war was fought in the fields outside Brihuega, as the Garibaldi battalion of the International Brigades, made up of Italian communists, republicans and anarchists, helped fight the Corpo Truppe Volontaire (CTV) to a standstill by 20 March. Almost 3,000 of Mussolini's men were dead, injured or captured. Some 500 were made prisoner.[4]

Il Duce's chest-puffing arrogance and that of Roatta now looked like hubris, as everyone from the international press to Spanish generals laughed at Italian pomposity. Officers at Franco's headquarters in Salamanca reportedly stopped saluting their Italian superiors and composed a song with the line: 'Guadalajara is not Abyssinia; here the reds chuck bombs that actually explode.'[5] It was as if, even on Franco's side, Spanish pride had been restored by a Republican victory.

German ground troops also enjoyed the Italian come uppance. 'Being friendly with several Germans in a nearby tank corps, I had heard the news about Guadalajara quickly, and the Germans were, paradoxically, since they are Italian allies, as pleased as we were,' said a legionnaire from Wales, Frank Thomas. In truth, German officers also regularly fell out with their Spanish counterparts, not least because they thought Franco overworked the Condor Legion's air crews.[6]

Herbert Matthews of the *New York Times* claimed 'Guadalajara is for fascism what Bailén was for Napoleon' – referring to Spain's 1808 defeat of a Napoleonic army during the War of Independence. He also recalled, however, that whenever the Republic looked to be winning, Hitler and Mussolini boosted aid. 'Sooner or later, it must either stop or be made so overwhelming so as to ensure a quick victory for

Franco,' he wrote. 'The other alternative is a European war.' Mussolini was outraged, partly by what he considered inadequate support from Franco's own troops during the battle but specially because Franco's propaganda machine did nothing to counter the narrative of Italian incompetence.[7]

Italian envoy Randolfo Cantalupo had hoped to find ways of shortening the war, perhaps by negotiating agreements with the Basques or Catalans. Franco was not interested. 'Everything will be decided by armed combat,' he said. He no longer cared if the war took him years to win. 'It is a war of Reconquista, more spiritual than military,' he told Cantalupo.[8]

Hitler and Mussolini, whose dynamic and ambitious political credos were reflected in their embrace of blitzkrieg and guerra celere, were immensely frustrated. Franco was, to them, a plodding general who constantly had his hand out, asking for more firepower and more credit to cover payments.[9]

As he tightened his grasp on power and built a personal dictatorship, Franco came to think that his own prestige and his side's morale were inseparable. His glory was Spain's glory, and vice versa. Indeed, Franco's chief of operations, Lt Col Barroso, admitted that his personal prestige was now a crucial factor in decision-making. Any Republican counter-attack or gain, in other words, had to be immediately pushed back – even if that meant abandoning other more strategically important projects that might bring a faster victory. Guerra celere, Barroso told an Italian, was too risky since any failure would damage Franco's reputation. Strategic retreats, likewise, were out of the question.[10]

Franco's greatest worry was that Mussolini would now pull out completely, taking his aircraft as well. In fact, Il Duce insisted his troops stay until they had 'made good' the damage to Italian prestige. Franco requested that, if this was so, they be placed firmly under his command and not operate independently. He was not ready for guerra celere. 'Give me aircraft, give me artillery, give me tanks and munitions,' he said. 'But above all, don't rush me.' In a war of attrition, Franco knew, whoever has the deepest stocks usually wins. He also needed to raise and train a much larger army.[11]

Just as importantly, Franco was now thinking about the Spain he wished to rule over. He did not just want victory, but to either annihilate opposition or intimidate it into silence. Since half of Spaniards were left-wingers, that required a protracted and intense purging of people and ideas. One German report stated that 'the number of politically unreliable people in White Spain [is] at about 40 per cent' while another fretted about 'opposition within the lower strata of the population'.[12]

Franco told Cantalupo that purging (or, in his words, 'redeeming' and 'pacifying') conquered territories was now as important to him as winning territory. In practice, that meant executing, jailing or otherwise terrifying opponents. It would be a thorough cleansing. 'We must carry out the task, which is necessarily slow, of redemption and pacification, without which military occupation is totally pointless. The moral redemption of the occupied zones will take a long time and be difficult, because the roots of anarchism are very deep in Spain,' Franco said. He would occupy Spain 'village by village' if necessary, giving himself time to cleanse them along the way. 'Nothing will make me abandon that gradual project. It will bring me less glory, but more inner peace.' This meant the Civil War might go on for up to three years, he admitted. By referring to his personal glory, of course, he was giving away how much that also mattered to him.[13]

From his rented room in Talavera de la Reina, American journalist John Whitaker discovered what 'redemption' might mean. 'I never passed a night there without being awakened at dawn by the volleys of the firing squads in the yard of the barracks. There seemed no end to the killing. They were shooting as many at the end of the second month as in my first days in Talavera,' he said. 'Any man who had held any office under the Republic was, of course, shot out of hand.' A Luger-touting local Falange leader in Toledo, José Sainz, boasted to him that he had personally shot 127 'Red prisoners' in four months.[14]

While accompanying Franco's Moroccan mercenaries, Whitaker had already witnessed what happened after a new town or village was taken. 'I stood at the crossroads outside Navalcarnero with this Moorish major when two Spanish girls, not out of their teens, were brought before him. One had worked in a textile factory in Barcelona and they found a trade-union card in her leather jacket. The other came from Valencia and said she had no politics,' Whitaker reported after accompanying Major Mohamed El Mizian, the senior Moroccan officer in Franco's army. 'After questioning them for military information, El Mizian had them taken into a small schoolhouse where some forty Moorish soldiers were resting. As they reached the doorway an ululating cry rose from the Moors within. I stood horrified in helpless anger. El Mizian smirked when I remonstrated with him. "Oh, they'll not live more than four hours," he said.' The 'prize' of Spanish women had been promised to the Moroccan mercenaries, Whitaker said, and officers in Franco's army knew it was official policy, though some occasionally argued that this was wrong.[15]

Queipo de Llano had already insisted that Red women deserved rape. 'Haven't they been playing at free love? Well, now they are going to find out what real men are like, rather than castrated militiamen. They won't be able to prevent it, however hard they struggle and kick.'[16]

The need to 'pacify' was one way of justifying Franco's decision, at the end of March 1937, to turn his attention away from Madrid in order to squeeze the large bubble of Republican territory in northern Spain. There were also obvious strategic reasons for closing down what was effectively the war's second front. After Franco informed him of the plan, Cantalupo succinctly summarised Franco's approach. 'This is absolutely how he prefers it: successive operations of limited reach but destined to achieve rapid and simple victories in order to produce frequent, morale-boosting results,' he said.[17]

The Condor Legion was especially active as, from 31 March onwards, the campaign in the north began with an attack on the Basque country in an attempt to besiege Bilbao. With the novel help of observer aircraft and mobile command stations, the Germans demoralised Republican defenders through bombing and strafing, though ground troops often failed to follow up. 'What can one do?' Wolfram van Richthofen, cousin to the famous World War One air ace and operational commander of the Condor Legion, wrote in his diary on 23 April. 'One cannot lead infantry which is not willing to attack weakly held positions.'[18]

German frustration helps explain the destruction three days later of Guernica, a town 10km from the front and considered the spiritual heart of the Basque country. Parliaments of various kinds had gathered under an ancient oak tree here since the fourteenth century and on 7 October 1936, after a semi-autonomous Basque Republican government was formed, regional premier José Antonio Aguirre had been sworn in under the same tree.[19]

On 26 April 1937 the town was packed with retreating troops and locals attending the weekly market. Richthofen had already been experimenting with tactics that needed little or no ground intervention, carrying out a first mass bombing of civilians at Durango on 31 March. Fighter planes there strafed survivors as some 250 people were killed, with 14 nuns and a priest dying alongside much of the congregation in one bombed church. On 26 April it repeated the operation more relentlessly at Guernica, adding incendiary bombs. Wave after wave of Heinkel 111s and Junker 52s bombed and strafed, provoking a firestorm that raged through the old town. Several hundred people died and, unlike in Durango, foreign journalists were soon there to witness the devastation. As he drove towards Guernica, the *Times*'s George Steer saw the flames from ten miles away. 'When I visited the town the whole of it was a horrible sight, flaming from end to end,' he wrote in a memorable dispatch. 'Throughout the night houses were falling until the streets became long heaps of red impenetrable debris.'[20]

Guernica became a scandal. Franco claimed his 'noble and heroic air force' would never commit such an 'atrocity' and that the town had been torched by its defenders. When quizzed about it in an interview published by the *Liverpool Daily Post* six weeks later, Franco repeated the lie: 'The Reds ... destroyed Guernica as an act of propaganda,' he said. In fact, it was a propaganda disaster for Franco. It inspired Picasso's famous *Guernica* painting, which became the centrepiece of the Republic pavilion at the Paris World Fair that summer. British foreign secretary Anthony Eden later identified Guernica as 'the first blitz' and fretted presciently that 'if that kind of thing is repeated and intensified on a larger scale, it is going to mean a terrible future for Europe.'[21]

If Franco was unmoved by Guernica, his legendary cold nature showed again six weeks later after an aircraft carrying General Mola crashed into a hillside. No-one survived. Mola's body was instantly recognisable by the general's sash around his waist. There was consternation and discussion over who should inform Franco. In the end, the task was given to Admiral Juan Cervera. The admiral entered Franco's office with a long face, announcing that he brought bad news. When told, however, about Mola's death, he seemed almost relieved. 'I thought you were going to tell me that the *Canarias* had gone down,' he said, referring to his navy's most potent heavy cruiser.

The German ambassador Faupel thought Franco probably also felt some relief: 'He told me recently: "Mola was a stubborn fellow, and when I gave him directives which differed from his own proposals he often asked me: 'Don't you trust my leadership anymore?' " '[22]

From then on, though, Franco stopped flying almost completely, travelling by road whenever possible.[23]

As Franco deliberately slowed the war, he also gave Republicans time to reorganise and transform their hotchpotch of militia and other units into a proper army. Italians and Germans had long feared that this would allow them to launch a counter-attack that could catch Franco unprepared. As Franco concentrated on the second front in the north, a surprise attack duly took place just 25 km west of Madrid, forcing his men back for the first time.

On the night of 5 July 1937 thousands of Republican soldiers descended from the wooded Sierra de Guadarrama above a plain dotted by small towns and villages occupied by Franco's forces, including Brunete and Villanueva de la Cañada. They marched in silence across the plain, surrounding the towns which they attacked as morning broke. Some were captured immediately, while others were besieged. Over the next few days, these were also captured and the Republicans began fighting their way up the eastern side of the Guadarrama valley, hoping to reach Boadilla and catch the Francoist army besieging Madrid from the rear.

Writers from across the world who were sympathetic to the Republic cause had gathered in Madrid for the Second International Writers' Congress for the Defence of Culture, organised by the Alliance of Anti-Fascist Intellectuals. Future and past Nobel prize-winners, including the Chilean Pablo Neruda and Spaniard Jacinto Benavente, were amongst the 100 or more delegates gathered in Madrid on July 6 when three helmeted men marched on to the stage, bearing a Francoist banner captured that morning, and declared to loud applause that the town of Brunete was now in Republican hands.[24]

Franco had been caught unawares. The Republicans had amassed 70,000 troops and unified their forces into a single command structure. A struggle to tame rebellious anarchists and Trotskyists had been won after a bloody internal encounter on the streets of Barcelona in May that inspired George Orwell, who took part, to write *Homage to Catalonia*. 'The Army of Madrid is the best; if we can't achieve success with such elements, then we can't achieve it anywhere,' President Manuel Azaña wrote in his diary.[25]

Franco had been about to set off for the northern front in his staff car from the Palacio de la Isla in Burgos when an aide rushed out to tell him the news. He cancelled the trip, got out of his car and returned to his headquarters.[26]

Franco was galvanised, ordering an immediate halt to an attack on Santander in the north and sending all aircraft, artillery and reserve units south to Brunete. As one of his generals noted at the time, the advance threatened his personal authority which 'depends on his [military] prestige'. Franco was at the battlefield himself by 8 July. 'The Madrid situation requires our full attention,' he wrote in a cable. 'It is indispensable that all our aviation acts on this front and that other projects are postponed.' He then made daily trips to the front, visiting generals and discussing battle plans.[27]

Condor commander General Hugo Sperrle – whom Hitler later promoted to field marshal – moved his entire legion of eight squadrons and anti-flak batteries to Brunete and took command of all air units. The skies over Brunete hosted the greatest air battle the world had ever seen with up to a hundred bombers and fighters in the air together, bombing, strafing and fighting duels. The newly arrived, speedy German Messerschmitt 109 proved superior to the Soviet aircraft that had triumphed at Madrid and Guadalajara. That helped stabilise the new lines by 12 July, while Franco readied his counter-attack.

Before dawn on 18 July, the Brunete battlefield awoke to a thunderous artillery barrage. It was the first anniversary of the insurrection and the day Franco chose to counter-attack. By now, his Axis-led air force had established dominance and he could also bombard Republican positions from the air almost at will. The resulting cacophony was heard in Madrid. Slowly the Republicans were driven back until, on 24 July, panic broke out. Harro Harder – a Condor Legion pilot who painted two large swastikas on his Heinkel-51 – picked out targets amongst the mass of disorganised units, vehicles and individuals below him. 'They ran from their positions in mindless flight,' he wrote in his diary. Above them, teams of Condor Legion aircraft set up strafing carousels, bobbing up and down in turn to machine-gun those out in the open. Harder boasted of killing one hundred men hiding in a single trench.[28]

Franco's men recovered what remained of Brunete but stopped before reaching Villanueva de la Cañada. This felt like victory and that evening his emboldened generals, thinking they had momentum on their side, gloated over the impending conquest of Madrid. Franco was not interested. He wanted to finish the conquest of the north. 'Stop the advance,' he told them. 'Remember that I am in charge.'[29]

The Republican offensive nevertheless showed that Franco's enemy was now more formidable. 'No, I didn't imagine that the war would last so long, nor do I know how much longer it will go on,' he wrote in an article published in a Belgian newspaper a few weeks later in August. In fact, Franco's reaction at Brunete set a pattern which continually slowed the war down. To the bewilderment of advisors and allies, he almost always replied to attacks by calling up reserves or diverting forces from elsewhere and trying to claw back all the territory lost – even when a tactical withdrawal might have been wiser. It happened again in August 1937 when the Republic attacked near Zaragoza, capturing towns like Belchite and Quinto, and then again when his enemy momentarily captured Teruel in December. On both occasions he regained some or all of the lost territory, though many men froze to death as they were obstinately pushed across the snow-covered battlefield at Teruel.[30]

Typically, this approach produced anguish in Mussolini and frustration from the Germans, who thought Franco stubborn and slow. In the end, his approach worked. At Zaragoza, Franco no longer felt the need to stop operations against the now shrunken northern zone of the Republic, which he conquered definitively with the capture of Bilbao, Santander and Gijón between July and October.[31]

By the end of 1937, he clearly held the advantage. He saw no military reason for speeding operations up. For political reasons, meanwhile, it suited him to go slow. That way he could establish his dominance over both friend and, above all, his conquered foe. People on both sides, and outside Spain, still wanted to know what he planned to do with such absolute power.

This was also haunting Franco. 'First I must be certain that I can found a new regime,' he had told Cantalupo before the ambassador was replaced in April 1937. Unification of the Carlists and Falangists had been a first step. It had been accompanied by promises of a 'New State' and totalitarianism. That meant either fascism or something like it.[32]

26

A New Regime

SALAMANCA, JANUARY 1938

The cramped and rudimentary administration that the generalísimo had set up to run his emerging state from buildings like the bishop's palace in Salamanca operated, according to Serrano Suñer, like a military encampment. While he concentrated on the war, Franco relied on an informal network of his family, fellow generals, military courts, his nascent mass party and the church to keep order and administer the territories he controlled. Between them they were sufficient to repress an enemy, ensure obedience, enforce unity and create the mystical halo of Franco as the saviour of Spain. They were not, however, enough to run a country efficiently. Finally, in January 1938, Serrano Suñer pushed Franco into forming a proper government by creating ministries and appointing ministers.[1]

This centralised power even further, and marked the end of Queipo de Llano's Sevilla-based fiefdom. 'Queipo was the most difficult to bring into line,' Franco complained later. It also meant the end of his brother Nicolás's period at the centre of his administration. Franco had wanted to make him a minister, but Serrano Suñer pointed out that having both a brother-in-law and a brother in the government would make it look too nepotistic. The industrious but erratic bon vivant now left for friendly Portugal as ambassador to Lisbon. There he became what one observer called 'a businessman ambassador', meaning that he used his position and influence to help others, taking commissions or shares in their companies. 'He set up a system where he could get rich by lending his name and support to people who offered him a share in what they were doing,' according to a biographer, Ramón Garriga. Indeed, in a regime that would soon be marked by corruption, cronyism and black-marketeering, Nicolás Franco was in the vanguard. 'He knew that he occupied a highly privileged position which meant he could do whatever he wanted without worrying about the consequences.'[2]

One British diplomat noted that a ministers' task in the new government was, first and foremost, to do as they were told. In fact, the new government was mainly put together by Serrano Suñer, who placed himself at its heart as Interior Minister, with responsibility for press and propaganda (later in the year, he added the Public Order Ministry to his portfolio). It was he, rather than Franco, who would be telling ministers what to do. The Italians were delighted, seeing fusty conservative generals and monarchists swept aside. With the Mussolini-admiring Serrano Suñer running civilian affairs, they imagined Franco would fully embrace fascism – a movement always excited and obsessed by its own forward-looking vitality.

Although fascism and socialism were now violently opposed, their origin stories overlapped. After all, Benito Mussolini had started out as a socialist while Adolf Hitler's Nazis were, in translation, 'National Socialists'. In much the same way, Spanish fascists owed part of their ideology to ideas originally developed on the radical left. That was reflected by the word 'syndicalist' (meaning a union of workers) in the single party's long-winded name. Indeed, the term was shared with one of its arch enemies – the anarchists of Spain's hugely popular Anarcho-Syndicalist movement. The anarchists were now part of the 'Red' enemy, but that did not stop the Falange from thinking of itself as a movement that also incorporated workers. In short, Spanish fascism labelled itself as 'national syndicalism' and Francoist Spain looked due to be organised according to its tenets – including some designed to combat capitalist overreach, which was sometimes explicitly associated with international financiers of Jewish origin.[3]

It was also to be strictly Roman Catholic and would repeal the Republic's 'secular legislation' – meaning lay schools, civil marriages, divorce, contraception and the nascent women's rights that had appeared over the previous years.

Franco's Labour Charter, written in March 1938, was his first major piece of legislation and, since it was inspired by its Italian equivalent, confirmed the fascist model. The charter showed that Franco's New State would be paternalistic, controlling and interventionist. Although it was largely a declaration of principles, the charter promised a minimum salary, guaranteed holidays, Sunday as a rest day and a future social security system for pensions or incapacity. It also banned strikes and created a so-called Vertical Union. This would be run by the party and represent entire industrial or service sectors, bringing together workers and business owners or managers – who were meant to be united, in a way far more marked than in Italian fascism, in their ambition to make their company a success and a contributor to Spain's economy. Its defining principles were 'unity, totalism and hierarchy'. That vertical hierarchy, modelled on the military, meant obedience and respect for the power of bosses and owners. This, Falangists claimed, was a way to eradicate class warfare and incorporate workers into the movement. It was also, of course, an instrument to control them. The bureaucracy of much of this was to be staffed by the single party, with newspaper editors instructed to inform their readers that 'the civilian life of Spain must run through the hands of the Falange.'[4]

A Press Law on 22 April 1938 formalised censorship and the obligation of newspapers to publish state propaganda – effectively turning newspapers and radio stations into government mouthpieces that constantly praised Franco, with the regime's different factions adding their own mark to the media they controlled. The law gave the interior minister power to appoint and sack newspaper editors and created a register of journalists. In Serrano Suñer's words, it was no longer permissible to 'argue about the Fatherland'. The 'National Revolution', he added, was just starting.[5]

By 18 July 1938, on the second anniversary of the insurrection, Franco was experimenting with openly describing himself as a 'fascist'. In notes for a speech that day, he wrote of 'Fascist Spain, with its missionary character [and] leadership by Caudillo'.[6] Only when Spain had swapped the leadership of true caudillos for parliaments and democracy had foreign ideas provoked its loss of glory. In other words, Franco was offering himself up as a new Philip II or Charles V – the mighty emperors of the sixteenth century.

But in the final version of his speech, the word 'fascist' disappeared - perhaps because it sounded too Italian and, hence, foreign. Given Franco's ardent nationalism, he preferred to explain himself in strictly Spanish terms. He also warned that he would not tolerate dispute. 'We must educate people and separate our youth from degenerate liberals ... we must deal harshly with youthful deviation,' he said. 'The spirit of criticism and having reservations is a liberal thing that has no place in our movement ... its character is military and monastic – to the discipline and patriotism of the former we must add the faith and fervour of religion.'[7]

That fervour was already being imposed through the purging of schoolteachers, whose numbers had increased dramatically under the Republic. In Burgos, for example, a quarter of teachers had been replaced. Some 15,000 teachers would eventually be punished, with 6,000 purged completely. A third of university professors were also sacked, executed or forced into exile. 'We must destroy this spawn of Red schools which the so-called republic installed to teach slaves to revolt. It is sufficient for the masses to know just enough reading to understand orders' said an unnamed count and major in Franco's army with whom American journalist Hubert Renfro Knickerbocker had spent time. 'We must restore the authority of the church. Slaves need it to teach them to behave.'[8]

Franco's new education officials were more enlightened than that, but by 1938 there was already a new course with textbooks that placed Catholicism at the core of Spanish identity and which sought 'to place greater value on the Spanish nature and to eradicate anti-Spanish, foreign-induced pessimism'.[9]

In practical terms, schooling soon began to reflect the military, religious and nationalist ethos of the new regime. Primary school was full of 'martial hymns, flags, physical punishments, national celebrations, uniforms and prayers', according to the memoir of a boy born into Francoism, Juan Miguel Batalloso, who sat in classrooms alongside 40 silent under-tens wearing grey gowns. Children marched into class in the mornings and were subjected to 'a large range of physical and psychological punishments', which included kneeling with arms outstretched, with books in each hand. 'Everything seemed to consist of daily repetitions of parts of the catechism and the *Sacred History* [a book of Bible stories], as well as endless exercises in arithmetic and handwriting,' Batalloso wrote. Teachers had to swear allegiance to the regime and the principles of the Movement, while young men who had served as volunteer officers in Franco's army were given preference when it came to entering the teaching profession. Not all teachers were sadists, of course, but the things they could teach were heavily prescribed by the demands of the church and of a state that demanded obedience and conformity.[10]

Children were also taught about Franco himself, whose life was sometimes told as if he had been predestined for sainthood, even with parts borrowed from the Jesus story. In one such book, the Virgin Mary appears to his mother Pilar, announcing the birth of a child 'with the heart of a Caesar and the wisdom of a sage'. Little Francisco, in this version, grows up knowing that the Virgin would one day give him an imperial sword and a white horse like those of St James in order to fight 'bad men from foreign lands who do not want us to pray'.[11]

The militant Catholic turn was reflected in both Franco's household and his decrees. In May 1938 he allowed the return of the Jesuit order, which had been expelled from Spain (for the third time in three centuries) in 1932, gifting it a legal standing that even the monarchy had not granted. 'The influence of the Catholic Church in Nationalist Spain has greatly increased in the last few months,' the German ambassador reported, putting this down to Franco's wife Carmen and the deeply religious Serrano Suñer.[12]

The Germans fretted about Vatican influence, but the Pope did not in fact share the unbridled enthusiasm of Spanish bishops for Franco's regime. The Vatican sought instead to broker peace between the warring sides while protesting against random bombing of civilian targets and mistreatment of the Basque church. It also mistrusted the Falange, which seemed too similar to the contemptuous Nazis. To Franco's immense frustration, the Vatican did not formally recognise his regime or allow him to send an ambassador until mid-1938.[13]

As the war slowly progressed towards victory, Franco's already considerable self-regard grew further. In October 1938, having promoted himself to Captain General of each branch of the armed forces – including the navy, in a return to family tradition – a ceremony in Burgos to mark the second anniversary of his elevation to the category of Generalísimo burnished the cult of personality. Franco spoke grandiosely of 'my people', 'my Movement' and 'my armies', asking Holy guidance as he sought 'to lead the Fatherland to the peak of power'.[14] The Bishop of Burgos thanked him for rescuing Spain from 'evil madness'.

With no-one to rein him in, Franco became increasingly enamoured of his own voice. He was already known for his irritating conversational habit of telling endless military anecdotes and opining on subjects about which he knew little. Now there was no-one to stop him, not even his ministers. 'Apart from being very talkative, he is a man for whom time has no limits,' complained Rodezno. Mostly, however, this meant expounding about battles and the operations that were under way, about which he was often indiscreet.

'This man has an enormous store of useless information,' added education minister Pedro Sainz Rodríguez. The latter's mordant sense of humour saw him sacked in April 1939, partly for making jokes at the expense of Serrano Suñer. He had also laughed at Franco's outlandish claim that the Dominican Republic, where Columbus had founded the first Spanish colony, was seeking to rejoin Spain. Franco was not amused. He accused Sainz Rodríguez of being a Freemason – in his mind, the worst possible accusation - and claimed to have shown generosity by not shooting him.[15]

To be accused of Freemasonry was civil death. Indeed, Franco's obsession grew unabated. In January 1937 he had ordered the War Ministry to expel any officers and non-commissioned officers who were Freemasons. Franco's own personal secretariat drew up secret reports, at one stage claiming at least one thousand Masons had infiltrated his administration and planned to destroy it from within. This was wildly fantastical, but a sign that acolytes were happy to feed Franco's obsession, creating a ballooning and self-fulfilling cycle of accusation and apparent 'evidence'.

This inquisitorial mindset saw Freemasons also targeted by two new laws that indicated, more broadly, how vengeance played a prominent part in the emerging, *sui generis* ideology of Francoism. The first of these, the Law of Political Responsibilities, came into effect in February 1939. The law reached back in time, punishing Franco's opponents for actions since 1934 that were legal at the time. The retroactive law was so sweeping, indeed, as to engulf almost anyone who had participated in left-wing, regionalist or separatist politics during and after the election campaign of February 1936.[16]

As if to prove that this was a political court, the special tribunals set up to try people under the law were made up of army officers, judges and officials from the 'single party'. The tribunals investigated 400,000 people, seeking reports from mayors, local police, the Falange and local priests. They punished some 200,000 people by requisitioning goods, purging them from their professions or sending them into internal exile. One in eighty adults were affected, and perhaps one in forty households. Many Republican families were, in effect, ruined and the dispossessed now formed part of the story of almost every town and village. Usefully, they served as a warning to others.[17]

This was not enough for Franco, however, as regards Freemasonry. In March 1940 he issued a decree for the 'repression of Freemasonry and communism' in which the two were treated exactly the same. Continued membership of either kind of organisation meant prison. Former members had to issue a formal retraction, but still risked being banned for life from public and some private jobs. Once again, the army and the Falange staffed the tribunals, though Franco's government had the final word on whether some people had redeemed themselves by serving their right-wing insurrection.[18]

The idea of a thorough purge was fully installed in Franco's mind by November 1938. By this stage, his battlefield advances meant he held many Republican prisoners and could cleanse captured lands of 'red' supporters. 'We have more than 2 million persons card-indexed with proofs of their crimes, names and witnesses,' he told the American UPI agency in November 1938. Spain's adult population was around 20 million people.[19] If half of these were 'reds', then Franco was claiming to have one in five of them on his card index. He was exaggerating, but it was a clear statement of intent. The 'reds' should expect punishment.

The culture of revenge created a society of suspicion and vigilance which was widely abused. The Falange and its single party, through its control of town and village administrations, was the conduit for much of this. It had its own parallel intelligence service, the Department of Investigation and Information Service, which reported to state intelligence. This found itself overwhelmed by false denunciations.

At least 130,000 Republicans were executed during the war (the other side accounted for around 50,000 behind-the-lines killings). Martial law was applied and new personnel drafted into the military juridical corps to deal with the deluge of cases that continued the system of declaring those who remained loyal to the Republic as having been involved in 'military rebellion'. Summary court martials saw the army appoint the judge, the prosecutor and the so-called lawyer for the defence – though many were officers with no legal training. In some cases the charges were not even read out. Circumstantial evidence could be enough to warrant a death sentence. 'Although there is no evidence that he took a direct part in looting, theft, arrests or murders, his beliefs make it reasonable to suppose that he did,' read one such sentence.[20]

On calling for the deaths of twenty men in Manzanares, the prosecutor stated that:

> My attitude is cruel and pitiless and it may appear as if my job is just to feed the firing squads so that their work of social cleansing can continue. But no, here all of us who have won the war participate and it is our wish to eliminate all opposition in order to impose our own order.[21]

The defence lawyer did not try to argue for their innocence. 'I can only plead for mercy. Nothing more,' he said.

Trials and shootings were just one way of repressing the defeated and defenders of the Republic. From now on, the label 'red' would pursue people whenever they applied for a job or asked for aid from the Francoist state. It was best to hide, if possible, a Republican past. Many of those who could not found themselves confined to a new underclass. The ever-vigilant Falange helped make sure of that, since it now ran town halls and other local entities, bringing the policy of revenge into people's daily lives. 'In every street there was a Falangist representative and that man reported on the good or bad behaviour of the neighbourhood,' was how one man from Valencia explained how anti-Franco opinions could be given in private. Such opinions were strongly held, with a British diplomat reporting enduring 'hatred' for the regime in the same city after it was occupied.[22,23]

A 'red' family with a father in prison was at the mercy of others, as a villager from Mijas, southern Spain, recalled:

> While he was in prison we were thrown out of our house. My mother rented it from a man who lived upstairs. One day he came

down and they started to talk, then to row. I was there, I remember it perfectly. Suddenly the man pulled a knife on my mother and – pssst! – he slashed her face. She ran screaming out of the house and my brother and I after her. She ran straight to the doctor and he had to put in twenty-six stitches, that's how big the wound was.[24]

In the lands ruled by Franco, then, it was soon apparent that there was a huge gulf between winners and losers. Reconciliation was not his way.

27

The Three Dictators

EBRO RIVER, 25 JULY, 1938

Early on the morning of 25 July 1938, Franco was woken at the Palacio de la Isla in Burgos by an urgent telephone call from Pacón. His troops had conducted a sweeping advance across Aragon and Valencia to reach Spain's Mediterranean east coast in mid-April, but now there was bad news. Despite repeated warnings about a Republican troop build-up, his forces on the right bank of the Ebro river in Catalonia had been steamrollered by a sudden counter-attack. Overnight, an estimated 30,000 Republicans had crossed the broad, swift-flowing river in boats with muffled oars, on rafts and over rickety pontoon bridges. 'The enemy has managed to overrun our defensive lines on the Ebro and seems intent on organising a vast bridgehead,' a first report read. 'That bridgehead has undoubtedly been broadly achieved.'[1]

The following morning, roads leading west from the river were full of fleeing Francoist troops and abandoned backpacks, blankets, clothes and arms. Confused peasants did not know whether to raise their arms in a fascist salute or clench their fists when the Republican forces suddenly arrived. By midday the Republicans were at the town of Corbera d'Ebre, where they were welcomed with Catalan cries of '¡Visca Catalunya! ¡Visca la República!' That evening they were finally halted within grenade-throwing distance of Gandesa, the main town of Tarragona's Terra Alta region. In two days, the Republicans had captured 800 square kilometres. Behind them stood the craggy, inhospitable Sierras of Pàndols and Cavalls. Their impenetrable gullies, rocky ridges and imposing crests were a magnificent natural defensive line.

Franco's troops had been trying to drive south along the coast to Valencia. Now they were redirected to the new front. Franco himself moved close-by as the war's bloodiest battle started. As ever, he wanted to win back the land that had just been taken away from him.

The wider political scene meant this attack came as Franco faced a level of jeopardy greater than at any moment since the early days of the insurrection. This was a direct result of his slow campaign and inability to read events in the rest of Europe, which now threatened to derail everything. In March 1938, Hitler had flexed the Third Reich's growing military muscle with the annexation, or Anschluss, of Austria. That made a new world war probable. Indeed, Franco's Republican enemies wanted this soon, since they would presumably be on the anti-fascist side of such a war with France and Britain as allies.[2]

Franco had already felt consequences from the Anschluss, since the French reacted by reopening the Spanish border to arms transfers – now clearly seeing Franco and Nazi Germany as a conjoined threat to them. Some 18,000 tons of material reached the Republic between March and June. That allowed for new Republican divisions to be formed, ready to strike back across the Ebro. After its lightning advance, this army was in a position to fight a long, protracted defensive battle designed to extend the war until, it was hoped, a wider European conflagration broke out. 'War is due in Europe by next summer at the latest,' noted Ernest Hemingway, who was a constant visitor to the Spanish war and a robust supporter of the Republic. 'It is possible that it will come now, in August [1938].'[3]

Franco, as always, accepted the invitation to battle. General Kindelán pointed out that by simply holding his defensive line and keeping the Republican army busy with attempted attacks, he could organise a quick conquest of unprotected Barcelona and ensure a rapid overall victory. That would leave him less exposed to events in Europe. Instead, Franco sent his troops to fight their way through the rugged sierras beside the Ebro. 'This is where the war ends,' he claimed.[4]

As summer temperatures rose, tens of thousands of Spaniards fought over a baked and war-blackened landscape of rocks, ravines

Francisco Franco, born on 4 December 1892, with his father, Nicolás Franco y Salgado Araújo (1855-1942) and his mother, María del Pilar Bahamonde y Pardo de Andrade (1865-1934)

Francisco, Pilar and Nicolás

Nicolás Franco Bahamonde (1891-1977), Secretary-general of the Technical Junta and Francisco Franco's older brother, October 1937

Ramón Franco Bahamonde (1896-1938), Francisco's younger brother, hydroplane squadron leader in Melilla, ca. 1923-24

Franco as a young officer in Morocco, 1916

José Millán Astray with Francisco Franco as leader and deputy leader of the Spanish Foreign Legion, 1925

Francisco Franco y Bahamonde (1892-1975) (first row, centre) and José Millán Astray (on his right) during the ceremony of giving the Honorary Sabre of the Legion to Franco, 1927

King Alfonso XIII of Spain (1886-1941) from last year of his reign, 1931

José Antonio Primo de Rivera (1903-1936), founder of the Spanish Falange

José Sanjurjo and Sacanell (1872-1936), Spanish general and coup plotter

General Franco accompanied by his officers in Tenerife, 17 June 1936

Moroccan soldiers from Spanish army regulares regiments boarding a German Junkers Ju 52 transport aircraft sent by Hitler to help Franco. The soldiers were to fly from Tetouan, Spanish-Morocco, to the Spanish mainland on 27 July 1936

Republican soldiers hiding with guns behind a barricade during the siege of the Alcazar of Toledo in the summer of 1936

Ruins of the embattled Alcazar of Toledo in the aftermath of combat

Madrid, 1936

Civilians fleeing Madrid, autumn 1936

Guernica after the bombing by German and Italian aircraft, 1937

General Francisco Franco and his wife, Carmen Polo y Martínez Valdés (1900-1988), during the Spanish Civil War

General Franco with his daughter Carmen Franco y Polo (1926-2017)

Ramón Serrano Suñer (1901-2003), Franco and Benito Mussolini (1883-1945) meet in Bordighera, 12 February 1941

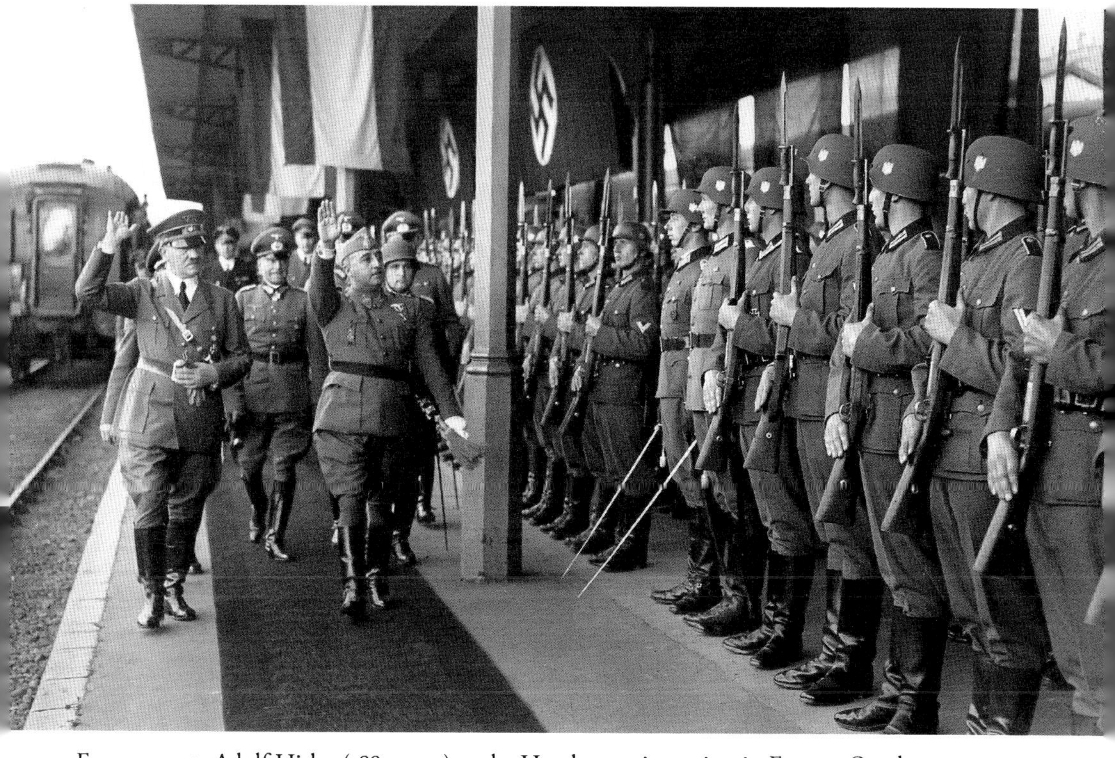

Franco meets Adolf Hitler (1889-1945) at the Hendaye train station in France, October 1942

Patriotic demonstration in Plaza de Oriente in support of Franco, against the UN's decision to withdraw the ambassadors accredited to Spain, 9 December 1946

Franco greets the United States President Dwight D. Eisenhower (1890-1961) at the Torrejón de Ardoz air base, 21 December 1959

Tourism flourishes on Spanish coasts. Playa de Benidorm, 1960

Franco poses with Movement secretary-general José Solís (2-R) and bullfighters Curro Girón (R), Curro Romero (2-L) and Santiago Martín, 'El Viti' (L), during a break in the traditional charity bullfight, at the Las Ventas bullring, in Madrid, 8 June 1961

Franco and Prince Juan Carlos, 5 June 1969

Damage in the road where Admiral-General Luis Carrero Blanco (1904-1973), prime minister of the Spanish government, was assassinated, 20 December 1973

Franco lies in state, November 1975

Adolfo Suárez and his wife Amparo cast their vote for a national referendum to approve the Political Reform Act of 1977 on 15 December 1976 in Madrid

Valle de Cuelgamuros, a Francoist monument to the Spanish Civil War and temporary resting place of Francisco Franco and José Antonio Primo de Rivera

A protester holds up a sign with people gone missing during Franco's dictatorship, March 2019

and escarpments. It was the largest and bloodiest battle of the war, as small stretches of harsh, charred terrain littered with corpses from both sides were gained and lost continually. 'Hill lost, hill retaken,' was the Republican refrain, whose spirit was mirrored on Franco's side. Progress was slow, with German and Italian observers blaming Franco's inability to coordinate infantry, artillery, tanks and air power. 'The losses on Franco's side are said to be great,' the Germans reported on 19 September. 'Violent scenes between Franco and his generals, who do not carry out attack orders correctly, are multiplying.'[5]

The cost in lives, munitions and equipment was such that Mussolini, once more, despaired. 'Write down in your journal that today, 29 August, I predict the defeat of Franco. This man either does not understand how to wage war, or does not want to,' he ordered foreign minister Ciano that day. 'The Reds are true fighters, Franco is not!'[6]

Franco, however, insisted that this was an opportunity to pummel the enemy, regardless of his own losses or how long it took. The Republic was short of troops and was now forced to draft 17-year-olds, while he boasted almost 1 million men in his army. 'They don't understand,' he said. 'I have the best of the Republican army shut into an area [along a front] of thirty-five kilometres.' He watched the battle almost daily through his binoculars, arriving at the command post early in the morning from a secret field camp near the town of Alcañiz. 'I am sure that the Republican army will be shredded, making the advance to Barcelona and the French border a stroll,' he told Pacón.[7]

His insistence on slow, attritional warfare continued to leave Franco exposed to events elsewhere in Europe. In September, this almost derailed him completely. The tension over Czechoslovakia's German-speaking Sudetenland built to breaking point. Franco fretted that Hitler might sacrifice his cause by sparking a wider war in which France and Britain immediately sided with the Republic. French troops might then descend into Catalonia and to the Ebro front, while Hitler withdrew his aircraft to fight elsewhere. Franco's slow campaign across Spain looked as though it might unravel. He worried that even his beloved Spanish Morocco might fall to France if he found himself enmeshed in a European war.[8]

Worse still, Franco was sidelined during the Czech crisis in September and October, with Germany refusing to share information. 'Franco wonders why Berlin maintains no contact with him at all. He said he knew nothing about the political and military intentions of Germany in the event of a European war or a war confined to Czechoslovakia; that, even if Nationalist Spain was not at present a great power, she was nevertheless in a position, as a friendly power, to help,' a German liaison officer reported. 'Franco seems somewhat hurt.' He even fell ill, which was unusual for a man of sometimes relentless work habits.

Franco's response was to inform the German ambassador that Spain would remain neutral if a European war broke out. Germans and Italians were furious. 'How disgraceful! Our dead in Spain must be wincing in their coffins,' Ciano wrote in his diary, while issuing instructions to study the withdrawal of Italian forces from Spain. A total of 2,794 Italians had died in Spain, along with 131 Germans. Promises that Franco would write to Hitler to explain his decision were not kept, confirming his personal aversion to imparting bad news. In a later conversation, the Condor Legion commander von Richthofen warned Franco of 'the great dissatisfaction aroused in leading circles in Germany' by his attitude. Franco answered that he had 'received no information from Germany and had been obliged to draw the conclusion that the intention was to exclude the Spanish ally completely'.[9]

In the event, the compromise signed by British prime minister Neville Chamberlain in Munich on 29 September averted war, at the price of allowing Germany to seize the Sudetenland without firing a shot. Franco wrote to Chamberlain, unctuously expressing 'sincere congratulations'. He had been saved, and knew it. Mussolini was gleeful: 'The end is approaching: the reds will give in, perhaps not immediately, but shortly, since the defeat in Prague also determines the defeat in Barcelona.'[10]

Franco, as usual, immediately asked his allies for more armaments to finish the task. On frequent visits to the front line he watched as his troops pursued a tactic of blasting small areas of Republican-held land to smithereens before sending infantry to occupy them.[11]

The tactic worked. By mid-November, the Ebro battle was over, with the Republicans pushed back across the river. More than 40,000 Spaniards had died, and the Republic had lost much of its fighting strength. In an attempt to pressure Franco into sending the Condor Legion and the Italian CTV out of Spain, the Republic had disbanded the International Brigades – a Quixotic gesture that few people noticed because 'the world was watching Prague, not the Ebro', according to the *Daily Telegraph* correspondent in Spain, Henry Buckley.[12]

Desertion from the Republican side became rampant since defeat now looked certain. This was more a question of survival than belief in Franco. Most deserters undoubtedly embraced the feelings of a Republican soldier who left a note before he was killed crossing the lines: 'I am not a fascist. I am leaving because we have lost the war. I am not stupid and don't wish to be cannon fodder,' he said.[13]

In the meantime, Italian bombers based in the Balearic Islands targeted Barcelona's civilian population, trying to break morale. It was another precursor to the Second World War. 'Terror is the most effective weapon of the air force,' an Italian general reported amid raids that killed 3,000 people. 'It should be launched against enemy populations, destroying cities, their centres and all means of life.'[14]

Franco's brother Ramón was among those flying bombing missions from Mallorca, and was killed over Valencia on 28 October. Franco received the news without showing emotion. He sent a telegram to his air force saying there was nothing tragic about 'a life joyfully sacrificed for the Fatherland', adding that 'I feel proud that the blood of my brother, Franco the pilot, is now joined with that of so many fallen aviators.' Their sister Pilar, who shared Franco's ability to conjure up conspiracies, was convinced that Freemasons had planted a bomb on his aircraft.[15]

Italian troops were to the fore again when, with fears of a French invasion now allayed, Franco drove the Republican army out of Catalonia in a campaign that ended on 10 February 1939. The Vatican had asked him to delay the offensive until after the Christmas celebrations, but Franco ignored papal entreaties and launched it on 23 December. Barcelona fell on 26 January 1939, with Franco's troops finding an eerily quiet city abandoned by its defenders. Southern France filled with refugees, including more than 200,000 disarmed Republican soldiers. Early in January, Franco sent an update to Mussolini – who was once more frustrated by his slow progress – which was so obsequious in its tone that Il Duce deemed it 'the report of a subordinate'.[16]

With victory now all but assured, Franco's allies began to demand returns on their investment. Chief amongst them was that he should join the 'Anti-Comintern Pact' that had already brought together the so-called Axis Powers of World War Two – Germany, Japan and Italy. Franco refused to commit. The German and Italian ambassadors tried to see him, but were constantly told 'the Generalísimo was extremely busy.' German ambassador Stohrer knew Franco was lying. 'The principal reason for the dilatory treatment of the question is surely Franco's aversion to giving a negative reply – even if only a temporary one – to the two representatives of the powers especially friendly to Spain,' he said.[17]

Typically, when Franco finally agreed to join the pact a few days later, he claimed to be overwhelmingly committed to it while demanding secrecy until the war's end. He did not yet want to attract the ire of Britain and France, who were on the point of recognising his regime (they did so early in March, effectively registering the death of the Republic). He was giving Hitler and Mussolini 'the egg today and the chicken tomorrow', Ciano noted after they agreed to his terms on 21 February 1939.[18]

The war, meanwhile, continued fitfully as the Republic crumbled. On 27 March Franco's men finally marched unopposed into 'evil-smelling and dirty' Madrid. 'A strange, unearthly silence met me at the gates of a great city which despite the strife around it had retained the silhouette rendered famous by Goya,' reported Luis Bolín, the man who had arranged Franco's flight to raise the Army of Africa three years earlier. 'Shabbily dressed people lined the thoroughfares and watched with bewilderment.'[19]

The anti-Comintern treaty was signed secretly by Franco's foreign minister, General Jordana, and the three ambassadors that same day. Four days later Jordana signed, in Franco's name, a German-Spanish Treaty of Friendship, in which the two countries also pledged to consult Italy on crucial matters. Pledges to 'exchange practical military experience' and that if one country 'should become involved in warlike complications with a third power, the other ... will avoid anything ... that might be disadvantageous to its treaty partner' were hardly onerous, falling short of a true military alignment. Franco seems to have missed the signing ceremonies, arguing that he was ill with flu.[20]

In fact, Germany had already extracted most of what it wanted from Franco by snapping up a large share of Spanish mining rights to help it wage so-called 'economic war' against Britain and France.

Göring called this his 'war booty'. With mines increasingly beholden to Germany, Spain became part of what one historian would call 'Hitler's shadow empire', or zone of economic domination.[21] Germany had accounted for just 10 per cent of Spanish exports prior to the war. By 1938, half of exports were going to Germany and Italy. Such dependency sat uneasily with Franco, whose fervent nationalism and hubristic belief in his expert knowledge of economics led him to imagine that Spain could be entirely self-reliant.[22]

The three dictators were finally in step, with Spain as the junior partner, or so some thought. 'We are establishing a strong system whose skeleton is the Rome-Berlin Axis and the Rome-Berlin-Tokyo triangle, a system which is being perfected by the alliance with Spain,' an elated Ciano told German diplomats. Franco encouraged such thinking, saying that his innate anti-communism meant joining the Anti-Comintern Pact had always been a certainty. The move had come 'from the heart' he told the German ambassador after overseeing a victory march through the streets of Barcelona. Typically, he then told the Portuguese ambassador something entirely different, playing the deal down as a mere sprinkling of 'rose water' that did not tie him to the Axis.[23]

Meanwhile, the Republic was collapsing. An internal coup saw supposedly 'moderate' Republicans and anarchists take power and seek a negotiated surrender. Franco refused. 'Delay in surrender and futile resistance to our advance will carry grave responsibilities, which we will exact on the grounds of blood spilled uselessly,' he announced. Republican soldiers deserted en masse and when Franco's troops advanced along the east coast on 26 March 1939, they put up little or no resistance. The ports of Alicante, Valencia and Almería filled with people desperately seeking berths on departing vessels to escape Franco's fury.[24]

The Republic died in the city of Alicante, which was the last place to fall. A handful of British steamers and fishing boats carried away the lucky last 5,146 passengers. The S.S. *Stanbrook* was so packed that it barely stayed afloat as it sailed precariously to Oran, in Algeria. Refugees crowded the port waiting for more boats that never came. On 1 April, at 2.45pm on the afternoon, Franco received a telegram telling him that Alicante, and hence Spain, were his.[25]

Shortly afterwards, Franco announced his absolute victory. 'Today, with the Red Army captive and disarmed, Nationalist troops have attained their final military objectives. The war is over.' Pope Pius XII was effusive. 'Lifting our hearts to God, we give sincere thanks to your Excellency for the desired Catholic victory in Spain,' read his message.[26]

In fact, the war was not entirely over. Guerrillas would continue to fight in country and mountain districts into the early 1950s, though without truly threatening Franco's new regime. They served as an excuse not to lift the formal state of war – giving the army a free repressive hand – until 1948. In parts of southern Andalusia, where the guerrilla problem was especially intractable, the war formally continued until 1951.[27]

Yet, if war is politics by other means then, as one historian of Spain has noted, 'terror is ... the continuation of war by other means.'[28] Many Spaniards were naturally relieved by peace. For those on the losing side, however, terror and vengeance were to become inescapable. A further 20,000 Republicans would be shot after the surrender. One side of the 'two Spains' typified by the split between Franco's own parents, had won. It would have its revenge.

28

Victory and Repression

MADRID, 19 MAY 1939

Franco had of course dreamed of receiving Spain's most prestigious medal, the Cruz Laureada de San Fernando, almost ever since he first donned a uniform. He had deserved it in Morocco, or so he thought, and was wounded by those who teased him for wanting it so badly. On 19 May 1939 he was finally able to award the medal to himself or, more accurately, permit his personally appointed government to pin it on him. 'The government, in the name of the Fatherland, decided to award the Cross of San Fernando for having saved the Fatherland,' foreign minister General Gómez Jordana intoned as grey clouds gathered over Madrid at the start of his victory parade on 19 May 1939.[1]

The medal he wore that day as he raised his arm in a fascist-style Roman salute to the 120,000 men who filed past him was secondhand. It had to be borrowed from the family of a deceased holder, since a new one had not been minted in time. Nominally, it was awarded for being 'the initiator and artifice' of the uprising against the Republic. It was not a time for recalling how he had, in fact, only properly joined the uprising at the last minute or had only become Caudillo because General Sanjurjo had been killed when his aircraft crashed in Portugal.[2]

His remarkable rise, then, had been a marriage of luck and relentless ambition. In short, Franco always pushed higher. That had driven him to the top of the army at a remarkably young age. His slipperiness over joining the insurrection reflected a determination to always be on the winning side. If the timing was wrong, he would not sacrifice himself foolishly. Even then, by his terms, it was a rare leap into the dark. With rivals like General Sanjurjo or Falange leader José Antonio Primo de Rivera fortuitously removed, this ambitious temperament had driven him to grab for ultimate power and turn it into something absolute.

After three years of war, the result was a personalist regime based on eradication of opposition and his belief that this was God's work. The diverse factions supporting the insurrection had lost autonomy. He had used the war years, and war powers, to impose discipline and obedience. All were now Francoists. Falangists, Carlists, monarchists and Catholic conservatives could squabble over their share of power, but these were scraps beside his own. Indeed, the extent of that power was on full display in Madrid's Castellana boulevard on that damp day in May 1939.

Those looking for clues about where Franco would take his country had only to look at the flags raised alongside those of Spain on his dais. The emblems of Nazi Germany, fascist Italy and the corporatist dictatorship in Portugal all hung limply in the drizzle. The march past was led by Mussolini's black-shirted Arditi – specially trained in hand-to-hand combat – holding their daggers upright, followed by an Italian motorcycle unit with feathers fixed to their helmets. The German Condor Legion trundled past in trucks towards the end of the five-hour parade. Despite the weather, people were expected to sit through the whole thing. 'Shortly after midday, with the arrival of motorised columns and artillery, the rain came down in earnest,' the *Times* reported. 'Spectators who hurriedly left the tribunes were sternly warned to return to their posts, where they remained, like the Generalísimo and his retinue of generals, in drenching rain for about an hour.'[3]

That night, in a radio speech, Franco uttered dark warnings about 'foreign agents' determined to undermine his victory. 'I cannot hide on this day the perils that still threaten us,' he said before denouncing 'the Jewish spirit that brought the alliance between rich capital and Marxism, which had so much to do with the anti-Spanish revolution [meaning the elected Popular Front government]'. American newspapers saw all this as a repeat of 'the Nazi-Fascist cry against the European "peace front" being built by Great Britain and France' as Europe marched ever closer to the Second World War.[4]

The following day, Franco handed over his sword to Cardinal Gomá, now primate of Spain, at a ceremony in Madrid's aristocratic Santa Barbara church as a symbol of crusading conquest. The cardinal blessed it, placed it on the altar and later ordered it displayed at his cathedral in Toledo. Franco himself already saw the war in the religious terms of a nation redeemed by the blood on its battlefields.[5] The war was the necessary price paid for Spain's earlier fall into sin, much like Jesus Christ's Passion, or suffering on the cross. Franco's victory was the resurrection. Spain, in other words, had been purified by violence.[6]

The medieval pomp of the church ceremony was even more elaborate than the previous day's parade, which had tried to imitate King Alfonso VI's entry into Toledo after taking it from 'the Moors' in 1085. Battle standards from historic victories were on display. 'Lord God, in whose hands is right and all power, lend me your assistance to lead these people to the full glory of empire, for thy glory and that of the Church,' Franco intoned, making empire now not just a national goal but a Christian one.[7]

Later in the day, Franco travelled to the ancient seat of empire, Philip II's vast El Escorial monastery and palace near Madrid, where he prayed before his tomb and that of the other sixteenth-century architect of Spanish global expansion, Carlos V. The implication was clear: Franco saw himself, and wanted Spaniards to view him, as their heir – or equal. He initially stayed at the enormous baroque former royal palace overlooking the river Manzanares from one side of the Plaza de Oriente in the centre of Madrid. Carmen wanted to live there permanently but Franco was urged by Serrano Suñer and others to be less obviously regal, partly to avoid conflict with monarchist supporters. Instead, he was loaned a country castle ten miles out of Madrid while a smaller but still grandiose royal palace, decorated with Goya tapestries, was being rehabilitated in hunting land in the city's Pardo district.[8]

This elevation of Franco to the effective status of absolute monarch aggravated a significant problem that grew continually during Franco's years in power. Sycophants gathered eagerly. Adulation only encouraged an already cold demeanour which few people could now penetrate. This was shared by his wife Carmen, now the first lady of Spain, whom he now demanded be referred to as 'the Lady'. He also insisted that the Marcha Real, Spain's wordless royal anthem, be played whenever she arrived at an official event – just like the queen consorts from before the Republic. It is not clear whether the idea came from Franco himself, or from his wife.[9]

The propaganda to raise Franco to such heights had begun during the war. 'The Press will be trained to serve the cause of truth in Spain,' the government had declared in February 1938. A press law written that year held for almost three decades and reflected the Falange view that 'newspapers and journalists will serve the state'. The level of censorship was such that newspapers had to send galleys of their pages to the censors for prior approval. Everything from news stories to advertisements and film or theatre listings were carefully scrutinised for conformity to the regime's rules. Serrano Suñer later said that the 1938 law was 'inspired by Goebbels' and one former propaganda official admitted that censorship became 'dogmatic, xenophobic and prudish'. At its most absurd, that meant not showing the knees of women tennis players or banning photographs of Rita Hayworth in *Gilda*, whose sensuous dance routines scandalised the church.[10] Bad news of all kinds was kept out of newspapers, from natural disasters and accidents to guerrilla attacks or the arrest and shooting of prominent leftists. Even rowdiness amongst bull-fighting crowds or fighting on the soccer pitch could be struck out by the censor's pen.

Under the terms of the 1938 press law, newspapers needed a license to print and their editors had to be approved by the government, while journalists had to apply to be allowed on to an official register, but only after being quizzed about their political leanings and past actions during the Republic. A whole raft of media were, in any case, in the hands of the government, the Falange or the church. Franco was explicit about how those who ignored the rules should be punished. 'Send him to jail, suspend his newspaper: let him go to ruin,' he said of one publisher.[11] Daily reports on the contents of newspapers sent from the provinces acted as a second filter to check if anything had slipped through.

At the same time, editors received constant instructions about what to print. In some cases, that meant obligatorily running news stories from state agencies. In others, it meant being told what stories to put on the front page (especially, for example, visits by Franco to their region) and even what size headlines and space to use on important stories. Editors were then instructed about what sort of comment pieces they should publish on those same stories, especially at moments when the regime was changing its narrative.

The glorification of Franco was unrelenting.[12] Foreign correspondents were censored until the end of World War II, after which their relative freedom often made them a more reliable source of news than the domestic press. Censors nevertheless banned specific editions of foreign newspapers – especially *Le Monde* – whenever they thought their reporting was damaging to the regime's reputation at home.[13]

The flood of propaganda painted Franco as the God-chosen saviour of a nation that now revered him absolutely. He could do no wrong. Censorship would make sure no-one found out if he did. Even Cardinal Gomá found himself targeted by the all-powerful censors who banned a pastoral letter he wrote in August 1939, apparently because it offended some members of the Falange.[14]

Everywhere the generalísimo went, he could expect to be met by crowds, usually organised by the Movement, shouting 'Franco! Franco! Franco!' In 1937, already, a first hagiographical biography had been published about 'the perfect soldier ... with the superior mastery of a leader' in whom 'courage and daring [were] united to brilliancy and will-power'.[15] More would follow.

The pomp and splendour of the May 1939 victory celebrations contrasted with the harsh reality of daily life in a war-broken country. While Franco was praying at the tomb of Philip II, heads of Spanish households were receiving ration cards – one for meat, one for other produce. They remained a part of daily life for the next 14 years.[16]

A long, anonymous opinion piece published over two days in May in the London *Times* by 'a correspondent lately in Spain' described the reality of life in Madrid that Spaniards could not read in their own newspapers. Much of the capital had been destroyed or damaged, the writer said, while factories remained shut because they lacked supplies. People returning to their homes had found floorboards and wainscoting torn out for firewood.

> Not a single shop is open, and the only crowds are those of the food queues. There is little traffic in the roadway, for no private cars are allowed to circulate. The only vehicles are ramshackle lorries carrying Government supplies, or unshaven soldiers lacking razor blades.

> The roadway itself, though it has well stood the strain of two years of war, is now worn into potholes, because there is no material or labour to repair them... Everything is covered with dust, and every house is devoid of windows and badly in need of a coat of paint. Here and there a house has disappeared altogether under an air raid, and its neighbours are twisted and dishevelled. Many of the houses which look quite whole from the outside are uninhabitable.[17]

It was, of course, dangerous in Spain to point out that all this was the result of an insurrection against an elected government and the subsequent three years of bloodshed. Rather than destroying Spain, according to the only permissible national narrative, Franco and his fellow army plotters had saved it.

Some places that had never seen war, or only a few days of it, were long used to the adulation Franco was now accorded by his own regime. For the previous three years, it had been quite possible to live a tranquil life in La Coruña, say, or Jerez, or Pamplona, reading only the Francoist version of the news and of the Caudillo himself. People in country areas around such cities, used to self-subsistence, had seen their quality of life change little – unless their men were called to war. Other parts of Spain were only just learning what Francoism meant. In the short-term, especially in big cities like Madrid, Barcelona and Valencia, or amongst the day-labouring peasantry of the south, it meant hunger as well as repression and the glorification of the caudillo.

While he toured Spain as the protagonist of repeated victory parades, Franco became increasingly convinced of his personal popularity, not least because the single party now had 650,000 members. In some places he was mobbed by over-enthusiastic Falangists, making Pacón worry for his safety. One evening in Zaragoza, a crowd of Falangist youths rushed at the cathedral doors just as Franco was entering. He stepped sideways and stood to attention by the honour guard's standard while the crowd pushed past him in the gloom, apparently thinking he was just part of the reception committee.[18]

Franco's usual sense of public caution abandoned him amid the euphoria of victory and the sycophancy of others. High-handedness was already obvious in his treatment of his enemies, but also occurred spontaneously when confronted by that other strange entity, foreigners. In May 1939, *Reichsmarschall* Hermann Göring had been snubbed when he sailed close to Spain and hurriedly asked for a meeting with Franco. As the man who had overseen the Condor Legion, he obviously thought it was his due. While Franco argued that his calendar was full, he almost certainly thought that, as head of state, he should not be at the beck and call of a mere reichsmarschall even if he was de facto second to Adolf Hitler in Germany.[19]

Similarly, when France had sent Marshal Philippe Pétain to Burgos late in March as its new ambassador to the regime it had just recognised, the reception was pointedly rude. Pétain was kept waiting for more than a week before he was received by the Caudillo for just 15 minutes. Petain was not impressed. 'Beside the don Quixote of his brother-in-law [the wiry and intense Serrano Suñer] the Generalísimo seems like [the small and fat] Sancho Panza,' he commented sarcastically.[20]

International relations mattered, not least because war-ravaged Spain needed aid, loans and trading partners. Franco, however, was convinced that Spain could be self-reliant, transferring his ideas of military pride and honour to the economy and Spaniards' stomachs. If the military mindset deemed it better to lose and die with honour than win without it, then it was a small step to thinking that Spaniards might risk eating less rather than bow to foreign pressure over food imports.

Spain's economic future now depended as much on who Franco supported in the forthcoming war as on its own ability to produce goods and food. A law issued on 8 August 1939 affirmed that his position was permanent and said that, with the war over, he would now exercise more 'direct and personal' control over government. 'General Franco and his brother-in-law are determined to push ahead with the fascist experiment,' the *Times* noted on 9 August. 'From whatever angle one regards the new reforms the clearest feature is the reinforcement of General Franco's powers. He is leader of the Empire, chief of the state, Commander-in-chief of the army, prime minister and Head of the Military Directorate,' it reported two days later. In Italy, Ciano noted with great satisfaction 'the distraught reaction of the French press' to these measures.[21]

The embrace with Mussolini tightened. In the first week of June 1939, Serrano Suñer sailed to Italy with Mussolini's returning divisions. He adored the Duce and felt close to his son-in-law and foreign minister, Count Gian Galeazzo Ciano. To his delight, the celebrations in Italy were almost as fabulous as those in Spain. Ciano found his visitor genuinely moved. Spain needed two to three years to recover from its Civil War, Serrano Suñer told him, but if a new world war broke out, as seemed likely, then 'Spain will stand by the Axis, guided by both sentiment and reason.'[22]

A new world war, indeed, might offer opportunities. Chief amongst them, in Franco's mind, were the chances of reclaiming Gibraltar from Britain and building a new Spanish empire by taking French Morocco from what Serrano Suñer called 'foul and dishonourable France'. Mussolini thought that a fine idea. 'Morocco entirely to Spain; Tunisia and Algeria to us,' he said. That way, the two allies would control the Strait of Gibraltar and entry into the Mediterranean Sea.[23]

When Hitler's tanks rolled into Poland on 1 September 1939, the next stage of his dream suddenly seemed possible. Hitler was a friend and ally. If he won the war, Franco's Spain would be on the right side of history. In Franco's mind, this meant it would have the opportunity to build an empire. That, to all effects, would make him an emperor.

29

The World at War

POLAND, I SEPTEMBER 1939

On 1 September 1939, on the five months' anniversary of Franco's Civil War victory, he was jolted by the news that Hitler had launched his armoured divisions across the Polish frontier. World War II had broken out and, like most other people, including Mussolini, Franco was initially stunned that Hitler had acted so boldly and apparently prematurely. 'I can't see why we should have a world war because of Danzig,' he said, referring to the German-speaking free city (now Gdansk, in Poland) that Hitler used as an excuse.[1]

Franco was still based at the Palacio de la Isla in Burgos, where he talked long into the night with Serrano Suñer about their plans for Spain and how the problems brewing across Europe would affect them. Like much of the world, Franco had been thrown by the non-aggression pact Hitler signed with Stalin nine days earlier. For him, this was a deal with the devil. His confusion deepened when Stalin also invaded Poland, taking a share of the country. The German ambassador had to explain to Franco that Soviet communism was heavily nationalistic and no longer considered global revolution a high priority. This contradicted what Franco, who had defined his uprising as an attempt to stave off an otherwise inevitable communist takeover, had long believed.[2]

Mussolini, meanwhile, had hoped that war would come only after he had fully armed his country, and initially opted to declare himself a 'non-belligerent'. This formula allowed him to support Germany without actually joining the war.[3]

Franco kept himself a step further back, declaring neutrality. He did not expect Hitler to prosper quickly, though the latter took just five weeks to quash Polish resistance. Always proud and verbose about his own military expertise, Franco soon congratulated the German ambassador on Hitler's 'brilliant military successes'. Although Pacón recalled him being surprised, Franco now claimed to have 'foreseen the swift annihilation of the Polish army' by the second day of war.[4]

Certainly, Franco fervently wanted Hitler to win, telling his ambassador that his was a 'benevolent neutrality' towards Germany and that an Allied victory threatened to derail his regime.[5]

But Franco was obviously not convinced that neutrality would always be the best policy. He moved troops to the borders of France and Gibraltar, while readying the Army of Africa to fight the French over Morocco if needed. Meanwhile, his press applauded Germany loudly, while his brother-in-law snidely told Pétain that Spain would be as 'sincerely' non-interventionist as France had been during the Civil War, referring to French arms deliveries to the Republic. As a result, Pétain boycotted the 1 October ceremonies in Burgos celebrating the anniversary of Franco's rise to head of state.[6]

On this occasion Franco wore his uniform of Captain General and his recently-acquired Cross of San Fernando for the cathedral mass and subsequent feast. Had Pétain assisted at what, from now on, became an annual act of self-homage and a public holiday as the Day of the Caudillo, he would have been subjected to what was becoming the established hyperbole about Spain's dictator. The essence of the day, *La Vanguardia* trumpeted on its front page, was: 'Unity with Franco. Unity under Franco's command. Unity towards the destiny of which Franco is the indivisible custodian before History – Franco, Generalísimo of the Armies; Franco, Head of State; Franco, supreme head of the Movement.'[7]

Franco watched Hitler with admiration as he attacked France in the spring of 1940, taking just three months to sweep French and British armies aside. By 14 June, German troops were marching through Paris. Mussolini had now joined the war by attacking France early in June. Soon Franco was telling people that the Third Reich was invincible.[8]

Mussolini wrote to Franco just before he joined the war, asking him for moral and economic support, naturally assuming that he would pay back the decisive aid received during the Civil War. Crucially,

Mussolini held out a prize which would come with the expulsion of the British from the Mediterranean. 'In the new reorganisation of the Mediterranean, Gibraltar will be returned to Spain.' The Rock of Gibraltar and the small isthmus attaching it to southern Spain had been in British hands since 1713, giving it a strategically valuable outpost overlooking the mouth of the Mediterranean Sea. To ultranationalists like Franco, such British presence on the Iberian peninsula was an insult and he was determined to recover it for Spain.

Franco therefore reacted with enthusiasm to Mussolini's proposal, giving Italian bombers permission to land and refuel in Spain if they bombed Gibraltar. On 12 June 1940, he officially shifted Spain from being neutral to non-belligerent. Since non-belligerence had no accepted meaning in international law and was exactly what Mussolini had declared in September 1939, this was seen as a step towards to a full-blown declaration of war against the Allies.[9]

In fact, Franco was still hedging his bets, though the idea that other countries would now assume he was preparing to enter the war was something to celebrate, according to an internal report. 'It will have a strongly coercive effect of fear in countries who may now feel threatened by our arms,' it stated. As if to prove the point, Spain now occupied the international city of Tangiers, nominally to maintain its neutrality but mostly to cement control over the southern side of the Strait of Gibraltar. Hitler applauded. He was also delighted to see the Francoist press enthusing about his victories.[10]

Hitler's joyful reaction was exactly what Franco sought. On 10 June 1940, as Hitler's armies swept through western Europe, he sent General Juan Vigón – one of his most talented commanders – to the Belgian fortress of Acoz bearing a fawning letter for Hitler. 'At the moment when the German armies, under your leadership, are bringing the greatest battle in history to a victorious close, I would like to express to you my admiration and enthusiasm,' he wrote. Spain and Germany shared enemies, he added, meaning that Spaniards saw Hitler's struggle 'as their own'.[11]

Both Franco's letter and Vigón's kowtowing make it clear that – with the wind now blowing firmly in Hitler's direction – Franco wished to share in the spoils. Vigón told Hitler when they finally met on 16 June 1940 that Spain would 'entrust her interests to Germany' once it had won the war, as now seemed inevitable to Franco. In fact, the real hope was to join the war just as it came to an end, reaping rewards without taking risks.¹²

To Franco's dismay, it was just as clear that Hitler did not need him. Six days after the interview with Vigón, Hitler forced the surrender of France, occupying most of it and leaving General Pétain – who had returned from his ambassadorial posting – to run the rump Vichy state in the south. Britain, some thought, would surely now sue for peace. With Hitler's prizes so large, Franco seemed irrelevant.¹³

In three separate reports delivered in August, German experts were unanimous that Franco's regime was weak, poor and incapable of fighting a war. 'We were ignored by Hitler,' Serrano Suñer said later. 'His state of euphoria released us from joining the fight, which otherwise would have happened and with great enthusiasm.'¹⁴

That sense of euphoria was shared by Franco. On 15 August he wrote to Mussolini, claiming that 'ever since the beginning of the present struggle it has been our intention to make every effort to prepare ourselves to intervene in the foreign war whenever a favourable occasion presents itself, to the extent permitted by our resources…' The shift to pro-Axis non-belligerence had carried a price, since the US and Britain responded by restricting exports to Spain, but that did not matter because Spain was looking forward to a new world order dominated by Germany. The following month he wrote to Hitler conveying 'firm faith in your imminent and final victory'.¹⁵

In September, with the situation now complicated by Britain's tenacious defence against German air attacks, he wrote to the Führer claiming to have agreed 'from the first day' with his view that 'the war will decide the future of Europe … [and] will also decide Spain's future, perhaps for centuries.' He sent Serrano Suñer to Germany as a personal envoy to start negotiations for Spain's entry into the war. His price was straightforward: he wanted Gibraltar and to found a new Spanish empire, starting with the handover of French Morocco.¹⁶

Serrano Suñer told the Germans that Franco was 'now willing to join the fight', not least because 'Spain itself also had a right to the position of a great power', according to the German record of the conversation. All Franco needed was material aid. He would be 'ready for the war' just as soon as Germany sent the heavy artillery he needed to attack Gibraltar. Hitler wrote to Franco saying that 'Spain's entry into the fight will help to show England even more emphatically the hopelessness of continuing the war.' Franco himself was now convinced that only a few minor technical details needed arranging. Otherwise, 'there is complete agreement between the Führer and ourselves', he told Serrano Suñer. Franco typically viewed his offer to Hitler as a stroke of fortune for the Axis powers, rather than the other way around. 'There are no doubts about our decision,' he said. 'Looking to the future, an alliance with Spain offers [Hitler and Mussolini] a strategically placed warrior nation.'[17]

With Franco making such promising noises, Hitler agreed to meet at Hendaye, a French border town, on 23 October 1940. Franco wrote to Hitler in advance thanking him for saying in his previous letter that he would 'recognise the Spanish claims to Morocco' so long as Germany could exploit its raw materials. In fact, the published version of Hitler's letter contains no such clearcut promise. A misunderstanding was brewing.[18]

It seemed, however, that Franco might get his empire. Serrano Suñer saw that the idea provoked in him a 'childlike wonder'.

30

My Friend Hitler

HENDAYE, 23 OCTOBER 1940

Franco was late and Hitler impatient as he stood in the autumn sunshine of south-west France shortly after 3pm on 23 October 1940. The Führer paced the platform of the railway station in the border town of Hendaye, wondering what had happened to Franco, whose official train eventually arrived ten minutes behind schedule. A smiling Franco offered a stiff-armed salute through the window before bounding down the steps from his wagon to meet, for the very first time, the man who had saved his insurrection by flying the Army of Africa to mainland Spain in 1936. Hitler, he believed, was an example of 'greatness, understanding and feeling'. He felt confident that his friend was about to help him found a new Spanish empire. That did not, however, mean it would be easy. Hitler needed persuading.[1]

The Führer was not used to being kept waiting. He had travelled here in the *Führersonderzug Amerika*, his special train and mobile headquarters with art-deco interiors and marble bathrooms, which was drawn up at the station. Inclusion of the word *Amerika* was reportedly a nod to Europe's colonisation of the Americas, which he viewed with the same awe as Franco. A German military band and honour guard were lined up on the platform, which was festooned with red-and-gold Spanish flags and Nazi swastikas. As he waited on the platform, Hitler muttered to foreign minister Von Ribbentrop about not making any concrete promises to Franco that might upset his important allies in Vichy France, since 'with these talkative Latins the French are sure to hear about it'.[2]

Franco's train, borrowed from the public works ministry, was a groaning, jolting, battered machine that rattled its way painfully over the shoddy, wider-gauge Spanish tracks that ended in Hendaye. The generalísimo was irritated by the delay, not least because they had only travelled from the Basque port town of Pasajes, just 20 kilometres away. Arriving late was not, Suñer admitted, 'the proper way to approach such a delicate and important interview … [and risk] irritating or putting in a bad mood the powerful man who awaited us'.[3] Suñer's comment referred to rumors about a one-hour delay, though it could also be applied to the ten-minute wait imposed on the Führer.

The two men nevertheless were genuinely pleased to meet. Once inside Hitler's train, they sat down to talk at the six-person table in his wood-lined salon. Their foreign ministers, Von Ribbentrop and Serrano Suñer (who Franco had appointed to this new role a week earlier) accompanied them, along with two interpreters. A further ten or so coaches housed Hitler's officials, their dining cars and bathrooms and his personal guard of SS soldiers.[4]

Both men had high, if differing, expectations for the meeting which had some almost comically odd elements. The German interpreter was a former export salesman who, according to Suñer, 'failed to understand more than half of what was said'. Hitler was both dramatically laudatory about Franco's performance in the Civil War and boastful of his own accomplishments. 'I am the master of Europe and as I have 200 divisions at my orders, people are left with no other option but to obey me,' he said. Only bad British weather, he claimed, had stopped him from invading England. In the meantime, his U-boats and Blitz bombers were inflicting such damage that victory was assured.

'We would happily be fighting alongside Germany already were it not for the economic, military and political problems that the Führer is already aware of,' Franco replied.[5] The move from neutrality to supportive non-belligerence showed how close Spain felt to Nazi Germany, he added.

The goodwill did not last. Having listened to Hitler, Franco embarked on a rambling, anecdote-laden and repetitive monologue that swung from sycophancy to expounding a long list of demands. In his quiet, high-pitched voice he insisted that he too wished to expel Britain from the Mediterranean and reclaim Gibraltar, but that his country was poor and short of basic foodstuffs and goods. He repeated a list of Spanish needs that had already annoyed German diplomats during negotiations over previous weeks. They included everything from grain and gasoline to lubricating oil and peanut seeds. He also demanded French Morocco, claiming it was part of Spain's natural zone of influence.[6]

Hitler, however, would promise only Gibraltar. Defeated France and the sympathetic Vichy regime were still more important to him than impoverished Spain. He could not award Franco French Morocco until he had beaten England, seen off the threat posed by Charles de Gaulle's exiled Free French and secured the absolute support of the Vichy leaders. The caudillo would have to wait until the war was over. First, however, they must act quickly to take Gibraltar for Spain and secure the Atlantic coast of northern Africa by establishing a German naval base in the Canary Islands – an idea that Franco did not like.[7]

The more Franco went on, the more bored Hitler seemed, barely repressing yawns. His eyes glazed over with impatience whenever Franco began expounding on military matters, incontinently blurting his opinion on how Germany should conduct its war and commenting on the battles fought so far. It was not a wise way to treat Hitler, who could be petulant about such things even with his own generals.[8]

In person, then, Franco was showing vastly reduced enthusiasm for joining a war compared to that shown by his envoy Serrano Suñer the previous month. After listening to Franco give endless excuses as to why he could not fight yet, Hitler told Von Ribbentrop to hand him a draft agreement and stood up to bring the meeting to an end. Franco could cross the platform to his own train and study it before returning for dinner.[9]

When Hitler extended a hand to say goodbye, Franco grabbed it with both of his and started making incontinent promises. 'Despite all I have said, if Germany really needs me one day I will be by its side unconditionally, with no demands,' he said.[10] Serrano Suñer noted, gratefully, that the translator missed that – since Hitler would have taken Franco's words at face value.

The first part of the meeting had not gone well. Hitler was a man of big, bold gestures and extravagant or theatrical action. Franco was cautious and mistrustful. 'We can't do anything with these people,' Hitler was overheard saying as they left (a staff member said he later commented that he would rather have his tooth pulled out than spend time with Franco again). 'It's not surprising he found the encounter painful,' observed Serrano Suñer.[11]

When he read the proposed protocol, Franco was stunned to see that it would be up to Germany to decide when Spain joined the war. 'That's intolerable,' he said, adding that the deal also failed to reward him sufficiently. 'They want us to join for nothing.' Hitler, undoubtedly, recalled that he had previously joined the Spanish Civil War for nothing more than economic deals. Franco, however, railed against not being awarded 'the basis of our empire', meaning French Morocco.[12] Ever mistrustful, he did not believe Hitler would give him this once he won the war unless it was written down in advance.

By some reports, the subsequent dinner with Hitler was an excruciating affair, made worse by the lack of a mutual language. After dinner, nevertheless, Franco returned to his own train in what one eyewitness said was a very good mood. He stood on the steps to his wagon, waving to Hitler as the train set off back to Spain with such a jolt that he was nearly hurled back onto the platform. Such was the scare that Serrano Suñer later wondered what would have happened if he had been killed – who would have decided whether Spain went to war, or not? After a few minutes, the train recrossed the bridge over the mouth of the river Bidasoa and he was back in Spain. Franco had barely moved more than 1km from the frontier. He later recalled Hitler's goodbye to him as 'glacial'.[13]

Franco now complained that the Führer had been rude and that the deal needed rewriting, staying up late in his rooms in San Sebastian to dictate changes so the decision on when Spain joined the war was mutual, rather than something Germany could dictate. Von Ribbentrop tried to steamroller the original version through early the next morning, sending a go-between to demand the signed agreement. Serrano Suñer had to wake Franco and they agreed to send back their altered version. Von Ribbentrop left Hendaye cursing Franco as an 'ungrateful coward'. The agreement would have to be painfully fine-tuned over the next two weeks, with Franco insisting it be kept secret in order not to provoke Britain into blocking urgently needed grain supplies due from Canada.[14]

The subservient press was sent an anodyne note simply stating that 'Spanish solidarity with the Axis powers had been strengthened'. The

Falange newspaper *Arriba* characteristically hailed proof that 'we are no longer victims but protagonists' thanks to 'the predestined chief whom Spain had desired for centuries'. Unlike newspapers in other countries, the Francoist press did not mention that, on the very same day, Jews in Warsaw had been given a week to move into the walled ghetto Hitler's occupying forces had built for them, or be dragged there forcibly. In fact, coverage of the meeting was tightly controlled, with newspapers instructed to use only stories written by the official regime news agencies and to avoid commentary.[15]

Ordinary Spaniards were already in no doubt about the regime's close embrace of Nazi Germany. While Hitler and Franco were talking, Gestapo chief Heinrich Himmler was ending a three-day tour of the country in Barcelona. His bespectacled face adorned the front pages of newspapers. Madrid had been bedecked with swastikas and Himmler had even been cheered by the crowd at a bullfight. But he was shocked by the scale of Franco's post-war repression, seeing a short-sighted attack on the working class. That repression was, at this stage, one of the most brutal seen in post-World War I Europe. Yet in some cases, the regime was receiving pressure to be even stricter, as when the families of those subjected to red terror in the town of Canal de Navarrès claimed perpetrators were being allowed home as some punishments were shortened in 1941.[16]

The cities Himmler visited were still partly in ruins and the misery of many people's lives contrasted with the grandeur of Franco's imperial dreams. An American visitor to Madrid looking for business opportunities in 1940 was shocked, especially after viewing the ruined University City campus. 'Bones and portions of skeletons lie exposed, and in one derelict building I saw the burnt remains of a "Red" now used by children as a toy—a nauseous spectacle!'[17]

At a Madrid lecture Himmler confirmed that 'all Jews from the Greater Reich' would soon be shut into 'a closed ghetto'. Those who listened to Franco's occasional radio speeches, which were faithfully reprinted in the press, were no strangers to antisemitism. Franco had started the year publicly applauding countries who 'combat and distance' themselves from the Jews, a race 'characterised by the stigma of greed and self-interest' and sensibly expelled from Spain by Queen Isabella and King Ferdinand in 1492.[18] In fact, Franco brought his three bugbears together into a single conspiracy that became known as the 'Jewish-Masonic-communist plot' against Spain. In this increasingly tangled conspiracy theory, many senior Masons were also Jews who combined the anticlericalism of Freemasonry with 'the atavistic hatred that the Jew has felt towards the true religion ever since the coming of Christ, his death and his resurrection'. He believed in the classic tropes of the Jews as child murderers – and could even recite a list of alleged killings in Spain before their expulsion in 1492 – and as 'an army of [financial] speculators'. The *Protocols of the Elders of Zion*, a fake document produced in 1905 that alleged to be a record of meetings held at a Zionist conference in 1897, remained, to Franco as to Himmler, proof of a Jewish plot to take ownership of the world's resources.[19]

Negotiations with the Axis powers ground on. Early in November, Canaris reported that Franco's fear of Britain was compounded by his pride and aversion to decision-making. 'Mutual understanding is handicapped by unwarranted hauteur,' he explained.[20] However, a revised version of the agreement was finally signed by Von Ribbentrop, Ciano and Serrano Suñer on November 11. Spain declared its 'readiness' to join at an unspecified date the Tripartite Pact which allied Germany and Italy with Japan. That pact recognised 'the leadership of Germany and Italy in the establishment of a new order in Europe'.[21] Spain expressed a similar intention to join the Pact of Steel that had sealed the German and Italian alliance just before the war in May 1939. Signees to the latter pact promised to intensify 'cooperation in the military sphere and the sphere of war economy' and cooperate in 'matters of press, the news service and propaganda'.[22]

The most difficult issues were fudged. Spain would join the war against Britain only after being given 'the military support necessary for her preparedness' and 'at a time to be set by common agreement'. In return, Franco could have Gibraltar. As for Morocco, the protocol included a convoluted promise of unspecified French lands in Africa, but required France to somehow be compensated with 'other territories of equal value in Africa'. The protocol was to be kept 'strictly secret' to avoid Allied retaliation against Spain. This was not surprising. No other non-belligerent country made such strong commitments to Hitler during World War II, though Franco saw nothing binding.[23]

In fact, another misunderstanding was brewing. Hitler saw this agreement as a firm promise to join the war. Franco did not. A week later, Serrano Suñer was summoned to Hitler's Alpine retreat in Berchtesgaden. Franco had agreed to join the war, Hitler said, and now he wanted to set the date. 'It is absolutely necessary to attack Gibraltar. I have decided,' he said. The Germans had an elaborate plan already worked out.[24]

But Hitler now discovered just how slippery Franco could be. Serrano Suñer produced a long list of excuses for not joining the war yet: Spain was hungry, he said, and needed grain shipments that only England and the US could guarantee, while Germany sent it no food. Franco was also waiting for Hitler to send 100 antiaircraft guns and three squadrons of seaplanes.[25]

As German enthusiasm for an attack grew, Franco's diminished. If Hitler delivered him an empire, Franco would follow him almost anywhere. Yet this had not been promised, and the failure to invade Britain added to his caution. When Canaris visited Franco on 7 December in an attempt to force his hand for a January attack on Gibraltar, he failed. When urged to name a date, Franco stonewalled. An exasperated Hitler postponed the operation.[26]

Franco had always found it difficult to commit himself to major new ventures. Now a young military tactician in the navy, Commander Luis Carrero Blanco, gave him strong reasons for waiting. Carrero Blanco pointed out that unless the Axis powers took control of the Suez Canal, allowing supplies to reach Spain via the Mediterranean, an attack on Gibraltar would create an internal crisis of huge magnitude since the Royal Navy could blockade its Atlantic coast. With no grain or goods from the Americas, it would depend on charity from Germany and Italy. The report not only persuaded Franco to postpone entry into the war, but also helped introduce the 36-year-old Carrero Blanco into his inner circle, where he would become a long-serving and highly influential character.[27]

In fact, Franco had growing and dramatic domestic problems that made dreams of building an empire or joining a war seem, at best, Quixotic. He was failing at the most basic task of government – to feed the people.

31
Famine

SPAIN, WINTER OF 1941-2

In Madrid people were dropping dead in the street from starvation late in 1940, diplomats reported. The situation was little better elsewhere in Spain, especially in the south, where visitors also saw people dying on the streets of Seville and Málaga. When Franco drove to Andalusia on one of his motorcade tours, the Falange was always there in large towns and cities to drum up crowds and mob him with admirers. In smaller towns and villages, however, especially in the provinces of Jaén and Málaga, reality came right up to his car window. Starving people approached and begged for food. 'Señor Franco, for God's sake, a piece of bread, we are hungry,' they said.[1]

By early September, Franco had seen estimates that grain production would fall short of what was necessary by a third, provoking widespread starvation. To make up the difference, he needed to import up to 1.6 m tonnes of cereals - some 270 shiploads. One of Franco's war slogans had been 'No home without a hearth, no Spaniards without bread.' He was failing to deliver that.[2]

'The poorer people in certain parts of Spain are even now going without bread again for days and sometimes weeks,' the German ambassador wrote on 14 November 1940. 'In several parts of Spain there is downright famine as a result of the simultaneous scarcity of oil.' By December 11, he considered the situation considerably worse. It was now entirely accurate to use the word 'famine', he insisted, as Spain careered towards 'catastrophe'.[3]

A British traveller found people living off acorns and chestnuts, stealing or eating cats and dogs, while in El Campillo, in Huelva province, they had torn at the carcass of a dead donkey. Out of desperation, people foraged for herbs and thistle stalks in the countryside around Málaga.[4] A poor boy from an Andalusian village whose Republican father was in prison, recalled the pain and despair:

> We were lucky if we ate twice a day... My brother and I would be crying with hunger and there was nothing anyone could do about it. Sometimes friends would give us something but they couldn't be handing out food every day, they needed it themselves.[5]

Hunger and unemployment, the German ambassador added, meant that 'dissatisfaction with the Government, or with the regime, is growing dangerously'. Yet three years of civil war had numbed people into apathy and given Spaniards an ability 'to perform astonishing things in enduring misery and suffering'. Wheat production in 1940-41 had fallen by a quarter from the previous year and overall farm production was at 74 per cent of its pre-war level, so the Civil War alone could not be blamed.[6]

When calculating whether to join the war, Franco had to balance this starvation against his dream of empire. A promise to deliver French Morocco might have made it worth it, but that had not been made. Britain, meanwhile, was applying carrot-and-stick diplomacy, leveraging Spain's economic woes. On 18 March 1940 it had given Franco £2 million credit to buy British goods, while cancelling another £2 million of debt. At the same time, it blocked German sea trade towards Spain. Britain exercised such tight control that Francoist officials complained it could turn on and off deliveries from countries like the US, Canada and Argentina at will. Franco's Spain was permitted stocks of up to two and a half months of gasoline, but no more. Effectively, Britain could decide whether Franco's regime fed its people, or not. He had fallen into a state of dependency on his allies' greatest enemy.[7]

This was a double bind for Franco. Obviously, he did not want Spain to be dependent on its enemies. More importantly, however, it spoiled his far bigger goal of shedding dependence on anything foreign. Autarky, or self-reliance, was his crucial economic aim. This was a logical progression of his ultra-nationalistic belief that Spain's fall from greatness had been provoked by foreign contamination. Just as Spaniards needed to shed foreign influence, so the Spanish economy must be weaned off foreign goods. It was as if all the economy needed was the same optimistic and patriotic mindset that had helped Franco win his war.

Franco had long been convinced of his expertise on economics, especially after his conversations with his wife's bank manager. The Civil War had shown him that 'economic theories that had been treated as dogmas until recently' needed changing.[8] Spain did not need other countries. It could make everything itself.

Franco was thus exultant about the news that was finally revealed to Spaniards on the front page of *La Vanguardia* and other newspapers on 8 February 1940. A factory was being built near Madrid to exploit a world-shattering scientific discovery which showed synthetic fuel could be made by mixing distilled water, fermented plants and a secret added ingredient. The 300 workers being hired for the factory would change Spain and its economy radically, producing three times more fuel than the country consumed. The magic fuel had supposedly been tested over six months in trucks that brought fresh fish from northern ports to Madrid. 'Within eight months Spain will have achieved autarky in fuel,' the newspaper reported, faithfully reproducing Franco's economic buzzword.[9]

Franco grasped eagerly at schemes that might magically turn his dubious theories into reality. The synthetic fuel scheme was one of these. It turned out, of course, to be a scam invented by a former Austrian artillery officer called Albert Filek.

Carmen Polo's brother Felipe, who worked in Franco's secretary's office and would make one of the many cronyist fortunes of the Franco period, appears to have introduced his brother-in-law to Filek. It is unclear whether he expected a cut of the new business, but Polo boasted he had already tried the fuel in his own cars. Franco constantly enthused about Filek's discovery to his finance minister, the economist José Larraz. 'It seems that he decomposes vegetable matter and then treats the product of this decomposition,' he explained. 'The key to it all is the secret ingredient.' Larraz later claimed to have had to repress his laughter when the matter was discussed at cabinet meetings.[10]

Filek had invented a perfect backstory for the Franco regime. A state news agency report marked for 'obligatory' publication revealed that Filek was 'Austrian by birth, but Spanish in his heart'. He had spent the war in some of the Republic's most infamous jails, resisting 'torments and persecution', arguing with his jailers and shouting the Francoist war cry '¡Arriba España!' every time they took away a prisoner's corpse. 'They said he was more fascist than Mussolini,' *La Vanguardia* reported approvingly.[11]

Some 200 hectares of land beside the River Jarama were requisitioned for his factory under the terms of an October 1939 decree which also gave tax cuts, reduced import duties on machinery and guaranteed profits to business projects of 'national interest'. The factory was due to be built in just ninety days. Workers' families would receive new houses complete with modern amenities like indoor bathrooms. 'All this at just 14 kilometres from Madrid, far from the coast and so with little risk of suffering an attack if war should happen,' *La Vanguardia* boasted. Soon Filek's factory would produce 3 million litres of fuel per day, meeting internal demand of 1 million litres and exporting twice as much.[12]

It took several months before Filek, a serial fraudster wanted in several countries, was exposed. American news agency reporter Charles Foltz found him in a Spanish prison camp five years later. 'He was rather proud of his hoax,' he reported. Franco, however, never stopped believing that some kind of fuel could be extracted or made in Spain. Portuguese finance minister João Pinto da Costa Leite listened in amazement a few years later as he outlined some of them. 'I prefer don Quixote in the original version,' he quipped afterwards.[13]

The caudillo also grasped eagerly at reports of Spanish mineral wealth. A month before news of the synthetic fuel revolution was revealed, Franco had announced in his New Year's radio speech, that 'Spain has vast deposits of gold ... [and] fabulous amounts of bituminous shales and lignite which can be used for distilling [oil] that can cover our consumption.' He even went in person to Extremadura to visit the site where gold had supposedly been found in mineable quantities. Both this and the oil distillation project proved commercially unviable. Grand plans for producing fertilisers and steel or to improve coal production, similarly failed – in part because, without imported machinery, the electricity infrastructure could not be upgraded.[14]

Despite these setbacks, Franco's belief in autarky was absolute. He objected not just to foreign aid and capital but also to imports. 'We have everything we need,' he had told a journalist during the Civil War. As a result, Spain would not return to pre-war levels of imports until the early 1960s, while its exports only hit pre-war levels in the second half of that decade.[15]

Autarky combined with Franco's hostility to the Allies to exact a terrible price in terms of lives lost. Estimates suggest some 200,000 people, and possibly three times as many, died of hunger or illness exacerbated by malnutrition or other post-war deficiencies between 1939 and 1942. Over the winter of 1941 to 1942, southern Spain was hit especially hard, with deaths surging 20 per cent. In the countryside around Cádiz the death rate doubled over the first three months of 1941 and Franco's government heard reports that the city was seeing forty or fifty deaths a day, instead of the usual ten.[16]

Shortages fuelled black market speculation and inflation, with basic food prices tripling from pre-war levels. Since around 90 per cent of a country labourer's income went on food, this was catastrophic. Deaths from pneumonia, typhus, diphtheria, tuberculosis and even malaria spiked as people's resilience was broken down. Epidemics and outbreaks of these diseases were silenced in the state-controlled press. The impact was so profound that the mean adult height of men in the Valencia region fell by three centimetres for those born in the fifteen years after the Civil War.[17]

Hunger drove people further into the black market, turning the consumer economy into a free-for-all in which nobody respected the rules. By 1940 almost half of all Spanish goods were being traded on the black market, with even 40 per cent of the wheat crop sold this way in 1942–3. The idea that the Falange somehow controlled civilian society and the economy for Franco in order to make it fairer seemed increasingly farcical. In Valencia, the traffic police ran much of the black market in tyres, for example, 'with their base in a bar called City, in front of the bull-ring', according to one report. In some cities, the feeling was of misery – with survival as the main aim.[18]

People flooded to join the Falange, which was seen as a safe berth from which to engage with a dog-eat-dog world. 'They find in the blue shirt and the loudest possible ostentation (with much chanting, slogans and national syndicalist saluting), security and a place for themselves,' read an internal report that Franco must have seen. Even the Nazi party's representative in Spain was damning about the state of the country. The Franco regime, he reported, had erected a façade of grandeza (grandiosity) with nothing behind it.[19]

That façade was maintained, despite the obvious evidence of widespread misery, by Franco's absolute control of the press and censorship of books and film. In fact, as changes to the education system already showed, Franco wanted to direct the way Spaniards thought about their country and, by extension, themselves. So keen was he, indeed, that as the country battled with hunger, he set about writing the outline for a film that – according to the regime's own propaganda – was meant to both change Spaniards' view of history and make the country's film industry join the drive to convert people to the Francoist worldview.

32

The Race

MADRID 1931

On 26 December 1941, newspaper editors received their daily *consignas* – the instructions over what they must and must not print in their papers. This was a routine part of the Francoist propaganda project under the 1938 press law that remained in place until 1966. The daily orders were sometimes based on handwritten instructions given by Franco himself to the head of the single party's press and propaganda department. On this day, newspaper editors were ordered to publicise and then give resoundingly positive reviews to an upcoming film called *Raza*, or *Race*.[1]

A similar set of orders were sent to the censors in Madrid and in Spain's provincial capitals. 'Censors will read reviews of *Raza* with special care, not permitting any that criticise the film in either its technical aspect or its script. For special reasons, reviews must be totally favourable and, if not, they must be removed,' they read.[2]

The 'special reasons' were not spelled out and there was no mention of why the film's scriptwriter, a previously unknown author called Jaime de Andrade (credited formally as having provided the *argumento*, or plot), deserved such special treatment. In fact, the secret screenwriter was Francisco Franco himself. He had sketched the outline for the film, in which different generations of a heroic Spanish family die while defending the nation's honour before finally triumphing under his own personal leadership. Secrets were not that easy to keep, however, in a small city like Madrid, especially amongst the even smaller circles of people involved in making cinema or censoring daily newspapers. The film's cast had previously attended a private viewing with Franco and his ministers at his Pardo palace home, so it is safe to assume that many people – especially the journalists and censors who jointly crafted the contents of newspapers – knew this was his film.[3]

The loudly enthusiastic reaction of the 'select audience' of army officers, officials and others at the first public screening in Madrid's Palacio de la Música theatre on 5 January 1942 suggests they also all knew of Franco's role. The film was constantly interrupted by clapping and, at the end, the audience 'leapt to its feet, shouting *vivas* to Spain', *La Vanguardia* reported.[4] The newspaper was obeying orders – knowing censors would rewrite anything that did not meet requirements – though the newspaper printed daily in Barcelona had become an enthusiastic mouthpiece for propaganda. Like most newspapers that did not belong to the single party or the church, it remained privately owned – but had to have a regime-approved editor, in this case the future Franco hagiographer Luis de Galinsoga. *Raza* was a 'magnificent film' that marked a 'huge leap forward' and a new era in Spanish cinema, *La Vanguardia* reported. In fact, this was the most successful first night ever for a film in Madrid, the newspaper claimed, which explained why foreign countries like Romania were buying copies.

La Vanguardia explained how the film contrasted the honourable but terrible defeats of heroic Spanish sailors at Trafalgar and in Cuba with 'the years of our glorious war of liberation from 1936 to 1939'. The civil war, which Franco preferred to call the 'war of liberation', had redeemed Spaniards and reawakened 'an exemplary race of people who, at that decisive moment, were magnificently reborn and rediscovered virtues that had lain dormant for many years'. Decades of Spanish decline, the film showed, had ended thanks to 'the invincible sword of the Caudillo'.[5]

This was an accurate description of Franco's intentions with *Raza*, in what was ultimately a romanticised rendition of his own idea of Spanish history. Just as revealing, however, was what the film said about Franco himself. The Churraca family of Ferrol is clearly a fantasy version of Franco's own family as he would have liked it to be. Instead of being naval accountants, his forebears are heroes of sea battles past. As a boy, Franco had played around a monument in Ferrol to the real Brigadier

Cosme Churruca, who died fighting alongside the French against Admiral Lord Horatio Nelson's British fleet at Trafalgar in 1805.

The paternal figure in *Raza*, who gives his life for his country in Cuba, is everything that Franco's errant and mercurial father was not – brave, loyal and noble. The saintly wife is an obvious version of Franco's cuckolded mother Pilar. The children are adaptations of his siblings, with a black sheep – like his brother Ramón – who initially backs the Republic. He eventually sees the error of his ways, thereby accepting the superior wisdom of the brother most like Franco himself – an army officer who joins the insurrection as a secret 'fifth columnist' in Madrid, survives a Republican firing squad and crosses into the Francoist zone.[6]

The young children are lectured on the heroism expected of Spaniards. 'Father, is it true ... that navy men and soldiers get dressed up before they die?' one son asks before Commander Churruca sails for Cuba. 'That's how it is. A navy man always gets dressed up for his biggest events. That's how he goes to his wedding. How could he not dress up for the most solemn day of his life, the day of his glorious death? When it is one's turn to die, one dies with all of the arrogance, all the acceptance and with all of the splendour.' In Franco's telling, heroes both know how to die and how to accept punishment. 'All navy men are good. He who commits an error is assigned a punishment, endures it and is then purified,' the father adds.[7]

Over two and a half hours, then, Spaniards were schooled in Franco's version of history, in which his own brilliant leadership ends centuries of gloom and provokes national renewal. They also, however, were given a glimpse of their own future. The film lays out the kind of conservative, religious domesticity that he thought true Spanish households should contain – with doting, pious mothers married to virtuous, virile fathers full of courageous vitality. The children are thus schooled in patriotism and religion, while learning how fortunate they are to belong to the magnificent Spanish race. Only a benign autocrat like Franco himself, they also learn, can make them – and Spain – properly great once more. It was a message that Spaniards were to hear repeatedly over the coming decades.

The film was, indeed, sold on to Romania and Germany – two Axis countries whose dictators were not just joined by Holocaust enthusiasm but by regimes that could see the wisdom of pleasing Franco this way. They clearly knew who had written the film's outline. There is no record of whether Franco thought the purchases reflected his own creative brilliance, or not.

Indeed, a cult of personality was being built around Franco himself. Instructions were frequently given for the names of officials below him to be kept out of news items, so that new measures appeared to come straight from him. Orders were given for his speeches to be reprinted on front pages, but also then glossed or commented on enthusiastically by commentators. Newspaper columnists duly likened Franco to Caesar, Napoleon, Alexander the Great, Joan of Arc, Hercules, don Quixote or Agamemnon. He was a 'genius of military science', who 'is adored and venerated by the public as their saviour', making him 'a legendary twentieth-century figure'. Even his thin, high-pitched voice became 'an iron voice' or 'bronzed and of diamond-like harmoniousness'.

While Franco's regime controlled what newspapers said and what Spaniards read, it had an even greater impact on them by deciding what they could *not* see or read. In many cases, this was the real 'news' of the day. Crimes, disturbances and trouble of all kinds were suppressed. So, in the 1940s, were ordinary train crashes. Even coverage of the accidental burning down of much of central Santander was kept to a minimum.

The trials, shootings and imprisonment of Reds were, after a while, also kept out of the newspapers – since Spaniards were meant to think that they lived in a country that was, thanks to Franco, at peace with itself. When the Nazis arrested former Republican leaders like the Catalan president Lluís Companys in occupied France and sent them back to be shot, Spaniards were not told. They were being pushed into a state of ignorance with the ultimate aim being to provoke apathetic obedience.

In country areas, many people were aware that guerilla groups known as maquis roamed nearby hillsides, visiting farms, demanding food and, occasionally, attacking soldiers or the Civil Guard. They did not know, however, that such groups existed across Spain, that they occasionally derailed trains or had shootouts with the police or assassinated Falangist officials. A farmer near Málaga recalled how a group would regularly visit their remote farmstead:

> Sometimes there were as many as nine together. They carried pistols, shotguns, sub-machine-guns and hand-grenades like those the

Guardia had. They were a lot better dressed than we were, with boots and good corduroy trousers and jackets. And they were always clean-shaven. We only managed to get our hair cut every three or four months when we got back to the village. It was we who looked like outlaws and they who looked like farmers.

They never stole anything; but they came to the farmsteads a lot to eat. They'd arrive without warning, put their rifles up against the side of the house, like the Guardia Civil, and start to chat. A couple always stayed on guard. When the farmer's wife had got the meal ready she would invite them to eat, as is the custom here. After the meal the outlaws told someone from the farm to alert the Guardia. It was for the people's own protection, because if the Guardia found out that someone had given them food he'd be put in jail and everyone was frightened of that.[8]

The Civil Guard pursued the maquis, often using a so-called Law of Evasion, or Ley de Fugas, as an excuse for shooting prisoners who were later deemed to have been trying to escape. Such acts did not make it into the press. Crime also disappeared from news pages, alongside such banal expressions of discontent as bull-fighting crowds booing bad matadors.[9] Franco had brought peace, according to the underlying message, and all forms of conflict had thus disappeared.

So, too, did news that showed some people were eating very well. In the early 1940s, coverage of banquets, receptions and society dinners were not allowed to include descriptions of lavish feasting.[10] Even the presence of Pedro Chicote, a celebrated cocktail-bar owner, was suppressed from reports on government events that he serviced. The silence, of course, extended to the existence of censorship itself – which was never commented on in the press.

Actors and intellectuals who had opposed Francoism found themselves erased from the public eye. Franco's regime, like Franco himself, did not forget its enemies. Foreign film stars who had publicly backed the Republic in the war, like Charlie Chaplin or Joan Crawford and Bette Davis, could not, initially, have their words quoted in the press.[11]

La Vanguardia was right when it suggested that *Raza* marked a new era in Spanish film-making, since this was now meant to be directed towards upholding the ideas of the Francoist state. As with newspapers, this involved censorship and obeying regime dictates with film scripts reviewed by censors.

In fact, films proved somewhat harder to control than newspapers, since fiction requires leeway, is open to interpretation and can even hide its messages. State funding, nevertheless, was most generous to those films deemed to be promoting the regime's message.[12] Few would enjoy as large a budget as *Raza*.

33

The Wrong Side of History

BORDIGHERA, ITALY, FEBRUARY 1941

Franco set off from Barcelona on an overland trip to Italy in response to an invitation from Mussolini on 11 February 1941. His convoy of sixteen vehicles crossed first into Vichy France, a place where Pacón admired the 'order and absolute tranquillity' of life in the middle of a world war. They drove north and then east along the French Riviera towards the Italian border. It was a rare trip abroad, suggesting Franco felt uncomfortable outside Spain. It was also a first encounter with a significant number of Spaniards who hated him and were free to show it.[1]

Accustomed to unceasing adulation, Franco must have been disturbed by the reaction of some people as they drove. Southern France was full of Spanish Republican army exiles. Many lived in camps, carefully policed by Vichy authorities, that Franco could see from his car window. As Franco drove past, the Republicans hurled insults. 'You could hear the shouts,' recalled Pacón. 'Everyone raised their hand with a clenched fist.' It was a reminder not just that many Spaniards detested the caudillo, but also that a good number were still gathered near the border and would be in a position to fight their way back into Spain if the Axis powers lost the war.[2]

Their convoy crossed the Italian border and drove a further twelve miles to meet Mussolini at the spectacular Mediterranean resort town of Bordighera. The encounter started well. Franco was charmed, deeming Mussolini 'the world's greatest politician' whose 'true Latin genius' and pragmatism elevated him above the 'mystical' Hitler. Mussolini's aim during their five-hour talk on 12 February was straightforward. Hitler had asked him to intercede with the 'hesitant and faithless' Franco so that the attack on Gibraltar could go ahead.[3]

It was a thankless task. Franco, as usual, did not refuse outright, but instead increased his demands. He now needed 100,000 tons of grain guaranteed every twenty days – equivalent to a 5,000-ton cargo ship almost daily. 'The Spanish people are eating bread made with the grain which comes into the country from day to day,' he explained. Once again, he demanded that Hitler agree to his 'colonial aspirations' by pledging him French Morocco.[4] The affable Mussolini did not seem upset. He could see Spain was wholly unprepared for war.

Franco's party also found the Italians fretting about their own war problems, with their invasion of Greece producing innumerable headaches. War had by now reached Italy itself: the Royal Navy had shelled Genoa while air raids targeted other cities. According to Pacón, Franco and his coterie detected a defeatist mindset that was hardly encouragement for joining the war. They drove back to Spain a few days later, stopping to meet Vichy leader Philippe Pétain along the way. Franco would never in his life leave Spanish territory or the Iberian peninsula again – his only other journeys being to neighbouring Portugal. That reflected, above all, his mistrust of anything foreign. Few heads of state have travelled so little.[5]

Once back home, Franco continued to delay and dissimulate until the whole shape of the war shifted with Germany's June invasion of Russia. Franco now felt undisguised glee. Communism was, along with liberal democracy and Freemasonry, his great enemy.[6]

The German attack, codenamed Operation Barbarossa, began early on 22 June 1941 and, before the day's end, Franco had offered to send 'a few volunteer formations of the Falange' to help. In fact, he and Serrano Suñer had seen the German attack coming and decided to raise a volunteer unit as soon as it started. This had the advantage of pleasing Hitler while avoiding formally joining the war.[7]

Within days, Franco had increased the offer to a full division of volunteers that was formed just four days after Operation Barbarossa started and began recruitment the very next day. The so-called Blue Division wore German uniforms and drew its initial 18,000 volunteers mostly from the Falange or Franco's officer corps, with leadership given to General Agustín Muñoz Grandes. Many volunteers were genuine enthusiasts. For others it was a way to recycle themselves as good Francoists. For workers of any political persuasion in starving, poverty-stricken Spain, it was a well-paid job – with money forthcoming from both the German and Spanish governments. Some 45,000 volunteers eventually joined, with one in nine dying in the snowy countryside near Leningrad or elsewhere in the Soviet Union. Newspapers were, nevertheless, banned from reporting on the oath of allegiance they all had to swear, of 'absolute obedience to the leader of the German army, Adolf Hitler'.[8]

The Blue Division served Franco both for internal propaganda and as a temporary way out of his dilemma about how to help Hitler. If all went well and Spain eventually joined the war, he could transform the Blue Division (formally a German army unit) into the shock troops of a new Spanish army. At popular rallies across Spain, Serrano Suñer often took the lead. 'Russia is to blame!' he told a rally in Madrid on 24 June. 'The extermination of Russia is a demand made by history and for the future of Europe.' Several hundred Falangists then marched to the British embassy and stoned it, with a German film crew conveniently on hand.[9]

This was soon followed by an interview in *Deutsche Allgemeine Zeitung* in which Serrano Suñer claimed that Franco's Spain had stepped deeper into the Axis camp by moving from non-belligerence to 'firm moral belligerence' in the attack on the Soviet Union. According to Franco's brother-in-law, Hitler was 'glorious', and the defeat of Russia would be the start of a great reorganisation of Europe in which a bankrupt Britain would sue for peace and the United States would have little or no say. The interview was faithfully reprinted by Franco's press, alongside slogans attacking the Soviet Union.[10]

Franco, however, again resisted German pressure to formally join the war, even just against the Soviet Union, fearing blockade by the Allies. As if to prove the point, two oil tankers due to sail for Spain were held up by the United States when news leaked that Serrano Suñer was travelling to Berlin late in November. It was a reminder that Franco's dalliance with Hitler brought immediate damage to the lives of ordinary Spaniards.[11]

These dynamics were demonstrated again when Franco donned the senior cadre uniform of red beret and white jacket of his FET y de las

JONS's single party before haranguing its National Council in Madrid on 17 July 1941. With ministers and diplomats in attendance, he was buoyant, boastful and belligerent. He publicly damned the United States, Britain and, above all, the Soviet Union. The attack on Russia was an extension of his own crusade again world communism and was bound to end in victory, he insisted. The truth about Soviet plotting against the rest of the world, he said, had long been hidden by 'the Jewish press'. His stated 'enemies' now appeared to include the Royal Navy and British convoys that were being bombed by German and Italian aircraft off Crete, Norway or in the English Channel, while the Allies 'had planned the war badly and lost it'. Falange blood was being spilled in support of the Axis Powers, he said, because 'Germany is directing the battle that Europe and Christianity had been wanting for so long.' He was cheered off stage with the now inevitable, triple cries of 'Franco! Franco! Franco!' He scolded Serrano Suñer, who was stunned that he would insult the British and American ambassadors so brazenly, for not joining in the adulation.[12]

Franco had revealed intentions that were best kept secret or vague, his brother-in-law believed, and such speeches should only be made by ministers who could be sacked if necessary. Spanish diplomats (including his brother Nicolás, now installed as ambassador in Lisbon) frantically tried to control the damage, claiming that Franco's speech had been for the internal consumption of radicals in the Falange. The damage was, however, done, with both Britain and the United States deciding to increase pressure on Franco – which mostly meant restricting food and other supplies, though Churchill also began to study seriously an attack on the Canary Islands.[13]

In fact, the speech had been written by the rising star of Franco's personal staff, navy commander Luis Carrero Blanco. He had already written a report claiming that President Roosevelt led a 'Jewish power block', in which 'democracy, Freemasonry, liberalism, plutocracy and communism' had become the key arms of international Judaism's attempt to destroy Christianity. Carrero Blanco was just one of several ferocious antisemites who stoked Franco's own prejudice and encouraged his extravagant belief in a triple conspiracy of Freemasons, Jews and communists.[14]

Such ideas were laughed at by, amongst other, Franco's father Nicolás – who was still living, now in retirement, with his girlfriend in Madrid. Don Nicolás was the only person in Spain who had full freedom to criticise the Caudillo in public. He did so with joyful abandon and colourful language. In the bars around his home in Madrid's Fuencarral street, he could be heard fulminating against the man no-one else dared to cross. His dictator son was 'inept', 'boastful' and a *'cabrón'* ('shit') who knew nothing of Freemasonry, which had attracted learned men who vastly outweighed him in intelligence and open-mindedness. He found regime descriptions of his son as a great politician and statesman 'laughable'. 'What do they think a politician is?' he asked. Police, when called and after seeing his identity documents, did not dare arrest the dictator's own father.[15]

In fact, his father had long been ill – though Franco never visited the 84-year-old. His brother Nicolás, on the other hand, flew over regularly from Lisbon. By now he had a reputation for holding up the Lisbon to Madrid flight, for which he often arrived late and crumpled after a night out. That did not stop him then entering the pilot's cabin and asking for a turn at the controls, since he also had a pilot's licence. 'Nicolás had a frivolous idea of life and did not worry himself about whether the things he was doing were good or bad,' says his biographer, Ramón Garriga.[16] Women learned to steer clear of him.

Their niece Pilar Jaraiz visited the elderly Don Nicolás and Augustina regularly, seeing someone as 'so… grumpy, that we ended up feeling great affection for him'. The dictator, however, bitterly resented the man who had abandoned his mother in Ferrol. With his loose morals, loud mouth and liberal politics, Don Nicolás continued to represent many of the things Francisco Franco hated. Don Nicolás's death in February 1942 may thus have come as a relief, though Hitler and Mussolini sent telegrams while newspapers claimed that 'the whole of Spain offers its condolences.'[17]

Franco's reaction to the death was spiteful. The body was forcibly removed from the home he had shared with Agustina Aldana for almost three decades, reportedly by a Civil Guard squad as she clung to the coffin. Don Nicolás was dressed up in his uniform and taken to Franco's own Pardo Palace on a cold and foggy night for the wake. Franco did not attend his father's burial, accompanying the funeral procession only as far as his own gates before the body was taken to be buried alongside his estranged wife in Madrid's Almudena Cemetery.

Agustina Aldana was banned from attending and Don Nicolás's name was not added to the tombstone.[18]

Franco's regime, meanwhile, seemed increasingly set to follow a fascist model. In March 1941 he had reorganised the police force with the stated aim of changing a 'depoliticised' force into an 'instrument of vigilance and repression'. That way 'the Spanish police can carry out the task of permanent and total vigilance that is indispensable for the Nation and which in totalitarian states is achieved through a combination of technical perfection and loyalty.' The FET y de las JONS single party was 'the political expression of the totalitarian state established in Spain', he declared in an August 1941 decree. This embrace of totalitarianism appeared again when he created a rubber-stamp parliament through the so-called Ley de Cortes (Law of Parliament), on 17 July 1942. 'In war, the totalitarian regime has shown its clear superiority; in the economy, it is the only way to save a nation from ruin, while in social affairs ... the working masses receive concessions and promises that totalitarians have as established norms,' he said. 'Very little of the liberal and democratic state can be saved.'[19]

Publication of the law was followed by enthusiastic glossing in newspapers which obediently echoed the official line. 'The totalitarian state is, then, an inexorable necessity,' declared the journalist and intellectual Eugenio Montes in his analysis on the front page of *La Vanguardia*, Barcelona's main daily newspaper.[20]

Open antisemitism, anti-Americanism, internal repression, praise for totalitarianism and eager support for Hitler now placed Franco as close as possible to the global fascist sphere. He had bet his future, and that of Spain, on an Axis victory followed by a world order largely dictated by Hitler. Ordinary Spaniards continued to pay for Franco's pro-Axis stance as supplies of food and goods from abroad were deliberately slowed down by the Americans and British. Reports sent to Madrid by the provincial delegations of the single party suggested that many were worried that he was about to lead them into another war, with the Bordighera visit to Mussolini increasing anxiety. However, people remained too exhausted, subdued, afraid or ignorant of what was happening to do more than bemoan their lot. In fact, their main concern remained the scarcity of jobs, of food and other goods, along with rationing and the corruption this provoked as the black market flourished.[21]

Newspaper celebrations of the key anniversaries of both Hitler and Mussolini's rise to power, praise for their regimes and reporting of their battlefield triumphs seemed to work on public opinion, according to reports from the Falange – which was itself passionately pro-Axis. The single party's imperfect polling suggested that three out of five young Spaniards saw Germany as their favourite foreign country in 1943. Almost three out of four chose Mussolini's fascism or Hitler's National Socialism as their preferred political regime, against 14 per cent who liked British or American-style democracy. The importance of such polls was not whether they reflected the truth at a time when many people were afraid to express their real and limited opinions but that the regime liked to believe them.[22]

The Allies' control of supplies was not just vengeful meanness. Spain had become a crucial blockade-busting country for Hitler, with some of his officials arguing against pulling it into the war since its role as a funnel for international supplies was more important than any direct military help it might provide. Fuel deliveries from the United States and elsewhere had to be carefully controlled to prevent them being reshipped to power the German war machine. A secret deal personally approved by Franco early in the war already meant German U-boats were using Spanish ports as refuelling and logistics bases, thereby dodging Allied vigilance while giving them greater range in the Mediterranean and off Africa. Refuelling facilities at the Canary Islands were especially valuable for patrolling the eastern Atlantic and the busy shipping lanes of west Africa, where U-boat 'wolf packs' attacked convoys. Franco also secretly allowed Germany to install nine infra-red detectors on the Spanish coastline around the Strait of Gibraltar, so that U-boats could be alerted to targets passing through. This provided a considerable threat to Allied operations in the Mediterranean from April 1942. A steady supply of Spanish wolfram, the crucial ore for the tungsten that toughened German armour (and armour-piercing shells), continued to flow north. Franco himself would justify Spain staying out of the war by arguing that supplying 'wolfram and other products is at this moment of greater value to Germany'.[23]

When Japan forced the United Sates into the war by attacking Pearl Harbour in December 1941, Franco did not change his attitude. In fact, Tokyo received formal congratulations from Madrid. The world war, meanwhile, was useful to Franco internally since it kept the army in a state of constant apprehension about whether it would have to start fighting again. 'Madrid was in its usual state of nerves,' British ambassador Samuel Hoare noted on returning from a period of home leave during the war. 'It mattered not whether the war went well or badly for us.'[24]

In fact, nerves frayed by World War II helped produce a first break-up between the pro-Franco factions, as army generals fretted that Serrano Suñer and the Falange were driving them into a war they could not fight, while Carlists worried about the Falange's support for godless Nazis. On 16 August 1942, a senior Falangist called Juan Domínguez carried hand grenades across the country to the annual service in memory of the Carlist Civil War dead at Virgin of Begoña sanctuary near Bilbao. When a crowd began chanting anti-Falange slogans, he hurled two grenades, reportedly injuring 100 people (true figures are impossible to establish, since the regime silenced the event).[25]

The hot-headed Minister of War General José Enrique Varela – who was present and may have been the bombers' target – resigned in protest and cursed Franco's lack of concern for the victims. 'I have listened to your speeches these last few days and you haven't said a single word of condolence to those poor victims, who are all working class, with many badly hurt and likely to die,' Varela scolded him after describing the bloody scene, with injured women and children.[26]

Franco, typically, did not act immediately. But within three weeks he had approved the execution of the grenade-thrower and sacked several factional leaders – including his brother-in-law Serrano Suñer. The sacking was typically cold, delivered with just a few words. By also accepting the resignation of Varela – who had led resistance by numerous generals to joining the war – Franco established a pattern of resolving disputes by sacking people on both sides.[27]

The Serrano Suñer sacking also revealed the emerging influence of someone even closer to Franco – his wife Carmen. Already, the Francoist media routinely covered her public outings with glowing reports. She was a notorious moraliser who had been scandalised by Serrano Suñer's personal behaviour: many people in Madrid knew that her brother-in-law was cheating on her sister Zita with the wife of an aristocrat in the army who had given birth to his unrecognised daughter in the week before his sacking. Even Zita, the offended party, was suddenly out of favour with her sister.

Not until late in life would Franco allow anyone else to accumulate as much power as his brother-in-law. He had needed Serrano Suñer as a political guide, but now considered himself fully qualified to judge alone what was right for Spain on all levels. Men who knew their place, like Carrero Blanco, could advise him from now on. The essence of his regime thus became even more starkly clear. It was a personal dictatorship, driven by his ideas and whims. These were soon to change as Franco realised he had made a terrible mistake. He had backed the wrong side in World War II.

34

End of Empire, Again

CASABLANCA, MOROCCO, 8 NOVEMBER 1942

Franco must have awaited with considerable nervousness the visit by US ambassador Carlton Hayes to the Pardo Palace at 9 a.m. on 8 November 1942. He already knew that a large Allied military operation was under way across Algeria and French Morocco, the territory he had demanded off Hitler. He nevertheless maintained his usual calm as Hayes handed him a letter from President Franklin Roosevelt explaining why, that morning, American troops had landed on beaches near Casablanca and elsewhere in French Morocco. Similar landings and airborne assaults were taking place in Algeria as the Allies wrested the French territories in North Africa away from the pro-German Vichy regime. That would place the German and Italian troops in north Africa in a pincer between the American forces and the British in Egypt. It would also leave Spanish Morocco surrounded by the Allies, with the nearby Canary Islands easy to invade and capture if Franco decided to join the war against them.[1]

Although Franco had almost certainly been woken earlier with the news and was rumoured to have spent time praying that Spain itself was not under attack, he showed no outward disquiet. 'These moves are in no shape, manner or form directed against the Government or people of Spain or Spanish Morocco,' Roosevelt reassured him. 'Spain has nothing to fear.' Franco was soon faced with a fait accompli, since the operation succeeded in just eight days. Yet this was a moment of deep humiliation. His dream of a new Spanish empire had been dashed and his Moroccan protectorate was now surrounded by enemies. Adding insult to injury, the operation had been directed from Gibraltar. Franco did not yet realise it, but the Allied victories in north Africa were changing the course of the war irredeemably.[2]

Preparations for the invasion, named Operation Torch, had been clearly visible to the Spaniards. The runway at Gibraltar had up to 600 aircraft crowded on to it at any one time. The target was not yet obvious, but Churchill himself fretted that all this preparation was 'in full range and in full view of the Spanish batteries'. German intelligence service agents had a clean view of the Rock, which they monitored with a powerful telescope from a Spanish villa across the Bay of Algeciras. It was just one of several German spying operations that enjoyed Franco's explicit support.[3]

General George S. Patton, who led the attack on the Atlantic beaches of French Morocco, called Operation Torch 'as desperate a venture as history has known'. German submarines often lay in wait for convoys forced to bunch up as they entered the Strait of Gibraltar. The secret U-boat refuelling facilities set up with Franco's permission in the Canary Island, Cádiz and Vigo ensured they could operate at will. Spanish surveillance from the mainland and Spanish Morocco made it difficult to sneak through unobserved. Admiral Harold Burroughs, the Royal Navy officer tasked with leading the support fleet into the Mediterranean, pronounced that he would consider this next job well done if half of his 100-vessel convoy survived.[4]

On the evening of November 5, the Abwehr agents in Algeciras spotted the blacked-out silhouettes of Burroughs' vessels passing into the Mediterranean. The following day, six B-17 Flying Fortresses landed at Gibraltar carrying Eisenhower and his staff. They installed themselves deep inside the Rock, setting up their headquarters in a secure but damp warren of tunnels.[5]

In the event, Operation Torch was a major success for the Allies, who quickly seized much of French Morocco while Franco remained inactive.[6] Three days later, as French troops there went over to the Allies, Hitler occupied Vichy France, bringing his army up to the Spanish frontier. Spain was now squeezed between two giant war machines and, in military terms, at the mercy of either. Franco mobilised troops but neither the Allies nor the Axis powers wished to become embroiled in what Churchill called 'guerrilla warfare with the morose, fierce, hungry people of the Iberian Peninsula'. In fact, the Allies did not need to go to war to tame Franco, since they already controlled his supplies of oil and other vital products. Germany, meanwhile, valued the raw materials that Spain already sent north more highly than Franco and his army. Part of the payment for these was now reaching the border railway station at Canfranc in the form of gold stolen from Jews or extracted from Jewish mouths in Holocaust death camps.[7]

Operation Torch was a fearful, humbling moment for Franco. It was also a tipping point. He could no longer be sure that the side he supported in the war was going to win. A mixture of caution, mistrust and Hitler's refusal to promise him an empire had kept him out of it until now. That now seemed fortunate or, in Franco's own terms, further evidence of his great wisdom. Franco still hated the liberal democracies and thought them doomed, but from now on played a duplicitous game. To the Allies, he said that his only real interest in the war was the defeat of communism. To Hitler, he repeated his belief in and desire for Nazi Germany's absolute victory and the founding of a new world order. Once more, he was hedging his bets.

Further setbacks followed quickly. The Blue Division fought bravely while sharing the disastrous outcome of the German campaign in Russia. The volunteer division had been a window through which Franco could peer into Hitler's dazzlingly successful army. That brilliance faded in the autumn and winter 1942 as overreach brought the destruction of German forces at Stalingrad by some of the same Russian generals who had helped Republican Spain as advisors in the Civil War. The course of the war was changing, and not in ways that Franco wanted.[8]

From now on, Franco became even more of a bit-player in the global drama of World War II as he sought to escape the hole into which he had dug himself by supporting Hitler and Mussolini. In fact, Franco spent the rest of the war in a desperate scramble to persuade the Allies that he had never been as pro-Axis as his words and actions had clearly shown.

The sacking of Serrano Suñer now seemed like a stroke of good fortune. As his hopes for fascism's victory soured, Franco could shift blame for his pro-Axis stance onto his former minister and congratulate himself on keeping his agreements with Hitler and Mussolini secret. In the meantime, the World War provided a further excuse for keeping Spain under martial law, arguing that the country was under constant threat. Censorship and propaganda meant Spaniards knew little about what was really happening, or why.

With the question of Spain's non-participation in the war seemingly settled after Operation Torch, internal tensions emerged – especially amongst army monarchists who had expected Franco to stand down at the end of the Civil War. General Kindelán, Spain's most senior active general, travelled to Madrid from his headquarters in Barcelona just three days after Operation Torch and told Franco that if he had a secret agreement to join the war on Hitler's side, he would have to be replaced. He also advised him to announce a restoration of the monarchy, with Franco as regent for the time being. (Alfonso XIII had died in 1941, leaving his son Don Juan de Borbón as designated heir). Franco, as usual, made evasive comments and bided his time before defenestrating Kindelán, who was sacked two months later. Meanwhile, he continued to sign secret deals with Germany. When Hitler held out the promise of fresh arms (something that always obsessed Franco) in February 1943, he signed an agreement obliging him to fight the Allies if they entered Spanish Morocco.[9]

For the first time, Franco found supporters abandoning him as they realised he had backed the wrong side. In June 1943, 27 senior members of Franco's rubber-stamp parliament signed a letter demanding he reestablish the monarchy. All were sacked. The following month Franco and his fellow conspiracy theorist Carrero Blanco claimed to have evidence of an international Masonic plot designed to produce a rift between the generalísimo and the army. It was further proof, they warned, that only a regime much stronger than the monarchy could withstand the multiple conspiracies against Spain. A group of normally loyal generals wrote to Franco in September, respectfully suggesting he had outstayed his time and should restore a monarchy acceptable to the Allies. His response was to announce the withdrawal of the Blue Division. This provoked complaints from the Germans, with Franco admitting that he was acting to save his own regime.[10]

Within a few months, Franco had taken down the pictures of Hitler and Mussolini that adorned his office, replacing them with the Pope and Portugal's President Oscar Carmona. Franco continued bargaining proudly with the Allies over supplies, often holding out so long that he was effectively swapping hunger for pride. British ambassador Samuel Hoare was driven mad by what he saw as Franco's 'staggering complacency' and inability to recognise when he was wrong. Franco, he noted, remained convinced 'that he had been marked out by Providence to save his country and to take a leading part in the reconstruction of a new world'.[11]

Franco's reaction was not to admit an error of judgement but to rewrite the narrative of what had happened during World War II. A set-piece interview with the American United Press International agency early in November 1944 was seen as key to this (in fact, it was not really an interview, but a set of written answers to questions agreed on with foreign ministry officials). Franco's answers were, in the words of historian Paul Preston, 'a disingenuous, not to say shamelessly mendacious, account of his policy during the previous five years'. Amongst other things, he denied any wartime collusion with the Axis powers, claiming that he could easily have invaded France as German troops marched on Paris, but chose not to. 'If the obligations concerning our alleged obligations with the Axis had been true this was the incomparable moment to have taken up arms,' he said. 'France had ceased to fight, leaving her territory easy prey.'[12]

A sign of the importance Franco gave to this interview was the flood of instructions to the Spanish press about how it should be used. They included demands that 'positive' coverage in the world press should be highlighted (though this was scarce) but also that Spanish newspapers emphasise that 'Spain is neither fascist nor Nazi, nor has it ever been.'[13]

Hopes of a possible military revolt from within the regime were dashed when several hundred armed Republicans who had fought in the French resistance crossed the Pyrenees in October 1944, hoping to spark a popular rebellion. This was doomed to failure, serving only to provoke a closing of ranks behind Franco. Hoare blamed these 'adventurers' for ruining his attempts to organise a proper opposition (in part led by generals who were receiving generous British bribes). Franco, meanwhile, still clung to the idea of either a German victory or a long fight to a mutual standstill, believing Hitler would invent a ray-gun or some other unbeatable new weaponry. The Allies eventually forced him, however, to reduce his wolfram deliveries to Germany to what Churchill called 'a few lorry-loads a month'.[14]

Franco was immensely pleased when Churchill publicly tried to keep him sweet with a 24 May 1944 House of Commons speech that irritated the more belligerent Americans. If Spain had entered the war when Hitler first wanted, Churchill pointed out, it was likely that 'the Strait of Gibraltar would have been closed and all access to Malta would have been cut off from the West. All the Spanish coast would have become the nesting place of German U-boats.' When Operation Torch happened, he added, 'Spain's power to injure us was at its very highest... However, the Spaniards continued absolutely friendly and tranquil. They asked no questions, they raised no inconveniences.'[15]

Franco used the speech, which was widely cited by the regime's press, to persuade Spaniards once more of his providential wisdom. In fact, he believed it himself. Such self-mythologising, bolstered by the adulators around him, was now part of the bedrock of his dictatorship. He wrote to Churchill claiming that 'once Germany is destroyed, England will have only one country left in Europe towards which she can turn her eyes – Spain.' Franco went on to list Spain's post-war attractions as 'a strategically situated country, sound, virile, and chivalrous, which has demonstrated her spiritual reserves and wealth of courage and vigour'.[16]

Privately, in a letter to Franco, Churchill set the record straight and gave his full opinion.

> I have not forgotten that Spain did not oppose at two critical moments of the war: the collapse of France in 1940 and during the Anglo-American invasion of North Africa in 1942. But I also recall that throughout the war German influence in Spain has been consistently allowed to hinder the war effort of Great Britain and her Allies and it is a fact that a Spanish division was sent to help our German enemies against our Russian allies...
>
> I must mention... the number of speeches in which your Excellency contemptuously referred to this country and other members of the United Nations [as the Allies saw themselves] and spoke of their defeat as desirable and unavoidable.
>
> Now that the war is coming to an end and plans are being made for the future of Europe and the world, his Majesty's Government cannot overlook the past record of the Spanish Government nor the consistently hostile activity of the Falangist Party, officially

recognised as the basis of the present political structure of Spain, nor the fact that the Falange has maintained a close relationship with the Nazi dictatorial party in Germany and with the Italian Fascists.[17]

In his post-war memoir, Churchill reaffirmed his overall opinion of Franco, stating that he was 'glad to place on record this testimony to the duplicity and ingratitude of his dealings with Hitler and Mussolini'.[18]

Franco's place in the world had been diminished, leaving him dependent on the sustenance provided to Spain by people like Churchill and Roosevelt – men who disliked him intensely. His dream of a radical shake-up of power across Europe and the rest of the world, with his regime joining Hitler's winning side at the last minute, had been thoroughly shredded. Famine, fortune and the Führer's refusal to promise him an empire had prevented him from overplaying his hand further but there was no escaping his broader error of judgement. When Berlin fell in April 1945 he was still in power, but was now utterly alone. Franco had turned Spain into a pariah state.[19]

35

Post-War Pariah

SPAIN, 8 MAY 1945

Franco presumably read the front pages of Spanish newspapers with great satisfaction on 8 May 1945, as Europe officially embraced peace. It was 'Franco's victory!', *La Vanguardia* trumpeted. The thesis was simple. Despite the strenuous efforts of both sides to tempt Franco into joining them in the war, he had held out. The death and destruction wrought across almost an entire continent over five years and eight months had passed Spain by. It was further proof of the Caudillo's providential genius. 'Once more Franco has done his duty. Once more Franco has saved Spain,' the newspaper said.[1]

This was exactly how Franco himself saw it. He had held out against German pressure. Sending the Blue Division to fight in Russia had not been a way of helping the Axis powers, but rather a demonstration of militant anti-communism. He invented his own theory of the war, which separated it into two parts. One of these wars was between Nazis and fascists on one side and the liberal democracies on the other. In that one, he claimed to have stayed resolutely neutral. The other war was against communism and he had been happy to participate. Even Churchill, he could and did claim repetitively, had praised him publicly.[2]

Convinced of his own providential role, Franco had ridden through Madrid on a thoroughbred horse during the annual parade and celebrations of his civil war victory on 1 April 1945. It was a flamboyant act of self-publicity and grandeur from a man who felt invincible and untouchable, even as the regimes of his allies disintegrated around him. Days after the fall of Berlin, his state-controlled press was highlighting the supposedly vast 'distance between the Spanish regime and imperialist totalitarian states' as if Franco had never mentioned, yet alone aspired to, an empire run on a Spanish version of totalitarianism.[3]

In short, Franco was convinced he had had a good world war. On one level this was unchallengeable. He had increased his power and emerged personally stronger. None of the factions that supported him, whether monarchists, Carlists, conservative Roman Catholics, army officers or the Falange were nearly strong enough to mount a challenge. In fact, they could usefully be played off against one another, with the Falange – robbed of role models and allies in Italy and Germany – now completely docile and dependent. He had also found that he could buy loyalty with jobs or other prebends. 'He must want something!' he would reply in frustration when told that someone's loyalty could not be bought.[4]

Franco's self-satisfaction and domestic strength contrasted with his position in the world. He was the only surviving pro-Axis, right-wing strongman in Europe (his bland Portuguese neighbour Oliveira Salazar had stayed neutral but favoured Britain). He had vocally supported the Axis powers. For much of the world his status was simple. He was 'the last fascist dictator'. By 1946, the US Department of State had published much of the correspondence with Hitler and Mussolini in which he showed himself ready to join the war on their side, under conditions, and signed secret agreements.[5]

One problem was the number of Nazis who were sheltering in Spain or passing through on their way to South America. French intelligence reported 100,000 of these by February 1946, while the Soviets claimed there were twice as many. The numbers were exaggerated but even a small percentage of that would have seemed outrageous to public global opinion as it digested the horrors of Hitler's Holocaust. The Soviet Union and its satellites also falsely claimed in 1946 that German scientists were helping Franco develop an atomic bomb.[6]

In a move designed to crown his apparent triumph and distract Spaniards, Franco chose the day after war ended in Europe to announce that a new law of rights and duties known as the Fuero de los Españoles, or the Charter of the Spaniards, would be presented to his rubber-stamp parliament. This was the third of what became known as the Fundamental Laws, which served as Francoism's constitution, after the fascist-inspired Workers Charter of 1938 and the Law of Parliament in 1942. It added some heavily constrained freedoms to the Francoist project, but stipulated that no rights could be used to threaten 'social, spiritual and national unity'. All rights could also be suspended if Franco deemed any kind of 'national emergency' was under way.[7]

The charter also saw the Francoist project embrace the Roman Catholic church as both its moral backbone and protector. This provided a more respectable face to his regime as Franco set about 'defascistifying' it now that he could no longer count on Hitler and Mussolini. The stiff-armed Roman salute stopped being the regime's official designated salute on 11 September 1945, though it was still used widely by the Falange.[8]

Franco's single party was now formally rebranded as the National Movement in an attempt to distance it from fascism. People still referred to it as the 'Falange' but even Serrano Suñer had by now recognised that it now had little to do with the party founded by his friend José Antonio Primo de Rivera. It was increasingly becoming what one historian called 'a tame bureaucratic instrument', charged with running everything from the trades' union to the youth and women's movements and social services. The Movement remained useful to channel or organise the apparent enthusiasm for his regime which, Franco insisted in 1945, 'I see on my journeys.' These were mostly visits to the provinces, with the small Franco cavalcade stopping off at towns and cities for him to deliver speeches. Eager to find a role for itself in adverse circumstances, the Movement organised a flurry of pro-Franco rallies across the country in 1946. Franco himself later compared the Falange to a 'claque', referring to paid clappers in theatre audiences. 'Haven't you noticed how, in a large group, it only takes a few people to start clapping before everyone else joins in?' he asked.[9]

Franco also saw the local networks of the Movement as a buffer against subversion, since 'they warn me of dangers.' At a local level, the Movement was about more than just vigilance since its members provided mayors and bureaucrats for the new institutions that intervened in everything from wages to food prices. Its more ideological members also provided ideas and leadership for the regime's social or labour projects. The Movement was a place for ambitious members to advance their careers or seek backhanders. For capable idealists who were genuinely interested in improving life for people in their village, town or workplace, it was also a place where they could make a difference. However, the Falange also upheld the division between winners and losers, ensuring that 'even the most modest [state] jobs' went to supporters. Above all, Franco pointed out, the Falange was a useful foil, since 'it receives the blame for the government's mistakes.'[10]

The word 'totalitarian', once present in Franco's speeches but soon explicitly denounced by the Vatican, was now considered alien. In fact, in a remarkable turnabout, it would be deployed by the Francoist press as a scornful term to describe communism or, even, Britain's Labour Party. By 1947, the president of parliament, Esteban Bilbao, felt free to denounce, with no apparent irony, the 'aberrations of Marxist totalitarianism'.[11] However, some totalitarian measures remained firmly in place, with one former minister observing in 1944 that 'even though we are informed by the caudillo that the current regime is not totalitarian, the methods it applies to the press and propaganda are.'

The exiled Borbón dynasty, now led by the 34-year-old prince referred to as Don Juan, posed perhaps the only real threat to Franco's power because of the broad support it enjoyed amongst conservative elites, including in the army. Franco had once been unctuously deferential to the monarchy. In private, he could now be viciously dismissive. The Borbón dynasty was loose in its morals, he explained, and who knew whether what emerged from a queen's womb was 'apt' for the throne? By 1946, he had effectively broken relations with Don Juan, who had moved his exiled court from Rome to neighbouring Portugal.[12]

But Franco soon devised a clever way to get ahead of the problem posed by the monarchy, following the suggestions of Carrero Blanco – who was emerging as the second most influential man in Spain. It was Carrero Blanco, indeed, who set the tone of the post-World War II period.

In March 1947, Franco dictated a Law of Succession (another Fundamental Law of the Francoist constitution, drawn up by Carrero Blanco) that allowed for the return of the monarchy if and when he decided. 'If the monarchy is to come, it must come because of Franco, or not at all,' said Bilbao when the law was waved through parliament. Franco made it clear that he would personally designate the new king – thereby choosing his successor as head of state. The future monarch would have to be Roman Catholic, aged over thirty and, crucially, vow to continue the Francoist regime by swearing to uphold the Fundamental Laws of the regime and the Falangist principles of the Movement. The law also devised a system whereby Franco himself could be removed for 'incapacity' in theory, but not really in practice. This required a large majority of ministers, parliamentarians and members of his new Council of State all to agree. Given that he personally appointed most of them, his dictatorship was entirely safe. It would last as long as he lived. 'I won't copy Primo de Rivera's foolishness. No resigning. When I leave this [job], I'll be going straight to the cemetery,' he told one of his generals.[13]

With this, the Francoist constitution of Fundamental Laws was almost complete, confirming Franco's power as absolute and lifelong. The pretender to the throne, Don Juan, angrily declared that Franco had broken all Spain's traditions of royal inheritance, but could do no more than that. Censorship, in any case, meant few Spaniards heard about this. Instead, the press was unleashed, damning Don Juan and his supporters as enemies of Spain. The British writer Gerald Brenan, returning to Spain, found newspapers devoid of real news. Readers, he said, 'might well suppose that nothing happens in the Peninsula except football matches, religious ceremonies and bullfights'. It was part of a political dumbing down of Spaniards, leaving them malleable, acquiescent and easier to dictate to.[14]

The law was approved at a referendum during which few people, for obvious reasons, dared show opposition. Turnout was officially 89 per cent, with a 93 per cent 'yes' vote. It was the kind of result that repressive regimes are expert at producing though Franco convinced himself that this was a genuine display of popular support. In fact, local officials were ordered to report a minimum 'yes' vote of 80 per cent, whatever the results. 'Whatever their contents, at least eight out of ten votes will be counted as "Yes", with one or two as "No",' secret instructions read. Falangists in some areas made voters bring their ration cards to be stamped. Those without stamps went without rations.[15]

The system of Fundamental Laws now provided a constitutional veneer for a system which Franco called 'organic democracy' but which, in reality, left political power in his hands. Organic democracy was deemed more natural and superior to 'inorganic' popular democracy (based on direct voting) by representing 'natural' elements of society such as the family, municipalities, Falange-controlled trade unions and the church. The fact was that, at its top tier, two-thirds of the deputies in the toothless parliament were appointees. The others were elected from a restricted list of candidates by the Falange's trade unions. The balance of members shifted over time, but that did not change the fact that they voted through all Franco's laws.[16]

None of these changes impressed the winners of World War II. In fact, few world leaders now wanted anything to do with Franco. A defanged Falange and intense wooing of the Vatican were not enough to persuade them that he was anything more than a Nazi-cheering, closet totalitarian running from his past. Churchill had been voted out of power in July 1945, to be replaced by the Labour Party's Clement Attlee. From Franco's point of view, it meant changing a man who had once fought for the Spanish imperial army in Cuba to a Labour leader whose name had been given to a British company in the International Brigades. France also lurched leftwards in January 1946 when De Gaulle lost power. Two months later, it closed the Spanish frontier.[17]

Franco's pariah status as head of a regime 'obnoxious to democratic opinion' (as *The Times* wrote) was confirmed at the United Nations. The USA, Britain and France declared that Spain could not join while he remained in charge. 'In origin, nature, structure and general conduct, the Franco regime is a fascist regime patterned on, and established largely as a result of aid received from, Hitler's Nazi Germany and Mussolini's Fascist Italy,' the UN's security council stated in June 1946. 'Incontrovertible documentary evidence establishes that Franco was a guilty party with Hitler and Mussolini in the conspiracy to wage war... It was part of the conspiracy that Franco's full belligerency should be postponed until a time to be mutually agreed upon.' On 9 December 1946, the United Nations political committee called on its members to withdraw their ambassadors in a decision ratified three days later by the full assembly. Most were gone by the end of the month. The feeling of dislike was mutual, with Franco later claiming that the victors had imposed democracy on Germany, Italy and other countries only because 'they were convinced that this would prevent them becoming prosperous.'[18]

In fact, the punishment meted out to Franco at the UN could have been worse. The United States had wanted it to formally exhort Spaniards to overthrow him while France had proposed a boycott on food exports. The final resolution, nevertheless, stated that the 'Franco Fascist Government of Spain, which was imposed by force upon the Spanish people with the aid of the Axis Powers… does not represent the Spanish people.' It would not be invited to UN events 'until a new and acceptable government is formed'.[19]

Franco's answer to this was to turn the United Nations' words on their head. On Monday, 9 December 1946, a massive demonstration was called in Madrid to coincide with the UN decision. Much of the city was shut down. Public buildings were dressed up with Spanish flags, banners and patriotic slogans, while shops were shuttered and streets closed to traffic. Falange members were ordered not to wear uniform, to disguise their organising role. One of the largest crowds that commentators could remember marched across the city in bright winter sunshine to the Oriente Palace, where Franco addressed them from its balcony. 'Nothing can spoil our victory!' he proclaimed, framing the UN decision as a communist-inspired attack on his civil war triumph. Hundreds of thousands of people were reported to have attended and, even though the Francoist press naturally tended to exaggeration, Franco himself must have been immensely pleased.[20]

The crowd was in festive mood, stirred by what *The Times* called 'jingoistic excitement' with students carrying 'placards inscribed with ribald slogans of defiance'. 'We'll do what the hell we like!' read one of the least offensive. Others referred to the potency of Spanish testicles. The protest lasted 'from 11am until the siesta hour', according to *The Times*.[21]

To the Spanish people, then, Franco proclaimed that this diplomatic boycott was an attack on them, rather than on him. This became a major theme of the coming years. 'What is being questioned by the Sanhedrin (a tribunal of Jewish elders) at the United Nations is not the Spanish regime, nor the person of Generalísimo Franco, but Spain itself,' *La Vanguardia* clamoured. Spain was the victim. By now, then, Franco had become Spain and Spain had become Franco. An attack on him was an attack on the nation. All Spaniards were meant to feel outraged if that happened.

If the 'anti-Spain' had been identified during the civil war with foreign ideas like communism and liberalism, now it was represented by supposedly vindictive foreign powers. Perhaps inevitably for Franco, he also deemed these to be in the grip of a global conspiracy against Spain run by the 'Masonic superstate' that sat 'above states and above the doings of governments'. This supposedly all-powerful cabal controlled broadcasters, newspapers and public opinion.[22]

Franco, then, had not lost his ability to conjure up conspiracy theories. In fact, he repeated his musings on Freemasonry frequently in the official Falange newspaper, *Arriba*, where he published columns under the pseudonym J. Boor. 'The secret about the campaigns directed against Spain lies in two words: "Freemasonry and communism"', he wrote in the first of these, on 14 December 1946. Elaborations on the theme appeared in book form in 1952, in a collection of J. Boor columns entitled *Freemasonry*. Surprisingly, the true identity of the author remained a well-kept secret – though the eccentric Falangist poet Ernesto Giménez-Caballero soon claimed that instead of a sword, Franco carried a black and silver pen that served as 'his staff of power, his magic wand, his cudgel, his incomparable phallus'.[23]

Franco's main hope for the future now lay in Churchill's repeated warnings that an 'Iron Curtain' was falling across Europe as Soviet-backed communist regimes were installed in the continent's east. Anti-communism, indeed, was the only common ground with the liberal democracies that he had so openly despised.

Another famine struck in the winter of 1945 to 1946, as harvests failed with wheat supplies below even the level of 1941 and overall farm production at just 58 per cent of pre-Civil War levels.[24] White bread, made with wheat, became less a luxury than an object of cultish desire. Years later, a villager from Mijas, on what would later be called the Costa del Sol of southern Spain, recalled the period vividly:

> I remember once we went nine days without tasting bread, any sort of bread, black or white. No one had white, but we didn't even have black. Some days we had nothing to eat at all.[25]

Once more, this was made worse by the Franco regime's pariah status which made international aid difficult to obtain. Help came from one of the few governments to collaborate with Franco, led by populist demagogue Juan Perón in Argentina, with a grain and foodstuffs deal signed in October 1946.[26]

A resultant visit by the glamorous and popular first lady of Argentina, Evita Perón, in June 1947 brought uncustomary exoticism to the impoverished, grey and struggling country she visited. The bottle-blonde, 28-year-old former actress stayed in the Pardo Palace with the Franco family, along with her court of attendants, costumers and hairdressers. Argentina's economy was booming and she represented a country whose people were more than twice as wealthy as Spaniards. The contrast was even greater in the dull and dour Franco household, which reserved its moments of regal magnificence for public display. Franco's daughter Carmen followed her around the house, enchanted by the brilliant contrast with her dowdy, if jewel-loving, 45-year-old mother. Carmen Polo appeared to respond to Evita's magnificence by donning increasingly flamboyant hats, but otherwise could not compete. In Argentina, Evita captivated the masses but Franco could not see why. 'How can you go and talk to the workers dressed like that?' Franco exclaimed when she appeared in a plumed hat and jewels.[27]

With fascism out of vogue, Franco now found that the Roman Catholic church provided a useful ethical cover for his authoritarianism. This chimed with his imperial ambitions and favoured version of Spanish history in which great Spanish monarchs converted the world to Christianity. By now he had taken up some of the religious customs of those same monarchs. Thus, he entered churches under a velvet canopy born by four carriers. The coins bearing his image were stamped with the words 'Caudillo by the Grace of God'. The church's embrace also allowed him to exercise moral authority over believers, while convincing some – and himself – of his providential nature.[28]

As the totalitarian dream subsided, Franco's co-opting of a mostly willing Spanish church thus saw his authoritarian ideology evolve into something that would later be known as National Catholicism. A handful of bishops were outraged by such a tight embrace between the church and the state. Since they were untouchable, the thin-skinned Franco found to his irritation that some felt free to criticise him in public – an option eradicated everywhere else. Chief amongst them was the archbishop of Seville, Cardinal Pedro Segura, who warned that the term 'caudillo' could also be applied to 'the chief of a gang of robbers'. Segura suspected that both Franco and the Falange were using the Spanish church. He refused the Falange permission to paint the names of its civil war 'martyrs' on church walls, as they were in towns and villages across the country with the words 'Fallen for God and Spain' daubed beside them. Nor would he permit outdoor masses at Falange rallies.[29]

When Franco visited Seville in 1948, his staff hoped he would inaugurate a new monument to the Sacred Heart, with an official banquet afterwards. When Segura was told that Franco would preside at one table and Carmen Polo the other, he explained that this was impossible – church rules required him to preside the second table, since a cardinal could only rank behind a king, queen, head of state, or heir to the throne. When Franco insisted, Segura said there were only three solutions: either his wife stayed home, or he did, or the event was cancelled. Franco chose to cancel. When he visited Seville again in 1953, the cardinal wrote saying that he would be shut away 'doing spiritual exercises' during the visit.[30]

Franco reportedly toyed with expelling Segura, a ferocious conservative who had previously been exiled for five years in 1931 by the Republic. Although he remained in Spain, he was eventually sidelined by the Vatican as a sop to Franco. Some conservative priests from Catalonia and the Basque country harboured similarly scornful thoughts about the nationalistic part of Franco's project, but generally remained quiet. Mostly, however, the church was delighted – especially as it was given extensive control over education. Conservative historians have called the laws that supported this 'the broadest assortment of religious regulations seen in any twentieth-century western state'. The Roman Catholic church in Spain had become, in effect, a part of the regime.[31]

36

Great Poisons

PARDO PALACE, MADRID

Pilar Bahamonde died before seeing her son become dictator of Spain, but her saintliness was clearly on his mind when he addressed a group of nurses in 1938. 'Great poisons have infected the Reds,' he told them. 'Yet the poison against the home, the family, and the saintly woman who brought us into this world did not infect the whole of Spain.' He was referring, mostly, to Republican laws that had brought what, in global 1930s terms, were radical new freedoms to women – from divorce and civil marriage to, in some parts of Spain, abortion. These were the poisons which good Spanish families had avoided taking, according to Franco.[1]

Apart from his mother, daughter and wife Carmen Polo, Franco had no close contact with women. He could even be stiff and uneasy around Carmen. At this stage of their life, he also frequently dismissed her opinions on matters of importance with an airy 'you don't understand such things.' Carmen Polo found nothing unusual in her husband's attitude. They had both been brought up in the conservative society of turn-of-the-century Spain, where a woman's place was mostly at home or at church. For Franco, such women were virtuous and 'true angels of the home' whose religiosity contrasted with the attitude of the men of his childhood, including his disappointing father Don Nicolás, for whom religion was 'women's business'.[2]

Franco believed absolutely in the social norms of the Roman Catholic church as practised by both his mother and his wife. The couple slept with the wizened relic of Saint Teresa de Ávila's arm on top of a bedroom cupboard. As the leader of what the Spanish church had called a crusade, Franco was determined to eradicate the Republican 'poison' and impose Roman Catholic norms. 'It is not enough for a people to be Christian,' he told his parliament. Laws, in other words, were needed to impose the church's rules.[3]

He immediately set about turning back many of the social advances of the Republic, especially for women. A law reestablishing the pre-eminence of canonical marriage, passed in 1938, was necessary as 'reparation of the Catholic conscience of the Spanish people'. Divorce was formally overturned in 1939, allowing only separations approved by the church. Abortion and the promotion of contraception were both banned in 1941. In 1942, the criminal code was rewritten to punish adulterous wives and their lovers with prison sentences. Errant husbands were treated far more leniently. This was welcomed in *La Vanguardia* as a 'wise, prudent, just and Christian law' that reestablished a right to defend personal honour which the 'nefarious Republic' had taken away.[4]

An early view of the Francoist attitude to women came from Doctor Antonio Vallejo-Nájera, an army psychiatrist and Africanista who set out to study Republican prisoners as a way of proving that Marxists were psychologically deficient. Left-wing women were a special interest. 'If women are usually peaceable, sweet and goodly, this is because of the social brakes on them,' he wrote. 'But given that the female psyche has much in common with the psyche of infants and animals, as soon as the brakes that restrain women socially disappear ... then an instinct of cruelty is awoken in women that surpasses anything imaginable.'[5]

Vallejo-Nájera's imagined expertise on women came, in part, from his study of fifty Republican women in Málaga jail during the war. This study simply confirmed the preconceptions of a man who went on to become the first university professor in psychiatry in Franco's Spain. The Republic had given them too much freedom, he claimed, turning them into bloodthirsty monsters who had aided the anarchists and others who committed atrocities against rightists, priests and members of the bourgeoisie before Franco's army conquered the city.[6]

The psychiatrist believed firmly in making recalcitrant Reds 'suffer the punishment they deserve, with death the easiest of them all … [or they will] lose their freedom, groaning for years in prisons, purging their crimes with forced work in order to earn their daily bread, and will leave their children an infamous legacy: those who betrayed the Fatherland cannot leave an honourable surname for their children.' In Málaga, this recipe had been applied liberally, with at least 55 women executed. Most of the female prisoners he met were there for 'inciting' support for leftist and Republican groups, or against the insurrectionists. This was linked, in his mind, to their sexual immorality, which he measured by asking about the 'age of deflowerment' of the single women who were not virgins (meaning most of them). Half had lost their virginity before their seventeenth birthday, he claimed.[7]

In the vengeful fury of the civil war, even pregnant women had been sentenced to immediate execution, according to the priest at Torrero prison in Zaragoza, who tried to persuade a judge to desist. 'Imagine if I had to wait seven months for each woman to whom we have to mete out justice,' the judge replied.[8]

Vallejo-Nájera had served as a military attaché in Berlin and knew of the 'advances' of Hitler's Nazi psychiatrists, who were sterilising tens of thousands of people deemed a threat to the Aryan gene pool. As a devout Catholic he could not go to such extremes but still wanted to purify a Hispanic race that, he claimed, had lost vigour after intermingling with Jewish converts to Catholicism five centuries earlier.[9] In Vallejo-Nájera's plan (never put into place) pre-selection of suitable breeding candidates would, he hoped, restore the lost 'nobility'.

Francoist judges took to a strict reading of Spain's civil code, which explicitly stated that 'the husband must protect his wife and she must obey her husband.' Women would find that they could not work, open a bank account, start a business, sign contracts or sue in court without their husband's permission. Children effectively belonged to the father and a woman could not stay away from her home for more than brief stretches without risking the loss of her children. The reformed penal code meant that adultery was punishable with prison sentences for women, but not for men – unless it happened in the family home or the man was openly living with the other woman. The singer-songwriter Mari Trini expressed the injustice in a song written shortly after Franco's death, called *Dear Judge*: 'Yes, your honour. I lied and cheated/but only once for every hundred times he did it to me.'[10]

In this atmosphere, it was also wise for women to go to church since priests oversaw education, distributed charity and acted as moral vigilantes. The fact that, for example, they were also to be consulted on cases to do with the Law of Political Responsibilities, shows how priests had become – along with the mayor, the police and the Falange – a cornerstone not just of the regime's moral compass but of its authoritarian structure.

Yet the return to church was not just down to fear. There was also a genuine surge in religiosity, perhaps partly due to the trauma of the war. Social conformity explained some of that, while the age-old rhythm of public religious events that marked village, town or neighbourhood social life had either never disappeared or had only done so briefly in some Republican areas during the Civil War.[11]

In the post-war prison camps where a quarter of a million Republican soldiers lived, attendance at mass was obligatory – part of an attempt at re-educating non-believing 'anti-Spaniards'. Priests appeared in regime institutions both high and low. Seven bishops were appointed to parliament and one sat on the seven-man Council of State that was nominally the highest consultative body in the land. Religious advisors appeared in state trades unions, ministries and other public bodies. No comparable religious restoration had been seen in Europe for decades, if not centuries.[12]

Apart from the church and courts, the most relentless indoctrinator of Spanish women was the Women's Section of the Falange, run by José Antonio Primo de Rivera's sister, Pilar. Membership and work in its Social Service branch was necessary for entry into some professions and a passport to regime acceptability. Jobs in the public administration, or entities funded by it, required women to have done Social Service work. From 1945, the obtaining of a passport, driving licence, membership of cultural and sports clubs and even hunting or fishing licences depended on having worked for the Social Service.[13]

Pilar Primo de Rivera's standing as sister of the martyred 'founder' – who had once declared that 'men are massively egotistical; while women almost always accept a life of submission, of service' – allowed her to exercise great power. All this was disguised behind her aspect as what one contemporary called 'a simple girl, not terribly concerned about appearance, agreeably shy, with a girlish voice'. That voice was used to pronounce speeches claiming that women were intrinsically inferior. 'Women never discover anything; they lack the creative talent for that, which God has reserved for male intelligence; we can do nothing more than interpret, well or badly, what men have already done,' she said in 1943. When Franco addressed the Women's Section at the end of the Civil War, he claimed that the heroics of 'the strong sex' meant nothing without their support. Their job now was 'the conquest of the home... to educate Spanish children and Spanish women.'[14]

Pilar Primo de Rivera urged her members to be discreet and never place themselves above a man. 'The less you are seen and heard, the better. Your contact with politics should not encourage you to get involved with intrigues and abilities that are inappropriate for women. Let's deal with our own things and leave the men alone, since they are the ones called upon to resolve the complications involved in the governing of the country.' Such was her standing amongst Falangists that one of them, the writer Giménez Caballero, even suggested to Joseph Goebbel's wife Magda that they should try to arrange a marriage with Hitler.[15]

The Women's Section's own magazine, *Medina*, gave weekly lessons in correct womanhood. 'Cheer yourself up. The only thing men cannot stand is boredom. And they are easily bored by unsmiling women whose eyes are red [from weeping]. Change your attitude. Offer yourself to his eyes as suggestive, entertaining, joyful,' the magazine's advice column suggested. 'A woman cannot feel fully happy unless she is protected by the shadow of something stronger,' the magazine said, referring to husbands. A wife's other obligation was to the nation. 'A woman's true mission is to give the Fatherland children.'[16]

An early sign that Franco would make Spaniards bow to the church had come just two months after the insurrection, when orders were issued for secondary classrooms in the Francoist zone to be sex-segregated and for textbooks to follow Catholic doctrine. The education ministry was placed in the hands of Catholic arch-conservatives. In 1938, Franco ordered that crucifixes be placed on all classroom walls, made lessons in Christianity obligatory and began planning a Catholic curriculum for secondary schools. Soon classrooms would also have his portrait and that of José Antonio Primo de Rivera on their walls. His 1943 university law gave supremacy to 'Christian dogma and morality' while demanding that 'the authority of sacred canons' should underlie all teaching. Primary school was, if anything, even more radically church-oriented. Schools provided the core of church's societal power, which now spread almost everywhere.[17]

Just as the church and the Falange controlled women's behaviour, so schools aimed to produce servile women and men who would defend the constantly threatened honour of Spain. 'The child must understand that life is like military service, meaning discipline, sacrifice, fighting and austerity,' read a 1938 set of instructions to teachers.[18]

Franco's first education minister, Pedro Sainz Rodríguez, was clear about his task. 'Our invincible Caudillo has said that Spain will be Roman Catholic in its culture,' he said. Conservative Catholicism was to be taught in all school years, along with 'an absolute prohibition' on 'anti-Catholic doctrines'. The outspoken Sainz Rodríguez did not always apply all the church's teachings to himself: he eventually found himself in trouble for using his ministerial car to take him to brothels. When found out, he saw no reason for shame. 'I wasn't going to walk, was I?' he said. A scandalised Carmen Polo, who kept an eye on the morals of her husband's closest collaborators, lobbied successfully for him to be sacked.[19]

In fact, prostitution boomed in the early years of Francoism as the wives and daughters of imprisoned or dead Republican soldiers and politicians found themselves forced to find new ways to support themselves. Single mothers who were rejected by their own parents also often found themselves resorting to prostitution. A law to ban brothels was eventually passed in 1956, but was never implemented. Abortion remained a messy and dangerous backstreet affair. Wealthier women could go to France or England – though they often had to make up other excuses in order to gain permission from their husband or father to travel.

While women were subjected from school age onwards to lessons about what femininity meant, boys were also taught the 'virility' which Franco considered such a vital part of the Spanish's man's character. 'And you, Spanish child: if anyone laughs at or insults God, Spain, or your own mother, don't hold back! Attack them with your fists, teeth and feet. If you do not, you are a coward!' urged a 1943 textbook. History, especially recent history, was rewritten to fit the Francoist narrative. The same book blamed 'Russia and Judaism' for promoting Basque and Catalan separatism as well as left-wing workers movements.[20]

Intolerance was also extended to homosexuals. After the poet and playwright Federico García Lorca was shot by a Falangist death squad in the hills outside Granada, one of his killers boasted that he had 'shot him twice in the arse for being a poof'. Such prejudices were common across Europe and the western world, but few placed homosexuality as a danger equivalent to Marxism, Freemasonry or Judaism. 'This book was written to demonstrate the danger that the sodomite poses to the Fatherland,' M. Carlavilla, author of a 1956 book called *Sodomites*, proclaimed. 'There is an undoubted affinity between the sodomite and the communist, both being aberrations against the family.' He went on to warn that a herd of 'wild beasts, thousands strong, has invaded the busy streets looking for its young prey... Your son may return home, corrupted, hiding his shameful secret.'[21]

Thousands of homosexuals were jailed, put in camps or locked up in mental institutions. Prison terms of up to three years were imposed under laws covering 'public scandal' or 'social danger'. Homosexuals were sent to mental hospitals and some suffered electric shock treatment. Introversion and self-doubt were deemed thoroughly un-Spanish attributes. Francoist optimism was meant to be the 'virile' essence of the natural Spanish character.[22]

Franco certainly loved the idea of Spanish virility and presumably saw himself as an exemplar. He was given to exclaiming about his regime's 'virile independence' from foreigners and considered Spaniards 'the most vigorous and virile people in the world'.[23] However, he lacked one of the old-fashioned proofs of virility – a son. Furthermore, no political successor had been appointed and nobody yet knew what was meant to happen on his death. Nor was there an answer to the question of whether Francoism would die with Franco.

37

The Sleeper Prince

LISBON, 8 NOVEMBER 1948

On 8 November 1948, a fair-haired ten-year-old boy boarded the overnight Lusitania Express at the Entroncamento station, 100 km north of Lisbon, reaching Madrid the following day. This was Prince Juan Carlos – or Juanito – the grandson of the now deceased King Alfonso XIII and son of his heir, Don Juan. Looking out of the window at the scorched, yellowed countryside of the Spanish meseta, he was surprised by the contrast with the green Atlantic coastline of Portugal. 'Is all Spain like this?' he reportedly asked, echoing the thoughts that Franco had when he had left Galicia as a fourteen-year-old boy.[1]

The journey was the result of an August 1948 meeting between Franco and Don Juan aboard the former's yacht, the *Azor*. The 41-metre *Azor* had been specially built for him and was mostly used for Franco's fishing trips – especially when he travelled to a country mansion bought for him by 'public donation' in his native Galicia, the Pazo de Meiras, or when he stayed during the summer in a hill-top palace overlooking the Basque seaside town of San Sebastian.. Although he mostly used it for tuna fishing, the *Azor* was also equipped with a harpoon gun.[2]

The two men met five miles off the coast of San Sebastian. Tears apparently came to Franco's eyes at the sight of Alfonso XIII's son, though his occasional weepy displays of emotion at moments of historic tension were hard to decipher. In this case, it may have been sentimentality (for the ordered, hierarchical days of the monarchy) or pure affectation. The crucial agreement reached during their three-hour meeting was that ten-year-old prince Juan Carlos would be sent to Spain for his schooling, under the dictator's watchful eye. The idea was to make a proper Spaniard of him, allowing him to grow up and make friends in a country that he might one day reign over. For the royal family it represented, at least, a return of a significant member to Spanish soil. To Franco it meant a large degree of control over another candidate to the throne – Juan Carlos himself.[3]

In fact, the relationship between Franco and Don Juan was mired in mutual mistrust. Don Juan was also flirting with the socialist party in exile, hedging bets in case the Franco regime crumbled, while the dictator had previously seemed to write him off as a pretender. The boy in the train was, in this respect, a pawn for both men. He would be educated together with eight other boys from elite or aristocratic families at a house in the countryside outside Madrid.[4]

Two weeks after arriving, the boy visited Franco – a meeting that must have been terrifying, given the hatred harboured for the dictator in his parental home. If he had read the regime's newspapers, especially those published by the Falange, the young prince would have realised that these were still spewing hatred towards his family. The appearance of a mouse scuttling out from under Franco's chair reportedly helped ease the tension. Franco, with no son of his own, appears to have liked Juan Carlos from the beginning, though the boy's welfare counted little in the tug-of-the-war with Prince Juan. Within weeks of his arrival, Franco and Don Juan were swapping angry letters, with Franco denying having promised him the crown and Juan threatening to call the boy home. In fact, he never did. Over time, Franco began to see the young prince as the son he had never had.[5]

One of Don Juan's closest advisors, Franco's former boss as Minister of War José María Gil Robles, believed that the man he called 'king' had lost his battle to sit on the Spanish throne by sending his son to Spain. 'There's no point in continuing,' he wrote in his diary. 'Given the danger posed by the Soviet Union, the Allies will eventually come to an understanding with Franco.' He was echoing the thinking of Franco, who believed a new world war was imminent in which Spain and the democracies would fight communism.[6]

Carrero Blanco had advised Franco to 'hold tight' until the Allies changed position, but how long would that take? In April 1949, they formed NATO, inviting Salazar's Portugal to join, but shunning Franco. That was like trying to make a tortilla without using eggs, the dictator complained.[7]

Meanwhile, Franco continued to write his newspaper columns under the pseudonym Jakim Boor, blaming the international boycott on Freemasons.

He even quoted his own speeches, praising himself for coming up with the theory that Britain had destroyed the Spanish empire by successfully setting 'Spaniards against Spaniards' since this 'allowed them to achieve in a few years what they had failed to manage despite all the wars they declared against us'.[8]

In these articles, Franco also felt free to refer to himself in the third person, using the standard propagandistic terms of his regime. He thus found himself praising his own 'firmness' against the United Nations and denouncing the 'masonic hatred towards our Caudillo and our regime' that animated it.[9] He even blamed President Roosevelt's wife, Eleanor, whom he called a 'well-known Freemason', even though she was not.

Two months later the Korean War broke out and international alliances shifted as fears grew of a third world war. Catholic politicians and military strategists in the United States urged that Spain be rehabilitated. The diplomatic boycott, some realised, had backfired by encouraging a section of aggrieved Spaniards to back the dictator, rather than overthrow him.

In November 1950, the United Nations finally lifted its diplomatic embargo and ambassadors began to reappear in Madrid. The new US ambassador even began negotiating for his country to set up military bases in Spain.[10]

The same year Franco's daughter Carmen married a playboy doctor called Cristóbal Martínez-Bordiú. To begin with, Franco and his wife worried that he was a gold-digger – though he won them over, reportedly with much flattery. For Carmen and her socially snobbish mother, the fact that Martínez-Bordiú was also a minor aristocrat with the title of Marquis of Villaverde (inherited via his mother) was undoubtedly part of the attraction.[11] Franco spent handsomely on the wedding of his adored only child, inviting 800 people who lavished the young couple with gifts.

With Spain having only recently emerged from famines and Spaniards still poorer than before the Civil War, the press was ordered to keep coverage of the event modest. It still made newspaper front pages and was accompanied by the now tediously routine praises of the bride's father. Photographs showed Franco in his full-dress uniform as captain general, complete with gold-tasselled epaulettes and adorned with medals. His son-in-law wore the extravagant white uniform (embroidered with a red cross on his chest), sword and plumed helmet of the chivalric Order of the Holy Sepulchre. The bride's long white silk dress was, the newspapers noted approvingly, 'totally closed at the cleavage' and her veil held in place by a diadem of jewels and pearls. A popular ditty went: 'The girl wanted a husband/the mother wanted a marquess/the marquess wanted money/so now they're all happy!'[12]

Given the dire state of the economy, it was wise to dampen coverage of the wedding. In the second half of 1951, Franco found himself facing the first serious popular demonstrations against his regime, after tram prices were hiked in Barcelona. Franco's repressive instincts were immediately awakened and he sent extra police units, complaining that local officials were not tough enough. When Don Juan wrote to him, blaming the regime's failures for the disturbances in Barcelona, Franco reacted furiously. The blame, he continued to insist twelve years after the civil war had ended, lay with the Republic.[13]

By 1951, Spaniards had lived under Franco's rule for anything between 12 and 15 years. Children leaving school that year might have no memories of the time before he took charge. It was only in 1951, however, that per capita income finally returned to 1935 levels. In comparative terms, Spain's economy had fallen further behind Italy and France, even though both had been ravaged by war more recently. In 1935, Spain's per capita GDP had been ten per cent below that of Italy. Now it was 25 per cent lower.[14]

Hunger, civil war and repression had drained Spaniards of political passion. A British traveller in the early 1950s, the writer V. S. Pritchett, found them 'politically tired out'. The Bloomsbury set's Spanish outlier, Gerald Brenan, thought the Civil War had left feelings of guilt about the embrace of fanaticism on both sides, with a rightist taxi driver telling him: 'Between us all we have brought disgrace on Spain.

Once it was a happy country; now it is a miserable one, racked from end to end with hatred.'[15]

In an attempt to prove the extent of the 'red terror' an investigative process called the Causa General was set up – which, although it exaggerated (giving 85,000 dead rather than 50,000), still produced a total number of victims far below the 470,000 dead which Franco had regularly touted. By contrast, the roadside mass graves of the victims of Francoist death squads were left unattended. In Piedrafita de Babia, Leon, flowers appeared once a year at the site of a mass grave containing the corpses of 14 men shot on 5 November 1937, having been secretly left there by family members at night. Such graves remained in the local memory as a menacing presence, as the sister of one those shot recalled more than half a century later.

> Everybody knew the bodies were here. Back then, even after they were killed and secretly buried, people from the village came across the bones after they were exposed by rain... The priest told them the rojos, the reds, were so vile that even the earth did not want them. Even now people remember the fear. They don't like to talk about it.[16]

Nevertheless, Spaniards found ways to settle into the new society Franco had created, ironing out some of its wrinkles. In many places, client relationships sprung up between civil war winners and losers. These were referred to in regime reports as 'adictos' (adherents) or 'desafectos' (malcontents) and were not to be confused with the growing mass of 'indiferentes'. The losers often needed someone from the winning side – who might simply have been drafted into Franco's army – to vouch for them if they sought work or any kind of relationship with the state. Since most Spaniards lived in villages, friends, relatives or neighbours were at hand as potential benefactors. A relationship of dependency was created, but the losers still did better as a result and, on a small local scale, it brought reconciliation.[17]

With imports heavily restricted, licences to bring goods into Spain became highly valuable – providing opportunities to trade in rare or high-quality goods. One of the best places to negotiate a licence was at the hunting parties where Franco now spent as much time as possible. In fact, Franco was becoming less and less interested in the day-to-day business of governing. That was what ministers were for. They still needed his approval for their plans and the Friday cabinet meetings were notoriously long, sometimes stretching into the night, but whereas he had previously done much of the speaking, he now mostly sat back and listened.[18]

Afternoons, whenever possible, were spent at his farm, from which he began to make large sums of money by raising cattle and planting everything from wheat, potatoes and garlic to cotton and tobacco (though Pacón noted that expertise was often provided by the agriculture ministry). He frequently hunted from Saturday through to Monday and often took whole weeks off for hunting parties. Fishing, either of river salmon or of tuna in the Cantabrian Sea, rivalled with hunting as a passion for which affairs of state could be put on hold. The outings on the *Azor* were one of the few places where the increasingly taciturn dictator remained garrulous. 'I have never had a dialogue with the general,' said Admiral Pedro Nieto Antúnez, a fishing friend who served as an aide de camp and navy minister. 'I have listened to very long monologues from him, though he wasn't speaking to me but rather to himself.'[19]

Official visitors, if invited to lunch or dinner at the Pardo Palace, found themselves subjected to an excruciating round of stiff, protocol-asphyxiated events in which often neither Franco nor his wife attempted to make conversation.[20]

The dictator was even less talkative when accompanied by his wife, whose presence seemed to make him uncomfortable and snappy. Pacón thought Franco had embraced silence as a way of avoiding people gossiping afterwards about what he had said. 'One is the master of what one does not say, and the slave of what one does,' Franco liked to say. However, the sight of his cousin chewing silently on wooden toothpicks even during more intimate dinners with family and friends also drove Pacón to despair. Many meals were punctuated by long stretches of silence, accompanied by the awkward scraping of cutlery against plates. It had not always been like that and Pacón wondered if the years of 'adulation and [church] incense' had turned them into bores who routinely followed protocol in order to avoid having to make any effort.[21]

Other members of the family also found the atmosphere asphyxiatingly dull. Even Franco's ebullient and plain-speaking sister Pilar could not break the ice. Franco's niece Pilar Jaraiz blamed Carmen Polo and her court of aristocratic sycophants. 'Her husband's family seemed small fry compared to those of her own category,' she said. Carmen Polo only became animated when talking about her husband's critics, 'cursing against all kinds of traitors and the ungrateful people who could be found everywhere'. One of the favourite phases uttered over post-lunch coffee with the family was 'we haven't fought a war so that any old liberal or Red can come along and steal our victory.'[22]

As the 1950s progressed, Franco spent more working days at hunts than at his desk during parts of the shooting season, which lasted from October to February. 'We all know that heads of state have always had a propensity to fall for the adulation of hangers-on who flatter them by finding ways to indulge their weaknesses and vices,' commented Pacón. 'The weak spot here is his love of hunting and fishing.'[23]

The other weak spot was his blindness to cronyism and corruption, with many of his closest collaborators now using their positions to do business deals or gain seats on company boards. Ministers, bureaucrats open to graft and businessmen seeking favours made sure they were also invited to the hunts attended by Franco. 'The hunts are a pretext for all the landowners' friends to make contacts and ask favours like tax breaks or import permits,' Pacón complained.[24]

Again, Franco's brother Nicolás was often connected to those seeking favours and there were also rumours that he was involved with currency smugglers who took cash out of Spain and converted it into dollars in Lisbon. By now Nicolás had a reputation for frivolity, lechery and rule-breaking that he could only get away with because he was the dictator's brother. He was also seen frequently in Mediterranean resorts, and was famously photographed on the beach at Cannes with the bikini-clad British model Nina Dyer – featuring in Italian and British magazines as a rotund playboy whose embrace of the loose morals of partying European aristocrats contrasted with the moral severity of his brother's regime, which disapproved of bikinis. Francisco Franco's reaction to being shown the photographs of his brother publicly behaving in a way that went against the regime's morals was said only to be: 'Look how fat Nicolás has got.'[25]

Even within his Pardo palace there were complaints about how his wife Carmen and her best friend Pura Huétor, wife of the aristocrat who was head of Franco's household, were using and abusing their position to demand gifts, pay knock-down prices for jewels or buy up real estate.[26] By the mid-fifties, Pacón was writing in his diary about how things had changed for the worse, with Franco surrounded by flatterers and deaf to useful or well-meant criticism. That, in turn, made it difficult to correct mistakes – especially since censorship prevented government failings from being aired in public, creating a wider atmosphere in which few people dared to criticise and people in power, however lowly, did not accept critiques. Even amongst regime backers, he had said in 1955, this was draining support.[27]

Carmen Polo's own family was amongst those who most benefitted from a combination of two of the Caudillo's weaknesses – his mistrust of people outside his close or family circle and his willingness to turn a blind eye to corruption. Her brother Felipe Polo had joined Franco's private office by 1942, became his personal secretary and ran his own family's business affairs. Franco's sister Pilar said that this was when the Polo family's fortune really began to grow. 'In reality, the family were farmers who lived off income from their lands. They were reasonably well-off. They didn't really become successful until her brother Felipe began to work with el Caudillo,' she said. Felipe Polo joined the boards of at least eight companies.[28]

The Franco family's fortune-seeking became especially blatant after his daughter's marriage to Cristóbal Martínez-Bordiú. Franco's son-in-law's family had made money during World War II as go-betweens with Nazi Germany, and his family now joined the Francos' self-enriching inner circle, with Villaverde's uncle José María Sanchiz helping the dictator buy the large farm estate at Valdefuentes, just outside Madrid, which he then administrated.[29]

The increasingly grandiose Franco, when asked by Sanchiz whether their family relationship after the marriage meant he could now address the dictator with the informal and affectionate 'tu', replied that he should keep using 'Your Excellency'. Franco's wife shared this shift to elaborate formality, and even began addressing Pacón as 'General' – 'and I've known her since she was a girl who had just left school', he sniffed. Franco's sister Pilar was one of the few to raise her voice against the Sanchiz clan, whose semi-aristocratic nature saw them more welcomed by Carmen Polo than her husband's surviving siblings, the abrasive Pilar Franco or the increasingly scandalous and womanising Nicolás Franco. Pilar nevertheless took it upon herself to issue warnings about how everyone else saw corruption emanating from the Pardo palace – even if it was not from the dictator himself. She was routinely told that this was all lies and that the rumours were the result of 'envy against successful people'. One otherwise admiring visitor pointed to Carmen Polo's 'imperiousness', while Pacón wondered whether this was a result of mixing her natural timidity with the sycophancy of those around her.[30]

Franco's son-in-law, Villaverde himself soon became known by various nicknames alluding to the wealth that allegedly piled up in his bank accounts. Although he continued to practise as a cardiologist (and carried out Spain's first heart transplant, in which the patient died), people soon came to him to do business, seeing the immense advantages of being closely associated to the dictator's family. He was 'Vayavida' (What a life!) or 'Vespaverde' (Green Vespa) because of his share in the importation of Italian Vespa scooters (all painted green). VESPA, wags suggested, now stood for Villaverde Entra Sin Pagar Aduana ('Villaverde passes through customs without paying'), since imports were heavily restricted by a regime given over to autarky.

Ministers inexperienced in shooting found themselves having to learn, with Manuel Fraga peppering Franco's daughter Carmen with a shot in her backside on one of his first partridge hunts. Both Carmen and the dictator were, he said, gracious about a 'gaffe' that obviously provoked no real damage. He soon noted in his diary that the hunts, some in the grounds of Franco's Pardo Palace, were 'a good place to talk politics'. Fraga judiciously started bringing along a screen to place beside him and prevent him shooting the next person along the line of participants.[31]

Hosts went out of their way to make sure there was plenty for Franco to shoot. On one hunt he claimed to have personally shot 5,000 partridges. It was, he boasted, 'a record'. He was capable of firing 6,000 cartridges in a single day, or so he told his doctor. He returned from tuna-fishing trips, where a navy minesweeper accompanied him and distributed bait, boasting of fighting 80 kilo tunas for hours or, even, of having harpooned a 20,000 kg whale that took 20 hours to land.[32]

He was behaving more like a king rather than as someone who had to govern, Pacón complained. 'It is sad that, when you reach such a high position you can become so blind. They think that they deserve whatever they get,' his cousin lamented. Austere, die-hard Falangists or army officers complained bitterly about the rampant cronyism. They could not understand how Franco, whose day-to-day lifestyle remained modest, did not see it and act. The dictator would simply change the conversation. 'Either he doesn't want to hear it because he already knows exactly what is going on, or is too trusting, or simply finds it easier not to listen,' Pacón lamented. 'And if it is the last of these, then he has to be exceedingly blind.'[33]

Franco's other pleasures, at this stage, were his private cinema, painting ('without artistic pretensions, but which distracts me'[34]) and his grandchildren – with Carmen giving birth to seven. All were born at the Pardo Palace and when a first grandson arrived in December 1954, he was not only given his grandfather's first name: parliament approved a change in his surnames so that these could be inverted, since Spaniards have two surnames, usually starting with their father's first surname followed by their mother's. Thus, a new Francisco Franco was concocted. The boy's ambitious father did not mind. He could see the distinct advantages of the Franco surname.[35]

Franco had done pretty much as he wanted with Spain, provoking global isolation and a malfunctioning economy. People were exhausted by war and poverty, while the post-war years of vengeful killing had laid down a memory of repression that kept fear alive during his entire dictatorship. Together with a watchful and violent security apparatus, that bought him time. Few people in Spain were in the mood to challenge him. Pritchett found them compliant and deeply sceptical. People he spoke to just wanted 'to forget the Civil War and its appalling personal losses; the business of surviving the terrible time after the Civil War, of keeping their heads above water, of getting enough to eat, has bewildered and exhausted them.'[36]

In fact, the baraka, or good luck, for which Franco had become famous as a death-defying young officer in Morocco was about to return. The post-World War II period had brought growing tension between, on the one hand, western democracies and their allies and, on the other hand, the Soviet Union and its communist satellites. The impact of the high stakes nuclear stand-off between the two blocs was about to sweep through Spain. The tide of history was changing in the generalísimo's favour. Franco was to become a Cold War winner.

38

The Grey Fifties

NEW YORK, 21 OCTOBER 1954

General Agustín Muñoz Grandes reputedly hung around his neck the Iron Cross with Additional Oak Leaves that had been personally awarded to him by Adolf Hitler before setting out to visit President Dwight Eisenhower at the Waldorf Astoria in New York. That, at least, is how a Spanish biographer reports the preparations of Franco's Minister of War before he met the president of the United States for a half-hour conversation on 21 October 1954. In fact, photographs of the meeting are too blurry to distinguish exactly which medal Muñoz Grandes is wearing and it was most likely the US military's Legion of Merit, which he had received a few days earlier. Even without the Iron Cross, however, it was still a sign of a remarkable change in the international status of Franco's regime that a US president should receive the former commander of the Blue Division from Hitler's army.[1]

The cantankerous, straight-talking Muñoz Grandes was a Francoist military archetype. As a young Africanista he had fought under Franco in Morocco. In 1936, he had joined the plotting for the insurrection, been detained, escaped from jail and then become a senior field commander. Given his closeness to the Falange, Franco had placed him in charge of the merged single party, or Movement, before choosing him to lead the Blue Division. On three separate occasions he had meetings with Hitler, who was delighted by a Spanish unit that embraced the disdain for danger typical of Africanistas. 'They and their general know the meaning of loyalty and valour in the face of death,' Hitler said before awarding Muñoz Grandes the Iron Cross. The Führer even thought of him as a possible replacement for Franco should the Axis countries win the war.[2]

Muñoz Grandes was the most prestigious military officer in Spain after the caudillo and Franco made him Minister of War in 1952. He inherited an impoverished, decrepit military – still using pre-World War II arms from Germany and Italy – that had fallen far behind its European counterparts. He also, however, was in place as Washington switched its stance on Franco, embracing him as part of a global anti-Soviet alliance. To Franco, this was justification for all he had done before. His propagandists now promoted him as the man who had saved the Western world from communism. 'By now it [communism] would have changed the face of the world,' *La Vanguardia* announced as he celebrated fourteen years in power in 1954. 'We are proud to have been the undefeated vanguard of the fight against world communism.'[3]

The spiky and surly Muñoz Grandes was an unlikely choice to be the face of Franco's regime as it tried to woo liberal democracies and distance itself from fascism. Early in April, he had stood at a Barcelona quayside to greet the last Blue Division prisoners-of-war released from the Soviet Union. When they were fêted by the city authorities of Madrid in December, one of the guests was the infamous Belgian SS officer Leon Degrelle, against whom Belgium had passed a death sentence in absentia. He was one of many Nazis and quislings who had found refuge in Spain and one of eight non-German officers, including Muñoz Grandes, to whom Hitler had awarded an Iron Cross with Oak Leaves.[4]

Amongst those who waved the general off on his trip to the US at the beginning of October 1954 was Pacón, who joked that most people were glad to be free of the ill-humoured minister for the next few weeks. At his first official interview with a fellow general after landing in the US, Muñoz Grandes was politely asked his first impressions. 'To be frank, it felt very strange ... to be visiting a great country like the USA, where up to a few hours ago I was convinced that I was considered a war criminal,' he replied. He followed up with a tirade about how Franco's Spain would remain a dictatorship 'with or without the help of powerful friends [like the US]'. His translator, the Spanish military attaché Colonel Carlos Iniesta Cano, watered down his replies, telling the Americans that the general had said he was delighted to be there.[5]

Eisenhower and the other American generals, all combat veterans of World War II or Korea, were not put out by Muñoz Grandes's brash manner. They shared his anticommunism and, as military men, found him easy to get on with. Muñoz Grandes had left Spain sharing the antipathy toward the US that was typical of Spanish military men, including Franco, brought up on tales of the shameful 1898 defeat in Cuba. He returned impressed by the most efficient military machine on earth and what he saw as an underlying culture of patriotism.

While Muñoz Grandes was meeting Eisenhower in New York, Franco was opening an exhibition in Madrid's Retiro Park, with press reports concentrating, as always, on the supposedly fervorous enthusiasm of the public for their caudillo. Ten days earlier, he had boarded the USS *Coral Sea*, the American Sixth Fleet's aircraft carrier, after it dropped anchor off Valencia. Wearing the uniform of the Supreme Commander of the Navy, Franco had observed flight and gunnery practice during what was billed as his 'first visit ever to a foreign warship'. It was part of the US charm offensive, designed to cement the new relationship. 'We've never put on such a display before, not even when the secretary of state visited us,' one US officer told the press. Franco was clearly impressed.[6]

In some ways, Spain itself had just become an aircraft carrier for the United States. The end of the diplomatic boycott, the Korea war and escalation of the Cold War brought an upheaval in international alliances. The 1947 Truman Doctrine, whereby the US had pledged support 'for democracies against authoritarian threats' would be waived for any regime considered anti-communist. A deal signed on 26 September 1953 gave the Americans joint air bases in Madrid, Seville and Zaragoza as well as a naval base at Rota, on the southern Atlantic coast. Given that the next world war was thought likely to involve nuclear weapons, this placed targets over three of Spain's most populous cities. Spain had not been used as a permanent base for a foreign army since Napoleon Bonaparte's troops arrived in the nineteenth century, provoking popular rebellion and the Peninsular War. In this case, Franco was eager to underline that Spanish sovereignty was not under threat – though war with the Soviet Union would have allowed the Americans to use the bases at will.[7]

The bases were the least important part of the package to ordinary Spaniards – though the impact of American soldiers, sailors and airmen on Spanish soil would eventually be felt not just in military terms, but also via radio stations and clubs in popular culture and music. More significant was the $226 million in aid for military and technological spending for a country which had looked on enviously at how money from the Marshall Plan – from which Franco had been excluded as punishment for his pro-Hitler stance – allowed Germany, Italy and other war-ravaged countries to rebuild after World War II and quickly pull ahead of Spain once more.

The aid, in turn, came with demands for the economy to be liberalised and opened up to world trade. One of Franco's most fervently promoted political ideas, of autarky, had to be heavily watered down. It had, in any case, proved a disastrous failure, with Spaniards poorer in 1950 than they had been in 1946 and a full 10 per cent poorer than before the insurrection against the Republic in 1936. Soon the Spanish economy was growing at rates unseen since before the civil war. In relative terms, this was still not spectacular: through the 1950s Spain would grow at the same rate as France but continue to lose ground to more directly comparable countries like Italy and Portugal. At last, however, some Spaniards finally found themselves becoming wealthier.[8]

A reduction of autarky was not the only price Franco paid for Spain's return to the club of world nations. In November 1955, US Secretary of State John Foster Dulles made a flying day-trip to Madrid. He had an hour and a half meeting with Franco, met with ministers and flew out again that afternoon. Dulles spent just seven hours on Spanish soil, but the symbolic message was clear: Franco could now be talked to. The regime's press, typically, claimed that Dulles had come 'seeking advice' from Franco. More importantly, Dulles held out the chance of United Nations membership, but only if Franco gave up the Spanish protectorate in Morocco.[9]

The following year, with Spain having been admitted to the UN in December 1955, he did exactly that – handing most of the protectorate over to Morocco's King Mohammed V. He was left with just the small area around Sidi Ifni on the Atlantic coast (eventually given up in 1969) and the barren Spanish Sahara. Apart from that, his empire was now reduced to Spanish Equatorial Guinea. It must have been a humiliating choice for a man who had made his name in Spain's

Moroccan wars and felt that 'without Africa I cannot explain myself'. His old dreams of empire now also lay in tatters. In a rare outburst of insubordination, two cadets at the officer's academy in Zaragoza burned a picture of Franco in protest.[10]

Such concessions to the outer world often provoked a rebellious streak in Franco, pushing him to tighten his dictatorship and double-down on its ideology at home. A new concordat signed with the Vatican in August 1953 had given him a gloss of legitimacy, underscored by Pope Pius XII decorating him with the Supreme Order of Christ. It also sealed the church's grip on education and social morality, while providing generous government funding. Greater economic freedoms, in other words, coincided with a tightened social straitjacket.[11]

The church's heavy hand was already visible in Spanish culture, where censors hacked away at books and plays. 'Intellectual life is certainly in eclipse – and literary society is so alive with malicious rumour and scandal that one cannot do more than crudely suggest the obvious reasons: political and ecclesiastical censorship,' reported V.S. Pritchett. 'Clerical censorship … is intensely disliked.'[12]

Flickers of protest against Franco's almost two-decade-old regime had begun to appear amongst university students. A study of student opinion, carried out in 1955 by psychology professor José Luis Pinillos and leaked to the *New York Times*, showed that most saw Francoism as a series of empty slogans. They viewed military officers as overwhelmingly incompetent, regime leaders as untrustworthy, priests as immoral and the church as out of touch and uncaring for the poor. Only a small minority approved of dictatorship, the Falange or totalitarianism. The conservative and concerned Pinillos observed that, although his interviewees were largely passive and apathetic about forcing change, they were natural 'radicals' who could easily be captured for leftist ideas. The report was censored in Spain, where only academics and politicians saw the results. When, however, it was reported on the front page of the *New York Times* on 4 January 1956, it became widely known that Franco's chosen apparatchiks were seen as 'lacking seriousness of purpose, amateurish, ignorant … comedians, ambitious without scruples, false'. His generals and other officers were 'ignorant, bureaucratic, worthless … libertines, brutal, heavy drinkers'.[13]

In 1956, student tension burst into lethal violence. Just as there was a single party (the Movement) so there was a single 'vertical' union for every sector run by the Falange. Membership of the Falange's Spanish University Union (Sindicato Español Universitario, or SEU) had been obligatory for students ever since 1939 but its grip was slipping, not least as Catholic student groups began to rebel and the clandestine Spanish Communist Party infiltrated both. Early in February 1956, a group of Falangist thugs that called itself 'the Centuria XX of Franco's Guard' armed themselves with cudgels and beat up law students and professors taking part in Madrid elections for student delegates that the SEU had not been allowed to control. During the angry confrontation, a picture of the untouchable Falangist founder and 'martyr' José Antonio Primo de Rivera was hurled out of a window and the Falange's yoke and arrows symbol defaced.[14]

On 9 February, Law Faculty Falangists were marking 'the Day of the Fallen Student' (in honour of a Falangist student killed by a socialist in 1934) when they again bumped into their rivals on Madrid's Gran Via. Street-fighting broke out, as fists were swung and stones hurled. Then half a dozen shots rang out and a 19-year-old Falangist fell to the ground with a gunshot to the head. Although the student's life was saved, it was an act of political violence of a kind almost unseen in such a public place for a generation. Falangists were outraged, though it turned out that the shots had come from their own side. The report to Franco detailing this was also never made public.[15]

The fact that armed Falangists were shooting on the streets shocked the military and those seeking to smooth the regime's reputation abroad. Yet Franco's instinct was to strengthen the Falange and ramp up repression. He immediately closed Madrid University and suspended some of the already weak freedoms guaranteed in the Charter of Spaniards. Almost two decades of power had not changed Franco's priorities. Control, obedience and unity remained his primary obsessions.[16]

In a government reshuffle the following week, he reappointed the die-hard Falangist José Luis Arrese as the Movement's leader. Franco tasked him with drawing up major new legislation. It was expected that this would, once and for all, define the Francoist constitution by cementing the Movement as the regime's backbone, increasing its power and ensuring it control over events after Franco's death. He seemed unconcerned that single party states in Europe were now mostly found behind the Iron Curtain. The Falange, in other words, was back.[17]

On the evening of 30 April 1956, Franco addressed 25,000 Falangists packed into the gardens of the Alcazares Reales in Seville, exhorting them to see themselves as the real powerbrokers in Spain. He pointed out that technically, since his succession law, Spain was 'a monarchy without royalty'. Under his guidance, this royal-free monarchy functioned 'like a pyramid in which one person sits at the top, where there is discipline and obedience'. Any future monarch, however, must bow to them. 'The Falange can live without a monarchy, but there can never be a monarchy without the Falange,' he said.[18]

By choosing Arrese, Franco had asked a strongly ideological Falangist to finally resolve the problem of what his regime actually stood for. He cannot have been surprised when Arrese presented a project in which the Movement's leadership would become Spain's dominant force, second only to Franco and above any future monarch. Alarmed critics noted that, like the Soviet Union, the party would govern the nation, above elected representatives or a weak head of state.[19]

The project was attacked by Carrero Blanco and others. Spain's three cardinals complained that it contravened Vatican doctrine, calling it an 'antichristian monstrosity'. The proposals were based on 'foreign totalitarianism' and embraced the idea of 'the dictatorship of a single party', they said. It took strong criticism to pull Franco back from the brink, but with the proposals receiving attacks from all sides, he withdrew support. The Falange never recovered.[20]

In February 1957, he appointed yet another new government, shifting direction yet again. It was led by technocrats, many of them linked to Opus Dei, a powerful, mostly lay Catholic organisation founded by the Spanish priest Josemaría Escrivá in 1928 and formally approved by the Vatican in 1950, which sought out powerful and well-educated members.

Franco had now watered down autarky while shedding imperialism and sliding away from fascism towards pragmatic autocracy in the dozen years since World War II. This was good for Spaniards, but left him with a project that – apart from the daily administration of a country – was about little more than law, order, repression of dissent and imposition of Roman Catholic morals. Some called it 'bureaucratic authoritarianism'. Muñoz Grandes, an ardent Falange supporter, resigned his ministerial post in disgust. A tepid new law of Principles of the Movement, passed in 1958, added little that was new. Francoism, it now turned out, was largely about maintaining Franco in power. That way he could ensure order and obedience. There would be no great idea to pass on after his death.[21]

Instead, the argument now became over how much Spain should open up to the world economy. Franco's decision-making in government was always painfully drawn-out. Typically, this took agonisingly long to resolve as two Opus Dei technocrats, Finance Minister Mariano Navarro Rubio and Commerce Minister Alberto Ullastres, urged him to liberalise and, eventually, devalue the peseta. In the meantime, the future European Union was formed, with Franco's Spain left out once again, when six countries set up what was initially known as the European Economic Community (EEC) in 1958. Franco, in any case, viewed 'Europeanism' with deep suspicion at this stage.[22]

While other European countries opened their trade borders to each other, Spain stood on the brink of bankruptcy. The economy had grown through most of the 1950s as trade restrictions were slowly relaxed, but tipped into recession in 1958. Inflation ran rampant. Gold and foreign exchange reserves fell close to zero. His new ministers found it hard to make Franco understand the need to devalue Spain's currency, which he saw as gifting money to foreigners. In fact, he was out of his depth. The complexities of international finance and economics had always escaped him. His inability to recognise this, indeed, had kept Spaniards poor. Fortunately, Spain had finally been allowed into the International Monetary Fund in September 1958. Yet in February 1959 Franco initially refused IMF help, convinced, as ever, that Spain could solve its own problems. He only acceded after Navarro Rubio warned that rationing may have to be reintroduced.[23]

The 1959 Plan of Economic Stabilisation delivered the death blow to autarky as the IMF came to the rescue, supported by the Europe-wide Organisation for European Economic Cooperation (OECE) that had successfully channelled US Marshall Plan funds to rebuild Europe's economy after World War II. The US provided $200m in credit. 'This insolvent nation is about to be rescued by an international consortium headed by the United States, Spain's main ally,' the *New York Times* noted.[24]

As if to underline Francoist Spain's inability to function alone, the devaluation was announced by the IMF in Washington on 18 July 1959, while Franco was busy celebrating the twenty-third anniversary of his insurrection in the triumphalist tone always employed on this public holiday. The peseta shed over 40 per cent of its value against the dollar overnight. While Franco watched an equestrian statue of himself being unveiled outside the housing ministry in Madrid, Spaniards remained unaware of the extraordinarily important event that had just happened. Measured in dollars, the value of the things they owned and the salaries they were paid had shrunk by 40 per cent. It was a huge readjustment and perhaps the most consequential moment since Franco's civil war victory. Yet they had to wait three more days for an official announcement.

The always slow-moving Franco had accepted the deal begrudgingly. He instinctively disliked the idea of Spain being rescued by foreigners. Like all rescue packages, this came with a price, measured in short-term austerity. Taxes were hiked, public spending cut and interest rates raised. Fears that this would provoke a lengthy recession and mass unemployment proved unfounded. Instead, foreign investment flowed and exports picked up (since Spanish products were now 40 per cent cheaper): by the end of 1959, indeed, Spain was building up its gold and foreign exchange reserves again.[25]

Despite what even the IMF had called 'radical measures', a relatively small dose of pain produced much gain. Cheap labour and the ability to import machinery made Spain a desirable place to build factories. The growth stymied by Franco's autarky policies was suddenly released and Spain finally joined a wider southern European boom, where 'miracle' economies like Italy had already been growing at an average annual rate of almost 6 per cent for a decade. With the blocks to growth removed, Spain could now start catching up. Former agricultural day labourers flooded into cities and women increasingly joined the formal workforce as the countryside emptied. A burst of emigration saw many people move to work in wealthier European countries. The mainly rural, and often conservative, Spain that Franco had conquered in 1939 was now changing in profound ways. In fact,

Spain was entering an entirely new economic and social era – even if this was overseen by a dictator who had already been in power for two decades.[26]

From Franco's perspective, the watershed year of 1959 was crowned in two ways. On 1 April, he was driven up a twisting road through a pine forest dotted with oaks and other deciduous trees into a fold in the Guadarrama Mountains outside Madrid known as Cuelgamuros. A rugged natural amphitheatre of mountainside was overlooked here by imposing walls of granite rock. It lay just four miles from the vast monastery at El Escorial, from where Philip II had run his sixteenth-century empire. Cuelgamuros was a beloved spot and he had been coming for eighteen years, sometimes on horse-riding outings with his daughter Carmen, to follow the progress of a monumental project called the Valley of the Fallen. On 1 April 1959, he was finally able to inaugurate a remarkable, 260-metre-long underground basilica. This was hidden below an imposing outcrop of lichen-clad rock, dotted with spindly, wind-tortured trees. A 150-metre-high granite cross sat atop this, ensuring the monument was seen from Madrid. Below it, a series of austere, arched galleries looked across a wide, featureless esplanade. Between the galleries two bronze doors gave way to the troglodyte basilica itself, where a 22-metre interior dome had been hollowed out and lined with gold mosaics. The resulting basilica was longer than St Peter's in the Vatican and almost as high.[27]

Doors in the apse opened onto the far side of the outcrop, where a large Benedictine monastery was built. The monks were charged with praying for those buried here – since Franco had ordered that the remains of 35,000 dead from both sides of the civil war be dug up and transported to the basilica. They were hidden away in walled-off side galleries. The only visible grave was that of Falange founder José Antonio Primo de Rivera, who had been carried here in procession from his previous resting place in the Royal Monastery of San Lorenzo at El Escorial, fourteen kilometres away, and buried beside the altar.

Franco had commissioned the work in April 1940, just a year after the civil war ended with a decree in which he argued that such a tremendous and transcendental event could not be marked by 'the simple monuments with which towns and cities commemorate the major events of our history'. Inspired by the El Escorial monastery (already described by one foreign visitor as 'the oppressive monument of the first totalitarian state in Europe'), Franco felt it needed to share 'the grandiosity of ancient monuments, which defy time and forgetting'.[28] Nineteen years later, after the deaths of fourteen workers and the employment of thousands of prisoners (some of them political), the architects had achieved that. This was nominally a monument to all the civil war dead but his inauguration speech was primarily about the 'glorious' martyrs from his own side and the wickedness of his enemies, including the International Brigades. 'Our civil war was not like other civil wars, but rather a true crusade,' he said. His enemies from the 'anti-Spain', he warned, were still a danger.[29]

Franco was still awaiting the pope's elevation of his underground church to the formal status of basilica (it arrived the following year) when, on 21 December 1959, he received definitive proof that he was no longer an international pariah. That afternoon, President Eisenhower touched down at the joint US-Spanish air base at Torrejón de Ardoz, outside Madrid, to be effusively welcomed by Franco. Ordinary Spaniards were even more overjoyed to see Eisenhower, who was greeted by one of the biggest crowds he had ever seen. People lined the route to Madrid in the largest turn-out since the victory parade at the end of the civil war. Franco, typically, saw it as approval for his dictatorship, telling Pacón it counted as a 'popular referendum on my foreign policy'.[30]

Eisenhower's translator was a polyglot army officer called Vernon Walters, who would later become acting director of the CIA. The visit was effectively an overnight courtesy call, with a formal dinner and a breakfast meeting with Franco in which nothing of great significance was discussed, but the Americans left feeling that the caudillo was quite popular and surprisingly able to appear in public with little fear for his life. Walters recalled a pleasant visit:

> It was getting dark but this did not dampen the enthusiasm of the crowds... The great Castellana Avenue was wall-to-wall people. We stopped on it to receive the keys of the city and be greeted by the mayor of Madrid. The two men got out of the car for the ceremony and they were not more than eight or ten feet from the people. If Franco was, as we are told, a hated despot, it certainly did not show on that day... Later on the aircraft, on the way to Morocco,

President Eisenhower expressed his surprise about Franco: 'He is nothing like the guy the press portrays.'[31]

Despite the impression taken away by Eisenhower, officials at Franco's Pardo Palace fretted that he was losing support. Pacón had already noticed a difference in the way Franco was received during their tours of the country. 'The reception was good, but it was not "triumphal" as the press proclaims. There is a huge difference compared to earlier years,' he noted after returning from two weeks in Andalusia the previous year.[32]

It was clear that – after two decades of peace, repression and poverty – Franco was still in absolute command. It had not proved difficult to impose absolute control as long as Spain remained closed in on itself. Now that he had opened the doors to the rest of the world, would that change?

39
Take-Off

BENIDORM AND BARCELONA, 1959–1960

In July 1959, a young Englishwoman called Judith Roberts was arrested by police in Benidorm after refusing to leave a beachfront bar because she was wearing a bikini. A municipal policeman who had swapped his usual job in Madrid for a summer patrol in the growing resort town had first ordered her to leave and then pulled a chair away from under her. Miss Roberts responded by slapping him twice in the face.

The case was taken up by the *Daily Express* in London and even by the *Sydney Morning Herald* in Australia. Naturally, local newspapers had nothing to say, but everyone from the civil governor of Alicante, the local bishopric and the mayor – a dynamic Falangist called Pedro Zaragoza Orts – became involved.[1]

Roberts was fined for slapping the policeman, but the incident reflected how important tourism was becoming to Spain and how much of a challenge it could be to Franco's Roman Catholic authoritarianism. Roberts had defied both authority and morals by wearing a bikini off the beach, but she also represented the desired object of a Spanish gold rush based on tourism.

Zaragoza Orts had been defending Benidorm against allegations that it was a den of vice for several years as the once poor fishing community began transforming itself into the capital of the new package tourism that brought northern Europeans flocking to Spanish beaches. He once claimed to have won the personal support of Franco after driving to Madrid for nine hours on his Vespa, with newspapers shoved down his shirt to keep the cold at bay. Although Zaragoza Orts was an unreliable storyteller, Franco certainly showered him with rewards and later gave him a seat in parliament.

'We have been told that there is an extraordinary number of Swedish, Finnish, German and British tourists in Benidorm this year and that their scandalous, shameless behaviour has turned that beach into a brothel,' an anonymous official report stated in July 1957. This and the arrival of 'numerous homosexuals' was, the report claimed, driving away decent Spanish families. 'The Nordic women holiday makers are characterised by their eroticism and man-hunting, especially chasing adolescent Spaniards and producing the most abject spectacle on the beach at night, near the little hotels, under trucks etc...' the report added.[2]

The idea of sex-hungry Swedish women hunting down young locals was a myth but also part of a culture clash that shook a Francoist society which was, in many ways, designed to faithfully reproduce the strict mores of the Franco household itself. The regime and the church were so paranoid about dangerous foreign morals that the local bishop of Orihuela issued constant warnings. Zaragoza Orts later claimed the bishop even threatened to excommunicate him, with Franco personally coming to his rescue.[3]

What was once a modest beach-side village of sailors, fishermen and farmers who cropped almonds, olives, carobs and citrus fruits had been transformed after Zaragoza Orts arranged for spring water to be piped in. Benidorm's spectacular three-mile-long, double crescent of golden sand had previously only been good for launching small, coastal fishing boats. Local men often spent months at sea as deckhands or setting out complex *almadrabas*, the maze of nets laid to trap tuna. The existing handful of small hotels and holiday homes were being replaced by multi-storey hotels as the mayor advertised the town's beaches as far away as Sweden and Finland. By 1959 the town was servicing tourists by the tens of thousands.

It would take several years, however, for bikinis to make it past cinema censors or to feature on the front cover of Benidorm town hall's own magazine, as they eventually did. Soon Manuel Fraga could comment that there were 'more bikinis than nazarenos' (the hooded members of religious brotherhoods who parade church statues through the streets) in Spain at Easter Week, while hardliners like the thuggish ultra-Catholic Blas Piñar complained that the nation was being corrupted. Others worried that ugly concrete hotels and high-rise apartment blocks were spoiling Spain's natural charm. 'Real estate dealers, foreign and national are allowed to ruin the beautiful eastern coast,' complained Salvador de Madariaga. With large sums of money to be made, rumours inevitably started that the Franco family had invested in Benidorm. They were false, but a sign of how much Spaniards realised that the wider Franco family was busy enriching itself in the dictator's shadow.[4]

The influx of foreign capital and Spain's new status as 'miracle' one of western Europe's fastest-growing economies meant Franco now frequently found himself inaugurating new buildings, factories and, above all, dams. The latter were designed to produce hydroelectric power, help redistribute water from the rainy north to the arid south and allow for new irrigation schemes. More than 600 dams would be built. As building picked up, they could be inaugurated at the rate of one every three weeks. With Franco so keen to be present, he was jokingly dubbed 'Paco the Frog'. Irrigated land did indeed increase by 40 per cent between 1950 and 1965 – though this mainly benefitted large landowners, who saw returns on their land leap up to twentyfold.[5]

For ordinary Spaniards, though, the arrival of electricity in their villages, along with tractors, television sets, extensive indoor plumbing and, after the state-owned Seat company signed a licensing deal with Fiat, the legendary but tiny Seat 600 car, felt like sudden and massive progress. Mateo Frias González, whose father was one of the 35,000-strong workforce churning out Seat cars in three rolling daily shifts, recalls his family taking 24 hours to travel from Barcelona in their first Seat 600 to the village in Granada where his parents had grown up. 'When this fantastic car looked down from above on the little village where its adult occupants had grown up, our mothers wept with emotion and in our fathers we could see the pride of returning home having made a better life for themselves,' he wrote.[6]

Elsewhere, the changes wrought by tourism, foreign investment, factory jobs, rapid urbanisation and a boom that brought sustained improvement in living standards were accompanied by a timid shedding of political apathy. Leaflets, for example, that circulated clandestinely around Barcelona in May 1960, as Franco spent almost an entire month based in the city, showed not just that his tours provoked less public enthusiasm than before but that they could also become a focus for underground opponents.

Franco was an oppressor, the leaflets said, who ruled through corruption, censorship and persecution of Catalan culture. Worse still, he was now amongst them. Police had no idea where the leaflets, written in Catalan and printed on orange-tinted paper, came from until the city's bourgeoisie gathered at the exquisitely tiled modernist Catalan Music Palace on 19 May 1960. The theatre was packed for a concert celebrating the centenary of the great Catalan poet Joan Maragall. Barcelona's most famous choir, the Orfeó Català, sang part of its repertory but was banned from performing a song based on a Maragall poem, the 'Cant de la Senyera' ('Song to the [Catalan] Flag'), since this was deemed to have separatist connotations.

The previous day, Franco had overseen a separate homage to Maragall, and pictures of him visiting the city's new zoo were on the front page of local newspapers. He looked perfectly healthy, but it was around now that doctors detected he was beginning to suffer from Parkinson's disease.[7] It was a first proper sign of physical frailty, and one that was duly kept secret.

Franco was not, however, at the concert, unlike several of the ministers who had joined him for his four-week sojourn in Catalonia. Jordi Pujol, the young businessman who had written the leaflets, was not at the concert either, but he had helped persuade some hundred Catalan activists to infiltrate the event. They began to sing the 'Cant de la Senyera' themselves and other audience members joined in. Plain clothes police in the audience then rose to their feet, swinging batons and arresting people. Many were taken to the infamous Via Laietana police station, a short distance away, where they were beaten and tortured in the manner routinely applied to suspected anarchists or communists. Pujol's name was mentioned, his home searched and it became clear that he was the author of the leaflets. He was detained, beaten, tried by a military court and sentenced to seven years in jail, though he only served two of them.[8]

Torture of political prisoners had not been a public issue in Franco's Spain, since arrests were not reported in the press and news of it only filtered out via underground publications or exiled party members. But Pujol was different. Trained as a doctor, the eminently respectable 31-year-old had gone into business. He had nothing to do with the left-wing radicals or the occasionally troublesome young university students who had broken with the Falange a few years earlier. He was close to the church, a member of the Catholic Institute for Social Studies and the son of a prominent city financier (who had just bought a small bank at his son's urging). He represented, in other words, the city's Catalan-speaking, traditional bourgeoisie. A few days later, Pujol's father filed a legal complaint for police mistreatment of his son.

Those who had not heard about the Catalan Music Palace incident could read about it in what, for some educated Spaniards, had become their most reliable source of domestic news – the foreign press, which was available at newspaper stalls if sometimes removed by the regime. The *New York Times* reported not only the concert fracas itself but also that Father Aureli Escarré, abbot of the Montserrat monastery, had sent a telegram to Franco in protest. 'Profoundly regret repression and tortures inflicted on young Catholics during Orfeó Català concert. Lamentable epilogue to your government's stay in Catalonia,' it said.[9] The newspaper noted that Escarré – whose monastery was the spiritual home of the Catalan church – was a 'revered figure amongst Spain's three million Catalan Roman Catholics'.

In private, Franco accused Escarré of 'defending the agitators', but a new level of opposition had suddenly become visible.[10] Previously, the opposition had been neatly divided between clandestine opponents from banned political parties, who were watched closely by police, and regime backers who pressured subtly for change and who were splintered into an ineffective range of modernisers, monarchists, Roman Catholics, Falangist die-hards, traditionalists and militarists. Now part of the church was openly defying Franco and doing it in the name of the sort of Catholic bourgeoisie that was expected to support the regime. The jailed Pujol became a figurehead to Catalan nationalists who – like their Basque counterparts – could always count on support from some local churchmen.

In fact, the Franco visit had itself been a reaction to a separate incident inside a Barcelona church. Shortly after his troops took the city in 1939, Franco had appointed his old friend Luis de Galinsoga as editor of the main local paper, *La Vanguardia* (rebaptised *La Vanguardia Española*). Galinsoga had written some of the early, laudatory profiles of Franco during his military career and had cowritten with Pacón a prize-winning 1956 hagiography of the dictator called *Sentinel of the West* that Franco's cousin eventually reneged on, suggesting that Galinsoga had overdone the colourful adulation. He also had a seat in Franco's rubber-stamp parliament.[11]

Some months before the incident at the Music Palace, Galinsoga had entered a Barcelona church, heard a service being conducted in Catalan and loudly hurled abuse at the priest, threatening punishment. 'All Catalans are shit!' he reportedly cursed when fellow worshippers argued with him, with the priest explaining that only one out of four services were in Catalan, even though this was the first language of many parishioners. Word of this outrage spread quickly and a boycott, partly organised by Pujol's group, saw copies of *La Vanguardia* snatched from newspaper kiosks and hurled to the pavement while advertisers received anonymous threats. As income dipped, the owner begged Franco to intervene, though it still took months for Galinsoga to be sacked in February 1960.[12]

The criticisms laid out in Pujol's leaflet all made sense. Corruption was so widespread, he had said, that anyone wanting to prosper had to join in by paying bribes and helping clients or suppliers to avoid tax, leaving themselves open to arrest and prosecution. 'He knows that a rotten country is easy to dominate,' Pujol had written. 'His regime wants everyone compromised, covered in the filth [of corruption].' Pujol may have been thinking of his father, one of 1,363 wealthy Spaniards whose secret Swiss bank accounts had been revealed in December 1958. He also criticised the hypocrisy of a regime that proclaimed itself 'democratic' when all elections – whether municipal, to syndicates or to a parliament 'with the same value of those in communist countries' – were meaningless. Censorship, suppression of non-political workers' organisations (unless run by the Falange) and the banning of even some Roman Catholic groups meant there was no cultural, intellectual or religious freedom. Priests and Christian youth groups were not allowed to stray into the social sphere, he complained, 'when the Popes wish us to be concerned about the common good in society and urge us to take responsibility for that'.[13]

Even shareholders were not safe, Pujol claimed, repeating reports that Franco's brother Nicolás had threatened to call the police on shareholders who complained about his stewardship of a company called Manufacturas Metálicas Madrileñas, where he was chairman. Nicolás was now on the board of many companies and was frequently held up as an example of regime corruption, including by those inside it. Several regime generals, indeed, were amongst those who prospered hugely in business, while Nicolás was famous for the letters of recommendation he wrote to officials so that they had to receive those he was personally in business with. 'Everyone knew that Nicolas felt that, as the elder brother of the caudillo – as he liked to call his brother every time that he needed to push past some obstacle – he was perfectly placed to operate with complete freedom,' says one biographer of Franco's brother. 'He believed, and nobody argued against him, that he was right to use for himself the privileges that fortune had endowed on the Franco family. All his energy went into making sure he was the member of the clan who got most out of life and the facts indicate that this personal philosophy worked well for many years.'[14]

Tired Spaniards, Pujol concluded, no longer knew anything else but Francoism. 'After twenty years of dictatorship there are people who find the world we live in natural, just as those who have always lived amidst pollution do not miss clean air,' he said.

Franco was used to brushing off criticism. Even the events at the Catalan Music Palace in Barcelona seemed small and inconsequential compared to the war he had won twenty-one years earlier. Such matters could easily be dealt with by repression or the co-opting of those who complained. 'Franco was always successful at judging the price of men. He thought: this one, a box of cigars; that one, councilman; that other, provincial deputy; to this man an import licence; this one, governor; that one, minister,' said his former education minister Pedro Sainz Rodríguez. Franco was irritated by those who rejected his offers and the former minister thought Franco's own constant lobbying for advancement in the army as a young, high-flying officer meant he expected everyone to always be jostling for personal advantage.[15]

Protest, in any case, could come from any direction. Later in 1960, after Pujol had been jailed, Franco was confronted by this himself during the Falange's annual homage to José Antonio Primo de Rivera in the Valley of the Fallen's echoing underground basilica. 'Franco, traitor to the Falange!' a young soldier shouted as Franco sat in his special gilt and scarlet chair by the altar. The caudillo was the centrepiece of these celebrations, kneeling for prayers 'lonely and austere in his gold-trimmed generalisimo's uniform, his aides ranged behind him, his face solemn, his eyes cast down, his hands folded', according to one observer. Many of the thousands of people present must have heard (and seen the soldier instantly detained), though Franco told Pacón that 'I only heard him call my name.'[16]

With guerilla opponents defeated, only the Falange and monarchists presented a potential threat from within Franco's regime – since both had military supporters theoretically capable of launching coups – but they had been co-opted long ago and were easy to manage. The events in Barcelona, however, showed that new alliances could spring up between rebels who opposed the regime from the outside and those who were tamely and obediently critical from within. For the church to ally with the rebels, indeed, represented a new and dangerous precedent.

When miners in Asturias went on strike in April 1962 and again in the summer of 1963, it seemed that the Falange's syndicates were losing control of their 8.5 million worker members and their employers. Once more, strikers found support amongst local priests, which scandalised Franco who was convinced that 'no Spanish government before this regime has ever been so concerned with workers' welfare.' The dictator did not generally fret much about strikes over pay or conditions (even though these were formally illegal), but was suspicious of the miners because of their revolutionary history. 'You have lived in Asturias so you know that labour unrest there is never about strikes and has always been about politics,' he told Pacón. 'They demand wage rises that the mining companies cannot possibly afford. So they go straight to a strike, then to a revolutionary confrontation and then to conflict with the forces of law and order.' He wished the miners would behave more like the largely passive, heavily religious workers of rural Old Castile. 'These days miners want for nothing. They and their families live well. But subversive propaganda is difficult to silence.'[17]

Franco had heard rumours that an exiled communist leader had slipped into Spain to organise the miners and blamed his secret police for not watching them closely enough. He even wanted bar owners paid to inform on those who plotted as they drank their Asturian cider:

> Nothing that happens in a mine should be allowed to avoid the vigilance of police or informers. That way you know whether a strike is

about labour conditions or is political. In the first case you have to rapidly study the reasons and deal with them within the conditions of labour legislation. In the second case you have to find the provocateurs and deal with them. The socialists and the communists are perfectly coordinated with their exiles. The proof is that, as soon as there is a strike, it is on the foreign radio stations.[18]

Foreign radio stations and newspapers were, in fact, the only media to cover the illegal strikes. As with certain veiled criticisms and the existence of groups who lobbied for change without challenging the regime, strikes could at times be tolerated, or not, depending on the whims of Franco and his officials. Such tolerance was often seen as generosity – a virtue that those who received it should feel grateful for, whilst also knowing that it could be removed and replaced by repression at any moment. In much the same way, a tame, easily controlled and highly constrained internal 'opposition' had emerged involving people unwilling to sacrifice careers or personal freedoms by publicly and vigorously challenging the regime. All this allowed Franco to imagine that he was not, in fact, a dictator, as he liked to tell foreign journalists. 'To me and all Spaniards, it is simply childish to call me a dictator,' he told a French journalist.[19]

While Franco remained delighted with Prince Juan Carlos and the princess he married in 1962, Sophia of Greece, the next challenge came from the monarchists who, for the most part, had long toed the Francoist line and its promise of a future restoration. The couple married in Athens in May 1962, with monarchists and aristocrats gathering at the wedding. Some of those guests appeared the following month in Munich at a European Movement meeting, where Spain's exiled opposition parties met on the sidelines. They drew up a public declaration demanding respect for human rights, proper democracy, freedom of expression and recognition that regions like Catalonia, the Basque country and Galicia formed their own 'natural communities'. It was signed by 118 people including prominent regime-friendly monarchists who were now loudly breaking with Francoism for the first time. This alliance of Social and Christian democrats with monarchists, socialists and Catalan or Basque nationalists represented the majority of pre-war political tendencies. Opposition to Franco had finally brought them all together. 'Today, the civil war is over,' the exiled writer and university professor Salvador de Madariaga said after signing the document. The socialists even agreed to accept a return to monarchy if this brought real democracy. Apart from communists and anarchists, the only people missing were the Falange, Carlists and those monarchists or Catholics on the extreme right.

Franco was furious at what the Falange newspaper *Arriba* dubbed 'the Munich conspiracy'. Amongst other reasons, he had been convinced that he had Don Juan's followers under control. Worse still, this was an alliance between the tame 'tolerated' internal critics of his regime and its banned militant opponents, mirroring the Catalan church's relationship with regionalists like Jordi Pujol. In other words, it broke the carefully constructed model of tepid internal criticism that could be used to pretend the regime was plural and tolerant.

Franco's reaction was, once more, to suspend the already restricted rights Spaniards enjoyed under the Charter of Spaniards for the next two years and to tell signatories who lived in Spain either to go into exile voluntarily or face being ordered out of the country. Almost two dozen prominent internal critics went into exile or were banished to the Canary Islands.

Franco now seems to have decided definitively that Don Juan could not be trusted and that the crown must skip a generation and go to his son Juan Carlos – though only after his own death. (In fact, Don Juan had nothing to do with the Munich meetings and had sacked members of his private council who signed the declaration.) Franco wanted someone he could control and Prince Juan Carlos, who had become skilled at nodding in agreement, was a safer choice. 'Why did I never say anything?' Juan Carlos said later. 'Because it was a period when nobody, not even me, dared speak.'[20]

In the meantime, Franco also decided to name a vice-president who could take over if he should die before choosing a monarch to follow him (though he was in no hurry to do that). His choice of Agustín Muñoz Grandes, the hardline, Iron Cross-wearing general who had led the Blue Division in Adolf Hitler's army made it clear that Franco had no intention of giving in to liberal democracy. In a characteristic carrot-and-stick manoeuvre, he also appointed an energetic young reformist, 39-year-old Manuel Fraga, to a refreshed government. Fraga became the Information and Tourism minister, a powerful post which gave him charge of the state's propaganda and censorship machinery, and he immediately began suggesting that censorship should be relaxed. The forthright and formidable Fraga sought reforms but was no liberal, with friends describing him as combining 'uncommon brilliance with uncommon imperiousness'. His main priority was to uphold Francoism, which he feared was doomed if it did not change. 'I've come here to defend the honour of Spain, which is above those who try to rubbish it from at home or abroad,' he said on taking charge in July 1962.[21]

Despite the excitement provoked by the Munich meeting, Franco was still in absolute control. The *New York Times* correspondent, Benjamin Welles, popped the balloon of enthusiasm of those who thought change was coming.

> Was General Franco really menaced by the sensationalised rally of a hundred or so political foes meeting in far-off Munich? He was not. Spain's Chief of State has 400,000 troops and police, an expanding economy, more than $1,000,000,000 in reserves, a defense treaty with the United States – and the acquiescence of most Spaniards more than 40 years old who recall the Civil War and want to be left in peace...
>
> He also enjoys the tacit or supine backing of a majority of the young citizenry who have grown up in an air-tight regime, know nothing of politics, are apathetic, cynical and more interested in economic security than in politics... For the moment General Franco is carrying on unruffled at the Pardo Palace.[22]

Although the Munich rebels were part of a sea change in the nature of opposition to Franco, neither they nor clandestine activists inside Spain were in a position to force change. Indeed, when Welles visited Franco at his Galician holiday house, the Palacio de Meirás, in August 1962, for a farewell interview after six years in Madrid, he found 'the dean of European rulers' calm and still absolutely certain that he had always been right. 'Our [civil war] victory saved Europe from falling under communism,' he said. 'Our political stability today is still helping to protect Europe's flank.'[23]

Welles found the dictator slightly thinner than in previous years, with a hand damaged in a hunting accident in December 1961 almost healed. He was 'relaxed, frequently breaking into laughter as he described the problems of ruling his volatile, quick-witted people'. These he governed 'as if they were headstrong children who required parental control'. Now that Franco had been saved by the Cold War, Welles observed, he remained blissfully convinced that 'his people, more than ever, need him; while Europe, more than ever, needs Spain'. The prize for his people was currently a booming economy, growing tourism and some of the lowest crime statistics in Europe. It was paid for with a lack of basic freedoms and political disenfranchisement.[24]

While Welles could see that the miners' strikes, Munich declaration and outbursts of song in Barcelona had failed to weaken Franco, a new and growing attitude of defiance from the church signalled that something was finally changing. Even Cardinal Pla y Deniel, who had so effusively praised the civil war 'crusade' was now lambasting the Falange for crushing church-affiliated workers' groups. That, in effect, was rebellion from within. Nor could Franco use force to threaten or oblige the church to shut up.

The Roman Catholic church as a whole was going through change. On 11 October 1962, it embarked on the three-year marathon ecumenical meeting known as Vatican II. No-one yet knew how that would end, but Pope Pius XII – with whom Franco had signed the concordat – had died in 1958 and John XXIII followed him in June 1963, giving way to the reformist Paul VI. The election of such a liberal pope, Franco remarked, was 'like an icy shower'.[25]

Before he died, John XXIII had written to Franco begging for clemency as he prepared to execute a political prisoner. The victim was Julián Grimau, a communist and former secret policeman during the civil war who had been caught after returning to Spain clandestinely. After being taken to the police headquarters in Madrid's Puerta del Sol square on 8 November 1962, Grimau mysteriously fell from a second-floor window, suffering injuries to his head and wrists. Police said he had hurled himself out. Grimau said he was hurled. Whatever the truth, he was charged with crimes dating back to the civil war when he allegedly took part in the persecution and torture of Francoist 'fifth columnist' spies. (In fact, Grimau had also been involved in repressing the POUM, the pro-Republican Trotskyist group which George Orwell joined in Barcelona and which later rebelled against the Republic for being insufficiently revolutionary.)

Franco was about to move responsibility for trying acts of 'subversion' from the military courts to a newly established, and soon to be notorious, Public Order Tribunal, or TOP. However, this was not yet in place and Grimau was subjected to a five-hour military hearing. 'I have never tortured anyone. It is not my nature to do such things. I carried out duties assigned to me by a legal government, I have been a communist for 25 years and I will die a communist,' he told the court. It sentenced him to death.[26]

The Pope was not the only person to write to Franco pleading for clemency. Letters came from world leaders as varied as the USSR's Nikita Krushchev (who lamented, in the first letter ever received by Franco from the Kremlin, that '25 years after the ending of the civil war a man can be tried in Spain under wartime laws') and the British government. 'Your goodwill is surprising in this case, given that Grimau is the author of horrendous crimes,' Franco answered the British, or so Pacón reported. He dismissed foreign complaints as another example of Spain being victimised. 'They are used to meddling in Spain's affairs, but say nothing when this happens in any other country,' he said.[27]

The director of the Civil Guard refused to let his men carry out the sentence, arguing that legally it was not their task and a firing squad was instead formed by army volunteers on 20 April 1963. Grimau calmly sent away a priest who tried to offer 'spiritual aid'. The firing squad failed to kill him outright and Grimau was finished off by a pistol shot to the head. Fraga told the international press that he had been a 'notorious torturer who came back to continue his crimes'.[28]

Franco still did not feel threatened or show much desire to soften his regime. In January 1963 a communist-sympathising writer, Manuel Moreno Barranco, died after allegedly throwing himself from a walkway into the patio of the prison in Jerez, southern Spain. In August 1963, Franco again ignored petitions for clemency when two anarchists, were garrotted. This ancient Spanish method of execution saw a metal collar, or garrotte, placed around their necks and tightened until it either snapped their spine or cut off the supply of air. Although one of the men had been found carrying explosives, their confessions were almost certainly extracted by torture and the two bombings they were accused of (including at a Madrid passport office where a 16-year-old girl was badly burned) were later claimed by a separate group.[29]

As the calendar turned into 1964, the economy was booming, and Fraga was organising marathon nationwide celebrations of Franco's quarter-century of rule. A canny campaign, inviting people to celebrate a lack of violence, as if the only options were Franco or permanent civil war, turned the usual 1 April annual celebrations of his civil war victory into a month-long propaganda push under the slogan of '25 Years of Peace' with its own specially minted commemorative medal for veterans from his side. Franco was presented as a wise and still vigorous leader, though officials and ministers noted that he now tired quickly, probably as a result of his developing Parkinson's disease. In fact, public appearances and speeches started to become shorter, occasionally revealing a man with 'a rigid stance, an unsure walk and a vacant, open-mouthed facial expression' in the words of Franco biographer Paul Preston.[30]

Since anyone under 40 had learned their history in Francoist schools, few were equipped to challenge the idea that a civil war that had killed half a million Spaniards had really been about creating peace. School children were being taught glorified and twisted versions of history, with Franco appearing in their textbooks as having 'planned the glorious National uprising' as if he had organised and directed it himself, rather than joining at the last possible moment. Those same textbooks claimed that Franco was 'a new El Cid, the saviour of Spain' and warned against the horrors of participative politics, comparing it to 'stimulants like coffee, tobacco, alcohol, newspapers... [that] undermine us and waste our bodies away'.[31]

Ever the cinema-lover, Franco received in 1964 a gift in the form of a biographical documentary made by the director of *Raza*, called *'Franco, That Man!'* The film was more of a success in cinemas than even the director expected. This and the crowds Franco saw on his 25 Years of Peace tours deepened his belief in his own popularity. It strengthened his resistance to change. In fact, he thought the world was finally working out just how right he had always been.[32]

40

Change

THE VATICAN-MADRID 1960–1964

'In Franco's eyes, it is not he who is changing; it is the world that is moving toward him,' the *New York Times*'s Benjamin Welles wrote in his 1965 book, *Spain: the Gentle Anarchy*. As an American newsman who had lived in Spain for six years, Welles sought to explain to a foreign audience how the 'despotic paternalism' of Franco's graft-ridden regime really worked. 'Nothing angers Franco more than charges that his is a naked military dictatorship with no freedom. He insists that his system, which he holds up as a model for underdeveloped nations in Latin America, Asia, and Africa, is democracy: democracy tailored to special conditions.' Change happened only at a snail's pace, Welles observed, but the opposition was toothless. 'Many millions of the voiceless Left still regard him as the archfiend of reaction. Yet he goes on preaching national unity, national togetherness.'[1]

A booming economy helped. Tourism had become one of the great motors of Spain's economic miracle and its main source of foreign currency, with more than 4 million people travelling to its sunny beaches in 1960, four times more than in 1954. By 1965 the numbers had jumped to 11 million and would reach 31 million in 1973, covering three-quarters of the trade deficit. More importantly, the influx of foreigners meant Spaniards were no longer isolated from the rest of Europe. That dynamic was amplified by a burst of emigration which saw one in ten workers, or some 1.12 million people, leave for more advanced economies in Western Europe from 1961 to 1975. The money they sent home covered 23 per cent of foreign debt.[2]

Emigrants returned each summer in flashy cars, with tales of lofty salaries and unimagined freedoms. 'All this is stirring up discontent among the local working class who feel inferior as a result,' read one police report on them.[3] 'Insults have even been proffered against the regime.' Other people, Spaniards discovered, enjoyed more freedoms and better living standards. That was not the sort of message they had been receiving from Franco's press for the previous 30 years. An old tourism slogan, 'Spain is different!', looked worryingly apt.

Rumblings of political dissatisfaction were growing slowly louder, though censorship dampened the noise. Student and worker protests were spreading with even a group of priests protesting outside one Madrid courthouse. Some thirty small explosive devices were set off around Madrid in 1964 and the Basque armed separatist group ETA (Euskadi Ta Askatasuna, Basque for 'Basque Homeland and Liberty', a revolutionary breakaway from the Basque Nationalist Party) had formally embraced violent insurrection. ETA had become a target for the police after failing to blow up a train carrying Falangists in 1961, but had probably first killed the previous year when a suitcase bomb blew up in a train station in San Sebastian, killing a 22-month-old girl.[4]

Even the Vatican was moving faster than Francoist Spain, declaring in December 1965 that it now believed in religious freedom, meaning governments should not prohibit or hinder the practice of other forms of Christianity. Franco's Charter of Spaniards merely spoke of 'tolerating' non-Roman Catholics, and mistreatment of Protestants had been a constant since the civil war (when several pro-Republican Protestant pastors were shot). Effectively, Protestants had been allowed to practice in private after 1945, but never in public. Everything from marriage to burial and even some bureaucratic paperwork was made more difficult for the 30,000 or more Spaniards (as well as for foreigners) who declared themselves to be non-Catholics. Such was the moral panic provoked by non-Catholics that a book called *New Customs, Old Sins* published in 1959 warned Spanish men against marrying foreign women since 'most are atheists, theosophists, spiritualists, protestants, quakers, Methodists, Anglicans or Mormons'.[5]

The Vatican's change provoked an apoplectic reaction around Franco's cabinet table, where the Opus Dei faction now dominated.

The idea that, as the Vatican now declared, 'the free exercise of religion in society' might be 'greatly in accord with truth and justice' was anathema to reactionaries like Carrero Blanco and, presumably, to Franco. In perhaps the most violently angry cabinet document circulated in the 1960s, Carrero Blanco declared that he would rather sink Spain than give way to religious freedom.[6]

Franco was now aged 73, surrounded mostly by other old men. Those closest to him, like Carrero Blanco and his law-and-order minister Camilo Alonso Vega (a childhood friend from Ferrol and the Toledo academy), still lived in a civil war mindset. Together with Muñoz Grandes, these were the four most powerful men in the land – with an average age of seventy. Carrero Blanco was the youngest at 61. Yet by 1965, nobody aged under 30 had any memories of the civil war, meaning half of the country. Fewer than a third of Spaniards had been adults during the war. In other words, Franco was losing touch with a rapidly changing nation. The younger, technocratic Opus Dei ministers spoke only of finance and the economy and were, in any case, from a deeply conservative corner of the church.[7]

An exception to this was Manuel Fraga, the young Information and Tourism Minister, who spent four years convincing Franco to relax censorship laws first imposed under wartime conditions in 1938. This had produced some bizarre decisions, especially in cinemas. In 1963 rules for film-makers had been published prohibiting 'the justification of divorce, adultery or anything that attacks the institution of marriage or the family' or anything that provoked 'low passions' or was 'lascivious, brutal, gross or morbid'. Already, Humphrey Bogart's lines about the Spanish Republic had been expunged from *Casablanca* while, in Robert Aldrich's *Dirty Dozen*, a no-good character called Franko was renamed, because his name sounded too much like that of the caudillo. In a celebrated faux pas, censors turned the protagonists of John Ford's *Mogambo*, played by Grace Kelly and Donald Sinden, from husband and wife into brother and sister. Their attempt to stop Kelly's on-screen affair with Clark Gable becoming adultery thus saw her marriage turned into incest.[8]

It was only in 1966, indeed, that reforms to censorship were approved. Essentially, this passed responsibility for prior censorship from state censors onto newspaper editors, who still faced fines and disciplinary action for overstepping boundaries. 'I don't [really] believe in this freedom, but it is a necessary step,' Franco told his ministers. Privately, he urged Fraga to remain as strict as possible. 'Let's not be too nice. Let us, like everybody else, exert indirect control,' he said. Magazine editors still had to send copies for pre-publication approval, which was withdrawn if they broke taboos like mentioning strikes. In the smoke-and-mirrors world of Francoism, strikes were both a regular occurrence and something that formally never happened. The Franco regime, after all, claimed to have resolved all class issues and strikes were illegal. 'That word does not exist,' the editor of one magazine was told after being banned from publishing an edition that contained a story about a strike at a car factory.[9]

Even so, the new law was too much for the old guard surrounding Franco, who complained bitterly about mild criticism of civil governors, the appearance of Don Juan in the *ABC* newspaper and reports about doctors unhappy with their pay. Fraga still stamped on those who broke the basic codes of Francoism. On 21 July 1966, he sequestered the popular monarchist *ABC* daily for an opinion piece saying that Spain needed 'a democratic monarchy' headed by Don Juan, rather than his son, Prince Juan Carlos. Police removed the newspaper from kiosks and reportedly even snatched it out of people's hands on the Madrid metro, while Civil Guard officers drove around country towns and villages hunting down copies. *Le Monde* claimed that more than a million copies of the piece were made for those desperate to find out what the fuss was about.[10]

Franco was furious about the article. He declared that 'not even the worst enemy of the monarchy and the regime could say such a terrible thing'. To Pacón, he ranted about the civil war and its million dead and wondered why former ministers were now backing Don Juan and, hence, his 'enemies'. This was revenge, he thought, for having sacked them. The journalist who wrote the piece was banished to Hong Kong as a correspondent. In fact, as the article pointed out, Prince Juan Carlos had himself recently been quoted in *Time* magazine as saying that he would 'never, never accept the crown as long as my father is alive'.[11]

By November, Franco was fed up with press freedom. 'I'm tired of the fact that the press wakes up every morning asking: "What shall we criticise now?"' he told Fraga. None of this, however, stopped Franco believing he was widely beloved. Another summer tour of

Catalonia, with cheering crowds, convinced him of this. So, too, did the approval at a referendum of a major new law, the Organic State Law. This unwieldy and frequently unintelligible text was designed to both complete the Francoist 'constitution' and take the fascist edges off the older Fundamental Laws that it modified. Mostly, it was a tidying up of a Francoist state to make its administration clearer and more efficient. The law separated out the roles of head of state and prime minister, allowing Franco to name someone to the latter post if he wished, though he did not do so for a further five years.[12]

When Franco presented the law in parliament, his Parkinson's disease was clearly visible. His head drooped, his voice descended into a monotone and he occasionally looked lost. That contrasted with his triumphal proclamation of the 'previously unequalled rhythm of perfection and progress' he had brought to the country. As one commentator noted, the loudest applause came when he stated that the law did not contain any fundamental changes to his regime.[13]

'I don't really believe in this,' Manuel Fraga wrote in his diary, seeing the law as a missed opportunity to give Francoism fresh life with bold reforms. Fraga was tasked with organising the referendum campaign, which was seen by the regime as a propaganda opportunity. Since it could ensure there was no campaign against the law, it could also use the inevitable 'Yes' vote to promote Franco at home and abroad as a wise, beloved and benevolent leader. 'A Yes vote is a vote for Franco,' one campaign slogan proclaimed. 'We are not being invited to choose between two possible outcomes, but to approve or reject a diktat presented in apocalyptic terms,' commented one critic.[14]

'Spanish cities are plastered with huge posters urging yes votes, stickers appear on taxis and private cars,' *New York Times* correspondent Tad Szulc reported. 'Mobile radio teams tour the countryside, helicopters rain leaflets, and radio and television conduct an unceasing campaign.' Two days before the referendum, Franco appeared on television – where all channels were run by the state – telling people to vote. Viewers saw an old man in a jacket and tie sitting at a desk, emphasising his words with brusque arm movements which highlighted how the thumb on his left hand was paralysed into an awkward curl. 'I was never motivated by a desire for power,' he claimed. In fact, he added, this had been thrust upon him, preventing him from 'enjoying life like so many other Spaniards'.[15]

Official results showed 96 per cent approval with 89 per cent participation, raising doubts about how such a majority had been achieved. The *New York Times* immediately compared it to the results routinely produced by totalitarian states, whether communist or fascist. As in the 1947 referendum, voting had been obligatory, with punishments for those who did not vote. The actual voting was overseen by regime officials. Fraga had recently established a government pollster, whose reports were distorted by Spaniards' fear of expressing themselves freely and openly. What polling it did carry out revealed ignorance and apathy. Only one in five Spaniards, for example, could name the Vice-President (Muñoz Grandes) and 84 per cent could not name any of the Fundamental Laws on which Francoism was based. Asked what the referendum was about, only 14 per cent mentioned the Organic State Law that they were supposed to approve, while 18 per cent thought they were voting directly on Franco. A full 45 per cent of voters could not even answer the question. That did not stop 84 per cent saying that they would vote. Most also admitted that the referendum was not something they had ever discussed with friends, though almost all had heard the daily propaganda in favour.[16]

Spaniards, in other words, did not know what they were voting for. The result probably did not need much fixing, though 10 per cent more people voted than were on the electoral registers.[17] A significant but unmeasurable number of voters undoubtedly believed that, as the propaganda repeated insistently, they were showing their support for Franco's great, paternalistic wisdom. The rest were guided by apathy, group think, passive acquiescence and an underlying fear of expressing opposition to Franco's will.

It was also true, however, that a No vote meant maintaining the status quo, while a 'Yes' at least nudged the regime slightly towards reform by allowing a prime minister to share some of the dictator's power and removing the overtly fascist elements. There was little reason to prefer the status quo. Many voters may simply have been pleased to be consulted. A 'large majority' actually wanted much greater change, Fraga admitted. Either way, Franco was delighted, once more seeing proof of his popularity. 'The huge majority of people are enjoying this peace and a level of personal well-being that they could never have dreamed of,' he told Pacón. He simply could not understand why the foreign press dared to question that.[18]

The historian Joan J. Adrià recalled his parents voting 'Yes' in the referendum even though, in private, they showed 'clear antipathy towards the dictator'. They were not interested in rocking the boat of Francoism. In public, they were 'passive, accommodating and apprehensive ... of any mistake that might make them "stand out" and be suspected of dissent in what was still a police state; and worried, too, about the possible appearance of anything unforeseen that threatened the existing stability.' After studying the Francoist history of his hometown, Llíria near Valencia, he concluded that his parents and people like them had voted as a result of 'the demotivating and lasting effect of police repression, the differentiation and discrimination between regime "adherents", "malcontents" and those who were "indifferent", the terrible memory of the civil war and the absolute need to have normality in their daily lives'.[19]

As usual, Franco balanced his small and mostly cosmetic steps towards liberalisation with measures to reinforce his long-term project of keeping the essence of Francoism alive after his death. With his Vice-President and political heir Muñoz Grandes now dying from cancer, he instead promoted Carrero Blanco to Vice-President in September 1967. It was a death blow to hopes that Spain might evolve into a normal, free democracy. Later in the year, Franco himself unwittingly helped explain why. 'I've been here so long that I don't know anyone anymore,' he said, referring to life in the Pardo Palace.[20]

In the meantime, the power of Opus Dei continued to grow as it embraced Spanish authoritarianism to please Franco and garner power. 'Though doubtless primarily religious, [Opus Dei] has in Spain gained more political power than any other order has done since the Templar in the Middle Ages,' noted one of the more knowledgeable observers of Spain, the historian Hugh Thomas. The group would, nevertheless, see its prestige take a hit after Franco pardoned three of its ministers before trial in a corruption scandal known as the Matesa affair.[21]

Franco remained convinced that Spaniards needed and wanted the hard and sometimes brutal hand of dictatorship. Growing evidence that this was not the case – from students rebelling in Madrid or Barcelona, striking miners or protesting leftist priests – was ignored. These were law and order matters, to be dealt with by the Social

Political Brigade of the police and the Public Order Tribunal. The infamous 'grises', as Franco's urban police force was known because of its grey uniforms, increasingly spent time fighting students and other protesters.

As his enemies became bolder, Franco's jails filled with political prisoners. The illegal communist-backed Workers Commission trades union had been founded in 1966 and emerged as a powerful opponent. It often led labour unrest, sometimes visibly. A university professor called Enrique Tierno Galván founded a clandestine party called the Interior Socialists. Franco knew that, as protests grew, left-wingers thought his regime was in terminal decline. 'They are completely wrong,' he told Pacón in March 1968.[22]

Five months later, as torrential summer rain fell on the Basque frontier town of Irún, the balding, jug-eared provincial head of the police's Social Political Brigade, Inspector Melitón Manzanas, stepped off an afternoon bus and walked towards the building where he lived with his wife and daughter. As 59-year-old Manzanas prepared to enter the main door, a pistol-carrying ETA member appeared from a basement stairwell and shot him half a dozen times. One of the most infamous police torturers in Spain died almost instantly. It was the first time ETA had planned and carried out an assassination. Franco's reaction was typically heavy-handed. The previous evening six Basque priests had been jailed for their involvement in protests. He now declared a three-month state of emergency in Guipuzcoa province, arresting more priests in an overnight clampdown that netted more than 100 people. The state of emergency was later extended for a further three months.[23]

Before the provincial state of emergency in Guipuzcoa ended, and with protests in the Basque Country and universities across Spain spiralling out of control, Franco ordered a nationwide state of emergency. Basic liberties were suspended and press censorship reestablished. Hundreds of dissidents were arrested. It was as if Spain was slipping backwards in time and, indeed, Franco turned to some of those who had helped him early in his rule, when it was at its most repressive. A new term, 'the bunker', began to be used to describe Franco's decision to dig himself in, accompanied by old hardliners. They found allies in Franco's close family, including Carmen Polo and their son-in-law Cristóbal Martínez Bordiú. Even for Franco's supporters, the crackdown was a reminder that the heavily curtailed 'freedoms' they enjoyed could be retracted at any moment and on the instructions of one man – the now 77-year-old generalísimo.[24]

The following week, Franco left his cabinet meeting before it ended, feeling unwell. It was a rare absence. 'It confirms the deterioration in his previously unbreakable physical state,' noted Fraga. 'There is a widespread sensation of crisis, of the end of an era.'[25]

41
Lost Years

MIJAS, 28 MARCH 1969

On 28 March 1969, 64-year-old Manuel Cortés listened to the radio in his hideaway in the southern town of Mijas – where he had once been the Socialist mayor – to hear that Franco had finally passed an amnesty for 'crimes' committed during the civil war. He wondered what to do. Cortés had left his hometown in February 1937, before Franco's troops conquered it, walking across country to join the Republican army. In November 1939, with the war lost, he had snuck back into town in the dark to the house where his wife Juliana was raising their only daughter, María. He had committed no crimes and had defended local landowners against anarchist mobs, but other former Republican politicians were being arrested and shot so he decided to stay in hiding. A first hideaway was built under a staircase with its entry covered by a picture of the Sacred Cross of Jesus. It was not spotted by the Civil Guard when they came looking for him.[1]

Cortés stayed hidden for the next thirty years. When they moved to a new house across the street, he dressed as an elderly lady and crossed at night – installing himself in an upper floor where nobody could see him. Only five other people, all close family members, ever knew of his existence – though there were several close runs, including encounters with two small children and a builder. Cortés had, in effect, watched the first three decades of Francoist rule go past by peeking through windows into the street, listening to the radio and, eventually, watching television. To begin with, the remarkable Juliana kept the family alive by walking 30 km a day to sell black-market eggs before building a business that included a small fleet of taxis and trucks. When his daughter María had married, Cortés had peeked at her in her wedding dress through a keyhole. María only told her husband about her hidden father after they had wed.

Knowing that he could no longer be accused of rebellion or any other crime, Cortés' family asked the town's Francoist mayor to accompany him to the Civil Guard police station in Malaga where he identified himself. He was told that he could go free. Juliana had suffered more than anyone else, he said later: 'To keep us alive she has had to work like a man.' Cortés was one of several men, known as 'topos' or moles, who crawled out of hideaways after the amnesty was passed. What was meant to be an act of clemency also served to highlight just how long Franco had punished people for serving the Republic.

Franco promulgated the amnesty to mark the thirtieth anniversary of his victory and it had been greeted by *The Times* of London as a measure 'that affects virtually no-one'. He spent the anniversary resting in a hotel in Santiago de Compostela. The day before, the Falangist newspaper *Arriba* had published an interview in which he blamed youth unrest around the world, following the May 1968 demonstrations in Paris, on 'the professionalisation of agitators' and 'lack of [Christian] faith'.[2]

A week earlier he had lifted the state of emergency in order to clear the way for an announcement which many Spaniards had seen coming. In January, Prince Juan Carlos had surprised his own father, Don Juan, by publicly declaring, in a staged interview printed in almost all Spanish newspapers, that he considered the Francoist constitution legitimate – effectively clearing the path to be named by Franco as the next head of state instead of his father.[3]

Three months later, on 22 July 1969, Franco formally named the young prince as future king in parliament. Carmen Polo had reportedly been pressurising her husband to do this, a sign that she was gaining political influence over her Parkinson's-stricken husband. As his energy flagged and his attention span dwindled, she was becoming a guardian of his legacy. He had increasingly left his ministers to do most of the governing, but his wife and his senior counsellors fretted about how Francoism would survive his death or incapacity. They now assumed that Juan Carlos would ensure that it did.[4]

Given the supposedly momentous nature of an event that Spaniards had speculated about for more than a decade, it was surprising that Franco did so little to publicise his choice of a successor to the position of head of state. He made the announcement in a week in which most Spaniards left for their summer holidays and, although he and parliament dressed in full pomp for the speech announcing Juan Carlos's nomination, it was not broadcast live. While *La Vanguardia* spoke in emotive, history-in-the-making prose of a large crowd gathering in 'the bright 7pm sun' at the colonnaded entrance to the parliament building, the *New York Times* reported that 'only a handful of people' watched Franco enter the building under a velvet canopy carried by four officials. Television viewers, meanwhile, were instead served an adventure series starring porpoises.[5]

Don Juan lived the appointment of his son as successor to the crown as a stab in the back. 'I have always told you this would happen,' the 31-year-old prince wrote in a letter to his father. Juan Carlos was sworn in as designated successor on 23 July 1969, vowing loyalty to Franco and 'fidelity to the principles of the National Movement'.[6]

With Franco showing no signs of wishing to step down and real power after his death seemingly set to lie in the hands of whoever he eventually appointed as prime minister (already expected to be Carrero Blanco), Spaniards as a whole seemed non-plussed. Among those who opposed the restoration were Republicans, Carlists (whose own foreign-born candidate as heir to the throne, Carlos Hugo de Borbón-Parma, had been expelled from the country in 1968 to remove all competition to Juan Carlos) and the small number of die-hard Falangists who stuck by their old 'we don't want stupid monarchs' slogan. None of these groups had the strength to change events. Franco's decisions remained unchallengeable.

The appointment of this 'inadequate young man' as successor of a dictator 'turned insane by decades of unchecked power' was greeted with dismay by people like the Oxford-based Salvador de Madariaga, who had led the so-called Munich Conspiracy:

> Franco's speech for the occasion left no one in doubt as to his intention never to retire before his death. His appointment of a successor

is yet another insult to the Spanish people, but worse still the whole operation amounts to a mere exhibition of autocracy in the void...

The regime lives by mendacity, corruption, censorship and vindictive punishment of its enemies, as well as by feeding what remains of the civil war spirit in the population.[7]

While Madariaga could speak freely from abroad, the political atmosphere surrounding Franco was best captured by a still relatively unknown author, the publisher Salvador Pániker. In May 1969, he wrote what he described as 'the book I wanted to read'. In it, he interviewed two dozen men from artists and bankers to politicians, including Fraga and the Opus Dei-aligned minister López Rodó, asking frank questions about the future. No women or dissidents were included. Surprisingly, the censors left the book untouched. Philosopher José Luís López Aranguren told him everybody was playing a game of blind man's buff in which the regime assigned the roles of 'liberal' or 'conservative' to its members as a way of pretending that some kind of real debate was going on. 'For the moment the game will continue – the game of not being able to tell where anyone really stands,' he said.[8]

A pro-Franco newspaper editor, Emilio Romero, fretted that the caudillo's longevity and refusal to share power meant 'the regime is deteriorating substantially, both intellectually and in its work.' The democratically inclined monarchist and diplomat, the Count of Motrico, said he felt like part of 'a group of men shut in a cage looking eagerly and in good faith for a way out, and not finding it'. When challenged on democracy, the minister López Rodó cynically asked: 'What is democracy?' while the supposedly liberal Fraga declared that 'political enemies [meaning dissidents] ... should be treated with the greatest severity.'[9]

Thirty years of indoctrination and quiet intimidation had largely delivered Franco's desire for obedience. A returning exile, the novelist Max Aub, found a country now profoundly apathetic and almost ignorant of its own lack of liberties. Spain was 'inconsequential, forgetful, unaware, far from any kind of rebellion', he said after his 1969 return. Even young people who declared themselves Leftists knew almost nothing about the Republic and the civil war, nor showed much interest.[10] They were far more excited by Fidel Castro and Cuba.

As a new decade began in 1970, rumours abounded about Franco's health. He was already suffering from Parkinson's disease, though this would not be made public for four years. One rumour said that Franco assumed God would not let him die while Spain needed him: 'When destiny needs a man, the laws of nature are suspended,' he had reportedly said. Other rumours spoke of hardliner generals preparing a coup in case Franco suddenly died or ceded to reformists.[11]

Carmen Polo worried that her husband was losing control of a country where a rebellious opposition was finally becoming visible. In this, Franco's wife was increasingly aligned with the hardline military officers and Falangistas of the so-called bunker. In many cases, they were old men she and her husband had known since the civil war. 'She doesn't like the way things are going, and sees Franco as more solitary and fretful than ever before,' Fraga wrote in his diary after a weeping Carmen Polo had expressed her concerns to Admiral Pedro Nieto Antúnez. Parkinson's disease and the medicines Franco was now taking to control it appear to have dented his previously unshakeable and inscrutable nature.[12]

Illegal strikes spread across the country, with some 400,000 people involved in around 1,500 work stoppages in 1970. In a church-run poll that same year, only 30 per cent of Spaniards said they wanted Franco's regime to continue after his death, while half wanted a republic and the rest opted for monarchy. Franco's support came mainly from the less-educated working class (13 per cent of Spaniards aged over 25 were still illiterate), where 55 per cent wanted the regime to continue. Overall, two-thirds said that they would like to be able to vote for Christian Democrat, Social Democrat or Socialist political parties. Only one in five preferred the Falange and Franco's National Movement. The 60-page poll was suppressed by censors and removed from a report on social conditions in Spain by the church's FOESSA SEEMS TO BE A FOUNDATION before it was published, but nevertheless it circulated secretly.[13]

In September 1970, *The Times* of London tried to untangle the situation:

> The security apparatus is said to be as strong as ever and there are no illusions about the willingness of the authorities to use it. The police are said to have effectively penetrated universities, making

it extremely difficult for students to organise any form of protest. Socialists are known to have been imprisoned for maintaining foreign contacts, which would be perfectly legal in a democracy. The treatment they received in prison is said to have been reasonably good, but is now deteriorating. Members of the opposition say that there are still about 1,000 political prisoners, including about 15 young priests in the special wing of the prison at Zamora, near the Portuguese frontier. Some are serving sentences of up to 15 years for hiding Basque activists. The priests in Zamora are completely cut off from other prisoners, and some are said to have been tortured ... last year five priests who contacted the United Nations Human Rights Commission about the Basque situation were each sentenced to 10 or more years in prison.[14]

Censorship continued to keep crucial information out of the press. Publishers now complained, in private, that strong-arm tactics included insisting on the sacking of writers, withholding newsprint subsidies and menacing phone calls demanding that sensitive topics never be touched again. Book censors were said to have become 'frightened and much more arbitrary' than at any time since Fraga's changes. While proper studies of the civil war could only be written from outside the country, many of the best were translated by a Spanish publishing house in Paris, Ruedo Ibérico, and circulated semi-clandestinely around Spain. The publishing house's first success had been a translation of *The Spanish Civil War* by Hugh Thomas – the first major history of the war – and it went on to publish work by Gerald Brenan, Herbert Southworth, Stanley Payne and Ian Gibson. Senior regime figures like Fraga and Pacón read them, even though they were banned.[15]

Censorship could also issue directly from the Franco family, with Carmen Polo allegedly behind the decision to sequester a copy of gossip magazine *Garbo* after it published cover photos of Luis Miguel Dominguín, a famous bullfighter, Falangist and frequent guest at the palace, canoodling with a bikini-clad girl twenty years younger than him. The girl was the married bullfighter's married cousin. Both had been regular guests at Franco's hunting parties, where the dictator would ask the bullfighter to tell him jokes and hangers-on waited to see if Franco laughed before joining in. Twenty years earlier the bullfighter had written to Franco to tell him that 'my fellow Spanish bullfighters, who are used to spilling their blood, offer to do the same in defence of their adored Fatherland and of the Caudillo they idolise'. The journalists who published the posed photographs of the bullfighter and his cousin-girlfriend were fined, but a court threw out charges that the couple were guilty of 'public scandal'.[16]

Spaniards who hoped the United States would apply pressure on the regime to democratise had their hopes dashed after the military bases agreement was renewed in 1970. In October that year, Franco welcomed his second US president, Richard Nixon, to Madrid. Again, the regime made sure he received a euphoric reception, claiming that 1.5 million people lined the streets at the start of a 21-hour visit. 'It was very exciting and it was the biggest crowd I have ever seen,' an overjoyed Nixon said. In fact, the regime had told employers to release madrileños early from work and, according to the *New York Times*, 'at strategic points ... busloads of out-of-town spectators were deposited along the sidewalks'.[17]

While Carrero Blanco insisted to Nixon that Western civilisation was collapsing and 'the barbarians are waiting outside the walls', Franco was more optimistic. He also admitted to the US president that he now delegated as much as possible and only decided on 'really vital matters'. The Madrid stopover nevertheless allowed Nixon to please Franco by declaring that he considered military cooperation with Spain to be a pillar of world peace. He did not, however, invite Spain to join NATO – from which it remained barred by European democracies.[18]

Excitement about Nixon's visit had barely settled when Franco found himself mired in a fresh crisis. On 3 December 1970, sixteen Basque prisoners – including two women and two priests – were brought before a military court in Burgos, accused of crimes (including two killings and several robberies) under a terrorism, banditry and military rebellion law. These included the 1968 shooting of Inspector Melitón Manzanas in Irun. Prosecutors accused 28-year-old Francisco Javier Izko of pulling the trigger and five others as his accomplices. They demanded death penalties for six of them. The trial sparked demonstrations across the country, especially on university campuses. In Madrid, where many faculties were already closed by strikes, students marched through the campus chanting anti-Franco slogans. Franco ignored calls from the Basque clergy for the trials to be held before civilian courts and instead cracked down on the demonstrators, arresting student leaders and prominent dissidents.[19]

Even before the trial started, Pope Paul VI called on Franco to 'show an attitude of clemency'. Franco responded by cracking down on the Basques even more, again declaring a three-month state of emergency in Guipuzcoa province. As police opened fire on demonstrators there, four people were wounded, one of them seriously. Elsewhere some 500 political prisoners went on hunger strike and a further 300 intellectuals and artists – including the world-famous painter Joan Miró - locked themselves into the Catalan monastery at Montserrat. Pablo Picasso refused to attend the opening of a museum for his work in Barcelona. ETA kidnapped the West German consul in San Sebastian, Eugene Beihl, as a way of applying pressure to the court and government. In a letter sent to a French radio station, Beihl tied his own life to that of the Burgos defendants. 'I am following with considerable fears the Burgos trial, on which my fate depends,' he wrote.[20]

A note published by the Vatican newspaper *L'Osservatore Romano* said: 'The Holy See trusts that, if the situation arises, the Spanish Government will make magnanimous use of the faculties which the law attributes to it in this respect.' Workers in France held stoppages to protest the trial, while the French government also pressed for no death penalties. As the world's attention settled on Burgos, Francoist newspapers denounced 'an international press campaign against Spain'. The Burgos trials generated headlines across the Western world, where they were seen as a test of Franco's repressive, authoritarian nature. Would he have them all shot or garrotted, or was the old dictator prepared to hold out against international opinion and stay true to his repressive and vengeful nature?

42

¡Viva Franco!

PLAZA DE ORIENTE, MADRID, 17 DECEMBER 1970

On 17 December 1970, 78-year-old Franco was meeting with Carrero Blanco in his office at the Pardo Palace when Carmen Polo marched into the room. Friends and relatives had phoned excitedly to tell her of a semi-spontaneous demonstration in support of her husband that had seen tens of thousands of demonstrators gather before the Oriente Palace, where Franco traditionally delivered speeches. The demonstration had formed after a mass said in the memory of Inspector Manzanas at a Madrid church on 17 December 1970, though it had actually been organised in advance by the Falange.[1]

Although his officials knew about the demonstration, they had not planned for Franco to attend it, and likely did not expect the numbers who arrived. After receiving a phone call from Pacón, who was at the Oriente palace and could hear people shouting Franco's name, Carmen urged him to travel into town to address the crowd. Franco soon appeared with Prince Juan Carlos at his shoulder and was greeted by a packed square chanting slogans like 'Franco yes! ETA no!'[2]

Dressed in an overcoat and trilby, Franco thanked them for their 'constant watchfulness ... faith and enthusiasm', while below him a sea of people waved white handkerchiefs and an airplane flew past dragging a '¡Viva España!' banner. He raised his arms in acknowledgement and Carmen joined the stiff-armed fascist-style salutes of the crowd as it sang the Falangist anthem 'Cara al Sol'.[3]

Although pro-regime protests like this were about the only ones allowed in Franco's Spain, this was an authentic display of support. It was clear that Franco had created a hardcore of supporters whose numbers, while unquantifiable, were significant. 'Once more, Franco triumphed resoundingly thanks to the people [of Spain], who remain faithful to the Caudillo who led them to victory,' wrote his cousin Pacón in a final diary entry before he became too frail to write in it anymore. He had used the previous pages to complain about how little Franco rewarded his most loyal collaborators while others grew wealthy through cronyism and corruption.

The German consul Beihl was released on Christmas Day, but three days later the Burgos military court passed death sentences on six of the sixteen defendants. Western European governments like Britain and Germany immediately urged Franco to commute the death penalties, while newspapers like *The Times* of London warned that this was Franco's worst internal political crisis since the civil war as hardliners exerted 'more influence ... than ever before.'[4]

Confounding everyone, and after two emergency cabinet meetings in two days, Franco uncharacteristically bent to the pressure and commuted their sentences on 30 December. He did not want this seen as weakness. That evening he gave his annual end-of-year speech on television, his words sometimes difficult to understand as his voice quavered. The demonstration outside the Oriente palace, he claimed, proved his government was beloved and strong. That was why he could afford to let the six men live. In reality, as one prominent journalist quipped: 'Franco, who until now had only felt responsible before God and History, also begins to be so before the foreign press.'[5]

Yet the Burgos trials exposed many of the splits that Franco had spent his life suppressing. In the Basque country, punishments were meted out to strikers and shop owners who closed their doors in protest at the original sentences. The clandestine, socialist-orientated General Workers Union and the Basque Nationalist party had been active in both protests, revealing a far wider opposition to Franco than that of ETA. Newspaper commentators began to call for the replacement of the Opus Dei government, while the senior general in Granada was sacked after publicly deeming the Catholic lay order 'a white Freemasonry'. Hugh Thomas, the historian, had already described Opus Dei's role as that of 'a Catholic sect in political power beneath the benevolent eye of an elderly dictator, aspiring to remain the determining force for the next generation, and hoping to do so with the agreement of the army ... Instead of an *apertura* [opening], therefore, there is *immobilisme* [stagnancy].'[6]

Tensions at the Pardo Palace were revealed when Franco's polo-playing son-in-law Doctor Cristóbal Martínez-Bordiú, Marquis of Villaverde, suddenly declared himself ready to join the political fray. A speech made in gratitude to a town in Guadalajara province that was naming a street after him was not reported in the controlled press, but copies circulated, with the buffoonish son-in-law stating that Franco was surrounded by traitors. A split was now opening between the Franco family entourage at the El Pardo Palace, including his wife Carmen, and the government. 'It is generally accepted that the Pardo group has influence,' *The Times* reported. 'It is also clear that the members of the [family] Pardo group are deeply opposed to Admiral Carrero, even though he is quite as conservative as they, and to the mildly evolutionary group he has brought into the government.' Martínez-Bordiú was reported to have got into a shouting match with the Opus-supporting Carrero Blanco. 'Sources close to the Cabinet say that the ministers fear that as General Franco grows older and feebler, his traditional independence from those immediately around him may diminish,' the newspaper added.

Cabinet sources were not the only ones to worry. While European governments looked on in desperation at the sluggishness of change, US President Richard Nixon still valued Franco as a military ally. In February 1971 he sent General Vernon, the CIA deputy director who had translated for both him and President Eisenhower on their visits to Madrid, on a secret mission to ask Franco what would happen after he died. On 24 February 1971, Walters found himself waiting alone in a second-floor room by Franco's office in El Pardo Palace that was lined with yellow silk and had five different clocks ticking away. ('Like [German chancellor Konrad] Adenauer, another old man, Franco was fascinated with time,' Walters noted). He proffered a personal letter from Nixon to Franco, who reached out with a hand which shook so violently from Parkinson's disease that foreign minister Gregorio López Bravo had to take it instead. Carrero Blanco had already warned Walters that Franco was showing his age and 'sometimes seemed feeble'. Walters found a man who looked unlikely to live much longer. 'His left hand trembled at times so violently that he would cover it with his other hand. At times he appeared far away and at others he came right to the point,' he noted.[7]

Franco guessed why Walters was there and dispassionately brought up the subject of his own death:

> He said that the succession would be orderly. There was no alternative to the Prince. Spain would move some distance along the road we favored but not all the way, as Spain was neither America nor England nor France. It was Spain. He indicated that the Armed Forces would never let things get out of hand, and expressed confidence in the Prince's ability to handle the situation after his death... 'Tell President Nixon that insofar as the order and stability of Spain are concerned, this will be guaranteed by the timely and orderly measures I am taking.'[8]

Franco's confidence contrasted with growing tensions on the streets. The extreme right, emboldened by the recent pro-Franco demonstration and knowing it had support in the police, armed forces and government, began holding its own demonstrations. The target of these was often the Opus Dei government. Old Falangists and young members of new radical groups like the Warriors of Christ the King (Guerrilleros de Cristo Rey) celebrated the April 1 anniversary of the civil war victory in 1971 by marching through Madrid, shouting insults and giving stiff-armed salutes. 'No Reds! No king! No Opus Dei!' they cried, as police detained journalists 'for their own protection'. The chants continued with 'The army to power!' and 'Franco, the Falange and the army!'. At the same time, the enraged Carlist movement turned on Franco for naming Juan Carlos, rather than an obscure Carlist candidate, as his heir, thereby creating an unlikely form of opposition on the extreme right.[9]

Rebellion from within the church also grew, with Spanish bishops voting down a new Vatican concordat proposal that kept church and state tied together. In Seville, even the conservative cardinal José Bueno y Monreal actively campaigned against the Social Political Brigade's zealous use of torture on local workers and activists.

Franco's reaction to all this was to clamp down further. In April 1971, a new public order law increased the fines that provincial governors, ministers and the cabinet could levy on outspoken dissidents. The press was soon inundated with warnings, threats and seizures, while film censorship meant two Spanish films put forward for the country's own San Sebastian International Film Festival had to be withdrawn.[10]

In July 1971, in an attempt to quell the growing instability, Franco decreed that Prince Juan Carlos would stand in for him if he ever became too ill to govern. This instead immediately led to speculation that he was gravely ill, which would continue unabated over the coming years. In fact, he was well enough to greet US Vice-President Spiro Agnew at celebrations marking his 1936 insurrection against the Republic that month – a sure sign that the US stood behind Franco. When *Time* magazine reported that Juan Carlos was expected to take over very soon, the issue was removed from Spanish newspaper stalls.[11]

The greatest blow of all came in September 1971, when the Spanish church formally apologised for its role in the civil war. 'We humbly recognise, and beg pardon for it, that we failed at the proper time to be ministers of reconciliation in the midst of our people, divided by a war between brothers,' it declared during an assembly of 94 bishops and 151 priests presided over by the Cardinal Primate of Spain, Vicente Enrique y Tarancón.[12] The declaration shattered Franco's long-standing affirmation that his insurrection had been a legitimate Crusade and effectively removed one of the main pillars of National Catholicism.

'What the Spanish church has now done is to recognise that it has sinned,' one priest explained. Conservative bishops complained, but there was nothing they could do. The previous year, the church had sent a questionnaire to priests, seeking their views. Only 11 per cent favoured the Francoist system. Some had become leftist 'worker priests' and gone to work in factories or settled in shanty towns on the outskirts of major cities. The day after the declaration, the police's Social Political Brigade raided a church in the slum neighbourhood of El Pozo del Rio Raimundo, on the outskirts of Madrid, where forty recently sacked workers were holding a sit-in. The police forced their way in, breaking the rules of the Vatican concordat, which required permission from the local bishop.

Franco himself attacked the church the following month, reminding a Falange meeting that the civil war had been 'fought in defence of the spiritual patrimony of Christian civilisation' and criticising those who 'try to give another interpretation'. The fact that a jailed priest had dug a 60ft tunnel in an attempt to escape the Zamora prison must have increased his irritation.[13]

On the thirty-fifth anniversary of his proclamation as caudillo on 1 October 1971, an apparently fit Franco declared he would hold on to power for 'as long as God gives me life and a clear mind'. His supporters again filled the Oriente Square by the palace, as if to show their strength in advance of his death and amid fear of a future reckoning. Once more, Franco took it as proof of his overwhelming popularity. 'The gathering was highly organised. Buses, trains and airliners were chartered to bring adherents, furnished with free tickets and lunch money, from all over Spain. The radio and television spoke of little else all week, and the press was full of interviews with old comrades of General Franco, who is 78 years old,' the *New York Times* reported. An amnesty that freed a quarter of Spain's prisoners, including many on political charges, was greeted as an underhand way to release government officials implicated in the Matesa corruption scandal. The following month 300 dissidents met in Barcelona, with police arresting their leaders.[14]

The backwards-forwards nature of an increasingly panicky regime constantly dashed hopes for a limited law of political associations that might permit some kind of formal oppositional debate. 'Political judgment is the exclusive competence of the Chief of State,' Franco told the opening of parliament in mid-November 1971.[15] 'Everything is tied down – well tied down – under the faithful vigilance of our Army' he said, implying no more change during his lifetime and very little afterwards. That dashed hopes that, for example, his regime would make the kind of changes that might allow Spain to join the EEC club of European nations. 'It was a state burial for the thesis that the regime can evolve while Franco survives,' an anonymous reformist deputy in parliament commented afterwards.[16]

In December 1971, Franco rowed back further by closing down one of Madrid's more adventurous newspapers and lashing out at the church during his end-of-year television speech. This was in reply to the church's Justice and Peace Commission, which had issued a lengthy indictment of his regime. 'A fight against the present Spanish social structure is necessary, because men cannot be asked to behave with justice if at the same time they are obliged to live under the inhuman weight of an unjust system,' it said.[17]

Franco was livid. 'One thing the state cannot do is stand by with its arms crossed in the face of certain attitudes of a temporal nature assumed by some clergymen,' he said.[18] Franco had, by now, petrified his regime. In public, officials talked about joining the European Economic Community, while in private they recognised this was impossible without proper democracy. In speeches, hardliners like Carrero Blanco repeated the mantra that Franco's unique 'organic democracy' was far superior. People now awaited the dictator's death with a mixture of hope and fear.[19]

His deteriorating health became clear to many of the 2,000 guests who attended the wedding of his eldest granddaughter – another Carmen – at the Pardo Palace in March 1972. The young Carmen married a cousin of Prince Juan Carlos, Alfonso Borbón y Dampierre, to the delight of her grandmother. 'A grandchild of king Alfonso XIII was marrying a Franco grandchild. She was beside herself with joy!' commented Franco's niece, Pilar Jaraiz, who was a guest. Carmen Polo embraced the family's new semi-royal status with fervour. Invitations referred to the groom, incorrectly, as 'his royal highness'. The bride was given away by her grandfather. Her grandmother even curtsied to her, expecting her friends to do the same.

Franco, however, did not look well. 'He could barely concentrate on the people there and almost did not recognise me when I said hello. He dragged his feet, held his mouth half open and looked terrible,' his niece recalled.[20] 'Everything had been prepared to honour him, more than the newlyweds, but the image was pathetic.' Franco had already accorded himself the royal prerogative of handing out noble titles (especially to close collaborators from the civil war). Under pressure from his wife and son-in-law, he allowed his granddaughter's husband to use the title of Duke of Cádiz.

In July 1972, under still more pressure to make succession plans clear, Franco decreed that his Vice-President Carrero Blanco would become prime minister on his death if he still had not appointed one by then. The future was thus left in the hands of the reactionary Carrero Blanco and the silent Prince Juan Carlos. The dour, bushy-eyebrowed admiral was described as 'a shy man, standing alone at social functions, sombrely dressed and rarely smiling'. The prince, meanwhile, frequently appeared in public at Franco's shoulder, vowing continued support, as he did again in July 1972 after his father Don Juan called for political plurality. 'I want to express once again my loyalty and adhesion to our Generalissimo,' Juan Carlos said. Mostly, the prince was 'more seen than heard', according to the *New York Times* which noted that 'few days go by without his appearance, on the television screen or in the press as he inaugurates a road, a school or an industrial installation, but he says almost nothing.' In fact, the newspaper added, the 'deeply introspective', 'naïve' and provincial prince was more 'like a carved figure on the bow of a becalmed ship, the faintly absurd emblem of movement for a regime that will not move'.[21]

The odd mixture of frustration and silence generated by the regime was captured by a snapshot of how political debate operated, published by the same newspaper in August 1972. Ordinary Spaniards could 'say anything they want [if] they keep their voices at a conversational level' but 'cannot shout it, print it, film it or act out'.[22] Political meetings were banned, it explained, but 'political dinners' with prior police approval were permitted and attended by what wags called the 'cenocracy' (from the Spanish word for dinner, cena). They brought together 'a carefully balanced melange of 40 or 50 people: officials of sub ministerial rank known for their moderation, a few ex-ministers who have turned assertively liberal since their fall from office, and members of the more respectable opposition'. Well-fed guests indulged in mild debate about the pace of reform and speculated about what would happen when Franco died. A plain-clothes policeman usually sat in. One dinner organiser described a typical scene:

> This man arrived and showed his police card. I invited him to take a seat in the audience, but he said he was sorry, but regulations required him to be on the podium. I said it would look ridiculous, but he insisted, so we sat him up there and he took out his notebook and started writing. At one point during the speeches we heard a tapping noise. We turned and saw him striking his notebook with his pencil. When he saw he had our attention he smiled and stopped – and the speaker switched to a safer subject. Afterward we all went to the bar for a drink and invited him along. He said he couldn't drink on duty, so I said goodbye. No, he said, drinks after a meeting were part of the meeting. So he stood there while we drank.[23]

These were self-important but impotent events. Reform had ground to a halt, repression was increasing and even regime officials were dismayed (and happy to say so, off the record). Everyone was waiting for Franco to die but lacked the energy to push for change. 'The 36 years since the beginning of the civil war have dulled everything: the regime's cutting edge and the passions of its antagonists,' the *New York Times* correspondent concluded.

In fact, many of those closest to the Franco family were now fretting about their personal futures. 'I can't go out anymore,' a tearful Carmen Polo told the family doctor in October 1972. 'Everyone asks me: "What's going to happen?" "What's going on?" "What will happen to us?" But Paco doesn't want to do anything at all.'

While Franco's regime froze into stasis, ETA flourished. Franco's repeated states of emergency in the Basque Country and accompanying police repression had grown support in villages and small industrial towns, especially where the unique and ancient language of Euskara was strong. Over August and September of 1972, a Civil Guard barracks was bombed, an office belonging to the Ministry of Information and Tourism was burned down, a so-called 'anti-Basque' man had his house blown up and some $190,000 was stolen during a raid on a bank truck. A municipal policeman died and a Civil Guard sergeant was wounded when trying to arrest four ETA suspects in the Basque town of Galdacano. The Civil Guard had, in effect, declared war, killing three suspected ETA members in the same shootout. A notorious new head of the Civil Guard, General Iniesta Cano, was deemed responsible for a shoot-to-kill policy. But ETA had been acquiring arms in Belgium and elsewhere and was preparing for a long campaign.[24]

By December 1972, Spain's bishops drew up a document that called for a rewriting of the 1953 concordat in order to properly split church and state. They wanted the Vatican to remove Franco's right to interfere in the nomination of bishops and for churchmen to refuse regime posts. The document, signed by most of the Spain's bishops, symbolised a final split between Franco and those who had originally hailed his insurrection against the Republic as a 'crusade'. In reply, Franco wrote to Pope Paul VI demanding he keep control of his Spanish priests. A furious pope cut short a visit from Franco's foreign minister when he repeated the same complaint.[25]

As he celebrated his 80th birthday on 4 December 1972, Franco remained nominally in absolute command of a Spain that was very different to the country whose government he obtained by force 36 years earlier. He had visibly slowed down, leaving Carrero Blanco to do most of the work. Franco still presided over cabinet meetings every other Friday, but these now lasted only three to four hours. Most decisions had already been taken at meetings between Carrero Blanco and individual ministers. Rather than sitting up late listening to ministers, Franco himself increasingly spent time watching television, especially sport and films. His wife Carmen, meanwhile, phoned the director general of the state television channels if she saw anything that she considered immoral. Carrero Blanco's weekly meeting with the same director general echoed her concerns. 'How was this week's programming? Any cleavages? Any rude expressions?'[26]

Carmen Polo had been a discreet political presence, but now meddled with the backing of the bunker old-timers and her son-in-law, who sided with them. Early in 1973, she called Carrero Blanco to see her, complaining that she was so worried about the political situation that she could barely sleep. She was particularly upset with Franco's foreign minister, the relatively youthful Gregorio López Bravo. 'He is not loyal,' she complained, 'He spoke badly about Paco [as she called Franco] in the embassy in Paris, without discretion ... He even said that Paco no longer counted,' she said. 'You have to persuade him to reshuffle his ministers. I've always said it: this government is full of incompetents and traitors.' Carrero Blanco was stunned. He had never heard her interfere that way. 'I'm worried: Who is pushing her to speak like that?' he wondered.[27]

Carrero Blanco could also see that, even within Franco's regime, support for the ageing dictator was flagging. He had set up his own spy service in March 1972, the Servicio Central de Documentación, which was based at an office in the building next to his own. Rumours quickly spread that this unit spied not just on students and the opposition, but also on ministers. Its agents appeared in ministries, drawing up reports on whether bureaucrats were trustworthy or too sympathetic with dissidents. They were also widely seen as behind the emergence of the thuggish Guerrilleros de Cristo Rey, who attacked left-wing meetings and protests. Like Carrero Blanco himself, it seems the secretive unit's aim was to prevent Francoism from being derailed, either by opposition in the street or in the administration.[28]

Evidence of how brutal Franco's police had become was presented by Amnesty International, which accused it of 'widespread, regular and virtually unrestricted' torture of imprisoned dissidents in August 1973. A 36-page dossier explained that political prisoners included students, priests, writers, workers, lawyers, Basque and Catalan nationalists, intellectuals and 300 Jehovah's Witnesses and pacifists jailed for up to twelve years for refusing to do military service. The crackdown continued, however, with 113 people – including two priests – detained in a raid on a Barcelona church hall meeting in October 1973. They had been trying to organise a larger meeting for Catalan dissidents of all types, including communists and conservative Catalan nationalists. Cardinal Jubany, the archbishop of Barcelona, complained that 'freedom of assembly and association' were basic human rights.[29]

Barcelona newspapers were initially prevented from reporting on the arrests, though reports appeared in media elsewhere in Spain. The workings of censorship had become another example of Francoist contradictions. State-controlled television and radio stations, whether private or public, mostly told feel-good stories about Spain while giving plentiful coverage of strife elsewhere. The aim was to show Franco's regime in the best light. While the rest of the world was assailed by war, terrorism and riots, it seemed that nothing of the sort ever happened in Spain. Only by buying newspapers could people find out basic facts about strikes, dissidents' arrests or price hikes – and then not always or rarely fully. Anti-Franco opinion pieces were still banned. The foreign press remained the only source of full, unbiased reporting and could normally be found on selected big city newsstands. Even when editions of foreign newspapers reporting on strikes and other protests against the regime were banned, these often circulated secretly and illegally. In fact, a circular news economy had evolved, in which Spanish journalists handed news items that they could not publish themselves to correspondents. Once the news was in the foreign press, it could then be repeated in a Spanish newspaper. At the same time, and given the lack of official news, reformists within the regime constantly leaked information to foreign correspondents in an attempt to influence both public opinion and Franco himself, who was fixated on what foreign newspapers said about him.[30]

When Franco finally named Carrero Blanco as his first prime minister on 14 June 1973, he immediately did Carmen Polo's bidding by bringing in a law-and-order hardliner, Carlos Arias Navarro as interior minister. Carmen Polo rang to congratulate him. 'Thank goodness they have appointed you. Now I can sleep at night,' she said.[31]

Once more, however, it seemed all was arranged so that a Francoist-style regime – nominally led by a monarch – would continue after the generalísimo's death. He had not counted on the increasingly violent tactics of ETA. These would soon, quite literally, blow his plans asunder.

43

Operation Ogre

MADRID, 20 DECEMBER, 1973

In November 1973, a 24-year-old Basque man called Javier Larreategi rented a basement apartment at number 104 Claudio Coello street, in the upmarket central district of Salamanca in Madrid. The building was across the street from a city block mostly occupied by a five-story building owned by the Jesuit order, which served as a residency for priests and housed the San Francisco de Borja church. A chauffeur-driven black Dodge Dart 3700 GT waited there every morning for Admiral Luis Carrero Blanco, who attended daily mass at the church. It then drove him to his office on the Castellana boulevard, close to Plaza de Colón. The way in which Carrero Blanco repeated this routine showed just how unconcerned Franco and his government were about violent opposition. With the still-minor exception of ETA, such opposition had disappeared long ago, after the defeat in the 1950s of the few remaining rural guerrillas.[1]

Eva Forest, a renegade communist based in Madrid, had told ETA about Carrero Blanco's daily routine and it began plotting to kidnap the admiral. The plans were changed, however, when Franco appointed him prime minister and an armed escort began to follow him in a separate car. When the basement flat at 104 Claudio Coello appeared for rent in November, ETA decided to rent it and dig a tunnel under the road, so that they could assassinate him by planting a bomb. In order to explain the noise, Larreategi pretended to be a sculptor who would use the apartment as a studio.[2]

On the icy morning of Thursday, 20 December 1973, Carrero Blanco left Mass at 9.30 a.m. and climbed into the back seat of the Dodge, which then took its usual route along Claudio Coello street. He had spent the evening before fretting about Franco's health and fading ability to govern. 'He is not the man he was,' he had repeated in worried tones. As Carrero Blanco left Mass, a member of the three-man ETA unit was standing on a ladder in an electrician's outfit, pretending to do some work further down the same street. At a sign from a second ETA member stationed nearby he pressed a button to detonate 75 kilos of explosives in the freshly excavated tunnel. The explosion blew the car a hundred feet into the air and over the roof of the five-storey Jesuit building, where it slid down into an internal patio. The ETA members ran off shouting about a gas explosion, in order to confuse people, until they reached their getaway car.[3]

Carrero Blanco, his driver and bodyguard were all pronounced dead on arrival at a Madrid hospital at 10.15 a.m. A 30ft by 21 ft crater, which soon filled up with water from burst pipes, was left in the road. That evening, ETA claimed responsibility. It was the group's first major attack outside the Basque Country. The following day, ETA announced that it would continue to strike against 'the fascist power'. The ETA unit hid at a safe house for a week before returning to the Basque Country and escaping across the River Bidasoa into France.[4]

Spain went into shock. Nothing of this magnitude had happened during Franco's 34 years in power. Three days of official mourning did little to calm the country's nerves. Franco's repeated boast was that he had brought Spaniards 'peace'. That had been shattered. 'The sadness and anxiety is deep,' *La Vanguardia* newspaper admitted.[5]

The day before Carrero Blanco was killed, US Secretary of State Henry Kissinger had been in Madrid. In fact, the assassination had been planned for that day, but ETA postponed it because of the special security measures. The postponement meant that the assassination coincided with the opening, just a mile away, of the Public Order Tribunal's trial of ten people, including the radical Jesuit 'worker's priest' Francisco García Salve, accused of leading the clandestine communist-related trades union, the Workers Commissions. The defendants in what was known as Case 1001 faced jail sentences of up to twenty years in the most important political trial since the Burgos hearings against ETA.[6]

US Vice-President Gerald Ford flew from Washington to attend the next day's funeral. Right-wing extremists turned this into an angry demonstration. They shouted 'Assassin!' at Cardinal Vicente Tarancón and demanded a return to military rule. 'Death to the Communist priests! Death to the Reds! Long live Spain!' they cried. Franco himself stayed at home, officially suffering mild flu. He seemed overwhelmed and did not eat, shutting himself into his office: that afternoon, he wept as he presided over a short cabinet meeting. He said nothing public about the assassination of a man who had worked closely with him since 1941. Carrero Blanco's coffin was paraded along the Castellana boulevard on an army caisson pulled by six black horses before being buried in a cemetery beside the Pardo Palace. Franco did not attend, though the sound of a 21-gun salute blasted into his rooms at the palace.[7]

The following day, Franco appeared at a Madrid memorial service officiated by Cardinal Tarancón. Dressed in his captain-general's uniform, now looking slightly baggy, with a black armband, he was cheered by a crowd outside the church. He then walked solemnly along the aisle under his customary canopy held up on four poles. 'Our brother Luis [Carrero Blanco] has been a victim of hatred, which is inhuman and, above all, antichristian,' said the cardinal before embracing both Franco and Prince Juan Carlos.[8]

In his televised end of year speech a few days later, Franco recalled their '32 years of direct and generous collaboration' and told Spaniards that Carrero Blanco had sacrificed his life for them. Casting around for someone to blame, he claimed the assassination had been planned on 'foreign' soil and was an attack on ordinary Spaniards and their love of peace and order. The armed forces, he reminded them, were standing by, willing to prove their 'devotion and discipline'.[9]

Carmen Polo started a campaign to have a hardliner appointed prime minister, ringing frantically around Franco's closest councillors. On January 2, 1974, Carlos Arias Navarro was sworn in to the role. The appointment of the tough interior minister pointed to a harshening of Franco's attitude. Arias immediately upgraded the new interior minister, José García Hernandez, to deputy premier and pledged to uphold order 'with severity and calmness'. As if to confirm the renewed toughness, the Case 1001 defendants all received prison terms of more than 12 years (later reduced on appeal).[10]

Further confirmation of the repressive turn came just a week later, when a military court handed 26-year-old Catalan anarchist Salvador Puig Antich the death sentence for killing a policeman. Franco was not in a mood for clemency and ignored appeals from bishops. Puig was garrotted on 2 March 1973 – making him the first political enemy executed by court order, and the first prisoner to be garrotted, for a decade. Several days of student protests and rioting followed, with universities in Barcelona, Madrid and elsewhere in near-paralysis as riot police patrolled campuses.[11]

Franco also took unprecedented steps in his fight against church liberals with his police placing the bishop of Bilbao, Antonio Añoveros, under house arrest for a homily demanding wider freedoms. Angry Francoists stormed out of some churches when the homily was read out. When Franco tried to expel the bishop, provoking a stand-off with the Vatican, the conservative *ABC* newspaper called it the worst split between state and church in contemporary history. Other bishops rallied to Añoveros, defending their right to preach at will while 12,000 parishioners and hundreds of priests signed protest letters.[12]

The next blow to Franco's world came from neighbouring Portugal. Early on 25 April 1974, listeners to the Rádio Renascença station in Portugal heard the folk protest song 'Grândola, Vila Morena' being played. This was the starting signal for a military uprising to unseat the 41-year-old New State dictatorship installed by António Salazar in 1930s. The so-called Carnation Revolution, in which rebel soldiers were given carnation flowers by supporters, brought sudden change with little violence (four people were killed by police) as the Portuguese people discovered that key members of their armed forces were strong leftists. A long-standing dictatorship similar to Franco's fell in less than a day.

For Spaniards, the Portuguese revolution could be visited by simply driving west or catching a bus. They immediately wondered whether Franco's regime might also crumble if given the requisite shove. More sensationally, some newspapers sounded excited about the coup, even printing unsubtle warnings about what happens when a rigid political system refuses to adapt. When Lieutenant General Manuel Díez-Alegría was replaced as chief of the defence staff in June 1974, the Madrid rumour machine immediately saw a move to stop army reformists imitating their Portuguese colleagues. The regime itself was split between reformers who saw Portugal as a warning and the bunker, which saw it as a threat. The latter remained in control.[13]

Franco was now an absolute anomaly, if not an aberration, in Western Europe – though his supporters correctly pointed out that Spaniards were freer, and better off, than people living in the communist regimes behind the Iron Curtain. The problem was not just that Franco was the sole remaining right-wing dictator, but that Spaniards were governed by a man from a different era. 'When he dies the nineteenth century will finally be over,' one prominent Spaniard told a foreign visitor in the summer of 1974. Who now, indeed, cared about the events from more than half a century earlier that had animated Franco's own worldview – from the war in Morocco to the loss of Cuba?

Spain's future, however, remained dictated by biology. Change would only come when Franco died. The dictator had spent much of June and early July slouched in front of his television, watching the football World Cup finals being played in West Germany. Spain had failed to qualify but he did not miss a single game. So much sitting down along with the accumulated pressure of hours spent holding a fishing rod to his leg, provoked an inflamed vein, or phlebitis, that hospitalised him on 9 July 1974. He failed to meet Henry Kissinger, who returned that day to sign a fresh declaration of military cooperation as he sought to keep US bases in Spain (though Franco had not allowed them to be used for refuelling aircraft taking supplies to Israel during the previous year's Middle East war).[14] Rumours began to circulate that his health was deteriorating rapidly.

44

He Listens but Does not Hear

PARDO PALACE, MADRID, 11 JULY 1974

On 11 July 1974 Franco missed a cabinet meeting for only the second time in thirty-five years. The previous occasion had been fifteen years earlier when, in a rare moment of ill-health, a bout of flu had stopped him attending. In recent weeks, though, ministers had noticed he had trouble concentrating. 'He listens but doesn't hear,' said one. Now he was in hospital, being treated for the phlebitis in his right leg.[1]

One of his most assiduous visitors in hospital was Prince Juan Carlos, who sat with him daily. Nobody knows what the two men spoke about after they were left alone by Doctor Vicente Gil, who gave Juan Carlos orders to call for help if anything looked awry. 'This lad amazes me,' Gil wrote in his diary.[2] 'He's so well-behaved.' Doctor Gil forbade Franco from travelling to the country palace at La Granja, near Segovia, for the usual celebrations to mark the 18 July anniversary of the insurrection. Instead, he walked him up and down a corridor in an attempt to get him fit again.

Ten days after being admitted to hospital, Franco's condition suddenly worsened. He had suffered what doctors called 'gastric complications' and vomited blood, since his Parkinson's medicines had been provoking ulcers. Outside his hospital room, his son-in-law Doctor Martínez-Bordiú began to argue violently with Doctor Gil about who was in charge and banned him from taking X-rays. When Martínez-Bordiú also started loudly boasting that he had personally saved Franco's life, Gil exploded: 'This morning when the caudillo started bleeding, we had to go and find him [Martínez-Bordiú] at the lake, where he was probably with some floozy, as usual,' he recalled. The so-called 'yernísimo', or 'super-son-in-law', then riled other doctors at the hospital and insults started flying. Carmen Polo had to send him away.³

The 81-year-old dictator signed a decree on 19 July from his sickbed announcing that, temporarily, he was relinquishing his role as head of state. Prince Juan Carlos was to stand in for him. Once again, Martínez-Bordiú intervened, trying to prevent Prime Minister Arias Navarro from entering Franco's room so that he could sign the decree. Gil had to push him aside. The super-son-in-law had hoped that his own daughter's husband, Alfonso de Borbón y Dampierre, still might take his cousin Juan Carlos's place as named heir. 'What a favour you have done to that big kid Juan Carlos!' he shouted at Gil. Juan Carlos immediately signed the joint military declaration with the US, while President Nixon did the same in California.⁴

The next day, the two doctors ended up scuffling outside the caudillo's room. 'I'll teach you,' shouted Martínez-Bordiú. 'Nobody talks to the caudillo's son-in-law like that!' After Martínez-Bordiú declined to step out into the garden for a fight, Gil recalled waiting to see 'if the moment came when I could beat him up'.⁵

After further rows, Franco's wife and daughter sided with Martínez-Bordiú and wanted Gil gone. 'There are lots of doctors, Vicente, but only one son-in-law,' Carmen Polo reportedly told Gil, who immediately resigned. Meanwhile, Martínez-Bordiú continued to rile Juan Carlos. 'It is intolerable. Neither the prime minister nor the head of state are in control. No-one is in charge,' said Gil.⁶

Spain soon closed down for the summer, however, and Franco was released from hospital at the end of July 1974, nine pounds lighter. He was not yet fully recovered and waited two weeks before travelling to Galicia for his usual summer holiday. The family had appointed a new doctor, Vicente Pozuelo, who Franco now insisted be always close at hand – which meant always sleeping in the same building. Franco, it seemed, was now scared of his own death. Pozuelo tried to relieve Franco's depression by playing him military marches, especially from the Legion. Franco was delighted. 'It was like a miracle,' recalled Pozuelo. To keep him fit, he marched the dictator around the room to the same tunes. Franco's daughter's family was away for the summer with their seven children, so once more it was Prince Juan Carlos who visited. With the country on holiday, there was not much for the prince to do, though he presided over two cabinet meetings. Meanwhile, Franco's family pressured the caudillo to return to work.[7]

On 2 September 1974, Franco announced that he was back in charge, though he remained at his holiday palace in Galicia. He had been away from power for forty-five days. A few days later he appeared on television playing golf. Spaniards were finally formally told that he suffered from Parkinson's. Many knew anyway. In fact, he was still not well and appears to have been pushed back into power by his wife and ambitious son-in-law. Franco reportedly fell asleep during his first cabinet meeting. Otherwise, life returned to normal. On 9 September, sixty-seven dissidents were arrested in Barcelona after meeting at a convent building.[8]

Rumours also circulated about rising tensions within the Franco family. A clique of hardliners headed by Martínez-Bordiú urged Franco to remove reformist cabinet members, especially the information minister Pío Cabanillas, who was deemed soft. Even Prime Minister Arias now publicly criticised Martínez-Bordiú as someone who 'believes he has found in the illness of the head of state, or in his recovery, a propitious occasion to promote his personal ambitions'. Arias, meanwhile, had begun to speak of passing a law that would finally allow 'political associations' to be formed outside the Falange's National Movement. Old political parties emerged from hiding, with the Spanish Socialist Workers Party (PSOE) even holding a press conference in a Madrid basement. The rival Spanish communist party was already well-established as a powerful dissident force thanks to years of clandestine activity, but was more circumspect about appearing in public.[9]

When Pío Cabanillas was sacked on 29 October 1974, it seemed that the bunker and the family clique surrounding Franco had triumphed. The minister's greatest crime may have been allowing newspapers to talk about sex, which was bound to anger Franco's prudish wife, but newspaper editors were now warned that any mention of illegal political groups could lead to prosecution. Arias continued to claim he would bring reform, while a group of regime officials or former officials who defined themselves as Christian democrats used the name Tácito to write newspaper commentary sniping at his lack of ambition.[10]

When Arias Navarro announced that a decree on political associations had finally been agreed, the details revealed a set of restrictions – including needing the approval of the National Movement – so strong that it seemed meaningless. Regime friends and moderate critics, after all, had long been able to debate and propose change amongst themselves, just so long as they remained discreet in public and did not form a political party.[11] The new law seemed tailor-made for those who were already part of Madrid's dinner-and-debate 'cenocracy'. It took several weeks for a first application for a new 'political association' to be made in January 1975: its ambition to represent small shopkeepers and artisans merely demonstrated how limited the new freedoms really were.[12]

None of this affected the real game being played almost invisibly, in which the minority of Spaniards who were not politically apathetic were already imagining a future democracy and trying to ensure it took a form that they liked. Christian democrats and monarchists wanted to conserve, or even expand, capitalism.[13] Left-wingers sought social reform, wealth redistribution and personal liberties. Catalan and Basque nationalists wanted decentralisation and regional governments.

'After all the speeches, debates, press articles and editorials, round-tables and public and private discussions of the last few years, it appears that nothing basic has changed,' the *New York Times* reported on 3 December 1974, after the text of the law was first made public.[14] 'Nor is it likely to change, in the opinion of a large number of liberals and leftists, as long as Generalissimo Francisco Franco, who will be 82 years old tomorrow, remains chief of state.'

While nothing had changed in the political structure of Francoism, the Roman Catholic social conservatism that he had tried to impose was beginning to crumble. The 1960s had brought a sexual revolution to neighbouring countries, which tourists and emigrants also brought into Spain. Elsewhere, women were demanding and gaining new rights. Spaniards now travelled frequently to France to see the films banned at home – including, or especially, pornography. Women seeking abortions also flew regularly to London or elsewhere, if they did not go to back-street clinics. In 1974 a Supreme Court Prosecutor's Office report on abortion put the number at 300,000 a year, or 40 per cent of live births. The true figure was possibly half of that, but still huge for a country where abortion was illegal but frequently carried out in insalubrious back-street clinics.[15]

Opinion polls, a carefully constructed and controlled novelty, began to appear in the press. In February 1975, *La Vanguardia* asked Spaniards what they thought of democracy. Almost three-quarters wanted it, with the poor and less educated more frightened by the prospect of change. This reflected apathy rather than opposition, since many working-class people admitted they did not know what they wanted. Explicit opposition to democracy ran almost equally through all classes, varying from 12 to 18 per cent.[16]

In the background, many regime figures began positioning themselves for a future without Franco. 'The rats are abandoning the regime's ship,' the conservative, monarchist journalist, Luis María Anson, wrote in May 1975. 'The cowardice of the Spanish ruling class is truly suffocating ... Already it has reached the beginnings of the sauve qui peut [each man for himself], of unconditional surrender.'[17]

Spain, like much of the Western world, was now suffering economically – in part because of the 1973–1974 global oil crisis. Inflation had stayed above 6 per cent since July 1970, reaching 15.6 per cent in 1974. As prices soared, so did workers' pay demands, and illegal protests spread across major cities like Madrid, Barcelona and Bilbao late in 1974, a year that saw some 2,200 strikes. The clandestine communist and socialist parties, along with their associated trades unions, grew amidst the turmoil. Arson attacks on car factories in Pamplona and Valladolid hinted at a return to class violence. Students, meanwhile, regularly fought with police and universities frequently had to halt classes. Housewives' groups and neighbourhood associations also began to agitate. Government austerity saw Christmas lights switched off to save on electricity bills. When the Supreme Court cut the jail sentences of the Case 1001 defendants by up to a third in February 1975, it was seen as a gesture towards workers' organisations. Arias kept promising, and failing to deliver, reforms as both the church and the communist party joined calls for an amnesty for political prisoners, with 160,000 people signing a petition sent to Franco.[18]

By now even many former loyalists were lobbying for change and quietly hoping Franco would hand over power or die. A rebellious Franco nephew called Nicolás (the son of his brother Nicolás and a go-between for Prince Juan Carlos with dissident leaders) appeared in the press saying he was 'against fascism and in favour of a peaceful egalitarian democratic coexistence, without privileges for any class'.[19] ETA, meanwhile, stepped up its violence, shooting two police officers in the space of four weeks. Franco reacted by ordering states of exception in both Guipúzcoa and Vizcaya provinces as hardliners vowed vengeance. Two priests were beaten by police and another roughed up in his church by the rightist Guerrilleros de Cristo Rey gang. Attacks by rightist thugs on pro-Basque businesses in Bilbao mysteriously stopped as soon as authorities showed concern. ETA nevertheless continued its violent campaign with one of its members, a Civil Guard lieutenant and two civilians dying in a shootout in Guernica on 14 May 1975.[20]

As Franco increasingly lashed out at the opposition, European countries made it clear that Spain must change or remain shunned. Attempts by the United States to win Spain membership of NATO were rebuffed by Germany and others. With Franco still in charge, membership of the European Economic Community (EEC, the future European Union) was impossible. It was a repeat of the 1950s, with Franco's presence as the main drag on Spain's economy.

Franco met his third US president when Gerald Ford made a one-day stop in Madrid on 31 May 1975 during a European tour. Ford, who had assumed the presidency after Nixon's resignation, was more interested in courting the English-speaking Prince Juan Carlos than the ancient, uniformed General Franco who accompanied him in an open-top car on the now-ritual trip past waving crowds of madrileños. The *New York Times* scolded Ford for the 'bestowing of such a spectacular blessing by the President on the last relic of pre-World War II fascism'. It deemed the trip 'emphatically unnecessary'.[21]

In the meantime, Franco's opponents became increasingly organised. In the summer of 1974, while Prince Juan Carlos was temporarily in control, a platform called the Democratic Council of Spain, or Junta Democrática de España, had brought together the exiled Communist Party of Spain with other pro-democracy groups, including monarchists and some people from Opus Dei. It had been launched simultaneously in Madrid and Paris, where the exiled communist leader Santiago Carrillo was one of its protagonists. Prince Juan Carlos even sent Franco's own nephew as an intermediary to talk to Carrillo. In June 1975, another democracy platform – the Platform for Democratic Convergence – was launched in Madrid. Amongst its leaders was Felipe González, a young lawyer from Seville who used the alias 'Isidore' and had pushed out the old guard of the Spanish Socialist Workers Party (PSOE) to take charge at a party congress in Suresnes, France, the previous year. Police were now being less active. 'The police know us,' one Communist activist said. 'They could arrest 5,000 Communists in a matter of hours. But they would provoke all kinds of upheavals, strikes, demonstrations.'[22]

As the state of exception in the Basque Country provoked more attacks on police there, Franco once more reached for the tools of repression, announcing a new antiterrorism law in August 1975. On 29 August 1975, executions were ordered of two ETA members. Half a dozen Basques were injured when police opened fire on demonstrations against the sentences, while some 13,000 workers joined protest strikes. Two weeks later, on 18 September, five members of the extreme left Revolutionary Antifascist and Patriotic Front (FRAP) were also handed death sentences. Isolated gun battles erupted in Madid and Barcelona over the next two days as police hunted suspected ETA members. On 27 September, Franco confirmed the death penalties of five people, two from ETA and three from FRAP. In an apparent attempt to dampen the inevitable outrage in the rest of Europe, the sadistic garrotte was not used. Instead, the five men were shot.[23] The change of method made no difference: European governments responded by withdrawing their ambassadors. A requiem mass for the five dead in a Madrid church saw twenty congregants detained, along with half a dozen journalists.

The regime now unleashed its own supporters as Arias Navarro stirred up patriotic hatred of foreigners, complaining that foreign protests against the execution were 'an intolerable aggression against Spanish sovereignty'.[24] Franco joined the finger-pointing, appearing as usual on the balcony of the Oriente Palace for the 1 October celebrations of his appointment as head of state, where another vast crowd waving white handkerchiefs had been assembled. The absence of European ambassadors at the reception underscored just how isolated he was. Dressed in his dark blue gala uniform with gold braid, a red sash and dark glasses, the caudillo gasped his way through a short speech denouncing a global 'leftist Masonic conspiracy' that supported 'Communist terrorist subversions'.[25] It was a return to the past. Spain was the victim, once more, of foreign plots. For Franco, it had always been so. Outrage about his use of the firing squad and the garrotte were just part of the same old phenomenon.

Firing squads, however, were no deterrent. Earlier on the morning of 1 October 1975, before Franco appeared on the Oriente Palace balcony, three policemen had been shot and killed in different attacks targetting those guarding Madrid banks. All were victims of a violent new group called the First of October Antifascist Resistance Groups (GRAPO) whose youthful members were inspired by leftist revolutionaries like Che Guevara in Latin America. At the police officers' funerals the following day, there were cries of 'Death to the Communists!' and 'No more clemency!' Franco's more thuggish supporters felt unchained, and a cycle of violence unseen since the civil war looked to be starting.

Fear of violence against European airlines and travellers by regime thugs saw flights to Rome, Milan and Copenhagen cancelled: trains were stopped from travelling to France or Switzerland and international bus services were disrupted. A football match between Barcelona and Italian team Lazio was called off. Most players from Denmark's national soccer team refused to travel to Spain to play a Nations Cup match. Some European vessels found themselves prevented from leaving ports and pro-Francoist demonstrators in cities in southern Andalusia cursed the countries they came from – while tourists from those same countries filled the region's hotels, beaches and bank accounts.

When ETA blew up a Civil Guard Land Rover and killed three guardsmen in the Basque country on 5 October, tension rose even further and a tough new commander, the ambitious former Blue Division officer Lt General Ángel Campano López, was appointed to head the well-armed force. Campano López was one of several generals also becoming wealthy from their business dealings. His appointment at the head of a force of 60,000 well-trained guardsmen was part of a plot by army hardliners, backed by Franco's family, to fill top positions in the military before the dictator died.[26]

Pro-regime thugs trashed the foyer of the Hotel Suecia in Madrid and, in a typically comical episode, Franco's son-in-law Martínez-Bordiú got into a fight with some Dutch tourists, one of whom was arrested for slamming a door against his nose. The EEC responded to the clampdown by suggesting talks over a new trade deal be suspended. Complaints about police torture continued to mount, whether from lawyers' groups, Amnesty International or the Roman Catholic church. The auxiliary bishop of Madrid, Monsignor Alberto Iniesta, had to leave the country for a 'holiday' in Rome after preaching against the use of physical or psychological torture 'to obtain confessions from defendants, which has occurred several times recently in our country'.

Attention then moved on to the armed services where, with the Portuguese revolution in mind, a dozen officers were arrested on suspicion of sedition. A small secret grouping of dissident young officers, the Democratic Military Union, had already been partly broken up. There were reports that several hundred officers were under investigation. In mid-October 1975, several generals felt it necessary to make public professions of loyalty to Franco. A feeling that Franco's end was close frayed the nerves of hardcore supporters and excited opponents. Change, everybody realised, would only come once the caudillo died.[27]

45

Last Gasp

MADRID, OCTOBER–NOVEMBER 1975

On 19 October 1975, Franco was reported to be resting at home after recovering from mild flu. In fact, his health was deteriorating rapidly. The following day he cancelled his engagements and on 21 October doctors said he was suffering serious heart problems. Two days later he suffered a further relapse and it was reported that he was too unwell to even sign a transfer of power to Prince Juan Carlos.

It was around now that Franco began to realise he was being manipulated by his close family and the bunker. He asked his dentist why his former doctor, Vicente Gil, no longer looked after him. 'Is it true that Vicente has gone mad and they have had to lock him up?' he asked. When the dentist told him that was not true, Franco replied that 'they have tricked me' and demanded that Gil visit him. He asked Carmen why they had lied to him. 'We said that so that you would stop worrying,' she replied.[1]

Rumours spread that he had received the last rites, but on 28 October he was reported to be eating once more. The improvement did not last and two days later 37-year-old Prince Juan Carlos took 'temporary' control of the government again. One foreign newspaper noted that, despite the many years spent standing at Franco's shoulder during public events, the young prince was still 'more expert in sports than in politics'.[2]

Spaniards now found themselves following a daily medical drama, in which rumours were interspersed with official bulletins on the dictator's health. On 4 November 1975, Franco's internal bleeding from a burst artery was such that doctors submitted him to a three-hour operation and the following day he was put on a kidney dialysis machine. On 7 November he was rushed to La Paz hospital and underwent another emergency operation to have much of a badly ulcerated stomach removed.[3]

Doctors claimed to be 'astonished' by his ability to recover from their operations but by 12 November 1975 he was showing symptoms of pneumonia and his condition again became critical. The medical team surrounding him was now made up of 32 doctors, including specialists of all kinds. They issued regular bulletins cataloguing the mounting problems of internal bleeding, oedema, lung congestion and the appearance of a respirator alongside the kidney dialysis machine.[4]

A small crowd gathered daily outside La Paz hospital, watching a stream of senior officials and dignitaries walk in and out. Some prayed, held arms open in the sign of the cross and shouted Franco's name or, occasionally, sobbed. Religious relics were brought and people offered blood or even their kidneys. By now, the generalísimo was being kept alive artificially. 'My God, that's enough!' his granddaughter María del Carmen reportedly exclaimed on seeing him hooked up to machines on 14 November. By the following day, at least one doctor was arguing that it is 'time to let this man died peacefully'.[5]

On 18 November Franco suffered another massive internal bleed, with doctors lowering his temperature by 7 degrees Fahrenheit to help stem the loss. Rumours began to circulate that Franco was really dead and the truth was being hidden. Hotels were full of foreign journalists who had flown in to cover the historic moment. The following day, doctors produced six different medical bulletins. These were read out by Franco's press secretary to journalists in the hospital lobby, starting at 7.35 in the morning with 'no change' and ending, almost tearfully, at 23.25 with 'unfavourable signs'. Old hardliners were seen weeping as they left the hospital. Soon after, Martínez-Bordiú gave the order to turn off the machines.[6,7]

By now, officials were more than prepared for the death of the man who had ruled Spain absolutely for thirty-six years. This was eventually announced as having happened at 4.30 a.m. on 20 November – the same day of the year that Falange leader José Antonio Primo de Rivera had died. Although the news had already been confirmed and broadcast on radio stations, Prime Minister Carlos Arias Navarro made a special television broadcast that morning, weeping as he declared that: 'It is true that Franco, who was our *caudillo* for so many years, is no longer with us, though his work and example remain.' Special editions of morning newspapers reached newsstands by 7 a.m. and sold in their millions. 'The Generalissimo died at 4.30 this morning,' they trumpeted. The formal death certificate eventually put 5.25 a.m. as the time of death.[8]

This was a lie. Those making the decisions about Franco's care – mostly Martínez-Bordiú – ensured that he died officially on the emblematic date of 20 November. That may, or may not, have been a coincidence, though by now everyone except Franco's brother-in-law Serrano Suñer had forgotten that the dictator and José Antonio Primo de Rivera never liked each other. In fact, he almost certainly did not make it to 20 November. The doctors charged with embalming his corpse had been called on the stroke of midnight and began work at 1 a.m. The body was already cold, as if Franco had been dead for a while. They pumped him full of embalming fluids, filling out and hardening the features. They finished shortly after 3 a.m. 'When we told them that the embalming was finished they asked us to dictate an official report to a typist saying that the embalming had been done between 5.30 and 10 a.m. on 20 November, which was obviously not true,' Dr Antonio Piga, one of the team, admitted later. He calculated that Franco probably died at around 22.00 the previous night. By 4 a.m., sculptor Santiago de Santiago had taken a plaster cast of Franco's face and hands. The body was then washed, dressed and taken to the Pardo Palace.[9]

On television, Arias Navarro read out Franco's posthumous message to the nation. In death, the man who had ruled and shaped Spain single-handedly for thirty-nine years added a final adjustment to the script of his life, by pardoning 'those who declared themselves my enemies, although I never considered them as such.' He still saw himself as a self-sacrificing servant to the nation, rather than someone driven by selfish desire.

He also left behind him words of warning: 'Don't forget that the enemies of Spain and of Christian Civilisation are on alert. You must also be watchful and place the supreme interests of the fatherland and of the Spanish people above all personal ambition.'[10]

Epilogue: Franco's Funerals

MADRID–VALLEY OF THE FALLEN, 20–23 NOVEMBER 1975

Franco's body was moved to the Oriente Palace in the morning of 21 November, where it lay in state for fifty hours as queues of people waiting to view the corpse stretched more than a mile uphill past the Puerta del Sol square. Mourners gawked, wept, prayed or proffered stiff-armed salutes. The open coffin eventually had to be moved to the palace's ground floor so the 300,000 or more people who wanted to see the uniformed corpse could file past more speedily. The embalmers claimed to have done such a good job that Franco's body would 'remain uncorrupted for thousands of years, just like the Egyptian mummies'.[1]

Those who came to view the body were not just, as the joke went, making sure that he really was dead. Historian Antonio Cazorla Sánchez was twelve years old when the generalísimo died and recalled his own sadness and that of his neighbours in the working class La Chanca neighbourhood of Almería, in south-east Spain:

> My parents went hungry after the civil war and some of my neighbours were punished by the regime. One was executed. When Franco died, however, I felt sad, even though there was no school on the morning of November 20. The sadness of that 12-year-old boy was shared at the time by millions of Spaniards, who believed that the man who had just died had been the best possible solution for a country that was difficult to govern. That is what they said at school, in the press, on the television etc... In 1975, maybe most of

us Spaniards believed that Franco had maintained peace in a country scalded by its past. We were happy with the progress in recent years, which we put down to the dedicated work of the old leader. It is not as though we had forgotten the misery of the forties and fifties, but rather that this was mainly blamed on the war and other things beyond his control.[2]

It took Cazorla, and many other Spaniards, time to overcome the years of conditioning by school and the media and to learn the truth about Franco. Yet it was also true that, as the French political theorist Jean-Francois Revel pointed out later, 'some important part of every society consists of people who actively want tyranny: either to exercise it themselves or – much more mysteriously – to submit to it.'[3]

A poll conducted in the days after Franco's death was fuzzy about the degree of support, not least because Spaniards were still not used to expressing themselves freely. Nevertheless, 29 per cent said they felt 'irreparable loss'. A further 53 per cent felt 'pained and saddened'. This was the polite reply to any enquiry about someone's death, but certainly it showed no major outpouring of joy.[4]

In fact, Franco's death provoked a mixture of fear and relief. Even amongst those opposed to him, celebrations were discreet. The Barcelona-based writer Manuel Vázquez Montalbán summed it up in his usual, ironic style. 'Above the skyline of the Collserola mountains, champagne corks soared into the autumn twilight. But nobody heard a sound,' he said.[5] A single question ran through everybody's mind: What would come next?

The special editions of newspapers that morning were mostly full of praise. After all, the Francoist regime was still in place. So were its censorship rules. *Doblón* magazine's special edition was sequestered by police for saying that Carmen Polo was 'good at business', a phrase taken as an accusation of cronyism and an unprecedented attack on 'the Lady'.[6]

'What's the rush? The generalísimo has only just died, and you people already want it all,' the information minister told *Doblón's* editor, José Antonio Martínez Soler. But Martínez Soler found the once all-powerful minister already diminished 'as if Franco's death had shrunken his body... and a little bit scared'.[7]

On 22 November 1975, Juan Carlos was sworn in as king before parliament. He asserted that Franco's regime had enjoyed 'the political legitimacy that emerged from 18 July 1936, amidst so much sad but necessary sacrifice and suffering so that our Patria could rejoin the path of destiny'. In other words, Franco had been right to overthrow Republican democracy and start a civil war. Juan Carlos praised Franco as an 'exceptional man' who had set Spain 'on the right path'. The caudillo's example, he added, would guide his own policy, while 'my hand will not tremble to do all that is necessary to defend the principles [of the Movimiento] and laws that I have just sworn.'[8]

That sounded very much like Francoism would continue. Yet Juan Carlos also spoke of a new era 'of emotion and hope', hinting at change. Nobody knew what that meant, or how fast change might come. At the following day's funeral in the Valley of the Fallen, Franco's coffin was lowered into the long-reserved niche under the marble floor beside the altar and covered with a weighty granite slab. A visibly moved and red-eyed Juan Carlos presided.

Foreign heads of state were scarce. Few wanted to be associated with the man damned as Europe's last fascist. General Augusto Pinochet, the murderous generalísimo of Chile, was the most prominent. Monaco's Prince Rainier and King Hussein of Jordan added glamour, but were mostly there to give moral support to King Juan Carlos.[9]

Formally, the dictatorship had not ended. It simply had a new head in the 37-year-old monarch. Franco's prime minister Arias Navarro underscored the idea of continuity by vowing that 'as long as I am here I will be a strict perpetuator of Francoism in all aspects.' Violence began to spread, with street demonstrations and terrorism from the far left and far right. Journalists remained cowed. They did not start referring to Franco as a 'dictator' until almost a year after his death.[10]

Francoist opponents and democrats faced a stark choice. They could pursue a high-risk strategy of rupture, demanding that the illegitimacy of the Franco regime be recognised and blame apportioned. However, that might provoke the army into rebellion. The only other path was the less profound one of change by reform, in which Franco's own institutions would be coerced to usher in democracy. That came with a price, in terms of dealing with Franco's legacy or seeking justice for its excesses, but was a far safer option. Even then, those in power were negotiating from strength. Manuel Fraga, who had become Arias Navarro's interior minister, had opposition leaders arrested. 'Remember that I am the power, and you are nothing,' he told Socialist leader Felipe González.[11]

Juan Carlos was viewed by many as a stop gap. '¡No al Rey impuesto!' ('No to an imposed King!') and '¡No al Rey franquista!' ('No to the Francoist King!'), the underground left-wing press clamoured. Some dubbed him 'Juan Carlos the Brief'. There were rumours that he was intellectually limited or spoke imperfect Spanish. 'Years of glum, mute appearances next to Franco had led to the widespread assumption that he had neither intelligence nor courage,' explains one biographer.[12]

In July 1976, however, Juan Carlos changed prime ministers, choosing an ambitious 44-year- old Movement apparatchik, Adolfo Suárez. The two men oversaw a remarkable transition in which the Francoist parliament – true to its rubber-stamp nature and amid promises that there would be no reckoning for having served Franco – dissolved itself. Political parties, including the communists, returned. Free elections were held in 1977 for a new parliament that drew up a democratic constitution. Suárez's own coalition of centrist parties, the Union of the Democratic Centre, won enough seats to govern. Years of obedience and inertia help explain why voters fell in behind the man appointed by the king to lead them.

The political extremes, meanwhile, did very badly. The communists, who had played a major part in opposing Franco, won just nine per cent of the vote as left-wing voters turned to the more moderate socialists. They now led the opposition. The Popular Alliance of former Franco minister Manuel Fraga won just eight per cent.

The new constitution was approved at referendum in 1978. The constitution represented all that Franco hated. It enshrined liberal democracy, freedom of speech, the existence of communist and separatist parties and the devolution of powers to Catalonia and the Basque country. More importantly, Spain continued to have a monarch as head of state, but with all real power vested in parliament. Juan Carlos had shed his powers while restoring his family's role and privileges. In fact, he continued to wield considerable influence from the shadows for the next few years.

Army 'sabre-rattling', as it became known, overshadowed and conditioned the whole transition to democracy, as rumours swirled of a coup to reimpose Francoism by force. On 23 February 1981, 200 armed police and soldiers duly burst into the parliament building in Madrid, machine-gunning the ceiling and taking the deputies hostage. This was the coup attempt that many had feared. A Civil Guard lieutenant colonel wearing a patent-leather tricorn hat, Antonio Tejero, brandished his pistol from the tribune and ordered the deputies to lie on the floor. A television camera kept rolling as Tejero ordered: 'Al suelo!'('To the floor!') and, more confusingly, 'En nombre del Rey!' ('In the king's name!'). They had been told the monarch was on their side. The coup leader, a mysterious figure known as 'White Elephant', was meant to appear shortly. In fact, he never did.

Instead, King Juan Carlos personally ordered senior generals not to support the would-be rebels, appearing on television in uniform to demand they lay down arms and helping ensure that it was all over in eighteen hours. No blood had been shed. The monarchy's popularity surged.

The failed coup liberated Spain from fear of a Francoist return, though another attempt was quashed in advance in October 1982. That year, Spaniards voted for their first left-wing government since the 1930s, led by Felipe González. Symbolically, this shift was enormous – completing the formal liquidation of Francoism. 'It may seem trivial to put it this way, but those elections were like the ritualistic death of the father,' historian Santos Juliá recalled.[13] 'The fresh air of freedom blew through all parts of Spanish society.'

González would stay in power for 14 years, overseeing a solid transformation of political culture. He tacked towards the centre, abandoning plans to leave NATO and appointing orthodox finance ministers who shuttered or sold off state industries and weakened Francoist labour laws that had made people almost unsackable. With Franco gone, Spain was welcomed into the European Economic Community (EEC, later the European Union) in 1986. Spaniards were delighted. They had longed to be accepted as 'normal' Europeans. A surge of European-driven growth brought Spain deeper into the club of advanced global economies. The trigger, then, for this burst in Spanish prosperity was the dictator's death, just as the spark for the 1960s growth spurt was his forced abandonment of autarky. It was further evidence of the ways that Franco's presence had held back material progress.

Less visibly, the move to democracy also brought about an apparent growth in national self-esteem. Ironically, once more, this was what Franco himself had wanted Spaniards to feel. His supporters now claimed that all this had happened because of, rather than in spite of, the caudillo. The theory they promoted was that by creating a large enough middle class and tempering the extremism of the 1930s he had created the ideal conditions for democracy. There was a secondary, self-justifying message inside that theory – which was that elites had been right to back Franco just as they were now right to back democracy.

The Spain that emerged from this process looked nothing like the country Franco dreamed of when he helped start a civil war that killed half a million people. Divorce, abortion, secularisation and a rapid shrinkage of church influence soon followed. Women won new freedoms, making up a majority of university students by the late 1980s. Social attitudes did not necessarily keep pace. 'Spain has leapt from pre-feminism into post-feminism without having really experienced the feminist upheaval which elsewhere took place in between,' John Hooper commented in *The New Spaniards* in 1987. 'As a consequence, profoundly sexist attitudes have survived into an era in which women are acquiring much genuine freedom and equality.'[14] Nevertheless, Spain eventually became amongst the most socially liberal countries in Europe. It would, for example, be the first to introduce marriage with full equality of rights for homosexuals. Its politics remained fractious and argumentative, but fully democratic.

For the first three decades after the dictator's death, the country looked steadily away from its Francoist past, treating the history of that period like a Pandora's Box that should never be opened. An amnesty passed by the first democratic parliament in 1977 freed the remaining political prisoners of Francoism and was greeted by the left as an opportunity to end the era of 'civil wars and crusades' and 'bury the sad, past history of Spain'. In fact, it also contained an amnesty for crimes 'against the rights of people' committed by 'authorities, functionaries and agents of public order' prior to December 1976.[509] That meant Francoist abuses, and abusers, could not be tried or revisited. The amnesty was hailed as 'a forgetting by everyone for everyone', promoting a form of amnesia that mainstream parties on both sides embraced.[15]

Felipe González admits silence was part of the price his generation paid for democracy. 'What we have is a change that is agreed between people coming from the old regime and the opposition ... That was very positive but it excluded, for example, an explanation (not to mention any demand that people be held responsible) for what had happened under Francoism, through truth commissions, as other countries have done. There was not sufficient strength to demand either justice or, even, any explanation for the past.'

This otherwise unwritten policy of amnesia was so generalised that it was even given a name: the pacto de olvido, or pact of forgetting. Amongst other things, it meant schoolchildren learned little or nothing about the civil war and the Franco period. It also prevented those who experienced the worst of Francoism from passing on their stories. Yet it was not an imposition. Spaniards genuinely did not want to rake over old coals. Their reasons varied. Some had good memories of Franco. Others were afraid of arousing old passions. Still more found it hard to shake off old fears and habits.

Opinion polls continued to tell a mixed story about Franco's reputation. A 1994 poll found a quarter of adults considered him one of the best leaders of Spain in the twentieth century. Almost half believed Franco had kept the peace and a third thought he had saved them from communism. That said, only 16 per cent thought Spain would have been worse off with democracy instead of Franco's dictatorship.[16]

Although Francoism was routinely denigrated in public debate, the fact that nobody was ever punished – or even shamed – for having been part of it after his death helped people believe that it had not been so bad. The early amnesties and the spirit of the pact of forgetting meant there was no formal condemnation of thirty-six years of lost freedoms. Spain, in that sense, was almost unique amongst the countries who threw off autocratic or totalitarian regimes of left or right at the end of the twentieth century. Even the Latin American countries that fell into the hands of military juntas – some of which sought inspiration in Franco – eventually rescinded their amnesty laws. Spain did not.

Prominent Francoists pursued major political careers in democracy. Suárez was just one of many. Fraga became one of the authors of the constitution and his conservative People's Party eventually alternated in power with the socialists. He was voted in by the people of his home region of Galicia as regional president four times over fifteen years. It was historically ironic that a former minister of Franco, who centralised everything and considered traitorous the regionalist parties that had operated in Galicia, Catalonia and the Basque country during the Republic, should lead one of the 17 semi-autonomous regional governments that emerged under democracy.

Franco had proclaimed Spain to be 'One, Great and Free' – an oft-repeated slogan that targeted the supposedly traitorous Catalan and Basque nationalists of the Republic. The new constitution recognised 'the right to autonomy of the nationalities and regions of which it is composed'. The term 'nationalities' was a fudge chosen to avoid the word 'nations'. In order to calm the military and the far right, the constitution also proclaimed the 'indissoluble unity of the Spanish nation, the common and indivisible country of all Spaniards', with the army obliged to defend Spain's 'territorial integrity'. Some in the military took that to mean they could intervene to prevent division of the country.[17]

During one of Fraga's political campaigns in Galicia, his party put out a statement saying that Francoism 'had not been as terrible as they want to make us believe'. Former regime apparatchiks rarely spoke about their work for Franco. 'The political class turned into angels, proud of the almost mafioso omertà when it came to talking about themselves,' observed writer Gregorio Morán, one of the few critics to point out the hypocrisy of switching from authoritarianism to democracy overnight.[18] A well-known Spanish psychiatrist called it 'a world-record in jacket changing'.

Old Francoists, meanwhile, continued to live well. In 1997, a silver-haired, elderly but fit 96-year-old could be seen off the beach at Marbella trying out a water scooter. This was Franco's brother-in-law Ramón Serrano Suñer, the architect of what he had hoped would become a totalitarian Spain in the early 1940s. He lived to the age of 101, dying in 2003. A chauffeur-driven black Mercedes took him to the beach from his summer house most days and he would take the sun or walk with his cashmere jacket, hat and stick. After Franco died, he continued with a successful legal practice and sometimes contributed to public debate. He presented himself as a moderate Franco opponent. 'He could not bear his own past and fought vainly to reconstruct it,' historian Javier Tusell said, when he had really been 'an indispensable instrument in the construction of Franco's dictatorship in its most totalitarian, fascist moment'.[19]

Policemen, Civil Guard officers, generals, judges and other enforcers of Francoism continued in their jobs. Nobody pursued members of the notorious Social Political brigade of the police like Antonio González Pacheco, aka Billy el Niño, or the infamous Juan and Vicente Creix brothers from Barcelona, for torturing political detainees. 'We, their victims, did not do anything to shine a light on them. The political reforms had already absolved those who owned the Creixes. Would it have been right to pursue their servants?' Vázquez Montalbán reasoned.[20]

The Czech writer, dissident and, eventually, president Vaclav Havel once said that the line separating collaborators from non-collaborators in totalitarian states mostly did not run between people but through them – since almost everyone is compromised. In Spain, few people were uncontaminated. Many prominent journalists, for example, had learned their craft serving Franco's state broadcaster or the newspapers of the Falange. Some now edited newspapers that delivered stern sermons about the importance of democracy to their readers, but never sought to explain to what extent they had been collaborators. Obviously, they were in no position to demand a national reckoning with the past.

The entire business and financial class remained intact, bringing the Franco-period habits of corruption and tax evasion with them. There was no immediate danger to the wealthy in a country where, thanks to Franco's low and inefficiently run tax regime, the richest 1.5 per cent of the population had as much wealth as the bottom 52 per cent. In terms comparative to their own nations' wealth, the top 10 per cent of Spaniards were two and half times richer than the top 10 per cent of people in the United Kingdom. That reflected the fact that Franco's state rarely took in as taxes, or spent, more than 13 per cent of GDP – well below the levels of neighbouring France or of other major European countries.[21]

Since the state bureaucrats remained the same, so did the culture of bureaucracy. Under Franco, this had been based on the idea that individuals should serve the nation, rather than the other way round. A significant change to that culture came with the disbanding of the Movimiento in 1977. It had been fashioned around Franco and few mourned its disappearance. Even sincere Falangists despised its lack of ideology. The civil governor of Barcelona ordered that the Movimiento's local archive be taken to an industrial oven and incinerated. 'Those archives smelt of the remote past,' he wrote in a memoir, as if Franco had died long before.[22] History was wiped away.

In fact, archive destruction had been happening since the mid-1960s and was not properly brought under control until 1985. 'Millions of documents were lost during those crucial twenty years, including the archives of the Franco regime's single party ... of provincial police headquarters, of prisons and of the main Francoist local authority, the Civil Governors,' the historian Paul Preston reported. 'Convoys of trucks removed the "judicial" records of the repression.'[23] Other archives were lost when town councils sold them for recycling.

The fall of the González government finally saw the question of how Spain should deal with the Francoist past emerge into public debate. His Socialist government had shown no interest in the matter. The change was, in part, a reaction to the election in 1996 of a right-wing elected government under prime minister José María Aznar of the People's Party, the first since Franco's demise. The Left was suddenly very keen to point out the right's political heritage.

Silence about Franco's regime meant that the victims of his death squads remained in roadside graves, gullies, wells and the other places they were disposed of. When volunteers began to search for these and dig them up, Spaniards woke up to the ghastly reality that they actually existed. The graves became the focus for a so-called historical memory movement, which demanded Spain finally condemn the ghastliness of Francoism.

In villages and towns like Poyales del Hoyo in Ávila province, women like Obdulia Camacho – whose mother had been killed by a death squad in 1936 – finally gave their executed relatives a decent churchyard burial. 'This thing has stayed in my mind all my life. I've never forgotten. I am reliving it now,' she said as her mother's corpse was disinterred in 2002. 'All the killers were from the village. They came with the intention of killing, and then they went off to confess ... I can pardon, but I cannot forget.'

Debate became increasingly fractious, with different socialist governments eventually passing so-called 'historical memory' and 'democratic memory' laws, in 2007 and 2022 respectively, to permit increased transparency and memorialisation of victims, while the Right accused them of once more trying to divide Spaniards.

Under the terms of the memory laws, Francoist street names and monuments mostly disappeared. For years, however, even socialist governments dared not touch the Valley of the Fallen, despite the fact that it was a state-owned monument. That changed in October 2019, when Franco's corpse was removed and taken to lie with Carmen Polo in a cemetery near the Pardo Palace. Conservative commentators had predicted that the enforced removal would provoke violent protests. In fact, only a few hundred demonstrators appeared, many of them more interested in praying than protesting.

Perhaps the most damaging inheritance of Francoism was corruption. This was not just about cronyism within the regime and Franco's wilful ignoring of corruption by friends and supporters. With low social spending, the ultimate fallback in times of economic distress was the family rather than the state. Nepotism, in such societies, is a sensible strategy, and it is easier to cheat the state through backhanders or tax evasion when it offers you little sustenance. 'In Spain, no one has ever been afraid to be corrupt,' judge Baltasar Garzón, a relentless pursuer of graft, lamented. 'Given that its existence was taken for granted, corruption is not something that has bothered the average citizen. This indifference has ensured that its roots have grown deep and solid and sustain a structure of interests that is very difficult to bring down.'[24]

This culture of corruption hit parties of all colours, from the socialists to the right-wing People's Party, to regional parties in Catalonia and elsewhere. A nadir was reached when the socialist head of the Civil Guard, Luis Roldán, was caught demanding kickbacks from construction companies and the governor of the Bank of Spain, Mariano Rubio, was arrested for tax fraud. 'The man in charge of the guards fled with the money and the man in charge of the money was in the custody of two guards,' one politician quipped. The People's Party proved no better, with three of José María Aznar's ministers ending up in jail.[25]

Juan Carlos, meanwhile, was forced to abdicate in favour of his son Felipe VI in 2014 after being discovered on a luxury elephant-hunting trip to Botswana with a former lover while ordinary Spaniards suffered through a prolonged construction and banking crash. By then, there were reports that Swiss bankers had been dropping off bags containing hundreds of thousands of euros at the royal palace. Questions were also raised about a $100 million payment from Saudi Arabia's royal family and Juan Carlos admitted owing back taxes worth 678,000 euros.[26] In fact, the close link between the royal household and corruption had already been exposed with the jailing of the king's son-in-law Iñaki Urdangarin in 2018.

Another damaging legacy of Francoism was terrorism. The same groups who emerged in his final years sometimes refused to go away. Other groups were created by his own supporters and were heirs to those same street-fighting Francoists who the bunker had encouraged to intimidate opponents. More than 591 people died in the seven years after Franco's death, including fifty-eight demonstrators killed by police or right-wing thugs.[27] When Fraga was asked to treat amnesty protesters in Valencia gently, he replied: 'Los voy a moler a palos' ('I shall beat them black and blue'). ETA blighted Spanish democracy for decades, finally dissolving in 2018 having killed 864 people.

The downturn that started in 2008 brought an end to a period of optimism based on change and escape from Francoism. Spain's political and financial elites were to blame. 'Mismanagement, hubris and greed, coupled with a banking system that lent according to political not financial criteria, proved disastrous,' according to Tobias Buck of the *Financial Times*.[28] The stresses provoked by that not only broke Juan Carlos, but also ushered in a new period of political extremism. Populist parties of the left and right, Podemos and Vox, appeared.

For decades, Spaniards looked on in amazement as other European countries voted for far-right parties. Francoism, commentators said, had inoculated them against anything similar. They shunned such parties until the 2010s, when the far-right Vox emerged. By 2019 it had 15 per cent of the vote. It was similar to the other far-right parties around Europe – socially illiberal, anti-immigrant and divided on whether to be liberal or protectionist about the economy. By 2024, it had shattered the political taboo of publicly defending Franco. 'The phase after the Civil War was not the dark period that the current [socialist] government tries to sell us, but rather it was a period of reconciliation, reconstruction and progress,' Vox deputy Manuel Mariscal told parliament.[29]

Catalan separatism also resurged with strength, throwing oil onto an already blazing political bonfire. A separatist Catalan government led by Carles Puigdemont held an illegal independence referendum on 1 October 2017. Voters were blocked or beaten by police. The polling results were meaningless, since only separatists campaigned and when Puigdemont unilaterally declared an ambiguous (and, ultimately, ineffectual) form of independence and promptly fled the country, the stand-off turned to farce.[30] All this was traumatic, but it happened without democracy falling apart or the army intervening. Spaniards clearly had no need of a strongman like Franco to resolve their problems.

Historians still puzzle over where to place Franco. His ideology does not fit the models of the twentieth century, when communism and fascism provided two easily identifiable extremes. That is because Franco's politics were born out of Spain's nineteenth-century history of imperial humiliation. His simplistic reactionary ideals were about righting that, as if everything from the French Revolution to the Enlightenment and the fall of the Spanish empire could be reversed.

Rewinding history is always an impossible task. If foreign ideas were to blame, however, the Spanish race and Franco's misguided belief in its exceptionality were the answer. That is why he tried to shut Spain off from the world and make it self-sufficient. It is also why his only ideological success was cultural, with the reimposition of the religious mores of the nineteenth century. In the end, Franco shed all he stood for, beyond control, anti-leftism and imposed social conservatism. He traded everything else away for order, absolute authority and political passivity.

A movement like Franco's ultra nationalist coalition which defines itself in negative terms – in this case against the supposed Masonic-communist plot against Spain – must always struggle to produce and deliver a vision of the future. Given his ideological barrenness, the regime became about holding on to power for power's sake. In part, this was because Franco was a soldier. Military hierarchies encourage a single overall commander. In the end Franco wanted power not so much for the excitement of wielding it, but in order to prevent others from doing so. He mistrusted everyone except himself. His sluggish approach to change, reform and law-making fit a man with little real interest in power as a transformative force.

With no big idea to impose on the Spanish people, Franco did not need the enforcement apparatus of, say, Hitler's Germany or of post-war communist East Germany. His early investment in terror, the survival mode that Spaniards were forced into in the early years of his regime and his long-term depoliticisation of people through schooling and a tightly controlled media were sufficient to dampen the desire for rebellion.

It is also true that just harnessing the transformative energy of Western capitalist economics, as he eventually did, produced such huge upheavals that he did not need to come up with or apply his own ideas to oversee enormous change. Two of his more admiring biographers consider this 'the real Spanish revolution':

> During the last fifteen years of his life Spain was transformed into a semiaffluent modern industrial society. Longstanding problems of nearly four centuries were being resolved, and this was infinitely more important than building another empire.[31]

But the fact that this 'miracle economy' phenomenon was happening elsewhere in southern Europe – and that Spain drifted further behind neighbours like Italy and Portugal – shows that forces much larger than Franco were at work. In other words, it would have been surprising if Spain had *not* experienced this economic leap forward, though that does not change the fact that any institutional merit goes to him directly (including a social security system built almost from scratch but only universal from 1972). It is also true that, especially in some rural areas, an ancient state of dependency on the whims and personal interests of aristocrats, landowners and *caciques* was turned into a dependency on the state which, amongst other things, strongly protected workers against dismissal. Even under Franco, that could be a far fairer regime.[32]

Two years before his death, a villager from southern Spain had told the oral historian Ronald Fraser why he liked Franco, pointing precisely to the social changes which took power away from landowners. His words were couched in the standard terms of political apathy encouraged by Franco:

> Although I've got no interest in politics, I'll say straight out that there's only one person for me: General Franco. He's called Franco and he's lived up to his name of being frank with the nation. Our regime is going ahead well, as I see it, and it's due to him. Though I

was young, I can remember what things were like under the monarchy. Four or five landowners here, another few in Casas Nuevas, a handful in Posadas and Benamali. Everyone else lived under their yoke. That should never have been allowed, he who has should succour the poor, that's what I say.[33]

The lack of a grand political idea beyond nationalism also prevented Franco from wreaking as much damage as those who clung to totalitarianism and the absolute wisdom of a single political idea. As a result, a Spanish man eventually lived both a freer and a wealthier life under Franco than, say, a Hungarian or a Pole under communism. A Spanish woman, on the other hand, was arguably worse off, while literacy rates also lagged far behind.[34] In religious terms, it is important to remember that the Roman Catholic church also enjoyed a huge and sometimes asphyxiating influence in a democratic country like Ireland.

Ideology is often blamed for the twentieth-century violence of what historian Eric Hobsbawm called 'the century of extremes'. Franco proves that was not the only cause. In the number of deaths it provoked, via a civil war and the civilian bloodletting that accompanied it, his regime was as destructive as, say, Mussolini's authentic fascism and its immersion of Italy in World War II. In fact, it may be better to see the Spanish Civil War and Franco's dictatorship through the lens of the First World War – where the tone and the ambition was unashamedly nationalist and classist, while those sacrificed in the name of patriotism, national status and the leader (whether king, kaiser or tsar) were mostly the working class. As in Spain, they were led to their deaths in the name of national exceptionalism by a proud officer class. In Britain, that class had memorised a line from the Roman poet Horace which read 'dulce et decorum est pro patria mori': 'how sweet and proper it is to die for one's country.' *Africanistas* like Franco agreed wholeheartedly. Yet while the two world wars also provoked surges in Britain and elsewhere in the political power and rights of the same working class that had been drafted to fight them, Franco continued to treat that class as unworthy of political influence except through the state-controlled voice of his 'vertical' unions.

It is notable that men like Mussolini's envoys or Holocaust inventor Heinrich Himmler were shocked by the killing and vengeance that accompanied and followed the Spanish Civil War. That was not because of the violence itself, but because it seemed foolish to attack Spain's working class this way. Yet this was part of Franco's plan. Ever since he had been a young officer, he had viewed exemplary punishment as a way of imposing discipline. It cowed people into obedience and served as a tool for eradicating the foreign ideas (of liberalism, Freemasonry or leftism) that Franco thought had poisoned Spain. It was also bankable terror, a dissuasive deposit of concentrated violence that paid out for years. A cold-blooded militaristic authoritarian, in that respect, can be just as ruthless as a hot-headed Utopian ideologist.

In many ways, Francoism worked by conjuring up ghosts. To begin with, these phantoms took the form of communists and Freemasons, neither of which had anything like the power that Franco attributed to them. By the same measure, the radical wing of the socialist party together with anarchists and others on Spain's far left helped produce a discourse of extremes – since they, too, saw fascists where very few existed. However, once Franco had grasped this form of discourse, he never let go. The enemies of Spain were to blame for all that went wrong. He was only responsible for the good things. In the post-war period, he blamed poverty, hunger and death on international boycotts and the Freemasons supposedly behind them rather than on his disastrous embrace of autarky. When Spain finally hit a boom in the 1960s, this was his own brilliance at work. Yet when industrial unrest, political protest and the violence of militant Basques or extreme leftists shook the country in the early 1970s, he turned once again to blaming Spain's enemies. They had become inseparable from his personal enemies.

By that stage, something unique had happened in Spain. An entire nation had been ruled by one man for so long that almost seven out of ten Spaniards could remember nothing else. The generalísimo had liquidated or expelled many of his enemies three decades previously. Fear kept the rest silent and in check. He had then shaped people through propaganda, schooling, societal pressure, church admonition, enforced political apathy and the weight of time itself. Franco and Francoism became normality, even if a significant part of the population wished they would vanish as quickly and quietly as possible.

This was long enough for communal memory itself to have changed. One side had been forced into silence and only the other had told its version of history. It is no surprise, then, that Spaniards avoided grappling with Franco's legacy for so long and that, when they finally did so three decades after his death, they found - and continue to find - it difficult. In a way, ignoring him in the early years of Spain's newfound and successful democracy had been the best way of reducing him in size. He was treated often as a nobody, or a cruel joke played on Spain. His lack of charisma, intellectual spark, ideological conviction or the kind of personal traits that Spaniards consider 'simpático' helped in that process.

Yet it is wrong to reduce Francisco Franco to a cartoon villain and historical mediocrity. Relentless personal ambition and considerable luck combined to allow him to occupy a commanding position in the history of Spain. An ability to grasp the moment, and then hold on to it for so long, are proof of ability, will power and abundant self-belief.

Such characters are by no means always good for their people or country, but they leave their mark. If anything, the surprise in Franco's story is that the legacy was not greater. He was once famously described as a sphinx without a secret. It may be better to think of him as a giant dam, determined to control the flow of the Spanish history – in part by holding back the societal and political changes that brought welfare and freedom to much of the Western world during his life. The floodgates that opened after his death released such a torrent of pent-up energy, communal will and progress that the towering figure of Spain's twentieth-century history almost disappeared below the waters. Fifty years after his death, indeed, what surprises is not the size of the dam that was opened after he died, but the ideological emptiness that lay behind it.

Many great figures from the past live on in our communal memory for the bold new ideas – whether good or bad – that they hatched or nurtured. Since Franco had no such big idea, he must be measured by his impact on the lives of ordinary Spaniards. Beyond the undoubted maintenance of order, the balance is overwhelmingly of harm: to the economic welfare, personal freedoms and cultural or intellectual life of the Spanish people. The transition to democracy after his death was hard, long and made more difficult by the deep-seated legacies of autocracy – especially the constant threat of military coups. Despite that, Spaniards eventually passed their own judgment on Franco by embracing many of the things that he most detested, beginning with liberal democracy. They show little or no nostalgia for the bullying nature of autocracy.

Given Franco's impact on Spanish history, attempts to rehabilitate him inevitably recur. These shift blame for the Civil War from those who started it to those who remained loyal to the Republic's battered and imperfect democracy. Essentially, they argue that Franco was right and a creeping Leftist revolution was under way. Yet while the Left shares responsibility for the Republic's failures, it was Franco who chose the carnage of civil war, embraced Hitler, turned Spain into a pariah state, inflicted autarky, returned women to an old-fashioned form of servility and took away basic freedoms.

It was Franco, too, who decided that Spaniards were too childish to govern themselves. Hence his obdurate refusal to ever step aside, whatever the cost to Spain. Yet it is a measure of both his stubbornness and his success that this simple, patronising idea produced one of Europe's most enduring dictatorships. For those seeking excuses for autocracy or tyranny, Francisco Franco will always provide a role model.

Acknowledgements

Many historians and archivists have, in person or through their work, helped in the writing of this biography. I would like to take the opportunity, however, to acknowledge two key resources for 'hispanistas' – as Spaniards call foreigners who write about the history and culture of the country. The first is the remarkably open archival policy of the Spanish state and its ongoing effort to digitise and democratise access via its Pares portal. The second is the support given to hispanistas of all kinds over decades by the Cañada Blanch Centre at the London School of Economics and Political Science, particularly during the years when it was directed with generosity and warmth by historian Paul Preston.

Invaluable editing help has come from Juliet Brooke, Eva Miller and Francisco Vilhena at Bloomsbury in London, from Miguel Aguilar and Julio Fajardo at Debate in Madrid and from Timothy Bent at Oxford University Press in New York. In-house editing and reading by Katharine Scott and Samuel Tremlett have proved equally as important.

Notes

INTRODUCTION

1 *El gran desfile de Franco en Madrid*, Radio Televisión Española, available at https://www.rtve.es/play/videos/archivo-historico/gran-desfile-victoria-madrid/2836276/.
2 Javier Rodrigo, 'Internamiento Y Trabajo Forzoso: Los Campos De Concentración De Franco', *Hispania Nova Revista de Historia Contemporánea*, Separata N° 6, 2006, pp. 5-6; Paul Preston, *The Spanish Holocaust: Inquisition and Extermination in Twentieth-Century Spain*, HarperCollins, London, 2013, Kindle Loc. 131.
3 Stanley G. Payne, 'Franco y los orígenes de la Guerra Civil Española' in *La Albolafia: Revista de Humanidades y Cultura*, N°. 1, 2014, p. 12.
4 *La Vanguardia*, 20 May 1939, pp. 1–4.
5 *La Vanguardia*, 31 March 1939, p. 1.
6 Juan Pablo Fusi, 'La cultura', in J. L. García Delgado (ed.), *Franquismo: El juicio de la historia*, Temas de Hoy, Madrid, 2000, p. 183.
7 *La Vanguardia*, 20 May 1936, pp. 1–4. See https://www.statista.com/statistics/1334182/wwii-pre-war-gdp/.
8 Antonio Cazorla Sánchez, *Franco: Biografía de un Mito*, Alianza Editorial, Madrid, 2015, p. 18.
9 Jaime de Andrade, *Raza, anecdotario para el guión de una película*, Delegación Nacional de Prensa y Propaganda, Madrid, 1942, p. 38.
10 Francisco Franco, *Marruecos: Diario De Una Bandera*, Editorial Pueyo, Madrid, 1922, p. 49.
11 L. Prados de la Escosura, *Spanish Economic Growth, 1850–2015*, Palgrave Macmillan, London, 2017, p. 42; see also Maddison Project Database 2023, University of Groningen, at https://www.rug.nl/ggdc/historicaldevelopment/maddison/releases/maddison-project-database-2023 and Fundación Rafael del Pino, *Series macroeconómicas históricas* at https://frdelpino.es/investigacion/category/01_ciencias-sociales/01_economia-espanola/02_economia-espanola-perspectiva-historica/.
12 Preston, *The Spanish Holocaust*, p. 473.

13　Justino Sinova, *La censura de Prensa durante el franquismo*, Espasa-Calpe, Madrid, 1989, p. 261; Alfonso Álvarez Bolado, *El experimento del nacional-catolicismo. 1939-1975*, Edicusa, Madrid, 1976.
14　Antonio Machado. *Proverbios y cantares*, Poem LIII.
15　Stephanie Wright, 'Out of the Ordinary: Confronting Paradox in the Historiography of Franco', in *Contemporary European History*, Vol. 30, Issue 1, pp. 136-146.
16　Stanley Payne, 'Spain's "Semi-Fascism"; Excerpted from *A History of Fascism, 1914–1945* by Stanley G. Payne, University of Wisconsin Press', *Slate*, 7 February 2017; Ismael Saz, *Fascismo y Franquismo*, Publicacions de la Universitat de València, Valencia, 2004, pp. 97–100, 192; Javier Tusell, *La dictadura de Franco*, Alianza, Madrid, 1988, p. 247; Enrique Moradiellos, *Franco: Anatomy of a Dictator*, I.B. Tauris, London, 2017, p. 183.
17　Francisco Sevillano Calero, *Ecos de papel: la opinión de los españoles en la época de Franco*, Biblioteca Nueva, Madrid, 2000, p. 44.
18　Paul Preston, *Franco*, HarperCollins, London, 1993, p. 563.
19　Stephanie Wright, 'Out of the Ordinary', pp. 136–146; Emilio Silva Barrera, 'Todos somos franquismo sociológico', in Asunción Esteban, Dunia Etura, Matteo Tomasoni, (eds.), *La alargada sombra del franquismo: naturaleza, mecanismos de pervivencia y huellas de la dictadura*, Editorial Comares, Granada, 2019, pp. 319–29.
20　Jessica Nogueira Castro, '«Salvaguardar dentro de la Ley el interés general». La declaración del estado de excepción durante la dictadura franquista', *História Unicap*, Vol. 9, No. 18, 2002, pp. 48–68.
21　*La Vanguardia*, 21 November 1975, p. 10.

I EL DESASTRE

1　Pilar Franco, *los Franco*, Planeta, Barcelona, 1980, p. 24; Bartolomé Bennassar, *Franco*, EDAF, Madrid, 1996, p. 20–21.
2　José Cervera Pery, *El Almirante Cervera, vida y aventura de un marino español*, Prensa Española, Madrid, 1972, p. 118.
3　Pascual Cervera y Topete, *Guerra Hispano-americana, Colección de documentos*, Diario de la Marina, Madrid, 1904, p. 159; Tomás Pérez Vejo, *3 de Julio 1898, El fin del imperio español*, Editorial Taurus, Barcelona, 2020, p. 20.
4　Sebastian Balfour, *The End of the Spanish Empire (1898–1923)*, Clarendon Press, Oxford, 1997, pp. 10–11, 14, 19.
5　Francisco Franco Salgado, *Mi vida junto a Franco*, Editorial Planeta, Barcelona, 1977, pp. 13–14; Balfour, *End of the Spanish Empire*, pp. 16, 20; Nigel Townson, *The Penguin History of Modern Spain: 1989 to the Present*, Allen Lane, London, 2023, p. 1.
6　Balfour, *End of the Spanish Empire*, pp. 2, 26–7, 31–2, 39; Townson, *Modern Spain*, p. 1; John Lawrence Tone, *War and Genocide in Cuba, 1895–1898*, University of North Carolina Press, Chapel Hill, 2008, p. 281.
7　Vicente Pozuelo, *Los últimos 476 días de Franco*, Editorial Planeta, Barcelona, p. 88; Francisco Franco, 'Los Mandos', *Revista de Tropas coloniales*, January 1924, p. 5.
8　Townson, *Modern Spain*, p. 4.
9　Balfour, *End of the Spanish Empire*, pp. 7–8, 20.

10 Hal Klepak, *Churchill Comes of Age: Cuba, 1885*, The History Press, Chicago, 2015; J. L. Francisco Martínez López, 'Testimonios sobre Franco y su familia', in *FerrolAnálisis: revista de pensamiento y cultura*, No. 14, 1999, p. 28; Francisco Franco Salgado, *Mis conversaciones privadas con Franco*, Editorial Planeta, Barcelona, 1976, p. 17, and introduction to 2005 Planeta edition by Julio Gil Pecharromán.
11 Franco Salgado, *Mi vida*, p. 13.
12 Manuel Baamonde Y Ortega, *La administración de la Marina militar española durante el reinado de la casa de Borbón y reformas que esta institución necesita*, Imprenta El Correo Gallego, El Ferrol, 1899, pp. viii–xii, 29, 66, 138; Francisco Franco, *Palabras del Caudillo, Abril 1937–19 Abril 1938*, Ediciones Fe, Madrid, 1938, p. 11; Pilar Jaraiz Franco, *Historia de una Disidencia*, Planeta, Barcelona, 1981, pp. 26–32.
13 Ramon Llorens Barber, 'Tres cruceros bilbaínos que también fueron ferrolanos', in *FerrolAnálisis: revista de pensamiento y cultura*, vol 13, pp. 58–60. Balfour, *End of the Spanish Empire*, p. v; Alejandro Anca Alamillo, 'El grave accidente del crucero Infanta Isabel ocurrido el día 3 de Agosto de 1900, En La Concha de San Sebastián', in *Revista de historia naval*, No. 150, 2020, pp. 33–48; Alejandro Anca Alamillo, 'Construcción naval y fuerza a flote en los primeros años del siglo XX', *Revista general de marina*, Vol. 263, No. 8–9, 2012, pp. 213–227; Franco, *Palabras del Caudillo*.
14 Mariano José de Larra, 'El día de Difuntos de 1836, Fígaro en el cementerio', in *El Español*, No. 368, 2 November 1836; José María Zavala, *Franco con franqueza: Anecdotario privado del personaje más público*, Plaza & Janes, Barcelona, 2015, p. 26; Franco, *Nosotros*, p. 27.
15 *Gaceta de Madrid*, 27 March 1885, p. 906, and 6 August 1903, p. 1793; *Guia Oficial de España, 1887*, Madrid, 1887, p. 601; *La Marina*, 25 January 1887, p. 1., 23 September 1887, p. 1, 6 December 1887, p. 1, 20 February 1890; *Anuario Militar de España 1922*, Ministerio de la Guerra, Madrid, 1922, p. 349; Pozuelo, *476 días*, p. 86; Carmen Díaz, *Mi vida con Ramón Franco*, Editorial Planeta, Barcelona, 1981, p. 22; Bartolomé Bennassar, *Franco. Enfance et Adolescence*, Editions Autrement, Paris, 1999, p. 32; Francisco Martínez López, 'Testimonios sobre Franco y su familia', in *FerrolAnálisis: revista de pensamiento y cultura*, No. 14, 1999, p. 38.
16 Jaraiz, *Disidencia*, p. 26–32; Stanley G. Payne and Jesús Palacios, *Franco. A Personal and Political Biography*, Wisconsin University Press, Madison, 2014, p. 18; Franco Salgado, *Conversaciones*, p. 174; Gonzalo Herralde (director), *Raza, El Espíritu de Franco*, (documentary film), minutes 6–7; Zavala, *Franco con franqueza*, pp. 14–1.
17 Franco, *Nosotros*, pp. 73–4; Franco Salgado, *Mi vida*, p. 14–15; Bennassar, *Enfance*, p. 38; Herralde (director), *Raza*, minutes 6–7.
18 Jaraiz, *Disidencia*, p. 54.
19 Jaraiz, *Disidencia*, p. 54; Franco Salgado, *Mi vida*, p. 14; Díaz, *Mi vida*; p. 22; Franco, *Nosotros*, pp. 39, 73; Geoffrey Jensen, *Franco: Soldier, Commander, Dictator*, Potomac Books, Lincoln, pp. 4–5; George Hills, *Franco: The Man and His Nation*, Macmillan, New York, 1967, p. 28; Herralde *Raza*, minute 6; Zavala, *Franco con franqueza*, p. 20; Francisco Martínez López, 'Ramón Franco visto por sus paisanos, parientes y compañeros', in *FerrolAnálisis: revista de pensamiento y cultura*, No. 21, 2006, pp. 187–8.
20 Franco, *Nosotros*, p. 70, 72, 74; Jaraiz, *Disidencia*, pp. 26–8, 32; Díaz, *Mi Vida*, p. 22.
21 Franco Salgado, *Mi vida*, p. 14.

22 Julio González Iglesias, *Los dientes de Franco: patobiografía del general Francisco Franco a través de las revelaciones de sus dentistas*, Fenix, Madrid, 1996; Palacios and Payne, *Franco*, pp. 12, 23.
23 Díaz, *Mi vida*, p. 22.
24 Pilar Franco, quoted in Herralde, *Raza, El Espíritu de Franco* (documentary film).
25 Franco Salgado, *Mi vida*, pp. 16–17.
26 Pozuelo, *476 días*, pp. 83–4; Benassar, *Enfance*, p. 39; Franco Salgado, *Mi vida*, p. 15.
27 Díaz, *Mi vida*, p. 20; Palacios and Payne, *Franco* (English ed.), pp. 12, 2020; Carlos Fernández Santander, *El General Franco, un dictador en un tiempo de infamia*, Editorial Crítica, Barcelona, 2005, p. 14.
28 Díaz, *Mi vida*, p. 20; Bennassar, *Enfance*, p. 35; Fernando Martinez Lopez, 'Recuerdos y semblanzas de la familia Franco', in *FerrolAnálisis: revista de pensamiento y cultura*, No. 20, 2005, pp. 20, 26; Zavala, *Franco con franqueza*, pp. 11–12; Pozuelo, *476 días*, p. 87.
29 Hermengildo Franco Castañón, 'Ferrol, Ciudad marítima en el siglo XIX' in *Cuadernos IHCN*, No. 29, 1996, p. 15; Pilar Franco, *Nosotros*, p. 11; Zavala, *Franco con franqueza*, p. 18.
30 José Álvarez Junco, 'Cultura y Libertad', *El País*, 4 February 2012.
31 Pamela Beth Radcliff, *La España contemporánea: desde 1808 hasta nuestros días*, Editorial Ariel, Barcelona, 2018, pp. 51–2, 54–5, 58; Townson, *Modern Spain*, p. 2.
32 Townson, *Modern Spain*, p. 38.
33 Townson, *Modern Spain*, p. 29–30.
34 Palacios and Payne, *Franco*, p. 18.
35 Balfour, *End of the Spanish Empire*, pp. 1–4, 7; Townson, *Modern Spain*, pp. 4–5.
36 Pozuelo, *476 días*, pp. 84–6; Palacios and Payne, *Franco*, pp. 18, 675.
37 Franco, *Nosotros*, pp. 17, 28–9, 33, 70, 74, 232–3.
38 *Guía oficial de España 1907*, Madrid, 1907, p. 489; *La Vanguardia*, 25 August 1908, p. 5, 8 Jan 1921, p. 10; Townson, *Modern Spain*, pp. 23–4; Luis Armando Roche, *'Que boten mis cenizas al aire y se olviden de mi', Luis Buñuel, cineasta de realidad y sueños*, Create Space, 2001, p. 15.
39 Franco Salgado, *Mi vida*, p. 16.
40 Jaraiz, *Disidencia*, pp. 54–5; Franco, *Nosotros*, p. 16; Díaz, *Mi vida*, p. 20.

2 CADET

1 *El Heraldo Militar*, 1 September 1911; Jensen, *Franco*, pp. 5–6; Jaime Antón Viscasillas, 'La Escuela de Ingenieros Navales de Ferrol: Academia de Ingenieros y Maquinistas de la Armada (1914–1932)', in *Revista de Historia Naval*, No. 133, pp. 102–7.
2 Jensen, *Franco*, p. 5.
3 Pozuelo, *476 días*, p. 89.
4 Pozuelo, *476 días*, p. 89.
5 Pozuelo, *476 días*, p. 91; Preston, *Franco* (Spanish), Kindle Loc. 315.
6 Zavala, *Franco con franqueza*, p. 52.

7   Pozuelo, *476 días*, p. 96; Jensen, *Franco*, p. 7; Geoffrey Jensen, *Irrational Triumph: Cultural Despair, Military Nationalism, and the Ideological Origins of Franco's Spain*, University of Nebraska Press, Lincoln, 2001, p. 104; Palacios and Payne, *Franco*, p. 23; Zavala, *Franco con franqueza*, p. 52, 54.
8   Jensen, *Franco*, p. 7; Zavala, *Franco con franqueza*, p. 55; Carlos Blanco Escolá, *Franco. La pasión por el poder*, Editorial Planeta, Barcelona, 2005, p. 89.
9   Jensen, *Franco*, p. 6, from Antonio García Pérez, *Consejos a los caballeros de la Academia de Infantería*, Viuda e Hijos de J. Pelaez, Toledo, 1910, pp. 10–11.
10 Pozuelo, *476 días*, p. 91.
11 Franco Salgado, *Mi vida*, p. 22.
12 Pozuelo, *476 días*, pp. 99–102.
13 'El extraño origen de la voz aguda y nasal de Francisco Franco: el rasgo del que se burló Hitler', *ABC*, 2 February 2021.
14 Pozuelo, *476 días*, p. 100.
15 Jensen, *Franco*, p. 9; Francisco Franco, 'Los Mandos', p. 5.
16 Pozuelo, *476 días*, pp. 100–1; Francisco Franco, 'La Maniobra', *Revista Tropas Coloniales*, February 24, p. 5; Sebastian Balfour, *Deadly Embrace: Morocco and the Road to the Spanish Civil War*, Oxford University Press, Oxford, 2002, p. 25; Jensen, *Franco*, pp. 9, 11.
17 Jensen, *Irrational Triumph*, p. 107; Pérez, *Consejos*, pp. 10–11.
18 Jensen, *Irrational Triumph*, pp. 102, 203; Geoffrey Jensen, *Cultura Militar Española*, Siglo XXI, Madrid, 2014, Kindle Loc. 4953.
19 Jensen, *Irrational Triumph*, pp. 127–80.
20 Franco, *Nosotros*, p. 73, 76.
21 Ginés Sanmartín Salona, 'La Compañía Española de Minas del Rif (1907–1984)', in *Aldaba: revista del Centro Asociado de la UNED de Melilla*, No. 5, 1985, p. 55–74; José Álvarez, *The Betrothed of Death: The Spanish Foreign Legion During the Rif Rebellion, 1920–1927*, PHD Thesis, Florida State University, 1995, p. 5.
22 Pozuelo, *476 días*. p. 102; Balfour, *Deadly Embrace*, pp. 19, 23–4; Jensen, *Franco*, p. 22.
23 Paul Southern, *Francisco Franco's Moroccan War Diary (1920–1922)*, Galago Books, Bromley, 2007, Kindle Loc. 309; Pozuelo, *476 días* p. 102.
24 Franco Salgado, *Mi vida*, p. 20.
25 Zavala, *Franco con franqueza*, pp. 59–62.
26 Ramón Garriga, *Ramón Franco, El hermano maldito*, Editorial Planeta, Barcelona, 1978, p. 25; Preston, *Franco* (Spanish), p. 47; Palacios and Payne, *Franco*, Kindle Loc. 308.
27 Palacios and Payne, *Franco*, p. 24; Jensen, *Franco*, p. 14.

3 WITHOUT AFRICA, I CAN SCARCELY EXPLAIN MYSELF

1   Jaraiz, *Disidencia*, p. 53; Franco Salgado, *Mi vida*, p. 23; Carmen Enríquez, *Carmen Polo, señora del Pardo*, La Esfera de los Libros, Madrid, 2012, pp. 29–30; Franco, *Nosotros*, pp. 39, 73–4; Pilar Franco in Herralde, *Ruzu*.
2   *ABC*, 13 February 1926, p 13; Luis Galinsoga and Francisco Franco Salgado, *Centinela de occidente (Semblanza biográfica de Francisco Franco)*, AHR, Barcelona, 1956, p. 79; Zavala, *Franco con franqueza*, p. 17.
3   Franco Salgado, *Mi vida*, p. 23.

4 Garriga, *Ramón*, p. 26.
5 Esteban Carvallo y González de Cora, *Hoja de servicios del Caudillo de España Excmo. Sr. Don Francisco Franco Bahamonde y su genealogía*, Editora Nacional, Madrid, 1967, p. 2; Southern, *Moroccan War Diary*, Kindle Loc. 253, Antonio Rubio, *El desastre del Annual a través de la prensa*, Libros.com, Madrid, 2022, p. 13; Balfour, *Deadly Embrace*, pp. 7, 11; Álvarez, *Betrothed*, p. 1; Jensen, *Franco*, pp. 15, 27.
6 Balfour, *Deadly Embrace*, p. 41.
7 Towson, *Modern Spain*, pp. 40–1.
8 *Correspondencia Militar*, 'Mirando al exterior', 16 March 1906, p. 1.
9 Vicente Blasco Ibañez, *Alfonso XIII Unmasked: The Military Terror in Spain*, Eveleigh Nash & Grayson Ltd, London, 1925, p. 75; Vicente Blasco Ibáñez, *Por España y contra el rey (Alfonso XIII, desenmascarado)*, Biblioteca de El Pueblo, Paris, 1925, p. 32.
10 Franco Salgado, *Mi vida*, p. 23; *Anuario Militar 1913*, Ministerio de la Guerra, Madrid, p. 398; *Anuario Militar 1914*, Ministerio de la Guerra, Madrid, p. 407; Salvador Fontenla, *Franco, caudillo militar: su historia en los campos de batalla*, La Esfera de los Libros, Madrid, 2019, p. 34.
11 Franco, 'Los Mandos', p. 5. Jensen, *Franco*, p. 27; Carvallo, *Franco, hoja de Servicios*, p. 2.
12 Barea, *The Track*, Fontana, London, 1984, p. 29.
13 Manuel Goded Llopis, *Marruecos. Las Etapas de la Pacificación*, Compañía Ibero-Americana de Publicaciones, Madrid, 1932, p. 95; Jensen, *Franco*, pp. 19–20.
14 Goded, *Marruecos*, p. 57; Jensen, *Franco*, p. 19.
15 Balfour, *Deadly Embrace*, p. 42. Sebastian Balfour, *Abrazo Mortal: De la guerra colonial a la Guerra Civil en España y Marruecos (1909–1939)*, Ediciones Península, Madrid, 2018, Kindle Loc. 659.
16 Southern, *Moroccan War Diary*, p. 503; Carvallo, *Franco, Hoja de servicios*, pp. 2–3; 'Hablando con el General Franco', in *La Zarpa: diario de los agrarios gallegos*, No. 1625, 14 March 1926, p. 1; Balfour, *Deadly Embrace*, p. 160.
17 Palacios and Payne, *Franco*, pp. 30–31.
18 Palacios and Payne, *Franco*, p. 30; Southern, *Moroccan War Diary*, p. 503; Carvallo, *Franco, Hoja de servicios*, p. 3.
19 Jensen, *Franco*, p. 23.
20 Preston, *Franco*, Kindle Loc. 472; Ramon Serrano Suñer, *Política de España*, Editorial Complutense, Madrid, 1995, p. 11.
21 Arturo Barea, *The Track*, Flamingo, London, 1984, pp. 19, 22. Álvarez, *Betrothed*, p. 29; Frank H. Mellor, *Morocco Awakes*, Methuen, London, 1939.
22 'Hablando con el General Franco', pp. 1, 5.
23 'Hablando con el General Franco', p. 1.
24 Franco, 'Los Mandos', p. 6; Francisco Franco, 'Pasividad e Inacción', in *Revista de Tropas Coloniales*, April 1924, p. 4; Balfour, *Deadly Embrace*, p. 47.
25 Southern, *Moroccan War Diary*, Kindle Loc. 488; Balfour, *Deadly Embrace*, p. 42.
26 Southern, *Moroccan War Diary*, Kindle Loc. 488.
27 Emilio Mola, 'Preparación de oficiales para prestar servicio en el ejército de Africa', in *Revista de Tropas Coloniales*, Jan 1924, p. 10; Pablo de la Fuente de Pablo, 'Sobre las circunstancias del ascenso a capitán por méritos de guerra de

Francisco Franco', in *Aportes: Revista de historia contemporánea*, No. 107, 2021, pp. 125–151; Benito Tauler Cid, 'La legión, historia de una organización para el combate', in *Revista de Historia Militar*, No. Extra 1 2020, pp. 26–46.

28 Carvallo, *Franco, Hoja de servicios*, p. 2; Francisco Franco, 'Las Unidades coloniales', in *Revista de Tropas Coloniales*, May 1924, pp. 58–9.

29 Carvallo, *Franco, Hoja de servicios*, p. 3. Franco, 'Las Unidades coloniales', pp. 58–9. *Anuario Militar 1913*, p. 196.

30 de la Fuente de Pablo, 'Sobre las circunstancias', pp. 135–43; Carvallo, *Franco, Hoja de servicios*, p. 2; Jensen; *Franco*, p. 29.

31 Jesús Palacios, *Las cartas de Franco: la correspondencia desconocida que marco el destino de España*, La Esfera de los Libros, Madrid, 2005, p. 41; Manuel Villatoro, 'Las cartas de amor secretas de Franco a una adolescente que le dio calabazas: 'Era un pelma'', *ABC*, 15 Feb 2021, updated online 28 Jan 2022; Zavala, *Franco con franqueza*, pp. 66–7.

32 Palacios, *Cartas*, p. 41; Manuel Villatoro, 'Las cartas de amor secretas de Franco'; Zavala, *Franco con franqueza*, p. 66–7.

33 Carvallo, *Franco, Hoja de servicios*, p. 2.

34 Carvallo, *Franco, Hoja de servicios*, p. 2; *Anuario Militar 1916*, Ministerio de Guerra, Madrid, 1916, pp. 376, 408–412; Jensen, *Franco*, p. 29; Daniel Macías Fernández and Sergio García Pujades, 'El africanismo castrense: un estado de la cuestión', in *Studia Historica. Historia Contemporánea*, No. 39, pp. 49–72; Palacios and Payne, *Franco*, Kindle Loc. 418.

35 Barea, *The Track*, p. 176.

36 Carvallo, *Franco, Hoja de servicios*, p. 4. Joaquin Arrarás, *Franco*, San Sebastian, Libreria Internacional, 1938, p. 38.

37 Carvallo, *Franco, Hoja de servicios*, Annex 2, pp. 35–6; Charles Esdaile, *The Spanish Civil War: A Military History*, London, Routledge, 2018, p. 359.

38 Zavala, *Franco con franqueza*, pp. 76–7. José Luis Sáenz de Heredia (director), *Franco ese hombre*, 1964 (documentary film).

39 Luis Franco de Espes, 'La Mujer en el hogar de los hombres célebres. El amor y la guerra. La esposa del general Franco', *Estampa*, 29 May 1928, pp. 19–21.

40 Carvallo, *Franco, Hoja de Servicios*, Annex 2, pp. 35–6.

41 Franco Salgado, *Mi vida*, p. 30; 'Los que viajan', *El Correo gallego*, 13 July, 1916, p. 1; 'Los que viajan', *El Correo gallego*, 10 August, 1916, p. 1; Garriga, *Ramón*, p. 27.

42 Carvallo, *Franco, Hoja de servicios*, p. 7; Esdaile, *Civil War*, p. 359.

43 Preston, *Franco*, p. 38; Pedro Sáinz Rodríguez, *Testimonio y Recuerdos*, Planeta, Barcelona, 1978. pp. 334–5.

44 Carvallo, *Franco, Hoja de servicios*, Annex 2, p. 36; Galinsoga and Franco Salgado, *Centinela de Occidente*, p. 30; Sáenz de Heredia, *Franco ese hombre*.

45 Barea, *The Track*, p. 12.

46 Carvallo, *Franco, Hoja de servicios*, Annex 2, pp. 35–7; 'Ley de 18 de mayo de 1862. Reformando los estatutos de la Real y militar Orden de San Fernando', *Gaceta de Madrid*, No. 142, 1862.

47 Carvallo, *Franco, Hoja de servicios*, p. 7; *Anuario Militar, 1918*, Ministerio de Guerra, Madrid, 1918, pp. 362–71; Palacios and Payne, *Franco*, p. 31.

48 Franco, *Palabras del Caudillo*, p. 31.

4 THE GIRL BEHIND THE LATTICE SCREEN

1 Alberto Bru Sánchez–Fortún, 'Los ascensos de guerra (1909–1922): su repercusión en el nacimiento de las Juntas de Defensa', in *Revista de Historia Militar*, No. 119, 2016, pp. 41, 45, 47–9; Balfour, *Deadly Embrace*, p. 57.
2 'En honor de un comandante', *El Día*, Madrid, 27 May 1917, p. 4.
3 Alas, *La Regenta* (English Edition), Penguin, London, 2005, Kindle Locs 106, 348–9, 400–405.
4 Alas, *La Regenta*, p. 29.
5 Franco Salgado, *Mi vida*, pp. 35–37.
6 Franco Salgado, *Mi vida*, pp. 35–37; Real Automóvil Club de Asturias, *Guía del año 1919*, Compañía Asturiana de Artes Gráficas, Gijón, 1919, p. 30.
7 Franco Salgado, *Mi vida*, pp. 35–37.
8 Preston, *Franco*, Kindle Loc. 610; Álvarez, *Betrothed*, p. 13; Real Automóvil Club de Asturias, *Guía del año 1919*, p. 1; Franco Salgado, *Mi vida*, pp. 35–37.
9 Preston, *Franco*, Kindle Loc. 605–31; Sánchez-Fortún, 'Los ascensos de guerra', pp. 17–19; Preston, *Franco*, Loc. 605–31.
10 Preston, *Franco*, p. 64.
11 Alas, *La Regenta*, Kindle Loc. 9499; Ramon García Piñera, 'Asturias 1917. Nace la leyenda', in *Atlántica XXII*, 27 September 2017; Preston, *Franco* (Spanish), p. 65. See also Carlos Arenas Posadas, *Por el bien de la patria: Guerras y ejércitos en la constitución de España*, Ediciones Pasado y Presente, Barcelona, 2019 and Daniel Macías Fernández and Sergio García Pujades, 'El africanismo castrense: un estado de la cuestión', in *Studia Historica. Historia Contemporánea*, No. 39, 2021, pp. 49–72; 'La Huelga de Agosto en Asturias', *España*, No. 134, 1 November 1917, p. 7.
12 Adeflor, 'La huelga última en Asturias', in *Asturias Revista Semanal (La Habana)*, 7 October 1917, p. 6.
13 Preston, *Franco*, Kindle Loc. 630. Francisco Franco, 'Antología de textos de Franco', *Revista de historia militar*, No. 40, 1976, p. 345; 'Discurso ante los mineros en Oviedo, 19 May 1946', in Gicara, 'Crónicas Ovetenses', *Asturias Revista Semanal (La Habana)*, 28 October 1917, p. 1. Townson, *Modern Spain*, p. 9.
14 Preston, *Franco*, Kindle Loc. 655; *The Man*, p. 105; 'Mio Marito, Parla La Signora Franco', *La Stampa*, 26 February 1937, p. 3.
15 'Discurso en Oviedo a los mineros Asturianos, 19 de mayo de 1946' in Franco, 'Antología de textos de Franco', p. 345; Townson, *Modern Spain*, p. 77.
16 Franco Salgado, *Mi vida*, pp. 31–2; Sánchez-Fortún, 'Los ascensos de guerra', pp. 23, 41; Preston, *Franco*, Kindle Loc. 610.
17 Mary Nash, *Mujer, Familia y Trabajo en España, 1875–1936*, Anthropos, Barcelona, 1983, p. 79.
18 Luis Franco de Espes, 'La Mujer en el hogar de los hombres célebres. El amor y la guerra. La esposa del general Franco', *Estampa*, 29 May 1928, pp. 19–21; Enríquez, *Carmen Polo*, p. 23–5.
19 Sáinz Rodríguez, *Testimonios y recuerdos*, pp. 323–4; de Espes, 'La Mujer', pp. 19–21; Paul Preston, *Palomas de guerra. Cinco mujeres marcadas por el enfrentamiento bélico*, Plaza y Janés, Barcelona, 2001, pp. 26–7; Francisco Martínez López, 'Testimonios sobre Franco y su familia', in *FerrolAnálisis: revista de pensamiento y cultura*, No. 14, 1999, p. 72.

20 Preston, *Palomas de guerra*, p. 469: de Espes, 'La Mujer', pp. 19–21.
21 Franco, *Nosotros*, p. 73; Sainz Rodríguez, *Testimonio y Recuerdos*, p. 323; Palacios and Payne, *Franco* (Spanish), Kindle Loc. 773.
22 Jaraiz, *Disidencia*, pp. 37–41; Preston, *Palomas de guerra*, pp. 471–2; Enríquez, *Carmen Polo*, p. 30.
23 Alas, *La Regenta* (English), Kindle Locs 310–311.

5 LOS NOVIOS DE LA MUERTE

1 Preston, *Franco* (English), pp. 46–7.
2 Millán Astray, 'Prologue', in Francisco Franco, *Marruecos: Diario De Una Bandera*, Editorial Pueyo, Madrid, 1922.
3 Franco Salgado, *Mi vida*, p. 43.
4 Hills, *The Man*, p. 144.
5 Allison Beeby and María Teresa Rodríguez 'Millán-Astray's Translation of Nitobe's Bushido: The Soul of Japan', in *Meta: Journal des traducteurs*, Vol. 54, No. 2, 2009, p. 224; Álvarez, *Betrothed*, p. 26.
6 Álvarez, *Betrothed*, p. 2; Southern, *Moroccan War Diary*, Kindle Loc. 2037.
7 Álvarez, *Betrothed*, p. 32.
8 Álvarez, *Betrothed*, p. 36.
9 Álvarez, *Betrothed*, p. 31.
10 Southern, *Moroccan War Diary*, Kindle Loc. 2012; Franco, *Bandera*, p. 17.
11 Álvarez, *Betrothed*, p. 34.
12 Southern, *Moroccan War Diary*, Kindle Loc. 2027; Franco, *Bandera*, pp. 17–18.
13 Álvarez, *Betrothed*, p. 32; Carlos de Arce Robledo, *Historia de la Legión Española*, Editorial Mitre, Barcelona, 1984, p. 24.
14 Barea, *The Track*, pp. 172–3.
15 Southern, *Moroccan War Diary*, Kindle Loc. 2053; Arturo Barea, *The Forging of a Rebel*, Pushkin Press, London, 2018, p. 452; *Revista de Tropas Coloniales*, February 1922, p. 12.
16 Barea, *The Forging of a Rebel*, p. 525.
17 Barea, *The Forging of a Rebel*, p. 525.
18 Barea, *The Forging of a Rebel*, p. 514; Álvarez, *Betrothed*, p. 44 fn.
19 Franco Salgado, *Mis conversaciones*, pp. 184–5.
20 Álvarez, *Betrothed*, pp. 48, 51–2; Esdaile, *Civil War*, p. 359.
21 Álvarez, *Betrothed*, pp. 50, 56–7.
22 Balfour, *Deadly Embrace*, pp. 60–1; Luis Togores, *Historia de la Legión Española: La Infantería legendaria. De África a Afganistán*, La Esfera de los Libros, Madrid, 2016, Kindle Loc. 1517; Álvarez, *Betrothed*, p. 33.
23 Gárate Córdoba, José María, 'Franco, escritor', in *Revista de historia militar*, No. 40, 1976, p. 11; Franco, *Bandera*, p. 37.
24 Franco, *Bandera* p. 37; Southern, *Moroccan War Diary*, Kindle Loc. 2663.
25 Southern, *Moroccan War Diary*, Kindle Loc. 2683.
26 Gárate Córdoba, 'Franco, escritor'; Emilio Mola, 'Preparación de oficiales', pp. 10–11.
27 Francisco Franco, 'Ruud... Balek!', *África*, February 1933. p. 5.

6 A NEW DISASTER

1. Luis Togores, '101 kilómetros: la marcha forzada de la Legión', *La Razón*, 5 October 2021.
2. *Expediente Picasso: Edición de su resumen publicado en 1931*, Agencia Estatal Boletín del Estado, Madrid, p. 500; Balfour, *Deadly Embrace*, p. 74; Álvarez, *Betrothed*, pp. 65–67; Southern, *Moroccan War Diary*, Kindle Loc. 2950.
3. Balfour, *Deadly Embrace*, p. 64; Álvarez, *Betrothed*, pp. 65–67, 86; Franco, 'Antología de textos de Franco', p. 290.
4. Álvarez, *Betrothed*, pp. 71–91; Balfour, *Deadly Embrace*, p. 83.
5. *Expediente Picasso*, Appendix, pp. 333; Álvarez, *Betrothed*, pp. 71–91; Balfour, *Deadly Embrace*, p. 81.
6. Álvarez, *Betrothed*, pp. 91–4; General Berenguer, *Campañas en el Rif y Yebala, 1921–2*, Editorial Voluntad, Madrid, 1923, p. 91; Togores, *Legión*, Kindle Loc. 1684.
7. Franco, *Bandera*, p. 47.
8. Berenguer, *Campañas en el Rif y Yebala*, pp. 91–2.
9. Barea, *The Forging of a Rebel*, p. 440.
10. Franco, *Diario*, p. 47.
11. Rubio, *Prensa*, pp. 30, 32, 39–41; Balfour, *Deadly Embrace*, pp. 69–70.
12. Balfour *Deadly Embrace*, p. 186.
13. Franco, *Bandera*, p. 67.
14. *Expediente Picasso*, Appendix, pp. 333, 381; Rubio, *Prensa*, p. 28.
15. Franco, *Bandera*, pp. 76–7.
16. Barea, *The Forging of a Rebel*, p. 523.
17. Togores, *Legión*, Kindle Locs 1517, 1824, 4370; Southern, *Moroccan War Diary*, Kindle Loc. 3147; Balfour, *Deadly Embrace*, pp. 82–4, 88, 87, 105; Joanna Bourke, *An Intimate History of Killing: Face-to-Face Killing in Twentieth-Century Warfare*, https://granta.com/products/an-intimate-history-of-killing/ Granta, London, 2000, pp. 160–5.
18. Franco, *Bandera*, p. 52.
19. Southern, *Moroccan War Diary*, Kindle Loc 3433; Franco, *Bandera*, p. 61.
20. Franco, *Bandera*, p. 62; Southern, *Moroccan War Diary*, Kindle Loc 3492.
21. Preston, *Franco* (Spanish), p. 76.
22. Balfour, *Deadly Embrace*, p. 88; Antonio Maura, 'Transcendental discurso pronunciado por D. Antonio Maura en el Congreso de los Diputados el día 10 de noviembre de 1921, exponiendo con clarísima precisión el pensamiento del Gobierno en el importantísimo problema de Marruecos', in *Francisco Silvela and Antonio Maura'*, Juan Pérez, Madrid, 1903.
23. Barea, *The Forging of a Rebel*, p. 443.

7 FAME

1. 'El "As" de la Legión', *ABC*, 22 February 1922.
2. El "As" de la Legión', *ABC*, 22 February 1922.
3. *El "As" de la Legión'*, *ABC*, 22 February 1922.
4. Balfour, *Deadly Embrace*, p. 111.

5 *El Globo*, Madrid, 23 February 1922, p. 2.
6 *El Carbayón, diario asturiano de la mañana*, 23 February 1922, p. 2.
7 *La Tribuna*, 7 March 1922, p. 5.
8 *El Globo*, Madrid, 23 February 1922, p. 2; Julio Gil Pecharromán, 'Prólogo', in Franco Salgado, *Mis conversaciones*; Fontenla, *Franco*, pp. 71, 77; Franco Salgado, *Mi vida*, pp. 61.
9 Carvallo, *Franco. Hoja de servicios*, pp. 12–13.
10 Juan José Amate Blanco, *La Legión en la campañas de Marruecos (1920–1927)*, Ministerio de Defensa, Madrid, 2022, p. 391; Ramón Diez Roja, *El desembarco de Alhucemas. La intrahistoria de una operación concluyente (1911–1925)*, Ministerio de Defensa, Madrid, 2022 (ebook), Section 6,3; Balfour, *Deadly Embrace*, pp. 65, 91.
11 Balfour, *Deadly Embrace*, p. 92.
12 Southern, *Moroccan War Diary*, Kindle Loc. 2663; Franco, *Bandera*, p. 37.
13 Daniel Macías Fernández and Sergio García Pujades, 'El africanismo castrense: un estado de la cuestión', in *Studia Historica. Historia Contemporánea*, No. 39, 2021, p. 66; Álvarez, *Betrothed*, pp. 167–8; 'Las Juntas Militares', *La Prensa*, 9 November, 1922, p. 2; Fontenla. *Franco*, p. 84.
14 Carvallo, *Franco, Hoja de servicios*, p. 14.
15 *Nuevo Mundo*, Madrid, 26 January 1923, pp. 13–4; Preston, *Franco* (Spanish), pp. 83–4.
16 *Nuevo Mundo*, Madrid, 26 January 1923, pp. 13–4; Preston, *Franco* (Spanish), pp. 83–4.
17 *Nuevo Mundo*, Madrid, 26 January 1923, pp. 13–4; Preston, *Franco* (Spanish), pp. 83–4.
18 de Espes, 'La Mujer' pp. 19–21; Fontenla, *Franco,* pp. 93–4; Carvallo, *Franco, Hoja de servicios*, pp. 14–5.
19 Preston, *Franco* (Spanish), p. 86.
20 Fontenla, *Franco,* pp. 94, 100.
21 *El Sol*, 14 July 1923, p. 8.
22 Fontenla, *Franco*, p. 95.
23 *La Vanguardia*, 1 October 1939, p. 2.

8 MY MUSSOLINI

1 Daniel Macías Fernández and Sergio García Pujades, 'El africanismo castrense' p. 71; Townson, *Modern Spain*, p. 90; Hills, *The Man*, p. 159; Balfour, *Deadly Embrace*, p. 93.
2 Townson, *Modern Spain*, p. 87.
3 Francisco Alía Miranda, *La dictadura de Primo de Rivera (1923–1930). Paradojas y contradicciones del nuevo régimen*, Los Libros de la Catarata, Madrid, 2023, p. 49.
4 Balfour, *Deadly Embrace*, pp. 94, 231; see also Rocío Velasco de Castro, 'De periodistas improvisados a golpistas consumados: el ideario militar africanista de la *Revista de tropas coloniales* (1924–1936)', in *El Argonauto Español*, No. 10, 2003.
5 De Castro, 'De periodistas improvisados'; Balfour, *Deadly Embrace*, pp. 93–4, 167–8, 170; *La Acción*, 24 October 1921, p. 1; General Miguel Cabanellas, letter

in 'La actuación contra las Juntas de Defensa', *La Correspondencia Militar*, 24 October 1921, p. 1; Fontenla, *Franco*, p. 83.
6   *El Comercio*, 23 October 1923, p. 1; Hills, *The Man*, pp. 134–5; Preston, *Franco* p. 67; Jaraiz, *Disidencia*, pp. 42–3; de Espes, 'La Mujer'.
7   Enríquez, *Carmen Polo*, p. 34. Luis Franco 'La Mujer', pp. 19–21. Preston, *Franco* (Spanish), p. 90.
8   Ricardo de la Cierva, *Francisco Franco: un siglo de España*, Editora Nacional, Madrid, 1973, p. 78.
9   *Anuario Militar 1924*, Ministerio de Guerra, Madrid, 1924, p. 180.
10 Emilio Mola, *El pasado, Azaña y el porvenir: las tragedias de nuestras instituciones militares*, La Crítica Literaria, Madrid, 2011, Kindle Locs. 245–68, 4255.
11 Balfour, *Deadly Embrace*, p. 188.
12 Javier Tusell and Genoveva Queipo de Llano, *Alfonso XII: el rey polémico*, Taurus, Madrid, 2001, p. 493; Eugenio de Santos Rodrigo, 'Franco en la Revista de Tropas Coloniales', in *Revista de historia militar*, No. 40, 1976, p. 23; Francisco Franco, 'Antología de textos de Franco', p. 182; *Anuario Militar 1923*, Ministerio de Guerra, Madrid, 1923, p. 433; Paul Preston, *Architects of Terror: Paranoia, Conspiracy and Anti-Semitism in Franco's Spain*, HarperCollins, London, 2023, p. 247.
13 Gonzalo Queipo de Llano, 'Nuestro proposito', in *Revista de tropas coloniales*, January 1924, p. 1.
14 Ramírez de Maeztu, 'Con el ejercito', in *Revista de tropas coloniales*, January 1924, pp. 4–5.
15 Franco, 'Los Mandos', p. 5.
16 *Revista de Tropas Coloniales*, February 1924, p. 7.
17 Díaz, *Mi vida*, p. 21; Ramon Franco, 'El Raid Larache-Canarias', in *Revista de Tropas Coloniales*, February 1924, pp. 29–33.
18 Franco, 'Pasividad e inacción', p. 4.
19 Franco, 'Pasividad e inacción', p. 4.
20 Franco, Francisco, 'Franco, escritor', *Revista de historia militar*, No. 40, 1976, pp. 182–3.
21 Víctor Ruiz Albéniz, 'Su Majestad el Rey y la "Revista de Tropas Coloniales"', in *Revista de tropas coloniales,* May 1924, pp. 6–7.
22 Balfour, *Deadly Embrace*, p. 98.
23 Luis Bolín, *Spain, The Vital Years*, Lippincott, Philadelphia, 1967, p. 77; Federico Martinez Roda, *Varela: el general antifascista de Franco*, La Esfera de los Libros, Madrid, 2012, pp. 62–64.
24 Philippe Noury, *Francisco Franco, la conquista del poder*, Cronicas, Gigon, 1976, p. 122.
25 Roda, *Varela*, pp. 63–64; José Calvo Sotelo, *Mis servicios al estado: Seis años de gestión*, Instituto de Administración Local, Madrid, 1974, pp. 164, 239; Balfour, *Deadly Embrace*, p. 101; '*Incidente de Ben Tieb*', Archivo Varela, Vol. 3.
26 De La Cierva, *Franco*, Vol 1., p. 225.
27 Roda, *Varela*, pp. 63–64.
28 'Luis Pareja Aycuens', *Diccionario Biográfico Español*, at https://dbe.rah.es/biografias/92857/luis-pareja-aycuens.

9 RETREAT AND REVENGE

1. Jensen, *Franco* pp. 47–9; Fontenla, *Franco*, p. 123.
2. Franco, 'Antología de textos de Franco', p. 177.
3. Álvarez, *Betrothed*, p. 277; Balfour, *Deadly Embrace*, pp. 90, 104; Jensen, *Franco*, pp. 47–9.
4. Carvallo, *Franco, Hoja de servicios*, pp. 16–22.
5. Antonio Goicoechea, 'El Coronel Franco', in *Revista de tropas coloniales*, March 1925, pp. 1–3.
6. Preston, *Franco* (Spanish), p. 98; de Espes, 'La Mujer' pp. 19–21.
7. Fontenla, *Franco*, p. 131.
8. Hills, *The Man*, pp. 134 5.
9. Tusell y Queipo de Llano, *Alfonso XIII*, p. 462; Hills, *The Man*, pp. 134–6.
10. Balfour, *Deadly Embrace*, p. 108. See also Diez, *El desembarco de Alhucemas*.
11. José E. Álvarez, 'Between Gallipoli and D-Day: Alhucemas, 1925', in *The Journal of Military History*, Vol. 63, No. 1, 1999, p. 90; Jensen, *Franco*, p. 53 Balfour, *Deadly Embrace*, pp. 110–2.
12. Diez Roja, *El desembarco de Alhucemas*, Fontenla, *Franco*, pp. 133–135; Franco, 'Antología de textos de Franco', pp. 230–2; Balfour, *Deadly Embrace*, p. 111; Pozuelo, *476 días*, p. 41.
13. Amate Blanco, *La Legión en Marruecos*, p. 333; Balfour, *Deadly Embrace*, p. 113.
14. Franco, 'Antología de textos de Franco', pp. 231, 232–6, 239–43.
15. Balfour, *Deadly Embrace*, pp. 112, 133.
16. *Revista de Tropas Coloniales*, January 1924; Fontenla, *Franco*, pp. 139, 145; Balfour, *Deadly Embrace*, p. 115.
17. Carvallo, *Franco, Hoja de servicios*, p. 25; Preston, *Franco* (Spanish) p. 100.
18. Radcliff, *España Contemporánea*, p. 281.
19. Balfour, *Deadly Embrace*, p. 117.

10 HERO BROTHERS

1. Preston, *Franco* (Spanish) p. 102; Carvallo, *Franco, Hoja de servicios*, p. 21; *New York Times*, 7 February 1926, p. 8.
2. *La Vanguardia*, 4 February 1926, p. 20; *New York Times*, 3 February 1926, p. 24, 7 February 1926, p. 8, 31 January 1926, pp. 1, 24.
3. de Espes, 'La Mujer'; *Anuario Militar 1927*, Ministerio de Guerra, Madrid, 1927, pp. 209–14.
4. Enriquez, *Carmen Polo*, p. 38; De la Cierva, *Franco*, p. 97; Díaz, *Mi vida*, pp. 58–9; Preston, *Franco* (Spanish), pp. 100, 516.
5. Preston, *Franco* (Spanish), p. 102.
6. Preston, *Franco* (Spanish), p. 102.
7. Preston, *Franco* (Spanish), p. 102; Townson, *Modern Spain*, p. 96.
8. De la Cierva, *Franco*, p. 97; Julio Gil Pecharromán, 'Prólogo', in Franco Salgado, *Mis conversaciones*.
9. Ramón Soriano, *La mano izquierda de Franco*, Editorial Planeta, Madrid, 1981, p. 61.
10. de Espes, 'La Mujer'; Julio Merino, *El Otro Franco: el Franco intelectual y el Franco de la república*, Espejo de Tinta, Madrid, 2005, p. 46.

11 Enríquez, *Carmen*, p. 39.
12 Stanley G. Payne and Jesús Palacios, *Franco, mi padre*, La Esfera de los Libros, Madrid, 2008, Kindle Loc. 2219, 11614.
13 Enríquez, *Carmen Polo*, pp. 40–41.
14 Carvallo, *Franco, Hoja de servicios*, p. 26; Preston, *Franco*, p. 87; Serrano Suñer, *Política de España*, p. 16.
15 Preston, *Franco* (Spanish), p. 109.
16 de Espes, 'La Mujer', pp. 19–21; Fusi, *Franco*, p. 35.
17 Fusi, *Franco*, p. 35; Hills, *The Man*, p. 128.
18 Luis Franco de Espes, 'La Mujer', pp. 19–21.
19 'Discurso de apertura de la academia general militar', 5 October 1928, in Franco, 'Antología de textos de Franco', pp. 333–4.
20 Jensen, *Franco*, p. 54; Fusi, *Franco*, p. 42; de Espes, 'La Mujer', pp. 19–21.
21 George Hills, *Franco, El hombre y su nación*, Madrid, San Martin, 1970, p. 153; Dora Lennard, 'Franco: A Close-Up Study of the Mind and the Nature of the Leader of Nationalist Spain by his English Teacher', *Spain: Semi-monthly Publication of Civil War Events*, Vol 1, No. 3, 15 November 15, 1937, p. 22.
22 Franco Salgado, *Mi vida*, p. 81; Preston, *Franco*, pp. 90–1.
23 Serrano Suñer, *Política de España*, p. 12; Franco Salgado, *Mi vida*, p. 147; Preston, *Franco*, p. 93.
24 Jensen, *Irrational Triumph*, p. 121; Jensen, *Franco*, p. 55; Garriga, *Ramón*, p. 178.
25 Hills, *El hombre*, p. 14.
26 Serrano Suñer, *Política de España*, pp. 10–11.
27 Serrano Suñer, *Política de España*, p. 13.
28 Soriano, *La mano*, pp. 154–5.
29 Serrano Suñer, *Política de España*, p. 14.
30 Serrano Suñer, *Política de España*, p. 14.
31 Palacios and Payne, *Franco*, p. 81–2; Palacios and Payne, *Franco, mi padre*, Kindle Loc. 2256.
32 FNFF, 26995, in 'Intercambio de correspondencia del Generalísimo con el Acuerdo International de Ginebra'; Palacios and Payne, *Franco, mi padre*, Kindle Loc. 2256; Stéphanie Roulin, *Un credo anticommuniste. La commission Pro Deo de l'Entente Internationale Anticommuniste ou la dimension religieuse d'un combat politique (1924–1945)*, Antipodes, Lausanne, 2010, pp. 261–4.
33 Hills, *El hombre*, p. 153; Hills, *The Man*, p. 157.
34 Sainz Rodríguez, *Testimonio*, p. 333; Radcliff, *España contemporánea*, p. 297.

11 OUT WITH THE OLD – THE END OF MONARCHY

1 Palacios and Payne, *Franco*, p. 77.
2 Carmen Díaz, *Mi vida*, pp. 20–1, 24–5, 72; *New York Times*, 23 February 1926, p. 20, 25 February 1926, p. 6.
3 *La Correspondencia Militar*, 2 July 1929, pp. 1–2.
4 *La Correspondencia Militar*, 2 July 1929, p. 1; Díaz, *Mi vida*, p. 90.
5 Díaz, *Mi vida*, p. 232.
6 Garriga, *Ramón*, pp. 173–4, 178; Zavala, *Franco con franqueza*, pp. 295–29;. Preston, *Franco* (Spanish), p. 98.

7   Zavala, *Franco con franqueza*, pp. 297–301.
8   Zavala, *Franco con franqueza*, pp. 297–301.
9   Garriga, *Ramón*, pp. 175–9; José María Pemán, *Mis encuentros con Franco*, Dopesa, Barcelona, 1976, p. 20.
10 *La Correspondencia Militar*, 10 June 1930. p. 1; Eugenio Vegas Latapie, *La frustración de la Victoria. Memorias políticas, 1938–1942*, Editorial Actas, Barcelona, 1995, p. 100; Franco Salgado, *Mi vida*, p. 89.
11 *La Correspondencia Militar*, 12 Oct 1930, p. 4; Preston, *Franco*, p. 99; Emilio Mola, *Obras completas*, Librería Santaren, Valladolid, 1940, pp. 389–95, 408–12, 454–5.
12 *La Correspondencia Militar*, 25 November 1930, p. 4; Díaz, *Mi vida*, pp. 114–5.
13 Alejandro Lerroux, *La pequeña historia de España (1930–1936)*, Ediciones Criticón, Madrid, 2016, p. 560.
14 Serrano Suñer, *Política de España*, p. 16; Preston, *Franco*, pp. 98–101.
15 Díaz, *Mi vida*, pp. 116, 130; Franco Salgado, *Mi vida*, p. 92; Palacios and Payne, *Franco*, p. 87; Preston, *Franco*, p. 102; Hills, *The Man*, p. 163.
16 Franco Salgado, *Mi vida*, p. 92.
17 Díaz, *Mi vida*, p. 123; Hills, *The Man*, p. 123.
18 Palacios y Payne, *Franco, mi padre*, Kindle Loc. 2298; Franco Salgado, *Mis conversaciones*, p. 440; Serrano Suñer, *Política de España*, p. 16.
19 Garriga, *Ramón*, p. 210.
20 Roda, *Varela*, p. 95.
21 José Ortega y Gasset, 'El error Berenguer', *El Sol*, 15 November 1930, p. 1.
22 Merino, *El Otro Franco*, p. 56; Franco Salgado, *Mi vida*, p. 100; Palacios, *Cartas*, p. 44.
23 Carmelo Romero Salvador, *Las elecciones que acabaron con la monarquía*, Los Libros de Catarata, Madrid, 2023, p. 124–5; Radcliff, *España contemporánea*, p. 294; Preston, *Franco* (Spanish), p. 103.
24 AHN, Tribunal Supremo Reservado, Exp. 46, No. 14, folios 2251–2258; Preston, *Franco* (Spanish), p. 127; Franco Salgado, *Mi vida*, p. 93.
25 Franco Salgado, *Mi vida*, pp. 93, 97.
26 Henry Buckley, *The Life and Death of the Spanish Republic*, I. B. Tauris, London, 2013, pp. 34–6; Romero, *Las elecciones*, p. 124–6; Palacios and Payne, *Franco*, p. 90; Townson, *Modern Spain*, p. 113; Radcliff, *España contemporánea*, p. 294.
27 Franco Salgado, *Mi vida*, p. 96.

12 ¡VIVA LA REPUBLICA!

1   Stanley G. Payne, 'Franco y los orígenes de la Guerra Civil Española' in *La Albolafia: Revista de Humanidades y Cultura*, No. 1, 2014, p. 12.
2   Andrés Padilla, 'Un dietario político de Josep Pla', *El País*, 2 November 2003.
3   Palacios and Payne, *Franco, mi padre*, Kindle Locs 2322–2324.
4   Preston, *Franco* (Spanish), p. 120, (English) p. 106; Franco Salgado, *Mi vida*, pp. 97–98; *La Correspondencia Militar*, 15 April 1931, pp. 2 3.
5   Clara Campoamor Rodríguez, *El voto femenino y yo: mi pecado mortal*, Espuela de Plata, Sevilla, 2018, pp. 21–22; *La Correspondencia Militar*, 15 April 1931.
6   *La Correspondencia Militar*, 20 April 1930, p. 3.
7   Franco Salgado, *Mi vida*, p. 100.

8 Franco Salgado, *Mi vida*, p. 102; Jensen, *Franco*, p. 60; Palacios and Payne, *Franco*, p. 90.
9 Norbert Bilbeny (ed). *La Segunda República Español: Textos Fundamentales*, Ediciones de la Universidad de Barcelona, Barcelona, 2021, pp. 205–7; *Gaceta de Madrid*, No. 113, 23 April 1931, p. 280; Fernando Puell de la Villa, 'Los militares ante la Segunda República', *Studia Humanitatis Journal*, 2022, Vol. 2, No. 1, pp. 153–74; Preston, *Franco*, p. 114; Franco Salgado, *Mis conversaciones*, p. 452.
10 Preston, *Gran Manipulador*, p. 359.
11 Joaquín Gil Honduvilla, 'Los Sucesos De Tablada De Junio De 1931 Y Sus Consecuencias', in *Revista de historia militar*, No. 110, pp. 11–50; Palacios and Payne, *Franco*, p. 101.
12 Franco, *Apuntes*, p. 7; Palacios and Payne, *Franco*, p. 86; Preston, *Franco* (Spanish), p. 110.
13 Francisco Sánchez Pérez (ed.), *Mitos del 18 de Julio*, Editorial Crítica, Barcelona, 2013, pp. 27–28; Charles Foltz, *The Masquerade in Spain*, Houghton Miffin, Boston, 1948, p. 21.
14 FFNF, Rollo 32, documents 02095–2120; Francisco Franco, '*Apuntes*', pp. 8–9. Francisco Franco (Jakim Boor), *Masonería*, CreateSpace, 2015, pp. 5–6, 51.
15 FFNF, Rollo 32, documents 02095–2120.
16 See Mola: *El Pasado, Azaña y El Porvenir*.
17 Franco, *Apuntes*, p. 7; Preston, *Franco* (Spanish), p. 109.
18 Franco, *Apuntes*, p. 8; Manuel Álvarez Tardío, *Anticlericalismo y libertad de conciencia: política y religión en la Segunda República Española, 1931–1936*, Centro de Estudios Constitucionales, Madrid, 2002, pp. 102–5.
19 Julián Casanova, *España partida en dos: breve historia de la Guerra civil*, Editorial Crítica, Barcelona, 2013, Kindle Loc. 139; Sánchez Pérez, *Mitos*, pp. 30–31; Fernando Puell de la Villa, 'Los militares ante la Segunda República', in *Studia Humanitatis Journal*, 2022, Vol. 2, No. 1, p. 160; Azaña, *Obra Completa*, Vol. IV, Ediciones Oasis, Mexico City, 1998, p. 447; Palacios and Payne, *Franco, mi padre*, Kindle Loc. 2362. Preston, *Franco* (English), p. 118, 137–8; Franco Salgado, *Mi vida*, pp. 101.
20 Franco Salgado, *Mi vida*, pp. 101, 107.
21 Franco Salgado, *Mi vida*, p. 102; Azaña, *Obras Completas*, Vol. IV, p. 35; Jensen, *Soldier*, p. 60; Franco, *Apuntes*, p. 8.
22 Franco Salgado, *Mi vida*, p. 103; Francisco Franco, *Discurso De Franco A Los Cadetes De La Academia Militar De Zaragoza. El 14 De Julio De 1931*, available at FNFF: see https://fnff.es/historia/discurso-de-franco-a-los-cadetes-de-la-academia-militar-de-zaragoza/.
23 Franco Salgado, *Mi vida*, pp. 11, 104.
24 Azaña, *Obras Completas*, Vol. IV, p. 33; Jensen, *Soldier*, pp. 60, 124; Merino, *El otro Franco*, pp. 124–5; Preston, *Franco* (Spanish), p. 148; Gómez Morato to Minister of War, 28 July, Archivo Azaña, Ministerio de Asuntos Exteriores, RE. 131-1.
25 Franco Salgado, *Mis conversaciones*, pp. 174–5; Preston, *Franco*, (Spanish) p. 123.
26 Manuel Azaña and Cipriano de Rivas Cherif, *Cartas, 1917–1935 (inéditos)*, Pre-Textos, Valencia, 1991, p. 116.

27 Azaña, *Obras Completas,* Vol. IV pp. 83, 95–6; Manuel Azaña, *Diarios de la República*, Ombú, Seville, 2021, pp. 100, 120–1.
28 Fernando Puell de la Villa, 'Los militares ante la Segunda República', in *Studia Humanitatis Journal*, 2022, Vol. 2, No. 1, p. 161; Franco Salgado, *Mis conversaciones*, p. 397; Franco Salgado, *Mi vida*, pp. 105–7; Julio Gil Pecharromán, 'Prólogo', in Franco Salgado, *Mis conversaciones*; Palacios and Payne, *Franco* (English), p. 10; Emilio Mola, *El pasado, Azaña y el porvenir*; Kindle Loc. 280.
29 *Diario de Sesiones de las Cortes Constituyentes*, 19 Nov 1931 p. 2530; Mercedes Cabrera, 'Los escándalos de la Dictadura de Primo de Rivera y las responsabilidades en la República: el asunto Juan March', in *Historia y política: Ideas, procesos y movimientos sociales*, No. 4, 2000, p. 12; Preston, *Franco* (English), p. 116; AHN, TRIBUNAL SUPREMO RESERVADO, Exp 46, No. 2, folio 213.
30 Franco Salgado, *Mi vida*, p. 108; Pemán, *Mis Encuentros*, pp. 18–22.
31 Sáinz Rodríguez, *Testimonio y recuerdos*, pp. 325–6; Palacios and Payne, *Franco* (English), p. 106.
32 Sáinz Rodríguez, *Testimonio y recuerdos*, p. 326.
33 Franco Salgado, *Mi vida*, p. 108.
34 Franco Salgado, *Mi vida*, pp. 108–9.
35 Townson, *Modern Spain*, p. 142; Pemán, *Mis encuentros*, p. 56.
36 Palacios and Payne, *Franco* (Spanish), Kindle Loc. 1695; *Franco* (English) p. 106.
37 Preston, *Holocausto*, p. 59.
38 Franco, *Apuntes*, p. 9.
39 Francisco Franco, 'Ruud… Balek', pp. 5–6.
40 Stanley G. Payne, The *Collapse of the Spanish Republic 1933–1936*, Yale University Press, New Haven, 2006, pp. 64–5.
41 Franco Salgado, *Mi vida*, p. 112; Payne, *Falange* (English), pp. 39–40; Buckley, *Republic*, pp. 205–6; Eduardo González Calleja, 'La radicalización de las derechas', in Francisco Sánchez Pérez (ed.), *Los Mitos del 18 de julio*, Critica, Barcelona, 2013, p. 306.
42 Campoamor Rodríguez, *El voto femenino*, p. 32.
43 Helen Graham, *The Spanish Civil War: A Very Short Introduction*, Oxford University Press, Oxford, 2005, pp. 10–15; Townson, *Modern Spain*, p. 146.
44 González Calleja, 'La radicalizacíon', pp. 295–8; Preston, *Civil War*, p. 62–4; Townson, *Modern Spain*, p. 146; *ABC*, 24 September 1973, p. 4; Julián Vadillo Muñoz, 'Julio Aróstegui Sánchez, Largo Caballero. El tesón y la quimera', in *Bulletin d'Histoire Contemporaine de l'Espagne*, No. 51, 2017.
45 Eduardo González Calleja, 'La radicalización de las derechas', in Francisco Sánchez Pérez (ed.) *Los Mitos del 18 de julio*, Critica, Barcelona, 2013; Payne, *El Camino*, Kindle Loc. 936.
46 Preston, *Franco* (Spanish edition), p. 165; Suarez, *Franco*, p. 262; Julio Gil Pecharromán, *Historia De La Segunda República Española (1931–1936)*, Biblioteca Nueva, Madrid, 2014, Kindle Loc. 2619–40: Townson, *Modern Spain*, p. 156; Ramiro Ledesma, *Conquista del Estado*, No. 1, 14 March 1931.
47 Townson, *Modern Spain*, p. 157.
48 Townson, *Modern Spain*, p. 158.
49 Stanley G. Payne, *Falange: A History of Spanish Fascism*, Stanford University Press, Stanford, 1961, pp. 13, 38–41; Victor Pradera, *Accion Española*, 16 December 1933, pp. 649–51; Nigel Townson, *La Republica que no pudo ser: política de centro*

en *España (1931–1936)*, Taurus, Madrid, 2002, pp. 423–4; Townson, *Modern Spain*, p. 159.
50 Garriga, *Ramón*, p. 265–9.
51 Mola, *El pasado, Azaña y El Porvenir*; Azaña, *Obras Completas*, Vol. IV, pp. 83, 95–6; Azaña, *Diarios de la República*, p. 44; Joaquín Gil Honduvilla, 'Los Sucesos De Tablada De Junio De 1931 Y Sus Consecuencias', in *Revista de historia militar*, No. 110, pp. 11–50.
52 Franco Salgado, *Mi vida*, pp. 112–3.
53 Zavala, *Franco con franqueza*, p. 40; Preston, *Franco* (Spanish), pp. 172–3.
54 Preston, *Franco* (Spanish), p. 143; Palacios y Payne, *Franco, mi padre*, Kindle Loc. 2391; Townson, *Modern Spain*, p. 195; Pecharromán. *Segunda República*, Kindle Locs. 3525–3532.
55 Sáinz Rodríguez, *Testimonio*, p. 324.
56 Townson, *La República que no pudo ser*, pp. 295–8; Franco Salgado, *Mi vida*, p. 114.

13 REBELS IN ASTURIAS

1 *Coventry Evening Telegraph*, 5 October 1934, p. 1; Preston, *Franco* (Spanish), p. 169; Joaquín Arrarás, *Historia de la segunda República española*, Editora Nacional, 1956–68, Vol II., p. 441.
2 Franco Bahamonde, *Apuntes*, p. 12; Franco Salgado, *Mi vida*, p. 116, 120.
3 Fuentes Aragonés, *Largo Caballero: el Lenin español*, Editorial Sintesis, Madrid, p. 248; Paul Preston, *La Republica asediada. Hostilidad internacional y conflictos internos durante la Guerra Civil*, Barcelona, Ediciones Península, 1999, p. 95: Sandra Souto Kustrín, 'Octubre de 1934 en Madrid: acción colectiva y violencia política', in *Hispania: Revista española de historia*, Vol. 59, No. 203, pp. 1082–93; Townson, *Modern Spain*, p. 169.
4 Stanley Payne, *Spain's First Democracy: The Second Republic, 1931–36*, Madison, University of Wisconsin Press, 1993, pp. 214–8; Franco Salgado, *Mi vida*, p. 119; Souto Kustrín, 'Octubre', p. 1088; 'El Eco de sus Voces', *Alcázar*, 19 November 1976; Arrarás, *Segunda República*, Vol. 2, p. 436–7; Thomas, *Civil War*, Kindle Loc. 3472; Preston, *Franco* (Spanish), p. 178; José Antonio Primo de Rivera, *Textos de doctrina política*, 4.a ed., Sección Feminina de FET y de las JONS, Madrid, 1966, pp. 297–300; Ramon Serrano Súñer, *Entre el silencio y la propaganda, la Historia como fue. Memorias*, Editorial Planeta, Barcelona, 1977, pp. 54–56; Franco Bahamonde, *Apuntes*, p. 9; Franco Bahamonde, *Palabras del Caudillo*, p. 132.
5 Julio Aróstegui, 'Los socialistas en la Segunda República: una victoria con alto costo', in Angel Viñas (ed.), *En el combate por la historia: la Republica, la Guerra Civil, el Franquismo*, Editorial Pasado y Presente, Barcelona, 2012, Kindle Loc. 2398; Sandra Souto Kustrín, 'De la paramilitarización al fracaso: las insurrecciones socialistas de 1934 en Viena y Madrid', in *Pasado y Memoria*. No. 2, 2003, p. 7; Townson, *Modern Spain*, p. 167; Preston, *Franco*, pp. 151, 153; Payne, *The Collapse*, pp 52–95; Julio Arostegui, *Largo Caballero, El Tesón y la quimera*, Debate, Madrid, 2013; Víctor Manuel Arbeloa Muru, 'El quiebro del PSOE en 1933 (del Gobierno a la Revolución) I', in *Estudios de Deusto: revista de Derecho Público*, Vol. 60, No. 1, 2012, pp. 13–55; Victor Manuel Arbeloa Muru, 'El

quiebro del PSOE en 1933 del Gobierno a la Revolución (y II)', Vol. 61, No. 1, 2013, pp. 39–86.
6   Townson, *Modern Spain*, p. 167; Aróstegui, 'Los socialistas', Kindle Loc. 2398.
7   Franco Salgado, *Mi vida*, p. 118; Townson, *Modern Spain*, p. 169.
8   Franco, *Apuntes*, p. 12.
9   Radcliff, *España contemporanea*, p. 330; Townson, *República*, p. 437.
10 FNFF 1514, p. 10 for Natalio Rivas's report of his own conversations with Hidalgo; Radcliff, *España contemporanea*, p. 331.
11 Payne, *Collapse*, p. 125; Payne, *Second Republic*, p. 218; Gil Pecharromán, *Segunda República*, Kindle Loc. 2640.
12 Townson, *Modern Spain*, p. 17.
13 Payne, *Collapse*, pp. 125–6; Payne, *Collapse*, pp. 89, 218; Radcliff, *España contemporánea*, p. 330.
14 'Las armas del "Turquesa"', *El Comercio*, 28 September 2009; Preston, *Guerra civil*, p. 95; Luis María Sala González, *Indalecio Prieto y la política española, 1930–1936*, PhD thesis, Universidad del País Vasco, 2015, p. 213.
15 Franco, *Apuntes*, pp. 11–12.
16 Franco, *Apuntes*, pp. 12–13; Jordi Palafox, *Atraso económico y democracia: La Segunda República y la economía española*, Editorial Critica, Barcelona, 2000, p. 318.
17 Claude Martin, *Franco, Soldado y Estadista*, Fermín Uriarte, Madrid, 1965, p. 129; Manuel Álvaro Dueñas, 'Los militares en la represión política de la posguerra: la jurisdicción especial de Responsabilidades Políticas hasta la reforma de 1942', in *Revista de Estudios Políticos*, No. 69, 1990, pp. 141–62; Preston, *Franco* (Spanish) p. 182.
18 Preston, *Franco* (Spanish), p. 182.
19 Preston, *Franco* (Spanish), p. 181; Payne, *Collapse*, pp. 126–7.
20 Preston, *The Spanish Holocaust*, pp. 83–4; Preston, *Holocausto*, pp. 133–4.
21 Nestor Cerdá, 'Political Ascent and Military Commander: General Franco in the Early Months of the Spanish Civil War, July–October 1936', in *Journal of Military History*, Vol. 75, No. 4, p. 1137; Ramón Garriga, *El general Juan Yagüe*, Planeta, Barcelona, 1985, p. 62.
22 Garriga, *Ramón*, p. 268.
23 Payne, *Collapse*, p. 128; Franco Salgado, *Mi vida*, p. 120; Preston, *Franco* (Spanish) p. 182.
24 Payne, *Collapse*, p. 138.
25 Franco Salgado, *Mi vida*, p. 121; Carlos Barciela López et al. (eds), *Estadísticas históricas de España siglos XIX–XX*, Vol.1, Fundación BBVA, Madrid, 2005, p. 1087; Payne, *Collapse*, pp. 135–36, 139–41; *Hoja clandestina de la Unión Militar Española haciendo un llamamiento a los militares tras la Revolución de Octubre de 1934*, Sociedad de Amigos de Laguardia at https://www.euskalmemoriadigitala.eus/handle/10357/58167; Casanova, *España partida en dos*, Kindle Loc. 208.
26 *La Stampa*, 26 February 1937, p. 3; Gabriel Jackson, *The Spanish Republic and the Civil War, 1931–1939*, Princeton University Press, Princeton, 1972, p. 167.
27 Franco, *Apuntes*, p. 11.
28 Franco, *Apuntes*, p. 12; Jackson, *The Spanish Republic*, p. 167; Preston, *Franco* (Spanish), pp. 180, 184.
29 Franco, *Palabras del Caudillo*, pp. 131–2.

14 THE PENDULUM SWINGS

1. Serrano Súñer, *Memorias*, p. 52; Franco Salgado, *Mi vida*, p. 121; Franco, *Apuntes*, p. 14.
2. José María Gil Robles, *No fue posible la paz*, Ariel, Barcelona, 1968, p. 230.
3. Franco, *Apuntes*, pp. 14–15.
4. Franco Salgado, *Mi vida*, p. 123–4; José María Iribarren, *Con el General Mola: escenas y aspectos inéditos de la Guerra Civil*, Librería General, Zaragoza, 1937, pp. 12–14; Fernando Puell de la Villa, 'La trama militar de la conspiración' in Francisco Sánchez Pérez (ed.), *Los Mitos del 18 de julio*, Critica, Barcelona, 2013, pp. 99–100.
5. Franco, *Apuntes*, pp. 14–15 Preston, *Franco* (English), p. 161.
6. Preston, *Franco* (Spanish), p. 192–3.
7. Preston, *Franco* (Spanish edition), p. 194. Franco Salgado, *Mi vida*, p. 124. Preston, *Franco* (English) p. 166.
8. AHN, FC-CAUSA_GENERAL,1563, Exp. 23 folios 73-81. Preston, *Franco* (Spanish), p. 193.
9. Gil Pecharromán, *Segunda República*, Kindle Loc. 3317.
10. Portela Valadares, *Memorias. Dentro del drama español*, Alianza Editorial, Madrid, 1988, pp. 168–9; Preston, *Franco* (Spanish Edition), pp. 194–95.
11. Karl Robson, 'Franco, A dictator in spite of himself', *Life*, 29 May 1939; Hills, *Franco*, p. 210; Preston, *Franco* (Spanish), p. 65. Barroso was speaking to Hills.
12. Niceto Alcalá-Zamora, *Asalto a la Republica*, La Esfera de los Libros, Madrid, 2011, p. 38.
13. Payne, *El Camino*, Kindle Loc. 949; Gil Pecharromán, *Segunda República*, Kindle Loc 3327; Arrarás, *Segunda Republica IV*, p. 42.
14. Franco Salgado, *Mi vida*, p. 127.

15 THE POPULAR FRONT – THE LEFT RETURNS

1. Alcalá-Zamora, *Asalto*, Kindle Loc. 1517; Franco Salgado, *Mi vida*, p. 127; Arrarás, *Segunda República*, p. 56; Eduardo González Calleja, 'La necrológica de la violencia sociopolítica en la primavera de 1936', in *Melanges de la Casa de Velázquez*, No. 41-1, 2011, pp. 37-60; Payne, *El Camino*, Kindle Loc. 950; Javier Tusell, *Las elecciones del Frente Popular*, Vol. 1, Cuadernos para el Dialogo, Madrid, p. 13; Manuel Alvaréz Tardío and Roberto Villa García, *1936. Fraude y violencia en las elecciones del Frente Popular*, Espasa, Barcelona, 2017, Kindle Loc. 678, 7282; Diego Caro Cancela, '¿Por qué perdieron las derechas las elecciones de 1936?', in *Revista de historia contemporánea*, No. 9–10, 1999–2000, pp. 329–344.
2. Alcalá-Zamora, *Asalto*, Loc. 1371; Arrarás, *Segunda República IV*, p. 56.
3. Franco, *Apuntes*, p. 26; Franco Salgado, *Mi vida*, p. 130; Arrarás, *Franco*, pp. 231-8; *El Sol*, 18 February 1936, p. 5; Preston, *Franco* (Spanish), p. 198; Alcalá-Zamora, *Asalto*, Kindle Loc. 1528.
4. Franco, *Apuntes*, p. 25.

5 Buckley, *Republic*, p. 146; See Helen Graham and Paul Preston (eds), *The Popular Front in Europe*, Palgrave Macmillan, London 1989, pp. 2–3; E.H Carr, *Twilight of the Comintern, 1930–1935*, Pantheon, New York, 1982.
6 Alcalá-Zamora, *Asalto*, fn. 178 at Kindle Loc. 5173.
7 *El Sol*, 18 February 1936, p. 5; Franco Salgado, *Mi vida*, p. 130; Portela, *Memorias*, pp. 184–5; Payne, *El camino*, Kindle Loc. 331; Preston, *Franco* (English), pp. 172–3. 'El general Franco, desmiente unos rumores', *El Pueblo (Valencia)*, 20 February 1936, p. 4; Alcalá-Zamora, *Asalto*, Kindle Loc. 1645.
8 Arrarás, *Segunda República* IV, p. 63; Fernando Puell de la Villa, 'La trama militar de la conspiración', in Francisco Sánchez Pérez (ed.), *Los Mitos del 18 de julio*, Crítica, Barcelona, 2013, pp. 99–100.
9 Franco, *Apuntes*, p. 27.
10 Franco Salgado, *Mi vida*, p. 129; *El Sol*, 18 February 1936, p. 1; Payne, *El camino*, Kindle Locs 950–86; Alcalá-Zamora, *Asalto*, Kindle Locs 1605–160; González Calleja, 'La necrológica', pp. 37–60.
11 Villa García y Álvarez Tardío, *1936. Fraude y violencia*, p. 621; Gil Pecharromán, *Segunda República*, Kindle Loc. 3340; Payne, *El camino*, Kindle Loc. 6301; Arrarás, *Segunda Republica* IV, p. 64.
12 Francisco Franco, '¿Dónde estamos?', in *La Revue Belge*, 15 August 1937; Payne, *El camino*, Kindle Loc. 6301.
13 Villa García y Álvarez Tardío, *1936. Fraude y violencia*, pp. 523–6, 549, 655, 658; Townson, *Modern Spain*, p. 182.
14 Fernando Hernández Sánchez, 'El Partido Comunista de España en la Segunda República', in *Bulletin d'Histoire Contemporaine de l'Espagne*, No. 51, 2017, pp. 85–100; Archivo del Congreso de los Diputados (ACD), *Documentación electoral*, 141, No. 16.
15 Franco Salgado, *Mi vida*, p. 131; Serrano Suñer, *Memorias*, p. 53; Serrano Suñer, *Política de España*, p. 33.
16 Franco Salgado, *Mi vida*, p. 132.
17 Franco Salgado, *Mi vida*, p. 132.
18 Serrano Suñer, *Memorias* p. 59.
19 Serrano Suñer, *Política de España*, p. 33; Serrano Suñer, *Memorias*, p. 56; Heleno Saña, *El Franquismo sin mitos: conversaciones con Serrano Suñer*, Grijalbo, Barcelona, 1982, p. 50.
20 Serrano Suñer, *Memorias* p. 53; Franco Salgado, *Mi vida*, p. 132; Ángel Viñas, 'La connivencia fascista con la sublevación y otros éxitos de la trama civil', in *Los Mitos del 18 de julio*, pp. 96–97.
21 Franco Salgado, *Mi vida*, p. 131; Preston, *Franco* (English), p. 136.
22 Franco Salgado, *Mi vida*, p. 132.
23 Franco Salgado, *Mi vida*, p. 132..
24 Ángel Viñas, 'La connivencia fascista con la sublevación y otros éxitos de la trama civil', in *Los Mitos del 18 de julio*, pp. 96–97; Preston, *Franco* (Spanish), p. 207; Franco Salgado, *Conversaciones*, p. 217.
25 Clara Campoamor, *La revolución española vista por una republicana*, Espuela de Plata, Sevilla, 2020, pp. 86–87.
26 Franco Salgado, *Mi vida*, p. 132; Preston, *Franco* (Spanish), p. 207.
27 Franco Salgado, *Mi Vida*, p. 135–6.

16 THE BIG DECISION

1. Franco Salgado, *Mi vida*, pp. 135–7, 150; *La Epoca*, 14 March 1936, p. 4; *La Vanguardia*, 14 March 1936, p. 31; *Ahora*, 14 March 1936, p. 33; *Siglo Futuro*, 14 March 1936, p. 14; Preston, *Franco* (Spanish), p. 208.
2. Campoamor, *La revolución*, pp. 85–6; González Calleja, 'La necrológica, pp. 37–60.
3. Archivo Histórico Nacional, FC-CAUSA_GENERAL, 1563, Exp. 23, p. 4; Carmen Franco, 'Mi Marito', *La Stampa*, 26 February 1937, p. 3; Dora Lennard, 'Franco', in *Spain*; Preston, *Franco* (Spanish), p. 209.
4. González Calleja, 'La necrológica', pp. 37–60. See table of 'Muertos por semana'.
5. Arrarás, *Franco* (English) p. 184, (Spanish) pp. 259–60; Hills, *Franco*, p. 220.
6. Arrarás, *Franco* (English) p. 184, (Spanish) pp. 259–60.
7. Franco Salgado, *Mi vida*, p. 146; Carmen Franco, 'Mi Marito', *La Stampa*, 26 February 1937, p. 3; Palacios and Payne, *Franco*, Kindle Locs 2300, 2314.
8. Franco Salgado, *Mi vida*, pp. 145, 347; Dora Lennard, 'Franco' in *Spain*, p. 22.
9. Franco Salgado, *Mi vida*, p. 139.
10. Preston, *Franco* (Spanish), p. 211; Ismael Saz, *Mussolini contra la II República*, Edicions Alfons el Magnanim, Valencina, 1986, pp. 179–180.
11. *El Siglo Futuro*, 14 April 1936, p. 14; Ángel Viñas, 'La connivencia fascista', pp. 97–98; Payne, *Life and Death*, p. 223.
12. Gil Pecharromán, *Segunda República*, Kindle Loc. 3562; Ángel Viñas, 'La connivencia fascista', pp. 97–98.
13. Franco, *Apuntes*, pp. 34–5; Preston, *Franco*, (Spanish), p. 213; Palacios and Payne, *Franco*, Kindle Loc. 2350.
14. Serrano Suñer, *Memorias*, p. 56.
15. Franco, *Apuntes*, pp. 34–5; Preston, *Franco* (Spanish), pp. 213–4; Franco Salgado, *Mi vida*, p. 138.
16. *La Vanguardia*, 9 April 1936, pp. 23–4; *La Vanguardia*, 12 May 1936, p. 23; Alcalá-Zamora, *Asalto*, p. 4.
17. Preston, *Franco* (Spanish), p. 215; Balfour, *Deadly Embrace*, pp. 261–3.
18. Martin Blinkhorn, *Carlism and Crisis in Spain: 1931–1939*, Cambridge University Press, Cambridge, 2011, pp. 240, 245–9.
19. Javier Tusell, *Franco en la Guerra: una biografía política*, Tusquets, Barcelona, 1992, p. 512.
20. Fernando Puell de la Villa, 'La trama militar y de la conspiración', in *Los mitos del 18 de julio*, p. 109.
21. Preston, *Arquitectos*, p. 296; Preston, *Franco* (Spanish), p. 221.
22. Saña, *Franquismo sin mitos*, p. 48; Franco Salgado, *Mi vida*, pp. 77, 147.
23. Francisco Franco '¿Dónde estamos?', in *La Revue Belge*, 15 August 1937.
24. Balfour, *Deadly Embrace*, p. 258; Preston, *Guerra Civil*, p. 116.
25. Serrano Suñer, *Memorias*, p. 52.
26. Preston, *Guerra Civil*, pp. 116–7.
27. Saña, *Franquismo sin mitos*, p. 48; Palacios and Payne, *Franco* (Spanish), Kindle Loc. 2455.
28. Sainz Rodríguez, *Testimonio y recuerdos*, pp. 232–5; Ángel Viñas, 'La connivencia fascista', p. 122; Saña, *Franquismo sin mitos*, p. 64; Preston, *Guerra Civil*, p. 113; Julio Gil Pecharromán, 'Un partido para acabar con los partidos: el fascismo

español, 1931–1936', in *Bulletin d'Histoire Contemporaine de l'Espagne*, No. 51, 2017; José Calvo Sotelo, 'Orden Público', in *Intervenciones de José Calvo Sotelo y otros diputados en las Cortes el 16 de Junio de 19*, available at https://www.retori cas.com/2010/07/jose-calvo-sotelo-discurso-antes-de-la.html; Serrano Suñer, *Memorias*, p. 50; 'Viaje al fondo de la noche', Infocatolica.com, 6 July 2015, available at https://www.infocatolica.com/?t=opinion&cod=24382.

29 Gil Pecharromán, *Segunda República*, Kindle Locs 3574–76., 3598–99; Joan María Thomàs, *José Antonio: realidad y mito*, Debate, Madrid, 2022, pp. 281–2, 303–5; Francisco Sánchez Pérez (ed.), *Los mitos del 18 de julio*, p. 516.

30 Martínez Roda, *Varela*, p. 117; Antonio de Lizarza Iribarren, *Memorias de la conspiración, 1931–1936: quinta edición*, Ediciones Dyrsa, Madrid, 1986, pp. 72, 78 for 8,400 figure; Puell de la Villa, 'La trama militar', p. 516; Gil Pecharromán. *Segunda Republica*, Kindle Locations 3569–73.

31 Balfour, *Deadly Embrace*, p. 267.

32 Preston, *Franco* (English), p. 196; Palacios and Payne, *Franco* (Spanish), Kindle Loc. 2412; Latapié, *Memorias Políticas*, p. 184.

33 Saña, *Franquismo sin mitos*, p. 66.

34 Sánchez Perez (ed.), *Los mitos*, pp. 513–4; Balfour, *Deadly Embrace*, pp. 262–4.

35 Balfour, *Deadly Embrace*, p. 266–7; Felipe Bertrán Güell, *Preparación y Desarrollo del Alzamiento Nacional*, Librería Santarén, Valladolid, 1939, p. 174; Preston, *The Spanish Holocaust*, p. 133.

36 Preston, *Franco* (Spanish), p. 227; Giles Tremlett, *The International Brigades: Fascism, Freedom and the Spanish Civil War*, Bloomsbury, London, 2021, pp. 56–57.

37 Serrano Suñer, *Memorias*, p. 121; Preston, *Franco* (Spanish), p. 227; Balfour, *Deadly Embrace*, p. 267.

38 Joaquín Gil Honduvilla, 'Los Sucesos de Tablada de Junio de 1931 y Sus Consecuencias', in *Revista de Historia Militar*, No. 110, pp. 11–50.

39 Sánchez Pérez (ed.), *Los mitos*, p. 509.

40 Sanchez Perez (ed.). *Los mitos*, p. 516; González Calleja, 'La necrológica', pp. 37–60; Payne, *El camino*, Kindle Loc. 950; Joaquin Arrarás, *Historia de la cruzada española*, Vol. III, Ediciones Españolas, Madrid, 1939, p. 456.

41 Julio Gil Pecharromán, 'Un partido para acabar con los partidos: el fascismo español, 1931–1936', in *Bulletin d'Histoire Contemporaine de l'Espagne*, No. 51, 2017, pp. 69–84; Sainz Rodríguez, *Testimonio y recuerdos*, pp. 232–5; Ángel Viñas, 'La connivencia fascista', p. 122; Buckley, *Spanish Republic*, pp. 205–6.

42 Preston, *Franco* (Spanish), pp. 229.

43 Dora Lennard, 'Franco: A Close-Up, Study of the Mind and the Nature of the leader of Nationalist Spain by his English Teacher', in *Spain: Semi-monthly Publication of Civil War Events*, Vol 1. No. 3, 15 November 1937; p. 22. Preston, *Franco* (English), p. 200.

44 Balfour, *Deadly Embrace*, p. 267; Franco Salgado, *Mi vida*, p. 150; Preston, *Franco* (Spanish), p. 229.

45 Francisco Franco '¿Dónde estamos?', in *La Revue Belge*, 15 August 1937, available at https://fnff.es/historia/donde-estamos-articulo-publicado-en-la-revue-belge-15-de-agosto-de-17/; Francisco Franco, 'Un Articolo Del Generale Franco', *La Stampa*, 26 February 1937, p. 3.

46 Bolín, *The Vital Years*, p. 34; Franco Salgado, *Mi Vida*, p. 152; Payne, *El camino*, Kindle Loc. 4883; Balfour, *Deadly Embrace*, p. 267.

47 Bolín, *The Vital Years*, pp. 12, 38.
48 Franco Salgado, *Mi vida*, pp. 145, 150; Preston, *Franco* (Spanish), p. 231; Moisés Domínguez Núñez, *En busca del general Balmes*, Librería Hispania, Madrid, 2015.
49 Franco Salgado, *Mi vida*, p. 145; Preston, *Franco* (Spanish), p. 231.
50 Hugh Thomas, *The Spanish Civil War*, Penguin, London, Kindle Loc. 3531; Anthony Beevor, *The Battle for Spain: The Spanish Civil War (1936–1939)*, Orion, London, 2007, pp. 55, 116; Bolín, *The Vital Years*, p. 42.
51 Beevor, *The Battle for Spain*, Kindle Loc. 1448; Thomas, *Civil War*, Kindle Loc. 3472; Payne, *El camino* Kindle Loc. 4883; Josep Clara Resplandis, 'Joan Seguí Almuzara (1885–1936), el figuerenc protagonista de la subversió militar a Melilla', in *Annals de l'Institut d'Estudis Empordanesos*, NO. 54, 2023, pp. 243–250.
52 Preston, *Franco* (Spanish), p. 233.

17 INSURRECTION

1 Julián Casanova et al., *Morir, matar, sobrevivir. La violencia en la dictadura de Franco*, Crítica, Barcelona, 2002, pp. 62–3, 311; Fernando del Rey and Manuel Álvarez Tardío, *Fuego Cruzado. La primavera de 1936*, Galaxia Gutenberg, Barcelona, 2024, pp. 191, 294, 325, 986, 1023; Preston, *The Spanish Holocaust*, p. 133; Francisco Sanchez Montoya, *Ceuta y el norte de Africa: Republica, Guerra y represión 1931–1944*, Nativola, Granada, 2004, p. 310; Preston, *Guerra civil*, pp. 113–115; Palacios and Payne, *Franco*, Kindle Loc. 2769; Preston, *The Spanish Holocaust*, p. 133.
2 Franco Salgado, *Mi vida*, pp. 161–2, 166–7; Balfour, *Deadly Embrace*, p. 268; Preston, *The Spanish Holocaust*, p. 133.
3 Franco Salgado, *Mi vida*, p. 155.
4 Franco Salgado, *Mi vida*, p. 156.
5 Joaquin Arrarás, *Historia de la cruzada española*, p. 70; Preston, *Franco* (Spanish), p. 234.
6 Arrarás, *Historia de la cruzada*, p. 70.
7 Franco Salgado, *Mi vida*, p. 155; Ángel Viñas, 'La connivencia fascista', pp. 109–12.
8 Franco Salgado, *Mi vida*, pp. 155–60; José Alcaraz Abellán, Luis Alberto Anaya Hernández, and Sergio Millares Cantero, 'Los extranjeros y la Guerra Civil en la provincia de Las Palmas (1936–1939)', in *VII Coloquio de Historia Canario-Americana*, Vol. I, 1990, pp. 99–131.
9 Carmen Franco, 'Mi Marito', p. 3; Palacios and Payne. *Franco*, Kindle Loc. 2785.
10 Preston, *Franco* (Spanish), p. 273.
11 Franco Salgado, *Mi vida*, p. 161; Bolín, *The Vital Years*, p. 47.
12 Bolín, *The Vital Years*, p. 48.
13 Franco Salgado, *Mi vida*, pp. 163–4; Balfour, *Deadly Embrace*, pp. 267–70; Preston, *Franco* (English), p. 210.
14 Bolín, *The Vital Years*, p. 53.
15 Preston, *Franco* (English), p. 210 for tearfulness; Franco Salgado, *Mi vida*, p. 170.
16 Sánchez Montoya, *Ceuta y el norte de Africa*, p. 310.
17 José Escobar, *Así* Guillermo del Toro, Madrid, 1974, pp. 119–24; Diego Martínez Barrio, *Memorias*, Planeta, Barcelona, 1983, p. 364; Beevor, *Battle*, pp. 62, 125–7.
18 Beevor, *Battle*, pp. 125–6.

19 Tremlett, *The International Brigades*, p. 44.
20 Franco, *Palabras del Caudillo*, p. 181; Beevor, *Battle*, p. 153; Michael Alpert, *The Spanish Civil War at Sea*, Pen & Sword Books, Barnsley, 2021, p. 26.
21 Alpert, *Sea*, p. 22.
22 Beevor, *Battle*, pp. 140–41; José Cervera Pery, *Alzamiento y revolución en la marina*, Editorial San Martin, Madrid, 1978, p. 44; Daniel Suero, *La flota es roja: Papel clave del radiotelegrafista Benjamín Balboa en Julio de 1936*, Ediciones Saliente, Guadalajara, 2009, p. 180; *Ahora*, 22 July 1936, p. 5.
23 Franco Salgado, *Mi vida*, pp. 172, 192; Francisco Velasco Hernández, 'El Crucero Libertad', in *Cartagena histórica*, Cuaderno monográfico No., 15, 2005, pp. 3–26; Alpert, *Sea*, pp. 23–4.
24 Bolín, *The Vital Years*, p. 53.
25 *The Times*, 20 July 1936, p. 12.
26 Casanova, *España partida en dos*, Kindle Loc. 358; Tremlett, *The International Brigades*, p. 42; Giles Tremlett, *Las Brigadas Internacionales: fascismo, libertad y la Guerra Civil Española*, Debate, Madrid, 2020, p. 38.
27 Barea, *The Clash*, p. 129; Tremlett, *The International Brigades*, p. 60.
28 Franco Salgado, *Mi vida*, p. 173.
29 Néstor Cerdá, 'Political Ascent and Military Commander: General Franco in the Early Months of the Spanish Civil War, July–October 1936', in *The Journal of Military History*, Vol. 75, No. 4, 2011, p. 1130.
30 Cerdá, 'Political Ascent and Military Commander', p. 1132; *La Vanguardia*, 5 February 1937. *La Nueva España*, 14 February 1937; *Chicago Tribune*, 26 July 1937, p. 4; *Chicago Tribune*, 27 July 1937, p. 1; Preston, *Civil War*, p. 115;. The word *franquista* was rarely, if ever, used in the press on either side until February 1937.
31 J. Prada Rodríguez, 'Rebelión militar y represión franquista en Galicia', in *Studia Historica. Historia Contemporánea*, No. 24, 2009, pp. 153–77; Preston, *Civil War*, p. 115.
32 Franco Salgado, *Mi Vida*, p. 176.
33 Michael Alpert, *The Republican Army in the Spanish Civil War, 1936–1939*, Cambridge University Press, Cambridge, 2013, p. 91; Esdaile, *Civil War*, p. 24.
34 Franco Salgado, *Mi vida*, p. 173, 175; Cerdá, 'Political Ascent and Military Commander, pp. 1130–2.
35 Jensen, *Franco*, p. 72.
36 Preston, *Palomas*, p. 42.
37 Cerdá, 'Political Ascent and Military Commander, p. 1130.
38 Preston, *The Spanish Holocaust*, pp. 134–5.
39 *La revolución*, p. 158.
40 Julius Ruiz, 'Seventy Years on: Historians and Repression during and after the Spanish Civil War', in *Journal of Contemporary History*, Vol. 44, No. 3, 2009, p. 116; *The Bristol Daily Courier*, 28 July 1936, p. 1.
41 Edoardo Mastrorilli, 'Spanish Civil War, Italian Intervention, and Total War', in *Revista Universitaria de Historia Militar*, Vol. 6, No. 6, 2014, p. 71.
42 DGFP, Series D, Vol. III, p. 4–8.
43 Tusell, *Franco en la Guerra*, p. 142.

44 DGFP, Series D, Vol. III, p. 10; Cerdá, 'Political Ascent and Military Commander', p. 1133.
45 Preston, *Franco* (Spanish), p. 264.

18 FASCISM'S TAILCOAT

1 Nicolaus von Below, *At Hitler's Side: The Memoirs of Hitler's Luftwaffe Adjutant, 1937–1945*, Hase & Koehler, Mainz, 1980, p. 19; Thomas, *Civil War*, Kindle Loc. 5571.
2 Thomas, *Civil War*, Kindle Loc. 5571; Pierpaolo Barbieri, *Hitler's Shadow Empire: Nazi Economics and the Spanish Civil War*, Harvard University Press, Cambridge, 2015, p. 139; Ángel Viñas, *Hitler y el estallido de la guerra civil. Antecedentes y consecuencias*, Alianza Editorial, Madrid, 2001, p. 414; Hugh Trevor-Roper, *Hitler's Table Talk: His Private Conversation, 1941–44*, Phoenix Press, London, 2000, p. 687.
3 Trevor-Roper, *Hitler's Table Talk*, p. 687; Preston, *Franco* (Spanish), p. 263.
4 DGFP Series D, Vol. III, pp. 14–15; Enrique Moradiellos, 'Caudillo de España: Franco, un dictador carismático y soberano', in Enrique Moradiellos (ed.), *Las caras de Franco. Una revisión histórica del caudillo y su régimen*, Siglo XXI, Madrid, 2016, p. 29.
5 Barbieri, *Hitler's Shadow Empire*, p. 139.
6 R. H. Haigh, D. S. Morris, Anthony R. Peters (eds.), *The Guardian Book of the Spanish Civil War*, Wildwood House, London, 1987, p. 20.
7 DGFP Series D, Vol. III, pp. 14–15; Roberto Cantalupo, *Embajada en España*, Luis de Caralt, Barcelona, 1951, p. 55; Renzo de Felice, *Mussolini l'alleato*, Vol II, p. 366; Cerdá, 'Political Ascent and Military Commander', in *The Journal of Military History*, p. 1133; Robert Whealey, *Hitler and Spain: The Nazi Role in the Spanish Civil War. 1936–1939*, University Press of Kentucky, Lexington, 1989, Appendix C; Preston, *Franco* (Spanish), pp. 260–3.
8 Cerdá, 'Political Ascent and Military Commander', pp. 1133, 1136; Whealey, *Hitler and Spain*, Appendix C; Preston, *Franco* (Spanish), pp. 263–271, 1331;. Esdaile, *Civil War*, p. 89; Trevor-Roper, *Hitler's Table Talk*, p. 687; Haigh, Morris and Peters (eds.), *The Guardian Book of the Spanish Civil War*, p. 24; 'Hitler's Hand in Spanish War Revealed', *Baltimore Sun*, 8 November 1945, p. 16; Preston, *Franco* (Spanish), pp. 263–271, 1331.
9 *News Chronicle*, 29 July 1936, 1 August 1936; *Chicago Tribune*, 29 July 1937, p. 2; Preston, *Franco* (English), pp. 222–3.
10 Joseph Goebbels, *Tagebücher 1924–1945* (vols. 1, 2, 3, 4, 5), Piper, Munich, 1992, p. 982; Payne, *Franco and Hitler*, p. 8.
11 Helen Graham. *The Spanish Civil War*, p. 33; Franco, *Apuntes*, p. 41.
12 Von Below, *At Hitler's Side*, p. 39; Trevor-Roper, *Hitler's Table Talk*, p. 607; Cerdá, 'Political Ascent and Military Commander', p. 1141.
13 Serrano Suñer, *Política de España*, pp. 18–9; Franco Salgado, *Mi vida*, p. 180; Cerdá, 'Political Ascent and Military Commander', pp. 1139, 1142–4; Manuel Rodríguez Barrientos, 'La Guerra Civil en Algeciras y su Entorno Geográfico', in *Revista general de marina*, Vol. 258, 2010, p. 399; Beevor, *Battle*, p. 61.
14 Cerdá, 'Political Ascent and Military Commander', pp. 1142, 1148; Preston, *Franco* (Spanish), pp. 266–7.

15 Pemán, *Mis encuentros*, p. 51; Cerdá, 'Political Ascent and Military Commander', pp. 1139, 1144; Preston, *Franco* (Spanish), pp. 266–7.

19 FIGHTING AT LAST

1 Saña, *Franquismo sin mitos*, p. 98; Cerdá, 'Political Ascent and Military Commander', pp. 1145–6; Preston, *Franco* (Spanish), p. 267.
2 Preston, *Holocaust*, p. 303; Ian Westwell, *Condor Legion: The Wehrmacht's Training Ground*, Ian Allen, Hersham, 2004, pp. 14–8; Esdaile, *Civil War*, p. 91.
3 *Censo de España 1930*, p. 339; Esdaile, *Civil War*, p. 92; Preston, *Holocaust*, pp. 308–9; Preston, *Franco*, (Spanish), p. 268.
4 Cazorla Sánchez, *Franco* (Spanish), pp. 102-3; Preston, *Franco* (Spanish), p. 270.
5 Enrique Moradiellos, 'Caudillo de España', in Enrique Moradiellos (ed.), *Las caras de Franco*, p. 29; Preston, *Palomas*, p. 371.
6 María de la Luz Mejías Correa, *Así fue pasando el tiempo. Memorias de una miliciana extremeña*, Editorial Renacimiento, Madrid, 2006, pp. 61–3, 64–5, 68; Esdaile, *Civil War*, pp. 90–2; Archivo Histórico Nacional, FC-CAUSAGENERAL, 1052, Exp. 2, p. 43; *Anuario estadístico de España 1936*, Ministerio de Trabajo, Sanidad y Prevision, Madrid, 1936, p. 19; Cerdá, 'Political Ascent and Military Commander', p. 1152; Francisco Espinosa, *La columna de la muerta. El avance del ejército franquista de Sevilla a Badajoz*, Editorial Critica, Barcelona, 2003, Kindle Loc. 2746, 3206; Mario Neves, 'Badajoz continuous hoje a ser bombardeada', *Diario de Lisboa*, 14 August 1936, p. 1.
7 Mario Neves, 'Badajoz esta entregue aos legionaries e aos "regulares" marroquinos', *Diario de Lisboa*, 15 August 1936, p. 1; Mario Neves, *Chacina de Badajoz*, Ediçoes O Jornal, Lisbon, 1985, excerpts accesible at https://silenciosememorias.blogspot.com/2017/08/1617-chacina-de-badajoz-ha-81-anos-por.html; Espinosa, *Columna de la muerte*, Kindle Loc. 5918; *Anuario estadístico de España* 1936, p. 19; Esdaile, *Civil War*, pp. 92, 118; Preston, *Holocaust*, p. 321; See also Mário Neves, *La matanza de Badajoz*, Editora Regional de Extremadura, Mérida, 1986.
8 Mejías Correa, *Así fue pasando el tiempo*, p. 81; Clara Sanz-Hernando, 'Crónicas de guerra: la matanza de Badajoz y la batalla del Alcázar de Toledo en la prensa portuguesa', in *Ler História*, No. 77, 2020, pp. 159–180.
9 Preston, *Franco* (Spanish), pp. 241, 271–2.
10 Franco Salgado, *Mi vida*, pp. 166–7; De la Cierva, *Un siglo*, Vol. 1, p. 27; Manuel Touron Yebra, *El General Miguel Campins y su época (1880–1936)*, PhD thesis, Universidad Complutense Madrid, 2002, p. 771.
11 Franco Salgado, *Mi vida*, pp. 185, 188, 359–50; Touron Yebra, *Miguel Campins*, p. 771.
12 Serrano Suñer, *Política de España*, pp. 12, 18–9.
13 Franco Salgado, *Mi vida*, pp. 352–3.
14 Touron Yebra, *Miguel Campins*, p. 545.
15 Touron Yebra, *Miguel Campins*, pp. 553–4, 556–7; Preston, *Palomas*, pp. 374–5. See also Aaron Shulman, *The Age of Disenchantments: The Epic Story of Spain's Most Notorious Literary Family and the Long Shadow of the Spanish Civil War*, HarperCollins, London, 2019.

16 *Archivo Gomá* Vol 1, pp. 227–8; Suñer, *Memorias*, pp. 243–6.
17 Cerdá, 'Political Ascent and Military Commander', p. 1153.
18 Preston, *Franco* (Spanish), p. 268.

20 ABSOLUTE POWER

1 Francisco Franco, pp. 268–70.
2 Álvarez, *Betrothed*, p. 389.
3 Franco Salgado, *Mi vida*, p. 196; Esdaile, *Civil War*, p. 93.
4 Tusell, *Franco en la Guerra*, p. 51; Arrarás, *Franco* (English), p. 210; *Anuario de España 1936*, p. 19.
5 'Hitler's Hand in Spanish War Revealed', *Baltimore Sun*, 8 November 1945, p. 16; Archivo Histórico Nacional, DIVERSOS-VICENTEROJO, Car. 2, No. 186, Recorte de prensa: 'Informe Auténtico sobre la Ayuda que Hitler dió a Franco', published in *El Excelsior*.
6 Preston, *Arquitectos del terror*, pp. 296, 584; Whealey, *Hitler and Spain*, p. 44; 'Hitler's Hand', p. 16.
7 Esdaile, *Civil War*, pp. 93–4; Beevor, *Battle*, pp. 284–85.
8 Serrano Suñer, *Memorias*, p. 215; Tusell, *Franco en la Guerra*, pp. 40–5; Franco Salgado, *Mi vida*, p. 196.
9 Franco Salgado, *Mi vida*, p. 197; Tusell, *Franco en la Guerra*, p. 50; DGFP, SERIES D, III, p. 107; Preston, *Franco* (English), pp. 255–56; Garriga, *Nicolás*, pp. 101–2.
10 Alfredo Kindelán, *La verdad de mis relaciones con Franco*, Editorial Planeta, Barcelona, 1981, p. 28.
11 Peman, *Encuentros* p. 19; Garriga, *Nicolás Franco*, pp. 110, 137; Hugh Thomas, *Historia de la Guerra Civil Española*, Círculo de Lectores, Barcelona, 1977, p. 619; Preston, *Palomas*, p. 375; Preston, *Franco* (English), p. 273.
12 Tusell, *Franco en la Guerra*, p. 52; Alejandro Pizarroso Quintero, 'La Guerra Civil española, un hito en la historia de la propaganda', in *El Argonauta español*, No. 2, 2005, at https://journals.openedition.org/argonauta/1195; Carlos Pulpillo Leiva, 'La Configuración De La Propaganda En La España Nacional (1936–1941)', in *La Albolea: Revista de Humanidades y Cultura*, No. 1, 2014, pp. 115–36.
13 Kindelán, *La Verdad*, p. 29.
14 Tusell, *Franco en la Guerra*, p. 53; Preston, *Franco* (English), pp. 256–257.
15 Preston, Franco (Spanish), pp. 289–90; Preston, *Franco* (English), pp. 260–61; Tusell, *Franco en la Guerra*, p. 53.
16 Preston, *Franco* (Spanish), p. 1335; Franco Salgado, *Mi vida*, p. 198; *La Unión de Sevilla*, 22 September 1936, p. 4; Preston, *Franco* (English), pp. 247, 251–52, 259–61.
17 *Revista Ejército*, No. 960, 2021, p. 70.
18 Alberto Reig Tapia, 'El Asedio del Alcázar: Mito y Símbolo Político del Franquismo', *Revisto de Estudios Políticos (Nueva Época)*, No. 101, 1998, p. 121.
19 *Diario del Alcázar*, 23 July 1936, at https://fnff.es/historia/dia-2-de-julio/.
20 Reig Tapia, 'El Asedio del Alcázar', pp. 113, 121–4; Preston, *Franco* (English), p. 236.
21 Franco Salgado, *Mi vida*, p. 199.
22 DGFP, Series D, Vol III, pp. 95–6. p. 97; Jensen, *Franco*, pp. 80–2.

23 DGFP, Series D, Vol. III, pp. 106–7; Preston, *Franco* (English), pp. 260–61.
24 *La Unión*, 29 September 1936, p. 14; *La Unión*, 30 September 1936, p. 18; Palacios and Payne, *Franco* (Spanish), Kindle Loc. 3111.
25 Arrarás, *Franco* (English), p. 212.
26 Armando Boaventura, *Madrid-Moscovo: da ditadura a republica e a Guerra Civil de Espanha*, Parceria A. M. Pereira, Lisbon, 1937, p. 212; Preston, *Franco* (English), pp. 260–61, (Spanish) p. 293; Palacios and Payne, *Franco* (Spanish), Kindle Loc. 3051.
27 Palacios and Payne, *Franco* (Spanish), Kindle Loc. 3075; Kindelán, *La Verdad*, p. 30.
28 Palacios and Payne, *Franco* (Spanish), Kindle Loc. 3075; Franco Salgado, *Mi vida*, p. 1877.
29 Guillermo Cabanellas, *Cuatro generales* (Vol. 2), Editorial Planeta, Barcelona, 1977, p. 338.
30 Julio Arostegui, *Por qué el 18 de julio... Y después*, Flor del Viento Ediciones, Barcelona, 2006, p. 420.
31 Preston, *Franco* (Spanish), p. 295; Julian Casanova, *República y Guerra Civil. Vol. 8 de la Historia de España*, Crítica/Marcial Pons, Barcelona, 2014, p. 344.
32 'Nombrando Jefe del Gobierno del Estado Español al Excelentísimo Sr. General de División don Francisco Franco Bahamonde, quien asumirá todos los poderes del nuevo Estado', in *Boletín Oficial de la Junta de Defensa Nacional de España*, No. 32, 30 September 1936; Preston, *Franco* (English), p. 265.
33 Tusell, *Franco en la Guerra*, p. 55; Fontenla, *Franco*, p. 201; Franco Salgado, *Mi vida*, p. 32.

21 HOLY WAR

1 Hilari Raguer in Viñas, Ángel, *En el combate por la historia*, Kindle Loc. 9952.
2 Hilari Raguer in Viñas, Ángel, *En el combate por la historia*, Kindle Loc. 9952; Pilar Franco, *Nosotros*, p. 66; *La Vanguardia*, 31 May 1952, p. 3; Palacios and Payne, *Franco* (Spanish), Kindle Loc. 334; Preston, *Palomas*, p. 357; De la Cierva, *Franco*, p. 61;. Francisco Torres, *Franco o la venganza de la historia*, p. 66; Serrano Suñer, *Política de España*, p. 11; Pozuelo, *476 días*, p. 86.
3 Giuliana de Febo in Moradiellos (ed.), *Las caras de Franco*, p. 153; De la Cierva, *Siglo*, Vol I, p. 531.
4 Glicerio Sánchez Recio, *De las dos ciudades a la resurrección de España: Magisterio pastoral y pensamiento político de Enrique Pla y Deniel Alicante*, Biblioteca Virtual Miguel de Cervantes, 2022, pp. 46–9: De la Cierva, *Siglo*, Vol I, p. 513.
5 Rodrigo, *Guerra fascista*, p. 113; Tusell, *Franco en la Guerra*, p. 132, citing *ABC*, Seville, 20 Jan, 13 Feb and 26 Feb 1937.
6 Preston, *Palomas*, pp. 364, 372; Preston, *Franco*, (English) p. 405.
7 María Merida, *Testigos*, p. 36; Carmen Martin Gaite, *Usos amorosos de la posguerra española*, Anagrama, Barcelona, 1994, p. 12; Preston, *Franco* (Spanish), p. 939; *La Vanguardia*, 31 May 1952, p. 3.
8 Gomá, *El Caso de España*, at https://www.filosofia.org/aut/001/1936goma.htm *Archivo Gomá, Vol 1*, pp. 286, 384, 412, 472; Beevor, *Battle*, p. 802; Preston, *Franco* (Spanish), p. 303.
9 Preston, *Franco* (Spanish) pp. 299–300; *La Union*, 2 October 1936, p. 12.

10 Cabanellas, *Cuatro generales*, pp. 4, 351.
11 *Movietone* at https://www.youtube.com/watch?v=O6iQ-Zq-sUk&abchannel=BritishMovietone
12 FNFF, *Discurso en Burgos de Francisco Franco* (1 October 1936) at https://fnff.es/historia/discurso-en-burgos-de-francisco-franco-1-de-octubre-de-16/, accessed 17 October 1923.
13 Tusell, *Franco en la Guerra*, p. 55; *La Unión*, Seville, 4 August 1936, p. 6.
14 DGFP Series D, Vol. 3, pp. 103, 106–7.
15 DGFP Series D, Vol. 3, pp. 102–3, 106–7.
16 Paul Preston, 'Franco as a military leader', in *Transactions of the Royal Historical Society*, 6:4 (1994), 29.
17 Preston, *Franco* (Spanish), p. 311.
18 AHN. FC-TRIBUNAL_SUPREMO_RECURSOS,125, Exp. 32; Garriga, *Nicolás*, pp. 115–6; Garriga, *Ramón*, p. 271.
19 Díaz, *Mi vida*, p. 224; Cabanellas, *Cuatro generales*, p. 429.
20 Whitaker, *We Cannot Escape History*, MacMillan, New York, 1943, p. 105; Franco, *Palabras del Caudillo*, p. 161.
21 Tusell, *Franco en la Guerra*, pp. 57–60.
22 Giménez Caballero, *Mi dictador*, p. 88; Preston, *Franco*, p. 406.
23 Preston, *Franco* (Spanish), p. 308; Seidman, *Republic of Egos*, p. 34, citing Casanova in *Víctimas de la Guerra Civil*, Sant Julia ed., p. 99.
24 Whealey, *Hitler and Spain*, pp. 27–8, 36. 'Hitler's Hand', p. 16; AHN, DIVERSOS-VICENTE_ROJO, Car. 2, No. 186.
25 Ros, in *Las caras de Franco*, pp. 122–3.

22 ATTACK ON MADRID

1 Claude Bowers, *My Mission to Spain: Watching the Rehearsal for World War II*, Simon & Schuster, New York, 1954, p. 320; Franco Salgado, *Mi vida*, p. 211.
2 Tusell, *Franco en la Guerra*, p. 133; H. R Knickerbocker, '"Kill'em All", Franco aide's philosophy' in *The Washington Times*, 10 May 1937, p. 7. See also Ian Gibson, *Paracuellos: cómo fue*, Plaza & Janés, Madrid, 1983, and Julius Ruiz, *Paracuellos, una verdad incómoda*, Espasa, Madrid, 2015.
3 Franco Salgado, *Mi vida*, pp. 212–5; Martin Minchom, *Spain's Martyred Cities*, p. 110; Beevor, *Battle*, p. 284.
4 Trevor-Roper, *Hitler's Table Talk*, p. 569.
5 *The Spanish Civil War*, pp. 40–1.
6 Arthur Koestler, *The Invisible Writing*, London, 1954, 2005 edn, pp. 336, 388–91; Tremlett, *The International Brigades*, pp. 76–7.
7 Mikel Aizpuru, *La presencia soviética durante la Guerra Civil en el Frente Norte*, p. 713; Esdaile, *Civil War*, Appendix 8; Reverte, *Madrid*, p. 234.
8 Knox, Premature antifascist, in *The Antioch Review*, Vol. 57, No. 2, p. 141; John Sommerfield, *Volunteer in Spain*, Lawrence & Wishart, London, 1937 p. 49; Manuel Vicente González, *Madrid Militarizado*, Kindle Loc. 2780; Reverte, *Madrid*, p. 234.
9 Knox, 'Premature antifascist', p. 141; Sommerfield, *Volunteer*, p. 49; Tremlett, *Brigadas*, p. 114.

10 RGASPI 545.1.401, *Rebière report*, pp. 32–3; Geoffrey Cox, *Eyewitness: A Memoir of Europe in the 1930s*, University of Otago Press, Otago, 1999, p. 33; Sommerfield, *Volunteer*, p. 85; Tremlett, *Brigadas*, pp. 118, 128; Franco Salgado, *Mi vida*, pp. 212–4.
11 Tusell, *Franco en la Guerra*, p. 133; H. R. Knickerbocker, *The Washington Times*, May 10, 1937, p. 7; Beevor, *Battle*, p. 35.
12 Reverte, *Madrid*, pp. 257, 265.
13 Bowers, *My Mission*, p. 320; Preston, *We Saw Spain Die: Foreign Correspondents in the Spanish Civil War*, Constable, London, 2009, Kindle Loc. 914; Michael Jackson, *Fallen Sparrows: The International Brigades in the Spanish Civil War*, American Philosophical Society Press, Philadelphia, 1994, p. 57, citing *Times*, 9 November p. 12.
14 RGASPI 545.3.73, pp. 2–4, 21–4; Bowers, *My Mission*, pp. 320–1; Louis Delaprée, *Morir in Madrid*, Raíces, Madrid, 2009, p. 170.
15 Franco Salgado, *Mi vida*, p. 214; Manuel Ros in *Las caras de Franco*, Moradiellos ed., p. 128.
16 *Manchester Evening News*, 12 Nov 1936, p. 16; *Leicester Evening Mail*, 12 Nov 1936, p. 7; Beevor, *Battle*, p. 101.
17 John Whitaker, *We Cannot Escape History*, pp. 103–4.
18 Franco, *Palabras del Caudillo*, pp. 11, 109, 266–7: Tremlett, *The International Brigades*, pp. 90–3; Franco Salgado, *Mi vida*, p. 214.
19 Franco, *Palabras del Caudillo*, p. 155.
20 Franco Salgado, *Mi vida*, pp. 214, 216.
21 Ronal Fraser, *Tajos: The Story of a Village on the Costa Del Sol*, Pantheon, London, 1973, p. 41.
22 Whitaker, *We Cannot Escape History*, p. 104; Franco Salgado, *Mi vida*, p. 215.
23 Muggeridge, *Ciano's Papers*, p. 54; Series D, Vol III pp. 154–6; Saz and Tusell, *Fascistas en España: La Intervención Italiana En La Guerra Civil A Través De Los Telegramas De La 'Missione Militare Italiana In Spagna'*, Consejo Superior De Investigaciones Científicas, Madrid, 1980, pp. 26–8; Viñas, *Franco, Hitler*, p. 454.
24 Saz and Tusell, *Intervención*, pp. 27–9.
25 Muggeridge, *Ciano's Papers*, p. 57, 60; *Baltimore Sun*, 8 November 1945, p. 16; AHN, DIVERSOS-VICENTEROJO, Car. 2, No. 186; Westwell, *Condor Legion*, p. 18; Whealey, *Hitler and Spain*, pp. 44–5; Basil Liddell Hart, *Other Side of the Hill*, Cassell, London, 1951, pp. 96–7.
26 Stefanie Schüler-Springorum, *La guerra como aventura: La Legión Cóndor en la Guerra Civil española 1936–1939*, Alianza, Madrid, 2014; Westwell, *Condor Legion*, pp. 12, 14, 23; Esdaile, *Civil War*, pp. 141, 339; Viñas, *Franco, Hitler*, pp. 452, 458; *Baltimore Sun*, 8 November 1945, p. 16; AHN DIVERSOS-VICENTEROJO, Car. 2, No. 186.
27 DGFP Series D, Vol. 1, pp. 36–7: Schüler-Springorum, *La guerra como aventura*, Kindle Locs. 298–307; Esdaile, *Civil War*, Appendix 7 and 8, pp. 338–45; International Military Tribunal, Avalon Project, Vol. IX, p. 281; Coverdale, *Intervention*, p. 163; Thomas, *Civil War*, Kindle Loc. 5571; *Baltimore Sun*, 8 November 1945, p. 16. AHN, DIVERSOS-VICENTEROJO, Car. 2, No. 186.
28 Saz and Tusell, *Intervención*, pp. 30–1, 112.
29 Rodrigo, *La Guerra fascista*, pp. 94, 98, 103–5; Antonio Navas Muñoz, 'La Italia fascista en Malaga', in *Tiempo y Sociedad*, 28 (2017). p. 83.

30 Preston, *Architects of Terror*, p. 278; Tremlett, *The International Brigades*, pp. 249–50; Rodrigo, *La Guerra fascista*, pp. 105–7.
31 Whitaker, *We Cannot Escape History*, p. 104; Rodrigo, *La Guerra fascista*, p. 105–9; Saña, *Franquismo sin mitos*, p. 117; Tremlett, *The International Brigades*, pp. 249–50.

23 THE ABSENT ONE

1 José M. Zavala, *La pasión de Pilar Primo de Rivera*, Plaza Janés, Barcelona, 2013, p. 226. See also Zavala, *La Pasión de José Antonio*, Plaza Janés, Barcelona, 2013; José Antonio Primo de Rivera, *Selected Writings*, Jonathan Cape, London, 1972, pp. 70–2; Foreign Relations of the United States Diplomatic Papers, 1936, Europe, Vol. II, pp. 563–9.
2 Pemán, *Conversaciones*, p. 59; Serrano Suñer, *Memorias*, p. 60; Saña, *Franquismo sin mitos*, p. 51; Preston *Franco* (Spanish), p. 313; DGFP, SERIES D, III, pp. 114–15; Foreign Relations of the United States Diplomatic Papers, pp. 563–9.
3 Pemán, *Conversaciones* p. 59; Saña, *Franquismo sin mitos*, p. 51; Preston, *Franco* (Spanish), p. 313; DGFP, SERIES D, III, pp. 114–15.
4 Tusell, *Franco en la Guerra*, pp. 126–8; 'Veintisiete Puntos de Falange Española de las JONS', in *ABC*, 30 November 1934.
5 Tusell, *Franco en la Guerra*, pp. 126–8; 'Veintisiete Puntos de Falange Española de las JONS', in *ABC*, 30 November 1934.
6 *El Liberal*, 19 Nov 1936, p. 2, 21 November 1936; *ABC*, 20 Nov, p. 7; *El Sol*, 21 November 1936, p. 1; *La Voz*, 21 November 1936, p. 1; *La Stampa*, 21 Nov 1936, p. 6; Thomàs, *José Antonio*, p. 427–432; *Diario de Las Palmas*, 21 Nov 1936 p. 2, 'Ha sido fusilado el jefe de fa lance española, don José Antonio Primo de Rivera'; Zira Box, *La Fundación de Un Régimen. La Construcción Simbólica Del Franquismo*, PhD thesis, Madrid, 2008, p. 157.
7 Thomàs, *José Antonio*. pp. 430–32.
8 DGFP, Series D, Vol III, p. 269; Tusell, *Franco en la Guerra*, pp. 124, 203, 430; Franco, 'En el II aniversario del alzamiento, Burgos, 18 de julio de 1938' in *Palabras del Caudillo*, pp. 12, 132.
9 Tremlett, *Ghosts of Spain: Travels Through A Country's Hidden Past*, Faber, London, 2012, pp. 19–21.
10 Whitaker, *We Cannot Escape History*, p. 106; Franco Salgado, *Mi vida*, p. 354; Tusell, *Franco en la Guerra*, pp. 117–9, 225; Franco, *Las cartas*, pp. 88–89, 96; Ricardo de la Cierva, *Don Juan*, pp. 104–5; Preston, *Franco* (English), p. 235; Tusell y Queipo de Llano, *Alfonso XIII*, p. 798.
11 Whitaker, *We Cannot Escape History*, p. 108; Tusell, *Franco en la Guerra*, p. 116.
12 H. R. Knickerbocker, *Washington Times*, May 10, 1937, p. 7.
13 Tusell, *Franco en la Guerra*, p. 116.
14 Sainz Rodríguez, *Testimonio*, p. 316.
15 F. H. Thomas, Robert Stradling (ed.), *Brother against Brother*, Sutton Publishing, Stroud, 1998, pp. 50–1.
16 DGFP, Series D, Vol. III, pp. 137–8; Tusell, *Franco en la Guerra*, p. 69.
17 Tusell, *Franco en la Guerra*, pp. 70–2; Beevor, *Battle*, p. 315; Blinkhorn, *Carlism and Crisis*, p. 222.

18 Tusell, *Franco en la Guerra*, pp. 62, 72.
19 DGFP, Series D, Vol III, p. 268. Tusell, *Franco en la Guerra*, p. 98; Blinkhorn, *Carlism and Crisis*, pp. 252–5.
20 Tusell, *Franco en la Guerra*, pp. 76, 96–7, 100; Blinkhorn, *Carlism and Crisis*, pp. 276–77.
21 Blinkhorn, *Carlism and Crisis*, pp. 276–277; Tusell, *Franco en la Guerra*, pp. 99–103, 159–60.
22 Tusell, *Franco en la Guerra*, pp. 100–1, 159–60; Manuel Martorell, 'Navarra 1937–1939: El Fiasco De La Unificación', in *Príncipe De Viana*, 2(244), p. 439.
23 Tusell, *Franco en la Guerra*, pp. 99, 577.

24 ENFORCED UNITY

1 Saña, *Franquismo sin mitos*, p. 58.
2 Serrano Suñer, *Hendaya*, p. 27; Saña, *franquismo sin mitos*, p. 61; Preston, *Palomas* p. 376; Carmen Polo, 'Mi marito', *La Stampa*, 26 February 1937, p. 3; Gimenez Caballero, *Memorias de un dictador*, p. 88; Crozier, *Franco*, p. 218.
3 Ciano, *Diario 1937–1943*, '5-6-7 GIUGNO 1939'; Saña, *Franquismo sin mitos*, p. 60; Ridruejo, *Casi*, p. 108.
4 Tusell, *Franco en la Guerra*, pp. 133–5, 348.
5 Tusell, *Franco en la Guerra*, pp. 133–5; Preston, *Franco* (Spanish), p. 360.
6 *La Stampa*, 26 February 1937, p. 3; Tusell, *Franco en la Guerra*, pp. 131–2.
7 Tusell, *Franco en la Guerra*, pp. 133–5; *El Faro de Ceuta*, 12 February 1937, p. 1.
8 Tusell, *Franco en la Guerra*, p. 156; Renzo De Felice, *Mussolini: Il Duce*, Vol. II, Einaudi, Turin, 1981, p. 379.
9 Victor Pradera, *Accion Española*, 16 Dec 1933, pp. 649–51; Blinkhorn, *Carlism and Crisis*, pp. 6–9, 18–22, 156–8.
10 Tusell, *Franco en la Guerra*, pp. 143–9, 174–6, 186; Joan Maria Thomàs, *El gran Golpe*, Debate, Madrid, 2013, pp. 99–170.
11 Tusell, *Franco en la Guerra*, pp. 169–70, 422–3; Thomàs, *El gran golpe*, p. 231; Preston, *Franco* (English), p. 380.
12 Angela Loureiro (ed.), *Estelas, laberintos, nuevas sendas: Unamuno, Valle-Inclán, García Lorca, la guerra civil*, Anthropos, Barcelona, 1988, p. 367.
13 Tusell, *Franco en la Guerra*, p. 177.
14 Ridruejo, *Entre literatura*, p. 206; Tusell, *Franco en la Guerra*, p. 422.
15 Boletín Oficial del Estado, Burgos, 20 April 1937, No. 182, pp. 1033–34: *Decreto de unificación de FET y de la JONS*.
16 Boletín Oficial del Estado, Burgos, pp. 1033–34: *Decreto de unificación*. Umberto Eco, 'Ur-fascism', in *New York Review of Books*, 22 June 1995.
17 Ridruejo, *Escrito en España*, p. 92; Serrano Suñer, *Memorias*, p. 173; Tusell, *Franco y la Guerra Civil*, p. 203.
18 Tusell, *Franco en la Guerra Civil*, pp. 353–5; Preston, *Franco* (Spanish), p. 620.
19 Julián Pemartín, *Teoría De La Falange*, Editora Nacional, Madrid, 1942, pp. 16–17; Tusell, *Franco en la Guerra Civil*, p. 193–4. See also Alberto Reig Tapia, *La crítica de la crítica*.
20 Tusell, *Franco en la Guerra Civil*, pp. 133, 195–6, 209.
21 Tusell, *Franco en la Guerra Civil*, pp. 198, 221.

25 SLOW WAR

1. Rodrigo, *Intervención*, p. 118.
2. Manuel Ros in Moradiellos (ed.), *Las caras de Franco*, p. 129; Preston, *Franco* (Spanish), p. 349; Rodrigo, *Intervención*, p. 115.
3. Tusell, *Franco en la Guerra*, p 262; Rodrigo, *Intervención* p. 127; Manuel Ros in Moradiellos (ed.), *Las caras*, p. 129.
4. Rodrigo, *Intervención*, pp. 115, 118.
5. Rodrigo, *Intervención*, pp. 127, 134; Cantalupo, *Embajada*, pp. 167, 170; Tremlett, *The International Brigades*, p. 337.
6. Stradling, *Brother against Brother*, p. 101; 'Hitler's Hand', p. 16.
7. Richard Rhodes, *Hell and Good Company*, Simon & Schuster, London, 2015, p. 167; De Felice, *Mussolini*, Vol. 5, p. 405.
8. Cantalupo, *Embajada*, pp. 99–100.
9. Tusell, *Franco en la Guerra*, p. 262; Viñas, *Franco, Hitler*, p. 451, 465, 518; Payne. *Franco and Hitler*, p. 46.
10. Moradiellos (ed.), *Las caras de Franco*, p. 152; Tusell, *Franco en la Guerra*, pp. 278–83, 299.
11. Cantalupo, *Embajada*, p. 168, 175, 193, 195; DGFP. Series D, Vol. III p. 261.
12. DGFP. Series D, Vol. II p. 662. Vol III p. 657; Whitaker, *We Cannot Escape History*, p. 111.
13. Cantalupo, *Embajada*, p. 192.
14. Whitaker, *We Cannot Escape History*, p. 111.
15. Beevor, *Battle*, p. 169; Whitaker, *We Cannot Escape History*, p. 114; Alejandro Fernández Pérez, 'Masculinidad Fascista Inspiradora Y Piedra Angular Del Régimen', in *Huellas del Franquismo*, Cuadrado Bolaños (ed.), Editorial Comares, Albolote, 2019, p. 42.
16. Fernández Pérez, 'Masculinidad Fascista', in *del Franquismo*, Cuadrado Bolaños (ed.), p. 42.
17. Cantalupo, *Embajada*, p. 185.
18. Beevor, *Battle*, pp. 357, 362.
19. Domínguez García, R., 'El juramento de José Antonio Aguirre, una toma de posesión en la Guerra Civil' in *Historia y comunicación social* 25(2), 2020, pp. 323–31.
20. Beevor, *Battle*, p. 357; *The Times*, 27 April 1937.
21. Beevor, *Battle*, p. 364; *Liverpool Daily Post*, 14 Jul 1937, p. 9; Franco, *Palabras del Caudillo*, p. 161.
22. DGFP Series D, Vol. 3, p. 410; Cabanellas, *Cuatro Generales*, Vol. 2, pp. 423–5; Serrano Suñer, *Política*, p. 30. Trevor-Roper, *Hitler's Table Talk*, p. 608.
23. Franco Salgado, *Mi vida*, p. 227.
24. Tremlett, *The International Brigades*, p. 443.
25. Beevor, *Battle*, p. 278.
26. Franco Salgado, *Mi vida*, p. 229.
27. Franco Salgado, *Mi vida*, p. 229; Severiano Montero, *La Batalla de Brunete*, Raíces, Madrid, 2010, pp. 70, 131–2, 178.
28. Montero, *Brunete*, pp. 175–97.
29. Tremlett, *The International Brigades*, pp. 446–469, citing Montero, *Brunete*, pp. 199–202.

30　*La Revue Belge*, 15 August 1937: Spanish translation at https://fnff.es/historia/donde-estamos-articulo-publicado-en-la-revue-belge-15-de-agosto-de-17/; Cabanellas, *Cuatro generales*, Vol. 2, p. 428.
31　DGFP. Series D (1937–1945), Vol. III, pp. 557–8, 576–7, 588, 917.
32　Cantalupo, *Embajada*, p. 194.

26 A NEW REGIME

1　Soriano, *La mano*, p. 156.
2　Garriga, *Nicolás*, pp. 59–60, 167, 191, 197; Tusell, *Franco en la Guerra*, pp. 318, 321, 331–3, 351 356, 585; Preston, *Franco* (Spanish), p. 1520; Preston, *Franco* (English), p. 420.
3　Payne, *Falange*, p. 12; Tusell, *Franco en la Guerra*, pp. 334, 356, 361.
4　BOE, 10 March 1938, pp. 6178–81; Tusell. *Franco en la Guerra*, p. 371; Glicerio Sánchez Recio, 'El Sindicato Vertical Como Instrumento Político y Económico del Régimen Franquista', in *Pasado y Memoria*, No. 1, pp. 19–32; Sheelagh Ellwood, *Spanish Fascism in the Franco Era*, Palgrave Macmillan, London, 2014, p. 59; Alejandro Andreassi Cieri, 'Trabajo y Empresa en el Nacionalsindicalismo', in *Fascismo en España*, eds Ferran Gallego Margaleff and Alejandro Andreassi Cieri, pp. 13–42; Sinova, *La censura*, p. 171.
5　Franco, *Palabras del Caudillo*, pp. 51–2, 138; Tusell, *Franco en la Guerra*, pp. 374–5, 359, 587.
6　Tusell, *Franco en la Guerra*, pp. 359, 587.
7　Franco, *Palabras del Caudillo*, p. 140.
8　Francisco Moreno Valero, 'La muerte de una ilusión: el Magisterio español en la Guerra Civil', in *Historia y Comunicación Social*, 2001, No. 6, p. 200; Francisco Moreno Valero, 'La universidad fascista y la universidad franquista', in *Cuadernos del Instituto Antonio de Nebrija*, 8 (2005), pp. 179–214, p. 195; H. R Knickerbocker, *Washington Times*, 10 May 1937, p. 7.
9　Tusell, *Franco en la Guerra*, p. 379.
10　Juan Miguel Batalloso Navas at https://batalloso.com/memoria-personal-de-los-60-8-la-educacion-en-el-franquismo/
11　Cazorla Sánchez, *Franco* (Spanish), p. 236, citing J. Manuel Useros, *El hombre en el paredón*, Bello, Valencia, 1957, pp. 54, 58, 59–61.
12　DGFP Series D, Vol II, pp. 600–1.
13　Tusell, *Franco en la Guerra*, pp. 387–91.
14　Tusell, *Franco en la Guerra*, p. 360; Franco, *Palabras del Caudillo 1936–8*, p. 67. Preston, *Franco* (English), pp. 438–39.
15　Sainz Rodríguez, pp. 327–30; Tusell, *Franco en la Guerra*, pp. 447, 450.
16　BOE, 13 February 1939, 'Ley de 9 de Febrero de 1939 de Responsabilidades Políticas', pp. 824–48; Julián Casanova, ed., *Cuarenta años con Franco*, Crítica, Barcelona, 2015, pp. 53–77.
17　Manuel Álvaro Dueñas, 'Los militares en la represión política de la posguerra: la jurisdicción especial de Responsabilidades Políticas hasta la reforma de 1942', in *Revista de Estudios Políticos*, Universidad Autónoma de Madrid, Madrid, 1990, pp. 141–162.

442   NOTES

18 BOE, 2 March 1940, pp. 1537–9, 'LEY DE 1 DE MARZO DE 1940: Sobre represión de la masonería y del comunismo.'
19 Herbert L. Matthews, 'Franco's Problems', *Foreign Affairs*, 17, 4 (July 1939), p. 725.
20 Preston, *Holocaust*, pp. 472, 475–6.
21 Preston, *Holocaust*, p. 474.
22 Saz in Saz (ed.), *El Franquismo Valenciano*, p. 206.
23 Saz in Saz (ed.), *El Franquismo Valenciano*, p. 207.
24 Fraser, *Tajos*, p. 82.

27 THE THREE DICTATORS

1 Franco Salgado, *Mi vida*. p. 263.
2 Igor Lukes, 'The Czechoslovak Partial Mobilisation in May 1938: A Mystery (almost) Solved', in *Journal of Contemporary History*, Vol. 31/4 1996, pp. 699–720.
3 DGFP, Vol 3, pp. 634–5; '6 April 1938', Ernest Hemingway, *By-line*, Simon & Schuster, New York, 2002, pp. 276–8; Preston, *Franco* (English), pp. 460–62.
4 DGFP, Series D, Vol. III, pp. 744–5; Franco Salgado, *Mi vida*, p. 264; Preston, *Franco* (Spanish), p. 480.
5 DGFP, Series D, Vol. III, pp. 744–5; Ciano, *Diario*, p. 174; Tremlett, *Brigadas*, p. 655.
6 Ciano, *Diario 1937–1943*, p. 175.
7 Reverte, *Ebro*, p. 219; Franco Salgado, *Mi vida*, pp. 263–6.
8 DGFP Series D, Vol. 3, pp. 742, 746–8; Preston, *Franco* (Spanish), pp. 480–2.
9 DGFP Series D, Vol. 3, pp. 746, 749–50, 818; Barbieri, *Hitler's Shadow*, p. 190; Ciano, *Diario*, pp. 191–2; Preston, *Franco* (Spanish), pp. 482–3; Esdaile, *Civil War*, p. 320.
10 DGFP Series D, Vol. 3, p. 760; Ciano, *Diary 1937–1943* pp. 211–2; Preston, *Franco* (Spanish), p. 484.
11 Preston, *Franco* (Spanish), p. 484; Franco Salgado, *Mi vida*, pp. 265–75; Jose Manuel Martínez Bande, *La batalla del Ebro*, Editorial San Martin, Madrid, 1988, pp. 252–268.
12 Preston, *Franco* (English), p. 447; Beevor, *Battle*, p. 358.
13 Michael Seidman, *Republic of Egos,* p. 107, citing Parte, 13 September 1937, ZR, a. 69, l. 1045, c. 17, AGM.
14 Mastrorilli, 'Spanish Civil War', pp. 79–80.
15 Preston, *Franco* (Spanish), p. 487, citing Díaz, *Mi vida*, pp. 17–19, 216–226; Franco, *Nosotros*, pp. 200–13; Giménez Caballero, Memorias, p. 80; Pilar Franco in Gonzalo Herralde's documentary film *Raza, El Espíritu De Franco*.
16 DGFP, Series D, Vol III. p. 851; Beevor, *Battle*, p. 410; Ciano, *Diario*, pp. 253, 275.
17 Ciano, *Diario*, p. 275; DGFP, Series D, Vol. III, pp. 839, 857.
18 DGFP, Series D, Vol. III p. 856; *Time*, 'War in Spain', 6 March 1939; Ciano, *Diario*, p. 275.
19 Preston, *Franco* (Spanish), p. 494; Bolín, *The Vital Years*, p. 324.
20 DGFP, Series D, Vol. III, pp. 880–1, 883–6, 884–6, 889; Preston, *Franco* (Spanish), p. 496.
21 Barbieri, *Hitler's Shadow Empire.*

22 Barbieri, *Hitler's Shadow Empire*, pp. 261, 188; DGFP, Series D, Vol III, pp. 502–3; Preston, *Franco* (Spanish), pp. 444–6.
23 DGFP, Series D, Vol. III, pp. 855–6; Preston, *Franco* (English), pp. 434–35, 502.
24 Beevor, *Battle*, pp. 585–6, 588, 593–6; Luis Romero, *El final de la guerra*, Ariel, Barcelona, 1976, p. 123.
25 Preston, *Holocaust*, p. 474; Preston, *Franco* (Spanish), p. 497.
26 Preston, Franco (Spanish), p. 497; *La Vanguardia*, 2 April 1939, p. 1.
27 Pau Casanellas, 'La defensa del régimen. Cambios y continuidades en la represión franquista más allá de la posguerra' in Damián A. González Madrid y Manuel Ortiz Heras (eds), *Violencia franquista y gestión del pasado traumático*, Sílex, Madrid, 2021.
28 Sandie, 'How did the Spanish Civil War end? Not so well, *The American Historical Review*, Vol. 120, No. 5, pp. 1767–83.

28 VICTORY AND REPRESSION

1 *La Vanguardia*, 20 May 1939, pp. 1–2; *The Times*, May 20, p. 12.
2 Franco Salgado, *Mi vida*, p. 278; *La Vanguardia*, 20 May 1939, pp. 1–3.
3 *The Times*, May 20 1939, p. 12; Pemán, *Encuentros*, p. 90.
4 *La Vanguardia*, 20 May 1939, p. 2; Preston, *Franco* (Spanish), p. 1219; UPI in *Orlando Sentinel*, May 20, 1939, p. 4; AP in *Baltimore Sun*, May 20, p. 4.
5 Zira Box, *La Fundación*, pp. 59, 116.
6 UPI in *Orlando Sentinel*, May 20, 1939, p. 4; AP in *Baltimore Sun*, May 20, p. 4; AP in *Cincinnati Enquirer*, 21 May 1939, p. 11.
7 Payne, *Catholicism*, p. 179; *La Vanguardia*, 21 May 1939, p. 1.
8 Franco Salgado, *Mi vida*, p. 287; Preston, *Palomas*, p. 378; Preston, *Franco* (Spanish), p. 531.
9 Preston, *Palomas*, p. 379.
10 Sinova, *La censura*, pp. 17, 19, 35 247–8.
11 Tusell, *Franco y los católicos*, p. 154.
12 Sinova, *La censura*, p. 169.
13 See Tobias Reckling, *Foreign correspondents in Francoist Spain (1945–1975)*, PhD thesis, University of Portsmouth, March 2016.
14 Zira Box, *La Fundación*, p. 98.
15 Arrarás, *Franco* (English), pp. 69–70.
16 Martín Gaite, *Usos amorosos*, p. 219.
17 *The Times*, May 19, 1939. p. 17.
18 Franco Salgado, *Mi vida*, pp. 279–80; Palacios and Payne, *Franco*, Kindle Loc. 4720.
19 DGFP, Series D, Vol. III, pp. 905–916.
20 DGFP, Series D, Vol. III, pp. 878–9; *La Petit Gironde*, 25 May 1939, p. 2; Franco Salgado, *Mi vida*, p. 295; Preston, *Franco* (Spanish), p. 513.
21 *The Times*, 9 August, 1939, p. 11; 11 August 1939, p. 10.
22 Ciano, *Diarios*, pp. 339–40; BOE 9 August 1939, pp. 4326–7.
23 Ciano, *Diarios*, pp. 339–40, 342–3.

29 THE WORLD AT WAR

1. Franco Salgado, *Mi vida*, p. 280.
2. Franco Salgado, *Mi vida*, pp. 284–5; DGFP, SERIES D, Vol. 8, p. 181.
3. DGFP, SERIES Vol. 8, p. 901; Knox, MacGregor, *Mussolini Unleashed, 1939–1941: Politics and Strategy in Fascist Italy's Last War*, Cambridge University Press, Cambridge, 1986, pp. 41, 44; Neville Wylie, 'Introduction', in *European Neutrals and Non-Belligerents during the Second World War* (Neville Wylie ed.), Cambridge University Press, Cambridge, 2001. p. 4.
4. DDI, Serie 9, Vol. 1, pp. 37, 174; DGFP, SERIES D, Vol. 8, p. 181; Preston, *Franco* (Spanish), pp. 506–7; BOE, 5 September 1939, 'Decreto de 4 de septiembre de 1939'; *La Vanguardia Española*, 2 January 1941, p. 4; Preston, *Franco* (Spanish), pp. 534–535.
5. DDI, Serie 9, Vol. 1 p. 155.
6. DGFP, SERIES D, Vol. 8, p. 100, 225; DDI, Serie 9, Vol 1., pp. 72, 107, 174, 176; Preston, *Franco* (Spanish), p. 529, citing *Arriba*, 5, 7 Oct and 19 November 1939.
7. *La Vanguardia*, 1 Oct 1939, p. 1.
8. Serrano Suñer, *Memorias*, p. 288; DDI, Serie 9, Vol. IV, p. 620.
9. DDI, Serie 9, Vol. V, pp. 6; *La Vanguardia*, 13 June 1940, p. 1; Sir Samuel Hoare, *Ambassador on Special Mission*, Collins, London, 1946, p. 4; Ángel Viñas Martín, *Sobornos: de cómo Churchill y March compraron a los generales de Franco,*, Editoria Critica, Barcelona, 2016, p. 92; Preston, *Franco*, p. 551; Serrano Suñer, *Memorias*, p. 294. British ambassador Samuel Hoare claimed it really signified a state of 'pre-belligerency'.
10. DGFP, Series D, Vol. XI, pp. 585–7; Moradiellos, 'España y la Segundo Guerra mundial 1939–1945. Entre resignaciones neutralistas y tentaciones beligerantes' in *Siglo: actas del V Congreso Internacional de Historia de Nuestro Tiempo*, p. 62; Preston, *Franco* (Spanish), p. 551.
11. DGFP, Series D, Vol. 9, pp. 509–10, 585–7; Franco, *Las cartas*, pp. 114–15.
12. Saña, *Franquismo sin mitos*, p. 164; Serrano Suñer, *Memorias*, pp. 193, 328.
13. Serrano Suñer, *Memorias*, p. 328.
14. *Halder War Diary 1939–1942*, Charles Burdick and Hans Adolf Jacobsen (eds.), Greenhill Books, London, 1988, p. 252; Moradiellos, *España de Franco*, p. 63; Serrano Suñer, *Memorias*, p. 328.
15. DGFP, Series D, Vol 10., pp. 484–6, Vol. XI, p. 63; Franco, *Las cartas*, pp. 117–120.
16. DGFP, Series D, Vol. XI, pp. 106, 153; Moradiellos, *España de Franco*, p. 65.
17. Serrano Suñer, *Memorias*, pp. 331, 335; DGFP Series D, Vol. XI, pp. 62–6, 83–90, 108; Franco, *Las cartas*, pp. 124–9, 137.
18. DGFP Series D, Vol. XI, pp. 106, 100, 118, 153: *The Spanish Government and the Axis: Statement by the Department of State*, released to the press by the Department of State on Mar. 4, 1946. No. 4. 'Notes of a Conversation Between the Fuehrer and the Spanish Minister of the Interior Serrano Suñer in the Presence of the Reichs Foreign Minister in Berlin on September 17, 1940'. Franco was likely misled by apparent promises made by Hitler's ministers in conversations with Serrano Suñer (see DGFP Series D Vol. XI, pp. 100, 118, 153). These promises included: 'the Foreign Minister said that Germany would take Morocco away from France in her peace treaty with that country and give it to Spain, with the exception of the bases of Mogador and Agadir and their hinterland as well as

certain economic reservations, to be determined by friendly agreement, in the form of German participation in the Moroccan sources of raw materials (phosphates, manganese)' (p. 100) and that; The Fuhrer was prepared, in spite of the sacrifice that this would mean for Germany, to supply Spain with grain, gasoline, and several other materials. In addition, he was prepared to use his influence so that by the treaty of peace Morocco would go to Spain' (p. 118).

30 MY FRIEND HITLER

1 *Arriba*, 24 October 1939, p. 1; *The Times*, 24 October 1940, p. 4; Paul Schmidt, *Hitler's Interpreter: The Secret History of German Diplomacy 1935–1945*, Heinemann, London, 1951, p. 194; vvideo at https://www.youtube.com/watch?app=desktop&v=BheYQfVM_EU&ab_channel=LaVanguardia; Saña, *Franquismo sin mitos*, pp. 112, 185, 193.
2 Paul Schmidt, *Hitler's Interpreter*, p. 194: video at https://www.youtube.com/watch?v=DpLUBjsSOWQ&ab_channel=laSexta, https://www.youtube.com/watch?v=BheYQfVM_EU&ab_channel=LaVanguardia
3 Serrano Suñer, *Memorias*, p. 290.
4 *The Times*, 21 October, p. 4.
5 Serrano Suñer. *Memorias*, pp. 293–4.
6 Serrano Suñer, *Memorias*, pp. 295–6; DGFP, SERIES D, Vol. 11, p. 82.
7 Saña, *Franquismo sin mitos*, p. 184.
8 Serrano Suñer, *Memorias*, p. 299.
9 Schmidt, *Hitler's Interpreter*, pp. 194–6.
10 Serrano Suñer, *Memorias*, p. 29.
11 Serrano Suñer, *Memorias*, pp. 298–9.
12 Serrano Suñer, *Memorias*, p. 299.
13 Serrano Suñer, *Memorias* pp. 299–301; Franco interview in *Le Figaro*, 12 June 1958; *ABC*, 23 Oct 2020, 'El relato inédito del "taquígrafo" de Franco en Hendaya: el protocolo secreto de España para entrar en la IIGM' at https://www.abc.es/historia/abci-relato-perdido-gimenez-arnau-taquigrafo-franco-hendaya-decido-contarlo-202010230117_noticia.html
14 Serrano Suñer, *Memorias*, pp. 300–1, 306.
15 Sinova, *La censura*, pp. 173–4; Serrano Suñer, *Memorias*, pp. 300–1, 306; *Arriba*, 24 October 1940, p. 1; *The Times*, 25 October 1940, p. 3.
16 J. Alberto Gómez Roda, *Percepciones de las instituciones y actitudes políticas de la sociedad en la posguerra*, Biblioteca Virtual Miguel de Cervantes, Alicante, 2017, p. 121; *La Vanguardia*, 22 October 1940 p. 2; 23 October 1940, p. 1, 24 October, pp. 1–2, 25 October, p. 3; *The Times*, 25 October 1940, p. Peter Longerich, *Heinrich Himmler: A Life*, Oxford University Press, Oxford, 2011, pp. 504–5, 510.
17 Neal Moses Rosendorf, 'Be El Caudillo's Guest, The Franco Regime's Quest for Rehabilitation and Dollars after World War II via the Promotion of US Tourism to Spain', in *Diplomatic History*, Vol. 30, No. 3 (June 2006), p. 377.
18 *The Times*, 25 October 1940, p. 3; *La Vanguardia*, 2 Jan 1940, p. 3; Preston, *Franco* (Spanish), pp. 534–35, 603; Longerich, *Himmler*, pp. 504–5, 510.

19 Preston, 'Franco y la represión: la venganza del justiciero' in *Novísima: II Congreso Internacional de Historia de Nuestro Tiempo* / coord. por Carlos Navajas Zubeldia, Diego Iturriaga Barco, 2010, p. 59; Boor, *Masonería*, pp. 47, 59–60, 106–8.
20 Schmidt, *Hitler's Interpreter*, p. 196; Halder, *Diary*, Vol 5., p. 4.; Franco, *Las cartas*, pp. 137, 140–1.
21 DGFP, Series D, Vol. XI, pp. 377, 383, 466–7, 479; De Felice, *Mussolini*, Vol. 6, p. 181; Payne, *Franco and Hitler*, p. 93.
22 Preston, *Franco* (Spanish), p. 619; Payne, *Franco and Hitler*, pp. 93, 269; De Felice, *Mussolini*, Vol. 6, p. 181; Viñas, *Sobornos*, pp. 182–192; Donald S. Detwiler, 'Spain and the Axis during World War II' in *The Review of Politics*, Vol. 33, No. 1 (Jan., 1971), pp. 36–53; Antonio Marquinal, 'The Spanish Neutrality during the Second World War', in *American University International Law Review* 14, No. 1 (1998), pp. 171–184; De Felice, *Mussolini*, Vol. 6, p. 181; Payne, *Franco and Hitler*, p. 93; DGFP, SERIES D, Vol. 11, pp. 377, 383 466–7, 479. In telegram No. 3823 of Nov. 11 (18/247), Stöhrer reported that Serrano Suñer had signed the three copies, and that the copies for Germany and Italy were being sent back by special courier.
23 DGFP, Series D, Vol. XI, pp 383; Payne, *Franco and Hitler*, p. 269.
24 Serrano Suñer, *Memorias*, pp. 305–7.
25 Serrano Suñer, *Memorias*, pp. 306–7; DGFP, Series D, Vol. XI p. 82.
26 DGFP, SERIES D, Vol. 11, p. 88, 814–7; Halder *Diary*, Vol. 5, pp. 60–1; Payne, *Franco and Hitler*, p. 103.
27 Téllez Molina Antonio, 'España y la IIª Guerra Mundial: los informes reservados de Carrero Blanco' in *Mélanges de la Casa de Velázquez*, Vol. 29-3, 1993, Epoque contemporaine, pp. 265–5.

31 FAMINE

1 Miguel Angel del Arco Blanco, 'Famine in Spain During Franco's Dictatorship, 1939–52', in *Journal of Contemporary History*, 2021, Vol. 56(1), p. 23–4; DGFP, Series C, Vol. XI, pp. 575, 848; Franco Salgado, *Mi vida*, p. 297.
2 Moradiellos, *España de Franco*, p. 64; *La Vanguardia*, 2 January 1940, p. 3.
3 DGFP, Series C, Vol. XI, pp. 575, 848; Roda, *Varela*, p. 531.
4 Del Arco Blanco, 'Famine in Spain During Franco's Dictatorship, 1939–52', p. 14.
5 Ronald Fraser, *Tajos*, p. 82.
6 DGFP, Series C, Vol. XI, p. 848; *Cosechas, comercio y consumo de trigo*, Servicio Nacional del Trigo (1963), p. c-7-1; Preston et al, *España en crisis*, p. 161.
7 Franco Salgado, *Mi vida*, p. 301; Moradiellos, 'España y la Segundo Guerra mundial 1939–1945', in *Siglo*, p. 59.
8 Josep Fontana, 'La utopía franquista: la economía de Robinson Crusoe' in *Cuadernos de Historia del Derecho*, 103 2004, Vol. Extraordinario, pp. 97–103; Martínez de Pisón, *Filek; el estafador que engañó a Franco*, Seix Barral, Madrid, 2018, pp. 112–3.
9 *La Vanguardia*, 8 Feb 1940, p. 1.
10 Martínez de Pisón, *Filek*, pp. 129, 131.
11 *La Vanguardia*, 8 Feb 1940, p. 1.
12 Martínez de Pisón, *Filek*, pp. 133–5; *La Vanguardia*, 8 Feb 1940, p. 1.

13　Preston, *Franco* (Spanish), pp. 775–77; Charles Foltz, *Masquerade in Spain*, p. 260.
14　Ana Fernández-Cebrián, *Fables of Development: Capitalism and Social Imaginaries in Spain (1950–1967)*, Liverpool University Press, Liverpool, 2023, p. 12; Preston, *Franco* (Spanish), p. 535; Franco, *Discurso leído por el Caudillo a las 10:30 de la noche del día 31 de diciembre de 1939* at http://www.generalisimofranco.com/Discursos/mensajes/00024.htm
15　Fontana, 'La utopía franquista', pp. 97–103; *La Vanguardia*, 2 January 1940, pp. 1–4; Del Arco Blanco, 'Famine in Spain', p. 23.
16　Del Arco Blanco, 'Famine in Spain'.
17　Del Arco Blanco, 'Famine in Spain', pp. 11, 13, 16; Antonio D. Camara, Javier Puche, José Miguel Martínez-Carrión, 'Assessing the effects of autarchic policies on the biological well-being: Analysis of deviations in cohort male height in the Valencian Community (Spain) during Francoist regime' in *Social Science & Medicine*, 273 (2021), p. 5.
18　Gómez Roda, 'Percepciones de las instituciones y actitudes políticas', p. 30; Ellwood, *Spanish Fascism*, p. 81.
19　Gómez Roda, 'Percepciones de las instituciones y actitudes políticas', p. 18; Ingrid Schulze Schneider, 'Josef Goebbels, «historiador» de la guerra civil española', *Historia y Comunicación Social* 2001, No. 6, p. 53.

32 THE RACE

1　Sinova, *Censura*, pp. 174–5; Pilar Franco, minute 2.39 in Gonzalo Herralde's documentary film *Raza, El Espíritu de Franco*.
2　Sinova, *Censura*, pp. 175–6.
3　Pilar Franco in Gonzalo Herralde's documentary film *Raza, El Espíritu de Franco*.
4　*La Vanguardia*, 6 Jan 1942, p. 3.
5　*La Vanguardia*, 6 Jan 1942, p. 3.
6　*La Vanguardia*, 6 Jan 1942, p. 3.
7　Andrade, *Raza*, pp. 41–2; Alejandro Yarza, *The Making and Unmaking of Francoist Kitsch Cinema: From Raza to Pan's Labyrinth*, Edinburgh University Press, Edinburgh, 2018, p. 26.
8　Fraser, *Tajos*, pp. 98–9.
9　Sinova, *Censura*, pp. 260–1; Fernández Pasalodos, A. (2022). '«Se dio la orden de no hacer detenidos». El Ejército rebelde y la dictadura franquista contra los guerrilleros republicanos y la población civil (1936–1952)', in *Historia y Política*, 47, pp. 127–161.
10　Sevillano Calero, *Ecos*, p. 48.
11　Sinova, *Censura*, p. 67.
12　Fatima Gil Gascón, 'Dossier: Censura ao cinema nas ditaduras ibéricas Censurar para evitar el peligro: las censuras cinematográficas durante el franquismo, 1939–1959', in *Ler História* 79 | 2021 Portugal e Espanha: histórias comparadas.

33 THE WRONG SIDE OF HISTORY

1. Franco Salgado, *Mi vida*, pp. 291–3; Ciano, *Diplomatic Papers*, pp. 419–27; DDI, Serie 9, Vol. 6, pp. 582–3, 604; Preston, *Franco* (Spanish), p. 647, citing Tusell y García Queipo de Llano, *Franco y Mussolini*, p. 120.
2. Franco Salgado, *Mi vida*, pp. 291–3.
3. Franco Salgado, *Mi vida*, pp. 291–3. Ciano, *Diplomatic Papers*, pp. 419–27; DDI, Serie 9, Vol. 6, pp. 582–3, 604; Preston, *Franco* (Spanish), p. 648 citing Tusell y García Queipo de Llano, *Franco y Mussolini*, p. 120; Balfour and Preston, *Great Powers*, p. 175.
4. Ciano, *Diplomatic Papers*, pp. 421–8.
5. Franco Salgado, *Mi vida*, pp. 294–5.
6. Ciano, *Diplomatic Papers*, pp. 442–4, 447; Preston, *Franco* (Spanish), pp. 619–22.
7. DGFP, Vol. XII, pp. 1080–1; Preston, *Franco* (Spanish), p. 668.
8. Sinova, *Censura*, pp. 60–1.
9. *The Times*, 26 June 1941, p. 4.
10. *La Vanguardia*, 3 July 1941, p. 1.
11. DGFP, Series D, Vol. XIII, pp. 16–17, 904–5.
12. *La Vanguardia*, 18 July 1941, pp. 4–5.
13. *BOE*, 2 June 1940, 'Otro de 29 de mayo de 1940 por el que se nombra Embajador Extraordinario en los Centenarios de Portugal a don Nicolás Franco Baamonde', p. 3783.
14. Preston, *Franco* (Spanish), p. 674.
15. Jaraiz, *Disidencia*, pp. 58–60.
16. Garriga, *Nicolás*, p. 197.
17. Jaraiz, *Disidencia*. p. 168; *La Vanguardia*, 25 February 1942, p. 1; Preston, *Franco* (Spanish), pp. 695–696, citing Jaraiz Franco, *Disidencia*, pp. 58–60 and 23, *Interviú*, No. 383, 14–20 September 1983.
18. Preston, *Franco* (Spanish), pp. 695–696, citing Jaraiz Franco, *Disidencia*, pp. 58–60, 23, *Interviú*, No. 383, 14–20 September 1983; Pilar Franco in *Raza, El Espíritu de Franco*.
19. BOE No. 288, p. 7987, 'DECRETO de 10 de octubre de 1941 por el que se dispone que los militantes del Partido que sean separados de la Organización, no puedan desempeñar cargos de mando o confianza en el Estado'; BOE, No. 65. p. 1627, 'DECRETO de 31 de diciembre de 1941 por el que se dispone la ejecución de la Ley reorganizadora de la Policía, de 8 de marzo de 1941'; BOE, 8 April 1941, 'Ley de 8 de marzo de 1941 por la que se reorganizan los servicios de Policía', p. 2340; *La Vanguardia*, 18 July 1942, 26 July 1942, p. 2.
20. *La Vanguardia*, 3 August 1942, p. 1, 28 July 1942, p. 1.
21. Sevillano Calero, *Ecos de Papel*, pp. 41, 52–7; Francisco Sevillano Calero, *Dictadura, socialización y conciencia política. Persuasión ideológica y opinión en España bajo el franquismo (1939–1962)*, PhD thesis, p. 410; Preston, *Franco* (English), p. 679.
22. Sevillano Calero, *Dictadura, socialización y conciencia política*, pp. 11–2, 470–1.
23. DGFP, Series D, Vol. XIII, pp. 628–630, 647–648; Herbert Feis, *The Spanish Story: Franco and the Nations at War*, W. W. Norton and Company, New York,

1966, pp. 186–7; Preston, *Franco* (Spanish), pp. 518, 536, 555–6, 672, 675–8, 692, 695, 702–3; Preston, *Franco* (English), pp. 706–7.
24 Hoare, *Ambassador*, p. 240; Preston, *Franco* (Spanish), p. 629.
25 Preston, *Franco* (Spanish), pp. 673–80, 685–6, 689–90, 711.
26 Martínez Roda, *Varela*, p. 540.
27 Martínez Roda, *Varela*, p. 540; Preston, *Franco* (Spanish), pp. 713–14.

34 END OF EMPIRE–AGAIN

1 Hoare, Ambassador, p. 179; Preston, Franco, pp. 725–6; Hayes, *Wartime Mission*, p. 91.
2 Hoare, *Ambassador*, p. 179; Preston, *Franco*, pp. 725–6; Hayes, *Wartime Mission*, p. 91.
3 William Breuer, *Operation Torch*, St Martin's Press, New York, 1986, p. 96; Hansard, FOREIGN AFFAIRS, HC Deb. 24 May 1944, Vol. 400 cc. 762–829.
4 Hoare, *Ambassador*, pp. 197–204; Breuer, *Operation Torch*, pp. 16, 72, 82, 84, 95.
5 Breuer, *Operation Torch*, p. 82, 94, 96, 98.
6 *Churchill and Roosevelt*, Vol. 1, p. 665; Franco, *Las cartas* pp. 91–192; Hayes, *Wartime Mission*, pp. 118–9.
7 *Churchill & Roosevelt*, Vol. 1, p. 298; *The Testament of Hitler, The Hitler-Bormann Documents,* ed. Hugh Trevor-Roper, Cassell, London, 1961, pp. 13, 47–9; Preston, *Franco* (Spanish), p. 729.
8 Franco Salgado, *Mi vida*, p. 303; Preston, *Franco*, p. 676.
9 'The Spanish Government and the Axis: No. 14', *Secret Protocol Between the German and Spanish Governments*, at https://avalon.law.yale.edu/subject_menus/spmenu.asp; Preston, *Franco*, (Spanish) pp. 727–29.
10 Preston, *Franco* (Spanish), pp. 749, 751–2, 754–5, 758, 760, 765–6.
11 Hoare, *Ambassador*, pp. 48–9; Preston, *Franco* (English), p. 729; Preston, *Franco* (Spanish), pp. 775–77.
12 Preston, *Franco* (English), p. 729; *The Fresno Bee*, 3 Nov 1944, p. 4.
13 Sinova, *Censura*, p. 169.
14 Preston, *Franco* (Spanish), p. 787; Hansard FOREIGN AFFAIRS, HC Deb, 24 May 1944, Vol. 400 cc762-829.
15 Hansard, FOREIGN AFFAIRS, HC Deb, 24 May 1944, Vol. 400 cc762–829.
16 Hoare, *Ambassador*, p. 301.
17 Hoare, *Ambassador*, pp. 304–5.
18 *Churchill and Roosevelt*, Vol. 1, p. 86.
19 Serrano Suñer, *Memorias*, p. 308; Payne, *Falange*, p. 241.

35 POST-WAR PARIAH

1 Galinsoga, *Centinela de Occidente*.
2 Hansard, FOREIGN AFFAIRS, HC Deb, 24 May 1944, Vol 400 cc762-829; Preston, *Franco* (Spanish), pp. 739, 743, 753, (English) pp. 618, 686.
3 *La Vanguardia*, 11 May 1945, p. 1; Palacios and Payne, *Franco*, Kindle Loc. 6317.
4 Sainz Rodríguez, *Testimonio*, p. 334.

5   'The Spanish Government and the Axis: No. 14', *Secret Protocol Between the German and Spanish Governments*, at https://avalon.law.yale.edu/subject_menus/spmenu.asp.
6   Palacios and Payne, *Franco*, Kindle Loc. 6209–19, citing D. W. Pike, 'Franco and the Axis Stigma', in *Journal of Contemporary History*, 17: 3, July 1982, pp. 369–407.
7   *La Vanguardia*, 9 May 1945; Palacios and Payne, *Franco*, Kindle Loc. 6361.
8   Palacios and Payne, *Franco*, Kindle Loc. 6414, 6425, 6469; Payne, *Fascism in Spain*, p. 402.
9   Payne, *Falange* p. 247, Palacios and Payne, *Franco*, Kindle Loc. 6425, 6425, 6458; *Pueblo*, 7 Feb 1977, citing interview with Antonio Garrigues Diez-Cañabate in *Ya*, held in Archivo Linz de la Transición española, R-39398.
10 Moradiellos, *España de Franco*, p. 111; Palacios and Payne, *Franco*, Kindle Loc. 6425. See also Gómez Roda, *Percepciones de las instituciones y actitudes políticas*.
11 *La Vanguardia*, 24 December 1949, p. 8, 15 December 1949, p. 10, 15 February 1949, p. 9, 15 August 1948, p. 6, 8 June 1947, p. 1.
12 Palacios and Payne, *Franco*, Kindle Loc. 6589.
13 *La Vanguardia*, 8 June 1947, p. 1; Palacios and Payne, *Franco*, Kindle Loc. 6295; Radcliff, *España contemporánea*, p. 418.
14 Palacios and Payne, *Franco*, Kindle Loc. 6612, 6645–67; Tremlett, *Ghosts*, pp. 56–7.
15 Fernando Romero Pérez, *Campañas de Propaganda en Dictadura y Democracia. Referendos y Elecciones de 1947 a 1978*, PhD thesis, Universidad Nacional de Educación a Distancia, 2009 p. 145, citing *AGA, (3)44/3.519*; Francisco Sevillano. 'El Nuevo Estado y la ilusión de la "Democracia Orgánica". 'El referéndum de 1947 y las elecciones municipales de 1948 en España', in *Historia Contemporánea*, No. 24., p. 371; Preston, *Franco* (English), p. 801; Radcliff, *España contemporánea*, p. 418.
16 Tusell, *La dictadura*, pp. 87–8; Townson, *Modern Spain*, pp. 282, 290, 316; Preston, *Franco* (Spanish), p. 745; Radcliff, *España contemporánea*, p. 417; Palacios and Payne, *Franco*, Kindle Loc. 6425.
17 Palacios and Payne, *Franco*, Kindle Loc. 6469.
18 UN General Assembly, *Relations of Members of the United Nations with Spain*, 12 December 1946, A/RES/39. *The Times*, 11 December 1946, p. 5.
19 Associated Press, 9 December 1946, p. 1); United Nations General Assembly, *Relations of Members of the United Nations with Spain*, 12 December 1946, A/RES/39.
20 *La Vanguardia*, 10 December 1946, pp. 1–3; *The Times*, 10 December, p. 3.
21 *Los sitios de Girona*, 10 December 1946, p. 3.
22 Preston, *Gran manipulador*, pp. 244–5.
23 J. Boor, *Masonería*, p. 3; Franco. *Las cartas*, p. 251.
24 *Cosechas, comercio y consumo de trigo*, p. C-7-1; Preston et al, *España en crisis*, p. 161.
25 Fraser, *Tajos*, p. 82.
26 Raanan Rein, 'Un Salvavidas Para Franco: La Ayuda Económica Argentina a la España Franquista (1946–1949)' in *ANUARIO del IEHS*, VUJ, Tandil, 1993; José Miguel Ruiz Morales, 'El convenio comercial hispano-argentino', in *Revista de estudios políticos*, No. 29–30, 1946, pp. 173–236.

27 Maddison Project, 2023; Palacios and Payne, *Franco*, Kindle Loc. 6535; Preston, *Palomas*, p. 384.
28 Preston, *Franco* (English), p. 870; Palacios and Payne, *Franco*, Kindle Loc. 6535–46.
29 Palacios and Payne, *Franco*, Kindle Loc. 6546–57; Payne, *Christianity*, p. 181.
30 Preston, *Palomas*, p. 384; Franco, *Las cartas*, p. 305.
31 Palacios and Payne, *Franco* (English), p. 300; Payne, *Catholicism*, p. 181.

36 GREAT POISONS

1 *Diari Oficial de la Generalitat de Catalunya*, No. 9, 9 January 1937, 'Decreto de regulación de la interrupción artificial del embarazo'; Patricia Gonzalez Prado, *Aborto y la autonomía sexual de las mujeres*, p. 136; *Sur*, 6 October 1938, 'Palabras del caudillo a una comisión de enfermeras de primera línea'.
2 Preston, *Palomas*, p. 407; Pozuelo, *días*, p. 86.
3 Preston, *Palomas*, p. 356; Enríquez, *Carmen Polo*, p. 94; Franco, *Discursos y mensajes de S.E. el jefe del Estado a las Cortes españolas 1943–1961*, p. 30.
4 BOE No. 500, 5 March 1938, 'Suspensión de pleitos de separación y divorcio'; BOE, No. 301, 23 October 1939, 'Ley de 26 de octubre de 1939 sobre procedimientos para el ejercicio de derechos y acciones derivados de la Ley derogatoria de la de Divorcio'; José María Rives Gilabert, Antonio Pablo Rives Seva, 'Evolucion histórica del sistema matrimonial español' in *Noticias Juridicas*, 21 December 2001; *La Vanguardia*, 12 June 1942, p. 7; Payne, *Catholicism*, p. 179; Florentina Rodrigo Paredes, 'El Regreso A La Tradición Durante El Primer Franquismo: La Mujer, La "Gran Olvidada" De La Normativa Legal' in *Las Huellas del Franquismo*, p. 39.
5 Rafael Huertas, 'La Psicobiologia del Marxismo como categoría antropológica en el ideario fascista español', in *Llull*, Vol. 19, 1996, pp. 116, 122, 124.
6 Huertas, 'Psicbiologia del Marxismo', p. 129.
7 Huertas, 'Psicbiologia del Marxismo', p. 129.
8 *El Periódico de Aragón*, 12 April 2014, available at https://www.elperiodicodearagon.com/opinion/2014/04/12/homenaje-fray-gumersindo-estella-47307777.html
9 Preston, *Holocaust*, pp. 471–2, 505.
10 Fernando Neira, 'Quince años sin Mari Trini', *El País*, 7 July 2024; Martin Gaite, *Usos amorosos*, pp. 14–15; Hooper, *New Spaniards*, pp. 126–7.
11 Payne, *Catholicism*, p. 183.
12 Martínez Roda, *Varela*, p. 528; Payne, *Catholicism*, pp. 171, 182, 185; 'Prólogo', e Josep Fontana, *Una inmensa prisión*, eds Molinero et al, p. xiii.
13 Martin Gaite, *Usos amorosos* p. 56.
14 Martin Gaite, *Usos amorosos* pp. 52–4, 66 citing *Primer Consejo Nacional del S.E.M.* (Servicio Español de Magisterio), Afrodisio Aguado, Madrid, February 1943, p. 72, and *Medina*, 25 April 1943; Dionisio Ridruejo, *Casi*, pp. 52, 103; *Revista Para La Mujer*, June 1939, p. 22.
15 Giménez Caballero, *Memorias de un dictador*, p. 149. Martin Gaite, *Usos amorosos*, citing Pilar Primo de Rivera, V Consejo Nacional de la SF, NASA, Serie Azul, Carpeta 1A, doc. 5 20.11.

16 Martin Gaite, *Usos amorosos*, pp. 35–6, citing *Medina*, 'Consúltame', 3 September 1944, and p. 46 citing *Medina*, 'Consúltame', 13 June 1943; *Medina*, 69, 12 July 1942.
17 Payne, *Catholicism*, pp. 172, 181–2; See also Sonlleva-Velasco, M. and Torrego-Egido, L. (2018), 'A mí no me daban besos. Infancia y educación de la masculinidad en la posguerra Española', in *Masculinities and Social Change*, 7(1).
18 Sonlleva-Velasco, M. and Torrego-Egido, L., 'A mí no me daban besos'; Martin Gaite, *Usos amorosos*, p. 15, citing BOE, 8 March 1938.
19 Joan Domke, *Education, Fascism, and the Catholic Church in Franco's Spain*, PhD thesis 2011, Loyola University Chicago, citing Redondo, pp. 522–23; Preston, *Palomas*, p. 380.
20 Ernesto Giménez Caballero, *España nuestra*, pp. 23, 149; Inmaculada Blasco Herranz, 'Género y nación durante el franquismo', in *Imaginarios y representaciones de España durante el franquismo*, eds Stéphane Michonneau et Xosé M. Núñez-Seixas, Casa de Velázquez, Madrid, 2014. See also A. Serrano, *Yo soy Español*, Editorial Escuela Española, Madrid, 1962.
21 Tremlett, *Ghosts*, p. 213.
22 Martin Gaite, *Usos amorosos*, p. 252; Hooper, *New Spaniards*, p. 126.
23 Boor, *Masonería*, pp. 5, 52.

37 THE SLEEPER PRINCE

1 Palacios and Payne, *Franco*, Kindle Loc. 6711; Preston, *Juan Carlos* (Spanish) p. 531.
2 Preston, *Franco* (Spanish), p. 876.
3 *El Pais*, 23 Mayo 1976, 'Franco y don Juan se entrevistan en el "Azor"'; Preston, *Franco* (Spanish), p. 876.
4 *Observer*, 10 October 1948, p. 1.
5 Palacios and Payne, *Franco*, Kindle Locs 6758, 6723.
6 José María Gil-Robles, *La monarquía por la que yo luché: Páginas de un diario, 1941–1954*, Taurus, Madrid, 1976, p. 276.
7 Palacios and Payne, *Franco*, Kindle Locs 6792, 6803, citing 'Entrevista con H. V. Kaltenborn', 24 March 1949, Archivo de Franco, 130: 103.
8 Boor, *Masonería*, p. 51.
9 Boor, *Masonería*, pp. 7, 51, 152.
10 Palacios and Payne, *Franco* (Spanish), Kindle Locs 6922, 13459.
11 *La Vanguardia*, 11 April 1950, 12 April 1950.
12 *La Vanguardia*, 11 April 1950, 12 April 1950; Preston, *People Betrayed*, p. 388; Preston, *Palomas*, p. 385.
13 Palacios and Payne, *Franco* (Spanish), Kindle Loc. 6878; Preston, *Franco* (English), p. 853.
14 Palacios and Payne, *Franco* (Spanish), Kindle Loc. 6890; *Spanish Economic Growth, 1850–2015*, p. 42., via Fundación Rafael del Pino, Series macroeconómicas históricas at https://frdelpino.es/investigacion/category/01_ciencias-sociales/01_economia-espanola/02_economia-espanola-perspectiva-historica/
15 Tremlett, *Ghosts*, p. 69.

16 Tremlett, *Ghosts*, p. xvii.
17 Joan Adria in *E El Franquismo en Valencia: Formas de vida y actitudes sociales en la posguerra*, Saz y Gómez Roda, (eds.), Episteme, Barcelona, 1999, pp. 144–5.
18 Preston, *Franco* (English), p. 1105.
19 Pemán, *Encuentros*, p. 9; Giménez Caballero, *Memorias de un dictador*, p. 292.
20 Franco Salgado, *Mis conversaciones*, pp. 48, 164, 173.
21 Franco Salgado, *Mis conversaciones*, p. 48; Tremlett, *Ghosts*, p. 56.
22 Jaraiz, *Disidencia*, pp. 162–4, 174.
23 Franco Salgado, *Mis conversaciones*, pp. 143–4, 148–9.
24 Franco Salgado, *Mis conversaciones*, p. 23.
25 Garriga, *Nicolás*, pp. 187, 281–3.
26 Franco Salgado, *Mis conversaciones*, p. 195; Jaraiz Franco, *Disidencia*, p. 41.
27 Franco Salgado, *Mis conversaciones*, pp. 11–2, 47–8, 125, 159.
28 Ignacio Martínez de Pisón, *Filek*, p. 131; Enríquez, *Carmen Polo*, p. 30; *La Vanguardia*, 3 May 1960, p. 5; BOE, 6 October 1942; BOE, 1 February 1938; BOE 2 April 1943; *Informaciones*, 5 Oct 1942, p. 3.
29 *La Vanguardia*, 11 April 1950, 12 April 1950; Preston, *People Betrayed*, p. 389, citing Carlos Collado Seidel, *España, refugio nazi*, pp. 184–5, 203–4.
30 Franco-Salgado, *Mis conversaciones*, pp. 127, 394–5; Crozier, *Franco*, p. 45; Preston, *Palomas*, p. 406 citing Jaraiz Franco, *Disidencia*, pp. 162–66, 174, 387.
31 Fraga, *Memoria breve*, p. 99.
32 Franco Salgado, *Mis conversaciones*, pp. 126, 270–1.
33 Franco Salgado, *Mis conversaciones*, pp. 126, 131–2.
34 *Le Figaro*, 12 June 1958.
35 Payne and Palacios, *Franco, mi padre*, Kindle Loc. 5984.
36 See V. S. Pritchett, *The Spanish Temper*, Chatto & Windus, London, 1954.

38 THE GREY FIFTIES

1 *Baleares*, 24 October 1954, p. 1; Wayne H. Bowen, *Truman, Franco's Spain and the Cold War*, University of Missouri Press, Columbia, 2017, p. 153; Luis E. Togores, *Muñoz Grandes, héroe de Marruecos, general de la División Azul*, Esfera, Madrid, 2014, Kindle Locs 4528–29, 4581–85, 6718–21.
2 Togores, *Muñoz Grandes*, Kindle Locs 244–47, 4109–11, 4430–33, 4528–29, 4581–85.
3 *La Vanguardia Española*, 1 April 1954, pp. 1–3.
4 Pablo del Hierro, 'The End of the Affair: The International Dispute over the Deportation of Degrelle from Spain to Belgium, 1945–1946' in *The International History Review* 2021, Vol. 43, No. 4, 761–80; *La Vanguardia*, 16 December 1954, p. 10; Palacios and Payne, *Franco*, Kindle Loc. 7008.
5 Togores, *Muñoz Grandes*, Kindle Locs 6629–38.
6 *La Vanguardia*, 22 October 1954, p. 3: Associated Press report in *Arizona Daily Star*, 11 Oct 1954, p. 6.
7 *La Vanguardia*, 27 Sept 1953, pp. 1–4; Preston, *Franco* (English), p. 872.
8 Viñas, Ángel, *Los pactos secretos de Franco con Estados Unidos: bases, ayuda económica, recortes de soberanía*, Grijalbo, Barcelona, 1981, p. 27; Fundación Rafael del Pino, *Series macroeconómicas históricas*; *Project Database*.
9 *La Vanguardia*, 2 November 1955; Palacios and Payne, *Franco*, Kindle Loc. 7116.

10 'Declaraciones de S. E. a Manuel Aznar', 31 December 1938, available at http://www.generalisimofranco.com/Discursos/prensa/00036.htm; Franco, *Palabras 1937 a 1938*, p. 314; Preston, *Franco*, Kindle Loc. 483; Palacios and Payne, *Franco*, Kindle Locs 7148, 7386.
11 Preston, *Franco* (English), p. 871.
12 See Pritchett, *The Spanish Temper.*
13 J. Bandrés, 'Las encuestas universitarias de José Luis Pinillos: un episodio en la pugna por la orientación sociopolítica del franquismo', in *Revista de Historia de la Psicología*, 41(1), pp. 12–28; Helio Carpintero, 'Psicología y Política en España: La Encuesta de Pinillos de 1955', in *Psychologia Latina* 2010, Vol. 1 No. 2, pp. 88–96; Lafuente, E., 'Las Memorias de José Luis Pinillos. Un documento para la Historia de la Psicología en España', in *Revista de Historia de la Psicología*, 41(3), pp. 23–32; *New York Times*, 4 January 1956, pp. 1, 3.
14 Mercedes Cabrera, 'El arte del derecho: Una biografía de Rodrigo Uría Meruéndano Sergio Rodríguez Tejada', in *Zonas de libertad (Vol. I): Dictadura franquista y movimiento estudiantil*, pp. 247–8.
15 Mercedes Cabrera, 'El arte del derecho', pp. 247–8; Preston, *Franco* (English), pp. 910–11.
16 Jesús M. Zaratiegui, 'El Falangismo en Crisis con la Crisis de Febrero de 1956', in *Falange, las culturas políticas del fascismo en la España de Franco (1936–1975)*, ed. Miguel Angel Ruiz Carnicer, Vol. 2, 2013, p. 619.
17 Franco Salgado, *Mis conversaciones*, pp. 130, 190; Palacios and Payne, *Franco*, Kindle Loc. 7180.
18 *La Vanguardia*, 1 May 1956, pp. 1–4; Zaratiegui, 'El Falangismo En Crisis' pp. 609–27.
19 Palacios and Payne, *Franco*, Kindle Loc. 7256; Preston, *Franco* (English), pp. 927–9; Zaratiegui, 'El Falangismo En Crisis', p. 623.
20 Zaratiegui, 'El Falangismo En Crisis', pp. 624, 627.
21 Palacios and Payne, *Franco*, Kindle Locs 7321–40.
22 Palacios and Payne, *Franco*, Kindle Loc. 7453.
23 *The Times*, July 20, 1959, p. 5; Navarro Rubio, 'La batalla de la estabilización', pp. 196–9; Navarro Rubio, *Mis memorias: testimonio de una vida politica truncada por el 'Caso Matesa'*, Cambio 16, Barcelona, 1991, pp. 124–6; Rafael Calvo Serer, *Franco frente al Rey*, Ruedo ibérico, Madrid, 1972, p. 79; Preston, *Franco* (English), pp. 949–50. See also figures at https://www.inflation.eu/es/tasas-de-inflacion/ipc-inflacion-1958.aspx, https://www.inflation.eu/es/tasas-de-inflacion/ipc-inflacion-1957.aspx and https://frdelpino.es/investigacion/category/01_ciencias-sociales/01_economia-espanola/02_economia-espanola-perspectiva-historica/.
24 *The Times*, July 21 1959, p. 5; *New York Times*. 18 July 1959, p. 2.
25 IMF, *Annual report for year ended April 30, 1959*, p. 117.
26 IMF, *Annual report for year ended April 30, 1960*, pp. 16–17. Maddison Project Database 2023.
27 See https://elvalledecuelgamuros.gob.es/es/cronologia/inauguracion-del-valle-de-los-caidos
28 Preston, *Franco* (Spanish), p. 541.

29 See http://www.generalisimofranco.com/Discursos/discursos/1959/00003.htm, https://fnff.es/historia/los-presos-politicos-del-valle-de-los-caidos-por-pablo-linares/
30 *La Vanguardia*, 22 December 1959, p. 1; see also https://fnff.es/historia/pio-xii-juan-xxiii-y-el-valle-de-los-caidos-por-pablo-linares/; Franco Salgado, *Mis conversaciones*, p. 274.
31 Vernon A. Walters, *The Mighty and the Meek*, St Ermin's Press, London, 2001, p. 130.
32 Franco Salgado, *Mis conversaciones*, pp. 173, 179.

39 TAKE-OFF

1 *Sydney Morning Herald*, 1 Nov 1959, p. 21.
2 Carlos Salinas Salinas, *Pedro Zaragoza Orts, Alcalde franquista y desarollista de Benidorm, 1951–1967*, PhD thesis, University of Alicante, pp. 281–3, 286.
3 Monica Moreno Seco, *La Diócesis de Orhuela-Alicante en el franquismo: 1939–1975*, PhD thesis, University of Alicante, 1997, p. 204.
4 Fraga, *Memoria Breve*, pp. 136, 144; *New York Times*, 9 August 1969, O. 24; Salinas, *Zaragoza Orts*, p. 286.
5 Erik Swyngedouw, *Liquid Power: Contested Hydro-Modernities in Twentieth-Century Spain*, MIT Press Boston, 2023, pp. 100–15.
6 Mateo Federico Frías Gonzalez, *La otra sombra de Volkswagen*, available at https://reader.digitalbooks.pro/book/preview/50412/id217
7 *La Vanguardia*, 30 April 1960; Palacios and Payne, *Franco*, p. 534.
8 *La Vanguardia*, 18 May 2020, p. 15; *El Periódico*, 15 April 2013, 'Las octavillas de Pujol'; *La Vanguardia*, 15 November 2007, 'Pujol relata en sus "Memòries" la tortura a la que fue sometido'.
9 *New York Times*, 2 June 1960, p. 9.
10 Franco Salgado, *Mis conversaciones*, p. 288.
11 Franco Salgado *Mi vida, p.* 345.
12 Benjamin Welles, *Spain: The Gentle Anarchy*, Pall Mall, London, 1965, pp. 84–6.
13 Palacios and Payne, *Franco*, Kindle Locs 8198 and 13646.
14 Garriga, *Nicolás*, pp. 189, 229; Franco Salgado, *Mis conversaciones*, pp. 40–2, 178–182, 294–5.
15 Sainz Rodríguez, *Testimonio*, pp. 334-5.
16 Welles, *Gentle Anarchy*, p. 45.
17 Franco Salgado, *Mis conversaciones*, pp. 389–94.
18 Franco Salgado, *Mis conversaciones*, pp. 389–94.
19 *Le Figaro*, 12 June 1958;. Welles, *Gentle Anarchy*, p. 186.
20 Tremlett, *Ghosts*, p. 75.
21 *New York Times*, 25 Jan 1969, p. 12. See https://www.eldiario.es/comunitat-valenciana/eldiario-de-la-cultura/25-anos-paz-franco-maniobra-inteligente-manuel-fraga-mentira-gigante_132_8974669.html
22 *New York Times*, 17 June 1962, p. 143.
23 *New York Times*, 23 Aug 1962, p. 143; Preston, *Franco* (English), p. 992.
24 *New York Times*,23 Aug 1962 p. 143.
25 Fraga, *Memoria breve*, p. 100.

26 *The Times*, 19 April 1963, p. 12; Armando Recio García, 'La prensa jurídica en el tardofranquismo: el Proceso 1001' in *Revista Historia y Comunicación Social* 2007, 12, p. 179.
27 *The Times*, 20 April 1963, p. 8; Franco Salgado, *Mis conversaciones*, pp. 378–82.
28 *The Times*, 20 April 1963, p. 8; Franco Salgado, *Mis conversaciones*, pp. 378–82.
29 *New York Times*, 3 March 1974, p. 1; *The Times*, 19 August 1963, p. 7; *La Vanguardia*, 18 August 1963, p. 9.
30 Fraga, *Memoria breve*, p. 107; López Rodó, *Memorias*, pp. 458–9; Preston, *Franco* (English), pp. 1008, 1305. See https://www.eldiario.es/comunitat-valenciana/eldiario-de-la-cultura/25-anos-paz-franco-maniobra-inteligente-manuel-fraga-mentira-gigante_132_8974669.html
31 Tremlett, *Ghosts*, p. 57.
32 Fraga, *Memoria breve*, p. 115, 120; Welles, *Gentle Anarchy*, p. 13.

40 CHANGE

1 Welles, *Gentle Anarchy*, pp. 30, 37.
2 Townson, *Modern Spain*, pp. 312–3.
3 Sebastian Balfour, *Dictatorship, Workers and the City: Labour in Greater Barcelona Since 1939*, Clarendon Press, Oxford, 1989, p. 148.
4 Fraga, *Memoria breve*, pp. 110–3, 128–135.
5 Rafael Escobedo Romero, 'Los Protestantes Españoles, El Franquismo y La Política Exterior Estadounidense, A Través De Las Páginas De *The Christian Century* (1947–1951)' in *Historia Actual Online*, 43 (2), 2017, pp. 105–116; Fraga, *Memoria breve*, p. 159; Salinas Salinas, *Pedro Zaragoza Orts*, citing Daniel Vega, *Costumbres nuevos y pecados viejos*, 1959, pp. 7, 51, 70–1.
6 Fraga, *Memoria breve*, pp. 116–17, 142, 147, 159.
7 See figures at https://datosmacro.expansion.com/demografia/estructura-poblacion/espana?anio=1965 (49.42 percent under 30) and https://datosmacro.expansion.com/demografia/estructura-poblacion/espana?anio=1965 (62.65 percent under 40).
8 Fraga, *Memoria breve*, p. 167.
9 BOE 67, 19 March 1966, 'Ley 14/1966, de 18 de marzo, de Prensa e Imprenta', pp. 3310–15; Fraga, *Memoria breve*, p. 159. See https://www.eldiario.es/politica/martinez-soler-transicion-hubo-generosidad-miedo_128_9112853.html
10 Fraga, *Memoria breve*, pp. 166–172. See https://www.larazon.es/espana/franco-ordeno-el-secuestro-de-abc-por-un-articulo-de-anson-GK13192026/
11 See https://www.larazon.es/espana/franco-ordeno-el-secuestro-de-abc-por-un-articulo-de-anson-GK13192026; *Time*, 21 Jan 1961; Franco Salgado, *Mis conversaciones*, p. 479.
12 Fraga, *Memoria breve*, p. 183; BOE No. 95, 21 April 1967, pp. 5250–5272, 'Decreto 779/1967, de 20 de abril, por el que se aprueban los textos refundidos de las Leyes Fundamentales del Reino'
13 Romero Pérez, *Campañas*, p. 266; Preston, *Franco* (Spanish), p. 1101–2; Payne and Palacios, *Franco*, Kindle Loc. 8978.
14 Fraga, *Memoria breve*, p. 181; Romero Pérez, *Campañas*, p. 266.

15 *New York Times*, 2 December 1966; *La Vanguardia*, 13 Dec 1966 pp. 4–5. See https://www.youtube.com/watch?v=OKFG3TgjKyM&ab_channel=PatriaTelevisi%C3%B3n
16 Romero Pérez, *Campañas*, pp. 287–95.
17 Romero Pérez, *Campañas*, pp. 287–95.
18 Fraga, *Memoria breve*, p. 181, 187–8; Franco Salgado, *Mis conversaciones*, p. 489.
19 Joan J. Adrià, 'Los Factores De Producción Del Consentimiento Politico En El Primer Franquismo En Valencia' in *El franquismo en Valencia*.
20 Fraga, *Memoria breve*, p. 214.
21 *The Times*, 30 October 1970, p. 10.
22 *Amnesty International Annual Report 1969–1970*, p. 13, and *Amnesty International Annual Report, 1970–1971*, pp. 57–8; Franco Salgado, *Mis conversaciones*, 23 March 1968.
23 *La Vanguardia*, 3 August 1968, p. 5, 3 August 1968, p. 8; *The Times*, 6 August 1968, p. 4.
24 Palacios and Payne, *Franco*, Kindle Loc. 10755; Preston, *Franco*, p. 1129; *The Times*, 27 January 1969, p. 1; Preston, *Palomas*, p. 399.
25 Fraga, *Memoria breve*, p. 214.

41 LOST YEARS

1 Ronald Fraser, *In Hiding: The Life of Manuel Cortes*, Allen Lane, London, 1972, pp. 5, 7, 22.
2 *The Times*, 2 April 1969, p. 4; *La Vanguardia*, 2 April 1969.
3 Fraga, *Memoria breve*, p. 243; *La Vanguardia*, 8 January 1969, p. 4; *The Times*, 15 Jan 1969, p. 5.
4 *New York Times*, 23 July 1969, p. 16; *The Times*, 23 July 1969, p. 6.
5 *La Vanguardia*, 23 July 1969, p. 6, 24 July p. 6; *New York Times*, 23 July 1969, pp. 1, 16. See https://datosclima.es/Aemethistorico/Meteosingleday.php
6 *La Vanguardia*, 24 July 1969, pp. 1–7; *New York Times*, 23 July 1969, p. 16; Payne, *Fascism in Spain*, p. 451; *The Times*, 23 July 1969, p. 6; Fernández-Miranda, 'El Movimiento como fundamento doctrinal y la organización política del régimen español', in *El hombre y la sociedad*, p. 162.
7 *New York Times*, 9 August 1969, p. 24.
8 Translation from Richard Eder *New York Times*, 29 May 1970 p. 12.
9 Translation from Richard Eder *New York Times*, 29 May 1970 p. 12.
10 Javier Muñoz Soro, 'Entre la memoria y la reconciliación. El recuerdo de la República y la guerra en la generación de 1968', in *Historia del Presente*, p. 83.
11 *The Times*, 12 October 1970, p. 4, 17 September 1970, p. 10; *La Vanguardia*, 25 July 1970, p. 3; Fraga, *Memoria breve* p. 268; Preston, *Palomas*, pp. 401, 419.
12 Preston, *Palomas*, pp. 401, 419.
13 *FOESSA Informe sociologico 1970*: see https://www.publico.es/politica/estudio-1970-muestra-20-espanoles.html; Payne in *Spain in the 1970s: economics, social structure and foreign policy*, William T. Salisbury and James Daniel Theberge (eds), Praeger, New York, 1978, pp. 88–90.
14 *The Times*, 17 September 1970.

15 *The Times*, 17 September 1970. See Fraga, *Memorias*, on Southworth and Franco Salgado, and *Conversaciones*, on Thomas.
16 Francisco Franco, *Las cartas*, p. 241; *El Pais*, 1 July 1976. Available at https://elpais.com/diario/1976/07/01/sociedad/205020008_850215.html. See also https://www.libertaddigital.com/fotos/luismiguel-marivi-1001385/ and https://www.lecturas.com/blogs/pilar-eyre/asi-era-marivi-dominguin-mujer-a-que-miguel-bose-mas-odia_110889; *Vanity Fair España*, 23 November 2023, at https://www.revistavanityfair.es/articulos/marivi-dominguin-amante-primo-luis-miguel-dominguin.
17 *The Times*, 3 October 1970, p. 3. *New York Times*, 3 Oct 1970 p. 1.
18 Vernon Walters, *Mighty and Meek*, pp. 131–2.
19 *The Times*, 26 November 1970, p. 5, 28 November 1970, p. 3.
20 *The Times*, 28 November 1970, pp. 3, 5 December 1970, pp. 1, 7 December 1970, p. 1, 15 December 1970, p. 4.

42 ¡VIVA FRANCO!

1 Franco Salgado, *Mis conversaciones*, p. 559.
2 Franco Salgado, *Mis conversaciones*, p. 559; *The Times*, 17 December 1970.
3 *La Vanguardia,* 18 December 1970 pp. 1–4; *Filmoteca española* available at https://www.youtube.com/watch?v=O-bFarZU-6w&ab_channel=LaEspa%C3%B1adelGeneral%C3%ADsimoFranco; Preston, *Palomas*, p. 402.
4 *The Times*, 29 December 1970. p. 1.
5 Miguel Angel Aguilar, cited in Tobias Reckling, *Correspondents*, p. 226.
6 *The Times*, 4 January 1971, p. 4, 13 January 1971, p. 4, 30 October 1970, p. 10.
7 Walters, *Silent Missions*, Doubleday, New York, 1978, pp. 551–7; Palacios and Payne, *Franco*, p. 534.
8 Walters, *Silent Missions*, pp. 551–7.
9 *The Times*, 2 April 1971, p. 6, 3 May 1971, p. 4, 23 February 1971, p. 4; *New York Times*, 7 March 1971.
10 *The Times*, 29 April 1971, p. 7; *New York Times*, 2 October 1972.
11 *The Times*, 17 July 1971, p. 4, 19 July 1971, p. 4, 20 August 1971, p. 4.
12 *New York Times*, 17 September 1971.
13 *The Times*, 30 October 1971, p. 4, 18 October 1971, p. 4.
14 *The Times*, 16 November 1971, p. 7; 19 November 1971, p. 7; *New York Times*, 2 October 1972, p. 8, 5 December 1971, p. 2.
15 *New York Times*, 5 December 1971, p. 2; *La Vanguardia*, 19 November 1971 pp. 3–5.
16 *New York Times*, 2 Oct 1971, 5 December 1971, p. 2.
17 *The Times*, 31 December 1971, p. 4; 1 December 1971, p. 6.
18 *The Times*, 31 December 1971, p. 4;1 December 1971, p. 6.
19 *New York Times,* 27 August 1972, pp. 111, 305, 334–45; Jaraiz Franco, *Disidencia*, p. 139.
20 Jaraiz Franco, *Disidencia*, p. 205.
21 *New York Times*, 9 June 1973, p. 6, 5 December 1972, p. 2, 27 August 1972, pp. 111, 305, 334–45.
22 *New York Times*, 27 August 1972, pp. 111, 305, 334–45.
23 Preston, *Palomas*, p. 406.

24 *La Vanguardia*, 30 August 1972, p. 6; *New York Times*, 24 September 1972, p. 2; *Público*, 1 September 2022: see https://www.publico.es/politica/garantizo-impunidad-guardias-civiles-franquistas-ejecutaron-jovenes-lekeitio.html
25 *New York Times*, 21 January 1973, p. 8; Suárez Fernández, *Franco*, Vol. 6, p. 678.
26 *New York Times*, 5 December 1972, p. 2; Preston, *Palomas*, p. 398; *New York Times*, 27 August 1972, pp. 111, 305, 334–45, 27 August 1973, p. 9, Preston, *Juan Carlos*, pp. 162–3.
27 Preston, *Palomas*, p. 407.
28 Preston, *Juan Carlos*, pp. 162–3.
29 *New York Times*, 4 November 1973, p. 2, 14 November 1973, p. 3.
30 Tobias Reckling, *Correspondents,* pp. 215–6; *New York Times*, 21 November 1973, p. 2.
31 *New York Times*, 9 June 1973, p. 6, 10 June 1973, p. 220, 12 June 1973, p. 7, 17 September 1973, p. 15.

43 OPERATION OGRE

1 José Luis Alcocer, *Fernández-Miranda, Agonía de un Estado*, Planeta, Barcelona, 1986, p. 40.
2 *El País*, 13 December 2013, 'El cráter del régimen'.
3 Alcocer, *Fernández-Miranda*, p. 62; *New York Times*, 21 December 1973, p. 1; *El País*, 13 Dec 2013, 'El cráter del régimen'.
4 *La Vanguardia*, 21 December 1973, p. 5; *New York Times*, December 21, 1973, p. 1, 23 December 1973, p. 3.
5 *La Vanguardia*, 21 December 1973, p. 5, 20 December 1973, p. 9.
6 *La Vanguardia*, 20 December 1973, p. 9.
7 *New York Times*, 21 December 1973, p. 1, 22 December 1973, p. 3.
8 *New York Times*, 23 December 1973, p. 3; *La Vanguardia*, 23 Dec 1973, pp. 5–6.
9 *La Vanguardia*, 1 January 1974, p. 5.
10 *La Vanguardia*, 1 January 1974, pp. 5, 31; *New York Times*, 5 January 1974, p. 9; Recio García, 'La prensa jurídica', p. 181.
11 *New York Times*, 10 January 1974, p. 7, 3 March 1974, p. 1, 7 March 1974, p. 2.
12 *New York Times*, 7 March 1974, pp. 2, 14, 7 March 1974, p. 2.
13 *New York Times*, 11 May 1974, p. 6, 16 June 1974, p. 7.
14 Julián Casanova, *Cuarenta años con Franco*, Editorial Crítica, Barcelona, 2015, p. 170,; Preston, *Juan Carlos I* (Spanish), p. 361; *New York Times*, 10 July 1974, p. 2.

44 HE LISTENS BUT DOES NOT HEAR

1 Fraga, *Memoria breve*, p. 330; Preston (Spanish), p. 1158; Gil, *40 años*, p. 170.
2 Casanova, *40 años*, pp. 170, 180.
3 Casanova, *40 años*, p. 184; *New York Times*, 20 July 1974, p. 65; Preston, *Juan Carlos I* (Spanish), p. 361.
4 Casanova, *40 años*, pp. 189–90. *New York Times*, 20 July 1974, p. 65.
5 Casanova, *40 años*, p. 194.
6 Casanova, *40 años* p. 192, 197; Preston, *Franco*, p. 1159.

7 Pozuelo, *476 días*, p. 38, 46; Jaime Peñafiel Núñez, *El General y su tropa: mis recuerdos de la familia Franco*, Temas de Hoy, Madrid, 1992, p. 158; *New York Times*, 2 September 1974, p. 2.
8 Pozuelo *476 días*, p. 30; Preston, *Palomas*, p. 419; *New York Times*, 10 September 1974, p. 13, 3 September 1974, p. 13; 22 September 1974, p. 204.
9 *New York Times*, 22 September 1974, p. 204.
10 *New York Times*, 30 October 1974, p. 3, 3 November 1974, p. 18.
11 *New York Times*, 22 December 1974, p. 4.
12 *New York Times*, 22 December 1974, p. 4, 14 January 1975, p. 29.
13 *New York Times*, 17 November 1974, p. 245.
14 *New York Times*, 4 December 1974, p. 3.
15 Gerardo Landrove Díaz?, *Política Criminal del Aborto*, p. 34; Tremlett, *Ghosts*, p. 193.
16 *La Vanguardia*, 15 February 1975, p. 6.
17 *ABC*, 20 May 1975.
18 *Inflacion de España en 1974*, https://www.inflation.eu/es/tasas-de-inflacion/espana/inflacion-historica/ipc-inflacion-espana-1974.aspx; *New York Times*, 9 March 1975, Section E, p. 4, 13 March 1974, p. 4, 17 November 1975, p. 38, 22 December 1974, p. 4, 16 February 1975, p. 13, 20 February 1975, p. 5.
19 *New York Times*, 4 April 1975, p. 2.
20 *La Vanguardia*, 15 May 1975, p. 5; *New York Times*, 24 May 1975, p. 4, 26 April 1975, p. 2.
21 *New York Times*, 28 May 1975, p. 11, 1 June 1975, p. 1, 26 May 1975, p. 30, 3 June 1975, p. 32.
22 *New York Times*, 12 June 1975.
23 *New York Times*, 24 August 1975, p. 7, 20 September 1975, p. 9, 28 September 1975, p. 1.
24 *New York Times*, 1 October 1975, p. 93.
25 *New York Times*, 2 October 1975, p. 81; see https://www.youtube.com/watch?v=qCpQocHBRFk&ab_channel=AveThomaz
26 *New York Times*, 15 October 1975, p. 6.
27 *New York Times*, 10 October 1975, p. 6.

45 LAST GASP

1 Preston, *Palomas*, p. 421.
2 *New York Times*, 31 October 1975, p. 1.
3 *New York Times*, 18 November 1975, p. 8, 20 November 1975, p. 85.
4 *New York Times*, 14 November 1975, p. 5.
5 Pozuelo, *476 días*, p. 240; *New York Times*, 16 November 1975, p. 1.
6 *New York Times*, 18 November 1975, p. 8, 19 November 1975, p. 3.
7 Pozuelo, *476 días*, p. 241; *La Vanguardia*, 20 Nov 1975, pp. 5–6; Palacios and Payne, *Franco*, Kindle Loc. 10796–817.
8 *La Vanguardia*, 21 November 1975, pp. 1, 2, 8, 10.
9 *Actualidad del Derecho sanitario*, No. 274, October 2019, pp. 951–5.
10 *La Vanguardia*, 21 November 1975, p. 10.

NOTES

EPILOGUE

1. *La Vanguardia*, 23 November 1975, pp. 8, 10.
2. Antonio Cazorla Sánchez, *Franco*, (Spanish edition), pp. 17-18, Giles Tremlett's translation.
3. *Wall Street Journal*, 1 May 2006, citing Revel in *National Review*, 2000.
4. Cayo Sastre García, 'La transición política en España: Una sociedad desmovilizada', *Reis* 80/97, p. 41.
5. Tremlett, *Ghosts*, p. 57.
6. Martinez Soler in *20 Minutos*, 27 June 2023. 27
7. *El Diario*, 24 June 2023, 000 https://www.eldiario.es/politica/martinez-soler-transicion-hubo-generosidad-miedo_128_9112853.html; Martinez Soler, *La Prensa Libre no fue un regalo*, pp. 240-44.
8. *La Vanguardia*, 23 November 1975, pp. 6-7; Giles Tremlett, *España: A Brief History of Spain*, Apollo, London, 2022, p. 288.
9. Juan Carlos I, 'Primer Mensaje del Rey' at Biblioteca Virtual Miguel de Cervantes; Preston, *Juan Carlos* (Spanish), pp. 398–400; *The Times*, 24 November 1975, p. 10; *La Vanguardia*, 22 November 1975, pp. 7, 11, 15, 23.
10. Preston, *Juan Carlos* (Spanish), p. 412.
11. Tremlett, *Ghosts*, p. 78.
12. Preston, *Juan Carlos* (English), Kindle Loc. 4446.
13. Tremlett, *España*, pp. 292–5.
14. Hooper, *New Spaniards*, p. 193.
15. *El Pais* 15 Oct 1977 at https://elpais.com/diario/1977/10/15/espana/245718002_850215.html; Tremlett, *Brief*, p. 299; Tremlett, *Ghosts*, pp. 78–79.
16. Antonio Cazorla Sánchez, *Franco*, Kindle Loc. 116.
17. Tremlett, *España*, p. 290.
18. Tremlett, *Ghosts*, p. 83.
19. Tremlett, *Ghosts*, p. 80–1.
20. Tremlett, *Ghosts*, p. 84.
21. International Monetary Fund (2023), *Public Finances in Modern History. Government revenue, % of GDP and Government expenditure, % of GDP* at https://www.imf.org/external/datamapper/exp@FPP/ITA/FRA; Our World in Data, *Government expenditure (% of GDP). Government spending as a share of GDP, 1800 to 1987. Total government spending, including interest government expenditures, as a share of gross domestic product (GDP)* at https://ourworldindata.org/grapher/historical-gov-spending-gdp?tab=table&time=earliest. 1987; Fundación Rafael del Pino, *Distribución de la Renta. El índice de Gini y su composición* at https://frdelpino.es/investigacion/distribucion-de-la-renta/; Palacios and Payne, *Franco* (English), p. 627.
22. Tremlett, *Ghosts*, pp. 84–85.
23. Preston, *Holocaust*, Kindle Loc. 236.
24. Tremlett, *España*, pp. 302–9
25. Preston, p. 520.
26. Tremlett, *España*, pp. 317–318.
27. Tremlett, *España*, p. 291; María Cristina Palomares, *The Quest for Survival after Franco: the Moderate Francoists slow journey to the polls (1964–1977)*. PhD Thesis, London School of Economics, p. 280.

28 Tobias Buck, *After the Fall*, Weidenfeld & Nicolson, London, 2019, p. 60.
29 El País, *Elecciones generales Congreso 2023 Vox* at https://elpais.com/espana/elecciones/generales/congreso/escanos-por-partido/vox/; El Plural, 26 Nov 2024, 'Vox legitima la dictadura de Franco en el Congreso'.
30 Tremlett, *España*, p. 320.
31 Palacios and Payne, *Franco* (English), p. 625.
32 Palacios and Payne, *Franco* (English), p. 625.
33 Fraser, *Tajos*, p. 75
34 World Bank, *Literacy rate, adult total (% of people ages 15 and above) - Spain, Poland, Hungary, Romania. UNESCO Institute for Statistics)*, accessed September 30, 2024, at https://data.worldbank.org/indicator/SE.ADT.LITR.ZS?end=2023&locations=ES-PL-HU-RO&start=2023&view=bar&year=1981

Bibliography

ARCHIVES

AGMAV Archivo General Militar de Ávila, Ávila
AHN Archivo Histórico Nacional, Madrid
BL British Library, London
BNE Biblioteca Nacional de España, Madrid
CDMH Centro Documental de la Memoria Histórica, Salamanca
FNFF Fundación Nacional Francisco Franco
HIL Hoover Institution Library & Archives, Stanford University, California
IISH International Institute of Social History, Amsterdam
IWM Imperial War Museum, London
NA The National Archives, Kew
PR Biblioteca Pavelló de la República, Barcelona
RGASPI Rossiisky Gosudarstvenny Arkhiv Sotsialno-Politeskoi Istorii (Russian State Archive of Social-Political History), Moscow
TL Tamiment Library, New York University, New York

NEWSPAPERS AND PERIODICALS

ABC, Madrid.
ABC, Sevilla.
Ahora
Arizona Daily Star Associated Press (AP)
Asturias Revista Semanal
Atlántica
Baleares
Baltimore Sun
Biblioteca
Bristol Daily Courier
Chicago Tribune
Coventry Evening Telegraph
Diario de Las Palmas

Diario de Lisboa
El Carbayón, diario asturiano de la mañana
El Comercio
El Día
El Español
El Globo
El Liberal
El Periodico
El Pais
El Pueblo (Valencia)
El Siglo Futuro
El Sol
Informaciones
La Acción
La Correspondencia Militar
La Época
La Marina
La Nueva España
La Petit Gironde
La Prensa
La Stampa
La Tribuna
La Vanguardia
La Voz
La Zarpa
Le Figaro
Liverpool Daily Post
Medina
Nuevo Mundo
New York Times
News Chronicle
Reuters
Siglo Futuro
Sur
Sydney Morning Herald
Observer
The Times
United Press International (UPI)

OFFICIAL DOCUMENTS

Anuario estadístico de España 1936, Madrid, Ministerio de Trabajo, Sanidad y Previsión, 1936.
Anuario Militar 1913, Madrid, Ministerio de la Guerra, 1913.
Anuario Militar 1914, Madrid, Ministerio de la Guerra, 1914.
Anuario Militar 1916, Madrid, Ministerio de la Guerra, 1916.
Anuario Militar 1918, Madrid, Ministerio de la Guerra, 1918.

Anuario Militar 1922, Madrid, Ministerio de la Guerra, 1922.
Anuario Militar 1924, Madrid, Ministerio de la Guerra, 1924.
Anuario Militar 1926, Madrid, Ministerio de la Guerra, 1926.
Anuario Militar 1927, Madrid, Ministerio de la Guerra, 1927.
Boletín Oficial del Estado (BOE) 13 febrero 1939. Ley de 9 de Febrero de 1939 de Responsabilidades Políticas, pp. 824–48.
BOE 2 de Junio 1940. Otro de 29 de mayo de 1940 por el que se nombra Embajador Extraordinario en los Centenarios de Portugal a don Nicolás Franco Baamonde.
BOE No. 288 p. 7987. DECRETO de 10 de octubre de 1941 por el que se dispone que los militantes del Partido que sean separados de la Organización, no puedan desempeñar cargos de mando o confianza en el Estado.
BOE No. 65, p. 1627. DECRETO de 31 de diciembre de 1941 por el que se dispone la ejecución de la Ley reorganizadora de la Policía, de 8 de marzo de 1941.
BOE, 8 abril 1941 p. 2340 Ley de 8 de marzo de 1941 por la que se reorganizan los servicios de Policía.
BOE 2 marzo 1940, pp. 1537–9 Ley de 1 de marzo de 1940. Sobre represión de la masonería y del comunismo.
BOE No. 182 de 20 de abril de 1937, pp. 1033–1034. Decreto de unificación de FET y de la JONS.
BOE No. 500 de 5 de marzo de 1938, 'Suspensión de pleitos de separación y divorcio'.
BOE No. 301 de 23 de octubre de 1939, 'Ley de 26 de octubre de 1939 sobre procedimientos para el ejercicio de derechos y acciones derivados de la Ley derogatoria de la de Divorcio'.
BOE No. 67, de 19 de marzo de 1966, Ley 14/1966, de 18 de marzo, de Prensa e Imprenta pp. 3310–15.
BOE núm. 95, de 21 de abril de 1967, páginas 5250 a 5272. Decreto 779/1967, de 20 de abril, por el que se aprueban los textos refundidos de las Leyes Fundamentales del Reino.
Boletín Oficial de la Junta de Defensa Nacional de España número 32, de 30 de septiembre de 1936. Decreto número 138. 'Nombrando Jefe del Gobierno del Estado Español al Excelentísimo Sr. General de División don Francisco Franco Bahamonde, quien asumirá todos los poderes del nuevo Estado'.
Cosechas, comercio y consumo de trigo, Servicio Nacional del Trigo (1963).
Documents Diplomatiques Français 1932–1939, 2e Série (1936–1939) XV (Paris, 1981); Tome XVI (Paris, 1983); Tome XVII (Paris, 1984); Tome XVIII (Paris, 1985); Tome XIX (Paris, 1986).
I Documenti Diplomatici Italiani, 9 serie, vol. VI (Rome, 1986); vol. VIII (Rome, 1988).
Documents on German Foreign Policy Series C, vol. XI (London, 1964); Series D, vol. III (London, 1951); vol. VI (London, 1956); vol. VII (London, 1956); vol. VIII (London, 1954); vol. IX (London, 1956); vol. X (London, 1957); vol. XI (London, 1961); vol. XII (London, 1964); vol. XIII (London, 1964).
Hansard FOREIGN AFFAIRS, HC Deb 24 May 1944.
International Monetary Fund (2023). *Public Finances in Modern History. Government revenue, % of GDP and Government expenditure, % of GDP* at https://www.imf.org/external/datamapper/exp@FPP/ITA/FRA
IMF, *Annual report for year ended April 30, 1959*.

IMF, *Annual report for year ended April 30, 1960*.
United Nations General Assembly, *Relations of Members of the United Nations with Spain*, 12 December 1946.
United Nations, Security Council, Official Records, First Year: Second Series, Special Supplement, Report of the Sub-Committee on the Spanish Question (New York – June 1946).
US Department of State, *The Spanish Government and the Axis*, Government Printing Office, Washington, 1946).
World Bank. *Literacy rate, adult total (% of people ages 15 and above) – Spain, Poland, Hungary, Romania. UNESCO Institute for Statistics (UIS). UIS.Stat Bulk Data Download Service*. Accessed September 30, 2024. at https://data.worldbank.org/indicator/SE.ADT.LITR.ZS?end=2023&locations=ES-PL-HU-RO&start=2023&view=bar&year=1981

NEWSPAPER AND MAGAZINE ARTICLES

'El "As" de la Legión', *ABC*, 22 February 1922.
'El extraño origen de la voz aguda y nasal de Francisco Franco: el rasgo del que se burló Hitler', *ABC*, 2 February 2021.
'El general Franco, desmiente unos rumores', *El Pueblo (Valencia)*, 20 February 1936, p. 4.
'En honor de un comandante', *El Día*, Madrid, 27 May 1917, p. 4.
'Hablando con el General Franco', *La Zarpa: diario de los agrarios gallegos*, No. 1625, 14 March 1926.
'Hitler's Hand in Spanish War Revealed', *Baltimore Sun*, 8 November 1945, p. 16.
'La actuación contra las Juntas de Defensa', *La Correspondencia Militar*, 24 October 1921 p. 1.
'La Huelga de Agosto en Asturias', *España* magazine, No. 134, 1 November 1917, p. 7.
'Las armas del "Turquesa"', *El Comercio*, 28 September 2009.
'Las Juntas Militares', *La Prensa*, 9 November, 1922, p. 2.
'Los que viajan', *El Correo gallego*, 10 August 1916, p. 1.
'Luis Pareja Aycuens', *Diccionario Biográfico Español*, at https://dbe.rah.es/biografias/92857/luis-pareja-aycuens
'Mio Marito, Parla La Signora Franco', *La Stampa*, 26 February 1937, p. 3.
'Viaje al fondo de la noche', at Infocatolica.com, 6 July 2015 at https://www.infocatolica.com/?t=opinion&cod=24382).
'La huelga última en Asturias', *Asturias Revista Semanal (La Habana)*, 7 October 1917, pp. 6–8.
Cox, Geoffrey, 'Eyewitness in Madrid', *Harper's*, 175, 1936, p. 34.
De Larra, Mariano José, 'El día de Difuntos de 1836, Fígaro en el cementerio', *El Español*, No. 368, 2 November 1836.
De Maeztu, Ramírez, 'Con el ejercito', *Revista de Tropas Coloniales*, January 1924, pp. 4–5.
Eco, Umberto, 'Ur-fascism', *New York Review of Books*, June 22, 1995.
Franco, Carmen, 'Mi Marito', *La Stampa* (Turin, Italy), 26 February 1937, p. 3.
Franco, Francisco, 'Ruud... Balek!', *África*, February 1933, pp. 5–6.
Franco, Francisco, 'La Maniobra', *Revista de Tropas Coloniales*, February 1924, p. 5.
Franco, Francisco, 'Las Unidades coloniales', *Revista de Tropas Coloniales*, May 1924, pp. 58–59.

Franco, Francisco. '¿Dónde estamos?', *La Revue Belge*, 15 August 1937 at https://fnff.es/historia/donde-estamos-articulo-publicado-en-la-revue-belge-15-de-agosto-de-17/.
Franco, Francisco, 'Los Mandos', *Revista de Tropas Coloniales*, January 1924, pp. 5–6.
Franco, Francisco, 'Pasividad e inacción', *Revista de Tropas Coloniales*, April 1924, p. 4.
Franco, Francisco, 'Un Articolo Del Generale Franco', *La Stampa* (Turin, Italy), 26 February 1937, p. 3.
Franco, Ramón, 'El Raid Larache-Canarias', *Revista de Tropas Coloniales*, February 1924.
Franco de Espés, Luis, 'La Mujer en el hogar de los hombres célebres. El amor y la guerra. La esposa del general Franco', *Estampa*, 29 May 1928, pp. 19–21.
García Piñera, Ramon, 'Asturias 1917. Nace la leyenda', *Atlántica XXII*, 27 September 2017.
Gil Honduvilla, Joaquín, 'Los Sucesos de Tablada de Junio de 1931 y Sus Consecuencias', *Revista de Historia Militar*, No. 110, pp. 11–50.
Goicoechea, Antonio, 'El Coronel Franco', *Revista de tropas coloniales*, March 1925, pp. 1–3.
Junco, José Álvarez, 'Cultura y Libertad', *El País*, 4 February, 2012.
Knickerbocker, H. R *The Washington Times*, May 10, 1937, p. 7 *"Kill'em All"*, Franco aide's philosophy.
Lennard, Dora, 'Franco: A Close-Up, Study of the Mind and the Nature of the leader of Nationalist Spain by his English Teacher', *Spain: Semi-monthly Publication of Civil War Events*, Vol 1. No. 3, Nov. 15, 1937.
Matthews, Herbert L. 'Franco's Problems', *Foreign Affairs*, 17, 4 (July 1939).
Mola, Emilio, 'Preparación de oficiales para prestar servicio en el ejército de Africa', *Revista de Tropas Coloniales*, January 1924, pp. 10–11.
Neves, Mario, 'Badajoz continuous hoje a ser bombardeada', *Diario de Lisboa*, 14 August, 1936, p. 1.
Neves, Mario, 'Badajoz esta entregue aos legionaries e aos "regulares" marroquinos', *Diario de Lisboa*, 15 Agosto 1936, p. 1.
Ortega y Gasset, José, 'El error Berenguer', *El Sol*, 15 November 1930, p. 1.
Padilla, Andrés, 'Un dietario político de Josep Pla', *El País*, 2 November 2003.
Payne, Stanley, 'Spain's "Semi-Fascism", excerpted from *A History of Fascism, 1914–1945* by Stanley G. Payne, University of Wisconsin Press', *Slate*, 7 Feb 2017.
Queipo de Llano, Gonzalo, 'Nuestro propósito', *Revista de Tropas Coloniales*, January 1924, p. 1.
Robson, Karl, 'Franco, A dictator in spite of himself', *Life*, 29 May 1939.
Togores, Luis, '101 kilómetros: la marcha forzada de la Legión', *La Razón*, 5 October 2021.
Villatoro, Manuel, 'Las cartas de amor secretas de Franco a una adolescente que le dio calabazas: «Era un pelma»', *ABC*, 15 Feb 2021.

JOURNAL ARTICLES

Aizpuru, Mikel, 'La presencia soviética durante la Guerra Civil en el Frente Norte', *Historia contemporánea*, ISSN 1130-2402, No. 35, 2007.

Alcaraz Abellán, José, Anaya Hernández, Luis Alberto, and Millares Cantero, Sergio, 'Los extranjeros y la Guerra Civil en la provincia de Las Palmas (1936–1939)', *VII Coloquio de Historia Canario-americana*, Vol. 1, 1990, pp. 99131.

Álvaro Dueñas, Manuel 'Los militares en la represión política de la posguerra: la jurisdicción especial de Responsabilidades Políticas hasta la reforma de 1942', en *Revista de Estudios Políticos*, Universidad Autónoma de Madrid, No. 69, 1990.

Alvarez, José E., 'Between Gallipoli and D-Day: Alhucemas, 1925', *The Journal of Military History*, Vol. 63, No. 1, 1999, pp. 75–98.

Anca Alamillo, Alejandro, 'Construcción naval y fuerza a flote en los primeros años del siglo XX', *Revista general de marina*, Vol. 263, No. 8–9, 2012, pp. 213–227.

– – –, 'El grave accidente del crucero Infanta Isabel ocurrido el día 3 de agosto de 1900, En La Concha de San Sebastián', *Revista de historia naval*, No. 150, 2020, pp. 33–48.

Arbeloa Muru, Víctor Manuel, 'El quiebro del PSOE en 1933 (del Gobierno a la Revolución) I', *Estudios de Deusto: revista de Derecho Público*, Vol. 60, No. 1, 2012, págs. 13–55.

– – –, 'El quiebro del PSOE en 1933 del Gobierno a la Revolución (y II)', Vol. 61, No. 1, 2013, págs. 39–86, Santos Juliá, *Historia del socialismo español (1931–1939)*, pp. 39–86.

Aróstegui, Julio, 'El quiebro del PSOE en 1933 del Gobierno a la Revolución (y II)', Vol. 61, No. 1, 2013, págs. 39–86, Santos Juliá, *Historia del socialismo español (1931–1939)*, pp. 39–86.

Bandrés, J., 'Las encuestas universitarias de José Luis Pinillos: un episodio en la pugna por la orientación sociopolítica del franquismo', *Revista de Historia de la Psicología*, 41(1), 12–28.

Blasco Herranz, Inmaculada, 'Género y nación durante el franquismo', in *Imaginarios y representaciones de España durante el franquismo*, eds Stéphane Michonneau et Xosé M. Núñez-Seixas, Madrid, Casa de Velázquez, 2014.

Bru Sánchez-Fortún, Alberto, 'Los ascensos de guerra (1909–1922): su repercusión en el nacimiento de las Juntas de Defensa', *Revista de Historia Militar*, No. 119, 2016, pp. 13–66.

Boyd, Carolyn P., 'Responsibilities and the Second Spanish Republic 1931–6', *European History Quarterly*, Vol. 14, 1984.

Cabrera, Mercedes, 'Los escándalos de la Dictadura de Primo de Rivera y las responsabilidades en la República: el asunto Juan March', *Historia y política: Ideas, procesos y movimientos sociales*, No. 4, 2000, p. 12.

Calero, Juan Pablo, 'Vísperas de la revolución, El congreso de la CNT (1936)', *Germinal*, No. 7, April 2009, pp. 97–132.

Calleja, Eduardo and Aróstegui, Julio, 'La tradición recuperada: el Requeté carlista y la insurrección', *Historia Contemporánea*, No. 11, pp. 51–5.

Calvo Sotelo, José, 'Orden Público', *Intervenciones de José Calvo Sotelo y otros diputados en las Cortes el 16 de Junio de 19*, at https://www.retoricas.com/2010/07/jose-calvo-sotelo-discurso-antes-de-la.html.

Camara, Antonio D., Puche, Javier, Martínez-Carrión, José Miguel, 'Assessing the effects of autarchic policies on the biological well-being: Analysis of deviations in cohort male height in the Valencian Community (Spain) during Francoist regime' *Social Science & Medicine 273* (2021).

Caro Cancela, Diego, '¿Por qué perdieron las derechas las elecciones de 1936?', *Revista de Historia Contemporánea*, No. 9–10, 1999–2000, pp. 329–44.

Carpintero, Helio, 'Psicología y Política en España: La Encuesta de Pinillos de 1955', *Psychologia Latina* 2010, Vol. 1 No. 2, 88–96.
Casanellas, Pau, 'La defensa del régimen. Cambios y continuidades en la represión franquista más allá de la posguerra', in Damián A. González Madrid y Manuel Ortiz Heras (eds.), *Violencia franquista y gestión del pasado traumático*, Madrid, Sílex.
Cerdá, Nestor, 'Political Ascent and Military Commander: General Franco in the Early Months of the Spanish Civil War, July-October 1936', *Journal of Military History*, Vol. 75, No. 4, pp. 1125–57.
Clara Resplandis, Josep, 'Joan Seguí Almuzara (1885–1936), el figuerenc protagonista de la subversió militar a Melilla', *Annals de l'Institut d'Estudis Empordanesos*, No. 54, 2023.
De la Fuente de Pablo, Pablo, 'Sobre las circunstancias del ascenso a capitán por méritos de guerra de Francisco Franco', *Aportes: Revista de historia contemporánea*, No. 107, 2021, pp. 125–151.
Del Arco Blanco, Miguel Angel, 'Famine in Spain During Franco's Dictatorship, 1939–52', *Journal of Contemporary History 2021*, Vol. 56 (1).
Detwiler, Donald S., 'Spain and the Axis during World War II', in *The Review of Politics*, Vol. 33, No. 1 (Jan., 1971), pp. 36–53.
Domínguez García, R., 'El juramento de José Antonio Aguirre, una toma de posesión en la Guerra Civil', *Historia y comunicación social* 25(2), (2020).
Dueñas, Manuel Álvaro, 'Los militares en la represión política de la posguerra: la jurisdicción especial de Responsabilidades Políticas hasta la reforma de 1942', *Revista de Estudios Políticos*, No. 69, 1990, pp. 141–162.
Escobedo Romero, Rafael, 'Los Protestantes Españoles, El Franquismo y la Política Exterior Estadounidense, a Través de las Páginas de *The Christian Century* (1947–1951), *Historia Actual Online*, 43 (2), 2017: 105–116.
Fernández Miranda, Torcuato, 'El Movimiento como fundamento doctrinal y la organización política del régimen español', en *El hombre y la sociedad*, 1960, Madrid, Doncel.
Fontana, Josep, 'La utopía franquista: la economía de Robinson Crusoe', in *Cuadernos de Historia del Derecho* 2004, Vol. Extraordinario.
Franco Castañón, Hermenegildo, 'Ferrol, Ciudad marítima en el siglo XIX', *Cuadernos IHCN*, No. 29, 1996, pp. 7–24.
Gil Gascón, Fátima, 'Dossier: Censura ao cinema nas ditaduras ibéricas Censurar para evitar el peligro: las censuras cinematográficas durante el franquismo, 1939–1959' en *Ler História 79 | 2021 Portugal e Espanha: histórias comparadas*.
Gil Pecharromán, Julio, 'Un partido para acabar con los partidos: el fascismo español, 1931–1936', *Bulletin d'Histoire Contemporaine de l'Espagne*, No. 51, 2017, pp. 69–84.
Gómez Roda, J. Alberto, 'Percepciones de las instituciones y actitudes políticas de la sociedad en la posguerra', in *Pasado y memoria: revista de historia contemporánea*, No. 1 (2002).
González Calleja, Eduardo, 'La necrológica de la violencia sociopolítica en la primavera de 1936', *Mélanges de la Casa Velázquez*, No. 41-1, 2011, pp. 37–60.
Hernández Sánchez, Fernando, 'El Partido Comunista de España en la Segunda República', *Bulletin d'Histoire Contemporaine de l'Espagne*, No. 51, 2017, pp. 85–100.

Sandie, 'How did the Spanish Civil War end? Not so well', *The American Historical Review*, Vol. 120, No. 5 (DECEMBER 2015).

Huertas, Rafael, 'La Psicobiologia del Marxismo como categoría antropológica en el ideario fascista español', *Llull*, Vol. 19, 1996.

Lafuente, E, 'Las Memorias de José Luis Pinillos. Un documento para la Historia de la Psicología en España', *Revista de Historia de la Psicología*, 41(3), 23–32.

Llorens Barber, Ramon, 'Tres cruceros bilbaínos que también fueron ferrolanos', *FerrolAnalísis: revista de pensamiento y cultura*, Vol. 13. pp. 58–61.

Lukes, Igor, 'The Czechoslovak Partial Mobilization in May 1938: A Mystery (almost) Solved', *Journal of Contemporary History*, Vol 31/4, 1996.

Macías Fernández, Daniel and, García Pujades, Sergio, 'El africanismo castrense: un estado de la cuestión', *Studia Historica. Historia Contemporánea*, No. 39, 2021, pp. 49–72.

Marquina, Antonio, 'The Spanish Neutrality during the Second World War', *American University International Law Review*, 14, No. 1, (1998).

Martínez Lopez, Fernando, 'Recuerdos y semblanzas de la familia Franco', *Ferrol-Analysis: revista de pensamiento y cultura*, No. 20, 2005, pp. 20–45.

Martínez López, Francisco, 'Testimonios sobre Franco y su familia', *FerrolAnálisis: revista de pensamiento y cultura*, No. 14, 1999, pp. 70–75.

Martínez López, Francisco. 'Ramón Franco visto por sus paisanos, parientes y compañeros', *FerrolAnálisis: revista de pensamiento y cultura*, No. 21, 2006, pp. 184–194.

Mastrorilli, Edoardo, 'Guerra civile spagnola, intervento italiano e guerra totale' ('Spanish Civil War, Italian intervention, and total war'), *Revista Universitaria de Historia Militar*, Vol. 3, No. 6, 2014, pp. 68–87.

Moses Rosendorf, Neal, 'Be El Caudillo's Guest, The Franco Regime's Quest for Rehabilitation and Dollars after World War II via the Promotion of U.S. Tourism to Spain', *Diplomatic History*, Vol. 30, No. 3 (June 2006).

Moradiellos, 'España y la Segundo Guerra mundial 1939–1945. Entre resignaciones neutralistas y tentaciones beligerantes' in, *Siglo: actas del V Congreso Internacional de Historia de Nuestro Tiempo*, p. 59.

Morente Valero, Francisco, 'La depuración franquista del magisterio público. Un estado de la cuestión', *Hispania*, Vol. 61, No. 208, 2001.

Muñoz Soro, Javier, 'Entre la memoria y la reconciliación. El recuerdo de la República y la guerra en la generación de 1968', *Historia del Presente* 1, 2, 2003, pp. 83–100.

Nogueira Castro, Jessica, '"Salvaguardar dentro de la Ley el interés general". La declaración del estado de excepción durante la dictadura franquista', *Historia Unicap*, Vol. 9, No. 18, pp. 48–68.

Payne, Stanley, 'Franco y los orígenes de la Guerra Civil Española', *La Albolafia: Revista de Humanidades y Cultura*, No. 1, 2014, pp. 11–21.

Pizarroso Quintero, Alejandro, 'La Guerra Civil española, un hito en la historia de la propaganda', *El Argonauta español*, No. 2, 2005.

Prada Rodríguez, J., 'Rebelión militar y represión franquista en Galicia', *Studia Historica. Historia Contemporánea*, No. 24, 2009, pp. 153–177.

Preston, Paul, 'Lights and shadows in George Orwell's *Homage to Catalonia*', *Bulletin of Spanish Studies*, 1–29, 2017.

Preston, Paul, 'Franco y la represión: la venganza del justiciero', in *Novísima: II Congreso Internacional de Historia de Nuestro Tiempo*, coord. por Carlos Navajas Zubeldia, Diego Iturriaga Barco, 2010.

Puell de la Villa, Fernando, 'Los militares ante la Segunda República', *Studia Humanitatis Journal*, Vol. 2, No. 1, 2022, pp. 153–174.

Pulpillo Leiva, Carlos, 'La Configuración De La Propaganda En La España Nacional (1936–1941)', *La Albolea: Revista de Humanidades y Cultura*, No. 1, 2014, pp. 115–136.

Reig Tapia, Alberto, 'El Asedio Del Alcázar: Mito Y Símbolo Político Del Franquismo', *Revisto de Estudios Políticos (Nueva Época)*, No. 101, 1998, p. 101–129.

Rein, Raanan, 'Un Salvavidas Para Franco: La Ayuda Económica Argentina a La España Franquista (1946–1949)' in *ANUARIO del IEHS*, VUJ, Tandil, 1993.

Resplandis, Josep Clara, 'Joan Seguí Almuzara (1885–1936), el figuerenc protagonista de la subversió militar a Melilla', *Annals de l'Institut d'Estudis Empordanesos*, No. 54, 2023, pp. 243–250.

Richards, Michael, 'Morality and Biology in the Spanish Civil War: Psychiatrists, Revolution and Women Prisoners in Málaga', *Contemporary European History*, Vol. 10, No. 3, 2001.

Rodrigo, Javier, 'Internamiento y trabajo forzoso: los campos de concentración de Franco', *Hispania Nova: Revista de historia contemporánea*, Separata No. 6, 2006.

Rodríguez Barrientos, Manuel, 'La Guerra Civil en Algeciras y Su Entorno Geográfico', *Revista general de marina*, Vol. 258, 2010, pp. 399–412.

Ruiz, Julius, 'Seventy Years on: Historians and Repression during and after the Spanish Civil War', *Journal of Contemporary History*, Vol. 44, No. 3, 2009, p. 449–472.

Ruiz Albéniz, Víctor, 'Su Majestad el Rey y la "Revista de Tropas Coloniales"', *Revista de tropas coloniales*, May 1924, pp. 6–7.

Sánchez Recio, Glicerio, 'El Sindicato Vertical Como Instrumento Político y Económico Del Régimen Franquista, *Pasado y Memoria*, No. 1, pp. 19–32.

Sanmartín Salona, Ginés, 'La Compañía Española de Minas del Rif (1907–1984)', *Aldaba: revista del Centro Asociado de la UNED de Melilla*, No. 5, 1985, pp. 55–74.

Sanz-Hernando, Clara, 'Crónicas de guerra: la matanza de Badajoz y la batalla del Alcázar de Toledo en la prensa portuguesa', *Ler História*, No. 77, 2020, pp. 159–180.

Sastre García, Cayo, 'La transición política en España: Una sociedad desmovilizada', *Reis* 80/97.

Saz, Ismael, 'Fascism and empire, fascist Italy against republican Spain', *Mediterranean Historical Review*, 1 June 1998, Vol. 131–2, pp. 116–34.

Saz, Ismael, 'El fracaso del éxito, Italia en la guerra de España', *Espacio, Tiempo y Forma*, Serie V, Historia Contemporánea, T. V., 1992, pp. 105–28.

Schulze Schneider, Ingrid, 'Josef Goebbels, "historiador" de la guerra civil española', *Historia y Comunicación Social* 2001, número 6, p. 53.

Sonlleva-Velasco, M. & Torrego-Egido, L. (2018), 'A mí no me daban besos. Infancia y educación de la masculinidad en la posguerra Española', *Masculinities and Social Change*, 7(1).

Souto Kustrín, Sandra, 'De la paramilitarización al fracaso: las insurrecciones socialistas de 1934 en Viena y Madrid', *Pasado y Memoria*, No. 2, 2003.

Souto Kustrín, Sandra, 'Octubre de 1934 en Madrid: acción colectiva y violencia política', *Hispania: Revista española de historia*, Vol. 59, No. 203, pp. 1063–1103.

Tauler Cid, Benito, 'La legión, historia de una organización para el combate,' *Revista de Historia Militar*, No. Extra 1, 2020, pp. 19–46.
Téllez Molina, Antonio, 'España y la IIª Guerra Mundial: los informes reservados de Carrero Blanco, in: *Mélanges de la Casa de Velázquez*, tome 293, 1993, Époque contemporaine.
Vadillo Muñoz, Julián, 'Julio Aróstegui Sánchez, Largo Caballero. El tesón y la quimera', *Bulletin d'Histoire Contemporaine de l'Espagne*, No. 51, 2017.
Vallejo Nágera, Antonio and Martínez, Eduardo M., 'Psiquismo del Fanatismo Marxista. Investigaciones Psicológicas en Marxistas Femeninos Delincuentes', *Revista Española de Medicina y Cirugía de Guerra*, No. 9, 1939.
Velasco Hernández, Francisco, 'El Crucero Libertad', *Cartagena histórica*, Cuaderno monográfico No. 15, 2005, pp. 3–26.
Viscasillas, Jaime Antón, 'La Escuela de Ingenieros Navales de Ferrol: Academia de Ingenieros y Maquinistas de la Armada (1914-1932)', *Revista de Historia Naval*, No. 133, pp. 93–114.
Wright, Stephanie, 'Out of the Ordinary: Confronting Paradox in the Historiography of Francoism', *Contemporary European History*, Vol. 30, 2021, pp. 136–146.
Zaratiegui, Jesús M., 'El Falangismo en Crisis con la Crisis de Febrero de 1956', in *Falange, las culturas políticas del fascismo en la España de Franco (1936–1975)*, ed. Miguel Angel Ruiz Carnicer, Vol. 2, 2013.

BOOKS AND PHD THESES

Abella, Rafael, *La vida cotidiana durante la Guerra Civil, La España Nacional*, Barcelona, Editorial Planeta, 1978.
Águila, Juan José del, *El TOP. La represión de la libertad (1963–1977)*, Barcelona, Editorial Planeta, 2001.
Alas, Leopoldo, *La Regenta (English edition)*, London, Penguin, 2015.
Alcalá-Zamora, Niceto, *Asalto a la República. Enero-abril de 1936*, Madrid, La Esfera de los Libros, 2011.
– – –, *Memorias*, Barcelona, Editorial Planeta, 1977.
Alía Miranda, Francisco, *La dictadura de Primo de Rivera (1923–1930). Paradojas y contradicciones del nuevo régimen*, Madrid, Los Libros de la Catarata, 2023.
Alpert, Michael, *El ejército republicano en la Guerra Civil*, 2.ª ed., Madrid, Siglo XXI de España, 1989.
– – –, *La reforma militar de Azaña (1931–1933)*, Madrid, Siglo XXI de España, 1982.
– – –, *The Republican Army in the Spanish Civil War, 1936–1939*, Cambridge, Cambridge University Press, 2013.
– – –, *The Spanish Civil War at Sea*, Barnsley, Pen & Sword Books, 2021.
Álvarez Bolado, Alfonso, *El experimento del nacionalcatolicismo (1939–1975)*, Madrid, Editorial Cuadernos para el Diálogo, 1976.
Álvarez Tardío, Manuel, *Anticlericalismo y libertad de conciencia: política y religión en la Segunda República Española, 1931–1936*, Madrid, Centro de Estudios Constitucionales, 2002.
– – –, and García Villa, Roberto 1936, *Fraude y violencia en las elecciones del Frente Popular*, Barcelona, Espasa, 2017.

Álvarez, José E., *The Betrothed of Death, The Spanish Foreign Legion during the Rif Rebellion, 1920–1927*, PhD thesis, Florida State University, 1995.
———, *The Spanish Foreign Legion in the Spanish Civil War*, Columbia, University of Missouri Press, 2015.
Amate Blanco, Juan José, *La Legión en las campañas de Marruecos (1920–1927)*, Madrid, Ministerio de Defensa, 2022.
Andrade, Jaime de (seudónimo de Francisco Franco Bahamonde), *Raza. Anecdotario para el guión de una película*, Madrid, Ediciones Numancia, 1942.
Andreassi Cieri, Alejandro, 'Trabajo y Empresa en el Nacionalsindicalismo', in *Fascismo en España*, (eds) F. Gallego Margaleff, Ferran, Madrid, El Viejo Topo, 2005, pp. 13–42.
Arenas Posadas, Carlos, *Por el bien de la patria: Guerras y ejércitos en la constitución de España*, Barcelona, Ediciones Pasado y Presente, 2019.
Aróstegui, Julio, *Largo Caballero, El Tesón y la quimera*, Madrid, Debate, 2013.
———, 'Los socialistas en la Segunda República: una victoria con alto costo', in Angel Viñas (ed.), *En el combate por la historia: la Republica, la Guerra Civil, el Franquismo*, Barcelona, Editorial Pasado y Presente, 2012.
Arrarás, Joaquín, *Franco*, San Sebastián, Librería Internacional, 1937.
———, *Historia de la Cruzada española*, 8 vols, Madrid, Ediciones Españolas, 1939–43.
———, *Historia de la segunda República española*, 4 vols, Madrid, Editora Nacional, 1956–68.
Ashford Hodges, Gabrielle, *Franco: a Concise Biography*, London, Weidenfeld & Nicolson, 2000.
Azaña, Manuel, *Diarios completos: monarquía, república, guerra civil*, Barcelona, Crítica, 2000.
———, *Diarios*, 1932–1933, 'Los cuadernos robados', Madrid, Grijalbo-Mondadori, 1997.
———, *Obras completas*, 4 vols, Mexico City, Ediciones Oasis, 1966–8.
———, and Rivas Cherif, Cipriona de, *Cartas, 1917–1935*, Valencia, Pre-textos, 1991.
Azcárate, Pablo de, *Mi embajada en Londres durante la guerra civil española*, Barcelona, Ariel, 1976.
Aznar, Manuel, *Historia militar de la guerra de España*, 3 vols, Madrid, Editora Nacional, 1969.
Baamonde Y Ortega, Manuel, *La administración de la Marina militar española durante el reinado de la casa de Borbón y reformas que esta institución necesita*, El Ferrol, Imprenta El Correo Gallego, 1899.
Bachoud, Andrée, *Franco*, Barcelona, Editorial Crítica, 2000.
Balfour, Sebastian, *Abrazo Mortal: de la guerra colonial a la Guerra Civil en España y Marruecos (1909–1939)*, Madrid, Ediciones Península, 2018.
———, and Preston, Paul (eds.), *Spain and the Great Powers in the Twentieth Century*, Abingdon, Routledge/Cañada Blanch, 2009.
———, *Deadly Embrace, Morocco and the Road to the Spanish Civil War*, Oxford, Oxford University Press, 2002.
———, *The End of the Spanish Empire (1898–1923)*, Oxford, Clarendon Press, 1997.
Baón, Rogelio, *La cara humana de un Caudillo*, Madrid, Editorial San Martín, 1975.
Barbieri, Pierpaolo, *Hitler's Shadow Empire: Nazi Economics and the Spanish Civil War*, Cambridge, Harvard University Press, 2015.
Barceló, Juan, *Brunete: El nacimiento del Ejército Popular*, Madrid, Viento Céfiro, 2018.

Barciela López, Carlos, et al., (eds), *Estadísticas históricas de España siglos XIX-XX*, Tomo 1, Madrid, Fundación BBVA, 2005.
Barea, Arturo, *The Clash*, London, Fontana, 1984.
———, *The Forge*, London, Fontana, 1984.
———, *The Forging of a Rebel*, (trilogy of *The Struggle*, *The Clash* and *The Forge*), London, Pushkin Press, 2018.
———, *The Track*, London, Fontana, 1984.
Barrio Gozalo, Maximiliano, *El clero en la España moderna*, Madrid, CSIC, 2010.
Baxell, Richard, *Unlikely Warriors: The British in the Spanish Civil War and the Struggle Against Fascism*, London, Aurum, 2012.
Bayo, Eliseo, *Los atentados contra Franco*, Barcelona, Bruguera, 1977.
Bayod, Ángel, *Franco visto por sus ministros*, Barcelona, Editorial Planeta, 1981.
Beevor, Antony, *The Battle for Spain: The Spanish Civil War 1936–1939*, London, Orion, 2007.
Bennassar, Bartolomé, *Franco*, Madrid, EDAF, 1996.
———, *Franco. Enfance et Adolescence*, Paris, Editions Autrement, 1999.
Berenguer, Dámaso, *Campañas en el Rif y Yebala, 1921–2*, Madrid, Editorial voluntad, 1923.
———, *De la Dictadura a la República*, Madrid, Editorial Plus Ultra, 1946.
Bilbeny, Norbert, (ed.), *La Segunda República Español: Textos Fundamentales*, Barcelona, Ediciones de la Universidad de Barcelona, 2021.
Blanco Escolá, Carlos, *Franco. La pasión por el poder*, Barcelona, Editorial Planeta, 2005.
———, *La incompetencia militar de Franco*, Madrid, Alianza Editorial, 2000.
Blasco Ibáñez Vicente, *Por España y contra el rey: (Alfonso XIII, desenmascarado)*, Paris, Biblioteca de El Pueblo, 1925.
———, *Alfonso XIII Unmasked: The Military Terror in Spain*, London, Eveleigh Nash & Grayson Ltd, 1925.
Blinkhorn, Martin, *Carlism and Crisis in Spain, 1931–1939*, Cambridge, Cambridge University Press, 1975.
Boaventura, Armando, *Madrid–Moscovo da ditadura à República e à guerra civil de Espanha*, Lisboa, Parceria A. M. Pereira, 1937.
Bolín, Luis, *Spain: the Vital Years*, Philadelphia, Lippincott, 1967.
Boor, Jakim (pseudonym of Francisco Franco Bahamonde), *Masonería*, Madrid, Gráficas Valera, 1952.
Bowen, Wayne H. *Truman, Franco's Spain and the Cold War*, Columbia, University of Missouri Press, 2017.
Bowers, Claude, *My Mission to Spain: Watching the Rehearsal for World War II*, Simon & Schuster, New York, 1954.
Box, Zira, *España, año cero. La construcción simbólica del franquismo*, Madrid, Alianza Editorial, 2010.
———, *La Fundación De Un Régimen. La Construcción Simbólica Del Franquismo*, PhD thesis, Madrid, 2008.
———, *Praetorian Politics in Liberal Spain*, Chapel Hill, University of North Carolina Press, 1979.
Brenan, Gerald, *The Spanish Labyrinth*, Cambridge, Cambridge University Press, 1943.
Breuer, William B., *Operation Torch*, New York, St Martin's Press, 1985.

Buchanan, Tom, *Britain and the Spanish Civil War*, Cambridge University Press, Cambridge, 1997.
Buck, Tobias, *After the Fall: Crisis, Recovery and the Making of a New Spain*, London, Weidenfeld and Nicolson, 2019.
Buckley, Henry, *The Life and Death of the Spanish Republic*, London, I. B. Tauris, 2013.
Cabanellas, Guillermo, *Cuatro generales*, 2 vols., Barcelona, Editorial Planeta, 1977.
———, *La guerra de los mil días*, 2 vols., Buenos Aires, Grijalbo, 1973.
Calvo Serrer, Rafael, *Franco frente al Rey*, Paris, Ruedo Ibérico, 1972.
Calvo Sotelo, José, *Mis servicios al estado: Seis años de gestión*, Madrid, Instituto de Administración Local, 1974.
Campoamor, Clara, *El voto femenino y yo: mi pecado mortal*, Sevilla, Espuela de Plata, 2018.
Cantalupo, Roberto, *Embajada en España*, Barcelona, Luis de Caralt, 1951.
Cardona, Gabriel, *Franco y sus generales. La manicura del tigre*, Madrid, Ediciones Temas de Hoy, 2001.
Carr, E.H., *Twilight of the Comintern, 1930–1935*, New York, Pantheon, 1982.
Carr, Raymond, *Spain 1808–1975*, Oxford, Oxford University Press, 1982.
———, *The Spanish Tragedy: The Civil War in Perspective*, London, Weidenfeld & Nicolson, 1977.
Carretero, José María, *El general Sanjurjo: Su vida y su gloria*, Madrid, Ediciones Caballero audaz, 1940.
Carroll, Peter N., *The Odyssey of the Abraham Lincoln Brigade*, Stanford, Stanford University Press, 1994.
Carvallo de Cora, Esteban (ed.), *Hoja de servicios del Caudillo de España, Excmo. Sr. Don Francisco Franco Bahamonde y su genealogía*, Madrid, Editora Nacional, 1967.
Casanova, Julián, ed., *Cuarenta años con Franco*, Barcelona, Editorial Crítica, 2015.
———, Espinosa, Francisco, Mir, Conxita, and Moreno Gómez, Francisco, *Morir, matar, sobrevivir. La violencia en la dictadura de Franco*, Barcelona, Editorial Crítica, 2002.
———, *República y Guerra Civil. Vol. 8 de la Historia de España*, Barcelona, Crítica/Marcial Pons, 2014.
Casas de la Vega, Rafael, *El Terror, Madrid 1936, Investigación histórica*, Madridejos, Editorial Fenix, 1994.
Castells, Andreu, *Las Brigadas Internacionales de la guerra de España*, Barcelona, Ariel, 1974.
Cazorla Sánchez, Antonio, *Fear and Progress. Ordinary Lives in Franco's Spain (1939–1975)*, Wiley-Blackwell, Chichester, 2010.
———, *Franco, Biografía del mito*, Alianza Editorial, Madrid, 2015.
———, *Franco, The Biography of a Myth*, Abingdon, Routledge, 2014.
———, *Cartas a Franco de los Españoles de a pie (1936–1945)*, Barcelona, RBA, 2014.
Cervera Pery, José, *El Almirante Cervera, vida y aventura de un marino español*, Madrid, Prensa Española, 1972.
———, *Alzamiento y revolución en la marina*, Madrid, Editorial San Martin, 1978.
Cervera y Topete, Pascual, *Guerra Hispano-americana, Colección de documentos*, Madrid, Diario de la Marina, 1904.
Ciano, Galeazzo, *Ciano's Diary* (1939–1943), London, Heinemann, 1947.
———, *Ciano's Diary, 1937–8*, London, Methuen, 1952.

―――, *Ciano's Diplomatic Papers*, edited by Malcolm Muggeridge, London, Odhams, 1948.
―――, *Diario (1937–1943)*, edición de Renzo De Felice, Milán, Rizzoli, 1980.
Cierva, Ricardo de la, *Francisco Franco: biografía histórica*, 6 vols., Barcelona, Editorial Planeta, 1982.
―――, *Francisco Franco: un siglo de España*, 2 vols., Madrid, Editora Nacional, 1973.
―――, *Historia de la Guerra Civil española*, Madrid, Editorial San Martín, 1969.
―――, *Historia del franquismo, vol. I: Orígenes y configuración (1939–1945)*, Barcelona, Editorial Planeta, 1975.
―――, *Historia del franquismo, vol. II: Aislamiento, transformación, agonía (1945–1975)*, Barcelona, Editorial Planeta, 1978.
Conforti, Olao, *Guadalajara: la prima sconfitta del fascismo*, Milán, Mursia, 1967.
Coverdale, John F., *Italian Intervention in the Spanish Civil War*, Princeton, NJ, Princeton University Press, 1975.
Cox, Geoffrey, *Defence of Madrid*, London, Left Book Club, 1937.
Créac'h, Jean, *Le coeur et l'épée: chroniques espagnoles*, París, Librairie Plon, 1958.
Crozier, Brian, *Franco: A Biographical History*, London, Eyre & Spottiswoode, 1967.
Day, Peter, *Franco's Friends: How British Intelligence Helped Bring Franco to Power in Spain*, London, Biteback Publishing, 2011.
De Felice, Renzo, *Mussolini il duce: gli anni del consenso (1929–1936)*, Turín, Einaudi, 1974.
De Felice, Renzo, *Mussolini il duce: lo stato totalitario (1936–1940)*, Turín, Einaudi, 1981.
De Felice, Renzo, *Mussolini l'alleato I. L'Italia in guerra (1940–1943), 1. Dalla guerra «breve» alla guerra lunga*, Turín, Einaudi, 1990.
De Felice, Renzo, *Mussolini l'alleato I. L'Italia in guerra (1940–1943), 2. Crisi e agonia del regime*, Turín, Einaudi, 1990.
De Felice, Renzo, *Mussolini l'alleato II. La Guerra Civile (1943–1945)*, Turín, Einaudi, 1997.
De Lizarza Iribarren, Antonio, *Memorias de la conspiración, 1931–1936: quinta edición*, Madrid, Ediciones Dyrsa, 1986.
De Vicente González, Manuel, *Los Combates por Madrid*, MK Editora, Madrid, 2014.
―――, *Madrid militarizado*, MK Editora, Madrid, undated.
Del Rey, Fernando, and Álvarez Tardío, Manuel, *Fuego Cruzado. La primavera de 1936*, Barcelona, Galaxia Guttenberg, 2024.
Diario del Alcázar, 23 July 1936, at https://fnff.es/historia/dia-2-de-julio/
Díaz, Carmen, *Mi vida con Ramón Franco*, Editorial Planeta, 1981.
Díez Álvarez, Luís, *La Batalla del Jarama*, Madrid, Anaya, 2005.
Diez Roja, Ramón, *El desembarco de Alhucemas. La intrahistoria de una operación concluyente (1911–1925)*, Madrid, Ministerio de Defensa, 2022.
Domínguez Núñez, Moisés, *En busca del general Balmes*, Madrid, Librería Hispania, 2015.
Domke, Joan, *Education, Fascism, and the Catholic Church in Franco's Spain*, PhD thesis 2011, Loyola University Chicago.
Ealham, Chris, Class, *Culture and Conflict in Barcelona, 1898–1937*, Oxford and New York, Routledge, 2004.
Ehrenburg, Ilyá, *Corresponsal en España*, Barcelona, Prensa Ibérica, 1998.
―――, *Eve of War, 1933–41: Volume IV of Men, Years-Life*, London, MacGibbon and Kee, 1963.
Ellwood, Sheelagh M., *Franco*, London, Longmans, 1994.

———, *Spanish Fascism in the Franco Era*, London, Macmillan, 1987.
Escobar, José, *Así empezó...*, Madrid, Guillermo del Toro, 1974.
Enríquez, Carmen, *Carmen Polo, señora de El Pardo*, Madrid, La Esfera de los Libros, 2012.
Escobar, José, *Así empezó...*, Madrid, Guillermo del Toro, 1974.
Esdaile, Charles, *The Spanish Civil War: A Military History*, London, Routledge, 2018.
Espinosa Maestre, Francisco, *La columna de la muerte. El avance del ejército franquista de Sevilla a Badajoz*, Barcelona, Editorial Crítica, 2003.
Esteban, Asunción, et al. eds., *La Alargada Sombra del Franquismo: Naturaleza, Mecanismos de Pervivencia y Huellas de la Dictadura*, Editorial Comares, Granada, 2019, 319–29.
Evans, Daniel, *The Conscience of the Spanish Revolution: Anarchist Opposition to State Collaboration in 1937*, PhD thesis, University of Leeds, 2016.
Expediente Picasso: Edición de su resumen publicado en 1931, Madrid, Agencia Estatal Boletín del Estado, 2021.
Feis, Herbert, *The Spanish Story: Franco and the Nations at War*, New York, Alfred A. Knopf, 1948.
Fernández-Cebrián, Ana, *Fables of Development: Capitalism and Social Imaginaries in Spain (1950–1967)* Liverpool, LUP, 2023.
Fernández Cuesta, Raimundo, *Testimonio, recuerdos y reflexiones*, Madrid, Ediciones Dyrsa, 1985.
Fernández Martín, Andrés and Brenes Sánchez, María Isabel, *1937: Éxodo Málaga Almería, nuevas fuentes de investigación*, Casabermeja, Aratispi Ediciones, 2016.
Fernández Santander, Carlos, *El General Franco, un dictador en un tiempo de infamia*, Barcelona, Editorial Crítica, 2005.
Ferrer Benimeli, José Antonio, *Masonería española contemporánea*, 2 vols, Madrid, Siglo XXI, 1980.
FOESSA Informe sociológico, Madrid, 1970.
Foltz, Charles, Jr., *The Masquerade in Spain*, Boston, Houghton Mifflin, 1948.
Fontenla, Salvador, *Franco, caudillo militar: su historia en los campos de batalla*, Madrid, La Esfera de los Libros, 2019.
Fraga Iribarne, Manuel, *Memoria breve de una vida pública*, Barcelona, Editorial Planeta, 1980.
Franco Bahamonde, Francisco (originally published under pseudonym Jakim Boor), *Masonería*, Madrid, Fundación Nacional Francisco Franco, 1982.
———, *Palabras del Caudillo 19 abril 1937–7 diciembre 1942*, Madrid, Ediciones de la Vicesecretaría de Educación Popular, 1943.
———, *Palabras del Caudillo 19 abril 1937–31 diciembre 1938*, Barcelona, Ediciones Fe, 1939.
———, *Textos de doctrina política: palabras y escritos de 1945 a 1950*, Madrid, Publicaciones Españolas, 1951.
———, *Diario de una bandera*, Madrid, Editorial Pueyo, 1922.
———, *'Apuntes' personales sobre la República y la guerra civil*, Madrid, Fundación Nacional Francisco Franco, 1987.
———, *Discursos y mensajes de S.E. el jefe del Estado a las Cortes españolas, 1943–1961*, Madrid, Sucesores de Rivadeneyra, 1961.

Franco Martínez-Bordiú, Francisco, *La naturaleza de Franco. Cuando mi abuelo era persona*, Madrid, La Esfera de los Libros, 2011.

Franco Salgado-Araujo, Francisco, *Mi vida junto a Franco*, Barcelona, Editorial Planeta, 1977.

— — —, *Mis conversaciones privadas con Franco*, Barcelona, Editorial Planeta, 1976.

Franco, Pilar, *Nosotros, los Franco*, Barcelona, Planeta, 1980.

Fraser, Ronald, *Blood of Spain: an Oral History of the Spanish Civil War*, London, Pimlico, 1994.

— — —, *In Hiding*, Verso, London, 2010.

— — —, *Mijas. República, guerra, franquismo en un pueblo andaluz*, Barcelona, Antoni Bosch, 1985.

— — —, *Tajos, The Story of a village on the Costa del Sol*, New York, Pantheon, 1973.

Fusi, Juan Pablo, 'La Cultura', in J. L. García Delgado (ed.), *Franquismo: el juicio de la historia*, Madrid, Ediciones Temas de Hoy, 2000.

Galinsoga, Luis, and Franco Salgado, Francisco, *Centinela de occidente (Semblanza biográfica de Francisco Franco)*, Barcelona, AHR, 1956.

García Pérez, Antonio, *Consejos a los caballeros de la Academia de Infantería*, Toledo, Viuda e Hijos de J. Pelaez, 1910.

Garriga, Ramón, *El general Yagüe*, Barcelona, Editorial Planeta, 1985.

— — —, *Juan March y su tiempo*, Barcelona, Editorial Planeta, 1976.

— — —, *La Señora de El Pardo*, Barcelona, Editorial Planeta, 1979.

— — —, *Nicolás Franco, el hermano brujo*, Editorial Planeta, 1980.

— — —, *Ramón Franco, el hermano maldito*, Barcelona, Editorial Planeta, 1978.

General Berenguer, *Campañas en el Rif y Yebala, 1921–2*, Madrid, Editorial Voluntad, 1923.

Gibson, Ian, *Federico García Lorca*, London, Faber & Faber, 1989.

— — —, *Paracuellos: cómo fue*, Madrid, Plaza & Janés, 1983.

Gil Pecharromán, Julio, *Historia de la Segunda República Española (1931–1936)*, Madrid, Biblioteca Nueva, 2002.

Gil Pecharromán, Julio, *José Antonio Primo de Rivera. Retrato de un visionario*, Madrid, Temas de Hoy, 1996.

Gil Robles, José María, *No fue posible la paz*, Barcelona, Ariel, 1968.

— — —, *La monarquía por la que yo luché*. Madrid, Taurus, 1976.

Gil, Vicente, *Cuarenta años junto a Franco*, Barcelona, Editorial Planeta, 1981.

Giménez Arnau, J. A., *Memorias de memoria. Descifre vuecencia personalmente*, Barcelona, Ediciones Destino, 1978.

— — —, *Yo, Jimmy: mi vida entre los Franco*, Barcelona, Editorial Planeta, 1981.

Giménez Caballero, Ernesto, *Memorias de un dictador*, Barcelona, Editorial Planeta, 1979.

— — —, *España nuestra*, Madrid, Literatura Vicesecretaría de Educación Popular, 1943.

Gironella, José María, y Rafael Borràs Betriu, *Cien españoles y Franco*, Barcelona, Editorial Planeta, 1979.

Goded Llopis, Manuel, *Marruecos. Las Etapas de la Pacificación*, Madrid, Compañía Ibero-Americana de Publicaciones, 1932.

Goebbels, Joseph, *The Goebbels Diaries (1939–1941)*, edited by Fred Taylor, London, Hamish Hamilton, 1982.

— — —, *Tagebücher 1924–1945* (vols. 1, 2, 3, 4, 5), Munich, Piper, 1992, p. 982.

———, *The Goebbels Diaries*, January 1942–December 1943, edited by Louis P. Lochner, London, Hamish Hamilton, 1948.
Gomá, Cardenal, *Por Dios y por España (1936–1939)*, Barcelona, Editorial Casulleras, 1940.
González Prado, Patricia, *Aborto y la autonomía sexual de las mujeres*, Buenos Aires, Didot, 2017.
González Calleja, Eduardo, 'La radicalización de las derechas', in Francisco Sánchez Pérez (ed.), *Los Mitos del 18 de julio*, Barcelona, Critica, 2013.
González de Miguel, Jesús, *La Batalla de Jarama*, Madrid, La Esfera de los Libros, 2009.
González Duro, Enrique, *Franco: una biografía psicológica*, Madrid, Ediciones Temas de Hoy, 1992.
González Iglesias, Julio, *Los dientes de Franco: patobiografía del general Francisco Franco a través de las revelaciones de sus dentistas*, Madrid, Editorial Fénix, 1996.
Graham, Helen, *The Spanish Civil War: A Very Short Introduction*, Oxford, OUP, 2005.
———, *The War and its Shadow: Spain's Civil War in Europe's Long Twentieth Century*, Brighton, Sussex Academic Press, 2012.
———, and Preston, Paul (eds), *The Popular Front in Europe*, London, Palgrave Macmillan, 1989.
Guía oficial de España, 1907, Madrid, 1907.
Guía oficial de España, 1887, Madrid, 1887.
Haigh, R. H., Morris, D. S., Peters, Anthony R., (eds.), *The Guardian Book of the Spanish Civil War*, London, Wildwood House, 1987.
Halder, Franz, *The Halder War Diary (1939–1942)*, edited by Charles Burdick and London, Hans-Adolf Jacobsen, 1988.
Hayes, Carlton J. H., *Wartime Mission in Spain*, New York, Macmillan, 1945.
Heiberg, Morten, *Emperadores del Mediterráneo. Franco, Mussolini y la Guerra Civil española*, Barcelona, Editorial Crítica, 2004.
Hills, George, *Franco: The Man and His Nation*, New York, Macmillan, 1967.
———, *Franco. El hombre y su nación*, Madrid, San Martin, 1970.
Hoare, Sir Samuel, *Ambassador on Special Mission*, London, Collins, 1946.
Hoja clandestina de la Unión Militar Española haciendo un llamamiento a los militares tras la Revolución de Octubre de 1934, Sociedad de Amigos de Laguardia at https://www.euskalmemoriadigitala.eus/handle/10357/58167
Hooper, John, *The New Spaniards*, Penguin, London, 2006.
Howson, Gerald, *Arms for Spain: The Untold Story of the Spanish Civil War*, London, John Murray, 1998.
Hughes, R. Gerald, *The Postwar Legacy of Appeasement: British foreign policy since 1945*, London, Bloomsbury, 2014.
Hurcombe, Martin, *France and the Spanish Civil War*, Farnham, Ashgate, 2011.
Iribarren, José María, *Con el General Mola: escenas y aspectos inéditos de la Guerra Civil*, Zaragoza, Librería General, 1937.
———, *Mola, datos para una biografía y para la historia del alzamiento nacional*, Zaragoza, Librería General, 1938.
Irujo, Xabier, *El Gernika de Richthofen: Un ensayo de bombardeo de terror*, Gernika, Gernikako Bakearen Museoa Fundazioa/Gernika-Lumoko Udala, 2012.
———, *Gernika 26 de abril de 1937*, Barcelona, Editorial Crítica, 2017.
Jackson, Gabriel, *The Spanish Republic and the Civil War, 1931–1939*, Princeton, Princeton University Press, 1972.

Jackson, Michael, *Fallen Sparrows: The International Brigades in the Spanish Civil War*, Philadelphia, American Philosophical Society, 1994.
Jaraíz Franco, Pilar, *Historia de una disidencia*, Madrid, Editorial Planeta, 1981.
Jensen, Geoffrey, *Cultura Militar Española: Modernistas, tradicionalistas, y liberales*, Madrid, Siglo XXI, 2014.
— — —, *Franco: Soldier, Commander, Dictator*, Lincoln, Potomac Books, 2015.
— — —, *Irrational triumph: Cultural Despair, Military Nationalism and the Ideological Origins of Franco 's Spain*, University of Nevada Press, Reno, 2001.
Juliá, Santos, et al., *Victimas de la Guerra Civil*, Madrid, Temas de Hoy, 1999.
Julio Merino, *El Otro Franco: el Franco intelectual y el Franco de la república*, Madrid, Espejo de Tinta, 2005.
Kantorowicz, Alfred, *Diario de la guerra civil española*, trans. Vicente Abella, Madrid, Constraescritura, 2018.
Karl, Mauricio (pseudonym of Mauricio Carlavilla del Barrio), *Sodomitas*, La Coruña, Editorial Nos, 1956.
Kemp, Peter, 'I fought for Franco', in *History of the Twentieth Century*, A. J. P. Taylor (ed.), London, Purnell, 1968, pp. 1604–09.
— — —, *Mine Were of Trouble*, London, Cassells, 1957.
Kindelán Duany, Alfredo, *La verdad de mis relaciones con Franco*, Barcelona, Editorial Planeta, 1981.
— — —, *Mis cuadernos de guerra*, 2.a ed., Barcelona, Editorial Planeta, 1982.
Klepak, Hal, *Churchill Comes of Age: Cuba, 1885*, Chicago, The History Press, 2015.
Knox, MacGregor, *Mussolini Unleashed, 1939–1941: Politics and Strategy in Fascist Italy's Last War*. Cambridge, CUP, 1986.
Koestler, Arthur, et al., *The God that Failed*, London, Hamish Hamilton, 1950.
— — —, *Invisible Writing*, Collins, London, 1954.
— — —, *Spanish Testament*, London, Victor Gollancz, 1937.
Koltsov, Mijaíl, *Diario de la guerra de España*, Barcelona, Planeta, 2009.
Lafuente, Isaías, *Esclavos por la patria. La explotación de los presos bajo el franquismo*, Madrid, Ediciones Temas de Hoy, 2002.
Landrove Díaz, Gerardo, *Política Criminal del Aborto*, Barcelona, Bosch Casa Editorial, 1976.
Laureau, Patrick, *Condor: The Luftwaffe in Spain, 1936–39*, Stackpole, Lanham, 2010.
Ledesma, Ramiro, *Conquista del Estado*, No. 1, 14 March 1931.
Lerroux, Alejandro, *La pequeña historia de España (1930–1936)*, Madrid, Ediciones Criticón, 2016.
Little, Douglas, *Malevolent Neutrality: The United States, Great Britain, and the Origins of the Spanish Civil War*, Ithaca and London, Cornell University Press, 1985.
Lizarza Iribarren, Antonio, *Memorias de la conspiración*, 4th edn, Pamplona, Editorial Gómez, 1969.
Longo, Luigi, *Las Brigadas Internacionales en España*, México, Era, 1966.
López Rodó, Laureano, *El principio del fin: Memorias*, Barcelona, Plaza y Janés, 1992.
— — —, *Memorias*, Barcelona, Plaza y Janés, 1990.
— — —, *Memorias: años decisivos*, Barcelona, Plaza y Janés, 1991.
— — —, *Testimonio de una política de Estado*, Barcelona, Editorial Planeta, 1987.
Loureiro, Angela (ed.), *Estelas, laberintos, nuevas sendas: Unamuno, Valle-Inclán, García Lorca, la Guerra Civil*, Barcelona, Anthropos, 1988.

Lowe, Sid, *Catholicism, War and the Foundation of Francoism: The Juventud de Acción Popular in Spain, 1931–1939*, Brighton, Sussex Academic Press/Cañada Blanch, 2010.
Luca de Tena, José Ignacio, *Mis amigos muertos*, Barcelona, Editorial Planeta, 1971.
Togores, Luis, *Historia de la Legión Española: La Infantería legendaria. De África a Afganistán*, Madrid, La Esfera de los Libros, 2016.
— — —, *Muñoz Grandes*, Madrid, La Esfera de los Libros, 2014.
Madariaga, María Rosa de, *Los moros que trajo Franco. La intervención de tropas coloniales en la Guerra Civil*, Barcelona, Ediciones Martínez Roca, 2002.
Maisky, Ivan, *Spanish Notebooks*, London, Hutchinson, 1966.
Maíz, B. Félix, *Alzamiento en España: de un diario de la conspiración*, 2.a ed., Pamplona, Editorial Gómez, 1952.
Maldonado Moya, José María, *El Frente de Aragón: La Guerra Civil en Aragón*, Zaragoza, Mira, 2007.
Manuel Azaña, *Diarios de la República*, Sevilla, Ombú, 2021.
Manuel Touron Yebra, *El General Miguel Campins*, PhD thesis, Universidad Complutense Madrid, 2002.
María Thomàs, Joan, *José Antonio: realidad y mito*, Madrid, Debate, 2022.
Martin, Claude, *Franco, soldado y estadista*, Madrid, Fermín Uriarte, 1965.
Martín Gaite, Carmen, *Usos amorosos de la posguerra española*, Barcelona, Anagrama, 1987.
Martínez Barrio, Diego, *Memorias*, Barcelona, Planeta, 1983.
Martínez de Pisón, Ignacio, *Filek. El estafador que engañó a Franco*, Seix Barral, 2018.
Martínez Roda, Federico, *Varela. El general antifascista de Franco*, Madrid, La Esfera de los Libros, 2012.
Matthews, Herbert L., *The Yoke and the Arrows: A Report on Spain*, London, Heinemann, 1958.
Maura, Antonio, 'Transcendental discurso pronunciado por D. Antonio Maura en el Congreso de los Diputados el día 10 de noviembre de 1921, exponiendo con clarísima precisión el pensamiento del Gobierno en el importantísimo problema de Marruecos' in *Francisco Silvela and Antonio Maura*, Madrid, Juan Perez, 1903.
McDermott, Kevin, and Agnew, Jeremy, *The Comintern: A history of international communism from Lenin to Stalin*, Basingstoke, Palgrave Macmillan, 1996.
Mejias Correa, Maria de la Luz, *Así fue pasando el tiempo. Memorias de una miliciana extremeña*, Madrid, Editorial Renacimiento, 2006.
Mellor, Frank H., *Morocco Awakes*, London, Methuen, 1939.
Mérida, María, *Testigos de Franco*, Barcelona, Plaza y Janés, 1977.
Merino, Ignacio, *Serrano Suñer. Conciencia y poder*, Algaba Ediciones, 2004.
Miguel, Amando de, *Sociología del franquismo*, Barcelona, Editorial Euros, 1975.
Minchom, Martin, *Spain's Martyred Cities: From the Battle of Madrid to Picasso's Guernica*, Brighton, Sussex Academic Press/Cañada Blanch, 2015.
Mir, Conxita, *Vivir es sobrevivir. Justicia, orden y marginación en la Cataluña rural de posguerra*, Lleida, Editorial Milenio, 2000.
Mola Vidal, Emilio, *Obras completas*, Valladolid, Librería Santarén, 1940.
— — —, *Tempestad, calma, intriga y crisis. Memorias de mi paso por la Dirección General de Seguridad*, Madrid, Librería Bergua, 1932.

Mola, Emilio, *El pasado, Azaña y el porvenir: las tragedias de nuestras instituciones militares*, Madrid, La Crítica Literaria, 2011.
Molinero, Carme, *La captación de las masas. Política social y propaganda en el régimen franquista*, Madrid, Ediciones Cátedra, 2005.
Montero, Severiano, *La Batalla de Brunete*, Madrid, Raíces, 2010.
Moradiellos, Enrique, *Francisco Franco. Crónica de un caudillo casi olvidado*, Madrid, Biblioteca Nueva, 2002.
— — —, *Franco: Anatomy of a Dictator*, London, I. B. Tauris, 2017.
— — —, *La España de Franco (1939–1975). Política y sociedad*, Madrid, Editorial Síntesis, 2000.
— — —, 'Caudillo de España: Franco, un dictador carismático y soberano', in — (ed.), *Las caras de Franco. Una revisión histórica del caudillo y su régimen*, Madrid, Siglo XXI, 2016, pp. 29–96.
Morán, Gregorio, *Adolfo Suárez: historia de una ambición*, Barcelona, Editorial Planeta, 1979.
Moreno Julià, Xavier, *La División Azul. Sangre española en Rusia (1941–1945)*, Barcelona, Editorial Crítica, 2004.
Morente Valero, Francisco, *La depuración del magisterio nacional (1936–1943). La escuela y el Estado Nuevo*, Valladolid, Ámbito Alarife, 1997.
Nash, Mary, *Mujer, Familia y Trabajo en España, 1875–1936*, Barcelona, Anthropos, 1983.
Nenni, Pietro, *España*, Barcelona, Plaza y Janés, 1977.
— — —, *La matanza de Badajoz*, Badajoz, Editora Regional de Extremadura, 1986.
Nourry, Philippe, *Francisco Franco, la conquista del poder*, Gijón, Crónicas, 1976.
Orwell, George, 'Looking Back on the Spanish Civil War', in *England Your England*, London, Secker & Warburg, 1953.
Orwell, George, *Homage to Catalonia*, London, Secker & Warburg, 1938.
Palacios, Jesús, *La España totalitaria. Las raíces del franquismo (1934–1946)*, Barcelona, Editorial Planeta, 1999.
— — —, *Las cartas de Franco. La correspondencia desconocida que marcó el destino de España*, Madrid, La Esfera de Los Libros, 2005.
— — —, y Stanley G. Payne, *Franco, mi padre. Testimonio de Carmen Franco, la hija del Caudillo*, Madrid, La Esfera de Los Libros, 2005.
Palafox, Jordi, *Atraso económico y democracia: La Segunda República y la economía española*, Barcelona, Editorial Critica, 2000.
Palomares, María Cristina, *The Quest for Survival after Franco: the Moderate Francoists slow journey to the polls (1964–1977)*. PhD thesis, London School of Economics and Political Science, 2002.
Palomino, Ángel, y Paul Preston, *Francisco Franco*, Barcelona, Ediciones B, 2003.
Payne, Stanley and Tusell, Javier (eds.), *La guerra civil: Una nueva visión del conflicto que dividió España*, Madrid, Temas de Hoy, 1996.
— — —, and Palacios, Jesús, *Franco. A Personal and Political Biography*, Madison, Wisconsin University Press, 2014.
— — —, *El camino al 18 de julio: La erosión de la democracia en España (diciembre de 1935 – julio de 1936)*, Madrid, Espasa, 2016.
— — —, *Falange: A History of Spanish Fascism*, Stanford, Stanford University Press, 1961.
— — —, *Fascism in Spain (1923–1977)*, Madison, Wisconsin University Press, 1999.

———, *Franco and Hitler. Spain, Germany, and World War II*, New Haven & London, Yale University Press, 2008.
———, *Franco y José Antonio: El extraño caso del fascismo español*, Barcelona, Editorial Planeta, 1997.
———, *Franco: el perfil de la historia*, Madrid, Espasa Calpe, 1992.
———, *Franco's Spain*, London, Routledge & Kegan Paul, 1968.
———, *Politics and the Military in Modern Spain*, Stanford, Stanford University Press, 1967.
———, *Spain's First Democracy: The Second Republic, 1931–36*, Madison, University of Wisconsin Press, 1993.
———, *The Collapse of the Spanish Republic 1933–1936*, New Haven, Yale University Press, 2006.
———, *The Franco Regime (1936–1975)*, Madison, Wisconsin University Press, 1987.
Pemán, José María, *Apuntes autobiográficos. Confesión general y otros*, Edibesa, 1998.
———, *Mis encuentros con Franco*, Dopesa, 1976.
Pemartín, Julio, *Teoría De La Falange*, Madrid, Editora Nacional, 1941.
Peñafiel, Jaime, *El General y su tropa, Mis recuerdos de la familia Franco*, Madrid, Ediciones Temas de Hoy, 1992.
Pérez Vejo, Tomás, *3 de Julio 1898, El fin del imperio español*, Barcelona, Editorial Taurus, 2020.
Portela Valladares, Manuel, *Memorias: dentro del drama español*, Madrid, Alianza Editorial, 1988.
Pozuelo, Vicente, *Los últimos 476 días de Franco*, Barcelona, Editorial Planeta, 1980.
Preston, Paul, *Architects of Terror: Paranoia, Conspiracy and Anti-Semitism in Franco's Spain*, London, HarperCollins, 2023.
Preston, Paul, *¡Comrades! Portraits from the Spanish Civil War*, London, Harper Collins, 1999.
———, *A Concise History of the Spanish Civil War*, London, HarperCollins, 1996.
———, *A People Betrayed: A History of Corruption, Political Incompetence and Social Division in Modern Spain, 1874–2018,*. London, William Collins, 2020.
———, *Doves of War: Four Women of Spain*, London, HarperCollins, 2002.
———, ed. (with Sebastian Balfour), *Spain and the Great Powers*, London, Routledge, 1999.
———, *La Republica asediada. Hostilidad internacional y conflictos internos durante la Guerra Civil*, Barcelona, Ediciones Península, 1999.
———, ed., *Revolution and War in Spain (1931–1939)*, London, Methuen, 1984.
———, *El final de la guerra. La última puñalada a la República*, Barcelona, Editorial Debate, 2014.
———, *El gran manipulador. La mentira cotidiana de Franco*, Barcelona, Ediciones B, 2008.
———, *Franco*, HarperCollins, London, 1993.
———, *Franco*, Barcelona, Debate, 2015.
———, *Juan Carlos: Steering Spain from Dictatorship to Democracy*, London, Harper-Perennial, 2010.
———, *La destrucción de la democracia en España: reforma reacción y revolución en la Segunda República*, Barcelona, Grijalbo Mondadori, 2001.
———, *La política de la venganza: el fascismo y el militarismo en la España del siglo XX*, Barcelona, Ediciones Península, 1997.
———, *Las tres Españas del 36*, Barcelona, Plaza y Janés, 1998.

———, *Palomas de guerra. Cinco mujeres marcadas por el enfrentamiento bélico*, Barcelona, Plaza y Janés, 2001.
———, *The Coming of the Spanish Civil War: Reform, reaction and revolution in the Second Republic, 1931–1936*, London, Macmillan, 1978.
———, *The Politics of Revenge: Fascism and the Military in 20th Century Spain*, London, George Allen & Unwin, 1990.
———, *The Spanish Civil War: Reaction, Revolution and Revenge*, London, William Collins, 2016.
———, *The Spanish Holocaust: Inquisition and Extermination in Twentieth-Century Spain*, London, HarperPress, 2012.
———, *The Triumph of Democracy in Spain*, London, Methuen, 1986.
———, *We Saw Spain Die: Foreign Correspondents in the Spanish Civil War*, London, Constable, 2009.
———, *¡Comrades!: Portraits from the Spanish Civil War*, London, HarperCollins, 1999.
Primo de Rivera, José Antonio, *Textos de doctrina política*, 4.a ed., Madrid, Sección Femenina de FET y de las JONS, 1966.
Pritchett, V. S. *The Spanish Temper*, London, Chatto & Windus, 1954.
Puell de la Villa, Fernando, 'La trama militar de la conspiración', in Francisco Sánchez Pérez (ed.), *Los mitos del 18 de julio*, Barcelona, Editorial Crítica, 2013.
Radcliff, Pamela Beth, *La España contemporánea: desde 1808 hasta nuestros días*, Barcelona, Editorial Ariel, 2018.
Radosh, Ronald, Habeck, Mary R. and Sevonstiananov, Grigory, (eds.), *Spain Betrayed: The Soviet Union in the Spanish Civil War*, New Haven, Yale University Press, 2001.
Raguer, Hilari, *La pólvora y el incienso. La Iglesia y la Guerra Civil española*, Barcelona, Ediciones Península, 2001.
———, *Réquiem por la cristiandad. El Concilio Vaticano II y su impacto en España*, Barcelona, Ediciones Península, 2006.
Ramírez, Pedro J., *El año que murió Franco*, Barcelona, Plaza y Janés, 1985.
Real Automóvil Club de Asturias, *Guía del año 1919*, Gijón, Compañía Asturiana de Artes Gráficas, 1919.
Reckling, Tobias, *Foreign correspondents in Francoist Spain (1945–1975)*, PhD thesis, University of Portsmouth, 2016.
Redondo, J. Crespo, et al., *Purga de maestros en la guerra civil. La depuración del magisterio nacional en la provincia de Burgos*, Valladolid, Ámbito Alarife, 1987.
Reig Tapia, Alberto, *Franco 'Caudillo': Mito y realidad*, Madrid, Editorial Tecnos, 1995.
———, *La Cruzada de 1936. Mitos y memoria*, Madrid, Alianza Editorial, 2006.
Renn, Ludwig, *La Guerra Civil Española, Crónica de un escritor en las Brigadas Internacionales*, Madrid, Fórcola, 2016.
Reverte, Jorge M., *La División Azul*, Barcelona, RBA, 2011.
Rhodes, Richard, *Hell and Good Company: The Spanish Civil War and the World It Made*, New York, Simon & Schuster, 2015.
Richards, Michael, *A Time of Silence: Civil War and the Culture of Repression in Franco's Spain (1936–1945)*, Cambridge, Cambridge University Press, 1998.
Ridruejo, Dionisio, *Casi unas memorias*, Barcelona, Editorial Planeta, 1976.
———, *Escrito en España*, 2.a ed., Buenos Aires, Editorial Losada, 1964.

———, *Entre literatura y política,* Madrid, Seminarios y Ediciones, S.A., 1973.
Roche, Luis Armando, *'Que boten mis cenizas al aire y se olviden de mí', Luis Buñuel, cineasta de realidad y sueños,* Scotts Valley, Create Space, 2001.
Rodimstev, Aleksandr Ilích, *Bajo el cielo de España,* Moscow, Progreso, 1981.
Rodrigo, Javier, *La Guerra Fascista: Italia en la Guerra Civil Española,* Madrid, Alianza, 2016.
Rodríguez Aisa, María Luisa, *El Cardenal Gomá y la guerra de España. Aspectos de la gestión pública del Primado, 1936–1939,* Consejo Superior de Investigaciones Científicas, 1981.
Rodríguez Tejada, Sergio, *Zonas de libertad (Vol. I): Dictadura franquista y movimiento estudiantil,* Valencia, Publicaciones de la Universidad de Valencia 2009.
Rojo, Vicente, *Así fue la defensa de Madrid Aportación a la Historia de la Guerra de España, 1936–1939,* Imprenta de la Comunidad de Madrid, 1987.
Romero Pérez, Fernando, *Campañas de Propaganda en Dictadura y Democracia. Referendos y Elecciones de 1947 a 1978,* PhD thesis, Universidad Nacional de Educación a Distancia, 2009.
Romero Salvador, Carmelo, *Las elecciones que acabaron con la monarquía,* Madrid, Los Libros de Catarata, 2023.
Romero, Luis, *Tres días de julio (18, 19 y 20 de 1936),* 2.a ed., Barcelona, Ariel, 1968.
Ros Agudo, Manuel, *La gran tentación. Franco, el imperio colonial y los planes de intervención en la Segunda Guerra Mundial,* Barcelona, Styria Ediciones, 2008.
———, *La guerra secreta de Franco (1939–1945),* Barcelona, Editorial Crítica, 2002.
Roulin, Stéphanie, *Un credo anticommuniste. La commission Pro Deo de l'Entente Internationale Anticommuniste ou la dimension religieuse d'un combat politique (1924–1945),* Lausanne, Antipodes, 2010.
Rubio, Antonio, *El desastre del Annual a través de la prensa,* Madrid, Libros.com, 2022.
Ruiz, Julius, *The 'Red Terror' and the Spanish Civil War: Revolutionary Violence in Madrid,* New York, Cambridge University Press, 2014.
Sainz Rodríguez, Pedro, *Testimonio y recuerdos,* Barcelona, Editorial Planeta, 1978.
Sala González, Luis María, *Indalecio Prieto y la política española, 1930–1936,* PhD thesis, Universidad del País Vasco, 2015.
Salinas Salinas, Carlos, *Pedro Zaragoza Orts, Alcalde franquista y desarrollista de Benidorm, 1951–1967.* PhD thesis, University of Alicante, 2021.
Salisbury, William T., and James Theberge, Daniel (eds.) *Spain in the 1970s: Economics, Social Structure and Foreign Policy,* New York, Praeger, 1976.
Sánchez Montoya, Francisco, *Ceuta y el norte de África: Republica, Guerra y represión 1931–1944,* Granada, Nativola, 2004.
Sánchez Pérez, Francisco (ed.), *Los mitos del 18 de julio,* Barcelona, Critica, 2013.
Sánchez Recio, Glicerio, *De las dos ciudades a la resurrección de España: Magisterio pastoral y pensamiento político de Enrique Pla y Deniel Alicante,* Biblioteca Virtual Miguel de Cervantes, 2022.
Saña, Heleno, *El franquismo sin mitos. Conversaciones con Serrano Suñer,* Barcelona, Grijalbo, 1982.
Sartorius, Nicolás, y Javier Alfaya, *La memoria insumisa. Sobre la Dictadura de Franco,* Madrid, Espasa Calpe, 1999.
Saz Campos, Ismael, *España contra España. Los nacionalismos franquistas,* Madrid, Marcial Pons, 2003.

———, *Fascismo y franquismo*, Valencia, Publicaciones de la Universidad de Valencia, 2004.
———, *Mussolini contra la II República: hostilidad, conspiraciones, intervención (1931–1936)*, Valencia, Edicions Alfons el Magnànim, 1986.
———, y Gómez Roda, J. Alberto eds., *El franquismo en Valencia. Formas de vida y actitudes sociales en la posguerra*, Valencia, Ediciones Episteme, 1999.
Schmidt, Paul, *Hitler's Interpreter: The Secret History of German Diplomacy (1935–1945)*, London, Heinemann, 1951.
Schüler-Springorum, Stefanie, *La Guerra Como Aventura*, Alianza, Madrid, 2014.
Serrano Súñer, Ramón, *De anteayer y de hoy*, Barcelona, Plaza y Janés, 1981.
———, *Política de España (1936–1975)*, Madrid, Editorial Complutense, 1995.
———, *Entre el silencio y la propaganda, la Historia como fue. Memorias*, Barcelona, Editorial Planeta, 1977.
Serrano A., *Yo soy Español*, Madrid, Editorial Escuela Española, 1962.
Sevillano Calero, Francisco, *Ecos de Papel: la opinión de los españoles en la época de Franco*, Madrid, Biblioteca Nueva, 2000.
———, Sevillano Calero, Francisco, *Dictadura, socialización y conciencia política. Persuasión ideológica y opinión en España bajo el franquismo (1939–1962)* PhD thesis.
Shulman, Aaron, *The Age of Disenchantments: The Epic Story of Spain's Most Notorious Literary Family and the Long Shadow of the Spanish Civil War*, London, HarperCollins, 2019.
Silva Barrera, Emilio, 'Todos somos franquismo sociológico', in Asunción Esteban, Dunia Etura, Matteo Tomasoni (eds.), *La alargada sombra del franquismo naturaleza, mecanismos de pervivencia y huellas de la dictadura*, Granada, Editorial Comares, 2019, pp. 319–329.
Sinova, Justino, *La censura de Prensa durante el franquismo*, Madrid, Espasa-Calpe, 1989.
Skoutelsky, Rémi, *L'espoir guidait leurs pas: Les volontaires français dans les Brigades internationales, 1936–1939*, Paris, Grasset, 1998.
———, *Novedad en el frente: Las brigadas internacionales en la guerra civil*, Madrid, Ediciones Temas de Hoy, 2006.
Soriano, Ramón, *La mano izquierda de Franco*, Madrid, Editorial Planeta, 1981.
Southern, Paul, *Francisco Franco's Moroccan War Diary (1920–1922)*, Bromley, Galago Books, 2007.
Stradling, Robert, *Brother against Brother: Experiences of a British Volunteer in the Spanish Civil War*, Sutton, Sutton Publishing, 1998.
Suárez Fernández, Luis, *Francisco Franco y su tiempo*, 8 vols., Madrid, Fundación Nacional Francisco Franco, 1984.
———, *Franco: la historia y sus documentos*, 20 vols., Madrid, Urbión, 1986.
Szurek, Alexander, *The Shattered Dream*, Boulder, East European Monographs, 1989.
Thomas, Hugh, *The Spanish Civil War*, 4th edition, London, Penguin, 2012.
Thomàs, Joan María, *El gran golpe. El 'Caso Hedilla' o cómo Franco se quedó con Falange*, Madrid, Editorial Debate, 2014.
———, *José Antonio. Realidad y mito*, Madrid, Editorial Debate, 2017.
———, *La Falange de Franco. Fascismo y fascistización en el régimen franquista (1937–1945)*, Barcelona, Plaza y Janés, 2001.

Togores, Luis E., *Yagüe. El General Falangista de Franco*, Madrid, La Esfera de los Libros, 2010.
———, *Muñoz Grandes: héroe de Marruecos, general de la División Azul*, Madrid, La Esfera de los Libros, 2007.
Tone, John Lawrence, *War and Genocide in Cuba, 1895–1898*, Chapel Hill, University of North Carolina Press, 2006.
Torres, Francisco, *Franco o la venganza de la historia*, Madrid, Criterio, 2000.
Townson, Nigel, *La República que no pudo ser: política de centro en España (1931–1936)*, Madrid, Taurus, 2002.
———, *The Penguin History of Modern Spain: 1989 to the Present*, London, Allen Lane, 2023.
Tremlett, Giles, *The International Brigades: Fascism, Freedom and the Spanish Civil War*, London, Bloomsbury, 2021.
———, *España: a Brief History of Spain*, London, Bloomsbury, 2022.
———, *Ghosts of Spain: Travels through a Country's Troubled Past*, London, Faber, 2012.
Trevor-Roper, Hugh, *Hitler's Table Talk: His Private Conversation, 1941–44*, London, Phoenix Press, 2000.
Trevor-Roper, Hugh (ed.), *The Testament of Hitler, The Hitler-Bormann Documents*, London, Cassell, 1961.
Turón Yebra, Manuel, *El General Miguel Campins y su época (1880–1936)*, PhD thesis, Universidad Complutense de Madrid, 2002.
Tusell, Javier and Queipo de Llano, Genoveva, *Alfonso XIII: el rey polémico*, Madrid, Taurus, 2001.
———, *Franco en la Guerra Civil. Una biografía política*, Barcelona, Tusquets Editores, 1992.
———, *Franco y los católicos: la política interior española entre 1945 y 1957*, Madrid, Alianza Editorial, 1984.
———, *España y la Segunda Guerra Mundial. Entre el Eje y la neutralidad*, Madrid, Ediciones Temas de Hoy, 1995.
———, *La dictadura de Franco*, Madrid, Alianza Editorial, 1988.
———, *Las elecciones del Frente Popular*, 2 vols., Madrid, Edicusa, 1971.
———, y Genoveva García Queipo de Llano, *Franco y Mussolini: la política española durante la Segunda Guerra Mundial*, Barcelona, Editorial Planeta, 1985.
Valadares, Portela, *Memorias. Dentro del drama español*, Madrid, Alianza Editorial, 1988.
Vallejo Nágera, Antonio, *Eugenesia de la hispanidad y regeneración de la raza española*, Burgos, Talleres Gráficos El Noticiero, 1937.
———, *La locura y la guerra. Psicopatología de la guerra española*, Valladolid, Librería Santarén, 1939.
Van Hensbergen, Gijs, *Guernica: The Biography of a Twentieth-century Icon*, London, Bloomsbury, 2005.
Vázquez Montalbán, Manuel, *Autobiografía del general Franco*, Barcelona, Barcelona, Madrid, Editorial Planeta, 1992.
———, *Los demonios familiares de Franco*, Barcelona, Dopesa, 1978.
Vegas Latapié, Eugenio, *La frustración en la Victoria. Memorias políticas, 1938–1942*, Madrid, Editorial Actas, 1995.
Vinyes, Ricard, *Irredentas. Las presas políticas y sus hijos en las cárceles franquistas*, Madrid, Ediciones Temas de Hoy, 2002.

———, Armengou, Montse and Belis, Ricard, *Els Nens Perduts del Franquisme*, Proa, Barcelona, 2002.
Viñas, Ángel, *¿Quién quiso la guerra civil? Historia de una conspiración*, Barcelona, Editorial Crítica, 2019.
———, 'La connivencia fascista con la sublevación y otros éxitos de la trama civil', in Francisco Sánchez Pérez (ed.), *Los Mitos del 18 de julio*, Barcelona, Editorial Crítica, 2013, pp. 79–182.
———, and Blanco, Juan Andrés, *La Guerra Civil Española: Una Visión Bibliográfica*, Madrid, Marcial Pons Historia, 2017.
———, *Hitler y el estallido de la Guerra Civil. Antecedentes y consecuencias*, Madrid, Alianza Editorial, 2001.
———, *Guerra, dinero, dictadura: ayuda fascista y autarquía en la España de Franco*, Barcelona, Editorial Crítica, 1984.
———, *La Conspiración del General Franco*, Barcelona, Editorial Crítica, 2011.
———, *La otra cara del Caudillo. Mitos y realidades en la biografía de Franco*, Barcelona, Editorial Crítica, 2015.
———, *Los pactos secretos de Franco con Estados Unidos: bases, ayuda económica, recortes de soberanía*, Barcelona, Grijalbo, 1981.
———, Sánchez Pérez, et al., *Los mitos del 18 de julio*, Barcelona, Editorial Crítica, 2013.
Von Below, Nicolaus, *At Hitler's Side: The Memoirs of Hitler's Luftwaffe Adjutant, 1937–1945*, Mainz, Hase & Koehler, 1980.
Walters, Vernon A., *Silent Missions*, New York, Doubleday, 1978.
Welles, Benjamin, *Spain: The Gentle Anarchy*, London, Pall Mall, 1965.
Westwell, Ian, *Condor Legion: The Wehrmacht's Training Ground*, Hersham, Ian Allen, 2004.
Whealey, Robert, *Hitler and Spain: The Nazi Role in the Spanish Civil War. 1936–1939*, Lexington, University Press of Kentucky, 1989.
Whitaker, John T., *We Cannot Escape History*, New York, Macmillan, 1943.
Wylie, Neville (ed.), *Introduction, in European Neutrals and Non-Belligerents during the Second World War*, Cambridge, Cambridge University Press, 2011.
Yarza, Alejandro, *The Making and Unmaking of Francoist Kitsch Cinema: From Raza to Pan's Labyrinth*, Edinburgh, Edinburgh University Press, 2018.
Ysàs, Pere, *Disidencia y subversión. La lucha del régimen franquista por la supervivencia (1960–1975)*, Barcelona, Editorial Crítica, 2004.
Zavala, José María, *Franco con franqueza: Anecdotario privado del personaje más público*, Barcelona, Plaza & Janes, 2015.
Zenobi, Laura, *La construcción del mito de Franco. De Jefe de la Legión a Caudillo de España*, Madrid, Ediciones Cátedra, 2011.

Index

ABC newspaper 68–9, 105, 112, 147, 189, 344, 373
Abd al-Aziz, Sultan 37
Abd el-Krim, Mohammed ibn 62–3, 65, 67, 84–6
abortion 297–8, 302, 378–9, 392
Abwehr 164, 281
Abyssinia (Ethiopia), Italian invasion 137, 173, 214
Adenauer, Konrad 360
'adictos' and 'desafectos' 308
Adowa, battle of 64
adultery 9, 298–9, 343
África 112
Africanistas 39, 42–3, 47, 52, 59–61, 67, 70–1, 73, 75, 77–81, 84–5, 87, 90, 92–3, 99, 101, 108–10, 113, 115, 119, 121, 139, 171, 174, 315, 401
Agamemnon 268
Agnew, Spiro 362
Aguirre, Hosé Antonio 217
Aizpuru, General Luis 76–7
Ajdir 85
Alas, Leopoldo 49
Alcalá-Galiano, Dionisio 24
Alcalá-Zamora, Niceto 107, 114, 119, 122, 124–6, 129, 132, 139
Alcalá de Henares 213
Alcañiz 233
Aldana, Agustina 27–8, 275–6

Aldrich, Robert 343
Alexander the Great 268
Alfonso VI, King 241
Alfonso XIII, King 16, 37–8, 46, 50, 62, 69, 96, 104, 142, 157, 179, 202
  death 283
  his grandchildren 304, 364
  letter to Franco 83–4
  letter to Mussolini 160
  and Primo de Rivera coup 74–5
  and Second Republic 97, 99, 101–3, 108, 111
Algeciras 38, 57, 143, 154, 159, 281
Algeria 246, 280
Alhucemas Bay 84–7
Alicante 130, 157, 175, 186, 199–201, 237, 327
Allen, Jay 157, 164–5, 199
Alliance of Anti-Fascist Intellectuals 219
Almería 37, 197, 237, 387
Alto de León pass 159
Amezian, Mohamed 40
amnesty 350–1, 363, 392–3
Amnesty International 368, 383
Anarcho-Syndicalists 154, 223
Andrade, Jaime de 265
Angiolillo, Michele 25
Angola 27
Annual disaster 61, 63, 70, 72, 74–6, 84
Añoveros, Bishop Antonio 373

Ansaldo, Juan Antonio 156
Anson, Luis María 379
anti-Americanism 276
anticlericalism 120, 159, 257
antisemitism 256, 276
    see also Jews
archive destruction 396
Arditi 240
Arias Navarro, Carlos 369, 372, 376–8, 381, 386, 389–90
Army of Africa 42, 61, 66, 77, 79, 82, 112, 124, 126, 140–1, 143–5, 147–8, 151, 153–5, 157–9, 161, 165–6, 168, 172, 175, 178–9, 189, 236, 248, 252
Army of the North 167
Arranz, Captain Francisco 161
Arrarás, Joaquín 136
Arrese, José Luis 320–1
Arriba 256, 294, 336, 351
Arruja, Hermengildo 155
Asturias 48–9, 51, 110
    miners' strike 334–5, 338
    uprising 119–22, 132, 136, 138, 141, 166, 187
atheism 27, 108, 342
atomic bombs 288
Attlee, Clement 292
Aub, Max 353
Austerlitz, battle of 91
Austrian Anschluss 232
Axis entente 188, 196, 236–7, 250, 257, 272–4, 277, 281–2, 284, 287–8
Azaña, Manuel 107–10, 112, 122, 130, 132, 135, 139, 199, 220
Aznar, José María 396–7
Azor 304, 309

Badajoz 167–8, 170–1
Bahamonde, Don Ladislao 18, 20, 89
Bahamonde, Manuel 18–19
Bahamonde, Pilar 14, 21–2, 27, 36, 45, 115, 226, 267, 297
Bahamonde, Major Ricardo de la Puente 120, 149, 152

execution 168–9
Balboa López, Benjamin 154
Baldwin, Stanley 163
Baleares 202
Balearic Islands 112, 131, 186, 235
Balmes, General Amado 147
Bank of Spain 191, 397
Barcelona
    anti-Franco sentiment 329–33, 338
    Catalan Music Palace 330–3
    disturbances and regime failures 307
    ETA attacks 381
    Himmler visits 256
    Liceu Opera House 25
    Nationalist assault 154, 156, 219, 232–3, 235, 237
    Picasso Museum 357
    post-war shortages 244
    Semana Trágica 34
    student unrest 347, 373
Barea, Arturo 39–40, 44, 46, 58, 64–5, 67, 156
Barranco del Lobo (Wolf's Ravine) 33–4, 52
Barroso, Lieutenant Colonel Antonio 126, 215
Basque Country 19, 50, 183, 203, 215, 217, 226, 296, 335
    devolution of powers 390, 394
    ETA campaign 342, 348, 356–7, 359, 366, 369, 371, 380–2
    Guipuzcoa emergency 348, 357, 380
    nationalism (separatism) 154, 303, 342, 368, 378, 390
Batalloso, Juan Miguel 225–6
Batet, General Domingo 170
Bautista Aznar, Admiral Juan 102–3
bayonet charges 40
Bebb, Captain Cecil 144, 152
Beigbeder, Lieutenant Colonel Juan 157
Beihl, Eugene 357, 359
Belchite 221
Benavente, Jacinto 219

Beni Hosmar 43
Benidorm 327–8
Ben-Tieb military camp 81
Berenguer, Colonel Dámaso 42, 96, 98–100, 102
Berlin, fall of 286, 288
Bernhardt, Johannes 161–2, 164
Bianchi, Tranquillo 197
Bilbao, Esteban 290
Bilbao 15, 130, 157, 217, 221, 278, 379–80
bishops 3, 103, 182–3, 226, 295–6, 300, 361–2, 366, 373
black markets 263, 276
Blasco Ibáñez, Vicente 38
Blasco Salas, Captain Enrique 46
Blue Division 272–3, 282–3, 287, 315–16, 336, 382
Blum, Léon 163
Bogart, Humphrey 343
Bolín, Luis 147, 152–3, 155–6, 160, 236
Borbón, Don Juan de, *see* Don Juan de Borbón
Borbón y Dampierre, Alfonso de 364, 376
Borbón-Parma, Carlos Hugo de 352
Borbón-Parma, Don Javier de 204–5
Brackenbury, Lieutenant Colonel Delgado 131
Brenan, Gerald 291, 307, 355
brothels 35, 43, 64, 111, 152, 302, 328
Brown, William 58
Brunete 219–21
Buck, Tobias 398
Buckley, Henry 103, 146, 235
Bueon y Monreal, Cardinal José 361
Bulart, José María 182–3
bullfighters 355–6
Buñuel, Luis 27
Burgos 156, 159, 163, 167, 183–4, 202, 212, 225–7, 245, 248
  ETA trials 356–7, 359, 371
  jail riots 130

Palacio de la Isla 207, 220, 231, 247
Burguete, Ricardo 51–2
Burroughs, Admiral Harold 281

Caballero, Giménez 301
Caballero, Largo 127
Cabanellas, Guillermo 179, 186
Cabanellas, General Miguel 132, 170, 173–5, 177, 179, 184, 186
Cabanillas, Pío 377
Cáceres, Palacio do los Golfines de Arriba 172
Cádiz 98, 154, 159, 164–5, 196, 263, 281
  monastery fire 132–3
Calderón de la Barca, Pedro 58
Calero, Francisco Sevillano 11
Calles, Plutarco Elías 112
Calvo Sotelo, José 95, 127, 142, 146, 199, 202
Camacho, Obdulia 201–2, 396
Campano López, Lieutenant General Ángel 382
Campeche 191
Campins, General Miguel 94, 141, 169–70
Campoamor, Clara 133, 135, 159
Canarias 218
Canaris, Admiral Wilhelm 164, 172, 257–8
Canary Islands 79, 131–2, 139, 142–5, 149–51, 153, 161, 254, 274, 277, 280–1, 336
Cánovas del Castillo, Antonio 18, 25
Cantalupo, Randolfo 215–17, 221
Cape Juby Strip 38
capitalism 27, 142, 184–4, 200, 378
Carabineros 112
Carlavilla, M. 303
Carlists 25, 34, 133, 140, 143, 158, 160, 174, 179, 182–3, 185, 192, 204–5, 209–12, 221, 240, 278, 288, 336, 352, 361
Carlos V 19
Carmona, Oscar 283

INDEX

Carrero Blanco, Luis 258, 274, 279, 283, 290, 305, 321, 343, 347, 352, 356, 358, 360, 364, 367, 369
  assassination in Madrid 370–2
Carrillo, Santiago 380
Casares Quiroga, Santiago 139–42, 153
Case 1001 371–2, 379
Castelar, Emilio 16
Castillo, Lieutenant José del 138, 145–6
Castro, Fidel 353
Catalonia 19, 74–5, 108, 170, 183, 203, 215, 296, 330–3, 335–6, 345, 397
  devolution of powers 390, 394
  fall of 231–5
  nationalism (separatism) 50, 90, 96, 119, 150, 154, 303, 330, 368, 378, 390, 398–9
  sacking of civil servants 9
Catholic Institute for Social Studies 331
Causa General 308
Cazorla Sánchez, Antonio 6, 387–8
'cenocracy' 365
censorship and propaganda 3, 8–9, 12, 71, 79, 136, 168, 205, 224, 242–3, 264–70, 283, 291, 311, 319, 328, 330, 332, 336–7, 342–4, 348, 353–5, 362, 367–8, 388
  see also Press Law
Cervera, Admiral Juan 218
Cervera, Admiral Pascual 15, 17
Ceuta 34, 37, 44–5, 58–9, 62–3, 71, 75, 77, 84, 148–9, 153
Chaplin, Charlie 269
Charles V, Emperor 224, 241
Charter of Spaniards 288, 320, 336, 342
Chefchaouen 82
Chicote, Pedro 269
Chile 12, 389
Chilton, Sir Henry 190
Churchill, Winston 18, 66, 274, 281, 284–7, 292
  'Iron Curtain' speech 294
Churruca, Brigadier Cosme 24, 266–7
Churruca 156

Ciano, Count Galeazzo 160, 196, 207, 233–4, 237, 245–6
Civil Guard 51–2, 92, 101, 105, 112, 121, 125, 129–30, 137–8, 150, 154, 176, 187, 268–9, 275, 339, 344, 350–1, 366, 380, 382, 391, 395, 397
civil marriage 186, 223, 297
Claverie, Madame 53
Coco, Atilano 187–8
coinage 295
Columbus, Christopher 1, 17, 88, 90, 227
Comintern 126, 129, 177, 190
  Anti-Comintern Pact 236–7
communism 27, 95–6, 106, 112–13, 120, 127–9, 131–2, 144, 158, 162, 164, 179, 181, 184, 186, 188, 194, 209, 228, 237, 247, 272, 274, 282, 287, 290, 294, 305, 316–17, 337, 393, 399, 401
Companys, Lluís 119, 268
Condor Legion 196–7, 214, 217, 220, 234, 240, 245
Confederation of Autonomous Right-wing Groups (CEDA) 113–14, 116, 124–5, 130, 160
conquistadors 1, 5, 17, 83, 90
Constitution of Cadiz 24–5
contraception 223, 298
Correspondencia Militar 38, 105
Corrochano, Gregorio 68–9
corruption
  army 18, 40, 52, 63, 70
  and Franco regime 6, 12, 56, 223, 276, 310–12, 329–30, 332–3, 353, 359
  legacy of Francoism 395, 397–8
  Matesa scandal 347, 363
  and 'peaceful turn' 25
  and Primo de Rivera regime 96
Cortés, Hernán 83, 90
Cortés, Juliana 350–1
Cortés, Manuel 350–1
Cortés, María 350–2
Crawford, Joan 269
Creix, Juan and Vicente 395

Crisis of 1917 50–1
Cuatro Vientos airfield 101
Cuba 7, 10, 15–18, 26, 32, 65, 75, 87, 106, 266–7, 292, 317, 353, 374
Cuenca 138
Czech crisis 233–4

Daily Express 178, 327
Danchik, Bernie 154
Dar Drius 66
Davila, General Fidel 204
Davis, Bette 269
de Gaulle, Charles 254, 292
de Haya González, Captain Carlos 177
death rates, post-war 263
Degrelle, Leon 316
Delaprée, Louis 193
democracy 4–5, 7, 13, 25, 74, 104, 113–14, 118, 150, 159, 186–7, 224, 272, 274, 277, 335–6, 341, 347, 353, 355, 364, 378–80, 389–95, 398–9, 403–4
  'organic democracy' 291–2
Democratic Council of Spain 380
Democratic Military Union 383
Department of Investigation and Information Service 228
Deutsche Allgemeine Zeitung 273
Dewey, Commodore George 16
Diario Oficial 73
Díaz, Carmen 97, 100
Díez-Alegría, Lieutenant General Manuel 373
Disaster of 1898 17–19, 21, 25, 29, 65, 68
divorce 186, 193, 223, 297–8, 343, 392
Doblón magazine 388
Dollfuss, Engelbert 118
Dómine 133
Domínguez, Juan 278
Dominguín, Luis Miguel 355–6
Dominican Republic 227
Don Juan de Borbón 202, 283, 290–1, 304–5, 307, 336, 344, 351–2, 365
don Quixote 245, 262, 268
Doval, Lisardo 121–2, 187

Du Moulin-Eckart, Count 185–6
Dulles, John Foster 318
Durango 218
Dyer, Nina 310

East Germany 400
East Timor 27
Ebro, battle of the 231–5
Echarri Martínez, Maria de 16
Eco, Umberto 211
economy 8, 11–12, 17, 245, 260–4, 321–4, 338, 341–2, 379, 391–2, 395, 400, 402
  autarky 12, 260–1, 263, 312, 318, 321–3, 391, 402, 404
  economic blockade 250, 255, 260, 273, 277, 308
Eden, Anthony 218
education 225–6, 301–2
Edward VIII, King 193
Eighth Regiment of Zamora 36
Eisenhower, Dwight D. 315, 317, 325–6, 360
El Carbayón 70
El Cid 1, 17, 58, 340
El Comercio 76
El Día 48
El Ducali 45–6
El Escorial 241, 324
El Greco 30
El Labyout 44–5, 47–8
El Mizian, Major Mohamed 216–17
El Sol 102
Enlightenment 5, 7, 17, 25, 160, 399
Enrique y Tarancón, Cardinal Vicente 362
Escobar, José Ignacio 167
Escrivá, Josemaría 321
Espes, Luis Franco de, Baron of Mora 92
Estampa magazine 92–3
ETA campaign 342, 348, 356–8, 366, 369–71, 380–2, 398
European Economic Community 322, 363–4, 380, 382, 391

European Union 322, 380, 391
Euskara language 366

Fal Conde, Manuel 204–5
Falange 95, 113–15, 199–202, 204–5, 216, 226, 228–9, 385
  and Axis entente 272, 274, 277, 285–6, 315
  civil war 131–2, 141–3, 151, 157, 159–60, 166, 174, 176, 179, 183, 185
  disbanding 395–6
  and Franco victory 240, 242–4, 256
  grenade attack on Carlists 278
  and political violence 135–6, 138, 145, 201–2
  and post-war conditions 259, 263–4
  and post-war Spain (National Movement) 288–94, 296, 300–2, 305, 319–22, 324, 331–4, 336, 338, 352, 354, 358, 361–3, 377–8
  Principles of the Movement 322
  recruitment 200–1
  and socialist uprisings 118, 120
  and succession 351–2, 361
  and unification ('the Movement') 209–12, 221
  Women's Section 300–1
  and workers 223–4
Falla de los Lobos 51
Fanjul, General Joaquín 125, 128, 131, 156–7
Farinacci, Roberto 209
fascism 4, 7, 75, 95, 113, 129, 136, 160, 173, 183, 214, 221, 223–4, 277, 282, 289, 295, 316, 321, 380, 399, 401
  Italian 200–1, 207–8, 211, 224, 286
fascist salutes 211, 252, 289, 358, 361
Faupel, ambassador 219
Felipe VI, King 397
feminists 53, 133, 159, 392
  see also women
Ferdinand of Aragon 182, 211, 256
Ferdinand VII, King (El Deseado) 24

Fernández de Córdoba, Gonzalo (the Great Captain) 31, 37
Fernández Silvestre, General Manuel 62–3
Ferragut, Juan 71–2, 83
Ferrol 14–15, 18–19, 23–6, 28–30, 33–4, 36, 45, 54, 68, 70, 89, 107, 110, 157, 168, 181, 207, 266, 275, 343
FET y de las JONS 115, 210, 273–4, 276
Filek, Albert 261–2
First of October Antifascist Resistance Groups (GRAPO) 382
First World War 27, 32–3, 49–50, 63, 84, 191, 217, 256, 401
FOESSA 354
Foltz, Charles 262
Fontilles Lepers Hospital 130
Ford, Gerald 372, 380
Ford, John 343
Forest, Eva 370
Fraga, Manuel 312, 328, 336–7, 340, 343–6, 349, 353–5, 390, 393–4, 398
France, fall of 250, 285
Franco, Carmen 23, 26, 91, 151, 295, 306–7, 311, 324
Franco, Francisco
  anti-communism 95–6, 112–13
  anti-Masonic paranoia 107–8, 113, 122
  appearance 22, 164, 337, 340, 345
  attains absolute power 173–80, 183–4
  bargaining with Allies 283–4
  and battle of Alcuhemas 85–6
  and 'the bunker' 348, 354, 384
  churlishness 172
  commander in Balearic Islands 112
  commander in Canary Islands 131–3
  control of militias 204–5
  corpse reinterred 397
  courtship 43, 52–5, 72–3
  and cult of virility 11, 29, 35, 80, 93, 171, 181, 302–3
  de facto leader of insurrection 143–8, 157, 163, 167
  death 3, 384–6

declares state of war 149–50
early life 14–28
and economics 90–1, 95
and executions 168–70
and founding of Spanish Legion 55–73
and golf 135–6
government by edict 187
hospitalisation and sickbed decree 375–6
hosts Primo de Rivera 80–1
and launch of *Revista* 77–80
lying-in-state and funeral 387–9
marriage 73, 76
meeting with Don Juan 304–5
meeting with Eisenhower 325–6
meeting with Hitler 251–8
meeting with Mussolini 271–2
meeting with Nixon 356
military career and Morocco 36–47, 55–74
military career in Oviedo 48–52, 71–3
and military honours 4, 32, 45–8, 50; *see also* Laureate Cross of San Fernando
military training 29–35
and Mola's death 218–19
Moroccan War Diary 8, 64, 71
and mother's death 115
newspaper columns 7, 294
nicknames 21, 89, 329
Parkinson's disease 330, 340, 345, 351, 354, 360, 375, 377
patriotism 32–3
personality cult 226–7, 268
photographs and portraits 211, 302, 307, 319
political candidate 138–9
and religion 26–7, 92, 181–3
'Rewards of Campaigning' article 60
and Sanjurjo coup 111–12
sense of honour 106
and socialist uprisings 117–23
sphinx without a secret 403
and succession 352–3, 361–2, 364–6, 369
trust in family 206–7, 308–13
Valley of the Fallen incident 333–4
victory parades and propaganda 1–5, 239–46, 248, 340
wounded in Morocco 44–5, 91
and Zaragoza military academy 89, 91–4, 105, 109, 136
Franco, Francisco (grandson) 313
Franco, Gilda 27
Franco, María del Carmen 364, 385
Franco, Don Nicolás 14, 19, 21–3, 26–30, 33, 49, 69, 76, 107, 115, 274–6, 297
Franco, Nicolás 21, 45, 138, 174, 179, 186–7, 206–8, 222–3, 274–5, 310, 312, 332–3
Franco, Nicolás (nephew) 379
Franco, Paz 14, 22
Franco, Pilar 20–2, 27, 91, 235, 311–12
Franco, Ramón 10, 20–2, 28, 35, 79, 83, 85, 88–91, 94, 97–101, 103–4, 115, 121, 125, 138, 144, 186, 235, 267
Franco, That Man! 340
Francoism 2–3, 6, 8, 10–13, 192, 208–12, 225, 227, 244, 269, 289, 302–3, 319, 322, 333, 335, 337, 344–7, 352, 368, 378, 389, 391–8, 402
'sociological Francoism' 11
Franco-Prussian War 37
Fraser, Ronald 400
Freemasonry 5, 7, 17, 27–8, 98, 107–8, 117, 120–2, 132, 144, 146, 149, 173, 186, 209, 227–8, 235, 257, 272, 274–5, 294, 303, 306, 359, 381, 402
French colonies 246
French Foreign Legion 56
French resistance 284
French Revolution 184, 399
Frías González, Mateo 329
Fundamental Laws 289–91, 345–6

Gabarda, Dr 147
Gable, Clark 343

Galán, Fermín 100–1
Galarza, Lieutenant Colonel Valentín 132
Galdacano 366
Galicia 6, 15, 20, 48, 121, 147, 157, 304, 335, 337, 376–7, 394
Galinsoga, Luis de 73, 266, 331–2
Gallipoli 50, 84–5
Garbo magazine 355
García Hernandez, José 372
García Pérez, Antonio 31, 33
García Salve, Francisco 371
Garriga, Ramón 223, 275
garrotting 339, 357, 373, 381–2
Garzón, Baltasar 397
General Workers Union (UGT) 25, 86, 116, 359
Genoa, shelled by Royal Navy 272
George V, King 126
German-Spanish Treaty of Friendship 236
Gibraltar 37, 75, 138, 152, 246, 248–50, 254, 257–8, 272, 281
Gibson, Ian 355
Gil, Dr Vicente 375–6, 384
Gil Robles, José María 114–15, 124–5, 202, 305
Giménez-Caballero, Ernesto 294
Giral, José 153
Goa 27
Goded, General Manuel 125, 130–1, 156–7
Goebbels, Josef 164, 242
Goebbels, Magda 301
Goiocochea, Antonio 83
Gomá, Cardinal Isidro 170, 183, 241, 243
González, Felipe 381, 391, 393, 396
González Pacheco, Antonio (Billy el Niño) 395
Göring, Hermann 197, 244–5
Goya, Francisco 236, 241
Granada 165, 169, 182, 202, 303, 329, 359
Grimau, Julián 338–9
Guadalajara 213–14, 220, 360

Guardias de Asalto 112, 138, 145, 150, 154
Guernica 217–18, 380
guerrilla warfare 238, 268–9, 281
Guevara, Che 382
Guinea Bissau 27

Haddu-Allalu-Kadur 40
Hannibal 31, 37
Harder, Harro 220
Havel, Vaclav 395
Hayes, Carlton 280
Hayworth, Rita 242
Hearst, William Randolph 16
Hedilla, Manuel 200
Hemingway, Ernest 232
Hernández, García 100–1
Hess, Rudolf 161
Hidalgo, Diego 116–18, 121
Higón, Luis 122
Hill of Trenches 44
Himmler, Heinrich 256–7, 401
HISMA 164
Hitler, Adolf 3, 5, 10, 75, 96, 114, 118, 272–3, 275, 277, 292, 299, 318, 336, 399, 403
  and Czech crisis 233–4
  Franco correspondence 288
  and Franco letter 259–60
  and Franco's victory 236–7, 245–6
  meeting with Franco 251–8
  and Muñoz Grandes 315–16
  Pilar Primo de Rivera marriage plan 301
  and Second World War 246–51, 281–3, 286, 288–9
  and Spanish civil war 160–3, 165, 172, 180, 185, 188, 190, 194–7, 199, 207, 211, 213–15, 220, 223, 232
HMS *Eagle* 98
Hoare, Samuel 278, 284
Hobsbawm, Eric 401
Holocaust 267, 282, 288, 401
homosexuality 303

Hooper, John 392
Hope Gill, C. G. 77
Horace 401
Huelva 165, 196, 260
Huesca 100–1
Huétor, Pura 311
Hussein, King, of Jordan 389

Iglesias, Pablo 25, 107
Iniesta, Monsignor Alberto 383
Iniesta Cano, General Carlos 317, 366
intendentes 20, 29
Interior Socialists 348
International Anticommunist Entente (IAE) 96, 113, 118, 129
International Brigades 177, 191–4, 214, 235, 292, 325
International Monetary Fund (IMF) 322–3
International Red Aid 133
International Writers' Congress 219
Ireland 401
Irún, ETA campaign 348, 356
Isabella of Castile 19, 182, 211, 256
Isabella II, Queen 20, 25
Islam 41
Izarduy, Captain Angel 42
Izko, Francisco Javier 356

Jaca rebellion 100–2, 104, 111
Jaén 259
Jaime I 155
Jaraiz, Pilar 24, 54, 275, 364
Jarama, river 213–14, 262
Jehovah's Witnesses 368
Jerez 244, 339
Jerrold, Douglas 144
Jesuits 226, 370–1
Jesus Christ 241
Jews 5, 7, 82, 165, 223, 240, 256–7, 274, 282, 293, 299
  see also antisemitism
Joan of Arc 268
John XXIII, Pope 338

Jordana, General Gómez 236, 239
Juan Carlos, Prince 304–5, 335–6, 344, 351–2, 358, 361–2, 364–5, 372, 375–7, 379–80, 384
  abdication 397–8
  and failed coup 391
  sworn in as king 389–90
Jubany, Cardinal 368
Juliá, Santos 391
Julius Caesar 268
juntas de defensa 50, 52
Juventedes de Acción Popular (JAP) 114

Kelly, Grace 343
Kert River 40
Kindelán, General Alfredo 144, 174–5, 177, 179–80, 186, 232, 283
Kissinger, Henry 371, 374
Knickerbocker, Hubert Renfro 159, 192, 203, 225
Knox, Bernard 191
Koestler, Arthur 190
Korean War 306, 317
Krushchev, Nikita 339

La Coruña 27, 29, 110, 157, 244
La Epoca 18
La Stampa 208
La Vanguardia 248, 261–2, 266, 269, 276, 287, 293, 298, 316, 331–2, 352, 371, 379
Labour Charter 224
Labour Party (Britain) 290, 292
Langenheim, Adolf 161–2
Largo Caballero, Francisco 191
Larra, Mariano José de 19
Larraz, José 261
Larreategi, Javier 370
Las Provincias 73
Laureate Cross of San Fernando 4, 32, 45–8, 50, 239, 248
Law of Evasion 269
Law of Parliament 276, 289

Law of Political Responsibilities 227, 300
Law of Succession 290
Le Monde 243, 344
League of Nations 83, 94, 194
Lennard, Dora 146
Lepanto, battle of 91
Leret Ruíz, Captain Virgilio 149
Lerroux, Alejandro 100, 114, 116, 122, 124
Lías Pequeño, Captain Fernando 45
Liberal Republican Right 107
liberalism 5, 7, 10, 23–4, 28, 33, 209, 274, 294, 402
  'democratic liberalism' 186
Libertad 121, 155
Libya, Italian invasion 173
Life magazine 126
Lindbergh, Charles 10, 88
literacy 26, 40, 354, 401
Liverpool Daily Post 218
Llíria 347
Logroño, fall of 159
López Aranguren, José Luís 353
López Bravo, Gregorio 360, 367
López Ochoa, General Eduardo 120–1
López Rodó, Laureano 353
Lorca, Federico García 202, 303
L'Osservatore Romano 357
Luftwaffe 162, 197
  see also Condor Legion

Machado, Antonio 10
Madariaga, Salvador de 329, 336, 352–3
Madrid
  Almudena Cemetery 275–6
  Carrero Blanco assassination 370–2
  Comedia Theatre 111, 113
  declaration of Second Republic 103
  El Pozo del Rio Raimundo raid 362
  La Gran Peña club 90
  Modelo prison 206
  Montaña barracks 156
  Nationalist assault 154, 156, 185, 188–98, 204, 213, 219–21, 236
  Palace Hotel dinner 48
  passport office bombing 339–40
  political violence 381–2
  post-war conditions 243–4, 259
  Retiro Park 317
  Santa Barbara church 241
  screening of *Raza* 265–6
  socialist uprising 117–18
  student unrest 347, 356–7, 373
  University City 193–4, 256
  victory parades 239–40, 287–8
Madrid University 320
Maeztu, Ramiro de 78
Málaga 143, 157, 182, 351
  executions 197–8
  guerrilla warfare 268–9
  post-war conditions 259–60
  women in jail 298–9
Malraux, André 173
Malta 285
Manufacturas Metálicas Madrileñas 333
Manzanares, executions in 229
Manzanares, river 192–3, 241
Manzanas, Inspector Melitón 348, 356, 358
Maqueda, fall of 175–6
Maragall, Joan 330
Maria Cristina, Queen 17
Mariscal, Manuel 398
Marshall Plan 318, 322
martial law 51, 122, 129, 228, 283
Martínez Barrio, Diego 153
Martínez-Bordiú, Cristóbal, Marquis of Villaverde 306–7, 311–12, 348, 360, 375–7, 382, 385–6
Martínez Fuset, Lorenzo 170
Martínez Soler, José Antonio 388
Marxism 5, 7, 165, 240, 303
Matthews, Herbert 214
Medina 301
Mejías Correa, María 168

Melilla 33, 37–8, 42–3, 61–7, 71, 73, 77, 80, 148–9
Memorial de Infantería 60, 71
'memory laws' 396–7
Méndez Núñez, Admiral Castro 15
Mérida, fall of 167
Mexico 190
Miaja, General José 191–2
Mijas 229, 294, 350
Millán Astray, José 56–8, 60, 64, 66–7, 70–1, 105, 175, 187
mining rights 236–7
Miró, Joan 357
Mohammed V, King, of Morocco 318
Mola, General Emilio 42, 77, 99–100, 109–10, 125, 131–3, 138–40, 142–6, 149, 153, 157–9, 161, 163, 167, 172, 174–5, 179, 186
  death in plane crash 218–19
monarchists 74, 99, 102–3, 105–8, 110–11, 116, 122, 126–7, 140, 142, 146–7, 156–7, 160, 174, 179, 183, 185, 202–4, 223, 240–1, 283, 288, 331, 334–6, 344, 353, 378–80
Montalbán, Vázquez 395
Montero Navarro, General Manuel 77, 106
Montijo, Eugenia de 53
Montojo, Rear Admiral Patricio 16
Montserrat monastery 331, 357
Moore, Sir John 24
Morán, Gregorio 394
Moreno, Colonel Martín 141
Moreno Barranco, Manuel 339
Moroccan mercenaries ('Moors') 4, 40, 64–5, 69, 77, 120–1, 166, 168, 194, 217, 213, 241
  and rape 216–17
Morocco
  arrival of Italian aircraft 163–4
  ceding of Spanish protectorate 318–19
  communist threat 112
  and Franco victory 246

French Morocco 147, 152, 164, 246, 250, 254–5, 257, 260, 272, 280–1
military government 70–1, 86
Nationalist insurrection 150–3
Nazi Auslands-Organization 161
pacification campaign 32–4, 37–47, 51, 57
'Rif Republic' 83
Rif war 62–70, 75–6, 167, 171, 182, 195, 239, 313, 374
  Spanish retreat and victory 75–7, 80–7, 90, 105, 110
  and war in Europe 233, 248
Moscardó, Colonel José 176
Moscardó, Luis 176
Motrico, Count of 353
Mount Arruit 65
Mount Igueriben 63
Movietone News 184
Mozambique 27
Munich Conspiracy 335–8, 352
Muñoz Grandes, General Agustín 315–17, 322, 336, 343, 346–7
Mussolini, Benito 2–3, 5, 10, 74–5, 94, 96, 114, 137, 262, 275, 277, 292, 401
  and Arditi blackshirts 240
  Franco correspondence 288
  and Franco victory 233–6, 245–6
  meeting with Franco 271–2, 276
  and Second World War 247–51, 282–3, 286, 288–9
  and Spanish civil war 142, 160–1, 163–4, 172–3, 180, 184, 188, 190, 194–9, 207–9, 211, 213–15, 221, 223

Nador 65
Napoleon Bonaparte 10, 24, 37, 91, 214, 268, 317
Napoleon III, Emperor 53
National Catholicism 9, 293, 362
National Defence Junta 163, 173, 175, 177, 183–4
'National Revolution' 224
National Socialism 173, 207, 223, 277

'national syndicalism' 212, 223
Nationalists' (the term) 164
Nations Cup football 382
NATO 306, 356, 380, 391
Navarro Rubio, Mariano 322
Nazi fugitives 288, 316
Nazi party 161–2, 211, 223, 226, 264
Nelson, Admiral Lord Horatio 267
Neruda, Pablo 219
Neves, Mario 168
'New State' 180, 187, 209, 211, 221, 224, 373
New York Times 88, 214, 319, 323, 331, 337, 341, 345–6, 352, 356, 363, 365–6, 378, 380
Nieto Antúnez, Admiral Pedro 309, 354
Nixon, Richard M. 356, 360–1, 376, 380
Nuevo Mundo 71

oil crisis 379
Operation Barbarossa 272
Operation Guido 196
Operation Magic Fire 162
Operation Torch 281–3, 285
Operation X 191
Opus Dei 321–2, 342–3, 347, 353, 359–61, 380
Order of the Holy Sepulchre 307
Orfeó Català 330–1
Organic State Law 345–6
Organisation for European Economic Cooperation (OECE) 322
Orgaz, General Luis 131, 151, 169
Ortega y Gasset, José 102
Orwell, George 219, 338
Oviedo 48–9, 51, 53, 55, 70–3, 76, 91, 94–5, 115, 119, 121

pacifism 94
Pacón, *see* Salgado Arauja, Francisco Franco
Pact of Steel 257
pacto de olvido (policy of amnesia) 393
Pamplona 138, 158–9, 204, 244, 379

Panero, Leopoldo 170
Pániker, Salvador 353
Pareja Aycuéns, Lieutenant Colonel Luis 47, 81
Paris, May 1968 351
Paris World Fair 218
Patton, General George S. 281
Paul VI, Pope 338–9, 357, 366
Payne, Stanley 355
Pazo de Meiras 304
'peaceful turn' 25, 74
Pearl Harbor 277
Pemán, José María 99, 212
Peninsular War 24, 317
People's Party 396–7
Perón, Juan and Evita 295
peseta, devaluation 322–3
Pétain, Marshal Philippe 3, 245, 248, 250, 272
Philip II, King 224, 241, 243, 324
Philippines 10, 16, 26, 32, 65
Picasso, Lieutenant General Juan 75
Picasso, Pablo 218, 357
Piedrafita de Babia 308
Piga, Dr Antonio 386
Piñar, Blas 329
Pinillos, José Luis 319
Pinochet, General Augusto 12, 389
Pinto da Costa Leite, João 262
Pius XII, Pope 238, 283, 319
Pla, Josep 104
Pla y Deniel, Enrique, Bishop of Salamanca 181, 183–5, 338
Plan of Economic Stabilisation 322
Platform for Democratic Convergence 380–1
plutocracy 274
Podemos 398
Poland, German invasion 246–7
Pollard, Major Hugh 144, 147
Polo, Carmen 53–5, 72–3, 76, 89, 91–2, 136, 151, 172, 181–2, 187, 206–8, 226, 397
and executions 169–70

and Franco victory 241–2
influence 278–9, 295–8, 302, 309–13, 348, 351, 354–5, 358, 360, 364, 366–7, 369, 372, 376, 384
Polo, Zita 95, 170, 278–9
Polo Flórez, Felipe 53, 206–7, 261, 311
Polo Flórez, Isabel 53, 207
Popular Alliance 390
Popular Front 126, 128–9, 132, 136, 141, 163, 240
Popular Olympics 154
pornography 378
Portela Valladares, Manuel 129–30
Portuguese colonies 27
Portuguese revolution 373–4, 383
POUM 338
Poyales del Hoyo 396
Pozuelo, Vicente 376
Press Law 224, 242, 265
Preston, Paul 284, 340, 396
Prieto, Indalecio 158
Primo de Rivera, Fernando 75, 206
Primo de Rivera, José Antonio 95, 113, 115, 118, 131–2, 138–9, 141–2, 157, 199–201, 206, 240, 289, 302, 320, 385–6
and Valley of the Fallen 324, 333
Primo de Rivera, Miguel 74–7, 79–84, 86–7, 90–1, 96–7, 101, 104, 108, 110, 119, 173–4, 203, 211, 291
Primo de Rivera, Pilar 300–1
prison camps, post-war 300
Pritchett, V. S. 307, 313, 319
pronunciamentos 24–5
prostitution, increase in 302
Protestants, mistreatment of 342
Protocols of the Elders of Zion 257
Public Order Tribunal (TOP) 339, 348, 371
Publius Cornelius Scipio 38
Puerto Rico 16
Puig Antich, Salvador 373
Puigdemont, Carles 399
Pujol, Jordi 330–3, 336

Pulitzer, Joseph 16

Queipo de Llano, Brigadier General Gonzalo 77, 79, 82, 124, 152, 157, 161, 163, 165, 167, 172, 174, 179, 186, 217, 222
and executions 169–70, 197
Quinto 221

Radical Republicans 114, 116
Radio Castilla 184
Rádio Renasceça 373
Rainier, Prince 389
Raisuni, Ahmed er 59, 62
rape 216–17
Raza (Race) 7, 265–70, 340
Reconquista 68, 177, 182, 215
Red Army 126, 177, 193, 237
Red Cross 66
referendums 291, 345–7, 390, 399
Regulares Indígenas de Melilla 42
Republican Action 107
Republican Left 130, 139, 153
Requetés 143, 158, 204–5, 210
Revel, Jean-François 388
Revista de Tropas Coloniales 77–80, 83, 85–6, 101, 112
Revolutionary Antifascist and Patriotic Front (FRAP) 381
Ribbentrop, Joachim von 252–5, 257
Richthofen, Wolfram von 217–18, 234
Ridruejo, Dionisio 211
Rio de Janeiro 88
Rivas, Cipriano 110
Rivas, Natalio 90
Roatta, General Mario 172, 213–14
Roberts, Judith 327
Roda, Dolores 169
Rodezno, Count of 192, 204, 210, 227
Rodríguez del Barrio, General Ángel 130
Roldán, Luis 397
Roman Catholic church 5, 13, 27, 92, 108, 177, 180, 209, 226, 289, 295–7, 338, 383, 401

and CEDA 113–14
civil war apology 362
decline in influence 392
and education 301–3
Justice and Peace Commission 363–4
see also Vatican
Romania 266–7
Romanones, Count of 103
Romerales, General Manuel 148
Romero, Emilio 353
Roosevelt, Eleanor 306
Roosevelt, Franklin D. 274, 280, 286
Roosevelt, Theodore 16
Rota naval base 317
Royal Navy 24, 258, 272, 274, 281
Rubio, Mariano 397
Ruedo Ibérico 355
Ruiz Albeniz, Víctor 79
Ruiz-Fornells, General Enrique 33, 94
Russian Revolution 52, 128
Russo-Japanese War 37

Sacred History 225
Saenz de Buruaga, Colonel Eduardo 152
St Cyr military academy 92
St James 226
Saint Teresa of Ávila 182, 197, 298
Sainz, José 216
Sainz Rodríguez, Pedro 111, 116, 227, 302, 333
Salafranca, Captain Juan 45
Salamanca 174–5, 178–9, 185–7, 194–5, 204, 206–7, 210, 214, 222
Salamanca University 187
Salazar, António de Oliveira 114, 168, 288, 306, 373
Salgado Arauja, Francisco Franco (Pacón) 18, 20–1, 23, 27, 31, 34–5, 37–8, 49–50, 52, 56, 70, 103, 105, 206, 316, 332, 339, 355
    aide-de camp to Franco 109–11, 113, 116, 118, 124, 132, 134, 136–7, 141, 146, 148–9, 151, 157–8, 170, 177–9

and battle of the Ebro 231, 233
and Eisenhower visit 325–6
and fall of Madrid 193, 195
and Franco victory 244
and post-war Franco 309–13, 334, 344, 347, 358–9
and Vichy France 271
Saliquet, General Andrés 157
Salvador, Santiago 25
Sampson, Commodore William 15
San Sebastian 100, 160, 255, 304, 357
    ETA campaign 342, 357
San Sebastian International Film Festival 362
Sanchiz, José María 311
Sangróniz, José Antonio 173, 203
Sanjurjo, General José 68–9, 105, 109, 133, 137, 139, 153, 155–6, 173–4
    attempted coup 111–12, 122, 132, 169
    death in plane crash 156, 239–40
Santander 220–1, 268
Santiago de Compostela 73, 351
Santiago de Santiago 386
Scheele, Major Alexander von 164
Seat company 329
Second Republic, proclamation of 103–4, 114
Seguí, Lieutenant Colonel Juan 148
Segura, Cardinal Pedro, Archbishop of Seville 295–6
Serrano Suñer, Ramón 91, 94–5, 100–2, 115, 120, 124, 131–2, 138–9, 141–3, 169–70, 198, 200–1, 226–7, 289, 386, 394–5
    cuñadísimo and totalitarianism 206–9, 211–212
    and Franco government 222–3
    and Franco victory 241–2, 245–7
    and meeting with Hitler 253–5, 257–8
    sacking 278–9, 282
    and Second World War 250–1, 272–4
Servicio Central de Documentación 367–8

Seville 112, 114, 152, 154, 157, 159, 165–6, 169, 172, 189, 190, 196–7, 222, 259, 296, 317, 321, 361, 381
Sidi Ifni 318
Simpson, Wallis 193
Sinden, Donald 343
Sino-Japanese War 171
Social Political Brigade 347–8, 361–2, 395
Socialist Workers Party (PSOE) 25, 75, 107, 116, 129, 377, 381
Socialist Youth 145
Sophia of Greece, Princess 335
Southworth, Herbert 355
Soviet Union 12, 113, 120, 136, 158, 163, 177, 190, 194, 247, 288, 305, 314, 316–17, 339
  German invasion 272–4
Spanish Agrarian Party 138
Spanish Communist Party (PCE) 131, 320, 377, 380–1
Spanish Equatorial Guinea 318
Spanish Legion 55–73, 76–7, 79–80, 82–3, 86, 92–3, 100, 120–2, 129, 135, 143, 153, 171, 175, 187, 203–4, 376
Spanish Military Union (UME) 146
Spanish Renovation 142, 202–3
Spanish Socialist Workers Party (PSOE) 377
Spanish University Union 320
Spanish War of Independence 10, 24, 214
Special Operations Executive 191
Sperrle, General Hugo 196, 220
SS *Stanbrook* 237
Stalin, Josef 12, 126, 129, 190–1, 247
Stalingrad, battle of 282
starvation 259–60, 263, 294
Steer, George 218
Stohrer, ambassador 236
Strait of Gibraltar 155, 246, 249, 277, 281, 285
strikes 25–6, 101, 116–18, 135, 142, 344, 354, 356, 359, 368, 371, 379, 381
  Asturias miners' strike 334–5, 338

banned 224
and Crisis of 1917 51–2
and Semana Trágica 34
student unrest 293, 319–20, 342, 347–8, 351, 355–7, 373, 379
Suárez, Adolfo 390, 393
Suarez Valdés, General Alvaro 18
Subirán, Sofía 43
Sudetenland 233–4
Suez Canal 258
Supreme Order of Christ 319
Szulc, Tad 345

Tácito 377
Talavera de la Reina 172–3, 216
Tarancón, Cardinal Vicente 372
Tefero, Lieutenant Colonel Antonio 391
Términus 182
Teruel 221
Tetouan 38, 42, 45, 59, 62–3, 77, 148–9, 153, 155, 164, 168, 171
Third Prince's Regiment 48
Thoma, Colonel Wilhelm von 196
Thomas, Frank 214
Thomas, Hugh 347, 355, 359
Tierno Galván, Enrique 348
Time magazine 344, 362
Toledo 176–7, 180, 185, 188–91, 193, 216, 241
  military academy 29–34, 37, 39–40, 45, 48, 54, 89, 93–4, 343
Tomás, Belarmino 121
Torrejón de Ardoz 325
totalitarianism 10, 12, 75, 158, 185, 200, 208, 211–12, 221, 276, 288, 290, 292, 295, 319, 321, 325, 346, 393–5, 401
tourism 327–9, 338, 341–2, 382
Trafalgar, battle of 24, 266–7
Trini, Mari 299–300
Tripartite Pact 257
Trotskyists 154, 203, 219, 338
Truman Doctrine 317
Tukhachevsky, Marshal 126
Tunisia 246

Turquesa 120
Tusell, Javier 200, 395
Two Spains 10, 13, 19, 26, 107, 238

U-boats 253, 277, 281, 285
Ullastres, Alberto 322
Unamuno, Miguel de 187–8
Union of the Democratic Centre 390
United Nations 292–3, 306, 318
UN Human Rights Commission 355
United States of America 10, 15–16, 273–4, 277, 293, 306, 315–18, 356, 380
  defence treaty 337, 376
  Spanish bases 317–18, 374
  and Spanish economy 322–3
Urdangarin, Iñaki 398
USS *Coral Sea* 317
USS *Maine* 16

Valencia 25, 130, 157, 191, 216, 229, 231–2, 235, 237, 244, 263, 317, 347, 398
Valenzuela, Lieutenant Colonel Rafael 71–3
Valladolid 159, 379
Vallejo-Nájera, Dr Antonio 298–9
Valley of the Fallen 324, 333, 389, 397
Varela, General José Enrique 81, 101–2, 131–2, 143, 193, 278
Vatican 12, 226, 235, 290, 292, 296, 321, 324, 342–3, 357, 373
  concordat 319, 338, 361–2, 366
  Vatican II 338
Vázquez Montalbán, Manuel 388
Vázquez Moro, Manuel 136
Vega, Camilo Alonso 18, 343
Vertical Union 224
Vichy France 250, 253–4, 271–2, 280–1
Victor Emmanuel III, King 74
Victoria, Queen 19, 50
Victoria Eugenia, Queen 50, 199
Vigo 281

Vigón, General Juan 249–50
Villalba Riquelme, Colonel José 38
Villanueva de la Cañada 219, 221
Virgin Mary 36, 92, 226
Virgin of Begoña 278
Virgin of Covadonga 182
Virgin of Pilar 92
Vizcaya 18
Vox 398

Wagner, Richard 161–2
Waldi 146
Walters, General Vernon 325, 360–1
Warlimont, Lieutenant Colonel Walter 172, 196
Warriors of Christ the King (Guerrilleros de Cristo Rey) 361, 367, 380
Warsaw ghetto 256
Welles, Benjamin 337, 341
Wellington, Duke of 24
Whitaker, John 168, 187, 194, 202, 216–17
Wilhelm II, Kaiser 50
wolfram 277, 281
women (and women's rights) 9, 105, 113, 223, 297–301, 392, 401, 404
Workers Charter 289
Workers Commissions 348, 371
World Cup football 374

Yagüe Blanco, Lieutenant Colonel Juan 120–1, 132, 141, 143, 149, 153, 166, 168, 177–9
Yanduri, Marchioness of 165

Zamora prison 355, 363
Zaragoza 157, 221, 259
  military academy 89, 91–4, 99, 103, 105, 109, 125, 136, 141, 176, 319
  Torrero prison 299
Zaragoza Orts, Pedro 327–8

Image Credits

Francisco Franco as a baby, with his parents: Alamy Stock Photo; Nicolás Franco Bahamonde: Alamy Stock Photo/Archivo ABC/Jalón Ángel; Ramón Franco Bahamonde: Alamy Stock Photo; Franco as a young officer in Morocco: Alamy Stock Photo/World History Archive; Franco and Millán Astray in the Foreign Legion: Universal History Archive/Universal Images Group via Getty Images; Franco receives honorary sabre: Bridgeman Images; Francisco, Pilar and Nicolás: Alamy Stock Photo; Alfonso XIII: Alamy Stock Photo/Everett Collection Inc; Primo de Rivera: Alamy Stock Photo; Sanjurjo: Alamy Stock Photo/Heritage Image Partnership Ltd; Franco in Tenerife: Alamy Stock Photo; Moroccan soldiers of the Spanish Foreign Legion: Alamy Stock Photo/Sueddeutsche Zeitung Photo; Republican soldiers during the siege of the Alcazar de Toledo: Alamy Stock Photo/Sueddeutsche Zeitung Photo; Toledo aftermath: Alamy Stock Photo/Sueddeutsche Zeitung Photo; No pasarán: Alamy Stock Photo/CPA Media Pte Ltd; Civilians fleeing Madrid: Alamy Stock Photo/Sueddeutsche Zeitung Photo; Guernica, the aftermath: Alamy Stock Photo/World History Archive; Franco and his wife: Alamy Stock Photo/World History Archive; Franco and Carmencita: Alamy Stock Photo/Lebrecht Music and Arts; Franco meets Mussolini: Alamy Stock Photo/Sueddeutsche Zeitung Photo; Franco meets Hitler: Alamy Stock Photo/Shawshots; Franco protests against UN intervention: KEYSTONE-FRANCE/Gamma-Rapho via Getty Images; Tourism flourishes: Alamy Stock Photo/SDGH Images; Franco at the charity bullfight: EFE; Franco and Juan Carlos: Alamy Stock

Photo/Niday Picture Library; Road damage after explosion that killed Carrero Blanco: Alamy Stock Photo/World History Archive; Franco's funeral: EFE; Adolfo Suarez votes in the 1976 referendum: STR/AFP via Getty Images; Protester in 2019: Alamy Stock Photo/Zuma Press, Inc; Valle de Cuelgamuros: Alamy Stock Photo/Brian Harris.

A Note on the Author

Giles Tremlett is a prize-winning biographer, narrative historian and journalist based in Madrid, Spain. He has lived in, and written extensively about, Spain almost continuously since graduating from Oxford University. He has been a Visiting Fellow of the Cañada Blanch Centre at the London School of Economics, writes opinion and long-form reportage for the *Guardian* and is a former Madrid correspondent for the *Economist*.

A Note on the Type

The text of this book is set in Linotype Stempel Garamond, a version of Garamond adapted and first used by the Stempel foundry in 1924. It is one of several versions of Garamond based on the designs of Claude Garamond. It is thought that Garamond based his font on Bembo, cut in 1495 by Francesco Griffo in collaboration with the Italian printer Aldus Manutius. Garamond types were first used in books printed in Paris around 1532. Many of the present-day versions of this type are based on the *Typi Academiae* of Jean Jannon cut in Sedan in 1615.

Claude Garamond was born in Paris in 1480. He learned how to cut type from his father and by the age of fifteen he was able to fashion steel punches the size of a pica with great precision. At the age of sixty he was commissioned by King Francis I to design a Greek alphabet, and for this he was given the honourable title of royal type founder. He died in 1561.